OUR PARTNERSHIP

Early Days of the Partnership

OUR PARTNERSHIP
BY BEATRICE WEBB

EDITED BY
BARBARA DRAKE
MARGARET I. COLE

WITH PLATES

LONGMANS, GREEN AND CO.
LONDON   NEW YORK   TORONTO

LONGMANS, GREEN AND CO. LTD.
6 & 7 CLIFFORD STREET, LONDON W.1
NICOL ROAD, BOMBAY 1
17 CHITTARANJAN AVENUE, CALCUTTA 13
36A MOUNT ROAD, MADRAS 2

LONGMANS, GREEN AND CO. INC.
55 FIFTH AVENUE, NEW YORK 3

LONGMANS, GREEN AND CO.
215 VICTORIA STREET, TORONTO 1

First published 1948

*This book is produced in complete conformity
with the authorized economy standards*

CODE NUMBER 12438

PRINTED IN GREAT BRITAIN
BY R. & R. CLARK, LIMITED, EDINBURGH

PREFACE

WE have been asked by Sidney Webb to prepare for publication this first volume of *Our Partnership* by the late Beatrice Webb, and to write a short preface. The book, which is a sequel to *My Apprenticeship*, first published in 1926, relates to the earlier years of her marriage, 1892–1911, and was originally intended by her, had she lived, as a first instalment of other volumes to follow, but this was not to be. The plan of the book, like that of *My Apprenticeship*, was to interweave extracts from her contemporary diaries with the narrative of events. The work was actually begun in 1926, immediately after the publication of the earlier volume, but was soon interrupted owing to the pressure of research and to the political activities connected with the second Labour Government. It was resumed in 1931, only to be interrupted again by the Webbs' visit to Russia, the work on *Soviet Communism*, and by periods of ill-health. The main lines and arrangement of the book were settled at the beginning and maintained; additions and alterations were made at intervals almost up to her death in April 1943, but the text was never finally revised.

We have ventured to omit from the book a chapter on " Round the English-speaking World " (1898). While the chapter contains much interesting matter, it has little or no bearing on the main concerns of the present volume. We have also omitted some passages from the diaries on technical subjects, which were either of great length or had appeared in substance in earlier publications; again, a few phrases are left out which we felt that Beatrice herself would have withdrawn as they might have given offence to persons now still living. Otherwise, and apart from minor verbal corrections and the addition of some explanatory footnotes, the text remains exactly as she left it.

My Apprenticeship, in its first edition, included a number of footnotes on the principal characters which appeared in it, and a few such notes had already been added by Beatrice to *Our Partnership*. We have appended instead, for the convenience of the student, a biographical index of the persons mentioned in so far as they are concerned with the matter of the book.

For the rest, we leave Beatrice herself to write her own introduction. The full book as planned by her, and of which *My Apprenticeship* and this volume are only the two first instalments, was originally to be called *My Creed and My Craft*, but in her desire to describe truthfully her lifelong pursuit of a living philosophy, her changes of outlook and ideas, her growing distrust of benevolent philanthropy as a means of redeeming " poor suffering humanity ", and her leaving of the field of abstract economic theory for the then practically unexplored paths of scientific social research, she felt it necessary to reveal something of her own experiences and personality, of the restless and lonely phase of *My Apprenticeship*, of the loving companionship and deep peace of *Our Partnership*. The book became, in fact, an autobiography.

" I mean ", she writes in her diary (May 1922), " to finish this book before taking up my other work, and I mean to write it according to my conscience, not shamefacedly in fear of scoffing remarks. The difficulty is to tell the truth without being self-conscious about it. I have been reading through my diaries and dictating extracts so as to base my autobiographical element on it, not on memories but on contemporary evidence exactly as if it were about somebody else. It is amazing how one forgets what one thought and felt in the past, and even what one did and with whom one was intimate. Reading of all our intrigues over the Education Bill (1902) was a shock to me, not so much the intrigues themselves as our evident pleasure in them! How far is intrigue permissible? "

She writes again (February 1923): " There is a certain morbidity in writing this book—it is practically an autobiography with the love affairs left out—the constantly recur-

ring decision of what degree of self-revelation is permissible
and desirable. The ideal conduct would be to treat the
diaries exactly as I should treat them if they were someone
else's—of course a contemporary person with the same
objective requirements about other people's feelings. But it
is almost impossible to get into that frame of mind—one's
self-esteem is too deeply concerned—also Sidney's feelings
have to be considered. On the other hand, many personal
traits and experiences may seem significant to the author
which are really uninteresting—mere flashes of personal
vanity."

Later, in 1926, when she had begun to prepare the present
volume, she records her difficulty in expressing her philosophy of life, her belief in the scientific method, but its
purpose guided always by religious emotion. " I am perpetually brooding ", she writes (April 1926), " over my
inability to make clear even to myself, let alone to others,
why I believe in religious mysticism, why I hanker after
a Church—with its communion of the faithful, with its
religious rites, and its religious discipline, and above all
with its definite code of conduct." She rejects " scientific
materialism " as a rival metaphysic or as a guide to human
conduct. " The trend of scientific thought is to discourage
the mind of man from searching for absolute truth with
regard to the meaning of life, and to regard metaphysics as
an aid to living rather than as an extension of objective
knowledge. . . . Then there is the complaint that what
seems right to-day seems wrong to-morrow and that the
great religions of the world have differed in their moral
codes. This uncertainty in the verdict is equally true of
science; what seems proved to-day is disproved and rejected to-morrow. Indeed, the ideal of infallibility is and
can never be realised by faculties that are evolving; each
stage and conclusion will be a jumping-off place for a new
departure. Why should not our discernment of *what ought
to be* become clearer and broader exactly as our own discernment of *what is true* becomes more extensive and complete
and more completely verified? What we have to consider

is not the occasional lapses in the development of morality through religion, but whether history shows any constant relation between the presence of religious mysticism and the progressive development of what we consider right living."

The appeal made to her later by Soviet Communism may be traced, at least partly, to the passionate, almost religious, faith of its founders in the " brotherhood of man "—" from each according to his faculty, to each according to his need "—and their deliberate use of science as a means of achieving this end. Its political intolerance and fanaticism during its bitter struggle against enemies, both at home and abroad, she was wont to compare with the religious intolerance and savage persecutions of earlier centuries. " When it is objected ", she writes again (April 1926), " that, as a matter of fact, religious mysticism has itself led to meanness and cruelty, I answer, this is only another way of saying that all human faculties are imperfect and that the religious faculty, like the faculty of observation and reason, is subject to degeneration and even to death by disease." A question that then perpetually vexed her was: " Can we have the moral results of a religious faith without religious rites and religious discipline, without a communion of the faithful pledged to practise these rites and to carry out a definite moral code, *i.e.* without a Church? I doubt it. And the longer I live the more doubt tends to become a settled conviction. Somehow or other we must have the habit of prayer, the opportunity for the confession of sin and for the worship of goodness if we are to attain personal holiness. Otherwise we suffer from a chronic devitalisation of the religious faculty. But how can we get a Church without a dogma—a dogma which will offend intellectual integrity and moral sincerity? No such Church seems within sight. Like so many other poor souls I have the consciousness of being a spiritual outcast. . . . I have failed to solve the problem of life—of man's relation to the universe and, therefore, to his fellow-men. But I have a growing faith that it will be solved by a combination of truth-seeking and personal holiness—of the scientific mind with the religious life. When will such a leader arise who will unite the intellect of an Aristotle, a Goethe or an Einstein, with the moral genius of a Buddha, a Christ or a St. Francis of Assisi? "

Beatrice continued to write her diaries—awake in the early morning hours—to within a few days of her death in her eighty-sixth year. She knew that her strength was rapidly failing and the end was near; but, even after the tragedy of the second World War, she never lost her faith in the power of man to follow the light within him and, by the use of science, to create a social, economic and international order which would bring out what was best in him—the spirit of co-operation and service—and so overcome the great stumbling-blocks of fear and greed. She herself was ready to go—sad only at the parting from her beloved—and to pass on her task to others. The *Partnership* has already left its mark on the social legislation of to-day, and the revolutionary ideas of the early campaigns are now the commonplaces of all political parties.

We are indebted to the Cambridge University Press for permission to use extracts from a Report of the Pilgrim Trust on *Men Without Work*; to Messrs. Cassell & Company, Ltd., and the Yale University Press for an extract from *Politics from Inside* by Sir Austen Chamberlain; to Messrs. Constable & Company, Ltd., for "Lord Rosebery's Escape from Houndsditch" from *The Nineteenth Century and After*, September 1901, and for an extract from *The Apologia of an Imperialist* by W. A. S. Hewins; to Messrs. J. M. Dent & Sons, Ltd., and E. P. Dutton & Company, Inc., New York, for extracts from *Pillars of Society* by A. G. Gardiner; to Sir William S. Haldane and Messrs. Hodder & Stoughton, Ltd., for lengthy extracts from *An Autobiography* by R. B. Haldane; to Mr. Alexander MacLehose for extracts from *From One Century to Another* by Elizabeth Haldane; to Messrs. Macmillan & Company, Ltd., for an extract from *History of the London County Council* by Gibbon and Bell, and for an extract from *Life of Joseph Chamberlain* (Vol. III) by J. L. Garvin; to the *Manchester Guardian* for two reports from the *Manchester Guardian*; to the *News Chronicle* for an extract by H. W. Massingham from the *Daily Chronicle*; to the Students' Union of the London School of Economics and Political Science for an extract from the *Handbook of the Students' Union* by Professor Graham Wallas; and to the *Times* for an extract from the report of the Conference of the National Union of Women Workers, October 29, 1897.

For assistance in compiling the Biographical Index our thanks are due also to the following: Lord Beveridge, George M. Booth, Ivor Brown, Miss Mildred Bulkeley, Sir Arthur Cochrane, Professor G. D. H. Cole, Dr. Alfred Cox, Dr. Hugh Dalton, F. W. Galton, Philip B. Dingle, Town Clerk of Manchester, G. E. Haynes of the N.C.S.S., Stephen Hobhouse, P. F. Jupe of the Establishment Board of H.M. Treasury, Commissioner David Lamb and Colonel Carvosso Gauntlett of the Salvation Army, Mrs. C. M. Lloyd, L. M'Evoy, Town Clerk of Leicester, Dr. J. J. Mallon, John Moss of the Kent County Council, Dr. Stark Murray, Edward R. Pease, Dr. Karin Stephen, Herbert Tracey of the Trades Union Congress, and Miss May Wallas.

B. D.
M. I. C.

LONDON
September 1947

CONTENTS

INTRODUCTION

xi

CONTENTS

CHAPTER V

CHAPTER VI

CHAPTER VII

CHAPTER VIII

PLATES

AN INTRODUCTION

THE OTHER ONE

IN the summer of 1926, a few weeks after the publication of *My Apprenticeship*, thinking that I might continue the story of my life, I set down my impression of the Other One; the circumstance of his upbringing, his personality as it appeared to me, and the character of his influence on his contemporaries. Other tasks intervened and it was not until 1931 that I started to write the first chapter of this book. To-day, after another lapse of time, bringing with it advanced old age, I insert without correction the informal sketch of 1926 as an introduction to *Our Partnership*.

Sidney Webb was born of parents neither rich nor poor, neither professional brain-workers nor manual workers, neither captains of industry nor hired hands. His people belonged to the part of England (Kent and Essex), and to the social class that had escaped out of the feudalism of the countryside, without being transformed by the industrial revolution. The social environment of his parents and grandparents was, in fact, typical of the industrial development of the first half of the nineteenth century; a somewhat stagnant population of traders and fisher-folk, of master craftsmen and little cultivators—all alike living outside the ancient chartered towns. His paternal grandfather, who brought up a large family and accumulated a fortune of something like ten thousand pounds, for fifty years kept the village inn that served a Kentish hamlet; a vigorous old Radical. His mother's family were little property-owners in Essex and Suffolk, cultivating land or sailing wooden ships between the ports of the East Coast, and occasionally venturing across the North Sea and the Channel, sometimes blossoming out into yeomen stockbreeders or owners of fishing smacks and trading vessels. So far as I have been able to ascertain, there was only one person within the family connection who was,

I

B

in any way, distinguished—a first cousin—Fred Webb, the famous jockey who won the Derby, afterwards becoming a well-known trainer. Among uncles, aunts and cousins, there were apparently no members of the older and more dignified professions; no beneficed clergyman, no physician or surgeon, no solicitor or barrister, no naval or army officer. The families concerned belonged almost exclusively to the lower middle-class; some rose temporarily to be small landowners and " rentiers ", others fell into dependence and poverty; but none became directors of great undertakings, whether of profit-making enterprise or in public administration.

The father and mother of Charles, Sidney and Ada Webb were thus what the worldly call " little folk ", without social influence, but with a certain amount of backing from better-off relations. The mother had been left an orphan at a tender age, to be brought up by one or other of her aunts. In 1848, a brother-in-law advanced her a few hundred pounds to open a retail shop in a street of shops in central London which became, after her marriage in 1854, the home of the little family and the principal source of the family income. Meanwhile, the father, who had gained sufficient education to become a public accountant in a humble way, looked after the neighbouring shopkeepers' ledgers and settled the affairs of little companies and societies which had got into trouble, thereby earning a small and irregular income. He gave the greater half of his time gratuitously to serve on the local vestry and the board of guardians, or to acting as trustee or executor for humble folk. I doubt whether the family income ever reached £500 a year, and I doubt whether the family expenditure ever went below £300, in an era of cheapness.

But the most important part of a child's environment is the character of its parents. The Webb parents were both of them beyond reproach; they were, in fact, the last word in respectability. The father, who died a few months before I became engaged to Sidney, was, from all accounts, singularly refined in character—modest and unassuming, remarkably public-spirited, always ready to do unpaid work either for public bodies or friends who were in trouble. He was a diligent reader of newspapers and political pamphlets. But throughout life he suffered frail health and was managed by his far abler and more energetic wife. For Sidney's mother was a woman of character and capacity; a clever shopkeeper and excellent housekeeper, giving her children good fare, open windows and cold baths, and training them in good habits. Graham Wallas, who knew her before her breakdown in health, described her as " wise and witty, with a remarkable memory ". It was she who, after consulting with a friendly customer, sent the two boys, at a considerable sacrifice of income, first to a Swiss school to learn French and then into the family of a German pastor at Wismar to learn German—an accomplishment which indirectly led to Sidney getting into the first division of the Civil Service, and to his brother becoming the foreign correspondence clerk in Marshall & Snelgrove and other firms, and eventually graduating into a successful profit-making venture of his own. The intellectual atmosphere of the home was made up of the Radical politics of the father—he was, for instance, an ardent supporter of John Stuart Mill's candidature at Westminster in 1865—and the broad evangelical religious feeling of the mother, who took the children to one church or chapel after another in search of an eloquent preacher free from sacerdotalism. It remains to be added that the family " kept itself to itself " and had few relatives in London, and practically no friends. The Webb family was not socially attractive: there was no margin of income for entertaining; the home, though comfortable, was cramped and ugly; its inhabitants, if not ugly, were homely and plain in appearance and manners; the sister attractively plain, the brother just commonplace. Though I never saw the father, and only saw the mother when she was aged and crippled, it was clear that neither one nor the other had a fine appearance or peculiar charm—except the charm of essential goodness, of honesty, personal kindliness and public spirit. But the outstanding characteristic of this family circle was the absence

3

of the " will-to-power ", or the desire to be conspicuous. Even Charles, who had not inherited the public spirit and intellectual interests of his father, who was just a clever and honest tradesman and a good family man, never wanted to make more money than was necessary to give him a small but comfortable home, a little rough shooting and a few weeks' annual tour on the Continent. When he had secured £1500 or £2000 a year, he retired from active business. As for exercising authority over other people, he quite obviously disliked it; neither had he been tempted by social ambition. This absence of any desire to climb up the social ladder, or to enjoy luxury, as distinguished from comfort, was to me the most attractive feature of the family life of the Webbs. They neither admired nor objected to social superiors—they ignored them. A life of distraction and luxurious leisure, of conspicuous expenditure, would have merely worried and bored them past endurance. Thus Sidney's environment did not encourage class bitterness, nor lead to the conception of class war; there was certainly no consciousness of family failure; and, as it happened, there was, so far as he and his brother were concerned, from their early youth upwards, a growing consciousness of personal success. The material and mental environment of the Webb family was neutral in its politics and economics, a neutrality shown by the subsequent opinions of the two brothers and sister. Charles became and remained a City Tory, Sidney became a Socialist and Ada a mugwump—predominantly progressive but not " Labour ".

So much for family circumstances. Edward Pease, who knew Sidney's parents and his brother and sister, more than once observed that Sidney was one of the few men whom he had known, whose remarkable brain power could not be explained by the brains of his parents or forebears: his far-reaching and always working intellect must have been a physiological freak. Superficially, he resembled his family. " Undistinguished and unimpressive in appearance " would be the verdict of a qualified reporter. In an English crowd he would pass unnoticed unless someone asked whether he was a foreigner. " At an International Congress ", wrote an

American journalist, " Sidney Webb might be found among the intellectuals of any nation's delegation." On the Continent, he is usually assumed to be French. At the Hamburg International Socialist Congress in 1923, for instance, he was followed and abused as such; and a hotel porter rudely refused to believe he was English until he showed his passport as a British M.P., when effusive apologies were tendered.

Regarded as a public personage, Sidney Webb has always been the delight of caricaturists. With his big head, bulgy eyes, bushy moustaches and square-cut short beard (it is this latter feature which gained him the name of " Nannie " in the House of Commons), small but rotund body, tapering arms and legs and diminutive hands and feet, he lends himself to the cubist treatment of the ridiculous. These ill-looks, however, are not represented in photographs; for the photographer always selects the profile or half-face. Taken in profile, with the disproportion between head and legs corrected by the falsified photographic perspective, he is not only remarkable but attractive in appearance. The massive head, covered with thick wavy hair (originally black, now streaked with white), the broad finely-moulded forehead, large kindly grey eyes, imposing Roman nose together with the afore-mentioned bushy imperial, would look well on a coin! Assuredly this head-piece indicates brain power—a fine intellect tempered by visionary idealism and lit up with benevolence.

As a speaker he is not prepossessing. He has a husky voice, made less articulate by a rapid delivery; at times, in his haste, he omits a syllable or clips his words. When he hesitates, either in talk or in public speaking, there are ugly intervening " ers " and " ums ". His diction, though fluent and coherent, lacks style; he has none of the graces or tricks of the orator; when addressing a popular audience he is apt to be prosy and monotonous. But he has his own kind of effectiveness. In argument he is ingenious and often convincing; he is always informative and logical. In short, he is a first-rate class lecturer; he raises rapidly, and in their right order, all the relevant issues, and either settles them there and then, or gives his students some notion how to do so; he insinuates wise thoughts and suggests subtle qualifications; with advanced students he is often witty. At question time he is overwhelming; no heckler has ever got the better of him! Whilst honest enquirers get what they want. And, if he says he does not know, he tells them where to go for the best information.

But it is as a committee man that Sidney Webb excels. He is always on the spot; he thinks twice as fast as his colleagues; he so foresees the drift of the discussion that he can lie in wait, and open or block the way according to his aims. He is the ideal draftsman; able to express the desired conclusion in a dozen different phrases so as to disarm suspicion or prejudice and to suit diverse temperaments. He can accept, or even suggest, amendments which satisfy troublesome opponents without achieving their hostile ends.

Have I made it clear that, admirable as a social engineer, Sidney Webb has not the make-up of a popular leader? He lacks personal magnetism; he has no liking for personal prominence; he is, in fact, not a public personage at all, he is a private citizen with public aims and expert knowledge. Hence, the continuous depreciation of him by journalists like H. W. Massingham, who specialised in the melodrama of public affairs, and amused themselves and their readers by setting up idol after idol for the people to worship. For Sidney Webb did not lend himself to this game; he has always been a " behind the scenes " man, and even on committees he has succeeded best with fellow-researchers and fellow-administrators, in fact, with his intellectual equals. For it must be admitted he has not always been able to suffer fools gladly; he has had neither the patience nor the itch for power, needful for manipulating coarse characters and common minds by deception and flattery. I will not say he has courted unpopularity—he has been too unselfconscious for that—moreover, he would have thought it silly. If he has courted any state of being, it has been anonymity and inconspicuousness. But he has always had the courage of his

opinions; and time after time he has " used himself up " for
a cause in which he believed.

Of course, he has changed in manner and method after
middle-life. When he was young and enthusiastically convinced that mass poverty could be abolished and the economic circumstances of the world transfigured by collective
control and collective administration, his keenness took the
form of persistent permeation; of endless intrigues to persuade those in authority to go his way. By friends and
enemies alike, he was acclaimed an accomplished wire-
puller. Perhaps the cleverest caricature—about 1900—was
a picture of Balfour and Asquith bobbing up and down at
the end of wires handled by the " wily Fabian ". But, in
later years, he has become too philosophical, too much the
researcher and, therefore, the doubter, to persist in getting
his own way—even behind the scenes. After sixty he gladly
took a back seat in all affairs, and on all the occasions when
his colleagues were in the limelight, he was busying himself
about matters which, though important, the other leaders felt
irksome and were inclined to leave undone. Hence, his
apparent failure in the House of Commons relatively to his
reputation on entering it as *the* Intellect of the Labour Party
—a reputation which served him ill, seeing that it roused
the vulgar insolence of the baser type of Tory. Hence, also,
the odd ups and downs in the esteem of well-known contemporaries. " Son Éminence Grise " was Camille Huysmans' nickname when that clever Belgian statesman was
resident in London during the last two years of the Great
War, observing the reconstruction of the Labour Party by
Henderson and Sidney. " I never can see what people see
in him," remarked John Morley to a friend—who forthwith
reported it! " The worst of Webb ", wrote G. D. H. Cole in
a character sketch, " is that he is *permanent*; when you think
you have disposed of him he confronts you in another part
of the field." There were times when " the Webb myth "
took the form of a sinister and hidden presence, manipulating the activities of Church and State, of the Tory and
Liberal press, of the Trade Union and Co-operative Move-

ments in the direction of fanatically held ideals. At other times he has been dismissed as a " back number ", as " an exploded myth ", as " a bourgeois pedant ", hopelessly out of touch with the virile democracy. As a matter of fact, the " all-powerful " and the " insignificant " verdicts were equally beside the mark; his influence has been limited but steady; it has varied little from time to time; and it has never taken the form of personal power; he has insinuated thoughts which fructified, he has never actively dominated other people's activities; he has never been (except to his wife!) *a man of destiny*. What he has achieved, either in organisation or in thought, has been slow but continuous constructive work, carrying out elastic but definite and consistent plans of social reconstruction. Public spirit, personal disinterestedness, tenacity of purpose, accurate knowledge and sound reasoning, have been the faculties whereby he has attained such success as he has had in bringing about, by propaganda, in legislation, or through administration, the social reorganisation in which he has believed. Fullness of knowledge, sense of proportionate value of facts and issues, lucidity in expression and a tireless industry, have been his peculiar contribution to our joint work.

So far I have described the Other One as a public servant —for a public servant he has been in the fullest meaning of the term. In his intimate relations, he is singularly free from faults and he has certain delightful gifts. He has always been healthy in body and mind, he has had no day-dreams, his very sleep is dreamless. He has had no vindictiveness and he has never been obsessed by particular persons or events. To use topical jargon, he never suffered from " suppressions " or "complexes "; he never felt himself to be either inferior or superior to other people; in his own eyes he is just one among equals. He has never claimed to be in the front rank; he does not push his way into the corner seat of a railway carriage—as I invariably do!—he watches the others seat themselves, and takes the place that is left. Likewise he is no respecter of persons, except in so far as one man may need more help or be better able to serve a common

cause than another. Such personal sensitiveness as he has
—and I think he is largely unconscious of the effect of his
own personality—takes the form of withdrawing from the
contest, retiring into the background to go on with his own
researches complacently. In his outlook on men and affairs
he is impersonal—an amused and amusing observer, giving
the benefit of the doubt to erring mortals, generous in
appreciation of moral and intellectual gifts, but not a hero-
worshipper. Indeed, he dislikes reputed heroes and heroines,
and he laughs at Bernard Shaw's " Superman ". He is on
friendly terms with many people; they trust him and he
trusts them; but he is too absorbed in disentangling questions and promoting causes to have intimate friendships.
This absence of friendships in his life has, I think, been a
loss to him. Perhaps Bernard Shaw and, some way down the
scale of frank intimacy—Haldane—but I can think of no
other but these two who have been lifelong friends as well
as colleagues. He is apt to be bored by women; especially
by sentimental or " temperamental " women and by professional beauties; they don't interest him and he resents
their claims to admiration and attention. When I placed the
handsome but metallic Lady Desborough beside him at a
luncheon at our house, he remarked afterwards that he
thought her " unpleasing with her artificial and insincere
talk and silly trick of shutting her eyes at you ". His absence
of mind with another charming lady was signalised by her
ejaculation, as she noticed him listening to the conversation
at the other end of the table, " And what is *she* saying now,
Mr. Webb ? " How he detested Mrs. Pat Campbell when
she was brought to see us by Lady Elcho! G. B. S.'s subsequent infatuation he regarded as a clear case of sexual
senility! Sophie Bryant, the hard-headed and accomplished
principal of the North London Collegiate School, who sat
with him on the Technical Education Board and on the
Senate of London University, is the only woman I remember
to have interested him, and the generous and noble-minded
Alys Russell the only one for whom he has expressed
affectionate concern. Casual conversation in truth does not

9

amuse him; he prefers reading and he dislikes " unnecessary communications " from those he lives with. If he married a chatterbox as a " second ", Heaven help her!

The plain truth is that his emotional life—all his capacity for personal intimacy, and for over-appreciation of another's gifts—has been centred in his wife and partner, and his wife just because she is also his partner. One of his most attractive gifts as a life companion is his gaiety of nature, he is nearly always happy. One refrain recurs continuously in his consciousness and he does not hesitate to express it—an almost childlike gratitude for his good luck in life. " We ought to do good work," he often says as we wander arm-in-arm together or I sit on his lap by the firelight, " we have been so amazingly fortunate." Content with his lot in life, enjoyment of the daily round of research and the writing of books, the interest of an observer in the tasks of an M.P. and party leader; a varied outlook on life, a pleasant sense of humour, above all a continuous helpfulness to other people, are delightful characteristics in a constant companion—they make life seem worth while. And, if there be a touch of absurdity in his adoration of a helpmate, it is a flaw in his reasonableness which she discounts to his credit! Also, he has her " on the lead " and, when she strays into morbid ways, or darts off in a panic, she is firmly but gently pulled back with deprecating chaff combined with soothing reflections on the relative unimportance of any particular happening and even doubts as to the significance of her own frame of mind. Thus the monstrous self fades off the screen of her consciousness to be replaced by refreshing vistas of the past history and future prospects of the human race, as if the life-force were as beneficent as he is himself. For the Other One is an unrepentant optimist in big things and small! Sometimes he mocks at his own confidence in the wellmeaning of the universe. " When I was a child," says he, " haunted by a future Hell, I remember casting out the fear once for all by thinking to myself—perhaps derived from Martin Elginbrod, if I had then read him—' If I were God, and He were I, I should forgive Him His trespasses '. He is not worse but better than I." And he adds, " In our criticism of Nature's doings why should we not give the Almighty God ' the benefit of the doubt '? But the doubt must be an honest doubt and not contrary to evidence."

The days of his absence are weary to get through; and the sleepless hours of the night are haunted, not by the fear of death, but by the dread of life without him.

CHAPTER I

STUDIES IN BRITISH TRADE UNIONISM
1892–1898

WE opened Our Partnership with certain assets. An un-earned income of £1000 a year, and a liking for the simple life, ensured unfettered freedom in the choice of a career. We were in the prime of life and in good health; we felt assured of loving companionship without end, a confidence which proved singularly well-founded; we shared the same faith and practised the same craft; we enjoyed laughing at ourselves and at other people. " Two second-rate minds but curiously complementary ", I had recorded in my diary on our engagement to be married. Sidney had unique aptitude for documentary research; he could rush through MS. and printed pages at an incredible rate, turning out sheafs of separate sheets whereon were methodically inscribed, in immaculate handwriting, tables of statistics, minutes of pro-ceedings, series of events, rival hypotheses as to causal con-nection, apt quotations, each paper complete in itself with reference and date—all essential material for the discovery of the attributes of various types of organisations. He was a good linguist; he spoke and wrote fluently. He had an amazing capacity for memorising facts, and developing, in logical sequence and lucid phrase, arguments and con-clusions. Skill in social intercourse was my special gift. An experienced hostess, I had never felt the sensation of shyness in any company of men and women, whatever their char-acter or intelligence, their status or occupation; I could in-sinuate myself into smoking-rooms, business offices, private and public conferences, without rousing suspicion. I may observe in passing that, in those days of unemancipated females, to be a woman and, therefore, at the start-off, not taken seriously, yielded better innings, whether through cross-examination, disguised as light conversation, or by a happy-go-lucky acquisition (by guile, not theft) of confidential documents. I revelled in observing and recording the sayings and doings of men and describing their reactions to particular kinds of industrial or political institutions; and I jumped quickly out of old categories into fresh lines of enquiry. The two together had a wide acquaintance with men and women of all grades of poverty and affluence—of varied occupation and professions. Sidney had graduated as a civil servant through three government departments—the War Office, the Inland Revenue and the Colonial Office. As successful journalist, lecturer and pamphleteer, he was acquainted with the newspaper world, with the Radical caucus of the metropolis and provincial towns, and he was intimate with many of the rising intellectuals of his own generation. A few months before our marriage, he had become one of the leaders of the Progressive Party then dominating the London County Council. Born and bred in the world of the big business of two continents, I had, as a young girl, dashed about the outer ring of London "society", spent week-ends at the country houses of bankers and brewers and, more rarely, in the homes of county magnates. In these delectable places, I had associated with men of science and distinguished ecclesiastics; with Cabinet Ministers and leading lawyers; with "society" dames and university dons. For the six years prior to our marriage, I had devoted my free time to getting an inside knowledge of the homes and work-places of representative groups of manual workers; as rent collector and "would be" sweated worker in the slums of East London, as collaborator in Charles Booth's [1] great enquiry into the *Life and Labour of the People,* as a welcome visitor in the homes of my cousins among the Lancashire cotton operatives; [2] and, most important of all, through friendly intercourse with the leaders of the co-operative and trade union movements.

There were, I must admit, disabling gaps in our knowledge of Victorian England. We ignored and were ignored by fashionable "society"—not to mention "the smart set".

---

[1] See *My Apprenticeship,* chapters v and vi.   [2] See *ibid.* pp. 152-71.

Our minds were blank about the professionals and the multitudinous amateurs of high and low degree, of sport, games and racing. Few and far between were the diplomatists who sought us out; and foreign affairs, generally speaking, were a closed book to us. And alas! owing to our concentration on research, municipal administration and Fabian propaganda, we had neither the time nor the energy, nor yet the means, to listen to music and the drama, to brood over classic literature, ancient and modern, to visit picture galleries, or to view with an informed intelligence the wonders of architecture. Such dim inklings as we had of these great human achievements reached us second-hand through our friendship with Bernard Shaw. Our only vision of the beautiful arose during our holiday wanderings, at home and overseas, sometimes walking, sometimes cycling, by river and forest path, over plain and mountain, in mist, cloud and sunshine.

Thus, we started Our Partnership with an agreeable independence of the world's opinion and delicious dependence on each other. From an old woman likely to know, an ingenuous youth enquired: " After love-making and sufficient income, what's necessary for a happy marriage? " " Identity of taste in seemingly unimportant matters," I rapped out somewhat heedlessly, " such as, open or closed windows, regular or irregular hours, simple or elaborate meals, spells of silent fellowship or continuous talk about nothing in particular." Then, after reflection: " Unity of temperament on the one vital issue, self-expression or self-control. Is the way of life to be governed by the impulse of the moment for or against particular persons or places, occupation or amusements; or is it to be determined according to an agreed plan adhered to by both parties, irrespective of momentary likes or dislikes? " " Oh! " retorted the youth, " the old quarrel of reason *versus* emotion? " " Not at all," I answered; " patterns of behaviour, codes of conduct, general plans, whether for ten years or a lifetime, arise, so far as I know, from unreasoning, though not necessary *unreasonable*, emotion. Is not a general plan of conduct inspired and dominated by emotion the epicentre of all religions? However that may be, living according to plan is a surer basis for happy marriage than the perpetual shifting desire for self-expression. The impulse of the moment, noble or ignoble, aesthetic or philistine, is apt to differ every time, and all the time, from individual to individual. Living according to a deliberately thought-out plan, however tiresome and thwarting it may occasionally be, is an automatic aid to continuous comradeship."

Now a plan of life involved in our view not merely a deliberately designed method or style of living, but also an object to be sought, and as far as possible attained, as the result of our living. This is what is sometimes called a philosophy of life. Fundamentally, we agreed about this, though minute introspection might discover from time to time some variation of emphasis, and even differences of outlook. From many of the common ends of life we were saved by circumstances. Our income sufficed for our needs; and we felt none of the usual temptations to increase our joint little fortune, and (as we realised) thus become entangled in the trammels and trappings of wealth. The fact that our marriage proved to be childless made easy what other people sometimes called our " financial disinterestedness ". We had no objection to receiving payment for articles or lectures when it was offered to us; and we welcomed, as enabling us to engage additional assistance, the few hundreds a year which, as time went on, accrued from the sale of our solid but unreadable books. Indeed, we sometimes sought payment when it did not hinder our work or prevent us from saying what we liked, especially at times when the expenses of our investigations threatened to exceed our current account. We even scrupled sometimes at " spoiling the market " for others whose livelihood depended on writing or lecturing. We enjoyed our work quite as much when it brought no cheque as when we peddled fragments for payment; for it was not only our vocation willingly rendered in return for our unearned income, but served also as our daily sport—the particular game of life we preferred to play. It remains to be added that Our Partnership was an indissoluble combination of two strong and persistent aims. We were, both of us, scientists and at the same time Socialists. We had a perpetual curiosity to know all that could be known about the nature and working of the universe, animate as well as inanimate, psychical as well as material, in the belief that only by means of such knowledge could mankind achieve an ever-increasing control of the forces amid which it lived. We were, both of us, secularists, in the sense that we failed to find in the universe anything that was supernatural, or incapable of demonstration by the scientific method of observation, hypothetical generalisation and experimental or other form of verification. Like other scientists, we were obsessed by scientific curiosity about the universe and its working. But, unlike the astronomers and the physicists, the chemists and the biologists, we turned our curiosity to the phenomena that were being less frequently investigated, namely, those connected with the social institutions characteristic of *homo sapiens*, or what is called sociology. We accordingly devoted ourselves as scientists to the study of social institutions, from trade unions to Cabinets, from family relationships to churches, from economics to literature—a field in itself so extensive that we have never been able to compass more than a few selected fragments of it.

At the same time, we were active citizens; and, as such, we had to have a practical policy of public life. Our growing knowledge of social institutions led us to a policy of transforming the organisation of wealth production and distribution, from its basis of anarchic individual profit-making to one of regulated social service. That is to say, our action as electors, administrators and propagandists was that of Socialists, instead of that of Liberals or Conservatives. Looking back on half-a-century of scientific investigation and public activity, it seems to us in retrospect that every discovery in sociology and, indeed, every increase in our own knowledge of social institutions has strengthened our faith that the further advance of human society is dependent on a considerably further substitution of institutions based on public service for those based on profit-making. We have, accordingly, had the enjoyment of harmony between the two halves of our lives, between our scientific studies and our practical citizenship. At the same time, it must be admitted that our reputation or notoriety as Socialists has more than once aroused obstruction or hostility to our efforts, whether as individual investigators, or as promoters of adequately equipped sociological research, as an essential condition for the progress of mankind to ever higher levels of individual distinction and communal welfare.

At this point some readers may question whether it is desirable to combine scientific research into social institutions with active participation in their operation. Is the professional administrator or legislator made more efficient or less efficient as such by being also a practised observer, reasoner and verifier in the domain in which he is temporarily an actor? Conversely, is the scientific investigator, concerned essentially to discover the truth about the working or development of a particular type of economic or political organisation, rendered more likely or less likely to arrive at verifiable conclusions because he finds himself temporarily " behind the scenes ", or at the very centre of the current activities of the social institution in question, by his membership of the elected authority, or his appointment to its executive staff? I am disposed to think that there is something to be said on each side of the question. But I suggest that, if the human unit in the case is not a single individual but an intimate and durable partnership, the balance is wholly in favour of the combination of purposes. If one partner is predominantly and continuously the scientific investigator, with only slight and occasional participation in active life, whilst the other partner is more continuously entangled in administration or legislation, with only secondary and intermittent personal work in investigation or research, their incessant intimate discussions may well increase the efficiency and augment the yield of both sides of each other's intellectual activities. I believe that, from time to time, we had evidence of this happy result in Our Partnership. In the earlier years, when I was almost wholly engaged in studying the records and the working of trade unionism, the Other One, whilst intermittently sharing in different parts of England in this absorbing quest, was chairman of the Technical Education Board, and (as described in a following chapter) was mainly engaged, during three-quarters of each of six successive years, in laying the foundations of a unified educational system for the whole of London, and watching very closely the reactions upon schemes of vocational training of all the trade unions of the metropolis. Our duality was, in this instance, of reciprocal advantage. In another instance, about quite a different social institution, the Royal Commission or Select Committee, our experience yields a similar result. Both partners devoted much time and thought to the voluminous records and published criticisms of a whole century of these bodies, of various types and diverse compositions. But we never got a satisfactory hold on the conditions and the expedients that determined success, or failure, in each of the hundred or more specimens that we studied, until we both had enjoyed brief and intermittent experiences of actual membership of these bodies—membership in which the knowledge gained from investigation of the past was joined with incessant watchfulness of the happenings in which we were taking part. This was markedly seen when, from 1905 to 1910, I was a member of the Royal Commission on the Poor Law and the Relief of Distress from Unemployment; and the Other One was free for incessant consultation and enquiry outside.

TRADE UNION ENQUIRY

For the first six years of our married life—the part covered by this and the following chapter—our energies ran in three channels. There was the enquiry into the British trade union movement and the publication of *The History of Trade Unionism* in 1894, and *Industrial Democracy* in 1898; there was Sidney's administrative work on the London County Council and the establishment and chairmanship of the Technical Education Board; and, towards the end of the time, there was the initiation of the London School of Economics and Political Science. Finally, always and everywhere, there was propaganda of Fabian collectivism. In the following pages I describe the first of these activities, our researches into the constitution and working of British trade unionism and our consequent association with trade union officials and representatives, as these experiences were reflected in the pages of my MS. diary supplemented by our joint memories.

And here I must revert to my unmarried days a few months before I met the Other One. In *My Apprenticeship*, I have described how my investigations into the sweated industries of East London had convinced me that if the capitalist system was not to lead to " earnings barely sufficient to sustain existence; hours of labour such as to make the lives of the workers periods of almost ceaseless toil, hard and unlovely to the last degree; sanitary conditions injurious to the health of the persons employed and dangerous to the public "—to quote the words of the House of Lords Committee on Sweating in 1889–90—capitalist enterprise had to be controlled, not exceptionally or spasmodically, but universally, so as to secure to every worker prescribed minimum conditions of employment. Even in the co-operative movement, which had been started by working-men in the interests of the producers, but had developed into a consumers' organisation bent on getting the best quality for the lowest price, some such control was clearly necessary. This control was, in organised industries, such as cotton and mining and, to a lesser extent, engineering and shipbuilding, already operative, either through the specific device of trade unionism—collective bargaining—or by the legislative enactment secured by the pressure of the trade unions and their advisers and sympathisers. But, brought up as I had been, in a stronghold of capitalism, under the tutelage of the great apostle of *laisser-faire*, Herbert Spencer,[1] I was

---

[1] Herbert Spencer (1820–1903), " the household saint and philosopher of the hearth " of Beatrice's youth. An uncompromising individualist, he cancelled her appointment as his literary executor on the announcement of her marriage to a Socialist. See Biographical Index. (Ed.)

fully aware of the various objections to trade unionism: how it prevented, or at least hindered, the introduction of new inventions and the better organisation of the workshop; how it had fomented strikes and compelled employers to resort to lock-outs; how it had restricted output, either by rule or indirectly by limiting the number of apprentices; and how it had thus checked the mobility of labour from place to place and industry to industry, and damaged Great Britain's capacity to compete in the markets of the world. And it so happened that, at the very time I was meditating on the virtues and vices of trade unionism, there broke out the great London Dock Strike of 1889, which, for the first time, united in one solid phalanx the thousands of casual labourers I had watched, day after day, at the gates of the dock companies, and in the tenement houses of East London. Moreover, this movement had secured an unusual amount of public sympathy among all classes of the community and financial support from the manual workers as far off as Australia. Hence it was not surprising that I used up a fortnight in August 1889 in attending the Trades Union Congress at Dundee, a Congress at which there was a battle royal between the " Old Unionists " and the " New ".[1]

Dundee, August 1889.—This morning, while I was breakfasting, Shipton—the chairman of the parliamentary committee of the Trades Union Congress, and secretary of the London Trades Council— joined me. His view of the Dock Strike is strongly adverse to the men; he is visibly biassed by his antipathy to, I might almost say hatred of, Burns. Ben Tillett is, he says, an enthusiast who, however, has " made a good thing " out of his enthusiasm. The way the strike was started, he told me, was illegitimate. No responsible official of a trade union which had funds of its own to lose, would treat employers in that fashion. Ben Tillett drew up a letter demanding certain concessions and sent it with a letter announcing that, if these demands were not con-

---

[1] " The leaders of the New Unionists (1884–89) . . . sought to bring into the ranks of existing organisations—the trade unions, the Municipality, or the State— such masses of unorganised workers who had hitherto been entirely outside the pale, or inert elements within it. They aimed, not at superseding existing structures, but at capturing them all in the interests of the wage-earners. Above all, they sought to teach such masses of undisciplined workers how to apply their newly acquired political power so as to obtain in a perfectly constitutional manner, whatever changes in legislation or administration they desired."—*History of Trade Unionism*, by S. and B. Webb, p. 404. (Ed.)

ceded by 12 o'clock that morning, the men would come out. " Just fancy," he added, " expecting a manager to decide a question of enormous financial importance without consulting his directors! " Then Burns came on the scene with his intense desire for notoriety and his foreign ideas of the solidarity of labour which he is trying to foist on British trade unionists. But it won't work. Each trade has its own interests and technicalities; and all organisation, to be permanently successful, must be based on the appreciation of these interests and on a knowledge of the facts of the special trade concerned. " Look how the ' Knights of Labour ' [1] have failed (in the United States)—that sort of thing is bound to break up in the end. The capitalist has only to sit still with folded hands. If the dock companies stand out—if they are able to resist the other capitalist interests which are using the strike to get their own way—if they are able to resist this pressure the whole organisation will break down and the workers will dribble back."

So spoke Shipton. Clearly, whatever may be his sympathy for dock labour, his dislike of a Socialist victory was the stronger feeling. . . .

Shipton is not an attractive man. Small, with a weasel-like body and uncertain manner, and an uneasy contorted expression; grey eyes without candour or freshness, and with that curious film over them which usually denotes an " irregular " life; deep furrows under the eyes and round the mouth; bald-headed with a black beard neatly trimmed; a general attempt at middle-class smartness completes the outward man. An ambitious disappointed man, a certain feeling of uncertainty as to his own position. Ability, divided aims, are the characteristics which seem most marked to the observer. I should imagine that in his heart of hearts he has little sympathy with the working-man, that he prizes his position as an official because of the power it brings. . . .

Tuesday. Dundee, Sept. 1889.—A battle royal at Congress between the supporters of Broadhurst and old-fashioned methods, on the one hand, and the Socialists led by Burns and Mrs. Besant, on the other. These two leaders, however, were absent: the Socialist Party was led by two somewhat foolish young men, delegates of the London compositors, and suffered in consequence. The battle raged round the personal abuse of Broadhurst. The Socialists have apparently spent the last year in spreading calumny of all sorts, besides trying to persuade the rank and file that Broadhurst is a reactionary. But I think they have

---

[1] Though trade unionism was legalised in the U.S.A. in 1845, the " Knights of Labour " were founded in 1869 as a secret organisation " to secure and maintain the rights of working-men against their employers ". They organised a general strike of colliers and railwaymen in 1887, involving some 50,000 strikers, but the strike collapsed before the end of the year. (Ed.)

carried it too far. Among English working-men of the better type there is a rooted dislike to desert old leaders; an intense suspicion of the mere talker who has not proved his faculty for steady work. Then the Socialist at present labours under the disadvantage of relying on outside money and outside brains. " Why should I be dictated to by an ex-artillery officer? (Champion) " was one of Broadhurst's most effective points. Trade unionists are jealous of interference and are intensely exclusive. (" Why are you here," I am frequently asked, " come with mischief in your pocket, to plot and plan? ")

So the whole Congress set its back up; the Socialists dwindled down to eleven while Broadhurst's supporters numbered 177. A brilliant victory for the conservative section—conservative, not in politics but in the methods and aims of their own organisation.

With Broadhurst I lunched afterwards, and smoked a cigarette. His suspicions of my intentions were completely dissipated when he heard I was an anti-suffrage woman: he immediately thought me sensible and sound. " When I hear a woman's name talked of I am immediately prejudiced against her; but I can see that you are as different as pitch from diamonds! " So he chatted on about societies, trade unionism, and his own complaints and showed every sign of becoming confidential. A commonplace person: hard-working no doubt, but a middle-class philistine to the back-bone: appealing to the practical shrewdness and high-flown, but mediocre, sentiments of the comfortably-off working-man. His view of women is typical of his other views: he lives in platitudes and commonplaces.

In spite of the prejudices and exclusiveness of the leading trade unionists, the frank fellowship, the absence of personal animus and personal rivalry, the general loyalty to leaders and appreciation of real work, as distinguished from talk, are refreshing. Then, among the veterans, the officials of the largest, oldest and most influential unions, there is a knowledge of facts, and realisation of industrial problems, an appreciation of commercial and financial matters, which makes one feel hopeful of the capacity for self-government in the working-class. Very different from the Socialist leaders, with the dirty personalities with which they pelt each other; with their envy and malice against any leader, and with their ignorance, one might almost say their contempt and hatred of facts. A crew of wrecked reputations, politicians on the make, and paid intriguers from the Tory caucus, interspersed, it is true, with beardless enthusiasts of all sorts and conditions, and redeemed by a John Burns, who seems to be a man with a conscience and a will. But is he not departing from the Socialist camp?

Another scene. Breakfast table. On my right Broadhurst, beaming over his ham and eggs and the delightful memories of yesterday's triumph over his enemies. " Yes, we are now going to take our stand against the intrusion of strangers into our body on false pretences. They blame us for being exclusive; they have made us ten times more exclusive. We have cleared the platform of outsiders, we will now clear the press table from intriguers."

All this muttered loud enough for my neighbour on the left to hear. Cunninghame Graham is pouring over the *Labour Elector*. (Cunninghame Graham is a cross between an aristocrat and a barber's block. He is a *poseur*, but also an enthusiast, an unmitigated fool in politics, I think.) " I have a letter from Kropotkin," Cunninghame Graham whispers to me; " he says, and I agree with him, if Burns with 80,000 men behind him does not make a revolution, it is because he is afraid of having his head cut off. Burns is a grand fellow tho', different from these miserable slaves of bourgeois trade unionists," he adds, with a wave of his hand towards Broadhurst, a wave of the hand which gradually settles down upon a loaf of brown bread which C. G. believes to be common property, but which, unfortunately, happens to be specially prepared for her great man's over-taxed digestion by Mrs. Broadhurst. The bourgeois slave watches with indignation the delicately tapering fingers of the anarchist clutch hold of his personal property, and with a large perspiring palm of the outstretched hand grasps the whole thing in his fingers. " No, no, Sir, not that," he roars; " this is my *own* bread, made by my *own* wife, in my *own* house, and carried here in my *own* portmanteau, that you cannot have." Cunninghame Graham withdraws with the apologies of a gentleman. " Not my bread; I'd rather he destroyed my reputation than took my bread," roared the dyspeptic but somewhat gluttonous Broadhurst. Cunninghame Graham looks unutterably disgusted, and wipes his aristocratic hand with soft cambric. . . .

Other scenes in the private smoking-room of the leading trade unionists, to which I was introduced by Broadhurst's favour. Not altogether a nice atmosphere; with a good deal of lobbying apparent in the background, resulting in the return of the old parliamentary committee with only one change. " Dirty work," said Burnett,[1] with a look of unutterable contempt in his clear grey eyes, " the sailor [2] brought twenty votes, practically exchanging them for a seat on the committee. Too much of that sort of thing."

Altogether the later scenes of the Congress did not impress me so favourably as the opening days, when only loyalty to the old leaders was apparent. The trade unionists are a fine body of men; but they

[1] John Burnett, former secretary of the Amalgamated Society of Engineers and afterwards Labour correspondent of the Board of Trade.
[2] Havelock Wilson, organiser of the National Sailors' and Firemen's Union.

are lacking in the naïve enthusiasm and open-hearted cordiality of the co-operators. They are officials, and officials who live by manipulating their constituents; they have the vices of officials combined with those of popular representatives. The majority of them are aiming at the dignity of the J.P., or the more solid preferment of the factory inspectorship. . . . The upshot of the Congress was the rehabilitation of Broadhurst and the old gang and the discomfiture of the Socialist outsiders. There are signs that the victorious leaders, warned by the Socialist attack, will try to tighten their hold by placing the Congress on a more representative basis with regard to members and payment. At present, every delegate has one vote; and a union may send any number of delegates irrespective of their membership and contribution. This gives undue influence to mushroom unions which may be created in order to swamp solid trade union organisations. On the other hand, if membership were duly represented, the great conservative unions of Lancashire would exclude from all power the new blood. The officials of these old standing unions have become intimately connected with the employers. Many of them are J.P.'s and most of them Conservative in politics. They believe in arbitration and conciliation and in dealing with each trade separately. All action is to be based on technical knowledge of the special trade. They are fully alive to foreign competition, and even versed in all the intricacies of the currency question. With them trade unionism is rapidly assuming the form of a union of all the producers in one trade against the outside world. The differences between the two great classes of producers, capitalist brain-workers, on the one hand, and on the other, manual wage-earners, are to be settled by experts from both sides. Mere ideas, such as the solidarity of labour, are to them absurd. " We lived through all that," said Birtwistle (the veteran leader of the cotton weavers); " they imagine themselves the advance guard, they are really the babies of trade unionism."

Thus, one of the cleavage lines in the Congress between the old and the new school was the question of sending representatives to foreign and international congresses. The younger school maintains that the very difficulty of foreign competition would be solved by the solidarity of labour; and that the fossil trade unions are diverted from vigorous action by the mere pedantry of technical knowledge of the " ins and outs " of one tiny specimen of industry.

The eight-hours question was fought on these lines and the specialists won by a fair majority.

The following two years were spent in nursing my father; using any free time in attending Co-operative Conferences and touring Co-operative Societies. Meanwhile, we had entered into an early phase of Our Partnership. As described in *My Apprenticeship*, we met for the first time in January 1890, and at Whitsun of that year we found ourselves together at the Glasgow Co-operative Congress. A telegram from a leading weekly, asking me to contribute a signed article on Lord Rosebery's presidential address, ended in Sidney helping me to write it. The joint article proved too long; the " editor " cut my stuff out and put his stuff in: consequence—mingled annoyance and pleasure! " I had no idea that Beatrice was such an accomplished journalist," observed one brother-in-law to another; " is she going to take to it as a profession? " At the Lincoln Co-operative Congress of 1891, we were privately pledged to marriage; and the following August holiday finds me caretaking Herbert Spencer's house in St. John's Wood (the philosopher being away in the country), a convenient meeting-place with a civil servant care-taking the British Empire from Whitehall!

St. John's Wood, August 14th, 1891.—A succession of trade unionists to dine here [I record in my diary]. Poor Herbert Spencer to think that his august dining-room is nightly the scene of Socialist talk, clouds of tobacco smoke aided with whiskey. Maxwell, Broadhurst's secretary, the shrewdest of mortals, who is friendly to me in the extreme, and anxious to help; but a cynic: the trade union world, according to him, is by no means lovely—more intriguing, it seems, than the co-operative world.

" I do not believe that there was a single secretary of a trade union that did not write to the governor (Broadhurst) to ask for an appointment as factory inspector " (Broadhurst had been Under-Secretary for the Home Office in 1885). By the way, the whole influence of the Home Office has been thrown against appointing working-men as factory inspectors. " You have no idea—working-men will do anything or give anything in order to be free of manual labour. There is no effort they won't make, no meanness they won't stoop to, to turn themselves into 'office men'. It is feeling conscious of this that makes them so suspicious of each other's effort."

He is fat and good-natured, with a detached intellect; never gives you his views, except about persons, and then he has humour and a sharp stinging tongue. He works for Broadhurst night and day; for very little pay, but with an apparent devotion; his motive is a riddle; he is unmarried, with no apparent convictions except a general scepticism of things divine and human.

I shall have some trouble to get my information. Most of the trade union officials are hard-headed, suspicious men, with an anti-feminist bias. Moreover, where they themselves are friendly, there is often on their part a dread of their assistant secretary. The latter is usually himself elected by the members as a sort of check on the general secretary. If you have one for you, you usually have the other against you. But we shall see. . . .

September 15th, 1891.— . . . And for Sidney [I note a few weeks later on, when I am again in attendance on my father, studying the material I had gathered], this enquiry will be of untold use. The politician of the future must understand all the details of industrial life; he must be, before all things, a practical economist. For economics in the widest sense are rapidly becoming the technical side of the politician's work. Also, he is learning through this wider intercourse with facts and men, a more proportionate sense and a wider judgement than was possible to a London civil servant. Thus, from a strictly personal point of view, an acquaintance with the leaders of working-class organisation throughout the country will be a highly-desirable connection, not to be despised. So that, in helping me, he does not feel, nor am I conscious, that this work is my particular concern. . . .

On New Year's Day, 1892, my father died and in a week's time our engagement was communicated to my family and friends.[1] But we were in no hurry to get married. Sidney had

---

[1] Here are three entries from the MS. diary of my sister, Kate Courtney, January 1892. The first from a description of her eight sisters, written whilst staying with me for my father's funeral; the other two a few days after hearing of my engagement to S. W.

". . . Beatrice—handsome and slightly Jewish-looking with a very intellectual face—gives herself up to investigating social questions—has written a book on Co-operation, is writing a larger one on trade unions—is in close alliance and friendship with the Fabian Socialists—particularly one of them—a great friend of Mrs. J. R. Green—she is much admired by many people though some of the family shake their heads a little over her emancipated ways and advanced views,—but with half admiration also. Father's death frees her to follow her own career without a tie of any sort. . . ."

". . . A letter comes from Beatrice, which is a great surprise to me and not at first quite a welcome one! She announces her engagement to Sidney Webb—the Fabian Socialist leader. The day before, in answer to a note from the *Pall Mall*, I had absolutely contradicted the rumour, supposing I should certainly have heard something if it were true. But Bee judged, rightly I think, that father's funeral should pass off without this new excitement. . . . On the Sunday night, Bee brought S. Webb to dinner and the A. Cripps came also. I had never seen him, but

resigned from the Civil Service and was busy writing the literature for, and helping to organise the victory of, the Progressives at the London County Council election of March 1892, at which he won by a large majority the Deptford seat from the Tories. Anxious to complete the enquiry into Lancashire and Yorkshire trade unions, I settled down in a lodging in Manchester and was immediately elected an honorary member of the club of trade union officials which met every Thursday in a Deansgate public-house. Aided by our newly engaged secretary, F. W. Galton, who was not only a bright and attractive youth but also the secretary of the trade union of highly-skilled silver crest engravers, I started out to attend trade union meetings whilst superintending Galton's work on trade union documents.

Manchester, February 11th, 1892.—Exactly three weeks since I set my foot in Manchester. Have been working hard; looking through minute books, interviewing and attending business meetings of trade unions. It was stupid of me not to think of this idea before. One learns so much more by observing men at their work, than by simply reading reports, etc. But it never struck me that I could get into the private executive meetings of societies and see for myself the sort of questions that arise. But, at present, it is difficult to see the wood for the trees; I am groping about, catching on first to one trunk and then to another; trying to follow the lines of growth of the branches, and the lie of the roots; and getting sadly mixed up in my ideas. But I am working hard and well. My engagement to S. W. has not injured me in the least; except, perhaps, with Birtwistle. . . .

There were, however, days of relaxation in the midst of all this drudgery, and I give two entries:

Manchester, February 28th, 1892.— . . . Two days utter exhaustion. Last Sunday was delightful; I need him once a week to rest me in the sublime restfulness of love, and he needs me to soothe him and

only heard various accounts not at all flattering. He was quiet, perhaps shy—but he looks strong and able though not much of a figure of a man, and I hope we may like him. Beatrice seems quietly happy and confident of the future, and she has a softness of expression and manner which looks as if her feelings were engaged."

" *Tuesday 19th.*—We met him again at Theresa's [Cripps] with Daniel [Meinertzhagen], W. Cripps, and Lallie [Holt], who was in great form in her most genial mood. Yes I *think* we may like this new brother-in-law whom we certainly should not have chosen. . . ."

reduce his world of cross-purposes to its proper calm. But alas! Our work keeps us apart. . . .

May 4th, 1892.— . . . Severe attack of influenza broke into my work; a fortnight in bed, just at the time of his triumphant return to the County Council, but the last week he was with me and we both went on to Liverpool. There I rested in the luxurious Holt mansion [my sister's, Mrs. Robert D. Holt] for a week and then back again to work. I found Galton working on the piles of material I had left. A good deal of his work had to be re-done, and the ensuing two weeks I spent in training him, he working all day under my eye. A sharp, attractive boy and assiduous worker, and as keen as a razor; a former pupil of Sidney's in economics. But all my appointments to attend [trade union] executive meetings had to be given up: a grievous disappointment to me.

Then a fortnight's holiday. . . . We spent four days at Arundel with Graham Wallas and the light-hearted Bernard Shaw, and then back again to our cosy lodging. Here for ten days: it seemed two. We have been working hard—shaping together the material into a rough history—and then he working at the reference library, whilst I casually interviewed trade unionists and superintended Galton. To-day, he left me and I feel a bit lonesome. . . . We are certainly supremely fortunate. We love each other devotedly; we are intensely interested in the same work; we have freedom and means to devote our whole lives to the work we believe in. Never did I imagine such happiness open to me. . . .

The last six weeks of solitary unmarried life were spent in Leeds attending the delegates' meeting of the Amalgamated Society of Engineers to revise their rules; to which I had been admitted by special resolution.

July 2nd, 1892.—The delegates sat (68 of them) for six hours a day. This delegate meeting will be a crisis in the history of the A.S.E. For some time past, under the guidance of a weak secretary, there has been trouble within and without. The spirit and aspirations of the New Unionism have infected even this conservative and aristocratic body which, until a few years ago, has been little better than a great benefit society. Not that the A.S.E. has not fought its battles. The nine hours' movement of 1872 was the beginning of a great revival of trade unionism and was initiated by the A.S.E. But, except for one or two pitched battles at long intervals, the even tenour of benevolent claims has been uninterrupted. The A.S.E. has appeared to its members, scattered about—some in remote country districts—simply as one more great friendly institution for mutual help in common needs. . . .

The scene has changed in the last two years. The two foremost figures in the Labour world, Tom Mann and John Burns, both happen to be members of the A.S.E. Though they won their reputation in organising unskilled workers, and in the political propaganda of the Socialist movement, their fellow-members have become proud of them and have been greatly influenced by their powerful cry of " Forward! " . . .

In the more populous districts, and especially on the North East Coast, the A.S.E. have been stimulated to strike for new privileges. This has led to serious friction between the local district authorities, with a definite trade policy, and the central and unrepresentative executive in London, fitted by its constitution only to administer a friendly society. No guidance and no control, yet irritating repudiations or dilatory acceptance of the already acted on decisions of the local district committees. The London council has, in fact, fallen into universal disrepute; and to make confusion worse confounded, the elaborate complicated local organisations, branches, local district committees, central district committees, grand committees, and joint committees, have thrown up a mass of divergent views for different and overlapping areas. Hence, the public discredit of the A.S.E. and the dissatisfaction and discord among its members.

The recent disasters on the North East Coast have ripened discontent into a determination to change the constitution of the Society fundamentally. Last year, the members voted, by a large majority, for a delegate meeting (the last one was in 1885), and for the past six months committees of revision have been sitting in all the centres of the engineering industry. The result is a " book of suggestions ", 258 pages of closely printed amendments to the present rules: emanating from all parts of the U.K., and even from America and Australia. The delegates are confined to these suggestions: they cannot propose an amendment which does not appear in the book. I listened to a six hours' debate on the subject (a proposal to create a permanent salaried executive committee, which was carried). One of the most level-headed discussions I have ever heard.

I omit the greater part of my report of the discussion on most of these suggestions, which lasted for some weeks.

There are half-a-dozen delegates who are quite admirable debaters: clear, forcible, concise. The language and arrangement of some of the subjects are quite excellent and I longed to see some of the speakers in Parliament. There is no limitation of time; but this freedom to prose and rant has not been abused and I listened for six hours with no sense of boredom or impatience.

The Conference is more or less divided up into sections or caucuses, pledged to a particular programme or reform—though, on the whole, there is a *bona fide* discussion of all the proposals. London and the North East Coast are found to stand for efficiency and inclusion; Manchester and Lancashire delegates represent a solid conservative reactionary vote and have opposed, tooth and nail, any radical change. Scotland would follow suit if it were not for a certain " home rule " tendency. Belfast is ultra Tory and has but one principle to promote—restriction of output in methods of work and exclusiveness in membership. The Midland delegates and the Yorkshire scatter their votes indiscriminately for and against progressive proposals. But, undoubtedly, the most level-headed as well as the ablest speakers are Socialists: for instance, Evans (Brighton); Sellicks (Woolwich); Barnes (Chelsea); Fletcher (Newcastle); Halston (Gateshead). This is altogether an agreeable surprise to me. Hitherto, my experience has been that the more feather-headed workmen are Socialists. But then Socialism is rapidly changing in character; it is losing its revolutionary and class-bitter character, and becoming constitutional effort based on hope and not on hatred. The Manchester men, and the Scotch and Irish, are for the most part individualists; but, with the exception of Fergusson of Glasgow who is a canny Scotsman, they have no remarkable men among them; though they exhibit a certain shrewd caution, they are narrow-minded and illiberal. In fact, they are not good examples of their creed. Whether this is chance, or whether it signifies a general conversion of the more generous-hearted and intellectual workmen to Socialist economics, is a moot question. Such Socialism as there is, is of a decided Fabian type; and one realises that the facts and figures and general arguments are taken from Fabian literature.

Some pleasant evenings I have had chatting with selected delegates. Yesterday evening I had a North East Coast man, an enthusiastic supporter of Sidney's possible candidature for the Gateshead vacancy when it occurs.

Altogether it has been a most fortunate coincidence—this A.S.E. delegate meeting and my visit to Leeds. Galton drudges away in the board room of the Co-operators (we always secure an office out of the Co-operators) at the minutes, etc., of local societies. He works very hard but he needs more training. Sidney is indulgent and flattering in manner, I have to be critical. . . .

The next entry is emphatic, and written in large letters:

Exit Beatrice Potter, July 23rd, 1892.
Enter Beatrice Webb, or rather Mrs. Sidney Webb, for I lose alas! both names.

Sidney Webb
(*Ætat circa 32*)

It certainly never occurred to me that, near forty years after-wards, I should be again asked to change my name and its prefix—and by the same man! [1] The answer has been in the negative, with the approval of the Other One.

The honeymoon was spent investigating on the spot the ramshackle trade societies of Dublin: nineteenth-century combinations of Catholic artisans, claiming direct descent from the exclusively Protestant guilds established in the seventeenth century by Royal Charter for the express purpose of preventing Papists gaining an honest livelihood. One of the societies, the Dublin Bricklayers' Society, paraded the old parchment charter, bereft of its seal, and apparently handed over by the lawyer's clerk to the society when the ancient companies were dissolved in 1843. Thence to Belfast, interviewing hard-fisted employers and groups of closely organised skilled craftsmen; many of them Scotch, veracious and cautious in their statements about their own conditions of employment, and contemptuous and indifferent to the Catholic labourers and women who were earning miserable wages in the shipyards and linen factories of Belfast.

The honeymoon holiday ended at Glasgow, attending the Trades Union Congress, collecting trade union documents and interviewing trade union secretaries.

August 1892.—Ugly certainly are the banks of the Clyde [I enter in my diary], and very hideous are the results of enormous earnings by certain sections of men, brutalised by want in bad times, and long hours of working during the spells of prosperity. The Clyde is the home of piece-work and contract work, of poverty, drunkenness, stupidity and competition. It is the paradise of the able, pushing man, who rises out of the slums to own a deer forest. . . .

This time the Congress meant eight hours and no mistake [I enter later on]; a large majority of delegates were pledged to it owing to change of front of the cotton operatives. . . .

The sting of the New Unionist movement has been effectively drawn out by the adhesion of the cotton officials to the eight-hour day; on all other points, stalwart Old Unionists. The fact that the

---

[1] When in 1929 Sidney was created Baron Passfield, Beatrice flatly refused to change her name and remained Mrs. Sidney Webb. (Ed.)

cotton unionists have always been legalists was overlooked. The labourers' unions too, are rapidly shrinking up with bad trade; while the Socialists, instead of being scurrilous and aggressive, are (under the influence of Fabianism) pursuing the policy of permeation—most successfully, I think. At the first Congress I attended, Dundee, only three years ago, Broadhurst reigned supreme, and the Socialists were at daggers drawn with all the Old Unionists, resorting to what Champion, with apparent approval, used to call " political assassination ", that is the destruction of personal reputation by slandering. Now Sidney hobnobs with all the older men, and we are as friendly with Mawdsley as with Tillett. The last bit of permeation—rather a joke—Mawdsley the Tory individualist, having been invited to address the Church Congress, begs us for hints. A Socialist discourse is promptly supplied him: it remains to be seen whether he accepts it.

The hopeful side of the Labour movement seems to me a growing collectivism of the Miners' Federation and the Cotton Unions. Here, at last, we are on solid ground and among men who, if they take a thing up, do it with the intention and capacity to carry it through.

Exactly four weeks at Glasgow—the last ten days a rush of work—Sidney working the whole day on documents except the hours he spends trudging out to the far-off suburbs to interview trade union secretaries. Out of the four weeks we have had two holidays—a Sunday on Loch Awe with Auberon Herbert,[1] and a week-end visit to R. B. Haldane.

Memory recalls the tall figure [of Auberon Herbert], wrapped in an old shawl, with vague blue eyes, soft high voice, flowing white beard—the Don Quixote of the nineteenth century, waving one hand at us, while pushing his sailing boat away from the shore; giving us his final blessing: " You will do a lot of mischief and be very happy in doing it."

But to resume the diary :

August 1892.—Sunday with Haldane was more remunerative. He is now an influential man: willing to stand in the background, to counsel the Ministers and act as go-between [I remind the reader that, in July 1892, the Liberal Party had taken office with a narrow majority]. Talked incessantly about the possibilities of reorganising the Home Office as the Ministry of Labour; perfecting the factory department. Ended in pressing us to write a memorandum for Asquith

[1] The Hon. Auberon Herbert: see *My Apprenticeship*, pp. 187, 188, 189, 190, 219, 322, 396.

(a request since repeated by Asquith). Wrote it the other day, but stress of work made us keep it over till Edinburgh. Haldane not hopeful of the future—" constituencies not converted to collectivism—at least not in Scotland ". Sunday afternoon a fair bevy of " Souls " [1] came over to tea. Haldane prides himself on hovering between the fashionable paradise represented by the " Souls " and the collectivist state represented by the Fabians. " Souls " good to look at; gushing and anxious to strike up acquaintanceship with an unconventional couple. A charming pair—the Alfred Lytteltons—graceful, modest, intelligent, and with the exquisite deference and ease which constitutes good breeding. But to me the " Souls " would not bring " the peace that passeth understanding ", but a vain restlessness of tickled vanity. One would become quickly satiated.

I leave Glasgow with no regrets. The working-men leaders here are an uninteresting lot; without enthusiasm or much intelligence. The Scotch nature does not lend itself to combination; the strong men seek to rise and push for themselves and not to serve others. And apparently the Co-operators have absorbed the finer intelligence and warmer hearts among the Scotch working-men of the official cast.

41 GROSVENOR ROAD

A " hard little house ", so H. G. Wells described, in *The New Machiavelli*, the home of the Oscar Baileys (*alias* Webbs) in Grosvenor Road, Westminster. To which I may add that it was ten-roomed, rent £110, served by two maids, and that we occupied it on lease for near forty years. I think I must have broken records in having had, during that period, only five separate servants, one of whom was with

[1] The following description of the " Souls " is taken from *An Autobiography*, by Lord Haldane (1928), pp. 120-21: " I began in 1893 to move a good deal in what is called London Society. There was a group of well-known people nicknamed the ' souls '. They sometimes took themselves much too seriously, and on the whole it is doubtful whether their influence was on balance good. But they cared for literature and art, and their social gifts were so high that people sought much to be admitted into their circle. Among the men were Arthur Balfour, the late Lord Pembroke, George Curzon, Harry Cust, George Wyndham and Alfred Lyttelton. Among the women were Lady Ribblesdale, her sister Margot Tennant (afterwards Mrs. Asquith), Lady Elcho, Lady Desborough and Lady Horner. Week-end parties at which the ' souls ' assembled were given at Panshanger, Ashridge, Wilton and Taplow. Among the hostesses on these occasions were Lady Cowper, Lady Brownlow and Lady Pembroke, older but attractive women, who were gratefully but irreverently called the ' Aunts ' of the ' souls '. One or two outside men were welcomed and were frequently guests on these occasions. Among them were John Morley, Sir Alfred Lyall, Asquith, and myself. We were not ' souls ', but they liked our company, and we liked theirs because of its brilliance." (Ed.)

me for over thirty years: another consequence of living
according to plan; housemates like to know exactly what to
expect, when and where? Our workroom on the ground
floor, which served also for meals, a long narrow room
running east to west, in early morning and late afternoon
welcoming sunshine, was lined with books and blue-books;
the space left over covered with engravings and enlarged
photographs of three generations of my family; from my
grandparents and their children, to a selection from among
a hundred or so nephews and nieces, with here and there a
portrait of a near friend: Herbert Spencer, R. B. Haldane,
Mandell Creighton, Bernard Shaw and Marie Souvestre;
and two brothers-in-law, Leonard Courtney and Alfred
Cripps (afterwards Lord Parmoor), I recall. On the half-
landing the secretary's office: oil-clothed floor, large deal
writing-table, from floor to ceiling shelved with pamphlet
boxes. As years went by, these hundreds of boxes, filled with
tens of thousands of quarto-sized research notes, overflowed
into an overhead box-room of identical shape. Not less
utilitarian in its furnishings was the conventionally shaped
sitting-room on the first floor; long seats fitted into alcoves
and, under the western window, an escritoire, table heaped
with books, three easy-chairs but no sofa: all designed to
accommodate the largest number of guests standing or
sitting. This harsh interior was redeemed by the unique
interest and beauty of the outlook. To spring out of bed on
a summer morning and see, spread out before you, the sun
rising behind Lambeth Palace, on clear days the Dome of
St. Paul's and the spires of the City churches, its rays lighting up the tiny waves breaking the surface of the swift-flow-
ing tidal river, whilst oar-steered barges, some with red or
yellow sails, drifting rafts of timber and steaming colliers
passed under the Vauxhall and Lambeth bridges, was a
joyful greeting to another day. Other scenes from the
balcony of the sitting-room I remember: on still autumn
days the river, in ebbing tide, sulking among the mud banks
and lapping the anchored river-craft; or, in full tide, losing
itself in fog, white, yellow or black, thus seeming as bound-

Beatrice Webb
(*Ætat 33*)

less in its expanse as the Mississippi; or, again, at night, city and river lights far and near, hardly distinguishable from the stars, sometimes the glow of brilliant moon-light, illuminating the moving waters, whilst blackening the bridges and their shadows. Other recreations were the walks along the Thames embankment, to the right past the Tate Gallery, the two Battersea bridges, the Royal Hospital and the Physic Garden, to the upper reaches of old Chelsea, where my sister Kate Courtney lived ; or to the left through the resort of Lords and Commons, the dwelling-place of the British Civil Service, the stately Inns of Court and their winsome gardens, citywards to the Cathedral of St. Paul's to seek peace in the music of old-world Christian rites. Or, again, an evening stroll, under St. Thomas's Hospital, watching the sun set across the river behind the terraced Houses of Parliament and the five towers of Westminster, secular and ecclesiastic. Even to-day, living in a delightful countryside, I sometimes feel homesick for the river Thames sweeping through the splendour and squalor of the birth-place of the nineteenth-century capitalist dictatorship.

Our plan of life was to spend eight or nine months of the year in our London home; working together in the mornings at the book; Sidney devoting a long afternoon to L.C.C. administration; the evenings either alone together, browsing over periodicals and light literature, or discussing research, municipal administration or Fabian propaganda with friends and associates. The other months, especially the long summer recess of the County Council, were spent either in some countryside working up our material or in provincial towns carrying on our investigations; whilst every two or three years, usually on the publication of another volume, we treated ourselves to a few weeks' complete holiday on the Continent.

Here are a few entries from the diary, mainly concerned with *The History of Trade Unionism* and *Industrial Democracy*, and our consequent association with trade union officials:

December 30th, 1892.—How gloomy other Christmas Eves have been: always the low-water mark of a year's despair; at best an arid time of family gossip, over-eating, preparation for heartless winter games. Now I have won a vantage ground of wonderful happiness: and, even when physical energy ebbs low, I still feel fundamentally happy. And Sidney also has found a resting place. No need now to struggle for happiness or success: all energy can be given to work. . . .

We have actually begun the book.[1] But, after writing the greater part of the first chapter, we are reading at the British Museum to get fresh ideas of eighteenth-century industry. It is still to be proved— the experiment of writing a book together—sometimes our ideas clash and we fall between the rival ideas; but on the whole we get on. My only trouble is that I can work such short hours compared to him and I feel a mere dilettante, but when spring comes I shall feel better. . . . Sidney for his part is enthusiastically happy. He seems to have settled down to the County Council administration work; at present largely engaged in planning the Technical Education Board. Parliament seems further off than ever; but we are getting used to the prospect of intellectual study, and the humble rôle of county councillor. But, I think, more is to be done by administrative experiment, on the one hand, and educating the constituencies, on the other, than by entering into the political game carried on in Parliament. . . .

The Argoed, Sept. 17th, 1893.—The first fortnight [I write nine months later when we are at The Argoed, our old Monmouthshire home: still in the hands of my father's executors], we spent finishing the sixth chapter of our book. Then Graham Wallas came, read our first chapter and severely criticised the form of it. He made me feel rather desperate about its shortcomings. So I took it and wrestled with it: writing out a complete new syllabus with a quite different arrangement of the subject. This Sidney "wrote to " with my help. Bernard Shaw came ten days after and has stayed with us the remainder of our time working almost every morning at our book. The form of the first chapter satisfied him, and he altered only words and sentences. The second chapter he took more in hand and the third he has to a large extent remodelled. Sidney certainly has devoted friends. But then it is a common understanding with all these men that they use each other up when necessary. That is the basis of the influence of the Fabian Society on contemporary political thought: the little group of leaders are practical communists in all the fruits of their labours. While Bernard Shaw was working on the book, Sidney and I set about separate tasks. I attempted to write a lecture on the sphere of trade unionism; he worked at Tom Mann's minority report.[2] My attempt

[1] *The History of Trade Unionism.*
[2] The Minority Report of the Royal Commission on Labour.

proved to be a hopeless fiasco. I struggled vainly under my great mass of information: historical lore, statistics, analysis—the stuff overwhelmed me. After five days' work I read to S. what I had written. He looked puzzled, and suggested that he should write it out. Then we had a bit of a tiff. For, when my miserable meanderings appeared in his clear hand, it was so obviously out of place for a lecture and that mortified me and I was in a devil of a temper. Next morning he sat down patiently to recast it, and we worked four days together and made a rough draft. Now I am working it up into lecture form. But my failure made me feel a bit of a parasite. So much for a holiday task. . . .

The Fabian Junta

As a relief from these entries about ourselves, I give my first impressions of S. W.'s friends and fellow-Fabians: Graham Wallas and Bernard Shaw, together with casual observations on John Burns and his relation to the Fabian Junta.

The Argoed, September 17th, 1893.—Graham Wallas—six feet with a slouching figure—good features and genial, open smile—utterly unselfconscious and lacking in vanity or personal ambition. Without convictions he would have lounged through life—with convictions he grinds; his natural sluggishness of nature, transformed by his social fervour into a slow grinding at anything that turns up to do. In spite of his moral fervour, he seems incapable of directing his own life, and tends to drift into anything that other people decide. This tendency is accentuated by his benevolence and kindliness and selflessness—almost amounting to a weakness. Thus, while his intimate friends love him and impose on him, superficial strangers of poor character often actually despise him. To some men and women he appears simply as a kindly, dull fellow—an impression which is fostered by a slovenliness of dress and general worn-out look. He preaches too, a habit carried over from his life as usher and teacher of boys. To his disciples he appears a brilliant man, first-rate lecturer, a very genius for teaching, a great thinker and a conscientious writer. It remains to be seen what else he will become beyond a successful propagandist and an admirable and most popular University Extension lecturer. He has two books on hand—but, owing to his constant running off on other people's business, they stand a poor chance of being finished within a year or so. If enthusiasm, purity of motive, hard if somewhat mechanical work, will make a man a success, then Graham Wallas has a great career before him. He has plenty of intellectual ability too; what he lacks is deliberate concentration and rapid decision what to do and how to do it. A loveable man.

Bernard Shaw I know less well than Graham Wallas, though he is quite an old friend of Sidney's. A fellow with a crank for not making money, except he can make it exactly as he chooses. Persons with no sense of humour look upon him as a combination of Don Juan and a professional blasphemer of the existing order. An artist to the tips of his fingers and an admirable craftsman; I have never known a man use his pen in such a workmanlike fashion, or acquire such a thoroughly technical knowledge of any subject upon which he gives an opinion. But his technique or specialism never overpowers him: he always translates it into epigrams, sparkling generalisations or witty personalities. As to his character, I do not understand it. He has been for twelve years a devoted propagandist—hammering away at the ordinary routine of Fabian executive work with as much persistence as Wallas or Sidney. He is an excellent friend, at least to men (" a perfect house friend ", I add two years later, " self-sufficient, witty and tolerant, going his own way and yet adapting himself to your ways "). But beyond this I know nothing. I am inclined to think that he has a slight personality; agile, graceful, and even virile; but lacking in weight. Adored by many women, he is a born philanderer; a " soul " so to speak; disliking to be hampered either by passion or convention and, therefore, always tying himself up into knots which he has to cut before he is free for another adventure. Vain is he? A month ago I should have said that vanity was the bane of his nature. Now I am not so sure that the vanity itself is not part of the *mise en scène*, whether, in fact, it is not part of the character he imagines himself to be playing in the world's comedy.

A vegetarian, fastidious but unconventional in his clothes; six feet in height with a lithe, broad-chested figure and laughing blue eyes. Above all a brilliant talker and, therefore, a delightful companion. To me he has not yet a personality: he is a pleasant but somewhat incongruous group of qualities. Some people would call him a cynic: he is really an idealist of the purest water.

These two men with Sidney make up the Fabian Junta. Sidney is the organiser and gives most of the practical initiative, Graham Wallas represents morality and scrupulousness, Bernard Shaw gives the sparkle and flavour. Graham Wallas appeals to those of the upper and educated class who have good intentions: no one can doubt his candour, disinterestedness, enthusiasm and extreme moral refinement. Sidney insinuates ideas, arguments, programmes and organises the organisers. Bernard Shaw leads off the men of straw, men with light heads—the would-be revolutionaries, who are attracted by his wit, his daring onslaughts and amusing paradoxes. He has also a *clientèle* among cynical journalists and men of the world. What the Junta needs to make it a great power are one or two personalities of *weight*; men of wide experience and sagacity, able to play a long hand, and to master the movement. If John Burns would get over his incurable suspicion and if he could conquer his instinctive fear of comradeship, I know no man who could so complete the Fabian trio and make it thoroughly effective. If Burns would come in and give himself away to the other three as they do to each other—the Fabians could dominate the reform movement. Burns is, in some respects, the strongest man of the four, though utterly ill-equipped in his isolation for leadership. But that contingency, I fear, is past praying for. Collectivism will spread, but it will spread from no one centre. Those who sit down and think will, however, mould the form, though they will not set the pace or appear openly as the directors. . . .

Grosvenor Road, October 17th, 1893.—Spent a whole morning with John Burns [I write when we are again in London] looking over the trade union documents he has. Our relationship with John Burns has never been a cordial one; it promises to be more so in future. I began with a prejudice against him. At the Newcastle Congress he seemed an intriguer who suspected everyone of intrigue. His unfriendly attitude towards Tom Mann also displeased me. Possibly, he heard of my dislike, for he treated me with marked suspicion. Of Sidney he has, until lately, been jealous and was anxious that he should not come on the L.C.C. But, for one reason or another, this unfriendliness has much lessened. On my part, I have long since seen reason to alter my opinion of him as a public man. His capacity, straightforwardness, power of reason, has given him a permanent position, which poor Mann forfeited by his light-headed change of front on all questions human and divine. Sidney has always had a high opinion of him. Burns, on his side, sees now that Sidney does not seek to play the rival Labour leader, and that his influence (Burns') will not be diminished by Sidney being on the L.C.C. If Sidney went into Parliament, it might be that the old jealousy would revive.

For jealousy and suspicion of rather a mean kind are John Burns' burning sin. A man of splendid physique, fine and strong intelligence, human sympathy, practical capacity, he is unfitted for a really great position by his utter inability to be a constant and loyal comrade. He stands absolutely alone. He is intensely jealous of other Labour men, acutely suspicious of all middle-class sympathisers; whilst his hatred of Keir Hardie reaches the dimensions of mania. He is a born ruler of barbarians, impressing his followers with his will and determination, not guiding them by reason. And yet he is essentially an intellectual man; one of his finest qualities is the constant testing of questions by intellectual methods rather than by sentimental considerations. It is pitiful to see this splendid man a prey to egotism of the most sordid kind; an egotism that seeks not so much to fill the world with its own doings as to diminish all other reputations in order that his own work may stand out in relief. . . .

ROYAL COMMISSION ON LABOUR

Meanwhile, Sidney had been helping trade union officials by drafting minority reports for royal commissions, notably for the much-advertised Royal Commission on Labour, about which I find the following caustic entry:

Grosvenor Road, December 24th, 1893.—Royal Commission on Labour a gigantic fraud.[1] Made up of a little knot of dialecticians *plus* a carefully picked parcel of variegated Labour men, and the rest landlords or capitalists, pure and simple. The dialecticians—Gerald Balfour, Frederick Pollock, Alfred Marshall and Leonard Courtney —have had it their own way: they have puzzled the workmen with economic conundrums, balked inconvenient evidence by crossquestions, and delivered themselves of elaborate treatises on economics, history and philosophy to bewildered reporters—equally in the form of questions. Spent a somewhat painful day there, the first day of Sidney's examination. He was irritated by the bad faith of the Commission, and treated them to a little of their own game. His answers read well, and were richly deserved; but his manner was objectionable and pained me. Also the Charles Booths, Kate Courtney, Mrs. Dugdale and others of that set were listening to him and, as they agreed with the dialecticians, they showed their disapproval markedly. However, the next day the dear boy made a pretty apology and bore the cross-examination with perfect good humour. It ended in an amicable discussion between him and Gerald Balfour for an hour-and-a-half, on abstract economics, pleasant to listen to, but fit only for after-dinner talk, and not the sort of questions and answers to be delivered at the public expense. Utter waste of time to all concerned except that it woke us up to the harm the Commission might do if their report is taken in good faith. Hence, the inspired article in the London [*Daily*] *Chronicle* written by Massingham after a long talk with us. . . .

[1] For an analysis of the defects of the Royal Commission on Labour, as a method of investigation, see *The Failure of the Labour Commission,* XIX Century, July 1894, by Beatrice Webb.

Grosvenor Road, Christmas Day, 1893.—Another chicken hatched here last summer—Tom Mann's minority report. . . . Sidney has spent quite three weeks on it; but, though we think it of importance, we cannot help regarding it as a practical joke over which we chuckle with considerable satisfaction. Poor Labour Commission, having carefully excluded any competent Socialists from its membership, having scouted the idea of appointing me as a humble assistant commissioner, will now find a detailed collectivist programme, blazoned about as the minority report of its Labour members! Dear old Leonard [Courtney], who told us with pompous superiority that they were all agreed: and that there was no prospect of any minority report—and we had it lying all the time on our table and had been putting the last touches to it that very morning. Certainly, persons with brains and independent means may have a rare good time. . . .

Grosvenor Road, March 13*th,* 1894.—Amusing afternoon. Mann came in in the morning to say that he was bringing Mawdsley, Austin and Abraham [1] to discuss the minority report at 5 o'clock—the excuse

[1] The scene at the Royal Commission when the Labour men produced their report was extensively noticed in the press.

" This report was produced at yesterday's sitting of the Commission [the *Westminster Gazette* of March 16, 1894, reports], and it created (says the *Manchester Guardian*) almost as much consternation as if a bomb had been exploded in Westminster Hall. The Duke of Devonshire was clearly unprepared for it. It altered the whole situation so far as his draft recommendations were concerned, and he suggested that the Commission should have time to consider the new report, for which purpose he then adjourned the Commission until after Easter. The minority report, it is reported, will propose among other matters a legal eight-hour day, with certain limitations, the amendment of the Factory Acts in the direction of the abolition of home work, the relief of the unemployed by empowering Boards of Guardians to acquire land and to till it by the labour of persons temporarily unemployed, the improving of the conditions under which female workers in certain trades are employed, the improvement of the lot of the dock labourers and other casual workers, and the amelioration of the condition of the agricultural labourer. The same report will also express regret that the nationalisation of the land cannot be dealt with. These questions bristle with opportunities for controversy, and it will not be possible to conclude the work of the Commission by the end of the month. It is expected that five members of the Commission at least will subscribe to this report."

Apparently Mawdsley was under no delusion about the authorship of the report. When a member of the majority of the Royal Commission observed with a sneer that the signatories had obviously not written the report, Mawdsley answered sharply: " Certainly not: nor has the Duke or any of you written the majority report. The only distinction between us and you is that you have paid your man, and we have been sharp enough to get it done without payment, and better done too." On the close of the Commission, Mawdsley insisted on the three Labour members, Tom Mann, Michael Austin and himself, signing a formal letter of thanks to S. W. for enabling them " to submit a report which we believe will prove to be of great value to the cause of Labour in the future, also in some sense a guide to the industrial and political policy to be endorsed by the workers ".

Among the other documents drafted for the trade union officials by Sidney Webb was the minority report presented by Broadhurst as a member of the Royal Commission on the Aged Poor, 1895.

being that he had left it with Sidney to look over it from a legal point of view. We were both rather taken aback: thinking that Mawdsley, whose adhesion was most important, would not only refuse to support it but would, perhaps, join the rest of the Commission in trying to keep it out altogether. We could not imagine Mawdsley, a staunch Conservative, adopting it " all of a heap ". When Mawdsley turned up early to write his copy for the *Factory Times*, I was relieved to find that he was supremely disgruntled with the majority report and felt in a fix as to what he should do. Sidney took the matter in hand, and asked leave, as a lawyer, to give the others the gist of Mann's report. Standing in front of the fire, he began reading out all the parts which would affect Mawdsley most, he making comments on it, Mann playing into his hand by suggesting more advanced statements, Sidney supporting Mawdsley in many of his criticisms. As he read on Mawdsley expressed his approval and was apparently delighted with the practical and detailed character of the suggestions. It ended by Mawdsley considering the report his own and taking it on himself to announce to the Commission that they were drawing up a minority report and would present it in a couple of days. The only alteration he insisted on was the omission of the word " Socialism ", though he agreed to the substitution of the words " public administration, national and local ". So much is in a word. . . .

INDUSTRIAL DEMOCRACY

Our first book—*The History of Trade Unionism*—was published in the spring of 1894, and we rewarded ourselves for the two years' work by a three weeks' holiday in Italy.

Grosvenor Road, April 30th, 1894.—It is the first complete break in our work that we have had since those happy days in Norway three years ago. Of course, I have had days and weeks of " lazing " from sheer incapacity to work—but I think I have used up all my energy during the last three years in work—I have never had sufficient over to enjoy anything but a somewhat depressed *rest*. The last weeks I have slacked off so that I may have plenty of spirits for our holy-day. We need to rid ourselves of the turmoil of the life here during the last three months, so as to set to our next bit of work with a clear head and clean conscience!

Grosvenor Road, May 21st, 1894.—Back from a delightful three weeks' holiday. Nine days in Venice. Charming rooms overlooking an Alma Tadema court, with canal and bridge between us and it and old marble gateway and well, whither Venetian women with their soft-coloured clothes went to draw water. Our days were spent on the water with an old gondolier whom we engaged by the day, and in St. Mark's Piazza and in St. Mark's itself—that vision of sumptuous beauty which it is a glory to recall. Very sweet hours of companion-ship—not thinking, but simply feeling the beauty around us—a true honeymoon of love and common enjoyment. Then to Como (Menaggio) where we met the Richard Stracheys—the General, an old experienced Indian administrator, and Mrs. Strachey, a strong, warm-hearted, enthusiastically literary woman. But, though our even-ings were spent with them, smoking cigarettes and sipping coffee on the terrace, our days were spent together wandering over the hills and in the lovely gardens of the Villas. Then a long journey back, and we are again in our little house, beautifully cleaned up by our two maids, and with Galton keenly anxious to be at the next volume. The holiday has been just what we needed; it has swept away all the cobwebs of secret minority reports, and all the tatters of the last bit of work, so that we can begin fresh and clear, a new subject. One day spent over our correspondence, and this morning I started off to plan the new volume. We propose to rough-hew the whole before either perfecting any part of it or completing our investigation; since we do not know exactly which points want clearing up. It will be a difficult and delicate piece of work, and need a great deal of hard hammering to weld it into anything like form. But we are encouraged—if, indeed, such a labour of love needed encouragement—by the appreciation of our labour and patience in the first volume. Perhaps I feel a bit of a humbug when the reviews talk of the " endless labour " entailed in the work—we have taken the work lightly, Sidney giving only half-time to it, and I the miserable few hours which I am capable of giving to any sort of work. But I must pull myself together and work harder at this volume—work hard and live simply.

To us *The History of Trade Unionism* seemed little more than an historical introduction to the task we had set before us: the scientific analysis of the structure and function of British Trade Unions, in order to discover the tacit assump-tions and social implications underlying their activities; and, what appeared to us of crucial importance, the relation of manual-working trade unionism to other forms of social organisation: notably, to profit-making enterprise, to political democracy, and to the consumers' co-operative movement. The following entries from my diary, scattered

43

over four years, reveal the intolerable toil of thought involved in working out a theory of trade unionism consistent with the facts we had observed and the hypotheses we believed we had verified.

Grosvenor Road, July 10th, 1894.—Not getting on with our book. It is a horrid grind, this analysis—one sentence is exactly like another, the same words, the same construction—no relief in narrative. And then the facts often do not admit of clear and definite classification—they are not grouped in distinct and separate classes, they are mixed up together in a fine tangle, and any attempt to place them in nice little maps seems purely artificial. No doubt the sequence involved in history writing is as artificial as are the groups involved in classification (how silly it is to suppose that facts *ever tell their own story*—it is all a matter of arranging them so that they may tell something—and the arrangement is purely a subjective process). I sometimes despair of getting on with the book—I feel horribly vexed with myself for loitering and idling as I do morning after morning; looking on while poor Sidney drudges along. London, too, is beginning to get on my nerves, with the heat and the continual noise and movement and the distraction of seeing one person and another. When we get to the country, it may be better: we must make an effort.

Borough Farm, Surrey, July 25th, 1894.—Overlooking a little country lane with heather-covered moorland on one side and a thicket of young trees behind, stands the farm-house we have taken for three months. The farmer and his wife, hard-headed, somewhat grasping folk, who make us pay more than London prices for all their produce, and whom I rather suspect of taking toll on our groceries! and a grim old labourer who serves them and does menial offices for us, and whom we meet in the late evening with a coat puffed out with concealed rabbits, are our co-occupants of the substantial red-brick old-fashioned house. Tho' only one hour and a few minutes by rail from London, it is too remote for postal delivery and we have to fetch our letters some 1½ miles from a village! But this and other drawbacks are outweighed by the exceeding charm of the country. Heather-grown moorland studded with firs and intermixed with broad expanses of wooded pasture, occasionally a grove of glorious forest trees with thorn and holly bush nestling under—all open and free to wander, mile after mile, without a single fence, ditch or " trespass board ". Here we shall be for three months resting, reading and writing as hard as we can at our book. These first ten days, Sidney has been working at his paper for the British Association, on *The Heresies of the L.C.C.*, and I have been somewhat despairingly spending my mornings over the chapter on "Apprenticeship". But he has been up and down to London, and even I had to rush up to two committees.

Borough Farm, Surrey, August 10*th*, 1894.—Either the Surrey climate is enervating, or I am no good at this analytical deductive work which goes to make up our second volume. Rightly or wrongly, we are writing our analysis of facts before we have completed our investigation, with a view of concentrating our attention, when we begin to investigate, exactly on those points which need clearing up and which we are certain to use. Consequently, we are perpetually working without sufficient or adequate material: our descriptive analysis lacks definiteness; the lines of our argument become shaky; each division, as we turn it out, seems unsatisfactory. Then our work suffers from being an almost unconscious attempt to unite three things: (1) a descriptive analysis of modern trade unionism with as much analytical history of separate trade unions as will light up the statistical account and show the direction of growth as well as the present structure; (2) a criticism of trade unions (for the good of the unionists!); (3) an apology for, or defence of trade unions (for the enlightenment of the middle-class and economists). These three objects do not amalgamate well. It spoils the descriptive analysis, which ought to be absolutely cold, for authors or readers to feel that these facts will presently be used to support a thesis. But this is not all. When we come to the thesis we find the facts, tho' they can be used as illustrations, are not much good as the basis of our structure—they are only the ornament. The whole structure of our argument turns out to be deductive in form, with psychological hypotheses or inductions used as its material. So the facts we have laboriously detailed seem somewhat *de trop*. Whether, that being so, we ought not to begin with the theory of trade unionism, instead of demonstrating the need for it, or whether we ought not to begin with the descriptive side—the facts— and then deal with the theory as a second division?

October 8th, 1894. *Borough Farm.*—It is some years since I have watched summer turn into autumn and felt the first breath of winter creeping over the country. This year the summer left us early, the sky closing over with cold grey clouds, only now and again they break, and the sun slants out and lights up the sombre blues and browns of the landscape. Perhaps, it is the rich tones of the heath and bracken which recall some of those lovely Rusland [my father's house in Westmorland] autumns; for, as I stand and watch the clouds drifting across the moor and try to fathom the glorious depths of colour of land and sky, memories of old days jostle each other and seem to take me back to the thoughts and feelings and daily life of struggling girl-

45

hood—the inevitable melancholy of the autumn months, the brooding over books, the long walks with Father, afternoon tea in the little hall at Rusland after a trudge in the mist, Mother's bright welcome to Father, her keen relish of her cup of tea before she went to her boudoir to study her grammars, or settled herself down to a talk with Father over his business affairs and the family prospects—all the strange medley of good and evil one lived through as a girl. But, in chewing the cud of those old memories, I am impressed, not with the *past-ness* of the old life but with the perfect continuity of the present and the past: these autumn months of years ago were always devoted to study, were always stimulated by a restless desire to conquer new strands of thought. After nearly twenty years of adult life, I am still living the same daily life, still using my whole energy in unravelling ideas and attempting to clear issues—the practical affairs which occupy most people's middle life are no more now than they were then—at least, not during our three months' holiday. There is an inexpressible delight in this consciousness of continuity, in feeling that those hours of lonely and painful study are linked on to the settled occupation—perhaps one might almost say the settled profession—of a productive brain-worker. If one could only have foreseen that this daily intellectual effort would one day be set in a frame of loving companionship and constant sympathy, one would have been less restless and morbidly self-conscious.

Of course, one gets discouraged at one's incapacity as of old. Each chapter of this book needs a certain amount of hard and vigorous thinking, and I feel dispirited when I have to knock off work an hour after I have begun, or when I have to lay by for a whole day. But it is vastly different working after one has some assurance of the worth of one's work and toiling, day after day, not knowing whether one has special capacity or not. And then what light love brings to the daily task: it turns that black despair of the over-strained brain-worker into calm quiescence. When first I was married, I feared that my happiness would dull my energies and make me intellectually dependent. I no longer feel that; the old fervour for work has returned without the old restlessness. Of course, my life in London, with its other claims, leaves me with less physical energy—but this, I think, is almost counterbalanced by the absence of any waste through mental misery. On the whole, then, I would advise the brain-working woman to marry—if only she can find her Sidney!

Borough Farm, October 11th, 1894.— . . . For all that, I leave this quaint little home with regret. The last months I have pulled myself together and done some hard thinking. We have roughed out four or five chapters of our book. I am beginning to see that, if we can only put enough work into it, this volume will be far more instructive than the *History*—a far bigger achievement. I dread the dullness that comes over me in London, the sheer incapacity to grapple with a hard bit of complicated analysis. However, I must save myself as much as I can for the book—I can only do my best. And I must, in order to be able to work, resolutely refuse to *worry*; otherwise I shall not do my share of the labour and shall be a source of fatigue and not of rest to Sidney. The next six months—with the vestry and L.C.C. elections added on to all the administrative business—seems likely to be somewhat trying for my Boy.

The last months of 1894 were largely taken up by the Westminster vestry elections, whilst our joint energies in the two first months of 1895 were completely absorbed in the London County Council election; all activities which will be described in the following chapter. Indeed, I gather from my diary that it was not until the August recess of 1895 that we disentangled ourselves from our political environment and returned to our special task of investigating the trade union movement.

The Argoed, August 8th, 1895.—I wonder whether other brainworkers make as many futile starts as we do. Here I have been painfully labouring to fashion a first chapter on the "Objects of Trade Unionism" and have wasted hours of Sidney's time in executing it and now the *idea* turns out not good enough—too thin and insignificant. It is hard to foretell the worth of an idea until you have expressed it fully with all its attendant facts in all their ramifications. After spending hours, if not days, on it, you find either that it is not true or absurdly insignificant and banal. It is this process, experimenting in working out ideas, that entails the length of time spent on analysis as compared with history. With history, the threads are supplied by the chronological order—you can weave these threads into any pattern; bring one of them to the surface and then another. But with analysis of facts, the threads are hypotheses: to be tested in strength and consistency before you dare weave them into conclusions and illustrate them with facts. . . .

Grosvenor Road, Sept. 9th, 1895.—At Cardiff [Trades Union Congress] we were in the usual whirl of talk. The hotel we were in was actually attached to the hall so that it was the centre where all the delegates congregated—especially as there were three entertainers quartered there—Lady Dilke [1] with her attendant ladies—Gertrude

---

[1] Representing the Women's Trade Union League, of which Lady Dilke was then president, and her niece, Miss Tuckwell, honorary secretary. (Ed.)

Tuckwell, Mary Abraham (factory inspector), Sir Hickman Bacon and ourselves. Lady Dilke entertained on a large, I might almost say gross scale—her young women asking every trade union official they came across to champagne lunches and elaborate dinners. The dear good baronet, with his doglike devotion to Sidney, provided us with a private sitting-room, where we had our trade unionists and he had the I.L.P.—we going in for little confidential lunches and suppers for the purpose of extracting information and insinuating useful suggestions. But all this is the background. The drama was fought out in the hall on the second day. The minority of the parliamentary committee inspired by Broadhurst, and led by J. Havelock Wilson, led the attack on the new " standing orders ". There was no defence—delegate after delegate got up and denounced the action of the parliamentary committee. No defence except bad language and abusive epithets from John Burns. But, when it came to the vote, the cotton and coal men showed their cards silently and with that vote collared the Congress and its organisation for their own purposes.

Mawdsley comes out now as the hero of the *coup d'état*.[1] Poor Burns has allowed himself to be used as the tool, his egregious vanity, virulent hatred of Keir Hardie and Tom Mann, suspicion of everyone else, prompting him to destroy the representative character of the Congress, to oust himself in order to oust certain other men, leaving Mawdsley and Cowey (Miners' Federation) in possession of the whole political influence of trade unions. Whether these men make anything of their power depends on whether the alliance stands good and whether Mawdsley shows more statesmanship than his predecessors. We had Mawdsley to dinner after the vote had been taken. Without disguising our opinion of the *coup d'état* we suggested to him that he might make the parliamentary committee a much more efficient instrument and that we should be glad to help. He rose to the suggestion, and I am not at all certain whether this parliamentary committee will not prove much more amenable to our influence than its predecessors. Mawdsley is a cool-headed man, quite aware of his own deficiencies and far too cynical to be suspicious. Whether or not we use Mawdsley, we may rest assured that he will use us: which after all is all we desire. Poor Burns, to have ousted Keir Hardie from the Congress and let in Sidney Webb to the parliamentary committee! Brought home a good deal of material. Must now turn to our book again. . . .

Now it so happens that this arbitrary alteration, by the parliamentary committee, without the consent of Congress, of the " standing orders " determining its constitution, re-

[1] See p. 49.

sulted in the domination of the " block vote " not only over the general policy of the trade union movement, but also, eventually, over that of the British Labour Party destined to become, from 1918 onwards, alternately His Majesty's Opposition and His Majesty's Government. Hence, I turn back the pages of my MS. diary to an entry, dated January 15, 1895, describing how this *coup d'état* came about.

Grosvenor Road, January 15th, 1895.—Meanwhile, there is an intrigue going on inside the P.C. which may affect the future of trade unionism, and which has already roused a storm in that little world. This much can be gathered from the newspapers. "Standing orders " have been issued to the trade unions which the parliamentary committee have declared shall govern the next Congress. Shortly stated, these orders amount to this: trades councils are to be excluded: the voting is to be on the plan of the Miners' Federation—the delegates of each trade, however few or numerous, are to have voting power according to the numerical strength of their society; one vote for every 1000 members; and, lastly, no man is to be a delegate who is not working at his trade, or serving as the *salaried* official of his union. Of course, this is a revolution in the constitution of Congress. These " orders " of the P.C. have been backed up by the *Daily Chronicle* and the *Factory Times*, denounced by the *Clarion* and the *Labour Leader*. So far as one can judge, they would mean that Congress would consist of a few salaried officials, each of whom would carry in his pocket the proxy of his whole trade.

It was on this question that Broadhurst came to consult us. He spent the first hour in giving us, with graphic but somewhat lengthy detail, the inner history of this *coup d'état*. How there had been a vague instruction by Congress to the parliamentary committee to consider all the resolutions with which Congress could not deal, how among these there appeared some minute alteration of " standing orders ", how Burns had got a sub-committee of five (himself, Woods, Mawdsley, Holmes and Jack) appointed to see what could be done, how at the November meeting of the P.C. these new " standing orders " were placed before the committee suddenly, without any notice, for their approval. So far Burns had had it all his own way. Broadhurst immediately rallied the other side and fought the question for three days. Six voted for, six against: Holmes gave his casting vote in favour of " revolution ". So far Burns had gained a hazardous victory; but relied on keeping back these "orders" until a month before Congress. Broadhurst waited till Burns and Holmes were gone to America, and having a majority at the P.C. insisted on circulating

E

the " standing orders " to all trade unions. " I wanted to issue a circular explaining their full nature, but that little vain imp Tillett would not stick to me. But I have taken care to let it be widely known that these 'orders' would exclude from Congress not only myself, but Keir Hardie, Tom Mann and Hammill; and would practically exclude from any say, not only the trades councils, but all the small trades of the country. Now Mr. Webb, I have told you the tale, let me know your frank opinion as to the orders in themselves? "

Then we set to, and discussed the whole constitution of Congress. Broadhurst had evidently come, not only to get Sidney's advice, but to get him to draft alternative " standing orders " to be submitted to Congress. It is going to be a duel between Burns and Broadhurst. Burns has acted in a very unwise if not a mean way. Seeing he cannot control the present Congress, and cannot work the parliamentary committee, he has decided to reduce both to the smallest dimensions, or (as he would say) to save them from becoming the instruments of " Labour politicians " and " agitators ". Of course, there is a good deal to be said against the present constitution of Congress; and, on the face of it, one of the " orders " is a self-denying ordinance on Burns's part, since he would be technically excluded. But, as Sidney says, it was a curious fact that the " self-denying ordinance " known to history did not exclude Cromwell who proposed it. And so with Burns. He is not technically a T.U. official; but, since he already receives £100 from the A.S.E., a stroke of the pen would make him one; whilst there is not the slightest chance of Broadhurst, Mann, Keir Hardie or Hammill getting a salary from the unions. That being the case, Sidney virtually agreed to Broadhurst's request to draw up suggestions for his private use. . . .

One cannot help admiring also the shrewdness of his [Broadhurst's] attitude towards us. He has read our book with minute care—he has swallowed our very severe criticism of his conduct of the P.C. between 1880–9 with perfect good temper. The fact that our account discredits him, and elevates Burns, has not apparently affected his determination to make full use of us. He is lazy, not quick in drafting, with no intellectual skilfulness; he realises that without some middle-class help he can do nothing—so finding no one he can trust more than us he unreservedly places himself in our hands and so doing places us in a very delicate position.

For Burns, though unscrupulous, incurably suspicious, and rather mean in his methods, has some splendid moral and intellectual qualities. So long as he does not fear any diminution of his personal prestige, his judgement is very fine—far more warmth, insight and intelligence than Broadhurst. We do not wish to detract from his influence. On nearly all questions he is instinctively on the right side. He honestly tries to think out problems. But, for the last year, it has been apparent that on all questions bearing on the trade union movement his intelligence and conscience have been completely *paralyzed* by a dominant terror that some other Labour leader will eclipse him by means of it. It looks as if he were deliberately trying to diminish the political force of the trade unions as great corporations. Of course, it would be possible to hold that that was a good thing to do from the point of view of the common weal—that associations of producers ought not to concern themselves with general politics. But that is not our view, more especially not Sidney's, whose whole political policy has been to stimulate this activity. It looks as if we should have to choose between backing Burns and backing the trade union world. He will not in any way consult us, or explain his meaning; he is never open with us; in spite of our genuine desire to work with him both on London and Labour questions, he always shows an undercurrent of jealousy and suspicion. For all these reasons, it will be almost impossible for us to refuse Broadhurst's appeal to help him to carry out our views. The hurry-scurry of politics and Broadhurst's discretion may save us from coming directly across Burns, but it will be rather of the nature of egg-dancing if we succeed in preventing him mischief-making without incurring his anger. . . .

Suffolk, September 16th, 1896.—Last day of our stay in the Suffolk rectory. For the first three weeks I was seedy—mooned and dreamed my life away, chatting with our visitors, or sitting in the little study watching Sidney work on with our chapter on " Apprenticeship ", or straining after the party on my bicycle—feeling all the time somewhat miserable and woe-begone. The last four weeks we have worked well together, and have really got within sight of the end of our book and the completion of our theory. Now that we have finished the elaborate technical analysis of each set of regulations—our own theory of trade unionism is emerging. It is exciting, this clearing-up of one's thought after two years of patient plodding. And, as far as we can tell, the ideas we are evolving seem to be fruitful and likely to breed others. Out of our study of trade unionism we are developing a new view of democracy and, I think, quite an original set of economic and political hypotheses. For the first time since we began this book I am feeling intellectually keen and absorbed in my work. . . .

The Argoed, January 18th, 1897.— . . . The hill enveloped in cold mist. But it has been a splendid time for work: have written the best part of two chapters. Have worked both together and apart, Sidney reading through the thirty volumes we brought with us on abstract economics and writing, with occasional suggestions from me, the chapter on the " wage fund ", whilst I spent hours scheming the chapter giving our synthesis of the " higgling of the market ". Then he and I would write it out clearly, he criticising my ideas; sometimes we would get at cross purposes, but our cross purposes would always end in a shower of kisses. I doubt whether two persons could stand the stress and strain of this long drawn-out work, this joint struggle with ideas, a perpetual hammering at each other's minds, if it were not for the equally perpetual " honeymoon " of our life together. These three weeks, with the peaceful grey days and long evenings, the wanderings over the moorland and up and down dale, the cosy evenings by the log fire, he reading *Brand* and *Peer Gynt* to me, have been a delicious holy-day—a relief from the noise, bustle and news of London. And, as if to reward us for being so happy enshrouded in cold mist, the sun, the last three days, has come out gloriously shining in red splendour over the whitened landscape; followed at sunset by an equally glorious moon lighting up in an absolutely still air the long lines of highland, their night's shroud of white mist creeping stealthily up from the village. I am so well and blessedly happy. Again those morbid troublings of last autumn seem to me amazing!

Looking back on the year, I am satisfied with our work. We are nearly through with our book, three months more grind of our little minds, and we shall have turned out all that they can yield on this subject. Of course, the worth of our work will be only temporary; all our hypotheses will be either truisms or fallacies in a generation's time. Still, I think, we shall have left a solid substratum of fact for others to reason on. Our descriptive analysis of special facts is, I believe, the best part of our work and likely to be most permanent. . . .

Dorking, May 1st, 1897.—I have been especially vigorous, completely absorbed in thinking out the last chapter of our book. To me the unravelling of a consistent theory of industrial regulation (in the chapter on " Economic Characteristics of Trade Unionism ") has been extremely exciting. Now that we have found our theory, every previous part of our analysis seems to fit in perfectly, and facts, which before puzzled us, range themselves in their places as if " by nature ". We alternate between thinking that the work will be as great, in its effect on political and economic thought, as Adam Smith's *Wealth of Nations*, to wondering whether the whole of it is not an elaborate figment of our imagination. Anyway, the elaborate analysis of the facts contained in the second part of the work, an analysis which we made by pondering over the facts and trying to get an exhaustive description of what actually exists, must be useful; for it was not until the whole diagnosis was complete that we began to see clearly the principles which seemed to spring from it. The companionship over the book in these latter parts has been delightful; the constant testing of the thought by the two minds, the act of *combined thinking* in which the experience and the hypotheses of the two intellects becomes inextricably mingled, so that we are both unconscious of what we have each of us contributed, has been extraordinarily stimulating. But I doubt whether the English reading public will understand or be impressed; if there is to be a *succès d'estime*, that appreciation will come from Germany.[1] The background of our lives—the pleasant friendships, the beautiful spring, with all its sweet sounds, sights and scents, and the pretty house and garden, the long hours of leisure—is luxurious almost to a fault. One broods at times over the question whether our work is worth all the happiness and well-being we are extracting from the life of the community, and at times one feels uneasy lest we are taking more than our share. Happily, the supreme luxury of love and close comradeship does not abstract from other people's chances of enjoyment. Our life at present is like the early summer, growth and delight in growing, love and the delight in loving. We are getting middle-aged, and yet we feel young in our intellectual life, always on the threshold of new discovery, and almost childish in our revelling in each other's adoration and tenderness. How full and brimming over with happiness human life can be. How could this happiness become universal or nearly universal—that is the problem. . . .

The Argoed, August 27th, 1897.—The first fortnight or three weeks Sidney and I struggled painfully with re-writing the " Economic Characteristics "—the stiffest chapter in the whole work—both of us feeling that we had " bitten off more than we could chew " in our *Theory of Trade Unionism.* At last we got into such a hopeless state of continuous argument that it was clear that we were wasting energy. So he agreed to go on by himself, whilst I should begin to plan out the last chapter. So he is grappling with it alone, I think, successfully. He is stronger-brained than I am, and can carry more things in his mind at once; I was getting hopelessly befogged with utter weariness. We are working really too hard to enjoy it: we are bent on getting the book done with and out with autumn; and this last chapter has proved far more complicated than we thought. The weather is one continual south-west rain storm which adds a touch of gloom to our overstrain. Bernard Shaw, too, is working continuously revising his plays. . . . We are a very middle-aged party this autumn—inclined to drudge at our work. For all that, Sidney and I are peacefully happy.

[1] Through the accident of a compositors' strike in the autumn of 1897, *Industrial Democracy* appeared in German a month before it was published in English.

Now that I feel the crucial chapter is really getting on, I can sit and calmly think out the last chapter and the preface. . . .

The Argoed, Sept. 10*th,* 1897.—The last day at the Argoed! Turned out to make room for a tenant and transplanting ourselves " over the way " to " Moorcroft " for the remainder of the vacation. Spent another ten days hammering away together at the " Economic Characteristics ". Sidney got over the kink, but his stuff was rough hewn and had to be polished up. Now, at last, we are sending the last instalment of the chapter to the printer. It has been by far the hardest bit of reasoning that I have ever attempted and it remains to be seen how much of it stands against hostile criticism. What will be said is that we have seized on certain characteristics of the " common rule " and magnified them out of all proportion to others that we have not even so much as mentioned. That is to some extent true. Our chapter is really " *an analysis of certain characteristics of the common rule* ". But then these are exactly the characteristics which have been hitherto completely overlooked and, therefore, want to be given all the prominence of isolated treatment. Other investigators will come along and set our little discoveries (if discoveries they prove to be) in their proper place. . . .

Grosvenor Road, December 10*th,* 1897.— . . . Also, the engineers' lock-out—Sidney constantly drafting letters and conditions, I sometimes egging him on. A wretched business! It is only those who know the rotten constitution of the A.S.E., and their guerilla policy, who realise the badness of the whole business, the hold that employers have over the public opinion of all classes in the general dislike of the A.S.E. This morning we drafted letters to the *Daily Chronicle* and the *Manchester Guardian,* and wrote private letters to the leading officials of the great unions begging them to take the matter up on the ground that collective bargaining is attacked. We may be on the eve of a big convulsion—a Conservative Government is always favourable to the growth of revolutionary feelings—and for the last five years working-class opinion has been lying dormant. Meanwhile, our portentous book is still in the press, will appear on January 4th. We must prepare ourselves for disappointment, or rather we must try not to think of success or failure, simply feel that we have done our level best and there it is—to be taken or left. Anyway, we have learnt enormously from our six years' investigation, and the life has been a happy one—full of love and interest. What more can we ask for? . . .

Grosvenor Road, December 14*th,* 1897.—Asquith called here this morning and spent half-an-hour discussing the engineering dispute. He has for the last few years been cold to the Labour movement, and unfriendly to us, so his anxiety to be informed was an interesting sign of the times. He is a shrewd able lawyer: coarse-grained and unimaginative, but sensitive like all politicians to the changes in the political atmosphere. Sidney explained the engineers' contention and also their weakness, and coached him up on the technical side of the question; gave him our chapter on the " Standard Rate ". We did our best: we shall see whether it bears fruit in his speech at Stockport. . . .

A month later I give the outcome of the engineers' lock-out:

Grosvenor Road, January 1898.—Sidney and I have spent much thought and time on the engineers' dispute, but all to no purpose. No sooner had we worked up public opinion against the original terms of the employers than the officials of the A.S.E. gave us all completely away by offering to accept practically the same terms if the employers gave 51 hours. The employers, of course, refuse the 51 hours, but point triumphantly to the men's proposal whenever it is suggested that these terms are inconsistent with the continuance of trade unionism. It is of no avail that the members reject these terms by overwhelming majority: public opinion, only too glad to escape from censuring capitalists, backs up the employers' logic. After the event Barnes comes and consults us—but it is useless advising when advice is not understood. This set of officials are hopelessly incompetent—feather-headed I.L.P. or obscurant old-fashioned unionists of the Allan type [1]—a type all right in its day but now bygone in usefulness. So the weary business drags on, and all friends stand aloof feeling that it is useless to move in any direction since the officials of the A.S.E. may drift in the other. The employers have, as regards immediate victory, played their cards with remarkable astuteness. But they are over-reaching themselves. Their victory, even if they attain their end of making the union agree as a corporation to their terms, will be a mere paper victory. It is childish to expect good results from a consent wrung from thousands of men by threats of absolute starvation. The best they can look for is that, under the stress and strain, the A.S.E. will go to pieces—discontented classes and districts breaking away and repudiating the society, its agreements and its debts. But that will be no advantage. Instead of one union to deal with, they will have a dozen irresponsible, semi-secret bodies fighting in guerilla wherever and whenever they get a chance. And they forget the polling booth! . . .

---

[1] William Allan, General Secretary of the A.S.E., 1851–74; typical of the " Old Unionist " official. An administrator of friendly benefits rather than a militant trade unionist. Consequently uninfluential in trade union politics. See Biographical Index and *History of Trade Unionism*, by S. and B. Webb, p. 458. (Ed.)

Here is the final entry, recording our partnership in the study of British Trade Unionism: the reader will forgive its naïve self-complacency.

Grosvenor Road, January 11th, 1898.—Our big book has had a brilliant reception. The *Times* gave us two columns on the day of publication; the *Standard* an abusive leader; the *Daily Chronicle*, the *Daily News*, and half-a-dozen big provincials were all properly enthusiastic. Other papers followed suit and produced their reviews the next day: the weeklies treated us quite handsomely. Altogether a small triumph in its way. The scientific character of the work is recognised, though of course the critics chaff us for our " pompous phraseology ". It is a big plant on the public: a new method and a new theory!

CHAPTER II

MUNICIPAL AND UNIVERSITY
ADMINISTRATION
1892–1898

AT this point in the narrative I turn aside from the narrow track of social investigation, which we pursued together, the direction determined by ourselves, to the broad and crowded highway of municipal administration. If the foregoing chapter recalls the habitual morning's work from 1892 to 1898, the following pages account for the Other One's afternoons. And here I fall from the status of equal partnership to that of a humble servitor of my lord, with the added zest of being an observer and recorder of his doings. But alas! this essay in biography will not be accepted as impartial so I give the portrait by the well-known editor of the *Pall Mall Gazette* of Sidney Webb as he first appeared at the L.C.C. election of 1892 before the footlights of municipal democracy.

Mr. Sidney Webb is a very remarkable man, much more remarkable than anybody thinks, excepting himself. Since Mr. Chamberlain arose in Birmingham there has been no man so like him as Mr. Sidney Webb, who aspires to be Mr. Chamberlain of London—only more so.[1] For to all the energy and perseverance and municipal spirit of Mr. Chamberlain, Mr. Sidney Webb adds a great literary gift and a philosophic conception of social progress to which Mr. Chamberlain can lay no claim. He is a socialist; but he is no utopian dreamer, he is a man crammed with facts. He is no fanatic, but a wily, shrewd,

---

[1] *The Elector's Guide*, p. 50. Edited by W. T. Stead. Beyond the fact that S. W. endorsed and developed Chamberlain's doctrine of " high rates and a healthy city ", I see no likeness in character, opinion or circumstances, of the social investigator and Fabian permeator to the outstanding politician, orator and imperialist statesman of the last quarter of the nineteenth century. There is, however, a superficial coincidence in political career. Alike, they entered the Cabinet for the first time without previous subordinate office, as President of the Board of Trade, and alike they retired from the Cabinet, when Secretary of State for the Colonies; the significant distinction being that S. W. entered the Cabinet at about the same age at which Joseph Chamberlain retired from it, when the great man became the propagandist of a new fiscal policy.

adroit wirepuller, whose hand is felt in a great many quarters where it is not seen. The next three years will be a test as to whether he is as capable in taking part in a public body as he has shown himself to be in writing pamphlets, inspiring editors, and in general wire-pulling. . . . At present there is some doubt as to whether he is not the most dangerous candidate in the field for the cause which he has at heart. His contributions to the Fabian Society and the *Star* newspaper, and his interesting book on *The London Programme*, are so many red rags to the Conservative bull; and there is no doubt that if Mr. Sidney Webb's programme could be fathered upon every progressive candidate in the constituencies, the moderates would sweep London. Mr. Webb is not a candidate for to-day, he is one for the day after to-morrow. But, for that very reason, it is urgently to be desired that he should be elected to the County Council without more ado. There is nothing like putting such a man in harness to take the nonsense out of him, and to make him understand the wisdom of the old adage, *festina lente*. . . .

THE LONDON COUNTY COUNCIL

The establishment of an elected governing body for the metropolis in the guise of a county council was incidental to the scheme of reform of county government throughout England and Wales, which the President of the Local Government Board (Ritchie) passed into law as the Local Government Act of 1888. For the administration of the justices of the peace in quarter sessions, there was substituted administration by a directly elected county council. In the metropolis, comprising, besides the ancient corporation of the City of London, parts of the counties of Middlesex, Surrey, Essex and Kent, the indirectly elected Metropolitan Board of Works, representing the congeries of vestries and district boards throughout London, had been established thirty years earlier (1855).[1] In 1888, Mr.

[1] The establishment in 1855 of the Metropolitan Board of Works by Sir Benjamin Hall (Chief Commissioner of Works in the then Whig Ministry) may be ascribed to the pressing necessity for a new Main Drainage authority to prevent the Thames becoming a common sewer, a task in which the Metropolitan Commissioners of Sewers, appointed by the Government in 1848, had lamentably failed. The new Board was, on the whole, an efficient body, largely directed by a salaried chairman (Sir J. McGarel Hogg) who was imposed on it by the Government. Besides a successful main drainage scheme which took nearly twenty years to complete the Board has to its credit, during its thirty years' life, the construction of the Thames Embankment; the systematic administration of the London Building Act which had

Ritchie saw no practicable alternative to the definite excision of these parts of four counties from the remainder of their areas, and the transformation of the indirectly elected Metropolitan Board of Works into a directly elected county council, corresponding to those which elsewhere superseded the justices in quarter sessions. This transformation, revolutionary as it seemed to the Conservative Party, was the more readily accepted because the Metropolitan Board of Works had recently been besmirched and discredited by the exposure of certain exceptional cases of graft in which one or two of its members, in collusion with one or two of its principal officials, had been implicated. This exposure led to a revulsion of feeling, which co-operated with the desire to give London a municipal government worthy of its pre-eminence, induced a number of distinguished men of philanthropy and goodwill to come forward as candidates for the new body. So outstanding a personality as Lord Rosebery agreed to stand for the City, with a view to assuming the chairmanship.

The first election, in January 1889, was, from the standpoint of the experienced politician, an unorganised scramble. Neither the Liberal nor the Conservative Party used the party electoral machinery. Candidates spontaneously offered themselves to the electors, mainly as advocates of " good government ".[1] There were no deliberately formulated party

---

been passed in 1855; the organisation of the Metropolitan Fire Brigade after 1866; the clearance of large areas of the worst slums, various great street improvements, and many minor services. In its last years, the Board's record was stained by the cases of graft mentioned above, which were investigated by a Royal Commission. It is only fair to say that these were shown to have been quite exceptional, and that most of the Board's administration was not only honest but also fairly well organised.

[1] Elizabeth Haldane in *From One Century to Another*, 1937, describes the rise of the Progressive Party in London administration: " The development of the social services was seen in the new London County Council, with its rather advanced programme. There were at least a majority of 'Progressives' and John Burns advocated what he called 'Practicable Socialism' which made a good cry, so that socialism thus became something less to be feared than it had been so far. Sidney Webb was its principal supporter and he gave it a certain intellectual flavour; though his programme was advanced enough. Sidney and Beatrice Webb became our friends, and visited us at Cloan. There was always great discussion as to which was the abler, but no conclusions were arrived at, for both were extraordinarily able and yet more extraordinarily diligent. They made one feel heartily ashamed of one's idle hours when one saw how they worked from morning to night, producing volumes of carefully verified matter. They had great influence on politics on both

programmes among which the voters could choose. Almost the only lead as to policy was given by what was then an obscure body of young men and women, the Fabian Society,[1] which, by what was then an original device, caused all the candidates to be importuned by showers of printed lists of questions, sent by electors demanding answers to every issue of what ought to be "municipal politics". These were accompanied by pamphlets explaining in detail the policy afterwards known as municipal Socialism. In the absence of any contrary policy, a large proportion of the candidates, who had thought only of "good government", found themselves subscribing to this programme.

The first three years' term of the London County Council was chiefly occupied in framing the elaborate constitution required for so great an administration, and with tentative efforts towards increased efficiency and avoidance of waste. When the second election approached (that of 1892 at which the Other One became a candidate for a seat held by a Conservative), party organisation on both sides became definite and powerful. The Conservative Party saw the importance of controlling so influential a local authority as the London County Council had become. Opposing the Conservatives were those councillors who called themselves the Progressives, with a view to uniting for municipal purposes, along with the Liberals (largely Nonconformists), also the Conservative and Liberal Unionist sympathisers with an active policy in London administration; the churchmen and Roman Catholic philanthropists who wanted the slums and the mean streets reformed; and the trade unionist workmen who sought to insist on fairer conditions of employ-

sides because they saw nearly as much of Balfour, the Bishop of London and the Conservatives as they did of Liberals like my brother, though there were indeed those like Asquith who turned a deaf ear to their theories " (pp. 135-6).

[1] The Fabian Society, the oldest living Socialist society in this or any country, was founded in 1884. Bernard Shaw and Sidney Webb both joined it in the first year of its existence, and Webb was a member of its Executive Committee for fifty years, from 1885 to 1935. Beatrice became a member of the Fabian Society shortly after her marriage. In the 1945 election, over 200 of the 394 Labour members returned to Parliament were Fabians. (Ed.)

ment. This heterogeneous host was marshalled by a professedly non-political body (the London Reform Union), and was supplied with a programme—the Other One says by the Fabian Society—a programme which, somehow or other, found its way into six months' issues of *The Speaker*, then the weekly organ of intellectual Liberalism.[1]

It is difficult to bring home to the perplexed, pessimistic and jaded mind of post-war England the mental climate of the London Progressive movement of the 'nineties. Honest indignation at the mass misery of the working-class quarters of London, ardent hopefulness of what might be, and assured confidence in the way of betterment—this union of pity, hope and faith underlies *The London Programme* of 1892.

First the rousing of the sense of shame in the better-off citizens of London:

Twenty thousand of its citizens fight in the fearful daily struggle for bread at the dock gates, and even after the Pyrrhic victory of the great dock strike of 1889, one-third of them, on an average, struggle in vain. Thirty thousand of its children are at school entirely breakfastless. One in every five of the five millions who began again to-day the weary round of life will eventually quit that life in the workhouse or the hospital, for want of a better refuge. One in ten of them had to accept the bitter bread of official pauper charity last year. And all this in the richest and most productive city in the world, paying an annual tribute, or ground rent, of fifteen millions sterling for mere permission to occupy the low hills and swampy marsh by the Thames, which labour alone has rendered productive! . . . The million households, immersed in constant toil, and for the most part pinched by sordid cares, have long had no common standard, no conscious common action. Without effective municipal or political organisation, without unity of taxation or representation, a mere loose aggregate of shifting sand, this great community has lain almost helpless in its anarchy before the forces of spoliation. . . . We dare not neglect the sullen discontent now spreading among its toiling millions. If only for the sake of the rest of the Empire, the London masses must be organised

---

[1] These articles were afterwards published in book form (*The London Programme*, by Sidney Webb, 1892). They had been preceded by the Fabian Society's *Facts for Londoners* (56 pp., 1889), described as " an exhaustive collection of statistical and other facts relative to the metropolis, with suggestions for reform on socialist principles ".

for a campaign against the speculators, vestry jobbers, house farmers, water sharks, market monopolists, ground landlords, and other social parasites now feeding upon their helplessness. Metropolitan reform has become a national, if not an imperial question.[1]

By himself [pleads the author of *The London Programme*] the typical Londoner is a frail and sickly unit, cradled in the gutter, housed in a slum, slaving in a sweater's den, and dying in the work-house infirmary. Collectively he is a member of the greatest and most magnificent city which the world has known, commanding all the latest resources of civilisation, and disposing of almost boundless wealth. Accepting the principle of municipal co-operation, which has proved so advantageous in the larger provincial towns, what can Londoners as citizens do for themselves collectively to make the metropolis a pleasanter home for its million families?[2]

The London County Council was, to quote from *The London Programme*, " born in chains ". The powers with which it had been endowed did not approximate to those of a provincial county borough:

It had nothing to do with paving, cleansing or lighting the streets; waterworks, gasworks, markets, and tramways were completely out-side its province; its police formed an army as alien as the Irish constabulary; it was functionless and almost powerless in valuation and assessment; it did not collect its own rates; it had no more control over the Thames than over the tides; it was neither the sanitary nor the burial authority; and it could not even prepare or supervise the registration of the voters who elected it. It was, in fact, simply a cross between the county justices and the Metropolitan Board of Works, and its chief occupations were a strange hotch-potch of lunatic asylums and the fire brigade, main drainage and industrial schools, bridges and baby-farms.[3]

The embittered conflict at each election between Pro-gressives and Moderates, usually backed up by the Liberals and Conservatives respectively, raged round the question of increasing the authority of the L.C.C., on the one hand, and, on the other, checking, if not superseding, its powers by establishing minor municipal bodies similar to the non-county boroughs scattered about the English counties. For it must be noted that *The London Programme* of 1892 did

---

[1] *The London Programme*, by Sidney Webb, p. 7 (1891).
[2] *Ibid*. p. 207.   [3] *Ibid*. p. 10.

not stop at improvements in the machinery of government.
The London County Council of the future was to make
energetic use of its existing and future powers. According
to the programme that was suggested, it was to become like
the Manchester or Birmingham County Borough Council, the
water authority, the gas authority, the tramway authority,
the market authority, the housing authority, the dock
authority and the hospital authority, and, most preposterous
of all—the police authority, for the metropolitan area. As I
shall describe in another chapter, one at least of the Progressives desired and intended, already in 1892, to unify
London education and, for this purpose, to make the L.C.C.
also the education authority for London, in supersession of
the directly elected London School Board, which was confined to elementary education.

New sources of revenue were to be secured by the equalisation of rates between rich and poor districts, by the taxation
of ground rents and by a municipal death duty. Above all,
the unearned increment, due to the mere growth of the
population or to public improvements, was to be partially
absorbed by the community, either through betterment
rates, or by the County Council having the power of compulsory purchase of land on the basis of a special valuation
as a source of revenue. To quote Joseph Chamberlain, the
London County Council of those days was a volatile body
" whose ambition soars far above those details of local
government upon which the health and happiness of the
people mainly depend ".[1]

Glimpses of the L.C.C. at work and of the reaction set
up by the doings and doctrines of the Progressives, at the
polls and in the press—extending even to the august circles
of the Cabinet and ex-Cabinet—appear in the MS. diaries
1892–98, and may interest the student of municipal institutions.

The Argoed, July 30th, 1893.—The London County Council
looms large in our lives because it takes up so much of Sidney's
energies. Every day he comes home he tells me about his various

[1] *The Speaker,* February 9, 1895.

committees and gives me glimpses of the internal working of the machine. Let me see whether I can sum up some of the impressions he leaves on my mind. First, the L.C.C. consists of the Progressive portion of it. The Moderates, as a party, are simply out of it. Individual Moderates become chairmen of committees, but only because in those particular departments they are more progressive than the Progressives. Indeed, the conversion of the abler Moderates to definite portions of the Progressive programme is one of the notable features of the County Council, and a token of the triumph of the idea of public administration as against private enterprise. That is, of course, the whole significance of the L.C.C.—the growing faith in and enthusiasm for public service. It is not that the L.C.C. does so much more than its predecessor the Metropolitan Board of Works, but that it does all its work efficiently and with zeal, and with a view to increasing and not diminishing its functions. There is no one man at the L.C.C. who dominates the organisation. I imagine in the last Council Lord Rosebery took a pre-eminent part. But, though Lord Rosebery continues a member, he seldom attends; and his swooping down on the Council, with regard to a proposed site the other day, was much resented. The Council is really run by various groups of county councillors, circling round the three office-holders—who are all county councillors—the chairman, vice-chairman and deputy-chairman of the Council. The most prominent of these groups is the one directing the parliamentary and political policy of the County Council—among whom are B. F. C. Costelloe, Sidney and J. W. [afterwards Sir John Williams] Benn. Then come the chairmen of the non-political committees—such as housing, parks, asylums, etc., all of whom are in touch with the chairman of the Council. John Burns occupies a quite unique position, owing, not to his committee work, but to his powerful personality and Labour following outside the Council. His influence, moreover, is diminishing since he has become an M.P.

It is, perhaps, a sign that the County Council is still young that the whole direction of its administration is in the hands of the councillors and not relegated to the paid servants. There are twenty or thirty men who make a profession of the Council, in the sense of spending their whole energies on its work. This, of course, means that the L.C.C. is a middle-class body; composed of men of sufficient means to work for nothing. And, even those working-men who are on it, contribute little to its government; they speak in the weekly meetings of the Council, but they take little or no part in committees.

The weekly Council meetings are, perhaps, the least important part of the Council's proceedings. The aim of the able chairman of a committee is to pass his reports through Tuesday's meeting without raising contentious questions. It is only the badly-managed committees that get their activities talked about and their policies discussed. The Council is a machine for evolving a committee; the committee is a machine for evolving one man—the chairman. Both alike a machine for dodging the democracy (in a crude sense) by introducing government by a select minority instead of the rule of the majority. . . .

Grosvenor Road, June 20th, 1894.—Haldane just been here: says the Unionist Party will make a determined attack on the L.C.C. and attempt to break London up into separate municipalities. That this has been in the mind of Chamberlain, Balfour and Salisbury is clear from their recent utterances. But Sidney says that it is an impossibility; you could not divest the L.C.C. of the great bulk of its powers though, of course, it would be possible to change its constitution and reinstate the Metropolitan Board of Works. But that would be too much to propose. Meanwhile, it is of the utmost importance to carry the vestries. I must see whether I can get the London Reform Union to take the matter up. Cannot help thinking that Chamberlain is leading his party very wrong and that he will knock his head against a blank wall both on the London question and on that of the trade unions. It looks like sheer political idiocy to throw the trade unions and the London Progressives into the arms of the Liberals—but, I suppose, he thinks he sees his game! Personally, one would regret being forced into the fight—as we shall both be if the attack is serious. It is so much pleasanter to investigate and write rather than organise and speak. Just now our life is so perfect; it might easily become strained, and dissipated in mere manipulation. But one thing is clear: we must live the plainest, most healthful life in order to get through the maximum of work; and one must economise on all personal luxuries in order to have cash to spend on anything that turns up to be done. With so much love and personal happiness, one ought to be able to do much for others.

The malignant desire of the Conservative Party of 1894 to destroy the County Council that its own Ministry of 1888 had set up, in order to break up the great metropolitan area into an unspecified number of independent municipalities, seems to have provoked us to widen our sphere of electioneering activity. For the triennial election of the London School Board in 1894, the Fabian Society threw itself into the " Fight against Diggleism ",[1] which our close friend,

---

[1] See p. 67. (Ed.)

Graham Wallas, was successfully organising, and which the Other One helped by various journalist activities. Our own main attention was given to the most neglected part of the electoral field, that of the five or six thousand members of the hundred or so vestries,[1] whose triennial term of office expired shortly after that of the members of the School Board. The vestry election campaign throughout London was taken in hand, not very efficiently, by the London Reform Union, the body formed primarily to look after the Progressive Party's electioneering for the County Council. We ourselves could do little more than lead the forlorn hope in our own Tory Westminster (at that time the united parishes of St. Margaret and St. John), where we both offered ourselves as candidates.

Borough Farm, Surrey, July 25th, 1894.— . . . We have the organisation of the vestry elections on our hands—I having instigated the London Reform Union to take it up, having got Sidney appointed as chairman of the sub-committee, feel that we must pull the fight through successfully. Also, started a " Citizen Sunday " for next October in the hope of drawing in the clergy of all denominations into London reform.[2] But all this casual work means taking time from our book, and I am glad to be down here to concentrate on this very tough bit of analysis. If we get on to the Westminster Vestry, that will take up even more time, and Heaven only knows when we shall

---

[1] It is hard to convey to the present generation the confusion and obscurity of the local administration of the several parishes of London outside the one square mile of the City Corporation during the whole of the nineteenth century. The ratepayers of the twenty-five large parishes elected vestries of 24 to 120 members, who administered (without any other supervision or control than, after 1871, that of the very perfunctory Local Government Board) the paving, lighting, cleansing and draining of the streets; all that existed of the sanitation of the dwellings and the removal of refuse, and many miscellaneous services. They had authority to levy an unlimited rate on the householders. Nearly a hundred smaller parishes were grouped in 1855 under fourteen district boards, of from 27 to 84 members, which were nominated triennially by the elected vestries of the constituent tiny parishes. When the London County Council was established in 1888, these vestries and district boards were spending nearly £2,000,000 annually.

[2] " Citizen Sunday ", a chosen day on which all churches and chapels are invited to unite in prayer for social reform, and to devote a sermon to some aspect of the citizen's duty, has since [1936] continued annually. It was at first sponsored by the Christian Social Union, which became the Industrial Christian Fellowship. A circular appeal, signed by about a hundred leading citizens, including, besides ministers of all denominations, prominent trade unionists, employers of labour and politicians, is addressed annually to all places of worship.

get the book to the printer: at present the thought of it undone and not visibly growing oppresses me much.

Grosvenor Road, December 1st, 1894.—Galton's little study turned into the central office of the Progressive candidates for the Westminster vestry elections. Certainly, we have created our organisation and selected our 90 candidates with singularly little trouble. The first stage was to create a branch of the London Reform Union—Sidney, chairman, Galton secretary; the second to call, in the name of the L.R.U. branch, a conference of all the temperance, trade union and political organisations and to form a Progressive council—Sidney chairman, Galton secretary; the final step to select our candidates and to form these into one organisation: Sidney chairman, Galton secretary. These three organisations, under their respective chairmen and secretaries, have worked with wonderful harmony; and have between them, at a cost of £30, initiated a really vigorous campaign. The Westminster Radicals, a poor down-trodden lot, perpetually licked at all elections, hardly know themselves with their 90 candidates. Sidney has drafted the address, Galton is acting as election agent, and the working-men candidates are doing the canvassing and even the clerk's work. If by some marvellous chance we get returned to-day fortnight, we shall have our work cut out to drill them into working shape.

Altogether we have been living in the atmosphere of elections. Graham's candidature for the School Board gave us a personal interest in the fight. Of course, the result of the School Board elections is most satisfactory, from the point of view of the Progressives generally, and most exasperating for the Progressive Party on the School Board. Graham Wallas is making friends with the " left wing " of the enemy in the hope of detaching the majority of them from the educational policy of Diggle, and turning the scale.[1] It is very curious, that both Sidney and Graham, though very advanced in their views, are better liked by the Moderates of the L.C.C. and L.S.B. than other members of the Progressive Party. " Wily Webb ", as Sidney is called on the L.C.C., is always colloguing with the more sensible of the Moderates with a view of getting them to agree to things *in detail* which they could hardly accept in bulk. That seems also to be Graham's policy which he is carefully beginning on the London School Board. The truth is that *we want the things done* and we don't much care what

---

[1] The School Board election in November 1894 resulted in the virtual defeat of the policy so long pursued by the Rev. J. R. Diggle, the leader of the Church party. But his opponent, the Hon. Lyulph Stanley (later Lord Stanley of Alderley), failed to secure a " Progressive " majority, though Graham Wallas came in with a notable reinforcement. This produced an almost evenly divided Board, in which a few enlightened and well-disposed churchmen often voted with the Progressives; a situation giving scope for skilful compromises!

persons or which party gets the credit; we are pretty confident that, if it comes to a fight, we know the arts of war as well as our enemies; but, between the battles, our cause may be advanced by diplomacy—even by a frank alliance with our former enemies if they be willing to take one little step forward in our direction. The Fabians are still convinced believers in the policy of permeation.

Meanwhile, the book hangs fire. With both Sidney and Galton completely absorbed, I feel helpless. Moreover, as a candidate myself for the vestry, I have caught a little of the election fever and am growing rapidly excited and perturbed. The L.C.C. elections, upon which so much depends, are looming in the distance. It might be better to give myself up frankly to electioneering and use these weeks as an opportunity for observing how elections are fought and won. It is all part of our subject-matter—democracy. Surely we shall end by constructing the great " Webb " chart of the modern democratic state?

December 1894.—Crushing defeat at Westminster vestry elections; only 5 Progressives out of 96! We had persuaded ourselves that we should at least carry St. John's II. solid, and make some show in St. John's I. and III.—the St. Margaret's Ward we recognised as hopeless. But, apparently, the slums of Westminster are as completely Tory as the palaces. I do not think there has been any lack of energy or even of skill in engineering such forces as we had. But it is obvious that our attempt to collar the constituency with three weeks' work—mostly amateur—was a fiasco, which we ought to have expected. Against us we had a perfect organisation with a permanent staff, a local paper and unlimited money, we had all the wealthy residents, nearly all the employers of labour, and the whole liquor interest—no fewer than ten publicans and five other persons connected with the Trade, running as Conservative candidates. We had a register from which every known Liberal had been knocked off, year by year, without a protest from the feeble flickering little Liberal Association. Behind all this, we had Burdett-Coutts's charities and churches. And to fight these potent powers Galton stood single-handed with a mob of working-men and small tradesmen candidates—some of them good talkers, but like most Labour men full of gassy optimism, caring only to fore-gather in the rooms of the Liberal Association and talk big of the victory they are going to win. Our one strong card was the corruption of the last vestry—" squalid jobbery amounting to corruption ". But the Conservatives very rightly preferred a little " jobbery "—infinitesimal burden on the rates—to a possible defeat of their party in one of its fastnesses. Deeply-rooted distrust of entrusting business to a lot of " small folk " of no standing operated, too, against our candidates; working-men—other things being equal—prefer an employer to a fellow-worker as a candidate; other things were in this case unequal—to our disadvantage.

Add to these causes the perfectly legitimate grudge the Westminster ratepayers have against the Progressives for the 6d. extra imposed by the Rate Equalisation Bill.

All that I have heard of vestrydom in this election and its doings, discourages me from hoping much from the new state of things. In London, there is no public opinion and no public knowledge about the government of these small areas. The L.C.C. has to submit itself to full publicity, its every action is scanned by a hostile press, its proceedings are witnessed by the whole metropolitan community. But in a vestry area there is no public supervision; you may live in a district 50 years and hardly know of the existence of your vestry—the ordinary working-man or professional man would not know any one of the vestrymen by name, will hardly know when and at what time they hold their meetings, still less what is the weekly or yearly record of work. It is only within three weeks of the election that we discovered that there had been an appalling amount of corruption and jobbery. The whole government is left practically in the hands of small tradesmen and one or two political wire-pullers largely interspersed with publicans and builders. Here the worst form of local feeling manifests itself—a local feeling which is in itself incipient jobbery. If there is a sanitary inspector to be appointed, a local man is most likely to be chosen quite irrespective of his qualifications. Of course, it does not stop at this comparatively innocent precept of "Westminster work for Westminster men" (to my mind a most rotten maxim), it soon degenerates into preference for a friend or relation of a popular vestryman. And, against this, the citizen has no chance of redress for the simple reason that he never knows what is going on. Probably the best governed London parishes are the purely aristocratic vestries—where the retired Indian civil servant, the officer, the rector, the medical man, rule undisputed. You cannot trust a democracy without any provision for *full and effective publicity*. That was why one felt half-hearted as to the results of this election. The little tradesmen or working-men whom we were supporting were no better than their Tory fellows. If they had got elected without a strong leader they would have sunk to the same level of mean local feeling and petty jobbery. Is it possible to create civic patriotism in a small *metropolitan* area, with no common life and no local press read, as a matter of course, by all classes of the community? I fear not—at least not in our day.

Grosvenor Road, February 10th, 1895.—Three weeks off the L.C.C. elections. Sidney spending all his mornings writing articles for all sorts of papers—especially the religious organs, such as the *Guardian*, the *Church Times*, the *Christian World*, the *Methodist Times*, etc. We are, in fact, making a vigorous attempt to get the Church, the Catholic and the Nonconformist ministers on our side. As all the " sinners " are against us, we might as well get the saints to support us. Moreover, we resolutely refuse to believe that any good person *properly informed* could be otherwise than a Progressive! If we are beaten—*i.e.* if a Moderate majority is returned—it will not be for lack of organisation. We are better *organised* than our opponents—if they win it will show that the common opinion is against us. . . .

Grosvenor Road, March 5th, 1895.—An anti-climax! After all the heat on both sides, after the blowing of both the big party trumpets, the calling to arms of saints and sinners by their respective champions, the rousing, on the one hand, of all the threatened interests, the appeal, on the other hand, to the forces of piety and democracy, London citizens send back an exactly even number of Moderates and Progressives—a bare half of registered electors taking the trouble to vote. In so many words, our constituents laugh in their sleeves, and say " tweedledee, tweedledum ". As far as Sidney personally is concerned, it is " as in 1892 ", his poll becoming fractionally higher, his majority fractionally lower. In a Conservative constituency, he retains a Progressive majority of eighteen hundred votes.

The loss of the second seat, too, means practically no change since it is fully accounted for by Keylock's stupidity and Elliott's [Social Democratic Federation candidate] superior poll.[1] In Deptford at least the mind of the electors is apparently unchanged. But, though this is most satisfactory, yet we do not disguise from ourselves that there is nothing like the enthusiasm of 1892. The same proportion of the electors went to the polling booth and voted for Sidney—largely because we insisted on it. . . .

Grosvenor Road, March 1895.—Sidney low about the L.C.C.— brooding over the defeat. It is not unnatural now that we should hear rumours of the magnificent organisation of our opponents—of £30,000 collected for the election, of an electoral council composed of delegates from the central Conservative Association and the Municipal Society, and the Moderate Party sitting daily receiving reports from constituencies; of swarms of convassers, of, in fact, a perfect electioneering kit for each candidate. There may be some basis for these reports—

---

[1] H. Keylock and J. Elliott split between them the Progressive vote and let in the Moderate candidate. H. Keylock represented Deptford on the L.C.C., 1892–95; he was said to be strong in support of municipal services, but timid in facing any consequent rise in the rates. (Ed.)

but, if all this happened, then why did not the Moderates poll a higher vote? No, there is no accounting for the defeat except the falling away of our supporters—in some cases, their transference to the other side, but usually their abstention. From reports, the explanation seems to be largely the lack of employment during a time of fearful cold—with the indifference and even savage hostility to all existing institutions which this state breeds. " Everybody is either out of work or only half employed and, consequently, out of sorts with everybody else, and some think if they could have a change of any sort, it must be an improvement." These words I read yesterday by chance in a report from a London branch of a great trade union; acting on this soreness—this feeling of quite unmerited misery—we have the I.L.P. abuse of the Progressives, and the cunning appeals of the Moderates for support to begin great public improvements without waiting for such fanciful reform as betterment rates. But the general conclusion that comes out of it is that an empty belly is, from our point of view, a bad politician. These times of physical want and mental despair are either the seed times of angry revolutionary feeling or of colourless despairing quietude. We forget that it was not until the dark years of 1881–85 were well over that *constitutional socialism*, as distinguished from *revolutionary socialism*, began to grow. It was no coincidence that the great Progressive victory came in the year of the greatest prosperity. We must educate and wait for fat years.

It has added to Sidney's discomfiture that the mercurial H. W. Massingham has turned against him. Massingham has had fits of admiration for Sidney, of more or less duration! Only the other day we heard of him dilating on his greatness, and asserting that any day he cared he could be in the Cabinet! All through the L.C.C. campaign he has been more than friendly—both publicly and privately. But the results of the fight have brought about a reaction against Sidney; and strangely enough it has been Sidney's personal success which seems to have tipped the balance. The fall of Burns' majority has angered Massingham, and the fact that Sidney—a middle-class collectivist— has not received the same snub from the multitude has made him still angrier. For Massingham has a hero-worship for John Burns. His excitable unstable nature has always been attracted by the boisterous vigour and immense self-conceit and assurance of our great Labour leader. As a dramatic critic, he has infinitely preferred the stalwart demagogue, with his picturesque language and bracing personality, to Sidney's quiet, unpretentious little figure, with its even flow of statistics, arguments and diplomatic persuasiveness (or as some would say evasiveness!), and, like a good critic, he is sore and angry that the audience do not take his view and favour his favourite. For the rest,

Burns has always disliked and suspected the pair of us and has instilled some of his prejudices into Massingham's mind. But Sidney will write a soft answer—and in a few months, perhaps weeks, the tantrum will be over.

There is no use blinding ourselves to the setback to our ideas. Tom Mann said that the victory of the Progressives would redound to the glory of official Liberalism. Quite the contrary, it is our defeat which will give them secret joy. " No more of your collectivism for us ", the Liberal capitalist will say—" it cannot even buy votes for our party." It will doubtless harden the heart of the old gang: militate against the reconstruction of the Liberal Party on the collectivist basis. And, while it will delay permeation, it will also weaken the chances of an Independent Labour Party becoming any force in the land. F. Hammill and Peter Curran have discredited themselves—by their success and failure. They have injured the Progressives, without showing any strength of their own. No class of Englishman can long tolerate the simple wrecker. . . .

Grosvenor Road, March 13th, 1895.—Yesterday at the L.C.C. was an exciting scene. When we arrived at half past two the entrance was crowded and all the galleries filled—the inside of the building leading to the Council chamber thronged with councillors and their immediate friends and relations. By Charles Harrison's kindness, I was passed on to the dais where I sat between Lady Farrer and Mrs. Beachcroft on the Moderate side of the chair. All the councillors were in their places before the clock struck three. To everyone's surprise Sir J. Hutton, though in the building, refused to take the chair, sulking at his non-re-election by his own party—Charles Harrison, vice-chairman, opening the proceedings in his hoarse guttural. The election of the chairman [Sir Arthur Arnold] was a foregone conclusion—the aldermen an agreed compromise. Both parties had their men in attendance, and they were ushered in by the two whips and welcomed by the new chairman. A distinguished company, three retired heads of great government departments, a bevy of peers— Ritchie, the stepfather of the Council, E. Hubbard, an aristocratic director of the Bank of England, Whitmore, the leader of the Tory M.P.'s for London and the organiser of the Moderate forces; in fact, only one nonentity among the new aldermen, the Progressive Hubbard, a rough and ready temperance member of the old Council. Certainly, if the Progressives have accomplished no other good, they have made the L.C.C. the most accomplished, distinguished, and even the most aristocratic, local body in the world! A strange effect of the Labour and Socialist onslaught on London! And we must admit that the Moderate victories have raised the standard of good looks of the L.C.C.

Slim aristocrats, well-fed and slightly dissipated-looking frequenters of London drawing-rooms and clubs, are, from a scenic point of view, welcome contrasts to the stunted figures of the Labour representatives and the ungraceful corpulence of the Progressive men of business. But the manners are as distinctly deteriorated. The " gentlemen's " party are loud and insolent in their ways—an insolence which is possibly a reaction from their long term of servitude to an overwhelming Progressive majority. Our side was subdued, sitting tight and forcing their way through, by their bare majority to the deputy-chairmanship—thus retaining the three executive offices. Over Dickinson's appointment raged a fierce debate—his rejection by Wandsworth, his partisanship, and finally his former acceptance of a salary, being alternatively advanced as arguments against his re-election. When Sidney rose to defend him (I noticed Ritchie turn round to scrutinize the speaker with quick curiosity), the interruptions of the Moderates reached their climax—Sidney being, for the nonce, the *bête noire* of the opposition. All we could do was to save Dickinson by promising a committee of enquiry into the whole subject of the deputy-chairmanship.[1] Whether we shall save him and his salary in the end, I much doubt.

It is quite obvious that the brunt of the battle will be over in a few months. The Moderates will make a determined attempt to reverse the policy of the late Council in all its controversial points. If they do not succeed in capturing, or, at any rate, obstructing the machine, they will tire in their efforts. Their party, though well equipped with able men, has no staying power—their attendance will fall off rapidly as the novelty wears off and the game of imperial politics becomes more absorbing, or the delights of sport and pleasure more enticing. Of course, there will still be powerful critics who are able to push us forward whither we do not desire to go, and pull us backward from our own course. All this will mean more strain, more temper, and more judgement. Whether, when the three years have elapsed, and the fourth Council takes its place in Spring Gardens, we shall have survived the ordeal, remains to be seen! But, whatever else

[1] The office of deputy chairman of the L.C.C. has an interesting history. Unlike the chairmanship, or vice-chairmanship, it was at one time a paid post. The appointment in its early form originated in the Progressive distrust of permanent officials, whom they suspected of being under Tory influence. A deputy chairman was, therefore, appointed from among the Council's members. He was expected to exercise personal control over the staff, and paid a substantial salary to enable him to give his whole time to the job. The post was first held by F. B. Firth, M.P., leader of the Progressive Party, and on his death by A. H. Haggis, 1889–91. The salary was abolished in 1895, when W. H. Dickinson completed his term, and a tradition has since then developed of appointing a member of the opposition to the post. See *History of the London County Council*, by Gibbon and Bell, p. 35. (Ed.)

may happen, we are not the kind of folk to say to the electorate, " Lord, let thy servants now depart in peace ". If we die, we will die fighting—and leave marks behind us!

Grosvenor Road, July 8th, 1895.—Meanwhile, the L.C.C. proceeds satisfactorily in spite of the fact that the Moderates have now a majority of one of the elected members. The Moderates have failed to wreck the Progressive Party policy—whenever they have been led out to do battle, they have ended in running away from the issue. Of course, new enterprise in the direction of municipalisation has been damped down; but, wherever the lines have been already laid, the machine runs smoothly on—with, perhaps, less friction than when the Moderates felt themselves a trampled down minority and cried out piteously to outside authorities, like the House of Lords, to help them. It is much more difficult for the peers to refuse to pass a proposal which is brought before them by Lord Cadogan than when it was promoted by Charles Harrison. And, if the truth must be told, the peers are the least reactionary of the new Moderate recruits and are apt to act as a centre between the Tory rump and the Progressive vanguard. So works our English society—progressivism may yet be saved by the priests and the lords. . . .

Grosvenor Road, March 2nd, 1898. [Three years later.]—A great meeting at St. James's Hall—Lord Rosebery to the rescue. I sat behind him and watched him narrowly. He had lost that drugged look—heavy eyes and morbid flesh—that he had as premier. He is at once older, healthier and *better* looking. His speech had vigour, astuteness and flashes of dramatic genius. But he was woefully full of himself; his whole expression and attitude was concentrated self-consciousness and sensitiveness—not sufficient of an actor to lose himself in his part, not sufficient of a patriot to lose himself in his cause. Throughout there was an undercurrent of complaint—of personal grudge against the political world. He is not a leader. Outside foreign politics he has no creed and only a scrappy knowledge; his very egotism is ineffective egotism—an egotism that shrinks from the world's touch, not the egotism that forces itself on the world. For my part, if a man is to be full of himself, I like him to have the will and the capacity to make the world full of him also!

No one knows how the L.C.C. election will turn out: both sides suffer in turn from hope and depression. The Conservative organisation is straining every nerve to get the Moderates in: whilst we, on our side, are beating up every available Progressive force wheresoever it is located. There is a good deal of beating of big drums over this election: the Conservatives say Lord Salisbury's Government is at stake, the Progressives that the L.C.C. is to be damned or saved. As a matter of fact, neither will happen: and sensible persons on both sides feel somewhat ashamed of the exaggeration. Apart from the result as a symptom of public opinion, it is doubtful whether it would not suit the Progressives that the Moderates should get a small majority, and the Conservatives that the Progressives should hold office on insecure tenure. An overwhelming defeat would naturally be disastrous to either side, but we imagine that public opinion is too divided for that. We incline to believe in a small Progressive majority; the Moderate whip, on the other hand, expects to win six seats. But there is no index to the public opinion of that anonymous creature— the London elector. . . .

Grosvenor Road, March 1898.—*The L.C.C. Election.* We sallied forth about 8.30 A.M. (Sidney having voted first in Westminster) laden with sandwiches, teapots and oranges, to fit up the committee rooms. It was a glorious morning, the Westminster buildings rising out of the blue atmosphere and the river dancing in the brilliant morning sun. At 9.30, I had settled down at one of the six committee rooms, spent an hour arranging the bringing-up cards, and learning my way about on the map of the district. Throughout the morning working-men helpers dribbled in, and voters turned up anxious to find out their polling district. About 3.30, the bringers-up trouped in; at 5, it was a crowd in the little room, each waiting to report progress. Then came on a heavy fall of snow; but the feeling of the Progressives was so hot that they trudged on through the sleet and the slush—not one of my fifteen workers gave up working. But I felt that the Lord had meant to test the strength of the conviction of the working-man and I trembled with doubt—would he go to the poll in spite of the rain? That was the question which agitated the heads of the organisation for the next two hours. Directly we learnt that the working-class districts had polled 60% we knew we were safe—and hoped that Deptford was a sample this time of London. Then the hurried dinner— nineteen of our West End helpers; then the exciting hours of the count; then the midnight visit to the National Liberal Club all aglow with Progressive victories—and then to bed, oh! so tired, far too tired to sleep.

The Moderates are hardly snowed under as in 1892, but they are soundly beaten, leaving us in a great majority for the next three years. They owe their defeat to the foolhardy attack on the L.C.C. led by Salisbury and Devonshire, to the apathy of the Conservative voter during a Conservative Government, and the negative character of the Moderate programme. Last time, the Moderates declared themselves in favour of Chamberlain's social programme: this time, as a Conservative Ministry was in power and doing little or nothing to carry out the programme, they could not pretend to be in favour of it. The workman, too, who is sentimentally attached to the Works Department (which represents his old shibboleths of standard rates and hours and direct employment), rallied to the defence of the Progressives with great enthusiasm. And the reaction against the Conservative Government was greater than the reaction against the Progressives. Probably, therefore, we are in for another six years' power—for so long as the Conservatives remain at Downing Street we shall not be turned out of Spring Gardens. It is a question whether the country does not advance more quickly with the Conservatives in power at the centre and the Progressives capturing local authorities, than with a weak Liberal Government, and a provincial reaction. . . .

THE TECHNICAL EDUCATION BOARD

It is a trite saying that it is the unexpected that happens in the development of institutions. The Progressive leaders of 1892 would have been mightily surprised if they had been told that the L.C.C. of the twentieth century would be far less concerned with material things such as gas and water, docks and markets, tramways and tunnels, than with the education and recreation, medical treatment and adequate maintenance of the five millions of inhabitants within the metropolitan area. And yet the main task accomplished by the Other One during his eighteen years' service on the L.C.C. was its development as the greatest educational authority in the world; its first beginnings being the establishment of the Technical Education Board covering alike elementary, secondary and university education by means of grants-in-aid and the establishment of a gigantic scholarship ladder; and then, through the 1903 Education Act, absorbing into itself as the practically unrestricted single education authority, for the whole metropolitan area, the School Board with its colossal network of elementary schools.

A series of accidents started the L.C.C. on its career as the education authority. The first of these was a mishap to the Conservative budget of 1890, which had included an addition to the spirit duties, to be credited to the county and county borough councils, partly for a scheme of police superannuation, and partly for the purchase of publicans' licences in order to get rid of redundant public-houses. To the latter proposal a storm of opposition arose, mainly from the temperance movement, which objected to such a recognition of property in licences. Towards the end of the session, after the increased taxes had been voted, and were in course of collection, the Government found itself constrained to abandon the proposed appropriation to the purchase of licences. The constitutional point was then pressed that the new tax revenue could not be left unappropriated in the same session in which it was authorised. At this stage, A. H. D. Acland,[1] a much underrated British statesman, an enthusiast for public education and one of the few adepts in the new subject of technical education, jumped in. For three days he fought to get the " whiskey money " definitely allocated, in England, to technical education, and in Wales to the execution of the Welsh Intermediate Education Act. In the end, the Government agreed to the proposal for Wales, and for England handed the money over to the county councils to expend as they thought fit; but with a distinct intimation that definite charges would hereafter be laid on them for educational purposes.

The newly established London County Council had not found time in its first term to take action under the Technical

[1] " A. H. D. Acland," writes R. B. Haldane in his autobiography (pp. 93 and 103), ". . . a real reformer in elementary and secondary education and to whom I was attracted on this account, was another of our members. Mr. Gladstone never cared for him much because, having once been a clergyman, he had renounced his clerical orders so as the better to be able to enter public life effectively. But, partly I think in response to the strong appeals some of us made to him, Mr. Gladstone, when he next came in in 1892, made Acland Minister of Education, a position in which he did splendid work. . . . Arthur Acland was also a stimulating personality, full of knowledge, particularly about primary and secondary education." To this appreciation I may add that from the first days of Labour representation and throughout the career of the parliamentary Labour Party right up to his death in 1926, Arthur Acland was a generous supporter of the new movement. In the general elections of 1918, '22, '23 and '24 he gave considerable sums to enable young university men to run as Labour candidates; and by a donation of £1600 he made possible the establishment of the National Labour Club in 1919. Finally, he left £10,000 on trust to enable young Labour men and women to pursue research in political and economic subjects. His lifelong connection with the consumers' co-operative movement is well known. Though he was not among the brilliant or dominant, he was assuredly the most enlightened and far-seeing of all the Liberal politicians of the last decade of the nineteenth and the first decade of the twentieth century.

Instruction Act; not even when in 1890 it found itself endowed with the funds thus vaguely allocated for the purpose. It so happened that S. W.'s first motion on the Council was one proposing that a committee should be appointed to consider whether the Council should not proceed under the Act. So cautiously worded a resolution, not taken seriously, was adopted unanimously; and the mover was left to choose the committee, subject to the usual exact representation of the party balance on the Council. S. W. has often explained how, in his anxiety to put on the ablest members from the various sections, he found he had not provided for a chairman, as practically all his nominees proved to be already chairmen of other committees. He was, therefore, virtually driven to preside himself. This committee was persuaded not to rely on its inner consciousness but to engage a young man—Hubert Llewellyn Smith— then acting temporarily as lieutenant to Arthur Acland in the promotion of technical education, to prepare a report, setting forth the existing position, and sketching out a possible policy for the Council. Within a year this comprehensive report—a volume in itself—was approved by the committee as a general outline. Meanwhile, the committee had been led to accept a new constitution. For the Council simply to add one more to its score of committees, wholly composed of members of the Council, would have antagonised the School Board and the City companies, and jeopardised the support of the teachers and the trade unionists. Far better, suggested Sidney, create a new instrument, which might conciliate opponents, and even enlist their assistance. This took shape in the Technical Education Board—a title not known to the law—composed of twenty members of the Council, with fifteen nominated outsiders. Moreover, explained the Fabian, if the Council was going to nominate outsiders at all, it was better to let the rival or sectional interests choose their own representatives than for the Council to impose its choice. Hence, the Council was recommended to allow the School Board, the City and Guilds Institute, the Head Masters' Association, the Head Mistresses' Association, the London Teachers' Association, and even the London Trades Council, to nominate their own representatives on what thus became a hybrid body. Incidentally, it seemed to follow almost automatically that this Technical Education Board, unlike the score of ordinary committees of the Council, had to be freed, once its annual estimates were approved, from the necessity of seeking specific approval of every expenditure exceeding £50, and even of reporting its proceedings more than once a quarter, and then only for the information of the Council.

One of the most effective instruments in the Board's policy of co-ordination was its elaborate scholarship system. In its popular aspect, this was an educational ladder of unprecedented dimensions. It was, indeed, among educational ladders, the most gigantic in extent, the most elaborate in its organisation of " intakes " and promotions, and the most diversified in kinds of excellence selected and in types of training provided, that existed anywhere in the world. But, in the policy of the T.E.B., the system of scholarships and bursaries was more than a " capacity-catching " device. The scholarships brought a steady stream of clever boys and girls to the languishing endowed secondary schools, to the expanding technical institutes and to the unfilled classes of the university colleges. Payment for these county scholars was made the basis of a system of annual grants to institutions under all sorts of independent administrations, justifying expert inspection of their work, and a carefully devised code of regulations to ensure their continued efficiency. What had previously been a chaos of isolated institutions, largely unaware of one another's existence, became gradually welded—without suppression of local administration by separate bodies of governors—into a graded educational system covering every part of London. Into such a system it became possible for the Council gradually to introduce new and additional secondary schools and technical institutes, to fill geographical gaps and relieve local congestion, without destroying or even weakening the older institutions, or arousing their opposition. Finally, in calling into being the Central School of Arts and Crafts and the London Day Training College, the T.E.B. set a standard in technology and pedagogy by which the whole kingdom has profited.

Under the initial inspiration of Arthur Acland and Hubert Llewellyn Smith, Sidney induced the Board to begin by appointing a bevy of highly expert officers—the scientist William Garnett as secretary and chief officer; Dr. Kimmins as chief inspector; G. J. Frampton and W. R. Lethaby as art advisers. Technical education was not to be cramped or fettered by limitations of grade or age or even of subject. The Board, indeed, could not go beyond the Council's statutory limitation. This, however, was found to be, when looked at in the right light, not unduly narrow! Every subject aided by the Science and Art Department was within the definition; and also any other subject that the Department might sanction at any time. Sidney chuckled when he described how he went to see Acland—then the Minister in charge of education—and represented that London was a kingdom in itself in which practically every occupation was represented. Would the Minister, accordingly, in order to save official time and trouble, at once sanction as " technical instruction in London " every subject that the department had already sanctioned anywhere? " I think we can do that, cannot we? " asked Acland of (Sir John) Donnelly, his permanent head. The outcome was an order adding, for London, a long list of subjects to the already lengthy array of the Science and Art Department, including all the sciences and all the arts, all foreign languages together with modern history, economics, geography, commercial education, domestic economy and what not. " We can now lawfully teach anything under the sun except ancient Greek and theology ", observed Sidney complacently.

The scope of the work thus defined, the most important issue, in the mind of the chairman of the Board, if not in that of the less observant members, was the method of organisation. It was important not merely to add odds and ends of classes and schools and institutes to the multifarious and diverse confusion of educational equipment already in existence. What was essential was to have in view, from the first, and to work steadily towards it, though not necessarily to talk about it, a scheme of education for London, as a whole, in which all grades and kinds of formal education, from the kindergarten to the university, in all subjects and at all ages, would find appropriate place, and be duly co-ordinated and connected. Such a vision involved an immediate decision at the outset; between a policy of utilising and assisting existing agencies as far as they could be made to go, on the one hand, and, on the other, a policy of confining the Council's work to setting up its own institutions in unabashed rivalry with established institutions, over which the Council would then gain no control. Needless to say, the Board was guided to the larger view of comprehension and control ; and the existing technical institutions, evening classes, secondary schools and university colleges, with any additions that philanthropic enterprise made to their numbers, were gradually brought into a systematic organisation. Some critics objected that the T.E.B. had, by its lavish subventions, saved the decayed endowed secondary schools from supersession by upgrowths from the elementary schools under direct public administration. Others declared that the T.E.B. had bought, by its grants, the recruiting, inspection, supervision, control and virtual direction of these ancient foundations, for which an unexpected *renaissance* in desirable variety was thereby assured.

I have set down rather fully what I have been told of the work of the T.E.B.[1] because, though the work of the Board was quite sufficiently praised by educational experts and uncritically applauded by the public, I do not believe that justice has been done to the amount of deliberate policy that underlay its multifarious decisions. The T.E.B. had the wisdom to equip itself from the outset with a considerable staff of the ablest experts it could enlist for love or money. The County Council had the sense to give the Board

[1] For an authoritative account of the T.E.B. and the development of the County Council into the Local Education Authority for London, see *A Retrospect*, by Dr. William Garnett, from the *Educational Record*, April 1929.

a free hand, and to receive its quarterly reports with due appreciation without party dissensions or hampering instructions. I recall with some pride that the Board, unlike the other committees of the Council which annually changed their chairmen, re-elected Sidney without opposition for six successive years (1892–98). I know that he attended every one of its meetings and nearly all the innumerable sub-committees. I have heard him say that, in the early years, he habitually wrote out before each meeting the exact words of the resolutions that he thought should be passed on all the subjects on the agenda—a practice which usually enabled him to steer the discussion to the desired conclusion, and at any rate gave him control over the drafting. It remains to be added that he insisted on signing every one of the thousands of cheques by which the Board's payments were made, in order, as he explained, to " look at each with the eye of the district auditor ", so that he might ensure (as throughout the whole six years he did ensure) that no payment was so described as to attract a surcharge—the bug-bear of inexperienced authorities working under indefinite powers.

Here is one of the few entries in the MS. diary referring to Sidney's afternoons at Spring Gardens:

Grosvenor Road, July 30th, 1893.—Five afternoons of the week he is engrossed in committee work.[1] Besides the general business of the

[1] The following list of committees on which S. W. served between 1892 and 1898 show that his afternoons were not entirely absorbed by the T.E.B. Throughout this period he was also a member of the party committee which acted as a sort of informal Cabinet deciding the policy of the progressives on all controversial subjects:

> Member of the Appeal Committee, 1892–93;
> Corporate Property Committee, 1895–98;
> County Rate Committee, 1896–98;
> Establishment Committee, 1892–93;
> Finance Committee, 1893–95;
> General Purposes Committee, 1892–98;
> Local Government and Taxation Committee, 1892–98;
> (Vice-chairman, 1892–94);
> Parliamentary Committee, 1892–98;
> Public Health and Housing Committee, 1892–93;
> Rivers Committee, 1894–95;
> Water Committee, 1892–95;

and of the Special Committees on—

> London Government, 1894–95;
> Thames Conservancy, 1893–94;
> Chairman of the Technical Education Board, 1892–98.

Council, he has been giving persistent work to starting the Technical Education Board and guiding its various sub-committees. Kind friends tell me he is an extraordinarily clever chairman of a troublesome Board of experts and obstructives. Besides this—his special work— he has had to draw up the plan to be submitted to the London Unification Commission and give constant attention to the special L.C.C. committee which has been somewhat at cross-purposes with the Commission presided over by our esteemed relative Leonard Courtney. . . . With his life I am more than satisfied. The work he is doing, creating machinery for collective action, is the work I desired to see him do: and the fact that his work is unostentatious, that it cannot be seen or estimated except by his fellow workers, makes it all the finer. . . . And as, in spite of this purely administrative effort, he still finds energy to think, reconstruct past history, to disentangle ideas—I do not feel that his life has been narrowed by becoming mainly practical. To adapt the present machinery to the facts of to-day, to think out the new machinery for to-morrow by the light of yesterday's experience —this combination of practice and theory is, I think, the ideal life for him. . . .

The Other One's work on the T.E.B., and Graham Wallas's service on the London School Board, seem to have led me to ponder over the question whether we were not putting the cart before the horse in concentrating on the education of the child and the training of the youth, without trying to solve the problem of the right breeding of the human race.

All this points [I enter in my diary in July 1894] to the endowment of motherhood and raising the " generation and rearing " of children into an art through the elaboration of a science. Sometimes, I imagine how the men and women of a hundred years hence will wonder at our spending all our energy and thought on the social organisation of adult men and women, and omitting altogether the vastly more important question of the breeding of the generation that is to succeed them. " How could you hope to improve (they will say) the organisation of society without attending to the quality of the men and women to be organised? The success or failure of your collectivist organisation depended on the characteristics of the democracy, and these characteristics you left to the chances of the unregulated and haphazard breeding of the slums." And their criticism will be true. What can we hope from these myriads of deficient minds and deformed bodies that swarm in our great cities—what can we hope from them but brutality, meanness and crime; whether they are struggling for subsistence at the dock gates, or eking out their days in the poor law or penal colony? To enlist the loafer at trade union rates, in the service of the community, will probably enable him to work less and eat more than under the lash of the slave-driver. On the other hand, the vigorous-minded artisans, with their well-educated wives, are abstaining from child rearing because it is an unpaid service rendered to the community, seriously impairing their strength for the struggle to gain their own bread. These facts will seem so obvious to the social reformer of 1994 that he will wonder at our endless discussions of present-day problems much as we wonder at the metaphysical politics which absorbed the whole energy of the French thinkers on the eve of the Revolution. But for all that, we cannot take up the woman's question. We cannot hope to attack individualism, or, as we prefer to call it, anarchy, in its stronghold of the home and the family, entrenched behind current religious morality and custom, before we have replaced it by deliberate collective rule in the factory, the mine— in the whole machinery of wealth production, where anarchy stands condemned by the great bulk of the people as meaning oppression and gross injustice between man and man. Possibly, too, woman will have to go through the same social stages as the labourer, on her way to freedom; she will have to exchange the servitude of *status* for the servitude of *contract*, to rise out of personal dependence before she gains social protection and recognition. We can but leave this problem reverently to our children: preparing their way by cutting at the roots of prejudice, superstition and rotten custom. Often, I wonder whether we do our full duty in this respect; whether we do not acquiesce timidly in the prevailing thought and feeling on these remote issues in order to diminish the friction for those reforms we have in hand? If so, we are short-sightedly practical—we attain our means but lose our end.

The London School of Economics

At this point I recall the first steps in what was perhaps the biggest single enterprise in Our Partnership—the initiation of the London School of Economics and Political Science.

An odd adventure! [I write in my diary on September 21, 1894]. A few weeks ago, Sidney received a letter from a Derby solicitor informing him that he was left executor to a certain Mr. Hutchinson. All he knew of this man (whom he had never seen) was the fact that he was an eccentric old gentleman, member of the Fabian Society, who alternately sent considerable cheques and wrote querulous letters about Shaw's rudeness, or some other fancied grievance he had suffered at the hands of some member of the Fabian Society. " Old Hutch " had, however, been a financial stay of the Society and the executive was always deploring his advancing age and infirmity. When Sidney heard he was made executor he, therefore, expected that the old man had left something to the Fabian Society. Now it turns out that he has left nearly £10,000 to five trustees and appointed Sidney chairman and administrator—all the money to be spent in ten years. The old man blew his brains out, finding his infirmities grow upon him. He had always lived a penurious life and stinted his wife and by no means spoilt his children—and left his wife only £100 a year which Sidney proposes should be doubled by the trustees. The children are all provided for and do not seem to resent the will.

The public-spirited attitude of the Hutchinson family deserves record. Owing to its extreme informality and the suicide of its author shortly after its signature, the will, we were informed, would probably not be upheld in a court of law, if the family chose to dispute it. But, with one accord, the widow and her children demanded that it should be carried out; one of the sons joining the Fabian Society to show his acquiescence. Moreover, the unmarried daughter, who had been given £1500 by her father, and who was one of the trustees, demurred to the proposed purchase of an additional annuity for her mother as inconsistent with her father's will, and, when overborne by the other trustees, made a will leaving her tiny fortune to Sidney and Edward Pease on a wide trust, practically in order to reimburse the original trust for the cost of the extra annuity. She died within a few months.

Now the question is how to spend the money [I continue]. It might be placed to the credit of the Fabian Society and spent in the ordinary work of propaganda. Or a big political splash might be made with it—all the Fabian executive might stand for Parliament! and I.L.P. candidates might be subsidised in their constituencies. But neither of these ways seem to us equal to the occasion. If it is mainly used for the ordinary work of the F.S., then it will merely save the pockets of ordinary subscribers or inflate the common work of the organisation for a few years beyond its normal growth. Moreover, mere propaganda of the shibboleths of collectivism is going on at a rapid rate through the I.L.P.—the ball has been set running and it is rolling down the hill at a fair pace. It looks as if the great bulk of the working-men will be collectivists before the end of the century. But reform will not be brought about by shouting. What is needed is *hard thinking*. And the same objection applies to sending nondescript Socialists into Parliament. The Radical members are quite sufficiently compliant in their views: what is lacking in them is the leaven of knowledge. So Sidney has been planning to persuade the other trustees to devote the greater part of the money to encouraging *research* and economic study. His vision is to found, slowly and quietly, a *London School of Economics and Political Science*—a centre not only of lectures on special subjects, but an association of students who would be directed and supported in doing original work. Last evening we sat by the fire and jotted down a list of subjects which want elucidating: issues of facts which need clearing up. Above all, we want the ordinary citizen to feel that reforming society is no light matter, and must be undertaken by experts specially trained for the purpose. . . .

To which contemporary account I add a reminiscence which Professor Graham Wallas contributed to the *Handbook of the Students' Union* in 1925:

So many causes go to every effect that it is generally impossible to assign the invention of any important institution to a precise date. There is no such impossibility in the case of the School. It was invented at Borough Farm, a couple of miles south-west of Godalming, early in the morning of a certain day in August 1894. . . . Mr. and Mrs. Webb, Mr. G. B. Shaw, and I were staying at the little farm. The day before, Mr. Webb learnt that, by the will of Mr. Henry Hutchinson, he had been given the duty of directing the expenditure of a sum of money. He and Mrs. Webb woke up early, had a long discussion, and at breakfast told us that part of the money would be used to found a school in London on the lines of the École Libre des Sciences Politiques in Paris.

For two relatively unknown persons, without academic distinction, holding outrageously heterodox opinions in the very branch of knowledge that they were intent on promoting, and provided with no other resources than the few thousand pounds that Sidney could allocate from the Hutchinson Trust—such an enterprise seemed an impertinence. The first step was to find a young economist, indifferent to the frowns of the orthodox, sanguine, enterprising, and, above all, sufficiently disinterested, to devote himself whole-heartedly to the creation of the proposed institution in return for a minute and uncertain salary. A queer accident had already marked out our man. A year or so previously, whilst writing *The History of Trade Unionism*, we had visited the Bodleian Library in order to discover whether among its miscellaneous collections it had happened to preserve any pamphlets, petitions or broadsheets making mention of combinations, other than those we had found in the British Museum, or in the well-equipped libraries at Dublin, Glasgow and Manchester. Although we had written in advance to Bodley's librarian, explaining our object, and also had provided ourselves with a personal letter of introduction from the Fellow of an Oxford College with whom we were staying, he received us with a discourtesy, not to say a downright rudeness, that we afterwards learned to be a personal characteristic. He, finally, repelled our enquiries with the remark that we should find all we required in Howell's *Conflicts of Capital and Labour*! At this point we were politely accosted by a young man, an obvious intellectual, with an attractive countenance and pleasant manner, who was reading in the library, and had noticed our discomfiture. He quietly took us into a corner, saying he would himself get out everything we wanted. We learned who he was and read with appreciation the volume that he had published on *English Trade and Finance chiefly in the 17th Century*. The mutual attraction between W. A. S. Hewins and the Webbs was not similarity in political outlook. His views sprang from an instinctive sympathy with mediaevalism which led him spiritually, in the course of a few years, to join the Roman Catholic Church, and politically into a lifelong advocacy of a scientific tariff. We were democratic collectivists, believing in the eventual triumph, in so far as social environment is concerned, of the principle of equality between man and man; if only by the roundabout way of the " inevitability of gradualness ". But there was a wide field of agreement for active co-operation. First, our common dislike of the so-called Manchester School, of its unverified deductive reasoning and abstract generalisations, of its apotheosis of " the economic man ", exclusively inspired by the motive of pecuniary self-interest, and of its passionate defence of the rights of property as against the needs of humanity. And, secondly, our common faith in the practicability and urgent necessity of a concrete science of society implemented through historical research, personal observation and statistical verification. I quote from the account that Hewins has himself given of his eight years' connection with the London School of Economics, at first a sickly infant, of doubtful parentage, born into an indifferent if not hostile world, for whose survival, through the first years of infancy and steady progress in size and stature, he was so largely responsible.

It was at the close of 1894 [W. A. S. Hewins writes], when I was giving a course of lectures at Hove on Social History, that Sidney Webb asked me if I would go and see him and his wife, as they wanted to consult me about the organisation of certain lectures. Sidney Webb was then chairman of the Technical Education Board of the London County Council. I found he had become executor of the will of a Mr. Henry Hutchinson, who had recently died leaving £10,000. . . . After consulting counsel, Webb had decided to devote part of this money to the foundation of an institution on the lines of the École des Sciences Politiques, Paris. Further, the Technical Education Board of the London County Council decided to organise lectures on higher commercial subjects, and Webb wanted my advice as to the way in which these two schemes might be combined to form a new institution in London for the higher study of economics and political science and training suitable for those engaged in administration or business. I drew up this scheme and we discussed it at 41 Grosvenor Road. There was then no idea that I should organise the proposed new institution; Webb consulted me as an outside expert, as I have no doubt he consulted other people. . . . On March 29th, 1895, I received another letter formally asking me to undertake the organisation of the proposed school, and accepted.

The work proceeded rapidly. This depended mainly upon Sidney and Beatrice Webb and myself, and I shall always look back on the period during which I worked with them as one of the happiest and most productive in my life. We met almost daily and never had a dispute during the eight years I was so closely associated with them. We desired that the lectures and investigations held at the School should be representative of all branches of economics and political science, and no differentiation against persons was to be allowed on the grounds of sex, religion, or economic or political views. Full provision was to be made for training for business administration, and for the central or local governments; for library work; the higher forms of research; the publication of monographs upon special subjects.

The first business was the acquisition of suitable premises. We began on a small scale and took the ground floor of No. 9 John Street, Adelphi, for class work, and official business, and obtained the co-operation of the Society of Arts and the London Chamber of Commerce for numerous courses of lectures. . . . Within two months of my acceptance of the Directorship of the School, we were in a position to announce provisional arrangements for the autumn session. . . . We quickly moved from No. 9 John Street, Adelphi, to 10 Adelphi Terrace. As we did not require the two top floors, we let them to a great friend and benefactor, Miss Charlotte Payne Townshend, who soon afterwards became the wife of George Bernard Shaw. The generosity of Mr. Passmore Edwards and Lord Rothschild then enabled us to build a new School in Clare Market. Since those days the building has been vastly extended and the entrance changed from Clare Market to Houghton Street, and there the work is still carried on. Mrs. Bernard Shaw and Bertrand Russell generously helped by enabling us to give research studentships. . . . When I think of the first days of the School of Economics at No. 9 John Street, Adelphi, and contemplate the great organisation which has grown from those beginnings, I can only feel that I was privileged, along with my colleagues, to take part in a great romance. Difficulties appeared from day to day, only to be overcome. Although we represented different schools of thought and were on different sides of politics, I cannot remember any incident which disturbed the harmony of our relations during those early years or which interfered in any way with the rapid progress of our great undertaking. . . .[1]

The truth implicit in W. A. S. Hewins' demure and discreet statement lies in the fact that he and we were far too absorbed in pushing the School into a sound position to have either the time or the inclination to quarrel over political and economic dogmas. For there were overt and hidden enemies, not a few of them, intent on blocking the way for this new departure in university teaching, this new laboratory of sociological research. They were beaten, bless

[1] *The Apologia of an Imperialist,* by W. A. S. Hewins, pp. 24-8.

them! so I won't mention names. If I did, the survivors might find themselves summoned to appear as defendants in a specially staged series of " mock trials ", for which high-brow performances, in aid of the funds of the London hospitals, the present London School of Economics [1931], with its 120 professors and lecturers and its 3000 students, has accidentally achieved a newspaper notoriety.

Stray sidelights on Sidney's day-by-day participation in building up the School appear in the MS. diary between 1895 and 1898. In the first of these, I introduce another of the founders of the School, described by a contemporary journalist as " the elusive personality of Mrs. Bernard Shaw ". An apt term, for this lady has hitherto escaped publicity by dexterously dodging, on all occasions, behind the figure of her famous husband. But she could not escape my mental camera, the imaginary snapshots being duly translated into words in the MS. diary.

Grosvenor Road, September 16th, 1896.—In person she is attractive, a large graceful woman with masses of chocolate-brown hair, pleasant grey eyes [" They are green," she observed, on reading this entry], *matte* complexion which sometimes looks muddy, at other times forms a picturesquely pale background to her brilliant hair and bright eyes. She dresses well; in flowing white evening robes she approaches beauty. At moments she is plain. By temperament she is an anarchist, feeling any regulation or rule intolerable, a tendency which has been exaggerated by her irresponsible wealth. She is romantic but thinks herself cynical. She is a Socialist and a Radical, not because she understands the collectivist standpoint, but because she is by nature a rebel. She has no snobbishness and no convention; she has " swallowed all formulas " but has not worked out principles of her own. She is fond of men and impatient of most women; bitterly resents her enforced celibacy but thinks she could not tolerate the matter-of-fact side of marriage. Sweet-tempered, sympathetic and genuinely anxious to increase the world's enjoyment and diminish the world's pain. . . . Last autumn she was introduced to us. We, knowing she was wealthy, and hearing she was socialistic, interested her in the London School of Economics. She subscribed £1000 to the library, endowed a woman's scholarship, and has now taken the rooms over the School at Adelphi Terrace, paying us £300 a year for rent and service. It was on account of her generosity to our projects and " for the good of the cause " that I first made friends with her. To bring her more directly into our little set of comrades, I suggested that we should take a house together in the country and entertain our friends. To me she seemed at that time, a pleasant, well-dressed well-intentioned woman; I thought she would do very well for Graham Wallas! Now she turns out to be an " original ", with considerable personal charm and certain volcanic tendencies. Graham Wallas bored her with his morality and learning. In a few days she and Bernard Shaw were constant companions. For the last fortnight, when the party has been reduced to ourselves and Shaw, and we have been occupied with our work and each other, they have been scouring the country together and sitting up late at night! . . .

To cut a long story short, the two married each other in the summer of 1898, while we were journeying round the world studying Anglo-Saxon democracy. This meant that for some years the Bernard Shaws were " at home " just one flight above the class-rooms and library of the new institution.

Here are other entries in the MS. diary between 1895 and 1897:

Grosvenor Road, April 9th, 1895.—Have settled down quite comfortably to work again, spending all mornings over our book and Sidney at the L.C.C. in the afternoon. Re-elected chairman of Technical Education Board, and giving a good deal of time to that and the starting of the London School of Economics and Political Science. Selected Hewins (a young Oxford don) as director, engaged Wallas and Schloss as Hutchinson lecturers, and Acworth and probably Foxwell as L.C.C. lecturers. Also, in treaty with Chamber of Commerce and Society of Arts for rooms free of charge. Great good luck that Sidney happens to be chairman of Technical Education Board, able to combine the two sources. Promises well just at present, but impossible to tell whether the old gang won't wake up and cry out before the institution is fairly started—which would delay, possibly baulk, our plans. . . .

Grosvenor Road, May 8th, 1895.—The London School looks promising. Hewins has talked over the principal economists including Marshall and Edgeworth; we have secured Foxwell; the Society of Arts and Chamber of Commerce are giving us their rooms free; the Technical Education Board has voted the £500 a year; the trustees are amenable—and apparently there is no hitch of any kind. I myself am anxious that the " show lecture " side should not be too much developed, and that we should concentrate on getting *research really done*. For that object, I should like to gather round us all the able young men and women who are taking to economics, free their minds of prejudices and start them with a high ideal of accuracy and exhaustiveness in work. If there is one thing I have believed " from the beginning to the end ", it is that no progress can be made except on the basis of ascertained fact and carefully thought out suggestion. Despite our theory, bias, creed and prejudice, we are all equally wandering in the labyrinth, searching for the clue of true facts to bring us out on the right side of each particular problem. It is pitiful to see the narrow sectarian view most Socialists take—binding themselves hand and foot by a series of shibboleths. The working-men are especially afflicted with the theological temperament—the implicit faith in a certain creed which has been " revealed " to them by a sort of inner light. " Why is it that I, a poor ignorant man," said [H. W.] Hobart, one of the I.L.P., to me yesterday, " have perceived ' the truth ' whilst educated men with leisure and brains are still adhering to the old errors; unless I am right in saying they are mostly knaves! " . . .

Welcombe, Christmas, 1895.—We have recovered from our feelings of depression at the widespread reaction—we have turned our hopes from propaganda to education, from the working-class to the middle-class. It is only fools who refuse to make to themselves a " Paradise "! Having been beaten back in our endeavour to make a London Progressive Party with a permanent majority, we are creating the London School of Economics and Political Science as a wider foundation than street-corner preaching. Hewins is making a success of the School— 200 to 300 students attending the different classes and lectures. It is honestly scientific—served, indeed, by more individualist lecturers than collectivists—because the individualists are still the better men. But collectivists are encouraged—and the younger men and women are brought under collectivist influence. We are to some extent trying our best to attract the clever men from the universities; Sidney and Wallas lecturing at Oxford and Cambridge; and letting it be known that any one coming up who is interested in economics will have a warm welcome at Grosvenor Road. Leonard Hobhouse recruits for us at Oxford, the young Trevelyans at Cambridge. All this means a good deal of expenditure of time, sympathy, and alas! money. One cannot keep open house and live economically.

Grosvenor Road, March 26*th*, 1896.—Our time, for the last five weeks, a good deal taken up with writing " begging letters " for the Political Science Library. This winter the rapid growth of the School of Economics made new premises inevitable. But how to raise the money? The Technical Education Board which, under Sidney's chairmanship, subsidises most of the lectures, could not be asked to find premises, the funds of the Hutchinson Trustees are not inexhaustible. A brilliant idea flashed across Sidney's mind. We needed, for the use of the students, books and reports—why not appeal to the public to subscribe to a Library of Political Science? At first we thought we could get a millionaire to subscribe the whole amount on condition that he called it by his own name. In vain I flattered Passmore Edwards; in vain Sidney pressed Sir Hickman Bacon; in vain we wrote " on spec " to various magnates. The idea did not impress them. So we decided to scrape money together by small subscriptions. Sidney drafted a circular; Hewins secured the adhesion of the economists and then began a long process of begging letter writing. Sidney wrote to all the politicians; I raked up all my old ball partners, and between us we have gathered together a most respectable set of contributions— a list which is eloquent testimony to our respectability! Next week the appeal goes out for publication to the press. Even if we collect a comparatively small sum, the issue of the appeal has been a splendid advertisement for the School; and whatever we do get is so much spoil of the Egyptians. Not that we want to deceive the contributors. We are perfectly *bona fide* in our desire to advance economic knowledge, caring more for that than for our own pet ideas. And anyone who knows us knows our opinions, and all the money has been practically sent to *us* personally—so that the contributors are fully aware in whom they are placing their confidence. [Eventually Passmore Edwards put down £10,000 for a new building and the L.C.C. allowed us to put it up on a vacant site.]

Here I may interpolate that there was another reason for starting the British Library of Political Science as a separate entity. Among the stray facts caught up in Sidney's memory was the little-known Literary and Scientific Institutions Act of 1843, by which the Prince Consort had endeavoured to lead the British public in the direction of " Wissenschaft ". This measure provided that such institutions should be exempt from local rates. The Treasury and the lawyers in due course saw to it that neither universities, nor municipal free libraries, came within the scope of the Act; but Sidney had observed that the London Library still enjoyed the exemption. Why not also a specialist library in economic and political science? On this precedent, exemption was actually granted for a number of years for the premises over which the library spread itself. Eventually, however, the local rating authority objected that the School, then become a constituent part of a university, was the dominant element in the occupation; and consequently withdrew the exemption.

Grosvenor Road, July 14th, 1896.—Making arrangements to start the London School in its new abode at Adelphi Terrace in October. Engaged a bright girl as housekeeper and accountant. Advertised for political science lecturer—and yesterday interviewed candidates—a nondescript set of university men. All hopeless from our point of view—all imagined that political science consisted of a knowledge of Aristotle and modern! writers such as De Tocqueville—wanted to put the students through a course of Utopias from More downwards. When Sidney suggested a course of lectures to be prepared on the different systems of municipal taxation, when Graham suggested a study of the rival methods of election from *ad hoc* to proportional representation, the wretched candidates looked aghast and thought evidently that we were amusing ourselves at their expense. One of them wanted to construct a " Political Man ", from whose imaginary qualities all things might be deduced; another wanted to lecture on " Land under the Tudors ", but had apparently read only the ordinary textbooks. Finally, we determined to do without our lecturer—to my mind a blessed consummation. It struck me always as a trifle difficult to teach a science which does not yet exist.

Grosvenor Road, October 5th, 1896.—The last fortnight we have been a good deal absorbed in preparing Adelphi Terrace for the opening of the School. Found Hewins in a state of nervous collapse threatening severe illness. Sent him away with his wife and child, and took over the work of preparing for the coming term. Poor Sidney trudges over there directly after breakfast and spends his mornings with painters, plumbers and locksmiths, interviewing would-be students to whom he gives fatherly advice—comes home to lunch and then off to the L.C.C. In the interval of arranging the details of the housekeeping of the School, I am getting on slowly with the book, preparing the ground for work with Sidney next week when Hewins is back. Obvious that this institution will take up much of our time for the next few years. We are convinced it is worth while, in spite of the harassing character of the work. We want to create a centre of intellectual work and comradeship from which our views will radiate through personal intercourse. It remains to be seen how we succeed.

Cliftonville, Margate, November 8th, 1896.—School promising, but not assured. Successful classes and lectures are those giving purely technical instruction to professionals—methods of statistics and railway economics—such subjects as commercial law and currency proving rather too abstract for the clerk to see in what way they make for his bread and butter. Pure learning and culture, such as growth of political theory, is at present a " frost " except for the attendance of the full student who has paid his guinea and attends all the lectures. It is this class we want to encourage—until we have a regular *clientèle* of 300 full students, our success will be problematic in the extreme. Hewins, who expected great things, has been depressed and irritable and it has taken all Sidney's good temper and tact to keep things smooth. Hewins is a sanguine enthusiast—pulls hard and strong when he feels the stream with him. . . . However, with the rise of the students to 220, Hewins' spirits have gone up and he is now again prophesying great things. But I see that this School, if it is to be made a permanent success, will mean a good deal of work and thought for Sidney and myself.

The Argoed, January 18*th*, 1897.—The London School is progressing. Sidney has contrived to edge it in to any possible London University. It is still a speculation in money, students and output, but it promises well.

THE LONDON UNIVERSITY

Out of the chairmanship of the T.E.B. and the founding of the L.S.E. sprang Sidney's collaboration, in so far as the metropolis was concerned, with that foremost pioneer in modern university education—R. B. Haldane. And here I recall a potent personality. As lawyer, politician and administrator, R. B. Haldane came to be recognised as one in the first rank. An ardent amateur in philosophy, his writings reveal a passion for deducing from given premises first principles, justifying an emotional faith in the vital as against the mechanistic interpretation of the behaviour of man. Thus, in the secret places of his heart, Haldane believed in the spiritual interpretation of the universe.[1] But it was pre-eminently as a big public personage, in some ways the

[1] The following passage from R. B. Haldane's autobiography bears out this view of his state of mind: ". . . My religious outlook was a genuine one. Its origin was a deep conviction that the more experience is spiritual the more it is real. My old master, Lotze, had influenced me towards this conviction, and so had Hegel, whom I had been studying as closely as the state of my then knowledge permitted. With all this had come the further conviction that not only in philosophy but in science it

95

biggest and most genial of his time, that he will be remembered by those who knew him. Plenitude, mental and physical, seemed to me his dominant feature, leading to a large intake and a like output. A big head on a bigger body —generous expenditure on the good things of life, not least among them choice edibles and the accompanying portions and potions of nicotine and alcohol, also of select quality; long hours of work; endless documents and books mastered and remembered; a multitude of interests, and an ever-widening circle of friends and acquaintances, extending from Emperors and Kings, distinguished diplomatists, and famous men of science and learning, to representative manual workers and scientific and administrative experts of all sorts and kinds: any adequate picture of his life would entail a large and crowded canvas. He had a thin small voice, he was no platform orator; he did not cultivate the press; he was not a fluent journalist; thus he never became a popular figure; he was, in fact, the exact antithesis of a demagogue. Though, successively, Secretary of State for War and Lord Chancellor in two Governments, he remained throughout his life a behind-the-scenes man. Unattractive as a young man, he became as he grew in years, owing to his wit and wisdom and courteous manners, a social charmer, equally at home in the smartest society set or in drab groups of professional men and women. He had a notable gift for manipulating his fellow-men and for the organisation of business; for getting the best out of his subordinates; mainly because, whilst being somewhat cynical, he was always good-humoured and considerate, tempering rebuke and approval with kindly humour. Thus, it was in personal intercourse that he excelled; in successful intrigue, always for public and not for private ends. About Haldane's personal disinterestedness there can be no doubt. He loved power,

was true that no systematic knowledge is sufficient in itself unless it leads up and points to first principles. This doctrine later became valuable to me even as a guide in work at the Bar. It did not help in the business of cross-examination. I was never good at that, nor in the conduct of *nisi prius* cases. But it was invaluable in preparation for the presentation of great questions to the Supreme Tribunals, where the judges were keen about first principles and were looking out for help from the advocate " (*Richard Burdon Haldane—An Autobiography*, pp. 29-30).

especially the power of the hidden hand; or shall I say of the *recognised* hidden hand? But he frequently sacrificed his own prospects if he could thereby serve a friend or promote a cause he believed in. To sum up my memories: a powerful and beneficent personality, a great citizen, above all a loyal and generous colleague.

Amongst all our common friends, R. B. Haldane takes precedence alike in the length of his friendship and in its bearing on the Other One's administrative and political career. He had known each of us before we knew each other; and, as he described, with a humorous gloss, in his autobiography, he had " covered " by the accommodating rôle of a desirable suitor, Sidney Webb's appearance in my father's house when we were, unbeknown to my family, engaged to be married. Our first intrigue with Haldane! After thirty years of uninterrupted friendship the two found themselves in 1924 colleagues in the first Labour Cabinet. It was Haldane who created and fostered the flattering " Webb myth " that flowered so agreeably and advantageously for us and our schemes in the first decade of the twentieth century. Even when the myth, being a myth, faded away, to be replaced by the myth of an " exploded myth ", he remained a steadfast fellow-conspirator for the public good. What bound us together as associates was our common faith in a deliberately organised society: our common belief in the application of science to human relations with a view to betterment. Where we differed was in the orientation of political power. Haldane believed more than we did in the existing governing class: in the great personages of Court, Cabinet and City. We staked our hopes on the organised working-class, served and guided, it is true, by an *élite* of unassuming experts who would make no claim to superior social status, but would content themselves with exercising the power inherent in superior knowledge and longer administrative experience.

Here is an entry in the MS. diary giving my contemporary impression of Haldane's personality before he had become a political personage:

H

Grosvenor Road, May 3rd, 1897.—Haldane here for a Sunday. Difficult to estimate what amount of influence that man exercises in public affairs. He has never held office; but during the last Liberal Government he was the chief instigator of their collectivist policy— serving to carry information and suggestions from specialists like ourselves to the heads of departments. He was also responsible for many of their appointments. In this Parliament he is in constant confidential intercourse with Balfour and other Conservatives over the many nonparty questions dealt with by a Government—and even in some purely political questions his advice is asked. He attracts confidence where he is at all liked—once on friendly terms, you feel absolutely secure that he will never use personal knowledge to advance his own public career to the detriment of any friend. The rank and file of his own party dislike him intensely; partly because he detaches himself from party discipline and acts according to his own inner light, and partly because he seems dominated by some vague principle which they do not understand and which he does not make intelligible. His bulky form, and pompous ways, his absolute lack of masculine vices or "manly" tastes (beyond a good dinner), his superiority and constant attitude of a teacher, his curiously woolly mind would make him an unattractive figure if it were not for the beaming kindliness of his nature, his warm appreciation of friends and a certain pawky humour with which he surveys the world. And there is pathos in his personality. In spite of the successful professional life, the interest and entertainment of constantly mixing with the most powerful minds and in the most stirring affairs, the enjoyment of luxurious living to a man with a first-rate digestion, he is a restless, lonely man—in his heart still worshipping the woman who jilted him seven years ago. All the sadder that genuine affectionateness—pleasure in intimate and entirely confidential relations, a yearning towards some sort of *permanence*— is really the strongest side of Haldane's character. He was made to be a husband, father and close comrade. He has to put up with pleasant intercourse with political friends and political foes.

When we are together we are constantly discussing hotly. He has been converted, in a sort of vague metaphysical way, to the principles of collectivism. But, whether it is that his best brains are given to his professional work, or whether it is that he is incapable of working out or even fully comprehending *concrete* principles, he never sees the right side of a question until you have spent hours dinning it into him. Even then he does not admit it, and will go on bringing entirely irrelevant matters wilfully into the discussion in order to "keep you off", so to speak. But it is quite worth while hotly debating the question with him, because he always comes right in the end, and when you meet him a month hence he repeats your own arguments. As a retort *he* would say that *we* were narrow and limited to our own questions, quite forgetting their proportionate value to other wider issues—and that it is impossible for the cultivated " representative " to do more than grasp certain large principles. Further, that mere logic and mere information are all very well, but they are of little service to move the world without a great personality and long-continued knowledge of affairs. With a pretty significant hint that we have neither, he always ends an encounter. " What *we* think to-day, *you* will think to-morrow " is usually my last hit. All the same, we two and he remain genuinely fond of each other.

Now it so happened that R. B. Haldane and Sidney, united by friendship, made a good combination for the task they undertook: to get carried into law the necessary Bill for the reorganisation of the London University. To begin with, they were, in their several ways, both entirely free from the subtly pervading influence of the Oxford and Cambridge of those days, with their standards of expensive living and enjoyable leisure, and their assumption of belonging to an aristocracy or governing class. Haldane had graduated at Edinburgh and Göttingen, among students living sparely in uncomfortable lodgings, undistracted by games, who looked forward to no other existence than one of strenuous brain-work. He believed intensely in the university, not only as a place for " great teaching " but also as a source of inspiration by " great minds ", producing, in the choicer spirits, a systematic devotion to learning and research. The Other One, on the other hand, with little formal schooling, had known what it was to gain education in adolescence whilst earning a livelihood; he realised the advantages of guidance and attraction that were, by a series of university examinations, brought to bear on myriads of lonely students, to most of whom a full-time undergraduate career, not to mention a residential university, was not within sight. Haldane, to gain his higher aim, would willingly have scrapped the system of external examinations by which alone London University awarded its coveted degrees. In his eyes, even the best-equipped public library, and the most highly organised evening classes, counted for nothing in comparison with the inspiration he had found in personal intimacy with Stuart Blackie and Lotze. But he realised, under Sidney's influence, if not the undesirability, at any rate the political unpracticability, of overthrowing what had already taken deep roots. He, accordingly, designed a scheme of combining in a single university, of a new type, all three elements, namely: the external students influenced by a system of examinations which could be improved; an organised hierarchy of evening classes which, so far as London was concerned, the Technical Education Board was raising to the highest grade; and the group of autonomous colleges, in which a professoriate in no way inferior to those of Germany and Scotland could be trusted to inspire self-selected groups of earnest students in every subject of study and research. For such a university in the greatest of all metropolitan cities, the two conspirators believed that the necessary millions of money would be forthcoming; and the experience of the past thirty years has justified their faith. Possibly, not without its effect on the negotiations (and these I leave Haldane to describe) was the promise which Sidney induced the London County Council to make that, out of the technical education " whiskey money ", the reconstructed university should be straight away endowed with £10,000 a year towards the support of four of its faculties, namely, science, the education side of arts, and two new faculties of engineering and economics, on condition that neither evening students nor the growing polytechnics were excluded.

For me [relates Haldane in his account of these years] the absorbing political subject was higher education. . . . I approached Balfour about the University of London. It was then a mere Board for examining outside students who got from it external degrees by means of examinations without teaching. Valuable as the work of extending degrees to external students had been in the past, it was no longer sufficient. The system lent itself to the purposes of the crammers, and the school teachers in particular used it for obtaining what were virtually little more than trade-marks. The real purpose of university training, the development of the mind in the atmosphere of the teaching university, where teachers and taught could come into close relation, was lacking. So strongly was this felt that many of the professors in the London colleges had set their hearts on the establishment of a second, the professorially-run university, with no external examinees at all. I knew that the opposition to so far-reaching a measure would be too strong to overcome in the then indifferent state of public opinion. I saw that, as a first step at all events, the only way was to pass an Act enlarging the existing University of London by giving it a powerful teaching side. This might be relied on in the end to absorb the other side by reason of its quality. Of this opinion, also, was my friend Sidney Webb, who as the successful chief of the Technical Education Board of the London County Council had great opportunities of studying the practical problem. Sidney Webb and I took counsel together. He was a very practical as well as a very energetic man. We laid siege to the citadel. We went round to person after person who was prominent in the administration of the existing University. Some listened, but others would not do so and even refused to see us. In the end, we worked out what was in substance the scheme of the London University Act of 1898. The scheme was far from being an ideal one. It provided by way of compromise for a Senate which was too large to be a really efficient supreme governing body for the new composite University, and it had other shortcomings of which we were well aware. But it did set up a teaching university, although Convocation, with its control of the external side, would remain unduly powerful. We saw that the scheme thus fashioned was the utmost we could hope for the time to carry, in the existing state of public opinion about higher education in London. I went to Balfour as soon as we were ready, and explained what we had done and why we had done it in this form. He was both interested and sympathetic, and, after consideration, said that his Government would take the matter up and introduce a Bill fashioned on our lines, although the Government could not pledge itself to stand or fall by it. The Bill was ultimately, after much consultation with me, introduced to the House of Commons by Sir John Gorst on behalf of the Government. He explained it to the House, and concluded by saying that it was on the whole a Bill which the Government recommended.

There was a storm. Sir John Lubbock, the member for the University, opposed it in the interest of the convocation by whose members he had been elected. Sir Charles Dilke and others attacked it fiercely on various grounds. For some time in the course of the discussion not a speech was made in its favour, and the prospects of the Bill seemed hopeless. I sprang to my feet when an opportunity at last offered, and I spoke for once like one inspired. I told the House of Commons of the scandal that the metropolis of the Empire should not have a teaching university to which students from distant regions might come as to the centre for them of that Empire. I showed how far we were behind continental nations, and what a menace this was to our scientific and industrial prospects in days to come. I knew every inch of the ground, and displayed its unsound condition. We were far away from the days in which a step forward had been made by calling into being the examining body named London University, a creation which had given degrees by examination to those whom the Church had in the old days shut out from university status. That reform was in its time a most valuable service to the state, but it was a service which had become superseded in the light of new standards in university education which demanded much more.[1]

In the course of the next few months, in circumstances which taxed to the uttermost Haldane's ingenuity and persuasiveness, the Bill became law. In the summer of 1897, the Government appointed a small executive Commission to draft the constitution and statutes—a vitally important body which happened to have as one of its leading members my old friend Dr. Mandell Creighton (the first President of the School of Economics), who had just been appointed Bishop of London; and, for its chairman, an old acquaintance, Lord Davey. In my diary, I find an entry summarising the doings of the spring of 1897.

Grosvenor Road, July 26th, 1897.—Sidney and Haldane rushing about London trying to get all parties to agree to a Bill for London University. If it goes through, it will be due to Haldane's insistence and his friendship with Balfour—but the form of the Bill—the alterations grafted on the Cowper Commission Report are largely Sidney's. He thinks he has got all he wants as regards the Technical Education Board and London School of Economics. The Commission appointed to carry the Act out is largely favourable, or at any rate " susceptible " to right influence. . . .

[1] *Richard Burdon Haldane—An Autobiography*, pp. 124-7.

CHAPTER III

SOCIAL AND POLITICAL ENVIRONMENT
1892–1898

HITHERTO I have described our specialised activities: first the joint enquiry into British Trade Unionism and the consequent publication of *The History of Trade Unionism* in 1894, and *Industrial Democracy* in 1898, and secondly the administrative work of the Other One on the L.C.C., his chairmanship of the Technical Education Board for six years, and the foundation of the London School of Economics and Political Science. I turn now to the outermost strand of our activities: the propaganda of Fabian collectivism, within the social and political life of our day.

Let me first remind the reader of the outstanding political events of Great Britain during the first spell of Our Partnership, 1892–98. For six years prior to this period the Salisbury administration held office, but it depended for its majority on the seventy Liberal Unionist members led by Joseph Chamberlain; and he, it is needless to add, gave the Government loyal support in return for an effective influence on home and foreign affairs. In July 1892, the month of our marriage, a general election left the Conservatives and Liberal Unionists in a minority in the House of Commons. " There never was so depressed an election ", one historian relates. " The country was tired of the Unionist Government, but without enthusiasm for its successors. The Irish quarrel had taken all the glamour out of Mr. Gladstone's crusade; British Radicals saw no prospect for the causes they had at heart. By heroic efforts Liberals and Irish scraped together a majority of 40 which, as their opponents pointed out, left them absolutely at the mercy of the Irish party in the teeth of a British majority against Home Rule."[1] " The

[1] *Great Britain, Empire and Commonwealth, 1886–1935*, by J. A. Spender, pp. 58–9.

interlude of Liberal administration from 11th August 1892 to 24th June 1895 ", we are told by another Liberal historian, " was only half the length of a normal Government's life in those days; and the two Cabinets which filled it were paralysed for want of any real majority either at Westminster, or in the constituencies." [1]

But this was not all. Mr. Gladstone, whom the Queen was compelled to accept as Prime Minister, was wholly out of sympathy with the projects of social reform vaguely adumbrated in the Newcastle Programme, upon which the election had been fought; proposals more clearly set forth by the little group of Liberal collectivists led by Haldane, Acland, Asquith and Grey.[2] Had not the great man asserted, during his last administration, that unemployment was actually an improper subject even for discussion by the representatives of the people, seeing that it was a necessary incident in profit-making enterprise, and, therefore, should not and could not be dealt with by the political state? Moreover, Gladstone was an anti-militarist and anti-imperialist, and objected to increasing expenditure on the armed forces almost as much as he did on social reform. Hence, when the Home Rule Bill was cast out by the House of Lords in the autumn of 1893, and his colleagues objected to a dissolution on that question, still more when in the spring of 1894 the First Lord of the Admiralty proposed an addition to the Navy, Gladstone threatened to resign: "He had supposed that there were several members of the Cabinet who shared his views and would follow his example, and it was a shock to him to discover in the end that he stood alone. ' Resigned! ' he said in after years, ' I did not resign, I was put out.' " [3]

There ensued a sharp and short struggle, reflected in the entries in my diary, between those Liberal M.P.'s who were at once collectivists and imperialists, who favoured Lord

---

[1] *England 1870–1914,* by R. C. K. Ensor, 1936, p. 209.

[2] Haldane was the only one who approached to a Socialist or remained a true collectivist. The others could more properly be termed "radical reformists". The same group, together with Lord Rosebery, formed the "Limps" or Liberal Imperialists. (Ed.)

[3] *Great Britain, Empire and Commonwealth, 1886–1935,* by J. A. Spender, p. 69.

Rosebery as Premier, on the one hand; and, on the other, the *laisser-faire* and anti-imperialist group, who insisted that Sir William Harcourt should not only lead the House of Commons, but also be Prime Minister. Apparently, the Queen took the matter into her own hands and sent for Rosebery. The Rosebery administration, with its chief standing aloof and resentful, lasted thirteen months and was terminated, in June 1895, by a catch vote on whether or not we had a sufficient stock of cordite! Whereupon Salisbury took office and dissolved Parliament, gaining a majority of 152 over the opposition (340 Conservatives and 71 Liberal Unionists, against 177 Liberals and 82 Irish Nationalists). The Liberal Unionist leaders accepted office in the Conservative Government, and for the next seven years the national policy at home and abroad was directed by Salisbury, Chamberlain and Balfour.

Such was the political framework within which we carried on our propaganda of Fabian collectivism. But what exactly was this peculiar brand of Socialism? In answer to this question, I give a few extracts from a lecture by Sidney Webb on " Socialism: True and False ", given to the Fabian Society in January 1894, on the tenth anniversary of its foundation.

Though we took the title of the Fabian Society [1] in January 1884, it was two or three years before we had quite found out what our instinctive choice of a title really portended. In 1884, the Fabian Society, like the other socialist organisations, had its enthusiastic young members—aye, and old ones too—who placed all their hopes on a sudden tumultuous uprising of a united proletariat, before whose mighty onrush, kings, landlords and capitalists would go down like ninepins, leaving society quietly to re-sort itself into utopia. The date for this social revolution was sometimes actually fixed for 1889, the centenary of the opening of the French Revolution. . . . It was against all thinking and teaching of this catastrophic kind that the Society gradually came to set its face—not, as I believe, because we were any less in earnest in our warfare against existing evils, or less extreme in

[1] The explanatory quotation of the name " Fabian " is given on the title-page of the early Fabian Tracts (see No. 7): " For the right moment you must wait, as Fabius did most patiently when warring against Hannibal, though many censured his delays; but when the time comes you must strike hard, as Fabius did, or your waiting will be in vain, and fruitless ".

our remedies, but because we were sadly and sorrowfully driven to the conclusion that no sudden or simultaneous transformation of society from an individualist to a collectivist basis was possible or even thinkable.

On the other hand, we had but little sympathy with schemes for the regeneration of mankind by the establishment of local utopias, whether in Cumberland or in Chili. To turn our back on the unearned increment and the machine industry seemed a poor way of conquering them. We had no faith in the recuperative qualities of spade husbandry, or in any devices for dodging the law of rent. In short, we repudiated the common assumption that socialism was necessarily bound up with insurrectionism, on the one hand, or utopianism, on the other, and we set to work to discover for ourselves and to teach to others how practically to transform England into a social democratic common-wealth. . . . What we Fabians aim at is not the sub-division of property, whether capital or land, but the control and administration of it by the representatives of the community. It has no desire to see the Duke of Bedford replaced by five hundred little Dukes of Bedford under the guise of enfranchised leaseholders, but prefers to assert the claim of the whole community to the land, and especially to that unearned increment of value which the whole community creates. It has no vain dream of converting the agricultural labourer into a freeholder, farming his own land, but looks to the creation of parish councils empowered to acquire land for communal ownership, and to build cottages for the labourers to rent. The path to its town utopia is that of Mr. Chamberlain's early career, though not of his political programme —unlimited municipalisation of local public services and a wide extension of corporate activity. London, in particular, has caught up the old Birmingham cry of " high rates and a healthy city ", but with a significant difference. Our modern economists tell us that the first source of public revenue for a rising city is the growing rental value of its site, which at present falls into private hands. Hence, the new demand for the gradual municipalisation by taxation of urban land values—a demand still so little understood by most of our statesmen that they fondly imagine it to have something to do with a division of rates between house-owner and occupier. It is coming to be remembered, in short, that Bentham himself, the great father of political radicalism, urged that taxation need not be limited to the supply of funds for the bare administrative expenses of the state, but that, wisely handled, it also supplied a means of gradually securing the great end of equality of opportunity to every citizen.

For the rest, the Fabian Society studiously avoided any quotations from Karl Marx, preferring indeed Robert

Owen; they translated economics and collectivism into the language of prosaic vestrymen and town councillors. They dealt largely in statistics; they talked about amending factory acts, and municipalising gas and water supplies. Above all, they were prolific of facts, ideas and practical projects of reform. They were, indeed, far more extreme in their opinions and projects than their phrases conveyed to the ordinary citizen. Their summary of Socialism, which was found in the ensuing decade to have a strong appeal, was put in the following terms. It comprised, they said, essentially collective ownership wherever practicable; collective regulation everywhere else; collective provision according to need for all the impotent and sufferers; and collective taxation in proportion to wealth, especially surplus wealth.[1]

At this point I had better confess that in the propaganda of Fabian collectivism, 1892–98, I was more an observer than a colleague. For it was with some misgiving that I joined the Fabian Society on my engagement to Sidney Webb. To discover the processes of social organisation, to observe and record the behaviour of man in society, had been my primary object in life; and it seemed to my cautious temperament that any pronounced views about social changes to be aimed at, might hamper these researches; partly

---

[1] Rather than give my own view of the place of the Fabian Society in British politics, I quote the estimate of G. M. Trevelyan in his well-known *British History in the Nineteenth Century*, p. 403:

" The third current of *fin de siècle* Socialism, and the most important, was the Fabian doctrine, specially connected with Mr. and Mrs. Sidney Webb. The Fabian Society was founded in 1883. Its name recalls a Roman general whose motto was ' slow but sure '. Eschewing revolution, and intent on the actualities of England at the end of the nineteenth century, Fabians exonerated socialists from the heavy obligation of reading Karl Marx. Without dogmatising as to the ultimate future of industrial organisation, they preached practical possibilities, here and now—municipal socialism and state control of conditions of labour. Equally far from Marx and Morris, they left the New Jerusalem alone, and sought to impregnate the existing forces of society with collectivist ideals.

" The Fabians became experts in bringing electoral, journalistic and personal pressure to bear on local bodies, and on the Liberal or Conservative government of the hour—somewhat after the methods of action of Francis Place, but with the added power of the democratic franchise. By the end of the century it is in Fabianism that we find the nearest approach to a body of doctrine directly affecting the laws and administration of the time, like the doctrines of Bentham and Mill in the past. The Fabians were intelligence officers without an army—there was no Fabian party in parliament—but they influenced the strategy and even the direction of the great hosts moving under other banners."

because it might bias my own selection of facts and hypotheses, but also because the way of discovery might be
blocked by those who held contrary opinions. As years went
by neither of these objections held good. I soon realised
that complete detachment from current politics was impracticable unless you were indifferent to the public welfare,
or had come to the conclusion that human society was
beyond human control. For the longer I studied the social
organisation in which I had been born and bred, the stronger
became my conviction that the distribution of power and
wealth among my fellow-citizens was being controlled, and
very deliberately controlled, in the interests of the propertied
classes, to the detriment of the vast majority of the people,
thus preventing any adequate rise in the health and happiness, the manners and the culture, of the community as a
whole. Nor did I find that Fabian collectivism stood in the
way of getting information. Students, as we happened to
be in those years, of working-class organisation and local
government, an avowed preference for legal enactment and
municipal development helped more than it hindered our
quest for knowledge. For the rest, the British governing
class of the 'eighties and 'nineties, enveloped in self-complacency and enjoying the consciousness of power and a
leisurely life in luxurious surroundings, was innately indifferent to the workings of the intellect. To the typical
politician and lawyer, landlord and financier, to the wealthy
manufacturer and trader, elaborate and accurate descriptions of the poverty of the poor, such as Charles Booth's
Life and Labour of the People in London, or carefully reasoned
arguments in favour of specific reforms, seemed equally
negligible. Men were, and always would be, governed by
their appetites or by conventional views of right or wrong;
if they were exceptionally self-controlled and intelligent,
they might be guided by their pecuniary self-interest and
their desire to found a family; in which case they would be
promptly enrolled in the governing class. Hence the group
of young intellectuals who were, between 1885 and 1892,
getting resolutions passed by Liberal associations and

Radical working-men's clubs, in favour of the eight-hour day, old-age pensions, a minimum wage for those in public employment, and increased health and educational services; or who were reading papers at the British Association and at other reputable gatherings on *The Difficulties of Individualism*, *The Necessary Basis of Society* and *The Transition to Social Democracy*, were welcomed with benevolent smiles and kindly words by distinguished members of the governing *clique*. Some Fabian phrases were actually incorporated in the platform speeches and election addresses of the leaders of the Liberal Party at the general election of July 1892. Had not Sir William Harcourt proclaimed from a public platform that " we are all Socialists now "? had not the rising Liberal lawyer, H. H. Asquith, solemnly stated in his election address: " I am one of those who believe that the collective action of the community may and ought to be employed positively as well as negatively; to raise as well as to level; to equalise opportunities no less than to curtail privileges; to make the freedom of the individual a reality and not a pretence "? [1]

The following entries from the MS. diary show rapid disillusionment with the policy of permeation leading to the publication, in the *Fortnightly Review* of November 1893, of the Fabian Manifesto entitled: " To Your Tents, O Israel ", drafted by Bernard Shaw.[2]

December 24th, 1892.—Have seen something of politicians [I write a few months after our marriage]. Haldane and Asquith to dinner; Sydney Buxton and Acland coming later on. . . . All the younger men in the Government hard at work introducing administrative reforms, yet uncertain whether the old gang will not dictate a policy of evading all legislative proposals. No leader to the new reform movement; a mere upheaval in favour of doing something, met by tight sitting on the part of the provincial capitalists. And when they do give way, they give way on the wrong points; they are as likely as not to skedaddle in face of some preposterous demand, whilst refusing even to consider some quite sound scheme. And the result is that the political world

[1] *Memories and Reflections*, by the Earl of Oxford and Asquith, K.B., vol. i. p. 113.

[2] But very considerably peppered by us with sallies which passed as characteristically Shavian.—G. B. S.

is simply chaotic at present, at least on the reform side. Men like Balfour know well enough what they are playing for and succeed in leading a compact party. If chaos continues they will have a still larger mass of voters. . . .

Grosvenor Rd., Christmas Day, 1893.—The excitement of the autumn [I write exactly twelve months afterwards] has been the issue of the Fabian Manifesto which for a week or so loomed large to us. With Shaw's reproduction of Sidney's facts, it boomed in the press: the Tory democratic papers quoted it freely; the Radical papers denounced it; only the *Spectator* and the *Standard* refusing to notice it out of sheer perplexity how to deal with it. I am not sure whether after the event I altogether approve of it. There is some truth in Graham Wallas's original observation that we were rushed into it by fear of being thought complacent and apathetic by the Independent Labour Party. Whether it is wise to do anything simply from fear of being left behind? But that was not the whole of the motive. All through the spring Sidney and Shaw have been feeling the need of some strong outspoken words on the lack of faith and will to go forward manifested by the majority of the Cabinet. They could hardly go on supporting the Liberals if these were deliberately fooling the Progressives with addled promises. Perhaps the Fabian junta chose the right time to speak: anyway they said only what they thought; they spoke to the world exactly what they had been saying in private. So far the manifesto was justified. . . .

It would be an impertinence to summarise the words of Bernard Shaw. Here are a series of extracts which give the gist of the Fabian Manifesto:

It is not for the Fabian Society to betray the secret history of the desperate efforts made from 1886 to 1892 to bring the Liberal Party up to the poll in some semblance of democratic condition. That red spectre, the Newcastle Programme, vanished on the morrow of the general election, having served its turn; and nobody now wants to hear the story of the infinite pains with which it was raised and brought to the uneasy bedside of Mr. Gladstone himself. The heroic speeches made by the Liberal leaders when, rallying to the revolutionary flag, blazoned with payment of members, death (by taxation) to the ground landlord and royalty owner, home rule for London and relief to the ratepayer, and municipalisation of every monopoly under the sun, they hauled it to the high top-gallant of the great Liberal Party amid the inspiring strains of " we are all Socialists now ", are not usually alluded to at present, having also served their turn; and it is not for the Fabian Society to spoil a stirring page of political history by bringing the public behind the scenes to see those eagle-eyed statesmen carried to the platform, kicking, screaming and protesting, in the arms of the collectivist radicals of London, who offered them the alternative of saying as they were told or spending another seven years in opposition. As the world knows, they said as they were told; and they just scraped through at the election by abandoning Home Rule to the Irish constituencies, and ruffing " Integrity of the Empire " and Tory democracy with collectivist trumps conveyed from the sleeves of the London Liberal and Radical Union and the Fabian Society.

There follows a detailed exposure of the reactionary doings of the Whig Ministers, notably in the administration of the Post Office under Arnold Morley, and of Public Works under Shaw-Lefevre: too long to quote.

Lord Spencer, at the Admiralty [proceeds the indictment], also had his opportunities. The scandal of the starvation wages at the Deptford and other victualling yards had become too great to be any longer ignored. . . . The Government's brand-new Labour Department made him a special report as to what he ought to pay, and brought forcibly to his notice the damning facts as to what he did pay. Like Mr. Acland in the Science and Art Department, he might frankly have accepted for all the dockyard workmen the recognised standard rates of the various trade unions concerned. Like the London County Council, he might have resolved to pay no wage on which a family could not decently exist. He might have put a stop to the practice, recently exposed in a tragic case, of not paying the labourers until their wages are a week overdue, thus driving them to the pawnbroker to borrow at heavy interest the money due to them by the British Government, which pays them no interest at all on the compulsory loan. He might have " abolished " the middleman who at Deptford drove poor Pluck to suicide at the very moment of the departmental enquiry, and taken all the Admiralty workmen into direct public employment. He might have established the eight hours' day in all the government dockyards. . . . Had Mr. Fowler been but a little less than a quarter-of-a-century behind his time, what a field he would have found in other directions! Had he been really in sympathy with the House of Commons' repeatedly expressed desire to put down sweating, what a circular he could have issued to all the local authorities in the kingdom, commending to their notice the model clauses of the London County Council; stimulating them to the establishment of an eight hours' day for all their employees; and urging them to follow the House of Commons in abandoning the competitive rate for a living wage! And with local authorities everywhere eager for guidance on the menacing problem of the unemployed, what really democratic president of the local government board would have let himself be put to open shame by ignoring the very existence of acts of parliament enabling the guardians to set the poor to work, or have refused to come to any decision as to whether local authorities should or should not be allowed to try their own experiments in this direction!

But all the Ministers are not found wanting: there are words of encouragement, or are they words of apology, for those members of the Cabinet who were deemed to be permeated with Fabianism:

Now Mr. Asquith and Mr. Acland, like Mr. Sydney Buxton, hold their portfolios as representatives of that Liberal dilution of collectivist radicalism which made itself felt in the last parliament on the memorable occasion when the three gentlemen in question, with Sir Edward Grey and Mr. Haldane, suddenly checkmated a reactionary Whig job put forward under the specious title of leaseholds enfranchisement, to the unspeakable astonishment and confusion of the Liberal leaders, whose sole objection to the measure was that it was too advanced. Without the collectivist movement outside parliament it is certain that Messrs. Asquith, Acland, Sydney Buxton and Sir Edward Grey would never have displaced members of the "old gang" in the ministry, and one can only surmise the intensity of the friction that must have been created in the Cabinet between administrators of their way of thinking and a reactionist like Sir William Harcourt holding the purse-strings. The situation is so obvious that the Fabian Society may, without indiscretion, say that when the secret history of Mr. Gladstone's administration comes to be written, it will be found that since the very formation of the Cabinet, the progressive party, led by Mr. Asquith and Mr. Acland, and joined by Lord Rosebery, Lord Ripon, Mr. Mundella and Mr. Bryce, has been hampered, blocked, and eventually overborne, firstly, by Mr. Gladstone's complete absorption in Home Rule; secondly, by the active hostility of such seasoned Whigs as Sir William Harcourt and Mr. Fowler; thirdly, by the doctrinaire "Manchesterism" and pettish temper of Mr. John Morley; and fourthly, by the ignorance, indifference and inertia of the Whig peers, Lords Spencer and Kimberley, backed by such obsolescent politicians as Mr. Shaw-Lefevre and Mr. Arnold Morley.

The Manifesto ends with a plan of campaign: the creation of a Labour Party securely anchored in the trade union movement.

To those working-men who look solely to the interests of labour we need not address any lengthy argument for putting the Reform Bill of 1885 to its proper use by largely increasing the representation of labour in parliament. The fact that, in the House of Commons, governing a country where four men out of every five are wage workers, only fifteen out of six hundred and seventy are labour members, is altogether disgraceful to our great labour organisations. . . . The case for the fifty candidates, the £30,000 and the prompt and energetic organisation of the labour vote, is unanswerable. The question is, who is to do it? There is, unfortunately, no such thing as completely effective and general organisation of the working-classes in this or in any other country. But there is one organising agency, which is so much more effective and advanced than any other, that its superior fitness for the political work in hand is beyond all question; and that is the trade union organisation. There is nothing in the labour world that can compare even distantly with it. . . . There is no other combination able to cope with a general election. Attempts have been made, and are still being made from time to time, especially by Socialists, to establish general societies of the whole working-class to relieve the trade unions of their political duty; but, at the present moment, if the unions polled their entire voting strength at a general election, they could put not less than two thousand voters into the field for every single voter in the ranks of the most successful of their rivals.

The money difficulty, which is the great bar to parliamentary representation of the working-class, does not exist for bodies which can raise a thousand pounds by a levy of from a penny to sixpence per member. A subscription of a penny a week for a year from every member of a trade union in the country would produce at least upwards of £300,000; and, though such a subscription is not completely practicable, the calculation shows how easily the larger unions alone, with their membership of a million, could provide £30,000 to finance fifty labour candidates at £600 apiece, and to force forward the long-deferred legislation for payment of members and election expenses.

On the whole then, we may take it that the representation of the working-classes at the general election will depend on the great national trade unions, and not on the Socialist bodies. Neither the Fabian Society nor the Social Democratic Federation, neither the Labour Electoral Association nor the society known as the Independent Labour Party, has the slightest prospect of mustering enough money to carry through three serious candidatures, much less fifty. Their part will be to provide the agitation which will enable the trade union leaders to obtain the support of the rank and file in rising to the occasion. [*Fortnightly Review*, November 1893.] [1]

The Fabian Manifesto, so I judge from a batch of letters from our personal friends among Liberal politicians and Liberal journalists, hurt feelings and roused anger.

The manifesto is a heavy blow to us [writes R. B. Haldane on November 2, 1893]. We younger men were striving to bring those with whom we were immediately in contact into relation with you. We were making an impression. The liberal machine was in course of modification. The work was very difficult. . . . It was easier to persuade the older men, like Harcourt and Fowler, than to coerce them. . . . It hurts *us* far more than the old gang, for weak as we were we could point, in the old days, the days of a week ago, to the support of your party. And now the Whig element will smile and go its way, and rely on what is really the substantial back-ground of the purely political working-man, who cares much where Liberalism is still comparatively strong, for things like Welsh Disestablishment and Home Rule.

Even more exasperated by the Manifesto was H. W. Massingham, the political editor of the *Daily Chronicle*.

Its appeal to trade unions is absurd and ill-timed; it is already being universally interpreted in the press (see the *Pall Mall* and the *Dundee Advertiser*) as a mere Unionist dodge, and it is in particular a retrogression (in the matter of the advice to trade unions—*who won't respond*) from every political principle that the Fabians have upheld. I think it a terrible mistake, which may have serious consequences. "Not that it is easy to discuss seriously a manifesto chock full of levity, of unreal and insincere argument, of unverified statements, and of purposeful exaggeration", he writes to G. B. S. ". . . You have perpetrated a schoolboy jest—a mere freak of mischievous tom-foolery." [I may observe in passing that within two years, as will be seen in the following pages, our correspondents had become as critical as we had been of the spinelessness of the Liberal Cabinet.]

I gather from the MS. diary that, during the next four years, we became increasingly intimate with politicians and

1 For details as to the organisation of the Labour Party and its relation to trade unionism see *The History of Trade Unionism*, S. and B. Webb, 1920 edition, chapter xi., "Political Organisation, 1900–1920" (p. 677). See also *History of Socialism*, by Thomas Kirkup, revised by Edward Pease, 1913, section on "The Labour Party" (pp. 384–92). (See, too, *British Working-Cass Politics*, G. D. H. Cole. Ed.)

civil servants. But, immersed as we were in our researches into British Trade Unionism and in S. W.'s municipal and educational administration, this contact with the greater world of politics has left few traces in our joint memory. So I restrict myself to giving, for the most part without comment, a long string of entries; which may well seem to the reader scrappy and inconsequent, unduly personal and therefore lacking in perspective and sense of proportion. As a set-off these contemporary notes will, at any rate, be free from the distortion of being " wise after the event ": the one irredeemable flaw, regarded as evidence of past states of mind, of all political reminiscences.

March 12*th*, 1894.—Last Thursday I was sitting down to work after breakfast when Haldane was announced. " I have come to see you and Webb about the political situation ", he began, looking grave and disturbed. I called Sidney in, and we both sat down feeling that we were expected to condole with some grievance but not quite certain which. " These are dreadful appointments ", he continued. " Shaw-Lefevre is fatal to the Local Government Board; couldn't be worse: George Russell at the Home Office, too." And then Haldane unburdened his soul to us. He described how the last ten days had been in reality a pitched battle between the old and the new Radicals. The common run of Liberal members were strongly in favour of Harcourt; the little gang of collectivist Radicals (which included Asquith, Acland, Sydney Buxton and Grey) had forced Rosebery on the parliamentary Radicals with the aid of such outside forces as the London Progressives and the *Chronicle*. John Morley had joined them from personal dislike of Harcourt, so that the hand of the Labouchere lot had been forced by the threat of the retirement of the most vital part of the Ministry. But the old gang had had their revenge. They had promoted Fowler, forced into the L.G.B. Shaw-Lefevre (Fowler and Harcourt's nominee), and effectually barred the way to Haldane's entry into the Cabinet. It was natural enough that poor Haldane, having sacrificed himself by incurring the hatred of the rank and file by his successful Rosebery intrigue, should not be satisfied with this result. He had come to us to suggest that the *Chronicle* should be more critical in its attitude towards the new Government, and that the Progressives generally should not give themselves away. It was a quaint episode, when one remembered his grave remonstrance about our hostile attitude last autumn, that he should be instigating us to be independent. I saw, however, that it was more the *Chronicle* that he was after than ourselves. So I arranged that he should meet Massingham here on Sunday night and talk it over.

Massingham came in before Haldane arrived, and confirmed his account of what had taken place. Asquith and Haldane, he says, are hated by the House of Commons Radical, who feels the ground slipping from under him without knowing why. Haldane incited Massingham to keep the *Chronicle* an independent force. They and Sidney more or less determined on a plan of campaign. . . . " It is war to the knife, now," said Haldane impressively, " either they or we have to go down." But what amused me was the way in which the present crisis had completely healed the strained feeling caused between Sidney and Massingham, and to some extent Haldane, by the Fabian Manifesto. Massingham, who had told us firmly that he would never work with us again, was now taking counsel about his conduct of the *Chronicle*, and his ultimatum to the nominal editor that he would stand no interference in the political editorship. It shows how right we were to treat his angry outburst of private and public abuse with imperturbable good temper, and turn our left cheek when he struck our right. I like Massingham immensely: I like him more than I respect him. His excitability, impressionableness, his quick appreciation of anything you say, and clever reproduction of it—all this is attractive —but one feels that to be safe with him one ought to keep him very much in tow. In that respect he resembles Tom Mann: he needs ballast.

Our little plan of writing the minority reports of the two Commissions[1] seems to be coming off all right. Tom Mann hands in his elaborate Socialist manifesto and programme to-morrow. Broadhurst swallowed his part quite complacently, and Sidney has prepared him an excellent document on old-age pensions and the reform of the poor law. But we tremble lest some inadvertence should spoil our little game and Sidney's work be wasted. But these sort of risks one has to run with these Labour men. They are not efficient. Broadhurst a good deal more so than Tom Mann; but then one likes him less in other ways, which makes working through him less pleasant. Whether we shall succeed in making our little home the intellectual headquarters of the Labour movement depends a good deal on the success, from the point of view of the two men concerned, of these minority reports. If it becomes generally known among the working-men leaders that Sidney is always ready to give them their stock in trade, and that no discredit comes to them from accepting his help, then we shall be able to direct the aims and methods of the popular party on the questions which we understand. This behind the scenes intellectual leadership is, I believe, Sidney's especial talent.

[1] Royal Commissions on Labour and on the Aged Poor.

Sidney is discouraged about the political situation [I write in July 1894]. Absorbed in the L.C.C. administrative work and in the book, he has little time for wire-pulling. He feels that there is a backwardation. The Conservative Unionist Party is now fully alive to the issue of individualism and property as against collectivism and labour legislation, and is making preparations to fight hard; whilst the Liberal Party, though vaguely collectivist, is not led by collectivists, and has even among its leaders the most bigoted individualists. We have to some extent roused our natural enemies without having secured our natural allies. The Independent Labour Party, with its lack of money, brains and, to some extent, moral characteristics, is as yet more a thorn in the side of the Liberals than an effective force on our side. Tom Mann is putting a good deal of steam into its propaganda and is lending to the cause some of his high character and personal purity; but at present there is no chance of its being more than a wrecking party, to some extent contradicting the permeating policy of the Fabians. Still, it has its uses: it may be a question of the surgeon's knife rather than of a sustained regimen.

I sometimes wonder whether I am right in inclining Sidney *not* to go into Parliament. Hardly a month passes but some constituency or other throws out a fly for him; but so far he resolutely refuses to consider it, and that largely because I discourage him. Personally, I feel that he is doing real work on the L.C.C., work which is not only useful to London, but useful to him, in that it gives him problems of administration to think out instead of pure wire-pullers' work. Is there any distinction? Is not all administrative work wire-pulling, with a clear conception of your ends? Perhaps the distinction is that in administration your ends must be practicable and desirable; in political wire-pulling, you may be highly successful in your machinery but have altogether misunderstood the object of it. I do not feel confident that he would be a big success in the House; I do not think the finest part of his mind and character would be called out by the manipulation and intrigues of the lobby. And then a parliamentary career would destroy our united life; would cut at the root of a good deal of our joint effort. Perhaps that is why I distrust my dislike of his going into Parliament; it would take so much away from me, personally, would add so many ties and inconveniences. Sooner or later I suppose he will have to make the sacrifice—but better later than sooner.

Borough Farm, Surrey, July 1894.—How far, I wonder [I write a few days later], will the collectivist principle carry us? The thinkers of fifty years ago believed as firmly in individualism as we believe in collectivism—probably more uncompromisingly; for the men and women of to-day distrust general principles even though they be prepared to use them. And yet it is easy to see now that the settled conviction of the individualists that government should be limited to keeping the ring clear for private individuals to fight in, was based on the experience of a one-sided and corrupt participation of the government in industrial organisation, and not on any necessary characteristic of state action. Face to face with the government action of their own day, they were to a large extent right. Is it not possible that it is the same with collectivism? Public administration is the alternative to private enterprise, and since private enterprise is corrupt and selfish we propose to supersede it by democratic control. But it is, on the face of it, as unlikely that the collectivist principle will apply all round as that the individualist principle would solve all the social problems of fifty years ago. I do not think that we Fabians believe in more than a limited application of the collectivist principle; though, as practical politicians, we think that we are as yet nowhere near the margin of cultivation, that we can cultivate this principle vigorously for all that it is worth, in all directions without exhausting its vitality. But of one thing I feel certain. The controversy which seems to us now so full of significance and import will seem barren and useless to our great-grandchildren; they will be amazed that we fought so hard to establish one metaphysical position and to destroy another. And that is why I value diagnosis so much more highly than controversy and propaganda. How eagerly one searches in old pamphlets, articles and speeches for the chance fact which has been used to illustrate some utterly bygone argument or principle; how much more highly one values accurate and vivid description to subtle argument and slashing logic. But even here one is discouraged. The selection of facts is governed by the hypotheses of the investigator. Just those facts, which would have been most illuminating to the student of the next century, may be overlooked, or even, if noticed, may be carelessly thrown on one side. One must be content to work for one's own day. . . .

December 29th, 1894.—Spent our Christmas at Parmoor, with Alfred Cripps, the children, the [Leonard] Courtneys and various Cripps nieces. Alfred's home is strangely attractive—with a dash of sadness in it—especially to Theresa's sisters.[1] A charming house, designed largely by Theresa, the soft luxurious colouring, the quaintness of the furniture, the walls covered with her portraits, all bring back to me the memory of her gracious personality, so full of sympathy, wit and vivid imagination. And yet the home seems complete without her—the children revel in high spirits and health, the servants are

[1] Beatrice's sister Theresa Cripps died in 1893, leaving five young children. (Ed.)

contented. Alfred himself has regained all the lightheartedness of his charming disposition. Possibly it is the rebound from the sadness of his most intimate thoughts, but to the mere spectator he seems more lighthearted than of old. He is again the young man—unattached— absolute master of his own life. And he is in the full tide of great prosperity. An enormous professional income (he told Arthur [1] that he made £1000 a week during the session) has enabled him to buy the family estate and sit down in front of a promising constituency. Doubtless he sees before him a brilliant career. Dear old Father used to call him " the little jewel of an advocate "—a term which just fits him. There is something jewelled in his nature; intellectual *skilfulness* raised to the highest degree, a perfect deftness in execution, a loving disposition, unruffled temper, a cheery optimism; all these bright qualities set in a solid determination that all things shall fit in with his view of what is desirable—for himself and others. He is a delightful father—the children obeying him implicitly with no consciousness of being ruled or regulated; a charming host—seeming to place his whole establishment at the service of his guests; a most indulgent master and landlord; and, yet for all that, he gets his own way in life, and takes a very large share of the good things of the world both material and spiritual. With this disposition he could hardly be a reformer. He has become of late years more and more a Conservative opportunist— bent on keeping the soft places of the world for his own class—but ready to compromise and deal whenever his class would lose more by fighting. He has almost a constitutional dislike of economic or social principle. In the management of his own estate he creates the maximum of personal dependence on himself, not only scattering his money freely, but almost preferring to give it when it is least deserved so as to get the greatest amount of personal gratitude. And yet he is a determined opponent of any kind of public help—opposes it on the ground that it would undermine personal effort; in his heart of hearts he feels that it would render impossible the exercise of that power which he loves—the love of binding people to you by ties of obligation and personal gratitude. I doubt whether Alfred ever thinks out an economic or political problem. Why should he? He knows on which side he is retained, and there will be time enough to get up the advocate's facts when the question turns up. This superficialism, of course, takes from his conversation all the deeper interest—he never weighs what you say, he simply listens to it to get the cue for a bright repartee or a quick turn of the subject. Discussion with him becomes a pretty play of words, he refuses to consider your position and will not permit you to look round his. Perhaps it is this part of Alfred's development

---

[1] Arthur Playne, married to Beatrice's sister Mary. (Ed.)

with which I am most disappointed. When I first knew him—for those three or four years I was intimate with him—he was *thinking* hard, trying to ascertain facts and draw conclusions. He has now ceased to think. All the intellectual energy he can spare from his money-making advocacy is spent in the enjoyment of his own prosperity, and in that baser form of advocacy—the manufacture of electioneering speeches. With his skill and charm he will succeed in politics as he has succeeded at the Bar—he will " make money or its equivalent "—and that is all. For all that, he remains an essentially lovable man. And without doubt he will one day find another mate, and then we shall lose sight of him.

It is curious to see the three brothers-in-law together. Each one has, for the opinions of the other two, tolerant contempt. Leonard Courtney likes Alfred far better than he does Sidney, thinks him a pleasant, attractive fellow with all the antecedents of a gentleman and a scholar. But for his opportunist Toryism—his demagogic anti-democratic attitude—he has, I think, an even greater intellectual contempt than for Sidney's collectivism. Alfred frankly defends class privileges and as frankly appeals to the prejudices of the masses— favours protection and publicans as well as priests and peers, and is as bitterly opposed to popular education, or even any stimulus to citizenship, as he would be to unlimited outdoor relief. Beyond all he is a purely party man and looks on every proposal as a move in the party fight.[1] All this is as intensely repugnant to Leonard as Alfred's lax management of his estate, or his scarcely veiled bribery of the Stroud constituency. To Leonard the means whereby you carry through a proposal, the arguments with which you support it, are as important as the end itself. And to do Leonard justice he is a democrat at heart, in that he honestly desires that the government of the country should be the reflection of the free desires and views of the whole body of the people. Possibly he is more of a democrat than we are ourselves; for we have little faith in the " average sensual man ", we do not believe that he can do much more than describe his grievances, we do not think that he can prescribe the remedies. It is possibly exactly on this point that Leonard feels most antagonism to our opinions. We wish to introduce into politics the professional expert—to extend the sphere of government by adding to its enormous advantages of wholesale and compulsory management, the advantage of the most skilled entrepreneur. Leonard agrees with us, I think, in believing that the happiness of the mass is the end to be aimed at, but he has no faith

---

[1] During the War 1914–18, Alfred Cripps, on the ground of pacifist principle, left the Conservative Party and later joined the Labour Party. See Biographical Index. (Ed.)

in our methods because he holds a radically different economic creed. Alfred, on the other hand, refuses seriously to discuss with us, because he recognises at once that we desire different ends—Leonard he holds to be a cranky faddist who cannot make up his mind which side of things he is really going to support. The attitude of the three brothers-in-law may therefore be described thus: Alfred looks on Sidney as a traitor to the brain-working and propertied class; Sidney looks on Alfred as a " kept " advocate of the *status quo*; Leonard looks on Alfred as a somewhat selfish, thoughtless and superficial conservative; on Sidney as a shallow-minded, self-complacent, half-educated democrat; whilst both Sidney and Alfred have much the same opinion of Leonard —an upright but wrong-headed man, dominated by a worn-out economic creed and shackled by lack of sympathy and quick intelligence. To some extent all opinions are equally true—as a summing-up of each individual they are all equally false.

January 20th, 1895.—Haldane, utterly discouraged with condition of the Liberal Party; says there is now no hope that the Cabinet will pull themselves through. With the exception of Acland, none of the Ministers are doing any work: Rosebery sees no one but Eddy Hamilton, a flashy fast Treasury clerk, his stud-groom, and various non-political fashionables; Sir W. Harcourt amuses himself at his country place and abroad, determined to do nothing to help Rosebery; even Asquith, under the dominance of his brilliant and silly wife, has given up attending to his department and occupies his time by visiting rich country houses and learning to ride! " Rot has set in," says Haldane; " there is no hope now but to be beaten and then to reconstruct a new party. If only you Progressives can hold your own at the L.C.C. elections, you would be a plank saved from the wreck upon which we could build a new combination."

The same strains from Massingham, now much under Haldane's influence. He spent three or four hours here the other day being coached for the *Daily Chronicle* on the L.C.C. election. Urged Sidney to go into Parliament and become one of the leaders of the reconstruction party. But Sidney will bide his time. At present, the L.C.C. is a better platform from which to bring about collectivism than the House of Commons.

January 23rd, 1895.—Last night we had an informal conference with the I.L.P. leaders; MacDonald and Frank Smith (who are members both of the Fabian Society and the I.L.P.), having been for some time harping on the desirability of an understanding between the two societies. To satisfy them Sidney asked a little dinner of Keir Hardie, Tom Mann, Pease and Shaw, and the two intermediaries. I think the principals on either side felt it would come to nothing. Nevertheless, it was interesting. Keir Hardie was reserved, and merely reiterated the burden of his speech to the Fabians. But Tom Mann gushed out his soul. The practical issue before us was the action of the I.L.P. at the L.C.C. elections. Tom Mann, with the concurrence of Keir Hardie, advised the I.L.P. to abstain from voting. The Progressives on the L.C.C., he said, were not convinced Socialists and, even those who were, chose to run as Progressives and not as purely Socialist candidates. Therefore, the I.L.P. should be hostile to their return. He would not support John Burns (or presumably Sidney), " because Jack played to get the vote of the mere Liberal ". " No one could get the votes of the I.L.P. who did not pledge himself to the nationalisation of the means of production, and *who did not run overtly in opposition to all who were not socialists.*" He would accept no alliance. When we cross-examined his reasons they amounted to this. First, even if the Progressives were trying their best to use the L.C.C. for socialist purposes, the I.L.P. of the provinces regarded them as mere Liberals; and, as a fact, if the Progressives were elected, it would redound to the credit of the official Liberals. Secondly, the amelioration brought about by the collectivism of the L.C.C. retarded the growth of the I.L.P. movement; set back the social revolution.

It was melancholy to see Tom Mann reverting to the old views of the S.D.F. and, what is worse, to their narrow sectarian policy. Keir Hardie, who impressed me very unfavourably, deliberately chooses this policy as the only one he can boss. His only chance of leadership lies in the creation of an organisation " agin' the Government "; he knows little and cares less for any constructive thought or action. But with Tom Mann it is different. He is possessed with the idea of a " church "—of a body of men all professing the same creed and all working in exact uniformity to exactly the same end. No idea which is not absolute, which admits of any compromise or qualification, no adhesion which is tempered with doubt, has the slightest attraction to him. And as Shaw remarked, he is deteriorating. This stumping the country, talking abstractions and raving emotions, is not good for a man's judgement; and the perpetual excitement leads, among other things to too much whiskey.

I do not think the conference ended in any understanding. We made clear our position. The Fabians in no way competed with the I.L.P. We were purely an educational body—we did not seek to become a political party. We should continue our policy of inoculation—of giving to each class, to each person, coming under our influence, the exact dose of collectivism that they were prepared to assimilate. And we should continue to improve and enlarge such machinery of government that came into our hands. Of course, this slow imperceptible change in men's opinions and in the national institutions, is not favourable to the growth of a revolutionary party. There is some truth in Keir Hardie's remark that we were the worst enemies of the social revolution. No great transformation is possible in a free democratic state like England unless *you alter the opinions of all classes of the community*—and, even if it were possible, it would not be desirable. That is the crux between us!

In the last chapter I described the stalemate of the London County Council election in the first days of March 1895; the Progressives deprived of their majority of elected members, and dependent, for their administrative control, on the Progressive aldermen overhanging from the outgoing Council. A fortnight later, there occurred an event which, because it affected one of the family group, lent acidity to the following entries in the MS. diary. My brother-in-law, Leonard Courtney, who had served for six years as Deputy Speaker, was pressed by Sir William Harcourt and his colleagues to accept the Government nomination for the Speakership: he felt compelled, out of loyalty to his own party, to enquire whether or not they wished him to accept it. The answer was decisively in the negative.[1]

March 19th, 1895.—Poor dear Leonard diddled out of the Speakership by his own party. A mean and discreditable intrigue of Chamberlain's, who has had an animus against him ever since I can remember—first because Leonard was too much of a Whig, then because he retained too much of the Radical. Most likely, however, it has been all through a personal animus dating from Leonard's refusal fifteen years ago to enrol himself as Chamberlain's follower. It is only fair to say that Leonard has had a contempt for Chamberlain's intelligence and character—and Leonard is not a man to hide his opinions. Leonard's bad manners, his supercilious depreciation of other people's claims, and his lack of graciousness, have been Chamberlain's opportunity. We are grieved not only for his and Kate's sake but because we really believe we have lost the most democratic Speaker available. For, with all his faults, Leonard has an honest desire for the maximum *efficiency* in democratic machinery; and he judges each change on its own merits and not on what it may lead to. He has *faith in democracy*— a quality which covers many sins.

[1] See *Life of Lord Courtney*, by G. P. Gooch, chapter xv., " The Speaker's Chair " (pp. 316-28).

March 26th, 1895.—Beatrice Chamberlain [1] paid me one of her annual visits, and we had a long talk on politics, carefully avoiding the L.C.C. and the Speakership. She was anxious to know our opinion of the Factory Bill—was it a good Bill—did it go far enough? I gather from her attitude that J. C. is friendly to regulation of private enterprise and has no prejudices in favour of free trade in labour. I told her that the Bill was excellent so far as it went, but might easily be made better by certain amendments. I felt inclined to offer to send her the amendments; but I am not sufficiently certain of J. C.'s *bona fides* to be completely confidential. One great advantage of the Bill is that at last we get recognised the principle I have been fighting for for five years, the responsibility of the *giver out of work* for conditions of employment: my own pet invention in labour legislation, I am glad to see it at last embodied in the black and white of a Government Bill.

May 27th, 1895.—A grey outlook in political situation, a heavy reaction setting in against the Liberal Government—the " haves " thoroughly frightened, the " have-nots " unsatisfied. Within the Liberal Party each man complaining of the other—no comradeship or cohesion—all at sixes and sevens with regard to opinions.

July 8th, 1895.—On the eve of the election, the Fabians are sitting with their hands in their laps [I write just before the general election]. From our point of view, no result can be satisfactory. The Liberals, on the eve of dissolution, show no signs of grace, they go unabsolved to their grave: if anything, rather inclined to repent their good deeds, not to regret their lost opportunities. Lords, Home Rule and Local Veto are their battle cries—Rosebery, Morley and Harcourt voicing each separately. The I.L.P. is splashing about in a futile ineffectual fashion, the S.D.F. turning all its energies into a fanatical crusade against John Burns! We wish the Liberals to be beaten, but we do not wish the Tories to win. A tie, or something near a tie, would suit us best. But it looks like a triumphant majority for the Tories. Nor does there seem much hope in the future. The Liberal Party is pledged to three measures which offend all the conservative instincts of the people—Home Rule, Local Veto and Church Disestablishment—without exciting the slightest enthusiasm among the advanced section of their party. Sometimes we think we are in for a long spell of strong Conservative rule beginning with 1895, and lasting possibly for another twenty years with only short interregnums of weak Liberal Government. For the Liberals have no leaders inspired with a new faith. Asquith has been ruined by marrying a silly ignorant wife; and

[1] Daughter of Joseph Chamberlain by his first wife and intimate friend of Beatrice before her marriage. (Ed.)

there is no other man who has at once capacity, character and conviction. The Labour men are mere babies in politics; judging from
our knowledge of the Labour movement we can expect *no* leader
from the working-class. Our only hope is in permeating the young
middle-class man—catching them for collectivism before they have
enlisted on the other side.

Though the situation looks bad for our side of things, it is impossible
not to be amused and interested in the political drama. Chamberlain
is the man of the moment. He has kept the little band of Liberal
Unionists separate and compact for ten years; and now, just before
they must of necessity melt away, he has deftly used them to ride into
power, dragging into the Government the faithful Jesse Collings, the
servile Powell Williams and the amiable youth, Austen. The humour
of the situation is the fact that the majority of the Liberal Unionists
in the House of Commons have been anti-Chamberlainites—more
hostile in their hearts to " Joe " than the bigoted Tories! It is a
testimony to the marvellous force of Chamberlain's personality that he
pervades this election—no one trusts him, no one likes him, no one
really believes in him, and yet everyone accepts him as the leader of
the united Unionists. His position in the Tory Party is, in fact, very
similar to his position in 1885 in the Liberal Party. Is it equally
unstable? Will he play again the rôle of the usurper to keep his seat
on the throne, or does he believe sufficiently in his new party to serve
it faithfully? I am inclined to think that, barring accidents from evil
temper, the cause of private property is sufficiently attractive to
Chamberlain's mind to keep him from wilful wrecking; and that, on
the whole, Salisbury has got a fair consideration in the bargain of the
last few days. But alas! for the poor dear Liberal Unionists—that
little company of upright, narrowly enlightened, well-bred men—who
drifted away from the Liberal Party ostensibly on Home Rule, but
mainly because of the shoddy social schemes Joe had imposed on
Gladstone. To be used as the ladder up which Joe climbs into a
Conservative Government, waving aloft his banner of shoddy reform,
then to be thrown ignominiously aside. A fit ending for a company
of prigs!

July 10th, 1895.—Attended London Trades Council meeting last
Thursday. Printed agenda of platonic resolutions on all manner of
questions. But the business done was exclusively on minutes of the
executive. For two-and-a-half hours some 100 delegates wrangled
over an accusation of *sweating* brought against the Salvation Army
by the Printing Trades Federation and reported by the printing trades
group of the L.T.C. Quite obvious that the delegates of the Printing
Federation had made numberless exaggerated statements: equally clear

that the printing trades group had given a clean bill of health to the Salvation Army in spite of manifold signs of sweating in the past, if not in the present. No conclusion—referred to another committee.

But the most astounding fact about this meeting was the total absence of any reference, or even a by-the-way allusion, to the approaching general election. It is almost inconceivable that a meeting of the representative working-men of London should be held within four days of the general election without taking apparently the slightest notice of it. It is another proof of the disastrous political incapacity of the present T.U. leaders. The T.U. world seems half-paralysed. The faked-up conference at Manchester on the 11th, held because it was ordered by the last Congress, has had not the remotest effect on any single election. The *Cotton Factory Times*, the organ of the cotton operatives, has dilated on cotton duties and bi-metallism, but not a word on the more general interests of the wage-earners; the I.L.P. journals—*Clarion* and *Labour Leader*—have published no programme, have given no lead [I record, as the returns for the long drawn-out election drop in], except Keir Hardie's futile suggestion that I.L.P. voters should spoil their ballot papers by writing the name of some woman as candidate. Even the miners seem to be in a state of political suspended animation.

Of course, this has meant a rout for the anti-Conservatives (really that is the only generic term wide enough to cover the numberless groups) all along the line—Sir W. Harcourt being smashed at Derby, and Keir Hardie at West Ham! The rout is quite indiscriminate: if the official Liberals have been extinguished, the Labour Party has certainly not won. Some dozen seats have probably been lost by Labour candidatures; but, where the Liberal has stood aside, the Labour man has failed to win the place.

To us the result is not altogether unsatisfactory. From our point of view the field had to be cleared. The official Liberals had rucked up. For the last year, there were numberless signs that our opinions were discounted—that there was a backwardation. This has been especially obvious since the L.C.C. elections—the Harcourts, Morleys, Hibberts and Fowlers have sneered, have as good as said that they were not any longer going to be bamboozled, that Home Rule, Local Veto, Church Disestablishment and anti-Lords were to be the only battle cries of the Liberal Party. The utter rout, the annihilation, one might almost say, of the Harcourt faction—the hopeless discredit into which such reforms as Local Veto, Home Rule, Church Disestablishment have fallen clears the field of a good deal of cumbrous débris. On the other hand, the I.L.P. has completed its suicide. Its policy of abstention and deliberate wrecking is proved to be futile and absurd; Keir Hardie has probably lost for good any chance of posturing as M.P., and will sink into the old place of a discredited Labour leader. So long as the I.L.P. existed as an unknown force of irreconcilables, the more reasonable policy of permeation and levelling-up was utterly checkmated.

I do not mean to say that events have gone as we wished. Two years ago we hoped not only to go on levelling-up the great body of Liberals, but also to weed out of the party, by a reasonable and discriminating Labour policy, the reactionaries; and thus possibly bring about a small Tory majority. But directly we discovered the ruck-up of official Liberalism, on the one hand, and the utterly unreasonable attitude of the I.L.P., on the other, we saw plainly that *our* game was up. *We were beaten* in the local elections of last autumn and this spring. From the general election we held aloof, refusing either to back the I.L.P. or support the Liberals. The rout of both, therefore, is no defeat for us. It leaves us free, indeed, to begin afresh on the old lines—of building up a new party on the basis of collectivism. Whether the English nation desires the change or can be brought to desire it; whether, if it does desire it, it will have the patience to work it out, is to my mind still an open question. In any case it will be a long business—and mainly dependent on the levelling-up of character and intelligence in the mass of the people. Meanwhile, the affairs of the nation are in the hands of an exceptionally able set of men who have been elected as trustees of the *status quo*. There is little danger of reaction, either in administration or legislation. The Conservatives are pledged up to the hilt to a policy of social reform, and the worst they can do is to stand still.

Grosvenor Hotel, Manchester, October 8th, 1895.—Sidney and I journeyed down here to cultivate Rochdale—Sidney speaking to the I.L.P. and I holding forth from the pulpit of a large Congregational church on the ethics of factory legislation. Rochdale, if ever Sidney thought of going into Parliament, is a possible constituency, at present held by a Tory owing to a split between Labour and Liberal. But Parliament seems further off than ever. We are loth to give up our quiet life of thought and enquiry, and we are discouraged by the hopeless state of progressive politics. Those who form the backbone of the Liberal Party, who dominate the party machinery, who own the wealth, who to a large extent monopolise the intelligence, have no convictions on the questions that interest working-men. At the best they are timid empiricists, who if they are assured that collectivism is the coming creed give it a faint-hearted support. For the most part, they are secretly hostile; they dare not proclaim their hostility so they remain dumb trying to evade the questions as outside practical politics.

These men would rather see a Conservative Government in power than allow the leaders of their own side to push forward social democracy. I am not sure that this hostile force is not still the strongest element inside the Liberal Party; none the less strong because they remain silent as regards the public, expressing themselves forcibly to the official leaders whom they surround like a body-guard keeping out all outside influence. The trick of forcing on the party an advanced programme, and then calling them traitors because they did not carry it out, is played out so far as we are concerned. It served its purpose; it was a wedge driven into the party and has discovered the true line of cleavage between the old and the new. But that is done and finished with. Now we collectivists have to assert ourselves as a distinct school of thought, taking up each question separately and reviewing it in the light of our principles. But the first need of a school of thought is *to think*. Our special mission seems to be to undertake the difficult problems ourselves, and to gather round us young men and women who will more or less study under inspiration. At present we have a certain set of young people all more or less devoted to the Fabian junta. Herbert Samuel, Charles Trevelyan, Bobby Phillimore, Bertrand Russell; all rich men of the upper or middle-class, and MacDonald, Martin, Macrosty of the lower middle-class. The London School of Economics should furnish others. But, in order to occupy this position, we must to some extent hold ourselves aloof; and, above all, we must be, and what is more or at least equally important, we must *appear* absolutely disinterested. At present that position seems inconsistent with any attempt to push forward a political career. If Sidney goes into Parliament he must go as an independent elected on account of his peculiar opinions and more or less the leader of a new party either within the Liberal organisation or outside it. No other position would compensate to the cause for his loss as an active thinker and administrator; no other position could make up for the personal sacrifice of giving up our joint work and the life of learned leisure for the inconvenience, separation and turmoil of a political career.

January 5th, 1896. *Parmoor*.—Two other visits, and we are back to-morrow at our work. Five days at Hadspen—Sidney's first introduction to the Hobhouse household. For Henry [1] he has always had an honest liking, admiring his public spirit and his refined view of life, and his painstaking industry. Henry's great lack is intellectual initiative and moral experience—he is narrow and limited—so to speak, blind to whole sides of life and quite incapable of discovering new lights and meanings. But he tries his level best to *be* enlightened, never

[1] Henry Hobhouse, married to Beatrice's sister Margaret. See Biographica Index. (Ed.)

consciously allows personal or class interest to bias him, and is quite incapable of unworthy motive. In this imperfect world these high and chivalrous qualities are admirable. Perhaps it has weighed with us that alone among my brothers-in-law he has welcomed Sidney with grave courtesy into the family, has always treated him with respect and friendliness, has apparently never felt that repulsion which most of my brothers-in-law have shown to him—either on account of his lack of social status or because of his opinions. Maggie,[1] of course, is the same high-spirited, rather vulgar and sharp-tongued woman—has cut her nature down to suit her husband's intellectual limitations without raising it to conform to her husband's moral standard. There is always therefore a jar in the house—Maggie protesting against Henry's quixotic principles—Henry silently resenting her plots and plans for social advancement and pecuniary saving. The family life suffers a little from this jar and loses in grace and charm. But this is only superficial. The two are honestly fond of each other, and Margaret is a capable and wholly devoted mother. Stephen, the eldest boy, now scholar at Eton, is a tall, lanky, ugly boy—unspoilt and simple-minded, with none of the public school boy's " side "—industrious, discreet and interested in men and things. No charm of body or mind—except an unsullied honesty and purity of nature. The little girls are correct and well-mannered, bright and happy, very pleasant to look at and quite sufficiently intelligent. The other children are too young to be judged. The most marked general feature of all of them is the lack of that introspective morbid character that distinguished most of us. Neither Stephen, nor the two girls, show any curiosity about religion, they all conform and never ask questions. They seem at present to have some of the limitations in intellectual and moral experience that is so marked a characteristic of their father. I should imagine that Stephen Hobhouse is destined by his character to be a civil servant— in which case we may hope to see something of this boy—to whom I feel drawn.

After five days at Hadspen we came on here. A charmingly attractive house—an atmosphere of "promise and expectation". Alfred [Cripps], after a brilliant professional career, is entering political life with all the self-assurance and ambition of the man who has never failed. And what a contrast to Henry! With a wide tho' superficial knowledge of human affairs, with the typical advocate's temperament, Alfred has chosen his political party and means to abide by it. No nonsense

---

[1] Margaret was Beatrice's most intimate companion among the sisters and, while they differed widely in outlook, Beatrice often expressed her admiration for her sister's intellectual integrity, her outspokenness and courage in defence of what she believed to be right. See Biographical Index. (Ed.)

about enlightenment, or any impartial study of the common weal. He deliberately shuts his eyes to the other party's case except in so far as knowledge of it will help him to controvert it. With infinitely more intelligence, knowledge and sympathy than Henry, he is far less capable of a sound political judgement. Whereas Henry in nine cases out of ten will be more enlightened than the rank and file in his own party, Alfred will probably range himself among the prudent and able reactionaries. He is, of course, far too clever not to compromise— but his compromise will always be the best compromise for his class and not the best for the community. He will never hesitate to start false issues and use false arguments in order to throw dust in the face of the people. Love of *truth*, at one time so prominent in his nature, now hardly exists; he is utterly uninterested in economic or political research. Sharp wits are all that are required to perceive an attack on the fundamental principles of " private property and the growth of the Empire "—sharp wits, and physical force are all that is needed to defend them. That being so, whether this evil, or that evil, prevails is an immaterial issue. Still more fantastic, to his mind, is that elaborate dissection and diagnosis of social and economic facts which enables a politician to deal with them. All this discovery and analysis are in his mind purely mischievous, not because *these evils cannot be cured* (Leonard Courtney's position), but for the far simpler reason that it is not worth while curing them. Having decided to stand by his class, being honestly (and no doubt justly) convinced that that class has everything to lose and nothing to gain by an alteration in the *status quo*, the one thing needful is to appeal to the popular suspicion, fear, prejudices and fallacies to keep back any further reforms. I do not mean this as a moral indictment. Alfred's original conviction that it is desirable that an upper class, owning most of the property and keeping the control of the nation, should exist is a proposition which can be perfectly well defended. But it is a proposition which, in face of a political democracy, it is impossible to state overtly and equally useless to attempt to prove. Foolish persons, like Auberon Herbert or Herbert Spencer, only injure the cause they are attempting to defend; since their conclusions render all their logic and all their facts suspect. That is, after all, not their fault, but the fault of the political public which is, let us admit at once, grossly biased. We, on the other hand, having arrived at the popular conclusion, are willing enough to uncover the facts and the reasonings which have led us there, and are supremely intent on finding out more facts so that we may proceed yet further. Alfred Cripps is far too clever not to perceive that the real interest of the people is hostile to that of the classes—to meander about like Henry Hobhouse attempting to discover the common weal argues simply, to his mind, a lack of capacity. There is no common weal—there is a solution which will suit the " haves ", and a solution which will suit the " have-nots ", and there is, of course, a compromise. It is this superior clear-sightedness which has transformed Alfred into a mere political advocate habitually ignoring facts and distorting issues. In a political democracy, no really intellectual politician who disagrees with the assumptions of democracy—still less one who agrees with the principles of a plutocratic or aristocratic state—can possibly remain an honest thinker and honest speaker. It is not the fault of Alfred's nature—it is the inevitable result of the conflict between his first principles, and the political circumstances in which he is forced to live.

Alfred's temperament and intellectual position is interesting because I think it is typical of the intellectual tone of the genuine conservative. And this means that the whole onus of economic discovery and political education will be thrown on those who desire complete democracy, still more on those who desire complete *social* democracy. This means a terrific intellectual strain on the progressive party. It is intensely difficult to be at once investigators and agitators—men of science and administrators. We are trying, in our humble way, to lead both lives— to keep our head clear to see the facts—without losing that touch of the political market which leads to effective propaganda. We shall probably fail at both pursuits—that is to say, we shall do each far less well than we might have done if we had specialised. Sooner or later there must needs be division of labour—if it comes in our time, we, I think, shall become investigators and not politicians.

The whole mind of the country is at present absorbed in foreign politics. There has been a dramatic interest in the Transvaal events. Secrecy in international matters has, I think, been finally discredited so far as England is concerned. And the occasion has found the man. Joe Chamberlain is to-day the national hero. Only a small section— the extreme Tories of the Alfred Cripps type—withhold their admiration for the swiftness and courage with which he has grappled with the crisis. Whether his Cabinet altogether appreciates the autocratic way in which he deals single-handed with every event is an interesting question of Cabinet politics. But his ways—his strong will, assiduity and reasonableness—have certainly given the nation confidence not only in his administration of the colonies but in the Conservative Government. In these troubled times, with every nation secretly disliking us, it is a comfortable thought that we have a Government of strong, resolute men—not given either to bluster or vacillation—but prompt in taking every measure to keep us out of a war and to make us successful should we be forced in it.

April 18*th*, 1896.—Whilst we were at the Lakes, we had furious letters from J. R. MacDonald on the "abuse of the Hutchinson Trust" in the proposal to contribute to the Library of Political Science. J. R. M. is a brilliant young Scot—lately I.L.P. candidate for Southampton—whom we [through the Fabian executive] have been employing as Hutchinson Trust lecturer in the provinces. These lectures are avowedly socialistic, but from the first Sidney has insisted that both MacDonald and Enid Stacy should make them educational: should issue an elaborate syllabus of a connected course, with bibliographies, etc. And, apparently, they have been extremely successful. But MacDonald is personally discontented because we refused to have him as a lecturer for the London School. He is not good enough for that work; he has never had the time to do any sound original work, or even learn the old stuff well. Moreover, he objects altogether to diverting Socialist funds to education. Even his own lectures, he declares, are too educational "to make Socialists"; he wants an organiser sent about the country. "Organise what?" asks Sidney. MacDonald dare not reply "I.L.P. branches", which he meant. Neither could he suggest organising Fabian societies as it has always been against the policy of the Fabians to organise people; its function being to permeate existing organisations. The truth is that we and MacDonald are opposed on a radical issue of policy. To bring about the maximum amount of public control in public adminis-tration do we want to organise the unthinking persons into Socialist societies, or to make the thinking persons socialistic? We believe in the latter process.

The Liberals being hopelessly out of court whilst the Conservatives seemed firmly established for many years ahead, the practical question arose, shall we or shall we not mend our fences on the Conservative side of the field of politics? From the following entries I gather that the answer was in the affirmative:

Whitsun, 1896.—Sidney much enjoyed colloquy with Sir John Gorst [acting Minister for Education], Michael Sadler, Llewellyn Smith and others about Education Bill. On the whole, he is favourable to the central idea of the Bill: that is, replacing *ad hoc* bodies by one set of representatives chosen to manage all the business of the locality (but doubtful whether the Bill, as it stands, will effect this): also, not against helping voluntary or denominational schools in return for a measure of control, which is bound to grow. Other clauses, enabling public authorities to subsidise private venture schools, he looks upon as radically bad. He, however, recognises that it is no good *for him* to oppose the Bill—far better to appreciate the good in it and, by appreciating it, get some influence in amending it in our direction. And he is fortunately placed for this purpose. As originator and chairman of the most successful educational authority in London, as a friendly acquaintance of Gorst's—as a friend of Llewellyn Smith and Sadler, and acquainted with all the educationalists in London, he is able to be constantly suggesting amendments which are favourably considered by those in authority.

This work, and pushing the London School and the Political Science Library, combine to force us more into political society on both sides. On Monday, for instance, we dined at the House with Haldane and Asquith and other Liberals; on Tuesday, with Sir John Gorst and Lord George Hamilton, two Conservative Ministers. Becoming too, every day more connected with the superior rank of civil servants, such as, Sir Alfred Milner, Sir George Kekewich, Henry Cunynghame and others (Sidney's old connection with the Civil Service stands him in good stead—he knows the ropes of almost every office). All this is in a way pleasant (I do not hide from myself that I am pleased and flattered that my boy is recognised as a distinguished man!), but it means less intellectual absorption in our work. Still we go plodding on with our analysis—making up our minds on each separate subject as we go along, more than ever convinced that we must write a *Textbook of Democracy*—crisp and authoritative—as our next work. We are always abusing the Liberal Party for not knowing its own mind—it would be more to the purpose if we made it up ourselves!

Whitsun, 1896.—Came back and found the Education Bill practically dead. . . . The discreditable failure of this complicated measure only another instance of how impossible it is nowadays to succeed in politics without technical knowledge of the great democratic machine. The last Liberal Government went out discredited because their members were mere prigs thrust into office—the present Government are going the same way. " In these matters I am a child ", says Balfour! We do not want clever school boys at the head of our great departments. We want grown men, " grown up " *in the particular business they have taken in hand*, doing their eight or nine hours' work for ten months in every year, whether in office or out of office; behaving towards their profession as the great civil engineer, lawyer or medical man behaves. In political life the standard of natural ability is remarkably high, the standard of acquirements ludicrously low. Who would trust the building of a bridge to a man who started with such an infinitesimal knowledge of engineering as Balfour or

Gorst have of national education and its machinery? There seems to be a settled conviction that any clever man, trained to any profession whatsoever, will succeed in politics whether or no he knows anything about the details of public administration, or the facts of the common life he has to attempt to reform. That impression we must try to destroy.

August 14th, 1896. *Saxmundham.*—A whole fortnight wasted in illness—rheumatic cold combined with general collapse. This must excuse the absence of the brilliant account which I looked forward to writing of the International Congress! To us it was, as we expected it to be, a public humiliation. The rank and file of Socialists—especially English Socialists—are unusually silly folk (for the most part feather-headed failures) and heaped together in one hall with the consciousness that their every word would be reported by the world's press, they approached raving imbecility. The confusion of tongues, of procedure, the grotesque absurdity of masquerading as " nations ", and you have all the factors for a hideous fiasco from the point of view of public opinion. The Fabians sat silent taking notes as reporters for the capitalist press; Sidney writing descriptive accounts for the *Manchester Guardian*, Shaw for the *Star*, Bland for a weekly paper, Clem Edwards for the *Daily News*, and another Fabian for the *Chronicle*. The Fabians at any rate write history if they do not make it!

But, though we were ashamed of the " British nation " as represented by the callow youths and maidens of the I.L.P. and S.D.F., the Socialists of other lands were exceptionally enlightening. The German political Socialists are substantial persons—their intellects somewhat twisted by their authoritarian dogmatism—but with strong sterling character and capable of persistent and deliberate effort. Among them, too, are thoughtful cultivated men such as Kautsky and Adler. The party is closely knit together, and apparently free of the frothy irresponsibility of our English movement. The Belgians in their responsible attitude resemble the Germans—both parties, one feels instinctively, are preparing themselves (perhaps prematurely) to become H.M. Opposition. Vandervelde, moreover, the leader of the Belgians, is a man of quite exceptional charm and distinction—a scholar and a gentleman. Among the French, Swiss, Dutch and Italians, there are individuals who are really " thinking ": we felt, perhaps, for the first time, how much the collectivist movement would gain by a quiet exchange of thought and experience between the cultivated and intellectual Socialists of all countries. Such a conference will be one of our likely plans for the future.

October 5th, 1897.—Had to attend Manchester Conference of Women. Usual large gathering of sensible and God-fearing folk—

dominated by the executive of Bishops' wives, who give to the proceedings an atmosphere of extreme decorum and dignity. I have resigned from the executive owing to their persistence in having prayers before all their business meetings which, I suggest, is wanting in courtesy to the Jewesses and infidels whom they wish to serve with them. Some of them agree but say that the Union would lose membership if it were not understood to be deliberately Christian. Very well: then I have no place on its executive. I remain on sub-committees and will keep the Union straight on industrial questions.[1]

The Bishops' wives are a nice lot—and I regret parting company with them. In spite of their piety they are large-minded—take broad views and have the pleasant manners of the great world. They are, in fact, " gentlemen " to deal with: very different from the narrow, intriguing, fanatical little Nonconformists who sit on the Council. Possibly it is the predominance of the Lyttelton family that gives the governing body of the conference such a sweet and wholesome flavour—there being at least three Lytteltons on the executive, whilst the sub-committees swarm with younger members of the family. The Lytteltons and Louise Creighton are the presiding spirits of the conference.

Louise Creighton now becomes—as wife of the Bishop of London —one of the great hostesses of London " society ". In spite of the fact that she is a fervent Christian and I an avowed agnostic, we have a warm respect for each other. She is an absolutely straight woman, who never swerves from what she believes to be right—is sometimes ugly in her brusque directness. She hides with difficulty her dislike or disapproval, and so has many enemies, or rather, persons who disparage her and call her " bourgeois " and thick-minded. To Alice Green, with her tortuous mind and uncertain ways, Louise is anathema,

---

[1] Report of Conference of National Union of Women Workers, *The Times*, October 29, 1897.

". . . Mrs. Sidney Webb moved a resolution to the effect that the business of the meeting should not commence with prayers as stated on the agenda. Speaking as a ' religious-minded agnostic ', she felt, when she saw the word ' prayers ' at the head of the agenda, that if she had not been elected on the committee on false grounds, she had been treated with discourtesy by the other members. While members of the Jewish persuasion did not object to be present at Christian prayers, the sect to which she belonged were not free to take part in them. Roman Catholics were differently placed. Agnostics were in an extremely difficult position; if present at Christian prayers they did not like to protest or leave the room or make themselves objectionable. She hoped those who participated in the business of the association would not be compelled to take part in the prayers.

" Mrs. Greenlees, in seconding, asked Mrs. Webb to substitute ' ladies of all shades of religious opinion ' for ' Christians '.

" Mrs. Webb : ' That will suit me better as it includes Roman Catholics '."

though possibly now that she is the wife of the Bishop of London Alice Green may see " quality " in her. A calm fine face, a cool manner, a somewhat dictatorial mind towards those whose intellects or characters she does not respect, Louise is not likely to become a popular woman—but she will raise " society " to a higher level of intellectual sincerity and warmheartedness, and make the world value sterling qualities rather than fashion and mere sparkle.

October 30th, 1897.—So ended my official connection with the Bishops' wives [I write afterwards, when my resolution to dispense with religious rites was rejected]. I felt, rightly or wrongly, that it was necessary to clear up the situation: either the association was distinctively Christian or not; if the latter, the executive had no right to impose the religious rites of a particular sect on a non-religious body; if the former, I was gaining influence on false pretences. It is difficult to know when and where it is wise to make a stand, and insist on equality of treatment as a matter of principle. But I have a distrust of slipping into a sort of quagmire of latitudinarianism, in which only the narrow-minded and uneducated persons are allowed to have strong convictions. And I feel one must fight against the temptation of pushing one's particular hobbies by sacrificing straightforwardness and intellectual honesty in all other issues. It is strange how a meeting is influenced by the *way of putting it*. My resolution had given great offence; and when I rose to move it I felt hostile feeling all around. But, with a few frank and gentle words, all the hostility vanished; and, though the meeting supported the executive, I had won their sympathy and respect, which again reacted on me and I felt rather a brute to object to their prayers! The association otherwise strikes me as doing good work: Louise Creighton has distinctly a statesmanlike mind—and the group of women who now control the policy are a good sort: large-minded and pleasant-mannered. The " screeching sisterhood " are trying to invade them, but Louise's battalions of hard-working religious and somewhat stupid women will, I think, resist the attack.

To return to the entry of October 5, 1896:

One reason I am so fagged is the growth of the social side of our work. We are perpetually entertaining—and the opening of the School has added a long list of students whom we feel it our duty to see and talk to. The usual visit to Oxford—48 hours talking— propaganda of collectivist views and the expediency of research— enjoyable enough this bright discussion with young dons and undergraduates, but oh! how exhausting. Sidney lectured twice and we both talked incessantly from the breakfast party to the last smoke late at night.

The Argoed, January 18th, 1897.—The Conservative Government finds itself paralysed. Except for its sordid grant to landlords it has not been able to move backward or to move forward. The Liberal leaders are as feeble and half-hearted as ever. But neither party are putting forward any alternative policy to collectivism—neither party *dare* take any step, or even make a proposal that contradicts this policy. The Conservative Government is being dragged by its own Arbitration Act into regulating the conditions of labour: it is being coerced by its promises into spending additional money on public education. It will presently have to confess itself bankrupt in proposals, or accept the collectivist solution of employers' liability and old-age pensions. In all probability it will do nothing in these matters, and the Chamberlain programme of social reform is becoming far too complicated for the actor-politician or the accomplished *littérateur*. That fact works our way: the collectivists alone have the faith to grind out a science of politics—and I think they will prove to have the capacity.

February 3rd, 1897.—Last night, being the second night of the education debate, Gorst entertained a lively party of young people at dinner, retiring afterwards to his private room where we laughed and smoked, whilst division bells were ringing and count-outs were threatening. As we sat on the sofa, Gorst became confidential in a curious spasmodic way. " The newspapers say this is a humiliation for me, the Education Bill. But it's the Duke [of Devonshire] who is humiliated. Salisbury told me from the first that I was to be under-secretary, and that the Duke would be responsible for the educational policy in the Cabinet. The Duke is quite as much against this Bill as I am. He told the Cabinet so: and when they insisted he shrugged his shoulders! " From the Education Bill, we passed to the general situation. I ventured to say that Balfour was discredited—at which Gorst looked pleased. " He doesn't know anything," he remarked contemptuously, " we are on the eve of a crisis: there will be a revolt presently of the urban Tories. They can't go on watching their seats being taken from under them. As for social reform: all chance of that is gone. When first this Government came into office, they honestly intended to do something. I know, as a matter of fact, that Salisbury said to Chaplin soon after the Government was formed, ' Chaplin, can't you do something for the unemployed? ' " At this my gravity gave way, and Gorst's eyes twinkled merrily; but, when the others looked up at my laughter, he checked himself and became demure and began to talk Indian administration and colonial policy.

February 6th, 1897.—A great gathering last night in Queen's Hall —900 L.C.C. scholars receiving their certificates from the Prince of Wales. Sat close to H.R.H. and watched him with curiosity. In his performance of the ceremony, from his incoming to his outgoing, he acted like a well-oiled automaton, saying exactly the words he was expected to say, noticing the right persons on the platform, maintaining his own dignity whilst setting others at ease, and otherwise acting with perfectly polished discretion. But, observing him closely, you could see that underneath the royal automaton there lay the child and the animal—a simple kindly unmoral temperament which makes him a good fellow. Not an English gentleman: essentially a foreigner— and yet an almost perfect constitutional sovereign. From a political point of view, his foibles and vices, his lack of intellectual refinement or moral distinction, are as nothing compared to his complete detach- ment from all party prejudice and class interests, and his genius for political *discretion*. But one sighs to think that this unutterably common- place person should set the tone of London " society ". There is something comic in the great British nation, with its infinite variety of talents, having this undistinguished and limited-minded German bourgeois to be its social sovereign. A sovereign of real distinction, who would take over as his peculiar province the direction of the *voluntary side of social life*, who could cultivate in rich and leisured society a desire to increase the sum of real intellectual effort and eminence, what might he not do to further our civilisation by creating a real aristocracy of character and intellect? As it is, we have our social leader proposing in this morning's papers, as a fit commemora- tion of his august mother's longest reign, the freeing of the hospitals from debt—the sort of proposal one would expect from the rank and file of " scripture readers " or a committee of village grocers intent on goodwill on earth and saving the rates!

My boy spoke a few words to the 900 children at the end, worth all the rest of the speeches put together—urging them to remember that, as London had helped them, they must seek, in their future lives, to serve London.

May 7th, 1897.—Accident Compensation Bill satisfactory—a sort of revolutionary proposal which only a Conservative Government could bring in. We should have preferred the state to find the money, but that is a detail. Moreover, there are plenty of objects to which our extra income-tax can be devoted directly it becomes feasible to exact it. The main point—*universal compensation without contribution from workmen*—is secured to a certain number of trades only, but extension only a matter of time. The limited application of a complete principle is far better than the universal application of a dwarfed or incongruous principle.

The Argoed, January 18th, 1897.—Christmas with Alfred Cripps. Last year he was starting his political life; this year he is well on the road to office. He is in splendid spirits: talks with easy critical familiarity of Balfour and other leading Conservatives, and gives one to understand incidentally that he is constantly consulted by them. He is, in fact, rapidly becoming a sort of legal adviser, "a little jewel of an advocate" (as Father used so affectionately to call him) to the Conservative Party. His tone is the same: save the *status quo* as regards property, and keep the Government in the hands of the upper classes, but compromise right and left on all immaterial points and don't let bigots and zealots get the upper hand. Vested interests must be curbed and regulated—but preserved. No nonsense from Church dignitaries about bossing education, or high-handedness from railway managers about their employees—preserve the world from sensations and then all will be well. Just at present he is irate about the Financial Relations Commission. "Another piece of Gladstone's mischief: setting commissions to work to make grievances." He is still as uninterested as ever in investigation. "Life is a process of cram from the university to the Bar, from the Bar to the Front Bench; of course you and Sidney who have the good fortune to be able to do original research," he pleasantly remarked, "are exceptions; but we practical men, who look to professional success, know that it is only a question of cram— of getting up your case—that is all there is time for." He is still making a large income at the Bar, and spending it lavishly on his constituency, home and children. The eldest boy, Seddon, is exhausting pleasures at a tremendous rate: this year his bicycle was discarded and he was driving about in the smallest dogcart covered with his initials, with rug, lamps, etc. to match. Ruth has become more thoughtful and looks on rather wistfully—the mother in her is creeping into view. A year's school has made Leonard commonplace: a year's home has made "Daddy"[1] more exuberant than ever. The Playnes were staying there; Arthur cross and uncivil; Mary extremely affable and uncomfortably anxious to be pleasant. Refused a half-hearted invitation to take Longfords on the way here.

Here follows the first entry about the series of dramatic events which led to the South African War; and, incidentally,

[1] The Rt. Hon. Sir Stafford Cripps at the age of eight. (Ed.)

to splitting of the Liberal leaders into two embittered factions: the Liberal Imperialists on the one hand, and, on the other, the pro-Boers, with Sir Henry Campbell-Bannerman balancing himself uncomfortably between the two. Meanwhile the Tories and the Liberal Unionists were finally merged in the powerful Conservative Party which swept the country at the general election of 1900.

June 25th, 1897.—Back in London. Imperialism in the air—all classes drunk with sightseeing and hysterical loyalty. Our morning, hard at work proof-correcting: in the afternoon and evening friends drop in to welcome us back—Sidney absorbed in catching up arrears of L.C.C. work.

July 8th, 1897.—Dined last night with Alfred Cripps and Margaret Hobhouse. Alfred full of Workmen's Accident Bill. He is organising opposition, and scheming with the employers to get in amendments. His feelings are a queer combination of anger at the Bill and at Chamberlain, helplessness in face of a Government majority, backed by the united forces of the opposition, and self-complacency that he, at least, perceived the danger and outrageousness of the proposal and was doing his lawyer's best to spike the wheels of this abominable legislation. " It is only the party's loyalty to Balfour that would carry it through," he said piteously, " not only is the principle of the Bill preposterous but the whole drafting of it is crude in the extreme." He asserted that it killed " contracting out "; " not one scheme of the many that I have seen will stand this Bill ". He admitted that it meant state compensation at no very distant date (I do not feel quite so cocksure about this, it *might* work out into trade groups). " It is a Trade Union Bill—it makes all in the direction of large establishments—I know you like that, I don't." Of course, I chaffed him—complimented him on the revolutionary character of Conservative reforms. " If the S.D.F. had proposed it, it would have been laughed out of court; and the Fabian Society would never have thought of such barefaced spoliation of one particular class." " You are a cynic, Beatrice," Alfred responded pleasantly, but looking extremely sore. " It is one of the triumphs of the underground force of the democracy," said I; " what we are now discovering is that a Conservative majority is a more effective instrument of this force than a Liberal Government." " It is those wretched urban towns—they are the force behind Chamberlain." How he dislikes and distrusts Chamberlain.

July 26th, 1897.—Spent Sunday with Alfred Cripps at Parmoor. Obviously disgusted with the ways of Parliament this session. " Balfour has no principle," he plaintively repeated. " He is perpetually asking ' why not? ' to the proposals of the Radical wing of the Unionist Party." " Chamberlain has beaten us; he twirls Balfour round his little finger and Salisbury is cynically indifferent to home affairs—except, perhaps, to the interests of the Church and of land." At other times, Alfred asserted that they had succeeded in getting 80% of their amendments into the Workmen's Accidents Bill—but it was quite clear that he felt the champions of liberty and property had been done in the play of the parliamentary hand. " It is hateful fighting your own party: you are not free to use the most telling weapons: if only I could have fought Chamberlain from the opposite side of the House! But the feeling is growing against him: he will break up the Unionist Party and you will have him back leading your side before this Parliament is out."

" He is much more useful to us fighting from within the Conservative ranks, my dear Alfred, we shall do our very best to keep him there. It is only Conservatives who can make revolutions nowadays, and they are, if anything, more susceptible to democratic pressure than the Liberals."

Alfred Cripps is, I think, beginning to discover that a Government will be flattering and considerate towards an able young lawyer who is ready to advise them and defend them whenever asked; but that these amenities cease when he begins to oppose them either overtly or privately.

He talked a good deal about the South African Committee, of which he is a member. He was against the production of the telegrams [1] on the ground that telegrams passing between co conspirators were not evidence! Throughout the proceedings he had evidently taken a somewhat tight-drawn legal view which had been combated by Chamberlain. He signified that Harcourt had first been led by Labouchere but, having been landed by the latter into some impossible position, he had turned round. " We were surprised at his attitude; but, of course, we did our utmost to meet him, it was all-important to get the two front benches to agree on one report." The two witnesses who left the worst impression on Alfred's mind were Hawksley and Flora Shaw. But he is evidently disgusted with the whole Rhodes party: in spite of his plea that now they are being unfairly treated as the result of the reaction.

July 29th, 1897.—This was a typical Haldane dinner on the night of the South African debate, typical of Haldane's weakness—his

---

[1] Probably a reference to the seven " missing telegrams " withheld by Cecil Rhodes from the Select Committee of Enquiry into the Jameson Raid. (Ed.)

dilettante desire to be in every set; and of his strength—his diffusive friendship which enables him to bring about non-party measures.

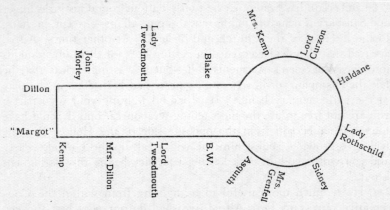

July 15*th*, 1897.—A great gathering of distinguished dames entertained at dinner a corresponding number of distinguished men.[1] It was a brilliant and polished set of people—representing a good deal of hard work. The dinner, the rooms, the flowers and the dresses were soberly luxurious and charmingly tasteful—the three speeches, Mrs. Steel, Lady Henry Somerset and the Bishop of London, were eloquent and witty—the Bishop excelled himself in the polished " man of the world " style. Strange person—my friend the Bishop—a scholar, a cynic, an admirable man of business, and a staunch believer in the Church—possibly also a believer in religion as a necessary element in society. But his faith is the other side of complete scepticism. His attitude towards all things is one of steady depreciation—no good in intellect, no good in sentiment, no good in science, no good in politics. Since " good " exists, there is only one place left for it—the Church! The faith that originates in cynical scepticism is not an altogether wholesome constituent towards the making of a church.

[1] The dinner referred to in the above entry was the Women's Jubilee Dinner and Soirée, July 14, Grafton Galleries, given by 100 distinguished women to 100 distinguished men, arranged by Mrs. Humphry Ward and the following ladies: Dr. Garrett Anderson, Miss Agnes Clerke, Mrs. Mary Davies, Mrs. Fawcett, Mrs. J. R. Green, Miss Jane Harrison, Lady Jeune, Miss Mary Kingsley, Lady Dorothy Nevill, Miss Flora Shaw, Miss Ellen Terry, Miss Maude Valerie White and Mrs. Flora Annie Steel.

Seeing that it was difficult to discover 100 distinguished women, some other ladies, among them myself, were called in to advise. I remember that my contribution was the principal factory inspectors and the heads of different educational institutions. My guest was the Bishop of London. What was remarkable in this dinner was that the 100 men were extremely distinguished, including practically all the leading politicians with the exception of Lord Salisbury, and many other persons of distinction; the difficulty being that so many distinguished men were left out, who in consequence were offended.

To which account I add another from the diaries of Sir Algernon West.[1]

On July 14th I was asked by Lady Henry Somerset to be one of her guests at the dinner of a hundred distinguished ladies of the Queen's reign. The interest was lost from the fact of my not knowing who was who, and I wished they had all been labelled! However, Lady Henry made a lovely speech and Dr. Creighton a very frivolous one, not at all suited to the occasion. Mrs. Annie Steel, the author of *On the Face of the Waters*, made a poor speech, and that was all, but the occasion was a remarkable one, and I fear there was some heart-burning among those who were not included in the chosen hundred.

July 30th, 1897.—Massingham dined here last night. Greatly excited about South African debate. " Superb rope dancing—Chamberlain's speech. Hawksley in the House ready to produce telegrams and letters unless Chamberlain repudiated condemnation of Rhodes. Harcourt completely taken in, consented to back up Government if they condemned Rhodes, and now Chamberlain declares that he accepted condemnation as a compromise and, as far as he was concerned, he always thought Rhodes a fine fellow. It is superb: it is a delight to watch such a man." And Massingham bubbled over with the joy of the political dramatic critic. " Chamberlain's career is extraordinarily interesting—every day brings its own trick. The career is more interesting than the man," added Massingham more gravely; " he has neither the knowledge nor the convictions to make him more than a great political artist." " Surely," I rejoined, " we shall look back on the last fifty years of the nineteenth century as the peculiar period of political artists: we have no statesmen: all our successful politicians, the men who lead the parties, are artists and nothing else. Gladstone, Disraeli, Randolph Churchill, Chamberlain, and the unsuccessful Rosebery—all these men have the characteristics of actors: personal charm, extraordinary pliability and quick-wittedness."

October 18th, 1897.—Met John Morley at a *tête-à-tête* dinner at the Courtneys. He and Sidney anxious to be pleasant to each other. A charming person for a talk on literature: but a most depressing spectacle as a Liberal leader. In sympathy with no single one of the progressive ideas, he clings to his old shibboleths of non-intervention and non-expansion abroad, and Church disestablishment and a sort of theoretical " home rule " at home. When I suggested that, if I had supreme power, I would hesitate before I disestablished the

---

[1] *Private Diaries of the Rt. Hon. Sir Algernon West, G.C.B.*, edited by Horace G. Hutchinson, 1922, p. 339.

Church he seemed aghast. And yet he dare not pronounce in favour of his own convictions: he feels instinctively the country is against him. To do nothing, and to say nothing, to sit and wait for the tide to ebb from this Government is the long and short of his policy. Naturally enough he is pessimistic: thinks that all things are going to the bad and that the country has lost its intellect and its character. On politics he is like a theologian who has begun to doubt his theology: in argument he always shrinks away from you, as if he suspected you of laying traps for him out of which he could not struggle. A closed mind and a lack of pluck in asserting the dogmas that dominate him, give a most unpleasant impression of narrow-mindedness and nervelessness. I shall send him our book: if he reads it, it may *antagonise* him into some living thought. Leonard Courtney, one felt instinctively, was infinitely more open-minded as well as more robust in intellect: was fully prepared to consider new propositions and not in the least inclined to run away because he might have to change his mind if he stayed to look at them. John Morley is a pitiable person as a politician; all the more so because he is conscientious and upright. It makes one groan to think of that moral force absolutely useless.

December 10*th*, 1897.—Perhaps part of my chaotic frame of mind is due to dabbling in " society ": thought it good opportunity to invite some people to dinner since it did not much matter whether I felt seedy or not the next day. [We had just passed *Industrial Democracy* through the press.] My little parties are said to be successful, but they don't please me. Directly you entertain for entertaining's sake, then they become hollow and unpleasant. An element of vanity enters in and you begin to wonder what impression you make; what your friends think of each other, and so on. My conclusion from this last month is that the dross in my nature is not yet eliminated! There is a good strong strain of the vain worldling left. Thank the gods, there is no trace of such feeling in Sidney. Work and love are the only gods he lives for. Oh! my boy, how I love you—past understanding!

March 1898.—Perhaps the most striking fact of the L.C.C. elections [I record a few days after the Progressive victory of March 1898] has been the complete eclipse of the Liberal leaders. The Progressive election committee has spurned their help, has fought the whole battle on the non-political line. And this contempt for the Liberal leaders has not sprung from the extreme left (Sidney thought they were carrying it too far and himself had down Lord Ripon at New Cross), but from the little knot of Progressive Radicals—Collins, McKinnon Wood, Dickinson, etc. Rosebery, it is true, came forward, but expressly as a past Progressive chairman of the L.C.C., and himself disowned any official connection with the Liberals. The official London Progressives, men who six years ago would have been only too proud of the patronage of an ex-Liberal Cabinet Minister, now stand completely divorced from their allegiance to the Liberal leaders, and talk of them with habitual contempt as men of no conviction and no knowledge. Even Rosebery, whom they are glad enough to use, has no influence with them. This victory will strengthen this feeling of independence, if not superiority, to the official Liberal leaders on the part of the L.C.C. Progressives. They will more and more regard themselves as able and experienced administrators, actually working out political problems, whilst they will look on men like Bryce, Asquith, Harcourt, Fowler, either as mere members of a debating society, or as London " society " men with whom they have little or nothing in common. Asquith especially has lost all his prestige in the eyes of the London Radical.

We gather, on the other hand, that there is no repentance on the part of the front bench Liberals, at least there was not before the L.C.C. election. Not a member of the front bench seems to be working at politics: they are either following their own professions or dancing attendance on London "society". Their whole attitude is certainly astounding: beyond cavilling at the Government, chiefly on foreign questions, no one is ever the wiser for their appearances in public. . . . I think most Progressives have ceased to read their speeches: even the I.L.P. find it precious difficult to criticise " a negation in opposition ".

We, therefore, close this portion of our life with considerable complacency and start on our long journey with a light heart.[1] Our book has been extraordinarily well received; our party has recovered a good working majority on the L.C.C.; the London School of Economics is growing silently though surely into a centre of collectivist-tempered research, and establishing itself as *the* English school of economics and political science. We can now feel assured that with the School as a teaching body, the Fabian Society as a propagandist organisation, the L.C.C. Progressives as an object lesson in electoral success, our books as the only elaborate and original work in economic fact and theory, no young man or woman who is anxious to study or to work in public affairs can fail to come under our influence. Massingham of the *Daily Chronicle* is again our friend: the *Manchester Guardian* and the *Echo* are practically our organs through Leonard Hobhouse and W. M. Crook, the provincial Liberal papers are extremely friendly. It is only the *Westminster*, the *Daily News*, the *Star* which remain somewhat cold and suspicious towards the rising of a new party. But all this does

[1] Between April and December 1898, Beatrice and Sidney were touring America and Australasia. (Ed.)

not mean that " our set " is anywhere near office or nominal political power. The crust of London Society Liberalism is, as yet, far too hard for us to break, and I doubt whether we are not always likely to work underground at foundations, upon which a younger generation will build, perhaps not quite in the form we intended!

To which hubristic passage I will add another entry from the diary, revealing the presence of personal vanity coupled with a sophisticated conscience:

February 1898.—The old " Eve " in me is delighted [I write a few weeks before our departure] with buying a trousseau for our nine months' journey. It is a long time since I have had a really good " go " at clothes: I am revelling in buying silks and satins, gloves, underclothing, furs and everything that a sober-minded woman of forty can want to inspire Americans and colonials with a true respect for the refinements of collectivism. It is a pleasure to clothe myself charmingly. For the last ten years, I have had neither the time nor the will to think of it. For this tour, I harmonise extravagance with my conscience by making myself believe that I must have everything new, and that I must look nice! I believe that it is a *deliberate* expenditure. For six months ago I determined that I would do myself handsomely. . . . But I daresay one or two of the specially becoming blouses are the expression of crude vanity; my delight in watching these bright clothes being made is a sort of rebound from the hard drudgery of the last two years. But it is rather comic in a woman of forty—40 all but two weeks. Forty, Forty, Forty! What an age! Almost elderly. I do not feel a bit old!

CHAPTER IV

ENQUIRY INTO ENGLISH LOCAL GOVERNMENT
1899–1905

ONCE again, in January 1899, we were back in our little home on the Thames Embankment, resuming our work in the triple capacity of investigators into social institutions, promoters of the newly established London School of Economics, and, in the case of the Other One, as chairman of the Technical Education Board, a determined organiser and agitator, intent on unifying all public education, whether elementary, secondary or university—more especially in the metropolis—under one local government authority—that of the London County Council.

In this and the following chapter, I shall attempt to describe successively these three separate activities from 1899 to 1906: a difficult task as they seem inextricably entangled together in the main sources of my information: the entries in my diary.

Why did we decide on English local government as our next subject for detailed investigation and analysis? Our main reason was that in the course of our previous investigations we had found ourselves coming to a new view of the scope and purpose of the compulsory association of men as citizens, whether national or local. Hitherto, we had investigated and described social organisation based on voluntary association: the co-operative and trade union movements. Already before my marriage I had studied a form of voluntary association lauded at the time by idealists of all classes, by leading trade unionists, by the more benevolent of employers, by Liberal and Conservative philanthropists and even by revolutionary Socialists—the ideal of Robert Owen, the self-governing workshop—as an alternative to the capitalist organisation of industry. This ideal was assumed to be the aim of the contemporary co-operative movement.[1] During my two years' enquiry into this remarkable manifestation of working-class organising capacity, I had made two separate discoveries. The Co-operators, who, with the assent of their intellectual supporters and admirers, kept on asserting that the object of their movement was the abolition of the wage system and the organisation of industry in the interest of the manual working *producers*, had, in fact, by 1889, built up a great industrial organisation of hierarchical character exclusively in the interest of the working-class *consumers*. In doing this, they had offered to the community a clear-cut alternative to capitalist retail and wholesale trading, and less completely, in the productive enterprises of the Co-operative Wholesale Society, to capitalist manufacturing. Unwittingly, the Co-operators had performed what is now known as the " Marxian operation ": they had cut out of the body politic the individual profit-maker, exploiting the producer and the consumer alike in order to build up his own fortune. Far from abolishing the wage system, what they had done was to extend it to the brain-worker. What they had abolished was the profit-making entrepreneur! Yet, at congress after congress, the Co-operators refused to recognise the transfiguration of

[1] For an analysis of the ideal of the self-governing workshop, and the reason for its failure, as an alternative to capitalist enterprise, not in Great Britain only, but also in France and Germany, in spite of a whole century of experiments, see *The Co-operative Movement in Great Britain*, chapter v., on " Associations of Producers " (pp. 127-69), by Beatrice Potter, 1891. It is instructive to note that this species of organisation flourishes in the industry of the USSR, whilst it is actually the dominant type in Soviet agriculture. The success of the industrial co-operatives (*artels*) as well as of the collective farm (*kolkhosi*) under Soviet Communism seems to be due (1) to the elimination from the environment of the private profit-maker, whether as financier, capitalist employer or wholesale or retail trader; (2) to the constant supervision and assistance of the collective farms by the USSR Commissar of Agriculture, the Communist Party and the local authorities, in the supply of water through irrigation, of unlimited tractors and combines and of plentiful fertilisers, supplemented by the continuous advice of scientific experts, almost irrespective of cost. The guiding principle is that wherever the self-governing association of producers is successful in fulfilling its obligations and in creating a peaceful and educational life for its members, it is left free to manage as it chooses; it is only interfered with when failure threatens, either through the break-up of the community through internal discord, or through the failure of its productive activities through lack of managerial ability, technical skill or the requisite machinery.

their own movement. What I did was to point out this trans-figuration, whilst at the same time I explained and justified it. My second discovery was that democracies of consumers, if they are to be a desirable as well as a practicable alternative to private profit-making, must be complemented by demo-cracies of workers by hand and by brain—that is, by trade unions and professional societies. Hence, when Our Part-nership was set up, our first job was to turn the searchlight of investigation upon the associations of producers, in their most obvious form of trade unionism.

Meanwhile, the Other One, who had already served thirteen years in three different departments of the Civil Service, including a whole decade of supervision of half-a-hundred separate governments overseas, became a leading member of the London County Council, one of the greatest of the world's social institutions divorced from the profit-making motive. It was borne in upon us, not merely that compulsory association in government had necessarily to be added to voluntary association both as producers and as consumers, but also that this inevitable compulsory associa-tion of man as a citizen was demanded for much more than national defence and the maintenance of internal order. We saw that to the Government alone could be entrusted the pro-vision for future generations, to which neither producers nor consumers would attend as such. Moreover, such obvious social utilities as public health and universal education, the provision for the destitute, the sick and the defectives, like that for the orphans and the aged—all of them based on pro-vision according to need—involved enterprises to which no profit-making could usually be attached, and which were, for the most part, outside the characteristic activities or desires either of the associated consumers or of the associated producers. In short, we were led to the recognition of a new form of state, and one which may be called the " house-keeping state ", as distinguished from the " police state ". This gave us a new vision of social development. The pro-vision of services according to need were, as we thought, destined to grow and develop. It was hard to imagine how this extension could possibly be undertaken and administered on the basis of the motive of profit-making, even if that motive was held to be essential to every undertaking of economic character. Moreover, the start had already been made on the contrary principle of a public service. The social institutions which had gradually undertaken most of what had been done in the way of provision according to need, notably for the destitute and the persons of unsound mind, were, in England and Wales, the parish vestries, the county justices and the municipal corporations, to which had been added in 1834 the boards of guardians— that is to say, they belonged to local rather than to national government. If social institutions based on the motive of profit-making were to be increasingly supplemented, or superseded, by social institutions conducted by a salaried public service—rewarded not by the making of private fortunes, but by public honour and special promotion; if local administration was destined to rival and even to surpass in importance the national Civil Service, it was important to discover by what means the various parishes and counties and municipalities were, in fact, governed; how their several administrations had arisen in the past and how they were now developing; and by what extensions and improvements these social institutions could be best fitted for the additional tasks that they would find themselves undertaking. Thus it was that we decided in 1898 to investigate the structure and functions of English local government, intending at the outset to concentrate our attention upon the period from the Municipal Corporations Act of 1835, and the Poor Law Act of 1834, to the present day.

So far, so good: but alas! at this point I had better confess that we failed to fulfil our plan of analysing and describing the local government of England from 1834 to the present time.

What we had contemplated was an analysis of the local government of this generation, with merely a preliminary chapter about the antiquities, anterior to 1835, which it had superseded. But, in the course of our journeyings up and

down the country, we found even the present local government so firmly rooted in the past, and the past so complicated
and obscure, that it became indispensable to us to make
a special study of the period immediately preceding the
reforms of 1832–35. At first, we intended to restrict ourselves to the first three decades of the nineteenth century.
Further study convinced us that we could neither understand
nor make intelligible by itself what was but the tag-end of a
period opening with the Revolution of 1688.

The century-and-a-half lying between the dismissal of
the Stuarts in 1688 and the Reform Parliament of 1832,
constitutes, for the historian of the internal administration of
England and Wales, a distinct period of extraordinary significance. For the first time, and perhaps for the last time in
English history, the national Government abstained from
intervention in local affairs, practically leaving all the various
kinds of local governing bodies to carry out their several
administrations as they chose, without central supervision
or central control. Even when Parliament was appealed to
for legislation, it allowed the different localities to have
practically whatever constitutions and whatever powers they
asked for; contenting itself with ratifying, in the innumerable local acts of the eighteenth-century statute book, the
particular projects and compromises of the local interests
concerned. The experiments in poor law and municipal
enterprise thus initiated were, we thought, instructive to the
reformers of to-day. But, besides these experiments in function, the diverse origins and varied constitutions of the
eighteenth-century local authorities seemed to us vital to
our understanding of the more uniform pattern of modern
local government, based on an electorate, at first restricted
by property qualifications, but becoming, as time went on,
practically inclusive of all adult inhabitants.

What sort of output grew out of this miscalculation, what
exactly did we fail to do, and what did we actually achieve,
during these six years of strenuous investigation?

Our initial purpose—an analysis of English local government as it existed in our own time for the use of would-be

reformers as well as students—was, as I have already indi-
cated, not carried out. At the beginning of 1906, we published a ponderous volume on the development of the parish
and the county between 1689 and 1834, to be followed in
1908 by two volumes on the manor and the borough for the
same period. It was not until 1920 that we issued the most
original and, certainly, the most significant of our series on
the constitution of English local government prior to 1834.
In this last volume—*Statutory Authorities for Special Purposes*
—we describe the gradual supersession of feudal institutions
based on mutual obligations of lord and tenant, and of the
newer mutualities of chartered corporations and guilds, of
craftsmen and merchants, all alike owing allegiance to the
King, by a new species of authority, arising directly out of
the needs of this or that section of the community: such as
the need for land drainage, and town sewers, for highways,
for street-lighting and policing, for the regulation of markets,
and last but not least, for the better relief of destitution
and the suppression of vagrancy. Many of these authorities
started as voluntary associations of the consumers of the
required services, to be subsequently transformed by local
Acts into compulsory associations of citizens. It was this
slow but fundamental change, alike in the organism, the
function and the environment of local authorities, that was
brought to a climax by the Reform Parliament in the Poor
Law Amendment Act of 1834, and the Municipal Corporation Act of 1835.

Apart from these four volumes, mainly concerned with
the constitutional development of local government authorities, and only incidentally with their activities, we published
from time to time during the next twenty years, special
studies of the doings of local authorities such as *The
Story of the King's Highway, English Prisons under Local
Authorities* and *The History of Liquor Licensing*. In only one
department did we complete our task of discovering and
analysing the structure, function and social environment of
a particular species of local government from its first inception in the dark ages to its latest development in our own

times. In this case, our own researches during the six years described in this chapter were continued as part of my work as a member of the Royal Commission on the Poor Law, 1905–9. In another chapter, I shall tell how I dovetailed our own enquiry into that of the Commission; thus enabling me to circulate to my colleagues reports on English poor law policy from 1834 to 1906, the municipal health service, and other matters, culminating in the Minority Report issued as part of the final Report of the Royal Commission on the Poor Law in 1909. But, owing to this and other distractions, it was not until 1925 that we published the first volume of *The History of the English Poor Law* (the old poor law), and not until 1929 that we were able to issue the second and third volumes (the new poor law), describing the doings of elected boards of guardians from their inauguration by the Poor Law Amendment Act of 1834 to their final abolition by the Local Government Act of 1929.

Such was the output from this long drawn-out enquiry into English local government. What were our instruments and methods of research?

Our first step was to find a colleague, free to leave London and carry out independently, but according to our plan, the investigation into the structure, activities and environment of local authorities in this or that part of England. We were singularly fortunate in securing straight away, and for six years, the services of F. H. Spencer,[1] to which were added

[1] Frederick Herbert Spencer, the son of a chargeman engineer at Swindon railway works, had graduated into the profession of elementary school teacher at the Borough Road Training College. During his time with us he took his LL.B., and afterwards, by a thesis based on his researches with us, on the Origins of Municipal Government, his D.Sc.(Econ.). He left us to become examiner for the L.C.C. scholarship system, and head of the commercial school of the City of London College. From that position he became one of the Board of Education inspectors on commercial subjects, and was stationed in Liverpool. After the war he was promoted to be H.M. Divisional Inspector of Schools for the N.W. Division. Subsequently he was appointed, at a salary rising from £1250 to £2000 a year, chief inspector for the whole educational service of the London County Council, from which he retired at the end of 1933. Even then he continued his work as educational adviser in more than one direction, being, for instance, invited in 1935–36 to lecture successively to all the universities of the Dominion of Canada, and to visit South Africa and Australasia to investigate certain educational problems.

He remained with us for some six years, and married our other research secretary, Miss Amy Harrison, a B.A. of the University of London, Aberystwyth College,

in the course of the following year those of Miss Amy Harrison. These two investigators settled down, together or separately, in town after town, taking elaborate notes of the minutes and reports of the local authorities, and making an equally detailed study of contemporary local newspapers and pamphlets, whilst attending the meetings of the local authorities concerned, and interviewing the representatives and officials. It is, perhaps, not surprising that, after one or two years of this close companionship, they married each other. " We have had constantly to put our heads together to read your illegible instructions; is it surprising that in due course our hearts grew together? " one of them wrote to us, in announcing their engagement. I may add that they became our lifelong friends.

At this point, it seems worth while to give to those readers who are interested in sociological research, a brief account of our method of note-taking. It is hard to persuade the accomplished university graduate, or even the successful practitioner in another science, that an indispensable instrument in the technique of sociological enquiry—seeing that without it any of the methods of acquiring facts can seldom be used effectively—is an exceptionally elaborate system of making notes, or what the French call *fiches*. This process serves a similar purpose, in the study of social institutions, to that of the blow-pipe and the test-tube in chemistry, or the prism and the electroscope in physics. That is to say, it enables the scientific worker to break up his subject-matter, so as to isolate and examine at his leisure its various component parts, and to recombine the facts when they have been thus released from all accustomed categories, in new

and joint author with Miss B. L. Hutchins of the *History of the Factory Acts*. On obtaining her B.A., Miss Harrison was for three years a teacher in a Welsh Intermediate School, after which she settled in London, at first attending evening lectures at the London School of Economics, and there being awarded the Lucy Rose Research Studentship enabling her to become a full-time student at the School. There her research into the effects of Factory Act regulation upon the labour of women resulted in a thesis with which she obtained the D.Sc.(Econ.) of the University of London.

From time to time we engaged extra assistants, and in 1905 Miss Bulkley, B.Sc.(Econ.) took the place of Mr. F. H. Spencer as our permanent research secretary, and continued with us in this capacity until 1912.

and experimental groupings, in order to discover which coexistences and sequences of events have an invariable and, therefore, possibly a causal significance. The first item in the recipe for scientific note-taking in sociology is that the student must be provided, not with a note-book of any sort or kind, but with an indefinite number of separate sheets of paper of identical shape and size (we found large quarto the most convenient form), and of sufficiently good quality for either pen or typewriter. The reason why detached sheets must be employed, instead of any book, is, as will presently be demonstrated, the absolute necessity of being able to rearrange the notes successively in different orders; in fact, to be able to shuffle and reshuffle them indefinitely, and to change the classification of the facts recorded on them, according to the various tentative hypotheses with which the investigator will need successively to compare these facts. Another reason against the note-book is that notes recorded in a book must necessarily be entered in the order in which they are obtained; and it is vitally important, in the subsequent consideration of the notes, to be set free from the particular category in which the note-taker has found any particular fact, whether of time or place, sequence or coexistence. In sociology, as in mineralogy, " conglomerates " have always to be broken up, and the ingredients separately dealt with. To put it paradoxically, by exercising your reason on the facts separately recorded and displayed in an appropriate way, on hundreds, or perhaps thousands, of separate pieces of paper, you may discover which of a series of tentative hypotheses best explains the processes underlying the rise, growth, change or decay of a given social institution, or the character of the actions and reactions of different elements of a given social environment. The truth of one of the hypotheses may, by significant correspondences and differences, be definitely proved; that is to say, it may be found to be the order of thought that most closely corresponds with the order of things.[1]

[1] The interested student will find deposited in the library at the London School of Economics a number of pamphlet boxes containing the sheet of notes, mostly

Guided by the subject-catalogue of our ten volumes on English local government and this summary account of our methods of research, my readers may find some interest in the following entries in my diary from 1899 to 1906, giving some more intimate and personal reactions of Our Partnership in this voyage of discovery.

March 7th, 1899. *Grosvenor Road.*—Now that I spend my time in taking notes vigorously all the morning from the minutes of town councils as well as writing such letters as are absolutely necessary, I have little inclination to make entries in my diary. . . . Meanwhile, we are well into our new enquiry and have elaborated a syllabus for the use of investigators. We have engaged as secretary a clever ambitious elementary school teacher—F. H. Spencer—about twenty-eight years old. We tried a nice young man straight from Oxford, but he was a dead failure, not realising what constituted a day's work, and presenting us with little essays instead of research notes. At present, we seem to be nibbling at the outermost corner of our subject. In a year's time, I suppose we shall feel that we have got some sort of grasp of it. I am aiming at living a student's life: withdrawing from any social excitement inconsistent with regular work, regular exercise, plain food and abundance of sleep.

April 28th, 1899. *Bradford.*—Sidney and I left London on our first investigating tour into local government on Thursday before Easter Sunday, and chose Leeds as our destination, as S. had promised to preside over a conference of elected persons to be held there on

in the handwriting of Mr. and Mrs. Spencer, and of other assistants, but also of the Webbs themselves, on the constitutions, activities and social environment of the town councils of Leeds and Leicester, of Newcastle and Liverpool, and many other boroughs, together with many Quarter Sessions and other county authorities. These slips of paper, which must number in the aggregate many tens of thousands, amount, in the case of Leeds, to about 800, and in that of Newcastle to 650; whilst in some cases there is a short summary of the development of the councils from 1835 to 1900. Even more voluminous are the notes relating to boards of guardians. These include an analysis, according to the type of pauper dealt with, the able-bodied, the sick, the children, the mentally defective, not only of the treatment afforded by the boards of guardians, but also of the policy laid down in the first instance by the Poor Law Commissioners and Poor Law Board, and by its successor the Local Government Board, whether in general or special orders, or in the private letters of the government inspector to the board of guardians concerned. This research enabled me to present to my colleagues a long memorandum on English Poor Law policy, 1834–1906, demolishing once and for all the fiction that the local government board had adhered, throughout this period, to the dogma of " less eligibility " laid down by the Royal Commission of 1834. (See the subsequently published volume entitled *English Poor Law Policy*, by S. and B. Webb, 1910.) For samples of these notes see Appendix.

Good Friday.[1] His speech and the conference were an unexpected success: all the papers giving full reports. Otherwise, the first week of our stay at Leeds was wasted seeing that all the officials were holidaying and the public offices—even the public library—closed. Sidney had an exceptionally bad cold, and the boarding-house we were in was dreary after our bright little home. On Thursday of Easter week we got to work, having persuaded the Lord Mayor to place a room in the Town Hall at our disposal and to give us free use of the minutes and reports. For another week Sidney, Spencer and I were hard at work on these documents. Then we tackled the West Riding County Council at Wakefield, and the Board of Guardians and School Board of Leeds. In the middle of my stay Sidney had to return to London, leaving me and our new secretary to finish up as best we might.

The personalities of Leeds public life are neither interesting nor attractive. Leeds and its inhabitants strike me as equally unlovely. " Getting on ", measured in money, is the dominant idea: the rich are conventional and purse-proud; the working-man dull, and without fight or faith. In fact the Tory squire and the Tory brewer are more public-spirited and more progressive than the lower middle-class Liberal. Leeds' Liberalism is the crudest individualism: negative and destructive—anti-state church, anti-public expenditure, the sweeping away of what they call " privilege " and the bringing in of political machinery for securing the equal value of all men's votes. No faith in any motive but that of pecuniary self-interest; no conception of any more complicated structure than the universalised ballot box. " There's not a man at this table, except yourself, that is not worth his £60,000 ", is the reported tactful remark of a Leeds alderman to a young London barrister who was dining with him. The saving grace, which has kept Leeds municipal government free from the grosser forms of corruption, has been the childish vanity which makes the ordinary Leeds shopkeeper desire to hear himself called " Alderman ", still more " my Lord Mayor ". Social ambition has prevented the motive of pecuniary self-interest from Americanising Leeds municipal life. After all, social ambition is a form of reverence for something better than yourself— the lowest form because the end aimed at is self-advancement—still a leaven because it means a recognition that some men are superior to yourself: which is true.

There will clearly be no difficulty in getting our material: our hardest task will be to determine what material to select, and where to stop. Between this diary and myself, I get on better at the actual

[1] Note, February 1920. This conference was held in connection with the I.L.P. Conference. I do not seem to have been interested in the latter.

investigation when Sidney is not there: he is shy in cross-examining officials, who generally begin by being unwilling witnesses and need gentle but firm handling: he hates life in provincial lodgings and seeing each day new people, and this repugnance reacts on me and I get disheartened and wonder whether I have not led him into a useless adventure. In dealing with documents he is far more efficient than I; but, in the manipulation of witnesses with a view of extracting confidential information, his shyness and scepticism of the use of it give me the advantage. And I am more ruthless in the exercise of my craft when he is not there to observe and perchance disapprove of my little tricks of the trade.

At the beginning of May 1899, I am back again in London recalling the six weeks' investigation into Yorkshire local government.

May 16th, 1899. *Grosvenor Road.*—Mrs. Gray of Gray's Court was my hostess at York. Almost a beautiful woman: fine features, queenlike figure, generous sympathy and warm-hearted public spirit— a perfection made less perfect by dramatic attitudes and an untrained mind. The old-world house, built into the city walls, and overlooking the Dean's garden, was a welcome change from the Leeds boarding-house with its ugly furniture and still uglier inhabitants. But, though unspeakably pleasanter, the few days I spent at York were less fruitful because I had to talk in return for my entertainment and came tired each day to work on the minutes. Mrs. Gray is a guardian, and her tales of the way in which outdoor relief is administered confirmed my observations of the relief work of the Leeds Board of Guardians, when I sat and watched them. The lay representatives of the ratepayers make a bad court to administer money payments which ought to be given according to definite principles—according to a code of law.

From York I went on to Beverley to look into the administration of the East Riding County Council. John Bickersteth, with whom I stayed, is the son of a Bishop, married to Lady Margaret, a pious old-maidish little woman. He is an athletic, attractive man of the country gentleman type, who bicycles into Beverley about 11 o'clock and comes out by the 3.30 train: takes life in a leisurely fashion and accepts with kindly tolerance the " little people " who have joined the country gentlemen in county administration since the election of the new county councils. He is a Yorkshire Whig, far too gentlemanly to share the old radical shibboleths, but quite unaware that there is a new school of radical collectivism growing up. Fortunately, he endowed me with all his reports, otherwise my visit would have been wasted, as he insisted on entertaining me the whole time; and, eventually despairing of getting to work, I went off for a ride with him and extracted what information I could about county government between pleasant gossip about men and affairs. He took me to see the town clerk of Beverley, a cynical, vulgar, but able man who was obviously delighted to call the aristocratic county clerk " Bickersteth ".

How much have I learnt in my six weeks' investigation? A vision of the tangle of local government: of the independence of the county boroughs, the recalcitrant defiance of the non-county boroughs, the shadowy authority exercised over them by the county councils; the grumblings of the district councils at the C.C.'s proddings, the appeals of the parish councils to the C.C. against the neglect of work by the district councils—the universal rivalry and sometimes actual litigation between various grades of sanitary authorities over incorporations and extensions of boundaries, over water catchment areas, tramways and hospitals. Then again, the mechanical grindings of the school board and the short-sighted stinginess of the boards of guardians, and in the dim and distant Whitehall the old-womanish L.G.B. threatening, obstructing, auditing and reporting—mostly without effect. It is not a vision of lucid beauty: but it is intensely human.

The town chosen for our next centre of investigation was Manchester, where I spent most of the summer, the Other One joining me now and again, and permanently for the August recess.

June 15th, 1899. Manchester.—The third week here. Sidney stayed for a fortnight, and has now returned to his L.C.C. work. We got straight away into our enquiry and we have been working every day, Spencer at the minutes of the Town Council, and Sidney and I at interviewing officials and abstracting reports lent or given to us. Two delightful Sundays we spent in the lanes of Cheshire: one night at Tarporley where, seven years ago, he and I stayed as an engaged couple with Mrs. [Alice Stopford] Green as chaperone. Those Sundays were very happy days, honeymoon rambles, dodging the high-roads and finding ourselves in farmyards.

At times we get discouraged at the bigness of our task: then we console each other by repeating " Well, if we cannot do it no one else can ", a conceited reflection. To-day I am feeling somewhat lonely in the little lodging—a whole fortnight away from him. . . .

Here I will insert an entry which does not directly concern the subject-matter of this chapter, but which gives a glimpse of the background of social distraction in which I lived.

July 24th, 1899. *Grosvenor Road.*—This last month of hot dry weather has been spent mostly in entertaining American and colonial friends. Some four mornings of each week have been spent at the British Museum scanning files of the *Manchester Guardian* and taking copious notes. Miss Fairchild, a charming Boston girl, has been staying with me and I have had a succession of little dinners for her entertainment. Our small circle of acquaintances is pleasant enough: easygoing, unconventional and somewhat distinguished. We are sought but do not seek—the most agreeable way of seeing people. Not that " society " pays us continuous attention: we are only casually found out by persons belonging to the great world—we live in a pleasant back-water of our own. But our social status, such as it is, is distinctly advantageous to the local government enquiry: it enables us to see any official from whom we want information. We are not going to have any trouble about getting access to facts: the task will be to select out of the mass of material submitted to us.

To return to our Manchester investigation, here is the impression I got from five weeks' work on workings of municipal government in that city:

September 9th, 1899. *Grosvenor Road.*—Five weeks in Manchester in a little rented house, with our own maids to look after us, and our secretary to help us—a peaceful happy time, collecting material and, by a well-regulated life, keeping fit for persistent work. We are more interested in this enquiry than in trade unionism: the problems are multitudinous and the machinery intricate. The least invigorating part of the subject-matter are the persons engaged in the work of local government: in the present administration of English provincial local government there is a singular lack of idealism and charm, of efficiency and force.

The Manchester Town Council turns out to be no better than that of Leeds. The most marked feature is the way in which the magnitude and importance of its work has outgrown its organisation. The different parts of the machine are out of joint; it rumbles on in some sort of fashion because it is pushed along by outside pressure, but it is always breaking down in the efficiency of its administration. The Council, judged by this test, would seem to be inefficient or corrupt or both. The men running the organisation are not a bad lot: one or two of the officials are distinctly able. But there is no head to the concern, no one who corresponds to a general manager of a railway company, still less to its paid chairman. The Mayor, elected for one year, has all his time absorbed by public meetings, social functions or routine administration: he is far more the ceremonial head of the city than the chief of the executive of the city government. The town clerk and his deputy are exclusively engaged in legal and parliamentary business; they spend most of their time in the lobbies of the House of Commons, in presenting the corporation's case at L.G.B. enquiries, in preparing leases and drafting agreements or in submitting bye-laws to government departments.

The suggestion that the town clerk of a great city like Manchester can be anything more than its solicitor and parliamentary agent—can fill the place of its chief executive officer—is, as things are at present, an absurdity. All the other city officers are technicians, accountants, engineers and medical men. The city surveyor and the M.O.H. are neither of them markedly competent and they have the status, not of administrators, but only of consultants called in whenever the chairman or secretary of one of the standing committees deems their advice necessary. The city treasurer is a promoted clerk; the chief constable a promoted policeman. With one exception, the administrative head of a department is the secretary of the committee supervising its work. Hence, the services of gas and of water, of tramways and markets, and even the rivers department, are all managed by promoted clerks with no professional training for their work. In fact, there is only one real executive officer who understands the technique that he has to supervise—a man named Rook, the superintendent of the sanitary department who, though he entered the Council's service at 30s. a week, has become a technician at his own job, and may be trusted to see that any given piece of work is carried through from its inception to its completion. To make confusion worse confounded, each committee considers itself like an independent company, and reports as little as it dare to the Town Council, which meets once a month, and is regarded by the chairman and members of each committee as a superfluous body which ought not to intervene.

These committees nominate their own members for election each year, and the tradition is that the committee must always be united in face of the Council. Hence, the atmosphere of secretiveness towards the Council, and of suspicious hostility on the part of those members of the Council who do not happen to be elected on the leading committees. Some of the committees are dominated by persons who are grotesquely unfit: for instance, the markets committee has had for years an illiterate tailor as chairman. In other cases the committee is run by a really able and upright man, but even he will pride himself on managing it " as I should my own business "; he resents mightily any criticism of his policy or methods. In short, there is nobody whose special business it is to see that all parts of the organisation are co-ordinated and working to a common end. Friction and petty scandals, accusations and recriminations, dog the Council's work. All this secretiveness and jealousy of control does not attain its object—if that be a quiet administrative life. Tales of peculation and jobbery, most of which are, I believe, untrue, get abroad through a malicious member or a resentful [elective] auditor who finds the accounts too much for his understanding. The rejoinder of the committees to all these stories, true or false, is always still more secrecy, with the result that the Council becomes enveloped in a permanent cloud of presumed stupidity and corruption.

So far as we have made the acquaintance of the councillors there are none very good, and none very bad. I have not picked out any who seem to be " rotters ". The abler among them are all old men— a little gang of Liberals who are still the salt of the Council. The social status is predominantly lower middle-class, a Tory solicitor and an I.L.P. journalist being the only men with any pretension to culture. The abler administrators have no pretension to ideas, hardly any to grammar: they are merely hard-headed shopkeepers, divided in their mind between their desire to keep the rates down and their ambition to magnify the importance of Manchester as against other cities. There is no cleavage on the Council according to policy—the Council drifts into subsidising the [Ship] canal or working its own tramways, or into " direct labour " in its public works, almost without deliberate thought, and certainly without any discussion either of principles, or of the special circumstances, which make for or against the proposal before the Council. The Council, in fact, fumbles along by the method of trial and error; but it has its head in the right direction pushed by outside force. But who is initiating this force? There seems no person, or group of persons, at work. It is more like the result of an impersonal current of ideas affecting all the persons concerned without their being conscious of them.

October 10*th*, 1899.—We saw little of the city government of to-day [I note after staying with Sister Holt in Liverpool], spending all our energies on the most interesting minutes of the old select vestry and on the documents of the town hall. Liverpool strikes us as more efficient than Manchester, a close ring of officials having replaced the petty incompetence of the committee system characteristic of Manchester town government. But there is a long tradition of corrupt dealing with publicans and other propertied sinners—at least so say the Liberal families of Holts and Rathbones. Munificent public work has been done at Liverpool by some of the wealthy Unitarian families, but these families are petering out, and the sons are not worthy of the fathers. Whether this is inevitable to all families, or the bad effect of two or three generations of luxury, I do not know. The present generation of rich folk want to enjoy themselves, find nothing to resist, no class or creed interest to fight for, so that they have ceased to consider anything but their pleasures.

October 1899. *Grosvenor Road.*—So far we see straight in front of us the way we shall go for the next few years. Our enquiry is stretching out before us, arduous, requiring patience and persistency, but by no means impracticable. For the rest there is the Economic Faculty to build up, and our share in administration and propaganda. Our finances are sound, our health good, and there is no reason for anxiety. We must spend, if need be, our capital on our work, and we must not be disheartened by its magnitude. We are fast becoming elderly, we have not so many years left, we must make the best of our talents and leave the future to take care of itself. And it is useless to be down-hearted because of the indifference and stupidity of the world, even as regards its own true interests. And it is childish to yearn after some sanction to the worth-whileness of human effort. For us who " know not ", this sanction is unattainable: we can but follow the still small voice of moral instinct which insists that we shall seek truth and love one another. Is the sanction the calm happiness in work: the peaceful delight in living?

November 30th. *Grosvenor Road.*—Immersed every morning in the reading of documents in some municipal office: can't manage more than four good hours. Two afternoons I am due at the School: to lecture or to see students. Another afternoon I am at home, and the other afternoons get filled up with calls, casual committee meetings and exercise. But we are sufficiently advanced in our work to contemplate beginning to write when we return from Plymouth in January.

December 14th. *Grosvenor Road.*—Spencer, Mildred Sturge and I spent a week over the St. Pancras vestry minutes. We have taken on Mildred Sturge, a Newnham graduate, as a sort of paid apprentice. She is not able, but accurate and painstaking. An expedition to Norwich in bitterly cold weather to start a Miss Watson on the Norwich records ends our autumn campaign. Next week we go to Plymouth for the Christmas recess to undertake the records there. I begin to grasp the character of local government at the beginning of this century. When we return we shall hew out of our accumulated material the first draft of our first chapter.

January 31st, 1900. *Torquay.*—Here for three nights attending an enquiry into borough extension.

A month at Plymouth at work together, with Spencer to help us, at the Plymouth records [I recall, before reporting on the extension enquiry]. For recreation we had two days' wanderings on bicycles over Dartmoor in mist and rain, one or two walks with Sidney on Mount Batten, and pacing alone over the Hoe watching the setting sun after the day's work was done. Otherwise, we stuck closely to our note-taking and interviewing. I remember when we were steaming through the tropics and I was visualising our work for the next few years, I dreaded the thought that we should have to spend all our time out of London in towns: I feared that my health and my spirits would break down with sedentary office work in places like Leeds, Manchester and Liverpool, without the long holidays in the country we were accustomed to. But our life during the last year turned out not half bad: the enquiry has been unexpectedly interesting: my health excellent, and the occasional 48 hour cycling in country lanes round about the towns, a joy and a delight—making up in intensity of pleasure for the longer holidays in the country. Sidney has been well, interested, and happy: every day brings greater confidence in the worth-whileness of this continuous study of facts and careful reasoning from them.

And here is a somewhat denigrating report of what seemed to me futile proceedings:

Three days sitting in bad atmosphere listening to the argument whether or not St. Mary Church and Cockington shall be included in the borough of Torquay. I had an introduction from T. W. Russell of the L.G.B. to the inspector who was holding the enquiry, one General Crozier; and I happened to light on the hotel where he and two of the leading counsel engaged in the case were staying. Unfortunately, the hotel was small and crowded, so that there was not much opportunity for confidential talks with judge and counsel; and the local men were too flustered to give me much information. But I quickly made friends with three out of the five counsel—Littler, Richards and Duke; Littler being a useful acquaintance seeing that he is chairman of Middlesex Quarter Sessions, the records of which we have to go through. General Crozier is a gouty and slow-minded old West End clubman, past his work, even if he were ever capable of it—a relic, I imagine, of the era of barefaced jobbery of appointments. I am not impressed with the quality of the legal ability present at the enquiry. Perhaps these extension cases do not lend themselves to a careful mustering of proven facts or to subtlety of argument. Hearsay evidence as to the wishes of this or that section of the population and jumbles of irrelevant considerations, the reiteration of stock arguments for or against extensions of boundaries in general, such as,

" the larger areas mean more efficient administration ", or, " a smaller area is more conducive to keen interest ", that a particular district is or is not the outgrowth of an older inhabited area, that borough government is more desirable than that of an urban district council, that the amenities of the borough are or are not shared with the surrounding districts—I felt that I could have reeled it all off mechanically if I had just been told on which side I was to plead. As to the evidence it was all of the nature of personal opinions, obviously *ex parte* opinions: no attempt was made to prove the truth or the falsehood of all this assertion, and counter-assertion. Then there is the silly badgering of inexperienced witnesses. " Will you answer yes or no, Mr. Jones? " when in the opinion of the nervous witness " Yes " would be misleading, and " No " inaccurate. It was easy to see that any facts obtained, and many not obtained, by this expensive process could have been got by a couple of experienced investigators examining witnesses quietly in their homes as well as documents which had not been faked for the occasion. Littler and Richards lent me their briefs to read and it was quite clear to me, as I sat and listened to the proceedings, that the K.C.'s drawing huge fees had added nothing whatever to the facts or the arguments prepared for them by the local solicitors. The culminating absurdity of the proceeding is that, if the decision of the L.G.B. inspector (who by the way took little or no interest in the talk of the counsel) is not accepted by the parties concerned, the whole case will have to be argued out again before a parliamentary committee. Personally, I came out of the court not having heard one of the issues raised adequately cleared up—certainly not the general issue of larger or smaller areas of administration. At present I am divided in my mind between the desirability of large municipal boroughs and the expediency of keeping alive the old historic county and, therefore, the minor local authorities under county jurisdiction.

June 12th, 1900. *Leicester.*—Staying in a rough boarding-house, the best in Leicester, for a fortnight's investigation. It is kept by a woman of character and intelligence but a bad housekeeper. House dirty, meals rough and monotonous, and service inefficient but willing. We pay £2 : 2 : 0 a week each and have a good bedroom and small sitting-room; our meals with some half-a-dozen other lodgers, four harmless business men and two women of the usual boarding-house type. Everyone is good-tempered and well-mannered; and the other lodgers either do not feel the roughness, or are too good-tempered to object to it. Sidney feels the discomfort more than I do. No doubt my greater intentness on the enquiry makes up for a good deal in my case. In his case the need for investigation is not a part of his personal life and aims, which are administrative.

In our MS. notes in Sidney's handwriting, I find the following summing-up of our general impressions of Leicester municipal government:

Summing up at the end of a fortnight, our general impression confirms our particular notes.

The new corporation started in 1835 with a remarkably able town clerk (Stone), and a set of able, honest and socially influential men—wholly Liberal and Nonconformist, mostly Unitarian—belonging industrially to the upper middle-class of the time—bankers, hosiery manufacturers and professional men. Partly in reaction against the prodigal and corrupt Tory administration, their dominant idea was to administer the public property honestly and economically—to pay low salaries, to contract wherever possible, to pay off debt by prudent sales of land. Notwithstanding this bias, and the hard times of the " forties ", when sanitation came up they were (under Whetstone) ahead of public opinion—appointed a medical officer and a staff of temporary inspectors to discover nuisances, which they peremptorily ordered to be abated. They had (under Whetstone) a horror of overgrown establishments, and thus shrank from enlarging functions—subsidised a Water Company (eventually taken over). They were, in fact, more like Leeds and Manchester.

Intensely political—always voting petitions in Liberal and Nonconformist interest—appointed all Liberal mayors and aldermen and, apparently, Liberal chief officials. The procedure was good, and reports of committees full; but it was adapted to a group of personal friends—Stone, town clerk, was friend and solicitor to all the leading councillors. The relationships would have been invidious, if they had not been men of high honour; they were simultaneously chairmen and directors of railway, water and gas companies, which they, as a corporation, had to control and deal with, they bought land of themselves, they were related with Stone and everyone else by marriage. But they left a tradition of highest integrity and always doing their best for the town.

This state of things continued certainly until Stone's death about 1870. After interregnum of unsatisfactory successors for a couple of years or so, the Council fell back on Stone's clerk (Storey), a shrewd but uncultivated man of no social position or professional status. He was assiduous in the office, attended all committees, and carried on traditions of Stone. During this 20 years (1874–1894) there was an involuntary expansion of corporate activity, taking over water and gas, flood prevention and sewerage works, etc., and finally in 1891 extending boundaries.

This was a period of great industrial expansion of Leicester; and, with the boot trade, the uprise of a new and somewhat rough class of employer. Gradually, the old families of Paget, Whetstone, Ellis, Johnson, etc., dropped out of municipal life—becoming M.P.'s and semi-county people—if remaining in Leicester, tending to become an aristocracy.

In 1891, with the election of the whole Council on the extension [of boundaries], the remnants of the above either retired, or were pushed on one side. Two new elements came to the front—the new capitalist traders and boot manufacturers (e.g. Hart, Wood, Lennard, Marshall), and the workmen. All evidence shows there was a great change. It is said that the new capitalists were more influenced by desire to improve their social position through municipal office than the old. At the same time, the workmen, as electors and as councillors, brought in motives of social improvement, propaganda, and conscious class interest.

The net result, since 1891, is that the Council has become much more progressive and democratic in sympathy; and, as the defect of this quality, more discordant and worse-mannered. This has been a further bar to any of the old " aristocracy " entering it.

The procedure, well enough adapted for a little party of friends, has not changed. The committees are now too secret, and have too much delegated to them—no provision for adequate publicity, or adequate control by Council. This leads to government by a clique (Wood, Lennard and Vincent), not on party lines, but on basis of satisfying personal power and ambition, and mutual protection. This has led to suspicions of the clique, and their friends getting indirect financial advantages, but no actual corruption is alleged.

Our impression is that the chief officers have, during the past decade, not been chosen on political lines, but rather for their probable subserviency to the clique. The ablest is evidently Colson, the gas manager. The new town clerk (Bell) did not improve on acquaintance; and we now judge him to belie his appearance of ability and solid qualities, by lack of experience, industry and zeal. He is, however, immensely thought of by many people in the town, and through his gentlemanly manners and good appearance carries great weight with rank and file of the Council.

The School Board is said to have begun in 1871, by having able educational enthusiasts and to have had two good chairmen in succession; then a steady-going business man, and now a weaker ditto— the clerk is a mere clerk. One great aim seems to be to avoid publicity. It strikes us as an inferior edition of Leeds.

The Board of Guardians has always been considered far inferior to the Council and School Board—is said now to be rather like the rank and file of the Council, several small men are on both. Rather a

rise since 1894—advent of six women, vote by ballot, and real election.
[S. W.'s entry.]

At this point I will again insert an entry which, while
reflecting my permanent interest in our joint investigations,
relates to our other activities and describes the social
environment of our daily existence.

May 22nd, 1900. *Grosvenor Road.*—The next eight years seem
likely to settle how useful we shall be to our generation. Our effort is
now directed to one end—to establish on a firm basis a science of
society. We are trying to bring this about partly by the School of
Economics. Sidney's persistent energy has attained at least a formal
success for the School. We have gained university status, we have
secured a building and a site, and we have the prospect of a regular
income; we have attracted students, and we are training teachers.
But how far the new activity will prove to be genuine science and not
mere culture or shallow technical instruction, remains to be seen. The
same doubt with regard to our own work. We are lavishing time and
money on the investigation, doing it in an extravagantly complete
manner. Shall we have the intellectual grasp to rise superior to our
material—or shall we be simply compilers and chroniclers? It is only
in rare moments that I have any vision of the book as a whole; at most
times I am dazed by the intricacy and technical detail of the subject.
Have we " bitten off more than we can chew "? It may be the time
is not yet come for a sound science of social organisation. Anyway,
we have faith that the beginning will be brought nearer by our effort,
even if it fails to attain for us any kind of personal success. But, if we
are to think out the development of local government in all its different
phases, from our chaotic notes, it is clear that I must be free from the
distractions of London life. Relations, old friends, continental and
American admirers, students and persons who can help us in our
investigation—all have to receive their due amount of attention. I am
on excellent terms with the family—the sisters have taken to us and
are beginning to wish that we should see much of them and their
children: this means the giving and taking of dinners, chaperoning
girls on bicycling parties, putting up public schoolboys on their trips
to London. The old friends seem to look reproachful when one evades
their offers to call or refuses blankly to lunch or dine with them. Then
again students. Here I acknowledge a duty—one is bound to do one's
little to helping forward younger persons, less fortunately placed than
oneself, to the pathway of research and investigation. Lastly, there are
a multitude of persons one ought to see in connection with local

government. And, as a penalty for possessing a social conscience, in the background of all other distractions, the ghostly forms of all sorts and conditions of men, who have helped me in the past to get information on the subjects I was investigating—employers, philanthropists, trade unionists, co-operators. The only way out of the whole tangle is to get out of London. This we will do next spring.

The eight weeks' recess from London County Council administration was spent in Northumberland.[1]

September 25th. Newcastle-on-Tyne.—Staying here to start Miss Kitson on the local minutes. Our vacation at an end. Five weeks in St. Philips Vicarage, the home of a high church Anglican priest, who is also a socialist, up on the high ground in a working-class quarter. The house was badly built and designed, but pleasantly appointed,

---

[1] After turning over the 650 or so separate pages of notes I recall our general impression of Newcastle municipal government between 1835 and 1900.

(1) The exceptional potential wealth in land ownership, in port facilities and in the right to levy town dues, which the corporation possessed when it started on its career as a representative body.

(2) Not unconnected with this exceptional corporate wealth was the continuous presence on the town council of distinguished local capitalists, including, for instance, chairmen and vice-chairmen, directors and shareholders of the railway company and of the local joint-stock companies that supplied the inhabitants with gas and water, with toll bridges and tramways; together with the principal local ship-owners, ship-builders and important traders.

(3) The outstandingly favourable terms which these business men habitually obtained from the corporation as buyers and lessees of its land and its port facilities, and in their arrangements for the composite payment of town dues, and in the control of the gasworks, waterworks and tramways.

(4) The absence of party politics and the infrequency of electoral contests, owing to the current agreement between the local Tories and the local Whigs not to contest seats on the town council unless the holders voluntarily retired.

(5) The complete absence of any consciousness, on the part of these eminent business men, that they were in any way acting otherwise than strictly honourably in their continuous stream of dealings with the corporation that they controlled in getting something for nothing at the expense of their fellow-citizens. In this way they contrasted with the "professional politicians" in New York and other cities, who were fully aware that they were selling " franchises " and other favours to big business, and failing to enforce the laws regulating the sale of alcoholic liquor and suppressing immorality.

(6) In contrast with the Birmingham Town Council, and in the last decade of the century also with the London County Council, the capitalists who dominated the Newcastle Town Council were honestly devoted to the doctrine of *laissez-faire,* which yielded conclusive arguments against undertaking improvements in the housing, education and sanitation of the poorer inhabitants of their city, as matters of public concern and common well-being. It was this naïve synthesis between their economic creed and their pecuniary self-interest which enabled them to carry out the policy of exploitation of the corporate wealth for private profit without self-condemnation, and even without public blame from their fellow-citizens. This self-complacency became impossible with the rise of a new political party inspired by the growth of municipal socialism practised in Birmingham and London.

with a good library of theological and devotional books. Our impressions of Newcastle local government, not flattering—even worse than Leeds or Liverpool—are given fully in our notes. The weather was detestable so that we had little temptation to desert our work; and, by the end of the time we were both of us ready for our delightful holiday at Bamborough.

Three weeks we spent lying in a tent on the sand, watching the sea, or cycling over moorland and mountain, or wading out to rocks or islands—a quite enchanting holiday. We took with us masses of books, chiefly works on the Oxford movement—a continuance of the theological taste we acquired at the Vicarage: also Perthes' memoirs, lent us by a remarkable Newcastle man, Dr. Merz (whose acquaintance we had made), and his own *History of Thought*.

I have found true refreshment in this theological reading—a change of thought and an exercise of feeling. Specially interested in the Catholic religion as mental hygiene and discipline of the emotions, an authoritative guidance to the *motive* of conduct. There is so much energy and happiness wasted in everyone's life through lack of single-heartedness, through the presence of evil or unworthy feelings. The Catholic discipline has a traditional—and no doubt empirical—wisdom in training of character and the direction of the emotions. I have no special sympathy with the ascetic saint, yet the world could do with a good deal more physical self-control, humility and disinterested love, without human beings losing their effectiveness. All this experience was, it seems to me, thrown clean away with the Protestant Reformation. Perhaps other qualities were gained: but it is easier for me to see the loss than the gain.

Sometimes Sidney and I feel that we can hardly repay by our work the happiness and joy of our life. It seems so luxurious to be able to choose what work one will do, according to one's faith in its usefulness, and do that work in loving comradeship. The next ten years will prove whether we are right in devoting our energies to the establishment of a science of society, and whether the amount of scientific work we have mapped out for ourselves is not beyond our powers. But all that we are responsible for is the single-hearted devotion of our talents, whether of capacity, means or position, to the work one believes in. With Sidney this is comparatively easy; with me it is always a struggle to keep my mind from wandering off into foolish romancings. It is in this self-discipline that I find the need and the truth of prayer.

From January 1901 to December 1905, the date of my appointment as a member of the Royal Commission on the

Poor Law and Unemployment, the MS. diary is mainly concerned with the two other activities of Our Partnership: the furtherance of the London School of Economics, and the propaganda, open and concealed, for the unification of all education from the infant school to the university, under the London County Council. But, in order to complete the tale of our local government enquiry before it was merged in that of the Royal Commission on the Poor Law, I give the following entries, which can be skipped by all those who are not interested in the tiresome struggle with masses of material involved in sociological research.

April 24th, 1901. *Churchfield, West Lulworth, Dorset.*—A large thatched cottage with low straggling rooms, plain, clean but not too comfortably furnished, has been our living place for the last three weeks. The village is in a hollow of the chalk downs, without trees, and cut off from the sight of the sea. From our sitting-room window we look on to the road, then a hedge and then an orchard, beyond—other thatched cottages. But, once on the downs, there are glorious stretches of well-shaped hill and abrupt chalk cliff, expanses of sea and sky, and, on the other side, the most beautiful plain of heath and moor and wooded promontory, with bright little rivers running in all directions except sea-ward. The colouring these last days has been exquisite, the sea—sapphire, amethyst, emerald, moonstone—the white chalk cliff rising out of it in mysterious lines of white, pink, grey, the brilliant yellow gorse in the foreground and, on the other side, the dark russet of the yet unfolded beech buds, the dull green-black of the fir, and the rich tones of heather and scrub covering the plain and creeping up the little valleys of the bare neutral-tinted chalk downs.

The first fortnight was wet and cold, and, beyond our regulation two hours' walk in the afternoon, we stayed in and worked at " the book ". We had brought with us ten pamphlet boxes of material, MS. minutes of vestries, etc. The first three days I spent struggling with the draft of our first chapter, rearranging each section and when I had rearranged it submitting it to Sidney. Then he would begin (I sitting by his side) to rewrite it: both of us breaking off to discuss or to consult our material. Indeed, this constant consultation of our " specimens " is the leading feature of our work. We are always handling our material: one of us will object, " that is not so ", or " that is not always the case ", and then forthwith it becomes a question of evidence, and how far the facts we have under our hands are representative of the whole. The last three or four days we have gone systematically through all the ten boxes over every specimen, so as to be sure that we have included all the facts and accounted for all the similarities and divergencies between our " specimen " vestries. At last our chapter on the parish is complete, and I sent it off to be typewritten this afternoon.

January 30th, 1902. *Grosvenor Road.*—I have been so hard at work on the book that I have had no energy left over for diary writing. . . . Then we went to Margate into lodgings taking the devoted Emily [1] with us—which made the lodgings quite homely. We worked well together and almost ended the difficult chapter on " Municipal Corporations ". The number of times Sidney and I have laboured through these four volumes of the Royal Commission Report of 1834 is tiresome even to think about, arranging and rearranging the evidence, and arranging our facts in endless ways so as to find coincidences and perhaps causes. Our conclusions from the evidence are almost too favourable to please us: they are hardly *vraisemblable.* Since we came back we have either been tidying up the chapters, or I have been at the Guildhall working with Spencer through the minutes of the Court of Common Council of the City of London.

April 25th, 1902. *Crowborough Beacon, Sussex.*—A pleasant four weeks here, camping out in the large rooms of a girls' school at Crowborough Beacon. We have had a happy and successful time here: writing the chapter on the " Commissioners of Sewers ", sorting the material from structure into function (a tiresome job which will have occupied one or other of us for ten days). I have been thinking out the " assumptions " underlying the working out of local government prior to 1834. At present, I have the following principles: obligation of all to contribute service; desirability of common agreement; supervision by superior authority, calling in the counsel of inferiors; and *co-option and nomination of successors* by the existing governing body. It is clear that the principle of " obligation " referred to old services or general statutory services; and the principle of " common agreement " to new services or pseudo-voluntary services. I shall doubtless see other principles when we come to work out the functions. The book is getting into the interesting and philosophical stage, and I am looking forward with hopefulness and happiness to the ten weeks with the Russells.

May 4th, 1902. *Friday's Hill, Fernhurst.*—Settled again for our nine weeks' sojourn with the Bertrand Russells. Hard at work on the

---

[1] Emily Wordley, for many years parlourmaid at 41 Grosvenor Road. (Ed.)

Poor Law Report of 1834. I had to break into the work to help Sidney through with his University of London article. . . .

June 1902. *Friday's Hill.*—I have worked well, but with small result in actual stuff written. Of the eight weeks we have been here, nearly two were spent on the university article—counting exhaustion and proof-correcting, another two in reading through and analysing the whole of the Poor Law Commission evidence of 1833–4. Another week has been more or less spent in entertaining and resting, so that not more than a fortnight has been actually consumed in writing. But what I have done is to get the whole poor law section planned out and about half written, as well as the general scheme of Part II. of the book conceived, so that now the work will go straight forward. Sidney has only been able to write out (he always elucidates and completes my rough draft) what I have done, spending only one or two days a week down here.

July 1902. *Grosvenor Road.*—Four fruitful weeks at Campden, Gloucestershire, whither we return for another three to-morrow. We have done good work completing our chapter on the Poor Law. We see now that our first work will be the history of English local government from the Revolution down to 1835, practically the eighteenth and nineteenth centuries. It has been impossible to separate the early nineteenth from the eighteenth century, of which it was a mere continuation, without any deliberate change in constitution. Administrative inefficiency was one of the features of the eighteenth century, and it was only in the reform movement of 1832–5 that we have the first sign of a desire for efficient administration; and that only in the minds of " cranks " like Chadwick. The reactionary and the radical parties were alike against efficiency, the first for corrupt and the second for doctrinaire reasons. Our work on local government will be a big indictment, not only of the eighteenth century, but also of the present-day local government.

November 10*th*, 1902. *Grosvenor Road.*—Meanwhile, we are hammering out our conclusions and throwing them at the head of the public in the form of massive historical analysis. It is a time, we think, for big artillery in the way of books. But hard thinking takes time. For a whole month I played about with propositions and arguments, submitting them, one after another, to Sidney, before we jointly discovered our own principles of poor law administration. And each of the services will have to be taken up in the same exhaustive manner! How could we do it, if working together were not, in itself, delightful? It is a curious process this joint thinking: we throw the ball of thought one to the other, each one of us resting, judging, inventing in turn. And we are not satisfied until the conclusion satisfies completely and finally both minds. It is interesting too, to note that we never discover our principles until after we have gone through the whole labour, not only of collecting, classifying and marshalling our facts, but of sitting down in front of them, until we discover some series of hypotheses which accounts for all the facts. This final process seems to me to be not at all unlike testing in a laboratory; or manipulating figures in the working out of a mathematical problem. It is experimentation, constantly testing the correspondence between the idea and the fact. I do most of this experimentation and Sidney watches and judges of the results, accepting some, rejecting others. It is he who finds the formula that best expresses our conclusions.

January 16th, 1903. Overstrand, Cromer.—The last afternoon here. . . . A happy time: spent the first ten days sorting and pondering over the material on vagrancy and classifying the subject under " devices "; Sidney, meanwhile, clearing up odds and ends of work— Technical Education Board, University and [School of Economics] business. Then we started work together, and roughed out the greater part of the vagrancy chapter—I lazing over the fire while Sidney did the real work. This would take up our mornings—four hours; in the afternoon, there would be a walk on the beach or more rarely a ride, and then a quiet read at 18th-century literature. Sidney must have devoured some fifty or sixty books: I only accomplished two or three together with a few novels borrowed from Lady Battersea. Half-a-dozen times we went in for a chat with our neighbours in their resplendent villa, or Lady Battersea came to see us. She is a good and true-natured woman, and quite intelligent, though like all these " society dames " quite incapable of anything but chit-chat—flying from point to point. . . .

January 1903. Grosvenor Road.—This year has been both happy and fruitful. We have got on well with the book—though the task grows bigger and more complicated as we toil to complete it. We find ourselves really writing the internal history of the eighteenth century —and for this purpose I am reading eighteenth-century literature— trying to discover what were the good features of the time. A certain kind of veracity seems its leading moral quality; a perfected form in prose, its intellectual achievement; and I suppose certain discoveries as to the contents of men's minds; appreciativeness of human motive, cynical, but at least open-eyed. In fact, short-sighted and limited truth-seeking. As to conduct, human nature seems to have sunk pretty low—at any rate in England. Selfish, self-indulgent, corrupt, and slack in all kinds of effort except dissipation—even cruel, at least compared to the present day. But what a lot of the eighteenth century survives in the twentieth! Progress seems to have been made chiefly by the lower middle-class and upper artisans.

March 2nd, 1903. *Grosvenor Road.*—I took the chair for H. G. Wells's lecture on " Areas of Administration " at the Students' Union. Like ourselves, he is impressed with the need for some scientific adjustment of units of administration to functions or services—the obvious absurdity of Newcastle and Jarrow, for instance, being separate units of tramway administration, instead of the whole of Tyneside. He suggested some ideal areas for all purposes based on the function of locomotion. In summing up the debate, I threw out, on the spur of the moment, the suggestion of sweeping away all fixed areas; of instituting one unit of representation: *e.g.* one representative for every 10,000 persons for all purposes whatsoever, and of combining these units with each other according to function in many different groups or governing bodies. Thus, the five representatives of Deptford would sit together for street cleansing and lighting purposes, would sit with the other London representatives for education, main drainage, and with these and those of the home counties for water, etc., etc. The grouping would be done by Order in Council according to the service and according to fixed or changing conditions with regard to population, industry, climate, etc. The local government through the country would thus be fluid, indefinitely elastic, the same units grouped in any number of ways. Each constituency would fix its eyes on the one man, and take precious care to get a good representative. This would involve a great development of statutory committees with co-opted members, as some of the groups would be too large in member-ship to admit of direct administration by the whole body. Also, it might be necessary in rural districts to provide for the election or nomination of purely subordinate administrative bodies, who would manage the local affairs under the supervision of a large body. G. B. S. was delighted with the suggestion. There may be some grain of use-fulness in it.

June 15th, 1903. *Aston Magna, Gloucestershire.*—Meanwhile, our big work on local government grows slowly and surely; but still there is a good deal of ground to cover. Since we have been down here—sixteen days—I have mastered the whole of our notes on licensing of public houses by the justices, and the evidence and reports of four parliamentary enquiries, and we have actually written the greater part of the section—some twenty pages of printed matter, I suppose. It reads a straightforward narrative now—but oh! the mental struggle of getting the facts disentangled and marshalled one after another! Four hours every morning have we worked either together or separately. I getting the scheme right and Sidney getting the details correct and revising my scheme. We have worked all the harder because we have been absolutely undisturbed and the weather has been bad, so that Sidney has worked on in the afternoon, and I have brooded over the chapters trudging in the rain along the dripping lanes. Some delightful rides we have had together in the few fine days—happy hours of light-hearted companionship, arguing about our book or plotting our little plans.

August 1903.—While I spend four whole mornings in mastering the contents of one little book, and rest the whole afternoon and evening in order to work again the next day, Sidney will get through some eight or ten volumes bearing on local government, or likely to contain out of the way references to it. . . . The continuous activity of his brain is marvellous: unless he is downright ill, he is never without a book or a pen in his hand. He says that he cannot think without reading or writing, and that he cannot brood; if he has nothing before him more absorbing, he finds himself counting the lines or spots on some object. That is why when he is in a street or a bus he sees and reads and often remembers the advertisements. If I would let him, he would read through meal times. A woman who wanted a husband to spend hours talking to her, or listening to her chit-chat, would find him a trying husband. As it is, we exactly suit each other's habits. Long hours of solitary brooding is what I am accustomed to, and without which I doubt whether I could be productive. It is restful for me to wander off in moor, in lanes and field, or even to sit silently by his side in our tent, or by the fire. I have my thoughts, and he has his book, and both alike go to complete and fulfil our joint task. Of course, it is exactly the eager effort, taken together, the discussion, the planning and the execution, the continuous mutual criticism of each other's ideas and each other's expression of these ideas—all this vigorous co-operation for three or four hours at a stretch—that makes the silent companionship possible, even when this last is continued, perhaps, for three or four days at a time. Sometimes I am a bit irritated because at some time he will not listen to what seems to me a brilliant suggestion—dismisses it with " that is not new ", or with a slight disparaging " hmm ". But I generally smile at my own irritation, and take back any idea to clear up or elaborate or correct with other thoughts, or to reject as worthless; sometimes I flare up and scold—then he is all penitence and we kiss away the misunderstanding. Our love gives an atmosphere of quiescent happiness (to use Rogers' classification), and our work gives us periods of restless or energetic happiness. And when we are alone in the country together there is no other thought or feeling to intrude on this peaceful activity. We have no incompatible desires, either together or apart; our daily existence and our ideal are one and the same—we sail straight to our port over a sunlit sea. But the point we make for seems sometimes an unconscionable way off!

November 1903. *Grosvenor Road.*—Exactly a month to-day we returned to London. I have worked regularly at the book, but until the last week my brain seemed like wool, and my daily effort was more painful than productive. The net result is half the chapter on prison administration written, and most of the material mastered— but Sidney has really done the better part of the work though occupied with other matters.

November 1903.—Becoming obsessed with my scheme of trans- forming English local government, by sweeping away all areas, paying skilled men as representatives and adding, by co-option, residents and expert amateurs for different purposes. Such a body—say 600 repre- sentatives for England—would make a Grand Council for all England's internal affairs—a similar Grand Council for Wales, Scotland and Ireland—breaking up into smaller units of local government according to function. Salaries of £1000 a year out of national funds.

Perceive now that it would be desirable to have a Part III. to our book on theory of local government, giving an analysis of the assump- tions upon which the 18th century and early 19th century local government was based—with the rise of new assumptions. With our mass of facts needful to have a brilliant and dogmatic theoretical part, quite apart from the concrete narrative, and based on a personal creed. Working well.

December 6th, 1903.—Finished the prison chapter to-day: for the last six weeks have worked well and hard at it—re-written it many times, improving it both in form and substance—Sidney the substance (which he is always adding to), I the form, which I model and remodel until I am satisfied with it. To-morrow I begin on another function— the suppression of nuisances. Meanwhile, Sidney will get out his little book on *London Education*.

January 17th, 1904. *Grosvenor Road.*—For the last fortnight— ever since I returned from our short Christmas holiday—I have been struggling with our material on municipal regulation. We have now decided to issue three volumes—I. on *Structure*, and II. and III. on *Function*—the two latter consisting respectively of poor law, police and prisons, and municipal regulation, municipal enterprise, and municipal finance. The two first volumes are done—in the first draft—and we have finished most of the separate chapters on municipal regulation, and the last chapter on the suppression of nuisances. The former I sketched and Sidney wrote out on Saturday—but I am still at work scheming the chapter on nuisances, without as yet seeing much light. It took a whole week pondering, analysing and indexing the material—then some days sorting out in my own mind the notions that belonged to a general introduction to regulation, and those belonging specifically to nuisances. This preliminary work is the hardest of all—one wanders far and wide in thought before one hits on exactly the right limits and right order of one's subject-matter. And it is work that one practically has to do alone, though directly one has got some limits and order satisfactory to oneself, Sidney's criticism or elaboration are an immense use. Indeed, I often feel that his " finish " is far more important than my preliminary framework.

October 1904. *Grosvenor Road.*—Since we returned a fortnight ago, I have been working for six hours a day, re-sorting the material back into structure—so that we may begin to re-write our first volume—and, by the way, clearing up my mind as to the arrangement of the subject-matter of each volume. It is hard driving work—a good deal is mere mechanical drudgery, but it has the advantage of a broad view of the whole subject-matter, structure and function, law and administration, origins and changes in the lines of development. . . . But, in the main, we lead the student's life—at least I do—the rest being taken as recreation in the odd times left over from the working day.

November 8th.—The sorting is finished—the two secretaries (Mrs. Spencer and Miss Crick) have completed it, working two days a week for the last six weeks. I, meanwhile, have superintended and helped—going over every page in the pamphlet boxes—and have looked up odds and ends of parish law in the British Museum. Now I have settled down to reconsider the chapter on the parish. I shall index the whole of the material under the four new heads of the parish and its office, the open vestry, the close vestry, the representative vestry, with innumerable subheads for each of the four chapters—varying the work with re-drafting the text of the chapter.

November 1904.—I am analysing all our material on vestries during the four morning hours and reading eighteenth-century literature for two odd hours in the afternoon—altogether I find I can manage six or seven hours' study now, as against the three or four hours of old days.

December 22nd, 1904.—Off to Felixstowe for a three weeks' recess —during which time we hope to finish off the parish chapter to be re-typewritten. We might do indefinitely more research, but it is time to be getting on if we ever are to complete our whole work on English local government up to the present time. Moreover, it is necessary for Sidney's administrative work to increase his reputation by publishing a big work of research.

January 1905. *Grosvenor Road.*—Since we returned ten days ago from our recess at Felixstowe, I have been hard at work analysing all our select vestry material, and reading at the British Museum everything that bears on it—Sidney going on to poor law pamphlets with occasional digressions to the matter I have in hand.

March 9th, 1905. *Grosvenor Road.*—Begun on the material for the county. Sidney another two weeks' work on the close vestry, annotating and completing it. . . .

March 15th.—Made an uncomfortable discovery this morning. In considering our material for our chapter on the county, I became aware that we have omitted to ask for and examine the presentments of grand juries, high constables, petty courts, etc. Also petitions from inhabitants and individuals. All we have looked at and abstracted are the orders of the quarter sessions. The mistake is due to our limited view at the beginning of our investigation: we started out with no systematic survey of our sources—merely allowed these to turn up anyhow. It is not too late, though troublesome, to remedy it. But I shudder at the thought of how bad our work was three years ago. We ought to have known better, with Cox's *Derbyshire* on our bookshelves. But I tend never to read a book until I actually want it, and Sidney does not regard discovering of sources as part of his duty. Damned stupid of me!

April 1905. *Grosvenor Road.*—Three or four weeks more after that spent either amassing new material at the British Museum for our chapter on the county, or in analysing our twelve boxes of material at home.

June 1905.—While we were at Aston, Sidney took the initiative and wrote hard at the chapter on county administration—I followed in his wake, supplying him, from my index, with all the instances in our material. But my work was mechanical. Now I have to pull the whole together—the county must be finished before we leave for Scotland a month hence. A strong sharp pull will do it.

July 1905.—Almost finished the county—but a few more pages to write—just the tag end of our last chapter.

October 1905. *Grosvenor Road.*—Five days' hard grind at MS. records of the Bristol Corporation of the Poor, and Municipal Corporation: encouraging Mrs. Spencer with my presence and leaving her to finish. Now at work sorting, indexing and scheming Book IV. of our work: seignorial franchises and municipal corporations. Sidney, meanwhile, gives all his spare time preparing *The Parish and the County* for the press, but much occupied with the L.C.C. work.

December 1905. *Grosvenor Road.*—Meanwhile, the thought of the work on the Royal Commission on the Poor Law added to the pressure of finishing our book, is not altogether a happy outlook. Our enquiry for Book III. is not yet completed—there are many gaps in our knowledge which I, aided by three private secretaries, am trying to fill up. But one hardly dare relax one's grip of the complicated subject, and how I shall manage to run a public enquiry side by side of our own, on a different subject, for a different period, I hardly care to think.

CHAPTER V

THE UNIFICATION OF LONDON
EDUCATION
1899–1902

" How can I produce the next act in Our Partnership? " I
ask the Other One. " So far I have disentangled and grouped
together all the entries in the diaries displaying our joint
investigation into English local government. But this uses
up a mere fraction of the diaries of 1899–1906. Here is a
mass of entries about your participation in the daily doings
of the London County Council; your continued work, as
vice-chairman, on the Technical Education Board, and the
further development of the scholarship scheme and the
co-ordination of the various grades and kinds of educational
institutions; the part you played in reconstructing London
University, and, as a senator, linking it up with the polytechnics, on the one hand, and the secondary schools, on
the other. More interesting to me is the record of our
devoted nursing of that delicate infant, the London School
of Economics; its rapid growth and admission into the
University of London, as part of the Faculty of Economics
and Political Science, a new faculty on which you had
insisted. And, last but not least, there are, from 1902
onward, all your manœuvres, which were certainly extensive
and peculiar, on the London County Council, in the lobbies
of the House of Commons, and even in the Tory press, to
make the London County Council the supreme authority
for the education of London citizens, whether elementary
or secondary, secular or denominational, technical or university. And, all the while, as a background to our personal
aims and efforts, there are entries about the South African
War, the discords within the Liberal Party, the triumphant
endorsement of aggressive imperialism at the polls in 1900,
the Nonconformist outcry against putting the Catholic and

Anglican voluntary schools on the rates, the break-away of Chamberlain from the Conservative Government in 1903, and the starting of the tariff reform campaign (which incidentally deprived us of Hewins as Director of the School of Economics)—all this political, economic and religious ferment, ending in the outstanding triumph of the Liberal Party at the polls early in 1906, giving us a firmly established Liberal Government right up to the outbreak of the Great War. How can I mould this medley of events into a single act in the absorbing drama of Our Partnership? "

" Why not have one chapter on the unification of London education, and another on the social and political environment in which this unification took place? " suggests the Other One. " That sounds sensible; also it follows the pattern of the three chapters dated 1892-8." Then, after a pause: "It might be possible, though difficult, up to 1901-2. But, when once you took to wire-pulling about the proposed London Education Act, our social environment changed. For good or for evil, we were compelled, if we wished to succeed, to seek out those personages who could help to carry out our policy. How else can we explain our association with Anglican bishops, other than Dr. Creighton who was an old friend, and even with Catholic priests? Why did we become intimate with Conservative Cabinet Ministers? And how else could we have secured Rosebery as second president of the School of Economics, and Lord Rothschild (of all persons in the world) as third president, with a handsome donation of £5000? Why did our dear friend Haldane insist on introducing us to other members of the Liberal League, even to the uncongenial Perks? The explanation is simple. It chanced that with all these personages we happened to find, during that particular period of Our Partnership—a common purpose—the unification of education, and its wide extension under a directly elected authority. No: I am afraid I must keep all the entries together for each successive year in chronological order. What I think I will do is to split the period of 1899–1906 into two chapters. The first, 1899–1902, will be concerned in the main with the unification of secondary, technological and university education, including scientific research, all departments which you happened to be administering in one way or another. The second chapter, 1903–5, will centre round your successful wire-pulling for the re-drafting of the London Education Bill, which proposed to make the metropolitan boroughs the education authority, into the London Education Act of 1903, which established the London County Council as supreme authority over all rate-supported or subsidised education and research throughout the metropolis. To which I shall add entries from the diary recounting your patiently pursued persuasion of the Progressive Party during the last three years of its dominance, 1903–6, in favour of working the Act whole-heartedly in the interests of maximum efficiency. Meanwhile, will you kindly sit down and write out exactly what you meant by the unification of London education? " Here is the slip he presently handed to me:

What we had dimly in view from the outset, although this was only gradually formulated, was the desirability of bringing about, so far as London's vast population was concerned, a three-fold unity of educational activity. It seemed necessary, if any substantial progress was to be made, to unify the government of London education, placing all of it under the direction of a single elected municipal organisation. It was equally important to bring all grades and kinds of educational institutions, literary and technical, academic and professional, elementary and secondary, university and postgraduate, into harmonious co-operation with one another, for what was, after all, a dominant purpose which they had in common. These two unities, horizontal and vertical, involved essentially problems and methods of administration. A third, and some would say, a more important unification to effect, concerned the substance and method of education, that of combining teaching with research, "pure" science with applied, intellectual development with artistic expression, instruction with training for life.

1899

For the first six months after our return to England,[1] we had to separate. Whilst I settled down in one provincial town

[1] The return home from their nine months' tour abroad. See p. 145 n. (Ed.)

after another, to start our colleague, F. H. Spencer, in our particular methods of research, the Other One resumed his various administrative activities in the metropolis. This enforced parting we found somewhat hard to bear.

" I have been horribly impressed all this week ", writes the Other One during one of our longer separations, " with the *loneliness* of life except when you are there. I can't bear to think of what it would be if there were an accident to your train, or when you were bicycling, which left me really alone. I get thoroughly nervous and depressed, and am miserable; unable to work, or read in the evenings, and wanting my colleague and companion, my helpmate and playmate. Fortunately, there is now little more than a week of it. . . ." Then again three days later: " The apparent advantage of dividing our forces is delusive, as I am afraid my work falls off by nearly as much as the gain. I have been able to do nothing towards the book this evil fortnight. Partly this must have been the case owing to the arrears of other business. But partly (and I am afraid in no small degree), it has been due to my own failure. I have been strangely incapable. It has been almost a failure of willpower. Of course, it is not easy to be sure this is not idleness. But, after all, if idleness is so strong as to incapacitate, it does not matter what you call it. What is annoying is that it is a miserable state. If one is idle, one ought at any rate to enjoy the idleness! I am afraid, therefore, we must not count on being able to increase our output by working apart. I am sure the very opposite is the case: a much more agreeable prospect! . . ."

Fortunately, there were the London County Council recesses: ten days at Easter and at Whitsuntide, a month at Christmas, and more than two months in the summer. Settled together in lodgings or in a rented house in a suburb of some provincial city, we spent the week-days in investigation and the week-ends in cycling in the neighbouring countryside; all of which is described in the preceding chapter. With these few words of introduction, I present the following entries of the diary of 1899, selected in order to give a vision of our life as a whole, apart from our specialised tasks of research. I begin with the very first entry in the MS. diary for 1899.

February 5th.—Since we returned to England I have been disinclined to write in my diary, having nothing to relate and having lost the habit of intimate confidences, impossible in a joint diary such as we have kept together during our journey round the world. One cannot run on into self-analysis, family gossip, or indiscreet and hasty descriptions of current happenings, if someone else, however dear, is solemnly to read one's chatter then and there. I foresee the sort of kindly indulgence, or tolerant boredom, with which Sidney would decipher this last entry! And this feeling would, in itself, make it impossible to write whatever came into my head at the time of writing without thought of his criticism. . . .

March 7th.—Sidney has been principally engaged in engineering the School of Economics into its proper place in the new University, bargaining alternatively with the Royal Commission to recognise it as a School of the University and to create a separate Faculty of Economics and Political Science, with the T.E.B. to endow the proposed Faculty with an income, and with Passmore Edwards to present a new building. Everything seems to be going excellently. . . .

May 15th.—Whilst I am mainly occupied in this enquiry, Sidney engineers the School and to a lesser extent the University. He is in the background of the County Council, partly because he has been so long away; partly because he is considered a specialist in education. On educational matters he leads without dispute; the T.E.B. and the Council doing anything that he asks them to do. He no longer evokes hostility: the Moderates respect him, the leading Progressives ask his advice, but do not regard him as a rival for the position of leadership. No doubt this is due to his growing disinclination to push himself forward for any position desired by anyone else; his refusal to take any steps to start a career of political advancement. His dislike of the personal struggle for leadership becomes, in fact, greater and greater. He is as energetic and persistent as ever, but his energy is perpetually seeking the line of least resistance for the cause he believes in—and the line of least resistance for his cause is the line of least advancement for himself. . . .

Haldane dined with us last night to talk over University affairs—especially the possibility of getting Carnegie to endow London University with some of his millions. We loathe what we saw of Pittsburg and explained that we could not possibly approach " the reptile ": but thought that others could do so who knew less or thought differently. John Morley for instance? So Sidney agreed to draft some kind of description of what might be done. Haldane was down-hearted, more down-hearted than I have ever seen him about the prospects of the Liberal Party. He tried to explain away Rosebery's last speech—crying quits to Home Rule, Socialism, Temperance and other social reforms, but could not do so even to his own satisfaction. The present situation —all the leaders of the party on strike—is becoming ludicrous—no one understanding what they are striking against unless they are striking against each other. Haldane brought a cordial invitation from Herbert Gladstone to Sidney to stand for Deptford, or any other London constituency, all expenses to be paid by the party: " a sign not of grace, but of dire necessity ".[1] " They think your standing would do them good," said Haldane, " but I told them ", he added in a half-bitter, half-playful tone, " that, like Rosebery, you would neither come in nor go out." " Until we know who is to be the company," I retorted, " we shall stand in the doorway and help to block the door by standing there."

Ten days in London have been dissipated by social duties. Three days I had to spend at Brighton with Herbert Spencer, he becoming insistent that I must visit him. Poor old friend: I verily believe that he thinks it is a treat for me to spend so many hours in his stuffy house, subsisting on his stingy housekeeping, so stingy that sometimes I spend no little time in considering whether I can manufacture an excuse to get a good

[1] In a letter 21/6/99, the Other One refers to this flattering desire to rope him into the Liberal Party:

" Last night's dinner was curious and interesting. Lord Tweedmouth had 40 to dinner, in his gorgeous house, on gorgeous plate. There were present Campbell-Bannerman, all the London Liberal M.P.'s except Stuart and Burns, Herbert Gladstone, and all the chosen Liberal candidates and probable candidates for London—including 24 County Councillors. I was given a very high place—put next to Sir H. Campbell-Bannerman at the main table! There was a most gorgeous dinner, and after it, to my surprise, and I think unexpected by others, Lord Tweedmouth invited us all to make suggestions how to win London. In response to cries Dr. Collins and Dickinson spoke, and then there were cries for me. So I rose, and being quite unprepared rather missed my opportunity I am afraid. It was difficult to say what one should have said. But I managed very politely to express my feeling that the leaders would have to make it clear that they meant business on London questions, especially taxation of Ground Rents and water: and that I was not myself a candidate. This led to rather a funny result—Causton, Herbert Gladstone and Bannerman in speaking later, all insisted with ludicrous iteration, that I *must* become a candidate. It became the ' note ' of the evening, to everybody's amusement. Steadman, Dr. Napier, Lawson also spoke, saying not much. The fact is we were all unprepared to speak, and of course rather hampered by our position as guests. I am sorry now that I did not say more ' for their good ', but I felt bound to try to be extra-courteous. Of course I told Causton and H. Gladstone afterwards very decidedly that I quite certainly would *not* stand—and I don't feel in the least inclined to do so. But it was evident that last night they meant to make a dead set at me."

meal out. However, on this visit there was no actual lack of nourishment. Two innocuous young women are in perpetual attendance—one a pianist, the other a housekeeper; the same secretary, half-secretary half-valet—three maid-servants, and a coachman—all at the call of the poor old man's money. He told me that during the last years he has been drawing from the sales of his books, eight hundred a year from England, and five hundred a year from America. All his savings are in the Linotype Company, in which he invested in order to break the trade union—an investment which yields high interest. So that he is more than well off considering his narrow needs. Notwithstanding all this mean living, there is the stamp of heroism on his daily life. At eighty years of age he still struggles on, in pain and depression, revising his biology in the firm faith that his words are the truth.

June 18th.—Spent Sunday with the Holts. Dear old Lallie most affectionate. Hers is a nature which improves with years—her character has softened, deepened, and she has gained in intellectual interests. At present, in the intervals of keeping a luxuriously comfortable house for a large family with many friends, she reads theology, trying to find a creed which combines rational thought with religious emotion. She has a strong mind, but she has neither intellectual training nor experience of thought, and it is pathetic to watch her struggling with wrinkled brow to reach conclusions which have been reached long ago by persons of her temperament. For the metaphysic we adopt is mainly a matter of temperament. She is a thorough-going puritan—pious but hating authority or intellectual or emotional self-subordination. Between her and us, there is a genuine regard: she admiring our persistency and strength of conviction, and we—Sidney especially—liking the orderliness and public spirit of the Holts. We go there again in September to study the Liverpool Town Council.

July 3rd.—Back in London in time for the International Women's Congress. The American and continental women took it quite seriously: but the more experienced English women, whilst organising it admirably, mocked at it in private: the press sneered at it, and the public generally ignored it—always excepting the entertainments of the duchesses and countesses who had been drawn in to patronise the Congress. It was not a failure, but hardly a success. The council meetings were stormy and unbusinesslike (I represented New Zealand owing to our recent visit to that land), resolving themselves into a duel between Mrs. Creighton, backed up by the N.U.W.W.[1] set of English women, on the one hand, and, on the other, Mrs. Wright Sewell (an

---

[1] National Union of Women Workers. (Not a trade union body, but a group of women interested in women's organisations. Ed.)

autocratic and self-assertive American), supported by Lady Aberdeen and the American and continental delegates. Great Britain and her faithful colonies were routed, which is what Mrs. Creighton desired, as she wished the National Council of Great Britain to withdraw from the International. It would have been better if the N.U.W.W. had refused to let itself be drawn into this adventure: it believed neither in Woman with a big " W ", nor in Internationalism with a big " I "; it is distinctly parochial and religious—most emphatically insular. To the well-bred and conventional ladies who dominate it, the " screeching sisterhood " demanding their rights represents all that is detestable. The public conferences were some of them informing and all of them decorous, and, owing to the predominance of the N.U.W.W. *clique*, the discussions were practical, even technical in character. I took the chair at one of the conferences and spoke at another, and turned up at the council meetings to support Great Britain. But with Mary Playne [my sister] in the house, and friends drifting in to see me, my week was wasted and my strength dissipated. Americans and colonials turn up and claim our attention, and the completion of our enquiry seems far off and unattainable.

October 10*th*.—This past summer [I note after staying with Sister Holt], so far as personal life is concerned, has been full of enjoyment of work, health and love. But it has been marred by the nightmare of the Dreyfus case and the Transvaal crisis. I took a feverish interest in the Dreyfus trial—Sidney grew impatient and would not read it, but to me it had a horrible fascination—became a morbid background to my conscious activities. Equally unsavoury have been the doings of our own people in the Transvaal—an underbred business, from the Jameson Raid to the South African Committee of Enquiry, from the hushing up of the Enquiry and the whitewashing of Rhodes, to the flashy despatches of Milner, and the vulgarly provocative talk of Chamberlain resulting in war with the Transvaal Republic, that remnant of seventeenth-century puritanism.

October 30*th*.—Haldane spent an hour or so with us this evening. Significant is the transformation in his attitude from a discreet up-holder of Liberal solidarity to that of a rebel against the views of the majority, determined to assert himself. " The Liberal Party is com-pletely smashed, Mrs. Webb ", and he beamed defiance. He had spent a month reading Transvaal blue-books and was convinced that Milner was right, and that war was from the first inevitable. The cleavage goes right through the Liberal Party into the Fabian Society, Shaw, Wallas and Whelen being almost in favour of the war, J. R. MacDonald and Sydney Olivier desperately against it, while Sidney occupies a middle position—thinks that better management might have prevented it, but that now that it has begun recrimination is useless, and that we must face the fact that henceforth the Transvaal and the Orange Free State must be within the British Empire.

Sidney lecturing at Oxford: I stayed here for my usual Wednesday afternoon at home. This is rapidly becoming a series of interviews with members of my class at the School of Economics. I enjoy lecturing every Thursday: the preparation of my lecture takes the best part of two mornings either in actual preparation or in resting so that my brain may be clear. The weekly class brings me into close connection with the work of the School: I see some half-dozen students every week and talk over their work with them. I am glad that our life becomes every day more that of students and teachers, our intercourse with general society shrinking up to occasional meetings with casual acquaintances. I sometimes long for more physical enjoyment, bright exercise and the still beauty of the countryside: for leisure as distinguished from the inertia of exhaustion. Indeed, when we are both a little weary we talk of the time when we shall be free to retire to the country and plan an ideal cottage with a large library, with lounges and room for endless book shelves, with a couple of spare bedrooms, and an open sunny verandah. Silence, beauty and physical exercise seem to me the supreme luxury; the mental superlatives we have already—mutual love and keen intellectual interest.

The Shaws have taken up their residence in Charlotte's attractive flat over the School of Economics, and Sidney and I meet there on Thursdays to dine sumptuously between our respective lectures. Charlotte and Shaw have settled down into the most devoted married couple, she gentle and refined, with happiness added thereto, and he showing no sign of breaking loose from her dominion. What the intellectual product of the marriage will be, I do not feel so sure: at any rate he will not become a dilettante, the habit of work is too deeply engrained. It is interesting to watch his fitful struggles out of the social complaisancy natural to an environment of charm and plenty. How can atmosphere be resisted?

December.—John Burns dined here last night. He is mellowed in temperament, he has lost his restless egotism and personal hatreds, and something of his force: lost his emphatic faith and his fierce sympathies with suffering. Of course, he will go on being " progressive ", and will back up anything that can be put into an Act of Parliament. But, like most untrained enthusiasts, experience of affairs has unhinged his faith and dulled his enthusiasm. All the common or garden objections to specific reforms, which were the trite commonplaces of one's child-hood, which one learnt to discount, realising the prejudices from which they sprang, seem brand-new truths to him. His special bugbear to-day is the pressure exercised on representatives by municipal and state employees to improve the conditions of their employment at the cost of the community (he having in his constituency some 3000 persons drawing maintenance from rates and taxes). These men and women might retort that John Burns, L.C.C., M.P., had become accustomed to postmen earning 18s. a week and denied the right of collective bargaining. His past utterances as a Labour leader—as a strike leader—hamper him in his reaction: it is assumed that he must necessarily be always on the side of the wage-earners, whatever their claims may be, and however fierce their resentment. When he insists on his freedom to judge the rightness and expediency of any demand he is denounced as a renegade. Certainly, there is no such pressure on Sidney. I do not think there is any danger of undue pressure. If public servants were to press for better conditions than were enjoyed by the majority of the voters, it would bring about its own reaction. These doubts and difficulties are fast paralysing Burns as a progressive leader.

December 1899.—Massingham, Vaughan Nash and Harold Spender have been dismissed from the *Daily Chronicle*; W. P. Reeves is out of spirits; and, generally, Liberals of all types are depressed and uncertain of themselves. The dismissal of Massingham from the editorship, and of the others from the staff, of the *Daily Chronicle* reflects the strong patriotic sentiment of its readers; any criticism of the war at present is hopelessly unpopular. The cleavage of opinion about the war separates persons hitherto united and unites those who by temperament and training have hitherto been divorced. No one knows who is friend and who is enemy. Sidney does not take either side and is, therefore, suspected by both. He is against the policy that led to the war, but that issue being past he believes in a policy of thorough in dealing with the Boers. And who can fail to be depressed at the hatred of England on the Continent: it is comforting and easy to put it down to envy and malice, but not convincing. To those who, like Massingham, Leonard Hobhouse and Frederic Harrison believe the indictment of British policy to be justified, the times look black, and the fact that those with whom they are accustomed to agree regard them as suffering from hysteria does not improve their temper. To my mind, given the fact that the Boers were fully armed, confident in their strength, and convinced of our weakness, war was inevitable. Whether this condition of affairs was in itself inevitable, or whether it was brought about by the impossible combination in British policy of Gladstonian sentimental Christianity with the blackguardism of Rhodes and Jameson, is another matter. But I doubt whether the partisanship of Milner, and the bad manners of Chamberlain, have had much to do with it. Chamberlain has injured himself with the thinking men of all parties by his lack of kindliness, courtesy and discretion, but he is still the " strong man " of politics: and the political " pit " of men from the street likes the strong man and has no desire that he should mend his manners. Besides, he has convictions and he expresses them honestly and forcibly—qualities at present rare in the political world. I should gather from the growing irritability of his speeches that his splendid physique is giving way.

1900

Kruger's ultimatum of the 11th October 1899, which demanded the withdrawal of British troops from any proximity to the frontiers of the two Boer Republics, produced immediately a state of war, beginning with an unexpected invasion of the Cape Colony by the Boer forces. British feeling was further embittered by the manifest pleasure of France and Holland, and by the even more humiliating episode of patronising advice from the German Emperor as to how we should conduct the campaign. Hence the year 1900 found British public opinion tense and angry, making even social intercourse difficult. The Conservative Party was solidly behind the determination of Chamberlain and Milner to " beat the Boers " and extend the British Empire. The Liberal Party, already enfeebled by a series of quarrels among rival leaders, was shattered by a definite split into three fiercely warring groups. The "Liberal Imperialists ", organised in the Liberal League under Lord Rosebery, and including Haldane, Asquith and Sir Edward Grey, gave full support to the Conservative Government in waging the war. A mixed group of distinguished individuals —the so-called pro-Boers—drawn equally from the Liberal Unionists and the Liberals—under the leadership of my brother-in-law Leonard Courtney, and enlisting many non-political intellectuals, upheld the right of the Boer Republics to complete independence, and denounced the policy and action of the Conservative Government as wicked aggression. An intermediate position was held by the newly chosen leader of the Liberal Party, Sir H. Campbell-Bannerman; supported by Sir William Harcourt and the central body of the Liberal Party, he found himself unable to deny the necessity of the war, but dissented alike from the policy which had led up to it, and from the objects and methods by which it was being pursued.

Looking back on this long and bitter controversy, and consulting the speeches and memoirs of the leading personages in all three camps, I am struck with an extraordinary omission, which seems to have passed unnoticed at the time. Amid all the angry argument as to whether the territories of the Transvaal and the Orange Free State should be governed by the resident Boer farmers or by the legislative assemblies at Capetown and Westminster; and as to whether or not the Boer farmers had an indefeasible moral right to independent sovereignty, or the Johannesburg [Uitlander] citizens a fundamental right to a vote, no one in Great Britain or South Africa seems to have remembered that these various claimants to power, whether Boer or British, agriculturist or gold-miner, were only a minority, a million or so strong, amid a vast majority of Kaffirs, five or six millions in number, amid whom this variegated white minority had intruded itself. With one exception, presently to be recorded, not one of the contending factions in Britain or South Africa—not one of the outstanding persons in the controversy—ever mentioned the claim of the native population whose conditions of life were at stake, even to be considered in the matter, let alone to be admitted to the government, or even to be given a vote, in the vast territories in which they had been living for generations.

How did the little group of Fabians react to this heated controversy? " The majority of the Society ", we are told by its historian and former general secretary, Edward Pease, " recognised that the British Empire had to win the war, and that no other conclusion to it was possible." But a considerable minority, including two members of the executive, J. R. MacDonald and J. F. Green, and George Barnes and Peter Curran, future Labour M.P.'s, together with Walter Crane, H. S. Salt, Mrs. MacDonald and Mrs. Pankhurst, were fervent pro-Boers. Hence, in December 1899, a special meeting of the members was called at which S. G. Hobson submitted a resolution—" That the Society should dissociate itself from the imperialism of capitalism and vainglorious nationalism and condemn the war ": the result being that the previous question was carried by a bare majority of 59 to 50. This inconclusive result reflected, we are told, " a great diversity of opinion in the Society, and the executive committee, for the first, and so far the only time, availed itself of the rule which authorised it to submit any question to a postal referendum of all the members ". As there was never any question of the Society issuing a pronouncement in favour of the war, the resolution submitted in February 1900, with arguments for and against, was: " Are you in favour of an official pronouncement being made now by the Fabian Society on imperialism in relation to war?" The membership at that time was about 800, of whom 50 lived abroad, and in all only 476 votes were cast, 217 in favour of a pronouncement and 259 against. Whereupon, as stated above, the MacDonalds and thirteen other members resigned from the Society.[1]

This, however, did not settle the matter. Within a few months of the secession which was jestingly referred to as " the Boer trek ", it became apparent that a general election in Great Britain would be forced by the Government. The Society would necessarily have to take a hand in a contest in which not the Boer War alone, but the whole policy of Joseph Chamberlain's imperialism, would be the dominant issue. The executive committee accordingly deputed a small committee to prepare the necessary election manifesto, and persuaded Bernard Shaw to act as draftsman. What, after prolonged discussion, he supplied, with incomparable skill, was a pamphlet of 100 pages, which brought out the Fabian position, but also did justice to the various valid criticisms and necessary qualifications expressed by all the most fanatical partisans of the Boers, on the one hand, and the patriots, on the other. The draft was again submitted to a full meeting of members, at which all sorts of criticisms

[1] *The History of the Fabian Society,* by Edward Pease, pp. 128-30.

were made and diligently noted by the draftsman, the meeting ending by adopting the statement by acclamation. The resulting pamphlet, published at one shilling as *Fabianism and the Empire*, was naturally ignored by the party newspapers and the rival parliamentary candidates. But it had its educational effect on those whom it reached, and it reads to-day, as, perhaps, the most prescient and permanently instructive public document of its date, notably as regards the relative rights and duties of the white and the coloured citizens of the Empire.

To this introduction I may add a domestic detail. My eight brothers-in-law, all of them more or less political-minded, represented every grade of opinion in favour of and against the war, from die-hard Tory imperialists to stubborn pro-Boers; we two sitting comfortably in the middle, speaking soothing words to each and all—an agreeable circumstance which tended to make our little house in Grosvenor Road, for the first time, a common centre for my sisters and their children.

Torquay, January 31*st.*—The last six months, and especially the last month at Plymouth, have been darkened by the nightmare of war. The horrible consciousness that we have, as a nation, shown ourselves to be unscrupulous in methods, vulgar in manners as well as inefficient, is an unpleasant background to one's personal life—a background always present, when one wakes in the night and in the intervals of leisure during the day. The Boers are, man for man, our superiors in dignity, devotion and capacity—yes, *in capacity*. That, to a ruling race, is the hardest hit of all. It may be that war was inevitable: I am inclined to think it was: but that it should come about through muddy intrigues and capitalist pressure and that we should have proved so incapable alike in statesmanship and in generalship is humiliating. I sometimes wonder whether we could take a beating and be the better for it? This would be the real test of the heart and intellect of the British race: much more so than if we succeed after a long and costly conflict. If we win, we shall soon forget the lessons of the war. Once again we shall have " muddled through ". Pecuniary self-interest will be again rehabilitated as an Empire-building principle. Once again the English gentleman, with his so-called habit of command, will have proved to be the equal of the foreign expert with his scientific knowledge. Once again our politicians and staff officers will bask in the smiles of London "society", and will chatter bad metaphysics and worse economics in country house parties, imagining themselves to be men of the world because they have neither the knowledge nor the industry to be professional administrators and skilled soldiers.

To us public affairs seem gloomy; the middle-classes are materialistic, and the working-class stupid, and in large sections sottish, with no interest except in racing odds, whilst the Government of the country is firmly in the hands of little cliques of landlords and great capitalists, and their hangers-on. The social enthusiasm that inspired the intellectual proletariat of ten years ago has died down and given place to a wave of scepticism about the desirability, or possibility, of any substantial change in society as we know it. There may be the beginnings of intellectual curiosity, but it is still a flicker and not a flame. And, meanwhile, the rich are rolling in wealth and every class, except the sweated worker, has more than its accustomed livelihood. Pleasure and ease are desired by all men and women: science, literature and art, even social ambition and party politics, have given way to the love of mental excitement and physical enjoyment. If we found ourselves faced with real disaster, should we as a nation have the nerve and persistency to stand up against it? That is the question that haunts me.

February 20th.—Meanwhile, our little schemes with regard to the new University of London prosper. We have got the School recognised as a Faculty of Economics, we have secured a site and a building, free of cost, and an income of £2500 devoted to economics and commercial science. Sidney will be a member of the Faculty and will probably represent the County Council on the Senate. Best of all he has persuaded the Royal Commission to recognise economics as a science and not merely as a subject in the Arts Faculty. The preliminary studies for the economics degree will, therefore, be mathematics and biology. This divorce of economics from metaphysics and shoddy history is a great gain. We have always claimed that the study of the structure and function of society was as much a science as the study of any other form of life, and ought to be pursued by the scientific methods used in other organic sciences. Hypothesis ought to be used, not as the unquestioned premiss from which to deduce an unquestioned conclusion, but as an order of thought to be verified by observation and experiment. Such history as will be taught at the School will be the history of social institutions discovered from documents, statistics and the observation of the actual structure and working of living organisations. This attainment of our aim—the starting of the School as a department of science—is the result of a chapter of fortunate accidents. There was the windfall of the Hutchinson Trust, then the selection of Hewins as director, the grant from the T.E.B. towards commercial education, the coming of Creighton to London as Bishop, and the successful packing of the University of London Commission. Then again we are humble folk whom nobody suspects of power; and Sidney's opinions on educational matters are considered moderate and sound as neither anti- nor pro-ecclesiastic. And we have had two very good friends helping us—Haldane and the Bishop of London, both of them trusting us completely in our own range of subjects. Of course, the School is at present extremely imperfect: its reputation is better than its performance. But we have no illusions, and we see clearly what we intend the School to become and we are convinced that the science will emerge.

February 23rd.—Beatrice Chamberlain came to lunch on Wednesday, ostensibly to tell me about poor Clara Ryland,[1] but really to find out what we felt about the Transvaal. She was as vigorous and attractive as is her wont, a fine generous nature, reflecting the best side of her father. Her tone about the Transvaal was far more moderate and magnanimous than I expected—not nearly so partisan as some of my sisters. Against Steyn of the Free State she was distinctly venomous and she was deprecatory of Schreiner and the Cape Government. " They have been deplorably weak, they have run from one side to the other, imploring each alternately to climb down. And, though Schreiner eventually slipped down on our side, he did so not out of loyalty but merely to save himself." All this I disputed with some warmth. When her carriage was announced, I noticed a look of nervous dissatisfaction on her face and she went to put on her veil, I following. With an effort she broke out: " You will congratulate Papa on having smashed his detractors last night? "[2] " We have never attached much importance to the telegram," I answered affectionately. " What other people say Mr. Chamberlain said is not evidence," I added. Her face brightened and she said something about misunderstandings of conversations when two persons were referring to different things—from which I gather that we are right in assuming that the telegrams are similar in character to those already published. If only Chamberlain

---

[1] Clara Ryland, youngest sister of Joseph Chamberlain. She had recently lost her husband. (Ed.)

[2] On February 20, D. H. Thomas (afterwards Lord Rhondda) moved in the House for a " full enquiry to be made into the origin and circumstances . . . of the incursion into the South African Republic of an armed force in 1895 ". To old arguments about the whitewashing of Rhodes and " missing telegrams ", the anti-war party added references to these documents stolen by a clerk from Bourchier Hawksley's office. Chamberlain's reply was volcanic. " It was a splendid exhibition of parliamentary genius ", reported the old *St. James' Gazette*, " and cannot fail to enhance even Mr. Chamberlain's reputation "; while the *Daily Chronicle*, which loved him not, described the speech as " a brilliant rhetorical feat, however much or little it answered the point of the indictment ". See *Life of Joseph Chamberlain*, J. L. Garvin, vol. iii. pp. 550-55. (Ed.)

had not whitewashed Rhodes! Though I am inclined to believe that his defence of Rhodes sprang from a defiant loyalty to a man in whose devotion to the Empire he has complete confidence, this explanation is not quite convincing.

March 8th.—A week with Herbert Spencer at Brighton. Combined a visit to him with some days' work at vestry and municipal records. The old man is better and more benign than I have seen him for years. But, about the world in general and England in particular, he is terribly pessimistic. " Heading straight towards military despotism: the people will get what they deserve. I remember ", he continued, " being angry many years ago with an Irishman for saying that the English were a stupid race. I should not be angry now, I should only add that they are brutal as well as stupid." He still retains his personal affection for me—more out of habit, I think, for every year he becomes more suspicious of our aims and of our power of reaching these aims. His housekeeping has become quite comfortable: two bright young persons as housekeeper and pianist respectively, three maids, a houseboy, coachman and a secretary, all dancing attendance on the old man. His secretary has not had a holiday for ten years and his two young ladies are kept close at it all day and every day, " making a pleasant circle for me ", he calls it. He is despotic—humanely despotic, anxious for their health and for his view of what ought to be their pleasures. But he is intensely suspicious that he is being done by his housekeeper or his servants, and certain that he is chronically cheated by his tradesmen. " Interests, interests, interests, that is what dominates the world: if you are to get your rights, you must be perpetually distrusting every one. And it is your duty to exact your rights ", he added with a snarl. Poor old man, it is pathetic to see a nature so transparently sincere, so eager to attain truth, warped by long-continued flattery and subordination of others to his whims and fancies into the character of a complete egotist, pedantic and narrow-minded—a true Casaubon.

March 16th.—Utterly done up with a week of dissipation. The day I came back I dined with Alfred [Cripps] at the House of Commons in a private room without ventilation—a veritable hole of Calcutta. Margaret Hobhouse had to leave, finding it unbearable. I struggled on, chatting with Carson, a clever, cynical and superficial Irishman—an ultra Tory on all questions. " Gerald Balfour, the worst Irish Secretary we have had: he and his brother have done more to make Home Rule possible than all the preceding governments put together. When he leaves, he will leave all parties united clamouring for Home Rule by making it clear that it is not worth while being loyal ", was his emphatic summing-up of the situation. It was not surprising to me that Carson thought that John Morley had been an admirable Secretary: " In all his administration he followed the advice of the Unionists ". On Friday, we had a little dinner of friends here: on Sunday, we supped with Willie Cripps: on Monday, I debated in the Chelsea Town Hall with an anti-regulationist; on Tuesday, we had to dine with us the Creightons and Professor Ramsay to talk London University, and on Wednesday, we dined with Haldane to meet a select party of Rose-berites including the great man himself. Haldane sat me down next Lord Rosebery against the will of the latter who tried his best to avoid me as a neighbour, but all to no purpose, Haldane insisting on his changing places. He is a strange being, self-conscious and sensitive to a more extreme degree than any mortal that I have ever come across. Notwithstanding this absurd self-consciousness, he has a peculiar personal charm, the secret, I imagine, of his hold on a section of the Liberal Party and of the public. At first he avoided speaking to me. But, feeling that our host would be mortified if his little scheme failed utterly, I laid myself out to be pleasant to my neighbour, though he aggravated and annoyed me by his ridiculous airs: he might be a great statesman, a Royal Prince, a beautiful woman and an artistic star, all rolled into one. " Edward," called out Lord Rosebery to Sir Edward Grey as the latter, arrayed in Court dress, hurried away to the Speaker's party, " don't tell the world of this new intrigue of Haldane's." And I believe Lord Rosebery winked as he glanced at me sitting by him. Which showed that he has at least a sense of humour. For the party *was* an intrigue of Haldane's—an attempt to piece together an anti-little-England combination out of the most miscellaneous morsels of political influence. " I feel deeply honoured at the place you gave me, Mr. Haldane," said I, as he saw me out of his luxurious flat, " but, if I were four-and-twenty hours in the same house with that man, I should be rude to him." Haldane is now amusing himself by weaving, from his gossiping imagination, a Rosebery-Webb myth.

Consequent on all this dissipation no work at the book and a feeling of disconsolate blankness when I look at our accumulating material. My brain is all wool, and my thoughts are woolgathering.

July 19*th.*—A month in London entertaining, especially seeing sisters, and snatching from the waste of energy two or three mornings at the British Museum over local newspapers. Longing to get back to quiet days of absorption in our subject. Sidney struggling on, engineer-ing the School, its site, its buildings, its income and its status as a university institution. Breakfast 8, sharp: reading together at British Museum from 9.15 to 1 o'clock: then back to lunch and he off to his committees, I to waste my time—always someone to lunch or to dinner, or dining out or calling—some distraction taking one's thoughts

from profitable brooding over local government. For our present work
—pushing the School, and our enquiry into local government—some
social connections are needful. The same old problem, how much
sacrifice of personal efficiency to personal influence? In England, all
power to establish new undertakings rests on your influence over the
various ruling cliques. The more cliques you are in touch with the
easier it is to lay broad foundations. On the other hand, your power
for good depends, in the long run, on the quality of your special
product; and this last depends on whole-hearted devotion to your
subject. The sort of compromise I make is to take the summer weeks
in London as my holiday, and to turn the times that would be holidays
into periods of sustained research. But we both look forward to the
time when long months in the country will give us at once time for
work and delightful recreation.

We have seen much of the Leonard Courtneys this spring. Leonard's
determined support of the Boers' plea for independence, even more
his denunciation of the war, has alienated him from both political
parties. The Tories regard him as a wholly unendurable person; the
vast majority of Liberals consider him to be a quixotic crank; even
the tiny group of pro-Boer Radicals think that his speeches and mani-
festoes are often out of season. It is only among the I.L.P. and S.D.F.
working-men that he finds enthusiastic followers in his anti-Govern-
ment crusade. A strange turn in the wheel of political popularity! He
is too absorbed in the consciousness of a great wrong done, too fervently
convinced that there is only one way out of the tragedy, to care much
for his own political career. What hurt him most, oddly enough, is the
social boycott: Leonard has always enjoyed the leisurely society of
persons of culture and position, and to-day he and Kate find themselves without the accustomed invitations.[1] The disinterestedness and
robustness of his convictions has impressed some of the elect; but a
cynical public has been annoyed and irritated by his tone of moral
indignation and his assumption of moral superiority. He has flung in

[1] Leonard Courtney was returned for Liskeard at a by-election of 1877 and held
the seat until the 1900 election, when he retired from the candidature owing to the
refusal of both parties, Conservative and Liberal, to support him. "When Courtney
was elected", wrote Justin M'Carthy, "I remember having a talk with an experienced Member of the House, who set himself up as an authority on all political
questions. 'Mark my words,' he said to me with an air of portentous wisdom, 'he
will be a dead failure in the House of Commons.' I did mark his words, and
Courtney was not a dead failure, but a very live success." (*Reminiscences*, ii. p. 369.)

"We are completely and entirely out of it", wrote Kate Courtney in her diary,
September 24, 1900: "my great man is in splendid isolation. To Ripon to stay
at Studley Royal. We were met by telegrams, and telegrams continued for the two
days we were there, mostly from various hopeless constituencies, suggesting he
should stand. Two requests for a speech from Exeter and Battersea, which we
acceded to after some hesitation."

the face of a nominally Christian, but really unbelieving world, Kruger's faith in God; and the majority of good citizens have resented it because they have not dared to answer back what they think, that such a faith in God unfits a man to be the ruler of an independent state. This very morning Kate produced from a blue-book a nobly felt and finely expressed letter from Kruger to an Englishman in January 1900, tense with religious fervour. " Kruger really believes in God, and God's government of this world ", I cheerfully admitted, a sentiment accepted by Kate as granting the whole case for the Boers. " Which proves to me ", I added sadly, " that he is an impossible person for the rest of this wicked world to treat with." Kate looked shocked, and almost asked me to leave the house on the spot. Dear Kate is an incurable sentimentalist and has no sense of humour: she gives happiness and increased self-assurance to Leonard; but she aggravates his one big fault—his inveterate mental habit of thinking everyone who disagrees with him immoral and unenlightened. All the same, there are few mortals for whom I have so continuous an affection and respect as I have for Leonard Courtney and his loving satellite.

Political parties become daily more chaotic. The Tories are, as a party, complete cynics bound together by a rampant imperialism, alternately protecting vested interests and appealing to demagogic passions they do not themselves share. But, at any rate, they understand the game of " follow the leader ". The great Liberal Party—" the engine of progress "—has lost its old faith and has no notion in which direction progress lies. The rank and file mete out contempt impartially to all their titular leaders. Captain Lambton, for instance, who believes neither in Home Rule nor Local Veto, still less in Disestablishment, and is an enthusiastic supporter of the Government's South African policy, is standing as Liberal candidate for Newcastle—John Morley's old constituency. Meanwhile, Leonard Courtney and John Morley are acclaimed as the only honest politicians by the recognised Labour leaders, who have one and all gone pro-Boer. The Fabian Society, it must be admitted, is completely out of it, the majority believing in the inevitability of the war, whilst the minority regard the majority as being the worst kind of traitors.

September.—On our way down to-day [from local government investigation up North] we found Haldane at Newcastle and travelled with him to York. He was full of political talk. " Not a single issue is being discussed at this election that will be remembered two years hence ", was his summing-up of the situation. For the last four months he has spent all his time, left over from his income-earning at the Bar, on building up the Liberal Imperialist Party. He obstinately maintains that no frontal attack on social and industrial evils is possible for the Liberal Party: they must gain the confidence of the electors on foreign policy and any social reform must come by " turning movements ". The Tory majority, he thinks, will be diminished; and the present Government will not last more than two or three years more. Balfour is tired of it, Chamberlain is the only strong man and he is universally distrusted as supreme ruler. " This Government is rotten: no young shoots and much dead wood. Moreover, it is tainted with jobbery and corrupt contracting: the Birmingham ring has made money out of the war: though little is said, the electors don't like it. It is only the emergency of the Transvaal settlement, and the uncertainty as to who and what the Liberal leaders are, that will make the elector continue the Tories in office." He intimated that the Liberals would reform after the election, with Rosebery as leader, Asquith as first lieutenant, and Perks as organiser. " Then money will flow in and everyone who dreams of a peerage or a baronetcy will send in his cheque ", added Haldane with a cynical shrug.

October 7th.—Haldane's anticipation of a diminished Government majority seems hardly likely to be fulfilled. The Liberal Party divided against itself, uncertain as to its policy, is being badly routed at the polls. The " strong man " of the Government has played it down low to the " man in the street ": the " street " has answered back with emphatic approval. And, in doing so, the electors have shown common sense. Who could trust a party with a lay figure as ostensible leader, and as the real leaders of its sections men who hate each other, and each other's ideas, more than they do the persons or the views of the enemy. And there seems little hope for the Liberals in the near future. To win back the large towns they have to give up Home Rule, Local Veto, and Disestablishment; they have to become imperialists and develop some kind of social programme. In giving up the old politics, they alienate the Celtic fringes, and all the provincial Liberal politicians: in imperialism, they cannot outbid the Tories: in all social questions, they lack knowledge or conviction and fear to lose their remaining rich men. So they will fall back on the Rosebery plan of " no policy ", hoping that they may be accepted as the only alternative to the Government gone stale. That may cause the adhesion, one by one, of men (mostly of the upper and middle classes) who are personally offended with the Government: or who belong to interests that are threatened by the expenditure and innovation of Tory democracy. But it will not bring back to their ranks the great mass of town workers who want some strong lead: something blatant and positive in return for their votes.

Meanwhile, we go on, little concerned with the stress and storms of politics. Now and again we have a qualm lest the huge Conservative majorities in London constituencies may mean a Moderate victory in L.C.C. elections in March. Otherwise a Conservative Government is as good for us as a Liberal Government, presided over by such men as Sir Henry Fowler. We realise every day more strongly, that we can never hope to get hold of the " man in the street ": we are " too damned intellectual ", as a shrewd journalist remarked. All we can hope to do is to find out for ourselves the actual facts and embody them in a more or less scientific form, and to trust to other people to get this knowledge translated into popular proposals. What is more probable is the silent use of this knowledge in the unperceived transformations of law and government by men and women of goodwill. Our business is to be friendly to men of all parties—to *try* to be charitable and unassuming, and to go on with our own work persistently and loyally. Sidney, in his administrative work, has considerable power to build up London secondary and university education on the lines he believes in; with the London School of Economics we have, in our own hands, the forming of the economic and political science teaching of the new university, and through the new faculty the gradual establishment of a new science and a new art. That, with our own research work, ought to be sufficient for our faculties, indeed, it may prove to be beyond them!

November.—One sad result of this election is the exclusion of Leonard Courtney from Parliament. He and Kate have fought splendidly for the cause they believe in, and though they accept the fact that the country is dead against them—they have accepted it with quite magnificent cheerfulness. And yet to Leonard it means probably an end to his career, the loss of an occupation which gave him public influence, agreeable society, and which minimised the results of his loss of sight. Fortunately for him, he has a devoted and sympathetic wife who lives for him and for his ideas, shares every feeling and every thought, and whose faith in his essential greatness is only increased by the world's neglect! And he has the staying power of strongly religious feeling, and a firm faith (though its particular form I have never been able to discover) enabling him to dismiss questions of personal gain as irrelevant alike in thought and action. If Leonard had been endowed with more intellectual humility and sympathy, with more desire for work, he might have become a great power for good. As it is, he has been " a voice crying in the wilderness ", ennobling and stimulating those who have chanced to hear and understand him.

December 9th.—A delightful Sunday with the Bertrand Russells and Haldane—talking philosophy, university organisation and politics.

Haldane still devotedly attached to Rosebery: trying hard to make friends for him even among such humble folk as ourselves and the Russells. And we used our opportunity to press for the adoption of this policy of a national minimum of health, education and efficiency, leaving free play to the competition between private enterprise and public administration *above* that minimum. " Rosebery has his back to the wall and will not be forced into a premature declaration of policy: all he is pledged to, is that there shall be no tampering with the Empire." But we are to meet Rosebery again: apparently, the great man is an admirer of *Fabianism and the Empire* and has sent various gracious messages to Shaw.

December.—Our autumn has been dissipated with odds and ends. Sidney has been absorbed in his administrative work. London University proves to be the most formidable addition to the L.C.C. and Technical Education Board. The Senate of 50 more or less distinguished folk, many unknown to each other, and drawn from all sections of society, without procedure and with extraordinarily incompetent officers inherited from the old " examining board ", is the most difficult body to get into working order. The Chancellor, Vice-Chancellor and Registrar are simple obstructionists, and represent respectively apathy, stupidity and ill-will, each carried to its *n*th. All that is done has to be done in spite of them; and, of course, as far as Lord Kimberley and Sir H. Roscoe are concerned, it is impossible to be otherwise than outwardly acquiescent and respectful. Sooner or later the running of the University will, I think, fall largely to Sidney and Hewins and one or two others: at present it is chaos. Meanwhile, we have been spending our substance on giving little dinners to diverse senators: trying to make them understand each other and accept Sidney's view of university organisation.

1901

January 2nd, 1901.—Back in London after a few days with the Playnes and Hobhouses. The sisters do not grow apart as years roll on: indeed, the last few years have seemed to bring us all nearer together. Blood relationship is a very tenacious tie: it outlasts many relationships of choice—wears better than any other relationship (except marriage), though it is seldom so close or satisfying as the special intimacy of the moment. For, as one gets middle-aged, intimate friendships seem to fade away, and one is too much occupied and, in a sense, too utilitarian, to make new friends. One sees persons who are for the time one's fellow-workers and these individuals are not necessarily sympathetic. Old friends die, or marry, or become estranged or indifferent: of my early friendships few remain: the Booths and Margaret Harkness estranged, Carrie Browne dead, the Barnetts, Ben Jones, Ella Pycroft, Alice Green, Bella Fisher and Marie Souvestre all extremely friendly when we meet, but we meet, perhaps, once a year: in the case of these latter, perhaps, two or three times a year. There is, it is true, Herbert Spencer whom I occasionally visit, out of piety towards an old sentiment. Then the " two dear comrades and friends " who for some half-dozen years regularly spent their holidays with us—Wallas and Shaw—are both of them married; and, though here again when we meet we meet as old friends, we seldom see each other. . . . And, possibly, they would all of them say that we were too much absorbed in each other to care for others and that our friendliness was more an overflow of our happiness than any special love for them. In fact, a sort of universal benevolence to all comers seems to take the place of special affection for chosen friends. It is only the persistent yet slack tie of sisterhood that seems to survive these inroads of indifference.

The man we see most of nowadays is Hewins: every Tuesday he lunches with us to discuss the affairs of the School. He is original-minded and full of energy and faith. Shaw always declares he is a fanatic. So he is. But he is also a born manipulator. We never know whether he is telling us his real opinion, or his real intention. We feel that we are being " handled " just as we watch him handling others. He ought to have been an ecclesiastic: and would have entered the Church if it had not been for the 39 Articles to be swallowed, just at a time when physical science and historical criticism made these tenets seem intellectually contemptible. In thought, he would be a reactionary if the present trend of Liberal opinion did not happen to be a reaction from the doctrine of " individual freedom ". He hates disorder; he detests protestantism; or following the " inner light ", or any other rebellion against the reasonable will of the community. He is a great admirer of Chamberlain; dislikes all the Liberal leaders equally; votes Progressive, and is a member of the National Liberal Club. He is a Churchman and an ardent believer in the scientific method in economics and politics. He is disinterested with regard to money: he is ambitious of power—altogether he is one big paradox. But the most characteristic paradox of his nature is the union of the fanatic and the manipulator. With such a character it is difficult to be intimate, however much it may excite one's admiration, liking and interest.

Naturally enough we have a large circle of friendly acquaintances, some of whom might be considered friends. Haldane, the Reeveses, the Bishop of London and Louise Creighton, the women factory inspectors, Lion Phillimore, the Bertrand Russells, the staff of the London School of Economics, the senators of the new University, the

Bishop of Rochester [Talbot] and his wife, Sir Alfred Lyall, the Richard Stracheys, and other more or less interesting folk—come and go: a still larger circle leave cards and force me, by so doing, to trudge to all the quarters of residential London. But, for the most part, we have been left to ourselves and allowed to spend our energies on our own special work.

At present, I am writing the opening chapters to a small book on *Factory Legislation: its Theory and Practice*, or rather adapting portions of our Part III. of *Industrial Democracy* to a more popular audience. I have also undertaken to edit the remaining chapters, and to see the whole through the press. It is to be a counterblast to the persistent opposition to factory legislation on the part of the " women's rights " movement reinforced by the employers' wives. This opposition has for the last ten years blocked all progress in the effective application of the Factory Acts to other industries. It is led by a few blatant agitators, who would not count for much if they were not backed up by many " society " women who belong to the governing clique, and by a solid opposition to further reform from vested interests. What we have to do is to detach the *great employer*, whose profits are too large to feel the immediate pressure of regulation and who stands to gain by the increased efficiency of the factors of production, from the ruck of small employers or stupid ones. What seems clear is that we shall get no further instalments of reform unless we gain the consent of an influential minority of the threatened interest. I feel sometimes in despair about the book. Beyond a little mechanical research, my mind has been entirely off the subject of local government, either preparing lectures on industrial competition, or on methods of research, or brooding over the religious question and the provision of a metaphysic and a mental hygiene. I have been reading at large on these questions: theology, saints' lives, James' *Will to Believe*, and his *Psychology*, various works on scientific method, and so on. The one subject my mind revolts at is local government. But we shall have to set to and *do it* directly the L.C.C. election is over. I am making elaborate arrangements for a good five months in the country, and hope to accomplish at least the first part (prior to 1835). We have masses of material, but all the thinking has to be done.

January 15th, 1901.—Mandell Creighton—Bishop of London— dead. One of our best friends. When we returned to London this autumn we found him invalided. He had broken down on his holiday, and was by the doctor's orders confined to the house. Three or four times I went down to Fulham to see him either with Sidney or alone. He was singularly gentle and sympathetic: eager to talk: the same delightful combination of banter and deep philosophy: the same strange enigmatical view of all things, whether of God or man. The very last time, in fact, just before Christmas, I had a long talk with him whilst the other guests were at tea. I told him our plan for reforming the Church; our idea of religion as mental hygiene, and the way in which we thought the High Church doctrine more consistent with it, than the Evangelical. To all of which he listened, and half seriously and half playfully agreed. Then I sent him James' *Will to Believe* and this note was the last word from him.

I first knew the Creightons in August 1887. I remember so well that visit to Worcester: my interest in the versatile and pleasant ecclesiastic and don, my attraction to the handsome and direct-minded Louise, so different from each other, and yet so completely complementary. From that time forward I remained a friend, and until they came to London used constantly to visit them. These visits to Cambridge and Worcester were among the happiest days of my life—during the long and trying time of Father's illness: the friendship, coming just at a time when I was suffering intensely, seemed a new opening into the world of distinguished men and women. And from the first they liked and trusted me—liked me for my best side. When I engaged myself to Sidney, they accepted him as their friend without hesitation; saw him through my eyes, and trusted him as they had trusted me.

Meanwhile, Dr. Creighton had changed the life of a professor and author for that of a bishop. There are many of his friends who regretted the step. The freedom of view, the brilliant dialectic, the subtle paradox, which often covered a daring hypothesis—all these were in place in a Cambridge don; they became impossible, or at any rate most baffling, in a bishop. Agnostic friends, sensitive to the proprieties of life, no longer dared to join in this intellectual adventure, with one who ought to feel himself to be a successor of the apostles. And, owing to a strange contrariness and rebellious audacity, a reaction possibly from the daily routine of a bishop's life, the change of position seemed for a time to accentuate the frivolous side of his intercourse with the outer world. Smart stories, somewhat cynical repartee, took the place of free and easy discussion of metaphysical questions. It was not possible to treat as " open questions " matters upon which a bishop had to lay down the law according to his pledges. On the other hand, he was not willing to give up his position as a member of the republic of letters, tolerant of all views and ready to be convinced by evidence. Hence, between him and the more serious-minded of his heterodox friends there arose a certain atmosphere of constraint. In our case, this was neutralised by his unfailing interest in our educational and research work. For, outside the spiritual side of life, Creighton believed implicitly in the scientific method of observation and verification. And he believed in organisation and machinery, in the regulation of conduct by law or public opinion, according to some deliberately conceived idea of social expediency. He had no faith in democracy; though he accepted it as necessary: his contempt for the politician amounted almost to intolerance. Lack of brains was to him the greatest social danger: with brains and goodwill no change was impracticable. Without intellectual leadership, the average man, however good his conduct, would remain in a state of squalor and mediocrity.

Is Dr. Creighton a convinced Christian? was the question perpetually canvassed by his friends. I always felt it an impertinence for an agnostic to raise the question. His tolerance, his desire to find a common basis with all his friends, made him deliberately stow away his Christian assumptions when he talked with heretics. " Let us find something on which we can agree, and argue on that basis ", was always his attitude of mind. He realised that the ultimate convictions of serious-minded persons could not be altered by a conversation: that they were rooted in their experience of life, or in the constitution of their minds. He never, therefore, tried to convert: all he did was to endeavour to sympathise and to justify. Probably this uncommon willingness to accept any person's fundamental assumptions, as a basis for argument, was the root of the feeling of many persons that he was intellectually insincere. Personally, I believe he had a firm belief in the validity of the Christian faith, and in its ultimate victory over other forms of thought.

Rightly or wrongly, Creighton believed that, for a state Church you must put forward a lay as well as a spiritual justification. " Baptism is the finest system of birth registration; Christianity is popular metaphysic; missions are a method of teaching the subordinate races the assumptions of their governors "—these and other sayings crept up in his conversation, addresses and charges. All this was sadly secular. The clergyman was not only a priest of the mystical body of Christ, he was also an extra official of the state charged with a certain supervision over education, poor law, and even sanitary work. Hence, during his reign in London, the Church was encouraged to throw itself bodily on the side of good, and even progressive, government in all local concerns. His own daughter he encouraged to become a manager, not of the voluntary schools, but of the board schools in Fulham. His conception was that the Church was to take its part in the secular affairs of the nation; its part being to keep up the standard of integrity, energy, scrupulousness and exact knowledge. In his short term of office he had assumed, to a large extent, the leadership of London life in secular as well as in spiritual matters; Nonconformists and secularists read his addresses with as much interest and, perhaps, even more edification than fervent churchmen. The last time I saw him he playfully remarked that he would resign his bishopric and retire to a cottage and " write messages to the English people ". These messages would, I am convinced, have mainly consisted in advice on secular matters.

Our intimacy with Dr. Creighton, and to a lesser extent with Dr. Talbot, has brought constantly before us the Church, its present difficulties and its future. Any outside demand for disestablishment and disendowment is dead at the present moment. A few political dissenters and Radical political workers in the smaller provincial towns still hold to the old doctrine of the iniquity of a union between Church and State. But, as far as the bulk of the people are concerned, this doctrine is obsolete. The town workman is now neither a Nonconformist nor a secularist, he is simply indifferent to the whole question of religion or metaphysic. On the other hand, he is inclined to think the hardworking curate, who runs his club, looks after his children on Sundays and holidays, stirs up the sanitary inspector and is sympathetic because acquainted with the struggle for better conditions of employment, a good fellow. He sees the dissenting parson moving out to the suburbs, the rich congregation preferring a new and fine building there to the old meeting-place down town. But the priest of the established Church remains in the old city parish, and is constantly abroad in the slums. The workman sees no distinction between the appropriation of the Church income by the clergy and the appropriation of mining royalties or ground values by the landlords, except in the expenditure of the income—a comparison immensely in favour of the clergyman. " The majority of them do a day's work for us and live among us, and it is precious poor pay they get for doing it ", is a frequently heard remark. " If we take to disendowing and disestablishing, we will deal with the landlords first ", is the half-conscious thought of the revolutionary workman. The educated classes who are not Church members are also losing their objections. " Nature abhors a vacuum: all metaphysic is equally untenable if you require scientific proof: the Christian metaphysic no more than the Hegelian. Why not leave the people with the old traditional faith? " are the dictates of the enlightened. " If the people wanted three state churches, I see no reason why they should not have them ", remarked Lord Rosebery. Moreover, state endowment, state control, state ownership, are all the order of the day.

Hence, there is no fear of destruction from without. But within there are disruptive tendencies. No man of culture can nowadays be a Protestant churchman of the old type—the dogma and doctrine, the written word of revelation are too ugly and impossible taken in their crudity. To be acceptable to the cultivated person the whole thing must be transformed by mysticism, by vague emotion, by the charm of tradition, on the one hand, and the hope of doctrinal development, on the other. Christianity must have its past and its future; and each alike must be different from its present. Hence, unrest in the Church and the initiation and elaboration of ritual and discipline, to cover up diversity of thought and feeling. " More room," cries the young churchman, " freedom from the limitations of the Elizabethan compromise." " Let us push forward where thought and feeling lead us." " Impossible," says the lawyer, " here are the 39 Articles, and I am charged as the representative of the state to interpret them, and eventually to enforce them."

Our suggestion is briefly this: we want no more vexatious prosecutions. Hence, abolish the right of the individual to prosecute, make prosecution the function of the vestry of ratepayers. If the inhabitants of the parish are satisfied with the clergyman, let him have absolute freedom to develop. If, on the other hand, he has failed to satisfy them, give them the power to prosecute him for breaches either of doctrine or ritual, or for non-performance of his duties. Let the court be, in the first place, his bishop, and ultimately the bench of bishops; if either party appeals, sweep away the bishop's veto on prosecutions—it is sheer nonsense to give a judge a veto on prosecutions and, unnecessary, if you otherwise provide against mere capricious prosecutions from individuals. Sweep away the civil jurisdiction over the Church. We do not want a lawyer's interpretation of the 39 Articles in the prayer book—we want a sympathetic interpretation by persons whose whole duty and life is to consider the national needs in the matter of religion. The secular state gets its control over the Church by the Prime Minister's nomination of the bishops and by parliamentary power to legislate. That is sufficient. Give such a Church, deriving its authority directly or indirectly from the people, freedom to develop along its own lines.

Of course, our object is to enable the Church to grow out of its present superstitious doctrine and obsolete form. We have faith that the development would be along the right lines. No doubt, at first, the direction would be sacerdotal and ritualistic. Personally, I do not altogether object to this. The more ritual, the more mystery, the more indefiniteness of thought, the greater the play for emotional purposes. Exactly, as in practical life, in the choice of ways and means, the scientific method, full and undefiled, must be exclusively relied on, so it seems to me in the higher ranges, in the choice of motives and ideals, it is a mistake to intellectualise, the expression must be obscure and elastic so as not to debase the purpose in the act of expression. And, though there are aspects of the priest which are distasteful, yet I desire to see the minister of religion practising the art of mental hygiene. I do not believe that the ordinary man is capable of prescribing for the diseases of the soul any more than they are for the diseases of the body. We need the expert here as elsewhere. Religion, to my mind, should consist in the highest metaphysic, music and ritual, and mental hygiene.

And I desire that the national life should have its *consciously* religious side. If, as a state, we are purely rationalistic and selfish in our motives and aims, we shall degrade the life of the individuals who compose the state. I should desire the Church to become the home of national communal aspirations as well as of the endeavour of the individual towards a better personal life. Meanwhile, I prefer the present Church, with all its faults, to blank materialism or competitive sectarianism.

To this short essay on Dr. Creighton, I add a more definite statement of my own outlook on life in the early years of the twentieth century.

January 25th, 1901.—Reading Leslie Stephen's *Utilitarians*. Always interesting to compare one's own point of view with that of one's parents! For Bentham was certainly Sidney's intellectual god-father; and though I have never read a word of him, his teaching was transmitted through Herbert Spencer's very utilitarian system of ethics, and his method through Spencer's deductive reasoning from certain primary assumptions. How has the position of the disciples shifted from that of their past teachers?

First, we agree that human action must be judged by its results in bringing about certain defined ends. There is no other sanction that we care to accept but results, though we should be inclined to give, perhaps, a wider meaning to results. For instance, the formation of a noble character, the increase of intellectual faculty, stimulus to sense of beauty, sense of conduct, even sense of humour, are all ends that we should regard as " sanctioning " action; quite apart from whether they produce happiness of one or all, or none. We altogether reject the " happiness of the greatest number " as a definition of our own end, though other persons are perfectly at liberty to adopt it as theirs. I reject it, because I have no clear vision of what I mean by happiness, or what other people mean by it. If happiness means physical enjoyment, it is an end which does not recommend itself to me—certainly not as the sole end. I prefer to define my end as the increase in the community of certain faculties and desires which I happen to like—love, truth, beauty and humour. Again, I have a certain vision of the sort of human relationships that I like and those that I dislike. But we differ from the Benthamites in thinking that it is necessary that we should all agree as to ends, or that these can be determined by any science. We believe that ends, ideals, are all what may be called in a large way " questions of taste " and we like a society in which there is a considerable variety in these tastes.

Science and the scientific method can be applied, not to the discovery of a right end, *but to a discovery of a right way of getting to any particular ends*. And here it seems to me the Benthamites fell lamentably short in their understanding of the scientific method. They ignored the whole process of verification. They deduced their ways of arriving at their own particular end—human happiness—from certain elementary observations of human nature: but they never sought to test this "order of thought " by the " order of things ". They never asked, Is it so? Now they were right in taking as their premiss an observation of human motive; they were right in forming a hypothesis deduced from this premiss. Where they went wrong, and most perniciously wrong, was in never attempting to verify and correct their hypothesis, and by this verification to discover other premises. Hence, they omitted from their calculation some of the most powerful impulses of human nature: reverence for mystery, admiration for moral beauty, longing for the satisfaction of an established expectation, custom and habit, tradition, sense of humour, sense of honour, passionate longing for truth, loyalty—besides a host of mean vanities and impulses none of which produce happiness or aim at producing it, but are just blind impulses.

February 9th.—Met Lord Rosebery at Haldane's again: Asquith, W. P. Reeves, Prof. Hewins, Prof. Massie and ourselves made up the party. I sat next to the great man who was gracious and less self-conscious than last time. But the entertainment was a futile business: we talked and laughed—" showed off "; we never got anywhere near a useful discussion on questions in which we were interested. Prof. Hewins, Sidney and I had hoped to talk about the School with Lord. Rosebery who is probably to be President, but we got nowhere near it. He is a strange capricious creature, always posing to himself and others, anxious only to attain right *expression*. I was angry with myself afterwards, and was strangely enough a bit vexed at being the only lady! That would not have mattered had we talked seriously—but in mere light banter—" the eternal feminine " will intrude, and in that case one likes companionship!

But, undoubtedly, our excursions into " society " advance the interests of the School. We are to have a meeting at the Mansion House with the Lord Mayor in the chair; Lord Rosebery to make a great pronouncement in favour of commercial education in the abstract and the School in the concrete, Lord Rothschild to act as treasurer and other great persons to play up—the whole intended to raise a building and endowment fund for the School. All this is Haldane's doing, partly out of friendship for us, partly because he wants to interest his chief in *uncompromising* advance movements. Also, he delights in intrigue, and is amusing himself with putting into one company the most unlikely co-workers. An institution which has united as its supporters ourselves, Rosebery, Rothschild, the Bishop of London and the Fabian Society, is just the sort of mixed party which Haldane revels in. " My dear Hewins," said Haldane, " you ignore the personal factor in politics." For Hewins, though he willingly accepts the result, does not wholly like this " society " development.

And, in truth, it has its unpleasant side. It is much wholesomer to win by hard work than by these capricious gusts of fancy in great folk. I feel that I am skating on rotten ice which might suddenly give way under me. I am not afraid of losing the support of the " personages ", because one does not count on its continuance and takes gratefully all one can get, knowing that it will come to an end. What I do fear is weakness in my own nature: incapacity to keep my intellect and heart set on our own work, undistracted by personal vanity or love of admiration. Fortunately, Sidney is absolutely single-minded. But, like Hewins, he does not quite like it.

March 8th.—Brilliant victory at the L.C.C. election. For the last three or four months (indeed since October) Sidney has been organising the election: writing the election literature, insinuating articles in the press, gathering up the Progressive forces all through London, as well as engineering the Deptford fight. We fully expected to lose seats in London, and a portion of our own Deptford majority. But the Water Companies, at the last moment, won our battle for us by their proposed water regulations.[1] Directly these appeared we knew the tide was in our favour; the only problem was to make it flow as swiftly as possible. Hence the articles contributed to all the halfpenny press, so that by the election day, every " halfpenny " was on our side and even the *Daily Telegraph* came out in our support! Still, the sweeping majority for the Progressives means that the London elector has confidence in the old gang which has now ruled London for twelve years; and that, in spite of the fact that the old gang are exclusively Radicals, whilst the vast majority of electors are Tories. It is a striking testimony to the industry and capacity of a small body of administrators. The Moderates, on the other hand, are mediocrities, the larger number of them will not work; as a party they suffer from the same fatal defect as the Liberal Party in national politics; the majority of them have un-

---

[1] These regulations imposed new and highly unpopular restrictions on what was already an inadequate water supply in many working-class districts. " *Vote for Monopoly and Bung—Unionist Candidates for the L.C.C.* ", ran a Progressive election pastor. (Ed.)

popular convictions and run away from them. To have unpopular convictions is bad enough: to run away from them is fatal.

And now that the election is over, we can at last turn to the book. I have already begun to sort both the material and my ideas for our country sojourn. I am not satisfied with myself, but hope to be more so after a course of country air and exercise and concentration on our subject. London life, with its constant clash of personalities—its attractions and repulsions, its manipulations and wire-pulling, is distracting and somewhat unwholesome. And this last year I seem to have passed into an emotional and imaginative phase, which, whilst it gives me a certain magnetic effect on others, knocks me to pieces myself. Indeed, I am becoming mediumistic. Country life and intellectual concentration will, I trust, bring back a saner frame of mind. Brainwork is a wonderful specific against the manifold forms of hysteria.

March 22nd.—Our long-planned meeting at the Mansion House came off yesterday. As far as we were concerned, there was no hitch in the arrangement. But, from Lord Rosebery's black looks when he came on the platform, something had evidently gone wrong, and afterwards we gathered that he had intended making the meeting an occasion to answer the somewhat futile remarks of Lord Salisbury on commercial education, but the Lord Mayor had intimated that such a course would be undesirable and that Lord Rosebery had, therefore, found himself cut off from the most effective part of his speech. It was not an able pronouncement but it sufficed, and has been a great advertisement for the School. Haldane spoke with real enthusiasm, and Harvey (of Glyn Mills) with knowledge of the subject. Lord Rothschild was unable to come but heads the contributions with £5000. The whole affair is an audacious advertisement and appeal. It will be a marvel if it does not provoke an attack on the management and teaching of the School. We are sufficiently firmly seated in the saddle to risk it. I feel that now we have done our utmost to give the School an independent life, it is time that it toddled out of our nursery and to some extent took its own line. Sidney is now turning his mind to the University and has drafted a scheme for its complete reorganisation as a great centre of applied science.

And now we can, or at any rate I can, turn my thoughts wholly to the book. Fortunately, my mind has become clear of the romancing which perturbed it a few weeks ago. One of those strange and mysterious alternations which go on seemingly uncaused in our mental life— a sudden regaining of complete control over thought and feeling and a positive *desire* to concentrate all mental energy on intellectual work. It is as if a hidden influence had been withdrawn and the mind again moved freely. But the mere physical exhaustion of London life prevents me doing good and sustained work. I am longing for our three months in the country.

Meanwhile, my boy is exceptionally well and happy. He is full of active thought and work: his health is excellent, he is conscious of success, and each day he seems more supremely happy in his love for me. All asperity and harshness has left him—he is always eager, but has lost the note of exasperation which used to characterise him. There is no slackening in his effort: he is perpetually working. He has as much if not more faith; though possibly faith in science has increased, and faith in any particular economic doctrine has decreased. He is less of a doctrinaire than of old, more of an investigator. He is not a leader of men, but he is an initiator of policies: his influence is not concentrated in his own personality, it ramifies through many organisations and persons, the outcome of multitudinous anonymous activities. And I think the setting I have given him, of simple fare and distinguished friends, suits him—both in reputation and taste. It satisfies his sense of consistency to adhere to a democratic standard of expenditure; and yet he reaps many of the advantages, in the scope and variety of social intercourse, of belonging to the inner circle of the political and scientific world.

April 2nd.—Hewins came as usual to lunch to-day: he was in thoroughly bad humour. No money to speak of has come in as the result of the Mansion House meeting, and he declares that the Mansion House meeting was a big failure. The plain truth is that, in the first place, he expected far too much from the meeting; in the second place, he managed with less skill than usual. He seems to have got on Rosebery's nerves, he failed to impress the Lord Mayor, and he delayed in sending out the appeal until five or six days after the meeting (we having understood that it went out on the very night of the meeting). Now he puts down the ill-success to the connection of the School with Lord Rosebery and the Fabian Society! We tried to calm and cheer him: suggested that Lord Rothschild's £5000 was more than we had originally thought of raising, and that at least the meeting had advertised the School. But he was not to be comforted. Hewins has three weak points: he suffers from attacks of quite unreasonable impatience and depression; he is a slack organiser of his staff; and he seldom takes his chiefs into his confidence as to what he really intends to do. This destroys any complete reliance on him. But he has a magnificent energy and persistence, loyalty to his own ideas (which are in the main the same as our own), and personal disinterestedness.

The three months between the first days of April and the beginning of July were spent, so far as I was concerned, with the Bertrand Russells at their house near Friday's Hill, working on our local government book: the Other One spending the mid-week in London on L.C.C. and other business. Here is a vision of the Bertrand Russells as they seemed to us in the spring of 1901.

July 1st. Friday's Hill.—The Russells are the most attractive married couple I know. Young and virtuous, they combine in the pair, personal charm, unique intelligence, the woman having the one, the man the other, in the superlative degree. Romantically attached to each other, they have diverse interests; Alys concerns herself with social reform, Bertrand with the higher mathematics. The scheme of their joint life is deliberately conceived to attain ends they both believe in, and it is persistently yet modestly carried out. The routine of their daily existence is as carefully planned and executed as our own. They breakfast together in their study at nine o'clock (we breakfast at 8!), then Bertrand works at mathematics until 12.30, then three-quarters-of-an-hour reading together, a quarter-of-an-hour stroll in the garden together. Lunch with us, 1.30; chat in our sitting-room or out of doors, over cigarettes and coffee. Then Bertrand plays croquet with Logan [Pearsall] Smith (Alys's brother who lives here) until tea at 4.30. After that mathematics until 6 o'clock, reading with Alys until 7.30, dine at 8 o'clock, chat and smoke with us until 9.30, another hour's reading aloud with Alys until 10.30. They sleep and dress in the same room, and they have no children. . . .

As individuals they are remarkable. Alys comes of an American Quaker family: she is charming to look at—tall, graceful, with regular features, clear skin, bright blue eyes, and soft curly nut-brown hair—always smiling, often laughing, warm-hearted and sympathetically intelligent. She has not the gift of intimacy except with her husband; her manner is the same to everyone—at least so far as I have seen. She has no arts of flirtation, if anything she prefers women to men—and I think really likes the womanly woman better than the professional. She has no moods, or they are controlled, she seems always happy and grateful for happiness and yet perpetually thinking how to make others happier. Since we have been here she has spent days away nursing a friend at Cambridge, with no consciousness of virtue, responding to a call of friendship as readily as most women respond to a call of pleasure. If she has a defect, it is a certain colourlessness of intellect and a certain lack of " temperament ". But in a woman are these defects?

So much for our hosts. Besides these two, Logan Smith, a refined and gentle-natured bachelor, with a pretty talent for turning out sentences and a taste for collecting bric-a-brac, is a daily visitor and chats with us over afternoon tea. He, like his sister, is tall, delicate-featured and always smiling. But, behind this smile there is a deep-seated melancholy, due to a long record of self-conscious failure to become an artist of words. The world has proved too complex for him to grasp—he is perpetually breaking off before he has mastered even the smallest portion of it. He was meant, like Alys, to be a complementary being: as a man he cannot find a career, or even a wife, to suit him.

Bertrand is a slight, dark-haired man, with prominent forehead, bright eyes, strong features except for a retreating chin; nervous hands and alert quick movements. In manner and dress and outward bearing, he is most carefully trimmed, conventionally correct and punctiliously polite: in speech, he has an almost affectedly clear enunciation of words and preciseness of expression. In morals, he is a puritan; in personal habits almost an ascetic, except that he lives for efficiency and, therefore, expects to be kept in the best physical condition. But, intellectually, he is audacious—an iconoclast, detesting religious or social convention, suspecting sentiment, believing only in the " order of thought " and the " order of things ", in logic and in science. He indulges in the wildest paradox and in the broadest jokes, the latter always too abstrusely intellectual in their form to be vulgarly coarse. He is a delightful talker, especially in general conversation, when the intervention of other minds prevents him from tearing his subject to pieces with fine chopping logic. He is always fruitful, especially in clearing up definitions and distinctions, or in following out logical conclusions. He is fastidious with regard to friends and acquaintances: he dislikes bores and hates any kind of self-seeking selfishness or coarse-grainedness. He looks at the world from a pinnacle of detachment—dissects persons and demolishes causes. And yet he recognises that, as a citizen, you must be a member of a party; therefore, he has joined the Fabian Society! He more or less accepts Sidney as his " representative " man. But the kernel of his life is research into the processes of reasoning. Of this new and highly abstract form of logic, more abstract than mathematics, I have no vision. All that one can say is that the effect on his own mind of these processes of pure reasoning is to make him singularly helpful in clearing up more concrete issues, even when he starts with no specialised knowledge of facts. To sum up, he is an expert in the art of reasoning, quite independently of the subject-matter.

A vigorous intelligence, at once subtle and honest, with the best kind of pride—the determination not to swerve from his own standards of right and wrong, truth or falsehood, are perhaps his finest characteristics. What he lacks is sympathy and tolerance for other people's emotions;

and, if you regard it as a virtue, Christian humility. The outlines of both his intellect and his feelings are sharp, hard and permanent. He is a good hater.

I observe in Bertrand a curious parallel between his intellectual and moral nature. He is intolerant of blemishes and faults in himself and others, he dreams of perfection in man: he almost loathes lapses from men's own standards. So in his thought he is almost violently impatient of bad reasoning: a right conclusion come to by bad arguments is offensive to him: it is the *perfection of the reasoning* that he seeks after, not truth of the conclusions. Now it seems to me that there is the same sort of connection between an intellectual concentration on applied science, and a tolerant, if not lax, judgement of men. Just as I am always striving to adjust my " order of thought " to the " order of things "—exactly as I am always looking to results as the test of right reasoning (power of prevision, for instance, as the result of shockingly bad reasoning?), so I am perpetually excusing myself and others for any lapses in morality. I analyse and describe my own and others' faults. But these faults seldom offend me in themselves, but only because they result in what is unpleasant and ugly. I have no "sense of sin", and no desire to see it punished. Bertrand, on the other hand, is almost cruel in his desire to see cruelty revenged.

July 9th.—Haldane spent yesterday at Friday's Hill, and brought us news of the Liberal split and enlisted Sidney on the Asquith side. We had been watching with half indifference, half annoyance, the " retreat " of the Liberal Party within the old lines of Gladstonianism, under the leadership of Campbell-Bannerman nominally, but of the pro-Boers actually. The whole of the spring, the vacuum left by lack of any clear thinking among those who can think has been filled with pro-Boer sentiment of an extravagant kind, and the old sort of secularist individualist Radicalism. Morley and Harcourt, supported by the *Daily News*, were showing signs of returning to political life; Campbell-Bannerman, a weak vain man who all along has been in his heart pro-Boer, had been entertaining Sauer and Merriman. The Liberal Federation meeting at Bradford had been strongly pro-Boer in sentiment, though passing lukewarm resolutions of the official type. Meanwhile, the Imperialist section—Haldane, Asquith, Grey—had been working at the Bar, enjoying themselves in London " society " and letting things slide. Suddenly, they woke up to find the Liberal Party in the House of Commons under the leadership of Lloyd George, declaring itself definitely against the war, accusing Milner and the army of gross inhumanity and asserting the right of the Boers to some kind of independence. Campbell-Bannerman had been captured.

Under the influence of his old friend Lord Milner (now in London),

Asquith came down heavily, declared that the war was inevitable, that there had been no wilful cruelty, and that independence, in any sense the Boers would understand it, was impossible. He followed up his speech by voting against Campbell-Bannerman and the Irish and Welsh contingent, and led out of the House some thirty Liberal M.P.'s (the bulk of the English Liberals seem to have abstained either by accident or with intent). Then to emphasise this protest the more enthusiastic Liberal M.P.'s insisted on giving a dinner to Asquith—to fête him for his defiance of C.B. Hence the uproar: the uncomfortable spectacle of Asquith, Grey, Haldane, supported by the Tory press, in flat rebellion against C.B., the chosen leader of the Liberal Party, supported by Morley, Harcourt and the whole force of pro-Boers. " We are fighting for our lives ", said Haldane to me: " both Asquith and I would attach much importance to Sidney being present at the dinner: we do not like to press it, because the whole movement may be a failure." A dilemma: Sidney is pro-Boer in sentiment: he agrees with Asquith and Haldane, by reason; but he has not thought out the question, has paid little or no attention to it. It suits him infinitely better to keep out of the whole affair: he has already made his position among the Radicals " suspect " owing to his attitude with regard to school boards. Moreover, in many details, such as the retention of Lord Milner as administrator, he is not convinced that he would be prepared to risk complete colonial self-government in the Orange Free State and the Transvaal. On the other hand, Haldane has always trusted him in matters he cared about, has been the most loyal friend in all educational projects. " I attach little importance to the dinner," Sidney said to me when I told him of Haldane's desires, " and no importance to my being there. If Haldane wants me to go, I certainly will. I would rather, of course, have kept out of the whole affair, but one must be ready occasionally to step forward for one's friends if one has no conviction to the contrary. As between the two sections of Liberals, my sympathies are with them. I think very little will come of either party, but Haldane and Asquith are at least not hostile to our views: the others are. I will go. But you need not imagine it of any importance, one way or the other."

And now that he has agreed to go I am worrying about it. First and foremost, I know he loathes the war; he thinks the whole episode of the Rand and the Chamberlain negotiations a disgrace to this country (though he attributes the inevitability of the war to the granting of the Charter to the S.A. Co., and the discovery of gold on the Rand); he distrusts Milner; above all he feels uncertain as to his own opinions, having carefully avoided reading anything on the subject. " It is not my show ", he has often said when I have suggested he should read blue-books. From a more selfish point of view, it suits him better not to be on either side so as to get what he can from both for his projects. Then I don't believe in the genuineness of the Liberal M.P.s' own questions: they live in the wrong atmosphere and are incurably lazy. They are desperately in awe of the City, consider the opinion of the *Times*, and have their eye on the goodwill of manufacturers—even on that of the brewers. Intellectually, they are more with us than the more Radical section: but they have no pluck and no faith. All these considerations rushed through my mind as I half deprecated Sidney accepting; but my instinctive wish was that he should accept in order to please Haldane, who has been so good to us. But no doubt, as Sidney says, his going or not going is of no importance.

July 28th.—On the night Rosebery issued his famous letter to the City Liberal Club and to the press, Sidney was pacing the terrace of the House of Commons with Haldane and Grey, explaining to them the attitude they ought to adopt on home affairs, having been called in to consult with them. At the time when the journalists in the lobby were humming with excitement about the letter, Rosebery's devoted lieutenants were absolutely unaware of its existence! "We are not in communication with Rosebery", Haldane had said to Sidney. Again on the Friday afternoon just before the Asquith dinner, I met Haldane in the House (whither I had gone to escort a young American lady) looking terrifically grave—almost agitated. "He has made a great speech to the City Liberal Club: has repudiated the Liberal Party, has announced his intention of 'ploughing his own furrow'—all within a few hours of Asquith's speech to-night—without a word of consultation. He is a Puck in politics", added Haldane with almost a note of exasperation.

The dinner, however, went off all right. It was a scratch assembly and Sidney was among the most distinguished of the guests. Margaret Hobhouse and I viewed it from the gallery. Asquith's speech was manly and sensible, finely phrased and spoken with considerable fervour. But, read in cold blood the next morning, it suffered in comparison with Rosebery's artistically sensational utterance. We did not take the tragic view of Rosebery's intervention taken by the little set of his immediate followers. If Lord Rosebery really means business, really intends to come forward with a strong policy, then he has done his lieutenants a good service by stepping boldly out of the ranks of an obsolete Liberalism. Asquith, Grey and Haldane can only proclaim their own freedom within the Liberal Party, they cannot denounce the other sections of it, for the simple reason that it is not business for them to step away from the front bench. To the front bench they must stick so long as they can stick also to their own principles. But Rosebery is bound by no ties, and can do the necessary work of the iconoclast of the Gladstonian ideals. Rosebery's business is to destroy Gladstonianism. Whether or not he is to become a real leader depends on whether he has anything to put in the place of a defunct Liberalism. Mere imperialism will not do: that the other side have. Now supposing he fails, as I think he will fail, to be constructive, then he leaves the field open to Asquith, Grey and Haldane with a good deal of the rubbish cleared away.

Whether this sort of reasoning glimmered into Haldane's brain, I know not. But when he came in on Monday evening he was in high spirits. Asquith and he had made it up with Rosebery (they are forgiving mortals!). It was agreed, he said, that Rosebery and Asquith were to plough parallel furrows. Meanwhile, G. B. S. writes urging us to plunge in with Rosebery as the best chance of moulding home policy. We have succumbed to his flattery; and now Sidney, with occasional suggestions from me, is engaged on an article entitled "Lord Rosebery's Escape from Houndsditch ".

What was the thesis displayed in "Lord Rosebery's Escape from Houndsditch ", published in the September number of the *Nineteenth Century*, 1901? The answer is: debunking Gladstonian Liberalism in order to clear the way for Fabian collectivism. Instead of ploughing his furrow in lonely grandeur, Lord Rosebery is respectfully incited to offer himself as titular leader to the progressive group of Liberals led by Asquith, Haldane, Grey and Acland, " a group of men of diverse temperaments and varied talents, imbued with a common faith and a common purpose, and eager to work out, and severally to expound, how each department of national life can be raised to its highest possible efficiency. If he does nothing but plough his own furrow," the author adds, " Lord Rosebery will, I fear, have to plough it alone " (p. 386).

Here are a few extracts, out of the twenty-paged article explaining its title and indicating the course to be taken by a reinvigorated and up-to-date Opposition to the Conservative Government:

Mr. Gladstone, as we now learn upon the unexpected testimony of Lord Tweedmouth, regarded the last twenty years of his life as having been spent in " patching up old clothes ". His achievements as a sartorial artist in politics approached, it must be admitted, the miraculous. But the patched-up suits of 1880, 1885 and 1892, though they served their immediate purpose, have, under the expanding conditions of contemporary politics, proved wretched wearing material. Not even Mr. Gladstone could have patched them up again. With amused dismay the new generation of progressives have lately witnessed Sir Henry Campbell-Bannerman piecing together the Gladstonian rags and remnants, with Sir William Harcourt holding the scissors, and Mr. John Morley unctuously waxing the thread. Mr. Asquith and Sir Edward Grey are sufficiently up-to-date resolutely to refuse even to try on the re-patched garment, but they are not in a position to decline to associate with those who still believe the Gladstonian cut to be fashionable. Lord Rosebery is the only person who has turned his back on Houndsditch and called for a complete new outfit. This is the first step towards the regeneration of the Opposition. I say the Opposition advisedly, for the political opportunity of the moment is not for a regeneration of Gladstonianism, or of " the Liberal Party ", or of anything else that had its day in the last century, but solely for a live Opposition. That Opposition, when it comes, may call itself the Liberal Party or any other name that may be convenient. But it is certain that it will not be the old Gladstonian party—quite the contrary, in fact—and that it will not become a political force until, meeting the new needs and expressing the new aspirations of the twentieth century —dealing, as Lord Rosebery rightly says, " in a new spirit with the new problems of the age "—it thereby makes itself into a practicable alternative to the Conservative Government.

What then is the matter with the Liberals? For fifty years, in the middle of the last century, we may recognise their party as " a great instrument of progress ", wrenching away the shackles—political, fiscal, legal, theological and social—that hindered individual advancement. The shackles are by no means wholly got rid of, but the political force of this old Liberalism is spent. During the last twenty years its aspirations and its watchwords, its ideas of daily life and its conceptions of the universe, have become increasingly distasteful to the ordinary citizen as he renews his youth from generation to generation. Its worship of individual liberty evokes no enthusiasm. Its reliance on " freedom of contract " and " supply and demand ", with its corresponding " voluntaryism " in religion and philanthropy, now seems to work out disastrously for the masses, who are too poor to have what the economists call an " effective demand " for even the minimum conditions of physical and mental health necessary to national well-being [pp. 366-7]. . . . The England of this generation is changing because Englishmen have had revealed to them another new world of relationships, of which they were before unconscious. This time it is not a new continent that the ordinary man has discovered, but a new category. We have become aware, almost in a flash, that we are not merely individuals, but members of a community, nay, citizens of the world. This new self-consciousness is no mere intellectual fancy, but a hard fact that comes home to us in our daily life. The labourer in the slum tenement, competing for employment at the factory gate, has become conscious that his comfort and his progress depend, not wholly or mainly on himself, or on any other individual, but upon the proper organisation of his trade union and the activity of the factory inspector. . . . The freedom for his trade union to bargain collectively, freedom for his co-operative society to buy and sell and manufacture, freedom for his municipality to supply all the common needs of the town, freedom, above all, from the narrow insularity which keeps his nation backing, " on principle ", out of its proper place in the comity of the world. In short, the opening of the twentieth century finds us all, to the dismay of the old-fashioned individualist, " thinking in communities ". . . .

Now the trouble with Gladstonian Liberalism is that, by instinct, by tradition, and by the positive precepts of its past exponents, it "thinks in individuals ". It visualises the world as a world of independent Roundheads, with separate ends, and abstract rights to pursue those ends [p. 369]. . . . Their conception of freedom means only breaking somebody's bonds asunder. When the " higher freedom " of corporate life is in question, they become angrily reactionary, and denounce and obstruct every new development of common action. If we seek for the greatest enemy of municipal enterprise, we find him in Sir Henry Fowler. If we ask who is the most successful opponent of any extension of *the common rule* of factory legislation to wider fields of usefulness, the answer is Mr. John Morley. And, when a leader is needed by those whose unalterable instinct it is to resist to the uttermost every painful effort towards the higher organisation of that greatest of co-operative societies, the state itself, who than Sir William Harcourt, at his most eloquent, can be more surely depended upon? Not that I have any right to reproach these eminent ones for standing by their principles. The principles were fresh once—in the last quarter of the eighteenth century. Their exponents' minds were fresh, too, about the middle of the nineteenth. But Adam Smith is dead, and Queen Anne, and even Sir Robert Peel; while as to Gladstone, he is by far the deadest of them all [pp. 370-71]. . . . And I confess that I feel the hopelessness, even the comic absurdity, of seeming to invite his more elderly lieutenants, at their ages, to change their spots—to turn over a new leaf and devote themselves to obtaining the greatest possible development of municipal activity, the most comprehensive extension of the Factory Acts, or the fullest utilisation of the government departments in the service of the public. I know too well that they quite honestly consider such aims to be mischievous. They are aiming at something else, namely, at the abstract right of the individual to lead exactly the kind of life that he likes (and can pay for), unpenalised by any taxation for purposes of which he individually disapproves. They are, in fact, still " thinking in individuals " [p. 370].

No leader will attract the support of the mass of unpolitical citizens —who in this juncture, at any rate, alone can give a decisive vote— without expanding his thesis of national efficiency into a comprehensive and definite programme. Nay, he must do more. He must understand his programme, believe in his programme, be inspired by his programme. He will, in fact, lead the English people—eager just now for national efficiency, they care not how—only by becoming a personified programme of national efficiency in every department of life.

Here Mr. Asquith is on the right tack: " What is the use of an Empire " (he asks) " if it does not breed and maintain in the truest and fullest sense of the word an imperial race? What is the use of talking about Empire if here, in its very centre, there is always to be found a mass of people, stunted in education, a prey to intemperance, huddled and congested beyond the possibility of realising in any true sense either social or domestic life? " [p. 375].

So far Lord Rosebery and Mr. Asquith, Mr. Haldane and Sir Edward Grey are right in their diagnosis. The nation sees that these men, in their different opportunities, have had the courage to cast off the old clothes. But, at present, we are all in the dark as to what is to be the new outfit. . . . What steps would their alternative government take to ensure the rearing of an imperial race? What action have they in mind for healing the open sore of the sweated trades: what do they intend to do with the poor law: what plan have they thought out for stimulating and directing the utmost possible municipal enterprise in sanitation and housing: what is their scheme for a comprehensive national system of education from the infant school to the university: what are their practical conclusions as to increasing the grants-in-aid, and assessing site values: how do they intend to transform the present silly procedure of the House of Commons: do they propose to simply neglect the military situation? It is on questions of this sort that they must, during the next few years, mark themselves out from their opponents, and convince us that they have a faith and a programme rooted no less in knowledge than in conviction. To think out such a programme is, of course, irksome, and, as every political Polonius will advise, to commit yourself to it is inconvenient—if you do not believe in it. But, to create a live opposition—still more, to construct an alternative government—this new thought and this new propaganda must be undertaken. If even one-half of the study and conviction, money and capacity, were put into such a campaign for the next five years that Cobden and Bright put into the Anti-Corn Law League, the country could be won for a policy of national efficiency. Without the pledge of virility which a campaign of this sort would afford, the nation will not be persuaded [pp. 385-6].

October 1st.—Sidney's article in the *Nineteenth Century* has been a brilliant success. No doubt there are some who found the self-assertiveness and contempt of others somewhat intolerable; but everyone has read it and found it new and full of substance (G. B. S. corrected the proof and inserted some of the brilliance). The Asquith, Haldane, Grey lot are delighted with it: Rosebery evidently pleased. The newspapers have taken it seriously, and it has improved his standing, I think, and made people feel that he is to be reckoned with. Now I am urging him to publish the positive side in a Fabian tract, and I intend to give the substance of it in a lecture at Oxford.

Meanwhile, we have no illusions about the Liberal Imperialists. We think that neither Rosebery nor Asquith mean to declare themselves in favour of our measure of collectivism. But they hold no views that are inconsistent with it—have nothing to offer but a refusal to take up the distinctive side of the old Liberalism. The time will come when, if they are to be a political force, they will have to " fill up " the political worker with some positive convictions. Then, we think, for the needful minimum of nourishment they will fall back on us and not on the other section.

But national affairs are not invigorating at present: the wretched war drags on, the newspapers nag and scold, and the Government seems helpless and the Opposition are more and more divided. The pro-Boers are very naturally rubbing their hands and saying " I told you so ". Personally, if there is no danger of intervention, I do not think the S.A. situation so intolerable as other persons do, and the longer and more determined the resistance, the more complete and thorough-going will be the collapse of the Boer nationality. And, with a race with so much patriotism, stubbornness and superstition, one wonders whether any more easy settling down would be permanent.

October 13th.—Sidney and Hewins in first-rate spirits about the School; building nearly complete and paid for, equipment provided from the hung-up grant of the T.E.B., a small but certain income from the same source and plenty of students. Hewins, who now sees before him a fine position and £600 p.a. secured, is somewhat elated and would, I think, tend to have a swelled head if it were not for the amount of skill and self-subordination required to engineer the business over the shoals of the university organisation. Again, one realises how, in a large and complicated society like the London educational world, the whole power of moulding events falls into the hands of the little *clique* who happen to be in the centre of things. Ten years ago Sidney could no more have influenced the teaching of economics and political science in London than he could have directed the policy of the Cabinet. But now no one can resist him: he wields the L.C.C. power of making grants, he is head of the one live institution; he is, on his own subjects, supreme on the University Senate (because he is thought to have the L.C.C. behind him), and he knows every rope and has quick and immediate access to every person of influence. Somehow I doubt whether such a state of things is quite wholesome: of course, one believes that in this case the hidden hand is beneficent and efficient! But the converse—the feeling of absolute helplessness against the doings of less efficient cliques!—is not so pleasant. One wonders whether it would be possible to conduct a country's government with efficiency and yet with free access and no favour to all concerned.

November 1st.—Asquith and Haldane dined here alone on Monday —the latter proposing to bring the former for a quiet chat. The talk did not come to much. They are, I think, somewhat depressed. Rosebery had " carted them ", so Haldane said, and was going to take his own line quite aloof from anything they might think or write. Asquith was preparing set speeches on social questions. But Haldane was still keen on winning the centre, a term which he always uses as synonymous with the non-political voter, in whose ultimate power we believe. In reality, these two sections—the centre and the non-political voter— are entirely different and to my mind very unequal in importance. What Haldane sees is the moderate politician: the capitalist or professional man who desires little social change and the Empire maintained. But the class we wish them to appeal to is the great lower middle-class and working-class, who want change, but don't know in what direction. Any party that knew its own mind as well as the facts, and had will to apply the one to the other, would succeed, in the long run, in getting hold of these classes for its policy of reform.

Rosebery is really on the same line as Haldane, though playing a different tune. Altogether the position seems somewhat hopeless.

Asquith impressed me with his manliness and unselfconsciousness, also with his shrewd open-mindedness; but he is a coarse-grained instrument and will never strike the imagination of any large section of men.

Q

The last entry of the diary is a preface to a new friendship which opened out in the following year:

December 1901.—Wells' *Anticipations*. The most remarkable book of the year: a powerful imagination furnished with the data and methods of physical science, working on social problems. The weak part of Wells' outfit is his lack of any detailed knowledge of social organisations—and this, I think, vitiates his capacity for foreseeing the future machinery of government and the relation of classes. But his work is full of luminous hypotheses and worth careful study by those who are trying to look forward. Clever phrases abound, and by the way proposals on all sorts of questions—from the future direction of religious thought, to the exact curve of the skirting round the wall of middle-class abodes.

1902

January 30th.—We spent Christmas with Alfred [Cripps] and the Courtneys. Our host was in splendid form: well in health and full of public affairs. He had been in close communication with Balfour and Chamberlain trying to arrange some sort of compromise between them with regard to the Education Bill. Joseph Chamberlain was against state aid, fearing the recrudescence of the " church-rate " crusade. Balfour felt the force of the Church's cry " now or never ". He and Sidney discussed the question: as usual the " little jewel of an advocate " had not thought out the position and, though he and Sidney agreed on main points, Cripps was inclined to leave all knotty points to be settled by the House: a counsel of despair when the knots are so complicated. Dear old Leonard kept out of all this confidential talk: he and Kate spending their time with the young people, while Alfred, Sidney and I sat over the library fire. I fancy that Alfred feels his feet again in politics, and sees office near at hand should the opportunity for a new man arise. We laughingly decided that, if the three brothers-in-law were in leading positions in the House, it would end in Sidney and Alfred arranging compromises between the two front benches, with Leonard always in opposition![1] The Courtneys were as self-righteously pro-Boer as ever, but more subdued. " We are passing through some smoke (effect of Lord R.'s speech)," said Leonard, " but it will clear off."

February 28th.—We are at present very thick with the " Limps ". Asquith, Haldane, Grey, Munro Ferguson and the [Jack] Tennants, form a little family group into which they have temporarily attracted Sidney by asking him to their little dinners and informal meetings.

---

[1] It is amusing to recall that Alfred and Sidney became fellow-members of the two Labour Cabinets of 1924 and 1929–31 (Oct. 1937).

Close acquaintance with them does not make one more hopeful. Asquith is wooden, he lacks every kind of enthusiasm, and his hard-headed cold capacity seems to be given, not to politics, but to his legal cases. His brother-in-law, Jack Tennant, and Haldane both assure us that he could retire to-morrow from the Bar if he chose and that he only stays at it " for an occupation ". Strange lack of imagination not to see that there is an over-abundance of hard persistent work ready to his hand in politics, alike in thinking out reforms and in preaching them, and organising a party to push them. That lack of imagination and sensitiveness to needs lies at the root of Asquith's failure as a leader of men. For the rest, he has neither charm nor personal magnetism: he has to gain his position by sheer hard work, and that work he is not inclined to do in politics. Grey is a slight person; he has charm of appearance, of manner and even of character; but he is I fear essentially a " stick " to be used by someone else! " Politics have completely changed," he said plaintively to me when he was last dining here, " formerly you had your cause made for you, all the politician had to do was to preach it; now you have to *make your cause*." Beyond foreign and colonial policy (whatever that may mean), Grey has no original ideas and finds it hard even to appreciate the ideas of others. And he has no notion of work as the main occupation of life; politics is merely with him an episode in his daily life, like his enjoyment of nature, books, society, sport (mostly nature and sport be it said). Neither Asquith nor Grey are, as politicians, well served by their respective wives. Margot is, I believe, a kindly soul; but, though she has in-telligence and wit, she has neither intellect nor wisdom. She is incurably reactionary in her prejudices: her two delights are hunting and other out-door exercises, and fashionable society. She is said to be ambitious for her husband; but, if so, her method of carrying out her ambition lacks intelligence as well as intellect. Lady Grey is a fastidious aristocrat, intensely critical of anyone to whom work is the principal part of life. She is clever enough to see that work alone counts, and yet knows, in her heart of hearts, that neither she nor her husband are capable of it. As for Haldane, to whom we are both really attached, he is a large and generous-hearted man, affectionate to his friends and genuinely enthusiastic about the advancement of knowledge. But his ideal has no connection with the ugly rough and tumble work-a-day world of the average sensual man, who is compelled to earn his livelihood by routine work and bring up a family of children on narrow means. Unmarried, living a luxurious physical but a strenuous mental life, Haldane's vital energies are divided between highly-skilled legal work and the processes of digestion—for he is a Herculean eater. He finds his relaxation in bad metaphysics and in political intrigue—that is, in trying to manipulate influential persons into becoming followers of Rosebery and members of the *clique*. Be it said to his credit, that he has to some extent manipulated us into this position. Munro-Ferguson is merely a pleasant young aristocrat. Perhaps, the most keen of the lot are the Jack Tennants. Mrs. Jack (formerly an inspectress of factories) is a fine-natured woman, with real knowledge and enthusiasm. She has inspired her husband with the same helpful attitude towards social questions. But Jack is a *little* man physically and mentally, and the notion of his being a force approaches the ridiculous. There remains the mysterious Rosebery. At present he is an enigma. Whether on account of his social position or of his brilliancy, or because of his streaks of wit and original thought, he can make all the world listen. He has imagination and sensitiveness, and he is a born actor. He is first-rate at appearances. Moreover, he seems to be developing persistency and courage. But as yet he shows no signs of capacity for co-operation, or even for leadership of a group of subordinates. All he has yet done is to *strike attitudes* that have brought down the House at the time, and left a feeling of blankness a few days later. To be a great leader, a man must either understand problems himself or be able to handle men who do understand them. Rosebery sees many persons, but only in order to extract from them the essence of public opinion so as to appear before the world in a popular attitude. He never asks how actually to work the machinery of government so as to get the best results. Has he any clear and definite view of the character of the results he wants to get? I fear not.

And why are we in this galley? Partly because we have drifted into it. These men have helped us with our undertakings, they have been appreciative of our ideas, and socially pleasant to us. They have no prejudice against our views of social reform: whilst their general attitude towards the Empire as a powerful and self-conscious force is one with which we are in agreement. Moreover, the leaders of the other school of Liberalism are extremely distasteful to us: we disagree with them on almost every point of home and foreign policy. Before we can get the new ideas and new frame of mind accepted, we must beat out the old. That is why we are not against the policy of the " clean slate ". We want to be rid of all the old ideals and enthusiasms —we want to stamp out the notion that the world can be bettered by abolition of some of the existing institutions; we want, on the contrary, to set people to work to build up new tissue which may in time take the place of the old. In Ireland, for instance, we don't want to abolish the union with England, but so to reconstruct the internal government that it will make the bond of union of secondary importance. We do not want to abolish or remodel the House of Lords, but to

build up precedents for their non-intervention with national expenditure—all collectivism coming under this head. We do not want
to disestablish the Church, but to endow science and secular ethics and
any other form of intellectual activity that may seem desirable. We
don't want to abolish or restrain the development of private enterprise,
but, by creating dykes and bulwarks, to control its mischievous effect
on the character of the race. We do not want to unfetter the individual
from the obligation of citizenship, we want on the contrary to stimulate
and constrain him, by the unfelt pressure of a better social environment, to become a healthier, nobler and more efficient being.

To these ideals the old Liberalisms of Leonard Courtney, Morley,
Campbell-Bannerman, and the bulk of Celtic members of Parliament,
are not only unsympathetic, but really hostile. Asquith, Haldane, Grey
and, I think, Rosebery, are sympathetic though timorous. They will
not themselves push these ideals (Rosebery is as likely as any to do it),
but they will follow any one who does, *if there seems to be the least
response from public opinion.* And, if Sidney is inside the *clique,* he will
have a better chance of permeating its activities than by standing aloof
as a superior person and scolding at them. So I am inclined to advise him
to throw in his lot with them in the days of their adversity and trial,
when an addition to their ranks from the democratic side is of great
value to them. Half the art of effective living consists of giving yourself
to those who need you most *and at the time of their most pressing want.*
And, seeing that politics is a mere bye-product of our life, our own
special work to-day being administration or investigation, there seem
few reasons against this course of action. If we came to throw our
main stream of energy into political life, we should have to choose our
comrades more carefully.

The Technical Education Board is a source of worry and anxiety
to Sidney. The hostility of the Conservative Government to the School
Board, and the threat to abolish it, have reacted on the Radical L.C.C.
and made it inclined to refuse to compete with the Radical School
Board for the administration of education. J. R. MacDonald, Sidney's
old enemy in the Fabian Society, slipped into the Council at an un-
contested bye-election and apparently spends his time in working up the
feeling against the Technical Education Board and Sidney's administration of it. He is anxious to get on to it, and Sidney is doing his best to
get him in, believing that an enemy is always safer inside than outside
a democratic body. But it means friction and a good deal of bickering.
MacDonald does not hesitate to accuse Sidney of taking advantage of
his position to favour the School of Economics [1]—an accusation which

---

[1] *July* 1921.—More than a year after this entry Sidney was told by a fellow-
member of the Technical Education Board that J. Ramsay MacDonald had been

is perfectly true, though we think absolutely harmless. In administration, you must advance the cause which you think right and are, therefore, interested in. The unpleasant sound of the accusation is conveyed by the double meaning of the word " interested " which in most men's mouths means *pecuniarily* interested. We believe in a school of administrative, political and economic science as a way of increasing national efficiency; but we have kept the London School honestly non-partisan in its theories. Otherwise " interested " we are not, unless the expenditure of our own energy and money on an institution be termed " interested ". And Sidney's energies have by no means been exclusively devoted to the subjects he is intellectually interested in. He has, I think, been quite exceptionally catholic in his organisation of secondary, technical and university education in London, alike in the class of students to be provided for and the range of subjects taught. Heaven knows there were arrears to be made up in politics, economics and the science of administration.

The Progressives are not very happy among themselves. The more eminent of them have served as chairman, or refused to do so; and there comes the question whether the hard-working little " cads " of the party shall succeed to the chair, or whether some well-bred nonentity shall be promoted. Sidney, though willing to back up the majority of the party in any course they think fit (he does not attach much importance to the whole business), is inclined to advise a frank recognition of the plebeian character of the L.C.C., and to take an excellent and devoted member who drops his *h*'s rather than an insignificant lord. The matter has been compromised by the choice of a plebeian as chairman and a lord as vice-chairman. But it has left heart-burnings and ill-feeling within the party committee: Sidney acting as peace-maker. By his colleagues he is considered a non-competitor: he has made education his province and rules over it undisturbed; he has no desire to be chairman or vice-chairman, or leader of the party in the Council itself.

We have seen something lately of H. G. Wells and his wife. Wells is an interesting though somewhat unattractive personality except for his agreeable disposition and intellectual vivacity. His mother was the housekeeper to a great establishment of 40 servants, his father the professional cricketer attached to the place. The early associations with the menial side of a great man's establishment has left Wells with a hatred of that class and of its attitude towards the lower

spreading a report that Sidney and I were making an income by lecturing for the School. As he was perfectly well aware that, far from taking money from the School, we had been spending our surplus on the School and the library, and that Sidney and I only lectured there in order to relieve the School from paying lecturers, this libel was inexcusable.

orders. His apprenticeship to a draper, his subsequent career as an assistant master at a private venture school, as a state student at South Kensington living on £1 a week, as an army crammer, as a journalist and, in these last years, as a most successful writer of fiction, has given him a great knowledge of the lower middle-class and their habits and thoughts, and an immense respect for science and its methods. But he is totally ignorant of the manual worker, on the one hand, and of the big administrator and aristocrat on the other. This ignorance is betrayed in certain crudities of criticism in his *Anticipations*: he ignores the necessity for maintaining the standard of life of the manual working population; he does not appreciate the need for a wide experience of men and affairs in administration. A world run by the physical science man straight from his laboratory is his ideal: he does not see that specialised faculty and knowledge are needed for administration exactly as they are needed for the manipulation of machinery or [natural] forces. But he is extraordinarily quick in his apprehensions, and took in all the points we gave him in our 48 hours' talk with him, first at his own house and then here. He is a good instrument for popularising ideas, and he gives as many ideas as he receives. His notion of modern society as " the grey ", not because it is made of uniform atoms of that shade, but because of the very variety of its colours, all mixed together and in formless mass; his forecast of the segregation of like to like, until the community will become extraordinarily variegated and diverse in its component parts, seems to us a brilliant and true conception. Again, democracy as a method of dealing with men in a wholesale way—every man treated in the bulk and not in detail, the probability that we shall become more *detailed* and less *wholesale* in our provision for men's needs—that again is a clever illumination. Altogether, it is refreshing to talk to a man who has shaken himself loose from so many of the current assumptions, and is looking at life as an explorer of a new world. He has no great faith in government by the " man in the street " and, I think, has hardly realised the function of the representative as a " foolometer " for the expert.

March 19th.—Met " Imperial Perks " at Mr. Haldane's—a repulsive being—hard, pushing, commonplace, with no enthusiasms except a desire to have his " knife into the Church "—a blank materialist although a pious Protestant, who recognises no principle beyond self-interest. I confess the thought that Perks was a pillar of the new Liberal League staggered me: how could we work with such a loathsome person! A combination of Gradgrind, Pecksniff and Jabez Balfour. And the choice of this man as their first-lieutenant throws an ugly light on Lord Rosebery. Anyway, we and Perks are incompatible in views, in tastes, and in all our fundamental assumptions as to ends and methods. This is no doubt an exaggerated statement; but regarded from a strictly matter-of-fact point of view, I doubt whether a leader who found Perks a delectable companion would really tolerate us and our ways when he came to know us and realise what state of things we were working to bring about. The situation is made worse by the fact that Perks is the only man in the group who is in deadly earnest and, therefore, *if the group succeeds*, is likely to come out top. To think of Perks as an English Cabinet Minister: Ugh! The very notion of it degrades political life.

Two months' sampling of the Liberal Imperialists has not heightened our estimate of them. Asquith is deplorably slack, Grey is a mere dilettante, Haldane plays at political intrigue and has no democratic principle, Perks is an unclean beast, and as for Rosebery, he remains an enigma. He, at any rate, has personal distinction, originality and charm; but he seeks only appearances, has no care for or knowledge of economic and social evils, lives and moves, and has his being, in the plutocratic atmosphere, shares to the full the fears and prejudices of his class. Moreover, he is a bad colleague, and suffers from lack of nerve and persistent purpose. As for the rank and file, they are a most hetero-geneous lot, bound together by their *dislikes*, and not by their positive convictions: they have no kind of faith in any of their leaders, and are in constant fear as to their political future and personal careers. And rising up against them is a force which will become apparent at the next election—Labour candidates officially run by the great trade unions, backed up by pro-Boer capitalists. That combination will have no constructive power. Here, again, the two elements are bound together, not by a common faith, but by a common hatred. But it will be able, in many places, to smash the Liberal Imperialists. Thus the Liberal Party seems cleaved into two equally unpromising sections—Rosebery appealing to the grey mass of convictionless voters on the broad and shallow ground of Empire and efficiency; C. B. relying on every description of separatist interest, on all the " antis "—anti-war, anti-United Kingdom, anti-Church, anti-capitalist, anti-Empire. Both combinations seem to me equally temporary and equally lacking in healthy and vigorous root principles.

Having done our little best to stimulate the " Limps " into some kind of conviction, and having most assuredly failed, we now return to our own work. Three months' peaceful and strenuous effort in the country seems a delightful prospect. And between me and this diary, I think the " Limps " will be glad to be rid of us! Our contempt for their " limpness " and our distrust for their reactionary views are too apparent.

April 25th. Sussex.—Poor Sidney is somewhat distracted with anxiety with regard to the future of the School, the development of opposition to the Technical Education Board and the L.C.C. His principal concern is the exact constitution of the educational authority for London to be proposed next year. It so happens that he can use the fear of the borough councils as the authority to frighten the opponents of the T.E.B. on the Council. It is an open secret that a strong section of the Cabinet is in favour of a joint-committee of the borough councils which would be a disaster of the first magnitude to the whole of higher education in London. To avert this disaster we are moving all the forces we have any control over—our friends in the Church, university educationalists, permanent officials and any one having influence over Ministers, against the proposal of an education authority elected by and from the borough councils.

It is, perhaps, fortunate that Sidney is known to approve the lines of the present Bill applying to the country outside London. Indeed, our Radical School Board friends scoff about " Webb's Bill "—which, of course, is an absurdity. They will scoff the more if next year we are hoist by our own petard! Meanwhile, he is writing an article for the *Nineteenth Century* for June on the London University in the hope of catching a millionaire! Beit is biting!

Friday's Hill, May 4th.—Settled again for our nine weeks' sojourn with the Russells. Hard at work on poor law reports of 1834. I had to break into this work to help Sidney through with his University of London article. . . . Sidney is somewhat distracted with his undertakings and feels himself at times unequal to them. " I am not a big man," he says plaintively to me, " I could not manage any larger undertakings." But, as I tell him, it is exactly this consciousness of imperfection, whilst others find him competent, that shows that he is more than equal to his task. We only feel completely complacent with our effort when we have ceased to grasp the *possibilities* of the situation.

Enjoyed my week's work on the University article, a relief from the grind of facts—a chance for scheming, an intellectual occupation I dearly love.

At this point I think it well to interpolate some explanation of our scheme for a reconstructed London University. The University of London, founded in 1837, was merely a corporation to confer university degrees. It had no professors; it gave no teaching; it conducted no research; it awarded its degrees to persons coming from all parts, on their passing examinations on papers set by examiners whom they had never seen. It is true that there were various colleges scattered over London's vast area; the oldest entitled University College, being (as the Anglicans declared) " godless ", at which my father, a Unitarian debarred from Oxford and Cambridge, got his academic education; and King's College, established avowedly in opposition to University College, in order that young men of Church families should not be tempted to resort to the " godless " college. To these had gradually been added a dozen hospital schools of medicine and surgery; and also colleges for teaching science, mostly in its practical applications, or for training science teachers. Many of the students of these London colleges sat for the London University examinations, and were awarded its degrees. But they had no better chance than students from other cities or other countries. All the graduates of the University of London were alike " external students ". Most of those responsible for the management of the University gloried in this " externality " of their graduates, and were proud of the fact that there was absolutely no contact between those who examined and the aspirants for degrees. And all London's millions lacked the encouragement, the fertilising influence of contact with educated minds, the intellectual direction and the development of research into the unknown, with all its inventions and discoveries.

Now this lack of university inspiration and direction to London's intellectual life had been complained of for many years by all sorts of people, and a whole generation of efforts had failed of achievement. There had been many plans for university reform, and more than one Royal Commission had reported on one scheme after another. At last the Government got through Parliament an Act re-establishing the University of London on the basis of a complicated compromise between the conflicting parties, combining the examining board awarding the external degrees with the various autonomous colleges giving the necessary instruction

to internal students.[1] This, however, came to little better than
formal binding together of college professors and university

[1] The passing of the Act was due to R. B. Haldane. " My great question ", he
writes in his autobiography, " was how to extend University organisation in
England. There were some excellent colleges, but outside Oxford and Cambridge
very little of University life.

" I approached Balfour about the University of London [1898]. It was then a
mere board for examining outside students who got from it external degrees by
means of examinations without teaching. Valuable as the work of extending degrees
to external students had been in the past, it was no longer sufficient. The system
lent itself to the purposes of the crammers, and the school teachers in particular used
it for obtaining what were virtually little more than trade-marks. The real purpose
of University training, the development of the mind in the atmosphere of the teaching
university, where teachers and taught could come into close relation, was lacking.

" So strongly was this felt that many of the professors in the London colleges
had set their hearts on the establishment of a second and professorially run university, with no external examinees at all. I knew that the opposition to so far-
reaching a measure would be too strong to overcome in the then indifferent state of
public opinion. I saw that, as a first step at all events, the only way was to pass an
act enlarging the existing University of London by giving it a powerful teaching
side. This might be relied on in the end to absorb the other side by reason of its
quality. Of this opinion also was my friend Sidney Webb, who as the successful
Chief of the Technical Education Board of the London County Council had great
opportunities of studying the practical problem. . . . Sidney Webb and I took
counsel together. He was a very practical as well as a very energetic man. We
laid siege to the citadel. We went round to person after person who was prominent
in the administration of the existing University. Some listened, but others would
not do so and even refused to see us. In the end we worked out what was in substance
the scheme of the London University Act of 1898. The scheme was far from being
an ideal one. It provided by way of compromise for a senate which was too large to
be a really efficient supreme governing body for the new composite University,
and it had other shortcomings of which we were well aware. But it did set up a
teaching university, although Convocation, with its control of the external side,
would remain unduly powerful. We saw that the scheme thus fashioned was the
utmost we could hope for the time to carry, in the existing state of public opinion
about higher education in London."

Some years later R. B. Haldane was again at work improving London University
education: " During this period the affairs of London University were approaching
a crisis, and in the end I undertook the Chairmanship of the Royal Commission,
which sat for four years and finally reported. I managed to carry this on through the
later period of my tenure of the War Office and during the earlier part of my Lord
Chancellorship until the Report was signed. That Commission was a very interesting
one. Among my colleagues were Lord Milner, Sir Robert Morant, Sir William
M'Cormick, my old friend the ex-judge Sir Robert Romer, and Mrs. Creighton.
. . . I ought to say that my investigations in Germany had at an early stage impressed me unfavourably with the separation which had been made there between
the universities and the great technical colleges, and when subsequently, after studying the organisation of Charlottenburg on the spot with the aid of my friend
Geheimrat Witt, the Professor of Chemistry there and head of the school, I set to
work in London, along with Mr. Sidney Webb and Sir Francis Mowatt, to found
the new Imperial College of Science and Technology, I decided to press for the
application of a different principle. The new college was to be fashioned so as to
be brought as quickly as possible into a reconstructed University of London. I
presided over the departmental committee which prepared the Charter, or rather
presided over it during the second and final year of the inquiry " (*Richard Burdon
Haldane—An Autobiography* (1929) (pp. 124-6 and 90-92).

examiners, under a composite Senate having the smallest possible financial endowment, or administrative control. The reorganised University started on what was little more than a formal existence, in which all the several parts wrangled over and largely counteracted each other's projects and proposals. Some fresh convulsion, amounting perhaps to a new birth, was required to give the organism a genuine life.

What exactly was our scheme for the reconstructed London University: what kind of university was possible in London? Here are a few extracts from the article by the Other One in the *Nineteenth Century*, June 1902:

Any practical policy for a London University has, it is clear, to have regard to the limitations, the needs and the opportunities of London life. It may at the outset be admitted that, for any university of the Oxford or Cambridge type, the metropolis is perhaps more unfit than any other spot that could be chosen. By no possible expenditure could we create at South Kensington, in the Strand, or at Gower Street, the tradition, the atmosphere, the charm or the grace of collegiate life on the Isis or the Cam. Nor is it possible to secure, amid the heterogeneous crowds of London and all its distractions, either the class selection or the careful supervision required by the parents of boys fresh from Eton or Harrow, with two or three hundred a year to spend in pocket-money. . . . With the exception of country students coming to study medicine or engineering, the undergraduate class of London University will, we may infer, be confined to London residents, and, among these, to students from the 99 per cent of London homes which are maintained on incomes under £1500 a year. . . .

What, now, should be the policy of the new London University? First and foremost we must accept, as the basic principle of its structure, an organisation by faculties, not by colleges or other institutions. Only on this principle can we develop a university structure adapted to the needs and opportunities of the metropolitan area. London, it is clear, can have but one university. For the small German town or provincial English centre, the university may suitably be of simple and, so to speak, unicellular type. Oxford and Cambridge, with their close aggregation of separate colleges of identical pattern, present us with what may be called a multicellular development of the same elementary type. By no such simple repetition of parts could we create a university for the huge area and dissimilar conditions of the metropolitan districts. Its unique combination of a widely dispersed undergraduate population and centrally segregated materials for research, its union of the most democratic student life with the most perfectly selected intellectual aristocracy of science, necessarily call for a more highly organised structure. This is found in the establishment, as the principal organs of the university, of separate faculties, each of them highly differentiated in structure, so as to fit it for dealing, in its particular department of learning, with all the teaching and all the research from one end of London to another, and capable of indefinite expansion, without interfering with any other faculty, to meet the requirements of every part of the area and every development of the subject-matter. So long as the several colleges or other teaching institutions regard themselves, and are regarded, as the units of university organisation, their instinctive megalomania is a disruptive force, creating internecine jealousy and competition for students, and impelling each particular institution, irrespective of its local conditions or special opportunities, to strive to swell itself into a complete university on a microscopic scale. Make the faculty the unit, and the same megalomania impelling the professors to work for the utmost possible extension and improvement of the faculty as such, serves only to extend the influence and enhance the reputation of the university as a whole. This is not to say that there is no place in the London University for separately organised institutions and autonomous governing bodies. It is impracticable and undesirable for the University Senate or the University faculties to undertake the vast business of managing all the colleges and other teaching institutions within the metropolitan area. Whether these institutions devote themselves to particular departments of research, to special grades of teaching, to distinct subjects of study, or to the local requirements of their districts, the University will with advantage leave to their governing bodies a large autonomy in business management and finance, and concern itself only with seeing that such portions of their teaching staff and students, their courses of instruction and equipment, as are recognised by the University, are properly organised and co-ordinated with the larger life of the whole. The lines along which this co-ordination must necessarily proceed are marked out by the subjects of teaching or research; that is to say, by faculties. At present there are eight such faculties—namely, arts, science, medicine, law, music, theology, engineering and economics. But the number of separate faculties will gradually increase, either by simple additions, such as pedagogy and philosophy, or, with the advance of the subjects, by the further differentiation into separate organisations of such large and comprehensive divisions as " science " or " arts ". . . .

Thus, instruction will have to be provided in the evening as well as in the day-time, and it should be carried on, with proper relays of teachers, practically continuously throughout the whole year. There is no harm, and indeed great advantage, in these University courses being attached to polytechnics or technical institutes whose other departments are of less than university rank. The University will, of course, take care to appoint or recognise none but thoroughly competent teachers; it will see that the courses of instruction are given the genuine university spirit: it will maintain a high standard in laboratory accommodation: and it will naturally admit, as university students, only those who satisfy its matriculation and other requirements. Subject to these conditions, there can be nothing but advantage in an indefinite multiplication of opportunities for undergraduate study in the whole of the vast area extending from Maidenhead to Gravesend, from Guildford to Bishop's Stortford. In the popular faculties of science and engineering, there will, not improbably, soon be an effective demand—measured by the presence of fifty to a hundred undergraduate students at each place—for complete degree courses at forty or fifty such centres. Even such a multiplication would give, for each centre, a population as great as that of Aberdeen or Plymouth. The teachers at these exclusively undergraduate centres, who will be chosen, it may be hoped, from the ablest post-graduates of London or other universities, must, of course, be members of the faculties and boards of studies in their respective subjects, and every possible opportunity should be given for them to meet, for the discussion of how best to advance their particular branch of learning, not only their contemporaries, but also their more distinguished colleagues, the chief university professors, whose pupils they will probably have been. Only by the frank acceptance of some such policy of extreme local dispersion of the mere undergraduate teaching, coupled with a highly organised intellectual intercourse between all the university teachers in each subject, can the London University rise to the height of its opportunity as the university for seven millions. . . .

But a university is, or ought to be, much more than a mere place for teaching. Its most important function in the state is the advancement of every branch of learning. . . . For the advancement of learning in this, the Baconian sense, the conditions of London life, far from being adverse, are, in reality, in the highest degree favourable. Even without the staff or equipment of a great university, London has always contributed much more than its quota to scientific discovery. It was by no mere accident that Davy and Faraday, Huxley and Tyndall, Sir Joseph Hooker and Herbert Spencer, had all worked in London. London's unparalleled wealth in " material " for observation and study necessarily makes it the principal centre for every branch of English science. The intellectual environment is no less favourable than the wealth of material. The fact that all the learned societies meet in London is significant. No place provides, in each subject of study, so highly specialised a society, in which the ablest thinkers and investigators in any department of learning can meet in friendly converse, not only their foreign colleagues visiting the great city, but also those who are, in the practical business of life, both needing and using the newest discoveries. Add to these natural resources of metropolitan life a university of the type required by London's needs—a large closely knit and highly specialised professoriat in each faculty directing the researches of assistants and post-graduate students in the different branches of each science—and we shall have created, in the very heart of the British Empire, an almost ideal centre from which future generations of investigators and inventors may explore new realms of fact, discover new laws, and conquer new applications of knowledge of life. In the whole range of the physical and biological sciences, in the newer fields of anthropology, archaeology, philology, pedagogy and experimental psychology, in the wide vistas opening out for applied science and the highest technology, in the constantly changing spheres of industrial and commercial relations, administration and political organisation, we may predict with confidence that a rightly organised and adequately endowed London University will take a foremost part in the advancement of learning. . . .

It may be that we must forego in London University the culture born of classic scholarship and learned leisure. But, if we can show that there is no incompatibility between the widespread instruction of an undergraduate democracy and the most effective provision for the discovery of new truth; between the most practical professional training and genuine cultivation of the mind; between the plain living of hardworking students of limited means and high intellectual achievements, we shall not, I venture to believe, appeal in vain. London University must take its own line. They are futile dreamers who seek to fit new circumstances to the old ideals; rather must we strive, by developing to the utmost the opportunities that the present affords us, to create out of twentieth-century conditions new kinds of perfection.[1]

April 1902. *Friday's Hill.*—Sidney had Morant to stay here. Morant is the principal person at the Education Department. He has occupied the most anomalous position the last six months. Taken into the office as a nondescript in a humble capacity some years ago, Gorst picked him out for his private secretary. In that way he became acquainted with the politicians—Cabinet Ministers and Conservative private members, who were concerned with Education Bills and educa-

[1] "London University: A Policy and a Forecast", by Sidney Webb, *Nineteenth Century*, 1902.

tion policy. Presently these folk—specially the Cabinet Ministers, found him a useful substitute for Kekewich (permanent head), who was deadly opposed to their policy, and even for Gorst with whom they were hardly on speaking terms, the situation being complicated by the fact that Gorst and Kekewich were complete incompatibles, having no communication with each other! So Morant has been exclusively engaged by the Cabinet Committee to draft this present Bill, attending its meetings and consulting with individual members over clauses, trying to get some sort of Bill through the Cabinet. Both Kekewich and Gorst have been absolutely ignored. Neither the one nor the other saw the Bill before it was printed. Just before its introduction in the House, Morant wrote to Gorst saying he assumed he " might put his name at the back ". Gorst answered: " I have sold my name to the Government; put it where they instruct you to put it! " Morant gives strange glimpses into the working of one department of English government. The Duke of Devonshire, the nominal Education Minister, failing through inertia and stupidity to grasp any complicated detail half-an-hour after he has listened to the clearest exposition of it, preoccupied with Newmarket, and in bed till 12 o'clock; Kekewich trying to outstay this Government and quite superannuated in authority; Gorst cynical and careless, having given up even the semblance of any interest in the office; the Cabinet absorbed in other affairs, and impatient and bored with the whole question of education. " Impossible to find out after a Cabinet meeting," Morant tells us, " what has actually been the decision. Salisbury does not seem to know or care, and the various Ministers, who do care, give me contradictory versions. So I gather that Cabinet meetings have become more than informal—they are chaotic—breaking up into little groups, talking to each other without any one to formulate or register the collective opinion. Chamberlain would run the whole thing if he were not so overworked by his own department."

Sidney and Morant discussed for many hours the best way of so influencing the Cabinet and its advisers that we get a good authority for London. Decided to send out the T.E.B. report widely with personal letters, and to set on foot quiet " agitations " among the Church folk and other Conservative circles. Among others, Sidney has written a short note to Chamberlain drawing his attention to the policy of " delegation " in the T.E.B. [report], leaving it to be understood that he would be prepared to delegate management of the elementary schools (properly safeguarded) to borough council committees. Also to Balfour—in fact, I think he has written to every prominent personage, to each according to his views and degree of influence.

May 30th.—Yesterday the formal opening of the new building of the School of Economics, a day of satisfaction to Sidney, Hewins and myself. Our child, born only seven years ago in two back rooms in John Street, with a few hundreds a year, from the Hutchinson Trust, despised by the learned folk as a young man's fad, is now fully-grown and ready to start in the world on its own account. There is the building and equipment, all admirably planned to suit the sort of work and life we have built up; there are the staff of teachers modestly but permanently endowed, there are the formidable list of governors, over which Sidney presides, and last but not least the School has attained university status with its own curriculum, its own degrees, and with even a prospect of its own gown. Meanwhile, Sidney's personal work has broadened out into the administration of university affairs as a whole, his position on the Senate is strong and seems destined to become stronger, since he is always mentally on the spot long before the others have arrived there. He and Hewins too are a strong combination among the warring atoms, and are reinforced by Dr. Robertson of King's and such outside members as W. P. Reeves, and Lord Davey, whilst Sidney is one of Dr. Rucker's (the new principal) more confidential advisers. Should he become one of the trustees of the fund that Haldane is trying to raise, still more should he persuade the L.C.C. to " go " a $\frac{1}{4}$d. or $\frac{1}{2}$d. rate, his influence with the Senate will become alarmingly strong and no doubt create anger and envy in various quarters. He will then have to walk warily, and not abuse his predominance. Fortunately for his work, he never suffers from inflation, he is too completely absorbed in getting things done and too sincerely modest to lose his head. All his aggressiveness has disappeared with his good fortune, that is his personal aggressiveness, he remains a good fighter when he has his back to the wall. In his opinion, fighting should always be the last resource before being beaten on some main issue of real importance.

Peace with the Transvaal: political burial of the pro-Boers. Immediate increase in popularity of Government: rise of Rosebery " futures ". He is playing the game of leading the Liberal Party on his own terms with consummate deftness.

June 5th. Friday's Hill.—Graham Wallas spent the afternoon and evening here without Audrey. He is more in his old form than I have seen him for years. The approaching abolition of the School Board, in which he acquiesces (on general grounds of objection to *ad hoc* bodies and I think on the particular experience of the L.S.B.), has detached his mind from the minute details of school management and left it freer to turn back to the student's life. He and I had a long discussion— walking on Marley Common—as to our respective position with

R

regard to denominational religion. He recognises but deplores the growing tolerance of it, if not sympathy with religious teaching, on the part of confessed agnostics. He distinguished with some subtlety between the old broad Church party, who wished to broaden the creed of the Church to one which they could emphatically accept, and those religious-minded agnostics who accept Church teaching, not because they believe its assertions to be true, but lest worse befall the child's mind in the form of a crude materialistic philosophy. " I cannot see the spirit of genuine reform, if there is no portion of the Church's teaching which you object to more than any other; if you cease to discriminate between what you accept and what you reject, denying all and accepting all, with the same breath, denying the dogmas as statements of fact, accepting them as interpreting a spirit which pleases you. Dean Stanley and the broad churchmen were in quite different position: they denied the Athanasian Creed and wished it ousted, they believed the Apostles' Creed and fervently and sincerely desired it to be taught." I admitted there was much in his contention. I could only shelter myself by the argument that the reform of the Church was not the work I had undertaken to do, or which I was trained to consider. The practical alternatives before us constituted a very simple issue; whether we were to throw our weight against the continuance of the present form of religious teaching and help to establish pure materialism as the national metaphysic; or whether we would accept, provisionally, as part of the teaching in the schools, the dogmas and ritual of the Christian Church of to-day. For my own children, and for those of other people, I deliberately believed the lie of materialism to be far more pernicious and more utterly false than the untruths which seem to me to constitute the Christian formula of religion. Moreover, we are face to face with the fact that the vast majority of the English people are, as far as they think at all, convinced Christians. By insisting on secular education, I should be not only helping to spread what seems to me a bad kind of falsehood, but I should be denying to others the right to have their children taught the creed they hold to be positively true. I see no way out of the dilemma, but the largest variety possible of denominational schools, so that there may be the utmost possible choice for parents and children, and, let me add, the widest range of experiment as to the results of particular kinds of teaching on the character of the child and its conduct of life.

June 5th.—For about three weeks out of the eight, Bertrand Russell has been away staying with his friends the Whiteheads, and poor Alys has been too unwell to be here. A consciousness that something is wrong between them has to some extent spoilt our sojourn here, both Sidney and I being completely mystified. We became so concerned about the situation that I suggested that I should take Alys off to Switzerland to complete her cure, and Sidney acquiesced out of affection for her and genuine admiration for Bertrand. It would be a sin and a shame if those two should become separated, and altogether wanton misery for both. Our impression is that they have both erred in sacrificing themselves and each other to an altogether mistaken sense of obligation to other people. It is quite clear to me that Bertrand is going through some kind of tragedy of feeling; what is happening to her I suppose I shall discover in the next three or four weeks. It is the wantonness of this unhappiness which appals me: saddens and irritates both of us.

Bertrand Russell's nature is pathetic in its subtle absoluteness: faith in an absolute logic, absolute ethic, absolute beauty, and all of the most refined and rarefied type—his abstract and revolutionary methods of thought and the uncompromising way in which he applies these frightens me for his future, and the future of those who love him or whom he loves. Compromise, mitigation, mixed motive, phases of health of body and mind, qualified statements, uncertain feelings, all seem unknown to him. A proposition must be true or false; a character good or bad; a person loving or unloving, truth-speaking or lying. And this last year he has grown up quite suddenly from an intellectual boy into a masterful man, struggling painfully with his own nature and rival notions of duty and obligation. His hatred of giving pain and his self-control will, I think, save him from the disaster of doing what he would feel afterwards to have been wrong. But it is always painful to stand by and watch a struggle one cannot help. The background of life here has, therefore, not been happy—especially for me, as I have had time and opportunity to observe and brood over it. Sidney, though most anxious and willing to give a helping hand (even to the extent of letting me leave him for three weeks!), is somewhat impatient with this quite unnecessary pain. However, the problems of human relationship have a way of unravelling themselves when those concerned are intelligent, warm-hearted and healthy in body and mind. The first thing to be done is to get Alys well. I am myself looking forward to the complete change and rest. My cure is not complete: I still suffer from eczema in one of my ears, due I believe to my greedy persistence in drinking coffee which I believe is rank poison to me. Also my recent attempts to companionise Bertrand so as to keep him here (which I believe to be Alys's desire) have meant more mental exertion than is consistent with regular work. And I have not always been quite faithful to the regimen: now and again a naughty greedy feeling overtakes me at a meal and I exceed! But I am improving in that respect; keep always before me the scale and the weights. I wanted, having spent yesterday in packing, to get back to the book, but I cannot stand the knocking and cleaning going on in the house—so off I go into the woods with *Mrs. Warren's Profession*—just sent me by G. B. S.

July 1902. *Friday's Hill.*—The last days of our stay—Sidney in London and I packing up our MSS. and blue-books preparatory to the advent of a large party of Berensens, etc.

I have worked well, but with small result in actual stuff written. Of the eight weeks we have been here nearly two were spent on the University article, counting proof-correcting, and another two in reading through and analysing the whole of the Poor Law Commission evidence of 1833–34. Another week has been more or less spent in entertaining and resting, so that not more than a fortnight has been actually consumed in writing. But what I have done is to get the whole poor law section planned out and about half-written, as well as the general scheme of Part II. of the book conceived, so that now the work will go straight forward. Sidney has only been able to write out (he always elucidates and completes my rough draft) what I have done, spending only one or two days a week down here. It has been a broken time for him, absorbed in University and T.E.B. committees, consultations, redrafting of Garnett's and Hewins's reports, writing memoranda for Haldane on university matters, for Conservative M.P.'s and Bishops on " The New Education Authority for London ", and keeping our eye on the Fabian Society and the Liberal League, altogether a somewhat distracted life. But he is very happy in his activity, feels ways opening out before him of getting at least some things done in the direction he believes right. Sometimes he is weary and longs to retire to " a cottage " with me and " write books ", but more often he is happily active—unconscious of anything but his desire to transact the business in hand, successfully. He has a delightful unselfconscious nature: he has (thank the Lord!) no " subconscious self ": when not at work, or asleep, or talking, he reads—reads—reads— always ready for a kiss or a loving word, given or taken. " I am frightened at my own happiness ", he often says.

July 21*st.*—Mr. Haldane came to lunch with us yesterday. He has been immersed in writing his Gifford lectures and was absorbed by his peculiar and personal vision of the " Absolute ". He is still keen on the University and full of energy and hopefulness. But much depressed about politics; does not evidently trust Rosebery. Thinks the Conservatives are going to pieces; that the leaders would even like to be defeated and retire for a year or two; that C. B. would grasp at office on any terms, and that it would end in the fresh discredit of Liberalism with the " Limps " forced into the position of Liberal

Unionists. If asked, Rosebery might accept a coalition with the younger Tories and leave his lieutenants in the lurch and the Liberals in a discredited opposition. For the present he is chiefly concerned to prevent the defeat of the Education Bill and came to consult Sidney about it. Sidney advised a demonstration in the *Nineteenth Century* of educationalists in favour of the Bill, to strengthen Balfour's hand, and again to urge the inclusion of London. Sidney has to write a memorandum on London situation to go through Hugh Cecil to Balfour.

Attended one or two meetings of the Trades Union Congress and had delegates to tea for three days. Dominant note of the Congress is determination to run Labour candidates on a large scale, and faith in the efficacy of this device for gaining all they require. The notion is to have Labour men in the field in a number of constituencies before the Liberal candidate is selected. There is no leadership in the Congress; little respect of one man more than another; but a certain unanimity of opinion among the delegates; less cleavage between trade and trade, or between Old and New Unionists than in any Congress I have before attended. Practically the Congress has been captured (as far as its formal expression of opinion is concerned) by the I.L.P. We find ourselves quite out of harmony with it collectively, though on cordial and confidential terms with many of the delegates.

Odd letter from Rosebery. I sent him a card for my trade union teas, more to let him know what we were doing than expecting him to come. Foolish of him not to have responded to the request from the trade unionists for an entertainment at his house. He needs strengthening on the democratic side, and it would have cost him so little! The half-heartedness of these leaders to their work of leadership annoys us. If it is worth our while at great inconvenience and expense to us— we who have nothing to gain politically—how much more is it their game. Asquith, too, with a house at St. Albans within one hour of London, cannot bestir himself to come up for one day for the Congress, let alone entertain the delegates in his empty house in Cavendish Square. He, too, with the memory of Featherstone to wipe out! Why play the game at all if you mean to play so carelessly, and with so little enjoyment of the process or concern for the result?

October 14th.—All our Radical friends bitter or sullen with us over Sidney's support of the Education Bill. Certainly, if he had political ambitions, it would have been a suicidal policy on his part. Fortunately, we enjoy the incomparable luxury of freedom from all care for ourselves. We are secure in our love for one another and we are absolutely content with our present daily life, as far as our own interest and happiness is concerned. Well we may be! I have a constant wonder whether we are earning our excellent maintenance. Sidney certainly does, assuming that his work is in the right direction, for he is at it from nine o'clock in the morning continuously until 7.30, and once or twice a week lectures in the evening as well. For myself, I peg along every morning at the book for three or four hours, sometimes putting in half-an-hour in the afternoon. But, generally, I find it pays better to do nothing in the afternoons except take exercise, especially as almost every day we have someone to lunch or to dine to talk shop. We have had the whole professoriate of the School (25) to dinner in detachments, and a selection of the students in afterwards. As president of the [Students'] Union, I am trying to develop the social side of the School and have arranged to be " At Home " to students on alternate Wednesdays next term.

November 10*th.*—The School has opened with éclat. There are now actually at work five hundred students and the staff is hard put to it to meet the new strains. The railway companies have at last come into it with a determination to make use of the lecturing both as an educational training and as a test of capacity of their staff of clerks. For the last three years the Great Western Railway has sent some thirty or forty and paid their fees, but the attendances have been perfunctory and usually tailed off towards the end of the term. This year Wilkinson (Great Northern) [?] took the matter up with vigour: selected groups of courses for each clerk, sent an inspector to see that they attended and to listen to the lectures, required shorthand notes of the lectures to be submitted to him, and gave it out that he would read the three best essays contributed by his staff submitted to him by the Director of the School. The writer of the best essay, an unnoticed clerk in a minor department, has been promoted to the general manager's office. The Great Northern general manager, at the instigation of Lord Rosebery (who is said to talk of " our School " at the meetings of the directors), has had a long talk with Hewins, and arranged to send a contingent to the classes and to require them to pass examinations before being promoted. If this precedent be followed by other business undertakings and by public bodies, we shall have done a good deal to promote efficiency in administration. Hewins, of course, is a little bit over-confident and elated, but that is his temperament. He inspires confidence in men of affairs and has, in fact, more the business than the academic mind; though sufficiently intellectual to state concrete facts in terms of general principles. His weak point is lack of accuracy and rapidity in the despatch of business; he is slovenly in such matters as proof-correcting and dilatory in getting certain things done. But there is usually method in his carelessness, and things left undone or mistaken are usually matters about which his judgement has been over-ruled or to which his aims are slightly different from those of the governors. His carelessness is, in fact, instinctively selective if not intentionally so. It is aggravating because he always agrees to do the job.

But he and Sidney, and to a lesser extent I myself, make a good working trio. The whole internal organisation of the School is left to him with suggestions from Sidney; the whole financial side is in Sidney's hands, whilst my domain has been roping in influential supporters from among old friends and connections. Every Tuesday Hewins lunches here and we discuss the affairs of the School in all its aspects; he consults Sidney about the curriculum; Sidney tells him the requirements for securing L.C.C., Technical Education Board and University support, I submit to both my little schemes for entertaining various persons likely to be useful. Almost every week since early in October we have had dinners of eight to ten—lecturers and governors, likely friends and supporters, and students to lunch. . . . The rest of our social life, which is both lively and interesting, is deliberately designed to help forward the University, the Progressive Party on the L.C.C., and to a slight extent to give Haldane and his friends a friendly lift whenever an opportunity comes that way. The Liberal League, notably Haldane and Rosebery, have been good friends to us, and we feel bound to return in kind.

Haldane and Sidney are constantly co-operating in educational matters. Haldane has taken a bold line in supporting the Government Bill (Education) and breaking from his political friends. His position as a party politician was so damaged before that I doubt whether it has been much worsened. Undoubtedly, if Rosebery goes under and the Campbell-Bannerman lot romp in, Haldane is pretty well done for, unless they should be desperately short of men. On the other hand, he has improved his status as a leader of opinion, has shown that he knows and is keen about the higher branches of education. And the higher branches of education are one of the coming questions. It seems likely that the beginning of the twentieth century will be noted as the starting point of the new form of university training and university research—the application of the scientific method to the facts of daily life, politics and business. In this movement, Haldane will have played one of the principal though unseen parts. His career is interesting as combining that of a considerable lawyer, an education reformer and an intriguing politician (though the intrigues are always to promote a cause, never to push himself). It is a paradox that a mind that is essentially metaphysical, laying stress on the non-material side of human thought and feeling, should have been, as a matter of fact, chiefly engaged in promoting applied physical science.

Rosebery is not making way in the country and is, I imagine, having a bad time with himself. He has no grip of anything except appearances. He is so intent on trying to find out which course will *appear right* to the ordinary man of affairs, that he forgets altogether to think out which course will work out best in social results. He seems positively frightened at the thought of any such enquiry. Publicly and privately Sidney has pressed on the Liberal League the necessity of its leaders making up their minds as to what they would do if they had the power. Rosebery and Haldane hang back—they do not want to be committed. " Quite so," says Sidney; " don't publish anything or decide on any course, but let us at least have the facts at our command and know all the alternative courses." He is, however, a voice in the wilderness.

November 15th.—I took the Prime Minister [Arthur Balfour] in to dinner! I say " took " because he was so obviously delivered over into my hands by my kindly hostess who wished me to make as much use as possible of the 1¼ hours he had free from the House. It was a little party of eight at the house of the charming Mrs. Horner—High Priestess of the "Souls", in their palmy days, now somewhat elderly and faded but gracious to those she accepts as distinguished. The other diners were Lady Elcho and Haldane, Mr. Horner and a handsome daughter.

Balfour has the charm of genuine modesty and unselfconsciousness, and that evening he seemed in earnest about education. He is delightfully responsive intellectually—a man with an ever open mind—too open, perhaps, seeing that on no question has it been sufficiently closed by study and thought to have developed principles. There comes a time in life when surely the mind should be made up conclusively as to the particular questions with which it is mainly concerned; man's work in life is action and not enquiry? Balfour's intellect has not the organic quality; there is no determinate result from the combination of his reason with his knowledge of facts. His opinions shift uneasily from side to side; the one permanent bias being in favour of personal refinement of thought and feeling. But I doubt whether he has any clear notion of how he would attempt to bring about this refinement in other people, except by personal example and influence. On the other hand, he has no bias in favour of *laisser-faire*. Action or inaction are open questions, and it is a chapter of accidents on which side he throws himself. But he *intends* to work on the side which at the moment he *thinks right*—not merely on the side that will appear right to other people—which I fear is Lord Rosebery's predicament. All this elaborate analysis based on one hour!

I set myself to amuse and interest him, but seized every opportunity to insinuate sound doctrine and information as to the position of

London education. Sidney says I managed skilfully, but then he is a partial judge! We found ourselves in accord on most questions. Perhaps that is only another way of saying that Arthur Balfour is a sympathetic and attractive person who easily tunes his conversation to the other minds. I can understand how colleagues in the House of Commons forgive his incapacity for transacting business: the flavour of his personality is delightful.

Three dinners and two evening parties at one's house in eight days is severe! But it seemed desirable to give a Conservative–L.C.C. dinner and a London University reception; and also a " Limp " dinner, and a " Limp " reception. Then there was a dinner to Lady Elcho to acknowledge her kindness to us in Gloucestershire and our introduction to Balfour; an introduction which may have good results. So I asked her to meet John Burns, the Shaws, H. G. Wells and Asquith. John Burns took the palm; his unselfconscious exuberance, dramatic faculty and warmth of feeling amounted to brilliancy; he gave us vivid pictures of prison and other episodes; views on the army; Eton and the aristocracy; on working-class and middle-class life; all fresh and interesting with a certain romantic sentiment for what was ancient and distinguished. Shaw and Wells were not at their ease—G. B. S. was jerkily egotistical and paradoxical, though he behaved well in encouraging Burns to take the stage; Wells was rather silent; when he spoke he tried hard to be clever—he never let himself go. Asquith was simply dull. He is disheartened with politics, has no feeling of independent initiative, and is baffled by Rosebery, snubs and is snubbed by C. B. He has worked himself into an unreal opposition to the Education Bill. He is not really convinced of the iniquity or unwisdom of the Bill he is denouncing. He eats and drinks too much and lives in a too enervating social atmosphere to have either strenuousness or spontaneity. Clearly he is looking to the money-making Bar for his occupation in life. As a lawyer he is essentially common quality; no interest in, or understanding of, legal principles; no ingenuity or originality in making new influences or adapting old rules to new conditions. However, he is under no delusion about himself; he has resigned himself to missing leadership.

The dinner was successful and thrilling to Lady Elcho, enjoying the new sensation of meeting such strange forms of distinction as Burns, Wells, Shaw at the house of the Sidney Webbs.

The " education " and " Moderate " dinner consisted of Sir Alfred Lyall and wife, Sir Owen Roberts (clerk to the Clothworkers and an excellent friend of ours) and wife, Sir John Dickson Poynder (L.C.C. Moderate and Conservative M.P., a simple-hearted, public-spirited country gentleman of attractive mien), Sir Lacy Robinson (L.C.C.

Moderate, former civil servant and a new governor of School of Economics), Mrs. J. R. Green, Beatrice Chamberlain and Charles Booth (whom I happened to meet in the street the day before). After dinner, we had some 30 or 40 of the educationists and University men-folk—Sir John Gorst and some eight L.C.C. Moderates. They all knew each other, or wanted to know each other, so that talk was incessant.

Finally, we had one " Limp " dinner yesterday—Sir E. Grey, Haldane, B. Russell, Wilberforce and Wiles (two L.C.C. Progress-ives), Harben (a promising young Liberal Leaguer), Isaac Mitchell (one of the ablest of the younger trade union officials) and Perry (the most influential of the university medicals and a Liberal Progressive). Lion Phillimore—the one lady to keep me company. In the evening some sixty men came in—trade union officials, L.C.C. Progressives, journalists and " Limp " M.P.'s. I introduced vigorously and they all chatted and chattered sometimes in confidential *tête-à-têtes*, sometimes in groups. Haldane, who had dined with us, chaffed me about the resurrection of the " Souls " in Grosvenor Road.

The interest of the evening to me was a long talk during dinner with Sir Edward Grey. Like Balfour he is a man of exquisite flavour; he is high-minded, simple, kindly and wise, without being able or clever—an ideal element in a Cabinet containing some strong master-mind. *But he is not the master-mind*: I doubt whether it would be physically or mentally possible for him to work eight hours a day, for, say, ten months of the year; he has neither the knowledge, the depth of feeling, nor the personal grip on life, to have a strong will or deeply-rooted convictions. His temperament is an exquisite poise—far above human passions and human prejudices—in an atmosphere rarefied by public spirit, fastidious honour and widely diffused human fellowship, essentially a passive and receptive nature, revelling in the beauties of nature, the interest of books, and the charm of one or two intimate friendships with men and women of like character in simple and refined surroundings.

The last entry in the diary of 1902 forecasts the leading preoccupation of the Other One during the following three years, 1903–5, signalised in the following chapter.

December 1902.—Morant dined here last night alone to talk over chances of London Education Bill. Wearied out with the autumn campaign and the prospect of having to superintend the working out of the new Education Act with a rotten staff and a hostile minority in each district determined to wreck the Act. He says that Balfour is furious with the Church, and the Church disconsolate with its bargain;

Londonderry a bull in a china shop, and Anson too academically clever to be a comfortable fifth wheel in the coach. He had drafted a Bill for London of two clauses applying the Act. " Quite satisfactory to you ", he observed. But alas! Walter Long, elated with his triumph over the constitution of the Water Board, says " he will be d——d before he sees the L.C.C. the education authority ". Morant doubts whether anyone wants any particular change sufficiently to get discordant views into line—the Church hesitates as to the worth-while of it, the Unionist members are terrified at the N.U.T., on the one hand, and the Tory political worker, on the other; no member of the Cabinet is keen to enhance the dignity of the L.C.C., though all except Long realise that the borough councils would be impossible. But Long is a loud-voiced persistent creature, who talks his colleagues down at Cabinet and committee meetings and is in touch with the commoner kind of obscurant Tory. So matters look dark and the present unsatisfactory situation is likely to persist, at least for the forthcoming year.

CHAPTER VI

THE LONDON EDUCATION ACT
AND AFTER
1903–1905

THE passage of the London Education Act of 1903 proved
to be a landmark in Our Partnership: a successful achievement which entailed some consequences that were unpleasant. Without the broad base of universal compulsory
elementary education, including within its ambit the denominational schools, the whole under the control of the
London County Council, the unification of London education would have been both incomplete and unsubstantial.
But this drastic reform involved not only the supersession
of the *ad hoc* school board, but also " putting Rome on the
rates ", not to mention also the Anglican established Church
schools abhorred by the more fanatical Nonconformists.
Hence, Sidney Webb's support of the Education Act of
1902, which abolished all school boards and handed over
not only the board schools with their undenominational
Christianity (subject to a conscience clause) but also the
denominational schools, Catholic, Anglican and Wesleyan,
to the provincial county councils and county borough
councils, nearly all of them Conservative outside the metropolis, had already offended both the orthodox Liberals and
the powerful Nonconformist element in the nascent Labour
Party. And this contradiction of orthodox Liberalism seemed
even more offensive when applied to the metropolis. Here,
at any rate, the Conservative Party was divided in its policy,
and there might be some hope of keeping the School Board
as the education authority. Gradually the Progressive Party
realised that the Conservative Cabinet was being encouraged
by a leading member of the party to go forward with the
abolition of the London School Board, with the important

qualification that the London County Council was to be substituted for the indirectly elected federation of metropolitan borough councils which had been the original Conservative proposal. This willingness to accept the placing of denominational schools on the rates, and thus give them a position of permanence in the British educational system, seemed to be all the more objectionable seeing that the Webbs were known not to belong to any Christian denomination, Protestant or Roman Catholic, but to be nothing better than agnostics.

How did we come to take up this position? We realised the strength of the common British objection to making the taxpayer maintain the teaching of a religion in which he did not believe, and which he often regarded as damnably injurious both to his children and to the community. But, rightly or wrongly, we were convinced that, at that time and probably for many years afterwards, there was no alternative way of securing for every child throughout the kingdom, irrespective of class or creed, the maximum duration and efficiency of educational facilities that the House of Commons could be induced to afford.

What were the alternative ways of solving this difficult problem of creating a universal compulsory system of elementary education, paid for out of rates and taxes, and administered by a public authority, without offending the conscience of parents or teachers? I may note in passing that, in the early years of the twentieth century, it was only rival religious creeds, concerned with man's relation to the universe and with life after death, which raised questions of conscience. It was at that time never suggested, as is the case in many countries to-day, that the child should be taught deliberately to prefer one political constitution or economic system rather than another. This absence of conscientious objection was in the main due to a general agreement among contemporary educationalists that political and economic problems were not fit subjects for children of school age. But it was also a sign that there was no practical objection among the inhabitants of Great Britain to the *status quo*, as represented in the school text-books, historical or geographical, which were used in the course of education.

So far as we knew there were three or four solutions actually practised in the Anglo-Saxon world. In England, part of the curriculum in all rate-supported schools included the teaching of undenominational Christianity—whatever that may mean—with a conscience clause for teachers and the children of conscientious objectors, the persons concerned being absolved from taking part in these particular classes. Outside the publicly supported and administered schools, there were the denominational schools which were aided by Government grants, though not by the rates. There was no provision from public funds for those parents or teachers who objected to the faith in the miraculous embodied in all Christian sects. In Scotland, on the other hand, where only two Christian sects were recognised, the Presbyterian and the Roman Catholic, the custom was that the head master should belong to the same denomination as the majority of the children, and the assistant master should represent the other recognised sect of Christians. In that way Presbyterian and Roman Catholic children alike had the specific religious dogmas in which their parents believed as part of their training.

In most of the states of the U.S.A. the schools were secular, and there was no provision of any kind for Catholics or Evangelicals, who desired that their children should be brought up in a religious faith. Hence, one or two million children were being brought up outside the state school system, mostly in Roman Catholic schools, without any public provision and with no public inspection, the result being, as we had discovered in our recent tour in the U.S.A., that both teachers and schools were disastrously below any decent standard of efficiency. The same principle was pursued in New Zealand and in some of the states of Australia: in its most rigid form in Victoria. In the Victoria of the 'nineties the Roman Catholics had succeeded, whilst maintaining their own schools, in preventing the publicly supported schools from teaching any history (which they asserted must be partial either to the Protestant or to the Roman Catholic religion), or reciting any poetry in which God was mentioned. When, for instance, Wordsworth's " Ode to Immortality " was objected to on the ground that it mentioned the Deity, the Minister of Education telegraphed: " Insert ' the Gods ' ". On the other hand, one of the American states insisted on " fundamentalist " Christian doctrine, and would not permit the teaching of biological science, because research into the evolution of life contradicted the Old Testament story of the creation of the world with all the living creatures it contains in six days, with God resting on the seventh, surveying with complacency the result of his creativeness.

What was proposed in the Acts of 1902 and 1903, applying to England and Wales only, was that all schools which provided elementary education up to a certain standard should come on the rates, and be controlled by the public authority; but that such of them as had been provided by a religious denomination should be permitted to choose teachers of their own creed provided that they were efficient in secular subjects, and that, subject to a conscience clause, there should be religious teaching according to the creed of the denominational school. This solution seemed to us, *in the then state of public opinion*, the most likely to be accepted and loyally carried out while maximising the efficiency and duration of the educational opportunities for the mass of the children of the United Kingdom.[1]

---

[1] It is a curious reflection that this unwillingness or inability to give religious instruction is far more common in council schools than in the avowedly denominational schools, where the teachers are chosen because they belong to the Roman Catholic or Anglican churches. This reluctance, on the part of teachers, leaves the child's mind in a state of bewilderment, leading in many cases to cynical indifference or hypocritical make-believe. The question arises: what is the alternative? It seems impracticable to teach a child how to behave—an important part of education—without some sincerely held scale of ethical values arising out of some definite conception of man's relation to man, and man's relation to the universe. Have we, in Great Britain, yet developed any genuine science of ethics arising out of observation, generalisation and verification, and based on a sincerely held vision of man's destiny? In the middle of the nineteenth century Auguste Comte and his followers believed that they had invented a religion of humanity, for which they actually started churches with rites and sermons. But this Comtist sect, though including some distinguished minds, petered out, perhaps because it was mixed up with economic and political speculations which failed to gain acceptance. In the past decade the USSR

1903

The narrative of our daily life, excluding our researches into English local government which have already been described in Chapter IV, will be found in the following entries in my diary, whether these relate to the administrative activities and the manipulation of public opinion by the Other One, or to our intercourse with relatives, friends and fellow-workers. To these I have added a few criticisms of books and my own reflections on the destiny of man and his instinctive reaction to the unknown or the unknowable. I do this, not because these casual notes have any value in themselves, but merely because they indicate a conflict in my mind between a conscientious desire to be strictly rationalistic, and an instinctive longing for some sanction other than scientific reasoning, for believing in the eternal worthwhileness of human life. For it was to this latent " religiosity " in one of the partners that some critics attributed our dubious association with Anglican bishops and Catholic priests, not to mention Conservative politicians and civil servants, in our pursuit of the educational policy embodied in the London Education Act of 1903.

January 16th. Overstrand.—For the first time for many years the three old friends—Sidney, Bernard Shaw and Graham Wallas—spent a week together with their wives as chorus—the Shaws at the big hotel nearby and the Wallases with us. Three delightful evenings we spent listening to G. B. S. reading his new work—*Man and Super-Man*. To me it seems a great work; quite the biggest thing he has done. He has found his *form*: a play which is not a play; but only a combination of essay, treatise, interlude, lyric—all the different forms illustrating the same central idea, as a sonata manifests a scheme of melody and harmony. I was all the more delighted with it, as I had not been impressed with the bits I had heard before, and Sidney had reported unfavourably of the play itself. Possibly, the unexpectedness of the success has made me over-value it—a reaction from a current in my mind of depreciation of G. B. S. Then I am so genuinely delighted at

thinks it has evolved in its political and economic structure, and its steadfast pursuit of science, in all its applications to social life, not only a fresh code of conduct, but also a new vision of man's future.

his choice of subject. *We* cannot touch the subject of human breeding —it is not ripe for the mere industry of induction, and yet I realise that it is the most important of all questions, this breeding of the right sort of man. G. B. S.'s audacious genius can reach out to it.

Graham was somewhat depressed, physically and mentally; and, though affectionate and pleasant to us, he has a deeply-rooted suspicion that Sidney is playing false with regard to religious education. He wants all religious teaching abolished. As Sidney is not himself a "religionist", Graham thinks that he too should wish it swept away. Politically, this seems to Sidney impossible, whilst I do not desire it even if it were possible. So between us we are prepared for a working agreement with the mammon of ecclesiasticism. Poor dear Wallas consequently sees this working agreement writ large in every act of the T.E.B., however irrelevant it may be to the religious issue (an issue which appears to Sidney to intervene as only a minute part of public education). Whether the T.E.B. takes action or omits to take action on any question there is always in Graham's eyes the priest behind the policy. This suspicion makes frank co-operation between Sidney and our old friend impossible—and though personal relations remain affectionate and appreciative, I fear there must be some official friction if not actual hostility. As Sidney's side is bound to win, though possibly Sidney himself will be sacrificed, it is to be hoped that Graham will retire from educational administration. He tried to talk G. B. S. round to his view, but failed. G. B. S. is too rootedly sceptical about all alternative philosophies to be inclined to oust Christianity by *force majeure*.

Meanwhile, we fear we shall lose on the question of the authority for London education. Inspired by Haldane the *Times* came down on our side and Sidney is seeing the *Daily Mail*. But the political Conservative is dead against the L.C.C. for London. . . . Moreover, the official opposition has declared in favour of an *ad hoc* body. The Progressives on the L.C.C. have not liked to claim education as their province; they have only been frightened by Sidney with the bogey of the borough council into holding their official tongue!

February 1st.—Sidney hard at work making public opinion as to the education authority. He interviewed Harmsworth and his "boy" editors, and the former handed over the direction of the campaign in the *Daily Mail* to Sidney.[1] He has seen Buckle of the *Times* and

---

[1] S. W. says (in 1937) that what he remembers is that, almost despairing of inducing the Cabinet to give London education to the L.C.C., he wrote at a venture to Harmsworth, whom he had never met, stating that he happened to know that the draft Bill proposed to entrust London education to a body formed by indirect election, like the old Metropolitan Board of Works. He said that he was convinced

Lawson of the *Telegraph* and Spencer Wilkinson of the *Morning Post*. He is stimulating the Church and educationalists generally to put pressure on Balfour. Haldane reports that it is still undecided, Walter Long holding out for a borough educational authority—or at any rate a majority of borough councillors on the L.C.C. committee. Progressives of L.C.C. sulky: some jealous of Sidney, others conscientiously opposed to any compromise with regard to Church schools. If L.C.C. finds itself the authority, it will be, I believe, entirely due to Sidney— to the excellent reputation of the T.E.B. under his guidance, and to his persistent efforts to stir up public opinion in favour of the L.C.C. But all this means Sidney's distraction from the book. And as it also entails a good deal of entertaining, it is a serious drain on my energy. However, the aim is worth the labour. From the standpoint of the book the worst is that, if we succeed, it will result in a big, difficult and continuous task for Sidney. All the more reason for me to keep in the highest degree of efficiency. Abstemiousness of body and calmness of mind the one way. . . .

Read through Haldane's *Pathway to Reality* on the journey to and fro—out of friendship for the author. To me his metaphysic seems an attempt to " intellectualise " the emotional assertion of a " beyond " which is bound to fail. What is called " verification " is impossible; there is no conceivable external test of the truth of your thought, and therefore no way of convincing those who do not think the same thought as you. If you are conscious of a great reality, this consciousness *may* be as valid as any other part of your consciousness? But its validity remains your own secret, not communicable to those who are not already in possession of it. Possibly, by attempting to put it into words, you rouse in other minds the knowledge that they *do* possess the secret somewhere—in the recesses of their souls—but for this purpose the emotional assertion of poetry and piety seem to me more effective than ratiocination. However, there are minds who can only accept the

---

that this would be disastrous for education, and what was more, he was sure that the London Conservative M.P.'s would not stand it. Hence the Government would have to give way; and why should not the *Daily Mail* have the credit of making the Government give way? To his intense surprise and delight, Harmsworth answered at once, asking him to call on Monday at 4.30 P.M. He was ushered in and found Harmsworth looking amazingly youthful, seated in conference with four still more boyish-looking assistant editors. Harmsworth asked several sharp questions, and then said, " Very well, Mr. Webb, we'll do it. But we don't know anything about the subject. You must come in every night at 11 P.M. for a week, and see that we say everything just right." Needless to say, S. W. jumped at the chance, and for a week sat with Thomas Marlowe, who was then the chief acting editor, and corrected the reports and paragraphs on London education. " I never revealed to anyone ", he laughingly said, years afterwards, " that one of my experiences had been to edit the *Daily Mail* for a week." How much this episode contributed to the formation of opinion on the Conservative side of the House of Commons no one can compute.

assertion when clothed in the form of a syllogism; and it is to these minds that metaphysics, I imagine, appeal. You must feel the need for this assertion, and you must have an intense predilection for reasoning and then you will find salvation in metaphysics. Emily Brontë's " Last Lines " are to me more convincing than the *Pathway to Reality*:

> " There is not room for death,
> Nor atom that his might could render void,
> Thou, thou art Being and Breath,
> And what thou art may never be destroyed."

February 25th.—A succession of dinners over the Education Bill, mostly Conservative and Church. Among our guests the Bishop of Stepney,[1] a remarkable man, who will go far. He is Creighton, without either his defects or his finest qualities; but, for that very reason, far more effective as an ecclesiastical statesman. The new kind of ecclesiastic with his eye on the *new social classes*, intent on winning for the Church democratic support. An Erastian in doctrine, anxious to see the 39 Articles and all other inconveniently obsolete documents regarded simply as formulae of historical interest, but not binding on the conscience. The Dean of Westminster, a scholar and mystic, is more attractive to me but not nearly so efficient.[2]

Met Sir William Anson at C. A. Cripps' (our brother-in-law has come out as an L.C.C. man), a pleasant subtle-minded don, a perfect head to a college, but singularly out of place in an administrative position.[3] Far more interested in discussing the relation of the Privy Council to the local authorities of the seventeenth and eighteenth centuries than the proper authority for dealing to-day with London's education. Indeed, one felt he knew so little of the elements of the latter subject, that it was barely worth while talking to him. Still it is desirable to have him not " agin us " and he must be asked to dinner. The interests of the School and the University and the smooth working of the L.C.C. have all to be considered in our little entertainments. Meanwhile, we try to get a morning's work, however perfunctory, at the book. We often long for that cottage in the country and the peaceful existence of a student life. We sometimes wonder whether such an existence would not be, in the long run, more useful. But then someone must do the rough and tumble work of government. It is a tiresome fact that to get things done in what one considers the best way, entails so much—to speak plainly—of intrigue. There is no such thing as spontaneous public opinion; it all has to be manufactured from

[1] Cosmo Gordon Lang. [2] Dr. Joseph Armitage Robinson.
[3] Vice-President of the Committee of Council on Education; M.P. for Oxford University.

a centre of conviction and energy radiating through persons, sometimes losing itself in an unsympathetic medium, at other times gaining additional force in such an agent as the Bishop of Stepney, or the *Daily Mail*. Of course, there is always the element of " sport " in this life of agitation: watching the ideas one starts (like, for instance, " the dominance of the National Union of Teachers over the borough councils ") wending their ways through all sorts of places and turning up quite unexpectedly as allies in overthrowing counter interests and arguments. It is fortunate when one happens to believe in one's own arguments: one always does so in a fashion, the most one does is to suppress the qualification. Is that " debasing the currency " or is it permissible to accept the position of an advocate to tell the truth but not the whole truth? As a matter of fact, with regard to administrative work, we plunge without hesitation on to the position of an advocate pledged only to display the arguments which tell in favour of the cause we believe in. In our scientific work, however, we honestly seek to tell the truth, the whole truth, and nothing but the truth; a distinction in standards which puzzles and perplexes me. . . .

March 14*th*.—The L.C.C. Progressives, or some of them, are playing the fool about the London education authority. So determined are they to " spite the Government " and so anxious for a good battle cry, that they are steering straight into a " Water Board " authority for education. A little *clique* headed by J. R. MacDonald and fighting all they know how Sidney's influence on the T.E.B.; some of the weaker of the rank and file, somewhat jealous of Sidney, are playing into their hands. Sidney thought it better to offer himself to the Progressive cause for election as chairman of the T.E.B. this year, in order to facilitate negotiations with the Government, but has given it to be understood that he does not wish to be chairman except with the full consent of the Progressive members of the Board. J. R. MacDonald has set to work to detach them from him and has succeeded with the Labour men (who are secularist, *ad hoc*, and anti-higher education) and one or two other middle-class members who are ambitious to be chairmen themselves. It remains to be seen whether he carries the caucus to-morrow. Sidney has refrained from canvassing and stood on his dignity—we both thought that, if the L.C.C. Progressives deserted him, it would be better to play for a " reaction " in his favour by having an inferior man elected chairman, under whom the Board would chafe. Of course, these dissensions will injure the chances of the Bill being on the right lines, as it will be open to the Moderates to say to the Government, that the one good man ready to carry out the Act has been rejected by his own party. It is strange that these personal enemies don't see that Sidney's position will be immensely stronger on a mixed board of borough councillors, L.C.C. and outsiders, than on a genuine L.C.C. committee, and that if he were playing for his own dominance he would go straight for that. Meanwhile, it will be a big misfortune for democratic government, even of the kind they believe most in, if the L.C.C. is put on one side as unfit to be the education authority.

I have been pondering over the question whether I could have done anything to stop the " slump in Webbs " on the Progressive side. Of course, our attention has been absorbed in getting hold of forces in the enemy's camp, and our frequent coming and going has excited suspicion in our own. They have not the wit to see that, if a Government is in power with an overwhelming majority, it is no use fighting it— at least not unless the other way has proved unavailing. Whether or not he is elected chairman to-morrow, I shall turn my attention seriously to the Progressive members of the T.E.B. when we come back from Longfords, and see what can be done to counteract J. R. MacDonald's machinations. I have suggested that whatever happens Sidney adopts an attitude of beneficent helpfulness. In only one eventuality would he fight the Progressive caucus—that is if J. R. MacDonald got himself nominated for chairman. In that case Sidney would propose Dr. Leaf, or failing him stand himself. But J. R. MacDonald is too shrewd to try that little game.

The complaint against Sidney resolves itself into this: (1) he is "in" with the Government; (2) he might sacrifice the interests of primary to secondary and university education; (3) he ignores the " religious " difficulty and is willing to be impartial between Anglican and " un-denominational " Christianity. Numbers (1) and (3) are true in essence; (2) is not true, at least in our most impartial moments we believe not. We don't believe you can raise the standard of elementary education and save it from mere mechanical efficiency unless you have the university in organic connection with it—unless you have mobility between all classes of teachers from the assistant master of the present elementary school to the research professor. The same with the students: the university must be open to them in fact as well as in theory. It lacks imagination to think that elementary education can be stimulating and progressive except as the broad base to the higher learning. Those who feel themselves specifically the representatives of Labour, fail through lack of ambition for their own clients and, be it added, through self-complacency with themselves as ideal reformers of society.

March 15th.—The " slump " in Webbs proves to be serious: Sidney was defeated by only four to three in a little caucus of Progressives on the T.E.B. But then, the others had not troubled to turn up, or had stayed away purposely, which means indifference if not hostility. The Board, after a little spluttering, acquiesced in the election of Shepheard and Leon, both *ad hoc* anti-voluntary school men, but not personally hostile to Sidney. There are indications, too, that this feeling of antagonism is not confined to this little group—the rank and file of the Progressives do not want the L.C.C. to be the authority and they think Sidney with his press and back-stair influence is bringing it about. The Crooks[1] election has swelled the Progressive head, and they feel inclined to fight for an *ad hoc* body and unsectarian education. The position has been worsened by an indiscretion of Dr. Garnett, the able secretary of the T.E.B. (which would not have occurred if Sidney had been chairman!), in circulating a memorandum in favour of a definite scheme of L.C.C. administration. Everyone believed Sidney to have had a hand in it.

But there is a very real cleavage between our views and those of the rank-and-file Radicals, and I do not see my way honestly to bridge it. We are not in favour of ousting religion from the collective life of the state; we are not in favour of the cruder form of democracy. And we *do* believe in expenditure on services which will benefit other classes besides the working-class, and which will open the way to working-men to become fit to *govern*, not simply to *represent* their own class; and we are in favour of economy as well as expenditure. But then what is the good of having means of one's own and some intelligence, unless one is prepared to advocate what is unpopular?

March 27th.—Matters not much mended. Hubbard, an honest Nonconformist rank-and-file member of the L.C.C., had put down a resolution in favour of *ad hoc* authority some weeks ago. McKinnon Wood and Collins, both in their hearts anxious for the L.C.C. authority as unifying London government, called a party meeting to try and get a decision against bringing the question up before the Government produced their Bill. With great skill Collins succeeded in getting the party to vote thirty to twenty on non-committal resolutions in favour of a directly elected body, understood to mean the L.C.C., but blaming the Government for attacking school boards and subsidising voluntary schools; and, by an overwhelming majority, for adjourning Hubbard's resolution. Meanwhile, the Government, scared by electoral results at bye-elections at Woolwich and Rye, took fright. Morant wrote begging Sidney to let him know the result of the meeting. Londonderry's private secretary came down to ask for permission to attend, with shorthand writer, the L.C.C. debate, so that the Cabinet might have a correct and complete version of the L.C.C. views. Last

[1] William Crooks, L.C.C., won a notable bye-election for Woolwich in 1903.

Tuesday the Council, as a whole, prevented the taking of Hubbard's resolution by talking at length on other matters. Sidney went at Haldane's request to see Sandars (the confidential private secretary to the Prime Minister) and the Conservative Whip, and to encourage them to introduce the L.C.C. Bill. But to-day we learn in confidence that the Cabinet yesterday decided that it would not introduce their Bill giving the L.C.C. the whole of education and complete control of its committee unless they could, by this means, secure the support of the L.C.C. Progressives. Failing this, it is to be the *status quo* and the settlement of London education left over to some future Government. Now it remains to be seen whether the official leaders of the Progressives are willing and able to get Hubbard's resolution negatived. Sidney does not believe that they can carry the rank and file with them, even if they plank themselves down on the policy of L.C.C. authority.

Haldane tells us that the rot has set in severely within the Cabinet. They are panic-stricken—all except Joe (Chamberlain) who holds himself somewhat detached from the rest and lets them stew in their juice of muddle and mistake. They have been so shaken by Woolwich and Rye, and the rising tide of Nonconformism (N.U.T. agitation in London), that they were actually considering the making of an *ad hoc* authority for London—a complete capitulation. However, they were shaken out of that by Sidney's assertion that not only would Dr. Clifford and Macnamara dominate such an authority, but it would light up the flame throughout the country against the 1902 Act, and encourage a persistent refusal to accept the Act by all sorts and conditions of malcontents. So they were prepared to throw themselves into the arms of the L.C.C., if they had been able, by so doing, to get a rest from virulent opposition. The L.C.C. has not been able to rise to the emergency. Possibly it has proved that it would not be equal to running the concern. The success of the T.E.B. is largely owing to the fact that Sidney removed it from the first out of the practical control of the L.C.C. But he lost consent in gaining efficiency.

Gave my presidential address to the Students' Union, which cost a good four days to prepare, on the relative function of the investigator, the man of affairs and the idealist. The upshot of the analysis was that the investigator or scientific man has to discover the process by which a given end can be obtained within a given subject-matter. This means specialisation and all the patient methods of observation, generalisation and verification. The man of affairs has to select the processes, to adapt and adjust them in order to bring about a " state of affairs ". This entails a knowledge of and capacity to control men, and perception of general ends, which would be actually obtained by the dovetailing of the processes of the various sciences. But neither the investigator nor the man of affairs could act, unless there was a conception of an end or purpose to be attained. This was given by the idealist. Where did he discover his ideals? Not in science, seeing that science can give processes and processes only. Not in affairs: that meant opportunism. In metaphysics or in religion? In choice of ideals within our own inner consciousness, or perhaps in communion with a higher and nobler life than that of common humanity?

April 3rd.—Listened from the Speaker's Gallery to (Sir William) Anson introducing the London Education Bill. Met with cold reception. Opposition jeering and supporters gloomily silent. An inept speech. As it stands the Bill is a bad one, though rather than the *status quo* or an *ad hoc* authority *we* would accept it as it stands. But it is clear to us that the borough council representatives on the central committee have been stuck in to be knocked out, and that the control of the L.C.C. over the local administration of elementary education will be indefinitely strengthened in committee of the House. If our prophecy be proved correct, the Bill is much what Sidney would have himself drafted, except that he would have defined in the Bill the outside element to be co-opted by the L.C.C. committee and not left it to the free will of the L.C.C. But this may be unduly distrustful of his Progressive colleagues! But, of course, the Bill as it stands has been received by every section of Progressives with contemptuous disapproval—almost delight, because it is considered so bad that it will not pass. Hewins and Pease have, however, been so indoctrinated by Sidney that they are almost enthusiastic about the present draft. Sidney goes up to-day to a meeting of the parliamentary committee of the L.C.C. to reconnoitre the position and see how far he can modify the outburst of L.C.C. disapproval.

April 29th.—L.C.C. Progressives rapidly coming round to notion of L.C.C. being the authority—the natural desire of a public body to increase its dignity and power overcoming the party feeling in favour of an *ad hoc* authority. Clear also that Government intend to give way if pressed. All the Conservative Party organs on our side agree as to strengthening of the L.C.C. position, though they differ about borough representative on the central committee, and the powers of the borough local committee. Looks as if Sidney would get his way all along the line even with regard to the constitution of the education committee.

June 15th. Aston Magna, Gloucestershire.—We left London seventeen days ago, tired out but with the restful consciousness that our plans had come off. The School gets its grant of £1100 from the T.E.B. renewed without opposition, J. R. MacDonald not being there. The Education Bill passed through committee the day before we left, in almost exactly the shape Sidney would have given to it: the L.C.C. absolutely supreme, the borough councils relegated to the quite subordinate part of selecting the majority of the local managers; but these latter having no more power than the L.C.C. choose to give them. In fact, the Bill endows the L.C.C. with rather more freedom of action than Sidney would have suggested as the ideal arrangement: he would have preferred a statutory constitution for the education committee, instead of leaving it open to the L.C.C. [as to co-option of] other outside interests. It was very easy to get the L.C.C. ten years ago to appoint a reasonably broad committee for technical education—when none of the Council were interested in the matter. It is another thing to persuade the Progressives, with their enormous majority and strong Nonconformist element, to be fair and sane about the outside interests. Hence, our anxiety is now passed from Parliament to the L.C.C. itself. So long as we can get the present Council to consent to frame a scheme under the Act, and so long as the scheme is not outrageously one-sided, that is as much as we can do. The working of the Act will be a matter for the 1904 Council. We are concerned now to see to it that this Council has the right complexion. The whole controversy between the Progressives and Moderates is stale and has lost its significance. The Progressives, beyond sticking to some old shibboleths, have lost all impetus to further action. The Works Department, the old symbol of collectivism, is a mere device for keeping the contractors in order; the taking over of the tramways has been accomplished in principle, if not in fact; but water is lost to the L.C.C., at any rate for the next decade or two, and with regard to asylums, to housing, to sanitary and building bye-laws committee, the work of the Council has become mere routine. In fact, it is asserted by some, that the old gang who ran the administrative departments have become cautious and economical to the last degree. On the other hand, while the Council has lost the impetus to do constructive work, it has accreted a good deal of destructive radicalism of the old type. Some thirty members of the Progressive Party are standing for Parliament, and owing to the latter-day developments they are, many of them, likely to get in. This will increase the disinclination of the Progressive leaders to a vigorous municipal policy, and identify them more completely than ever with parliamentary Liberalism. And all these general considerations have been enormously heightened by the raging controversy over the Education Bill. In this, the old nihilistic spirit of the 1843–1870 Nonconformist who deliberately preferred *no education* to the teaching of a rival dogma, is rampant. A powerful rump of L.C.C. Progressives imagine themselves to be in favour of education, with a big E, but at best it is only primary education of the most mechanical and uniform type that they want to promote. Behind them, and working with them, are two other more sinister forces—the Labour men who want no money spent on secondary or university education, and the N.U.T. who want all appointments—secondary as well as elementary—to fall into the hands of the superior elementary school teachers.

Meanwhile, the Moderate Party has become even more stale than the Progressives. Beaten down and divided by their last crushing defeat, they no longer have any heart for their work of opposition. Moreover, there is nothing for the most moderate of the Moderates to oppose in the thoroughly businesslike cautious and economical ways of the Progressive administrators. Just as the Progressives have permeated the Moderates with all that was immediately practicable in their schemes, so the Moderates have permeated the Progressives and forced them to adopt economical and businesslike methods. This mutual permeation is exactly what is accomplished by the English system of committees, in which party cleavages are lost sight of, the actual outcome being always a compromise—in a good body the " better reason " of both parties. All this, from the point of view of efficiency, is very encouraging but, when both sides feel that they have got a good deal of what they wanted and have persuaded themselves to give up the remainder, the spirit both of reform and of criticism is apt to go dead.

Now it is a question which Sidney and I have been mooting between ourselves, whether out of these elements we can produce a new party— formally or informally held together by a broad catholic and progressive educational policy. The planks would be (1) fairness to the voluntary schools, complete freedom for them to teach their religious doctrine in their own way; (2) unsectarianism in the board schools— these latter constituting, broadly speaking, the supply for the Nonconformist and secularist children—and, as regards all kinds of elementary teaching, thorough efficiency in staff and structure; (3) development of secondary and technical education on the present lines of independent governing bodies aided and inspected by the L.C.C. and kept up to the mark on their educational side; but completely free to be as denominational or anti-denominational as the governing body chose. And, last but not least, a great London University— independent of L.C.C. but subsidised and influenced by it—not only a leading university organised on a democratic basis, but a great centre of the highest and most useful science, scholarship and metaphysics.

Meanwhile, our own little schemes have been submerged, even in our own minds, by the new ferment introduced by Chamberlain into imperial politics. Protection *versus* free trade is going to supersede all other political issues for many years to come. From the public point of view, we do not regret the advent of the new ferment. Here again controversies between parties had got stale. This issue at least will force people to think, will force them to consider new facts, and to apply new assumptions. The absurd notion that the " natural " channels of trade are necessarily the best will be quickly given up; the notion that " cheapness " is the only aim in a nation's commerce will also be demolished; the need for investigation and the desirability of deliberate collective regulation will be enormously advertised. All this is to the good and makes towards economic science, and, we think, collectivism of the best sort. To Joe's specific proposals—a tax on food and eventually " protection all round ", we are, as at present advised, opposed, as politically impracticable, unnecessarily costly to the consumer and likely to lead to international friction and internal uncertainty. We do not agree, however, with the extreme hostility to these proposals; our trade depends on quite other considerations than tariffs or no tariffs. But we think Chamberlain's aim, the Empire as a unit, could be better and more cheaply and conveniently attained by other devices. Sidney, at present, inclines towards bounties on colonial imports as a likely compromise between the British consumer, the British manufacturer and the colonial producer. Viewed from the standpoint of our own little projects, the diversion of public interest from the educational controversy to the tariffs is wholly to the good. It will require, however, careful steering to prevent the School of Economics from being indiscreetly identified with either side. Hewins, somewhat impetuously, has decided to throw in his weight with Chamberlain; this will mean that Sidney must be, as he fortunately is, against the new proposals. All he will do is to get the Fabian Society at work to prepare the ground for some intermediate plan combining imperialism with sound national economy.

Just before leaving London Sidney was appointed on the small expert Royal Commission to enquire into trade union law.[1] This was our friend Haldane's doing—made easy by Mr. Balfour's kindly view

[1] This small Royal Commission, presided over by Graham Murray, afterwards Lord Dunedin, proved a fiasco. The Parliamentary Committee of the Trades Union Congress, hurt at not having been invited to nominate one of themselves as a member of the Commission, and rightly regarding it as a political device for staving off a difficult problem, resolved to boycott it, and to prevent any trade unionist from giving evidence. This did not matter much, as the problem was dealt with entirely as one of law. As the Conservative Cabinet did not want any immediate decision, or indeed any report at all until after the general election, the Commission went to sleep for a couple of years, and eventually (in 1906) made a unanimous report, with a lengthy reservation signed by me only. The Liberal Government brought in a Bill on the lines of the report; but the trade unions had utilised the general election to get most of the M.P.'s to commit themselves simply to a reversal of the Taff Vale judgement, which the Government was compelled to adopt,—a too sweeping legalisation which led, in after years, to an inconvenient reaction. [S. W.]

of us. The job is eminently one for him to do, and will have the incidental advantage of bringing us again into communication with the trade union world. Sidney's relation with the Labour men of the L.C.C. having been strained by J. R. MacDonald's ill service, it is all the more necessary to be on good terms with other sections. The parliamentary committee of the Trades Union Congress has never forgiven us our scathing description of them and their doings in *Industrial Democracy*. With John Burns we are very friendly; but this is only because he is jealous of Macnamara and Crooks, and has an old grudge against MacDonald. Next spring we shall resume our intercourse with the Co-operators in preparation for an official history of the movement.

July 8th.—Fagged with combination of work and entertaining. Before the " Charlottenburg " scheme [1] was launched, we spent ourselves, money and energy, in tuning the press and trying to keep the Progressives straight. But, of course, they unconsciously resent having situations " prepared " out of which there is only one way—*i.e.* ours! But there is so little statesmanship in the party that it is only by an elaborate preparation of the ground that they can be induced to take up the right position. Latterly I have been sampling the Progressive members—they are not much to be proud of—a good deal of rotten stuff; the rest upright and reasonable but coarse-grained in intellect and character. Even the best of them are a good deal below the standard of our intimate associates—such as Hewins, Mackinder, Haldane, Russell, etc., and the ordinary Progressive member is either a bounder, a narrow-minded fanatic, or a mere piece of putty upon which any strong mind can make an impression, to be effaced by the next influence—or rather the texture is more like gutta-percha, because it bounds back to the old shapeless mass of prejudice directly you take

[1] S. W. writes (1937): What was called, for short, " Charlottenburg ", needs explanation. Haldane, in his enthusiasm for German scientific education, had been immensely impressed by the success of the great technical Hochschule at Charlottenburg, near Berlin, to which Great Britain had nothing similar. Meanwhile Sir Julius Wernher (of Wernher, Beit & Co.), a South African millionaire who had bought a large estate and settled in England, was prepared to give a large sum to promote technical education of the highest degree. Haldane induced the Government to hand over the Royal College of Science and the School of Mines; and the City Companies to transfer the City and Guilds Institute which they had founded at South Kensington, to form, with the half-a-million which Wernher was to contribute, what we called, in intimate discussion, " Charlottenburg " but which eventually became the Imperial Technical Institute, now a constituent college of the reformed London University. It was part of the scheme that the London County Council, through its Technical Education Board, should contribute £20,000 a year to create additional professorships and equip laboratories, etc. All this took years to arrange, including a lengthy enquiry by a Departmental Committee, on which I sat, before the various complications were smoothed out.

your will away. It is very tiring for poor Sidney and he comes back from the L.C.C. or T.E.B. meeting exhausted though usually victorious, always so when he has had time to prepare the ground—when he does this the enemy usually don't turn up or collapse immediately and his trouble seems thrown away.

Hewins has complicated matters of the L.C.C. and School by his vehement adhesion to Chamberlainism; not only " letting out " his authorship of the *Times* articles, but resigning sensationally from the National Liberal Club. Fortunately the articles have been ineffective —but the fact of his partisanship makes our position more difficult and has necessitated Sidney flying the free trade flag. He would have preferred to keep quiet and not to take part, but that is impossible in view of Hewins' and G. B. S.'s indiscretions. Meanwhile, we struggle on in a lame way every morning; for three days I have been off with strained eyes—strained not with work but with dissipation of strength at four dinners last week. My diet saves me from worse ills than mere fatigue. Unfortunately, I don't always stick to my regimen—specially when I am bored.

Went into dinner with Winston Churchill. First impression: restless—almost intolerably so, without capacity for sustained and unexciting labour—egotistical, bumptious, shallow-minded and reactionary, but with a certain personal magnetism, great pluck and some originality—not of intellect but of character. More of the American speculator than the English aristocrat. Talked exclusively about himself and his electioneering plans—wanted me to tell him of someone who would get up statistics for him. " I never do any brainwork that anyone else can do for me "—an axiom which shows organising but not thinking capacity. Replete with dodges for winning Oldham against the Labour and Liberal candidates. But I daresay he has a better side—which the ordinary cheap cynicism of his position and career covers up to a casual dinner acquaintance. Bound to be unpopular—too unpleasant a flavour with his restless, self-regarding personality, and lack of moral or intellectual refinement. His political tack is economy: the sort of essence of a moderate; he is at heart a little Englander. Looks to *haute finance* to keep the peace—for that reason objects to a self-contained Empire as he thinks it would destroy this cosmopolitan capitalism—the cosmopolitan financier being the professional peacemaker of the modern world, and to his mind the acme of civilisation. His bugbears are Labour, N.U.T. and expenditure on elementary education or on the social services. Defines the higher education as the opportunity for the " brainy man " to come to the top. No notion of scientific research, philosophy, literature or art: still less of religion. But his pluck, courage, resourcefulness and great tradition may carry him far unless he knocks himself to pieces like his father.[1]

July 24th.—One sometimes wonders whether all this manipulating activity is worth while: whether one would not do almost as much by cutting the whole business of human intercourse and devoting oneself to thinking and writing out one's thoughts. It would certainly be far pleasanter, because a far less complicated life, with fewer liabilities for contraventions against personal dignity, veracity and kindliness. It is so easy to maintain these qualities in a vacuum! In rubbing up against others, one's vanity, one's self-will and any strain of spite gets uncovered and revealed in all their ugliness to oneself, one's friends and one's opponents. But someone has to do this practical work: and possibly it is just as well that it should be done by those who have the other life to withdraw into, so as to keep up their standard of thought and feeling. That disgust with oneself which always follows a time of turmoil—the consciousness that one has lamentably fallen short in dignity, gentleness, consideration for other people's lives and feelings, and in transparent truthfulness, is a wholesome reminder of one's own radical shortcomings. If one frankly realises one's own moral incapacity during spells of activity, it makes one more careful not to admit unworthy desires and thoughts in the times of withdrawal from the world—and the whole level of one's mental life is raised and supported by the wholesome fear of the eternal fall of the man of action. From an intellectual standpoint it is good, too, because one is constantly testing one's hypotheses by the course of events; proving whether a given social process does, as a matter of fact, bring about a given social result. Nevertheless, it is with a sigh of relief that we look forward to some months of restful intellectual work before the hubbub of next spring, and if Sidney *is* turned out of London administration, the lot will bring its compensations. It would be a mental luxury to give the whole of our joint strength to the completion of our big task, especially if we felt that we had fought hard and were in no way responsible, by carelessness, for affairs taking the wrong turn—that we had not resigned the heavier and more disagreeable work but had been dismissed as " not wanted " by the people of London.

Our season ended with a brilliant little dinner here to meet Mr. Balfour. Naturally enough I talked almost exclusively at dinner to the guest of the evening. A man of extraordinary grace of mind and body —delighting in all that is beautiful and distinguished—music, literature, philosophy, religious feeling and moral disinterestedness—aloof from

---

[1] This hasty estimate was reconsidered when W. C. became a Cabinet Minister in the Liberal Government, 1906–15; in that administration he was one of the ablest and most progressive.

all the greed and grime of common human nature. But a strange paradox as Prime Minister of a great Empire! I doubt whether even foreign affairs interest him: for all economic and social questions, I gather, he has an utter loathing—whilst the machinery of administration would seem to him a disagreeable irrelevance. Not a strong intellect and deficient in knowledge; but I imagine ambitious in the sense that he feels that being Prime Minister completes the picture of the really charming man—gives tone to the last touch of colour— piquancy to his indifference as to whether he is in or out of office. I placed Charles Booth next him—I doubt from his manner whether he knew who Charles Booth was—wondered perhaps that a Salvationist should be so agreeably unsettled in his opinions! Bright talk with paradoxes and subtleties, sentiments and allusions, with the personal note emphasised, is what Mr. Balfour likes—and what I tried to give him! From 19th-century schools of philosophy to 18th-century street life, from university to tariff, from Meredith to G. B. S., we flashed assertions and rejoinders; and " Bernard Shaw, the finest man of letters of to-day ", was one of his dicta. But he did not read *Mrs. Warren's Profession*: " It is one of the unpleasant plays. I never read unpleasant things ", he added apologetically, and looked confirmed in his intention when I asserted that it was G. B. S.'s most " serious work ". " I am reading Haldane's *Pathway to Reality* and should like to answer it; but somehow or other I don't get any time for philosophy ", he added with a note of graceful surprise. " I had hoped that the tariffs issue would turn us out, but I am beginning to doubt it." Then I explained to him with much benignity the powerful forces of the cotton trade and the Co-operative Union which would, I thought, bring about his release from office. Haldane and he returned to the House soon after 10.0, and I had a pleasant chat with Sir J. Wolfe Barry—the engineer.

July 25th.—Sidney got through the £20,000 grant to the " Charlottenburg " scheme, having drafted a careful report. Of the leading Progressives, some really approved, others dare not refuse Rosebery— only eight of the rump actually went into the lobby against it. J. R. M. made long and virulent attack on Sidney. " Mr. Haldane and Mr. Sidney Webb had presented a pistol at the head of the Council." He was supported by the Labour men. The farce of Sidney not being the chairman of T.E.B., when every agenda or report is obviously drafted by him, is becoming glaring and will make J. R. M. more angry than ever. Massingham and Macnamara too are trying to work up opposition to him in London. But Macnamara, in laying down authoritatively the issues upon which the L.C.C. election next March is to be fought, has overshot himself and disinclined the Progressive leaders to follow him.

The I.L.P. is making the Liberals very angry: and in that direction J. R. M. will not increase his influence. Meanwhile, the Moderates show some signs of working to capture Sidney for their side; and the moderate Progressives are beginning to fear they may lose him and are inclined to be more on-coming. It looks as if the rump would try to turn him out of the party, the Moderates would try to claim him, and the centre Progressives make some sacrifices to keep him. So long as he keeps his temper and head, and goes on quietly asserting his own education policy, his position is a strong one. But it is clear that the next election will be a scrimmage and we may go under. What would suit us least well (assuming that Sidney keeps his seat) would be a large Nonconformist majority; what would suit us best would be either a small Moderate or small Progressive majority—perhaps the former best of all. At this juncture the Progressive forces are really against a constructive policy or a large expenditure on education—more particularly in that direction in which it is most needed—higher education. Class, sectarian and professional jealousy leads them to a desire to stint education. Labour, Nonconformity and the N.U.T. dislike the advent of the university professor as part of publicly maintained instruction.

Our general social policy is to construct a base to society in the form of a legally enforced " minimum standard of life ", and to develop all forms of shooting upwards—whether of individuals or of discoveries and refinements. Doubtful which party in the state will help us most; protection is all to the bad, so is Nonconformist fanaticism —that is to say the positive policy of both Chamberlain and Campbell-Bannerman is bad and retrograde: and they are equally indifferent if not hostile to our programme. We have, in fact, no party ties. It is open to us to use either or both parties.

August 26th.— . . . Meanwhile, we have been entertaining and being entertained. We cycled over to the Elchos and spent a couple of hours chatting with them and Mr. Balfour and a clever Cambridge doctor—the P.M. charming as usual, but absorbed in the state of the weather and the chance of getting his golf, also awaiting sadly the death of his great-uncle (the Marquess of Salisbury). Then the Playnes came for two days, and we took them to see the Ashbees at Campden and to a formal lunch at our neighbour's, Lord Redesdale, afterwards spending a tiring afternoon standing about in his pretty gardens of bamboos. A melancholy household—this handsome, vain and autocratic elderly gentleman absorbed in his hobbies and somewhat hazardous enterprises—his wife mad at intervals, and usually away, and a family of nine young people. The two elder girls simple, attractive, but living an isolated and useless life shut up in their great house and park, kept too short of money to see life as aristocrats, and too dignified to see it as ordinary folk. When we asked them to tea at the home of their own tenant, within half-a-mile of their gate, they thought it necessary to drive here—a carriage and pair with footman—keeping it for two hours awaiting them. And yet clearly not able to go up to London for more than a week in the year!

On Monday, Sidney and I went to dine and sleep at Bishops House, Worcester. Dr. Gore, a delightful-natured pious ecclesiastic—without guile, with extraordinary fervour and earnestness—a mystic, a reformer, a preacher—but with no natural turn for administration or Church politics. He is not a wholly satisfactory bishop in the ordinary English sense. Refuses utterly to take up his position as a social magnate: he has given up his palace (Hartlebury) and settled in a large plain villa on the outskirts of Worcester, where he lives, with three other priests, a life of austere work and fervent worship. We found him deeply depressed, hating the administrative drudgery of the Bishop's position, not caring for its dignity and feeling how hard it was to be a simple missionary when clothed in bishop's purple. Into this monk's abode Sidney and I broke for one long evening's talk about the Education Bill, and the position of the Church generally. It was a strange proceeding—we non-Christians talking with these " true men of God " as to possible co-operation between them and us in any reform of society. When we woke in the morning we heard mass being said in the room beneath us, and when we came down to breakfast three out of the four were robed sacerdotally. But they were eating a hearty breakfast, whereas I was fasting, and I amused myself by upsetting their consciences on the simple food question, and the desirability of living on six ounces a day. So, in spite of my heterodoxy, I left in an odour of personal abstemiousness akin to an odour of sanctity!

On our way home, we picked up Beatrice Chamberlain, who had come to discuss the question of London school management. In the afternoon, a party assembled itself in our little parlour for tea—Lady Elcho bringing Mrs. Pat Campbell (the actress), the Freeman-Mitford girls, the Ashbees—a gay and talkative affair developing an antagonism between the actress and the economists. This morning Beatrice and I wandered over Lord Redesdale's garden and during the walk she formally proposed that I should make the acquaintance of her stepmother—she would " bring her to call ", etc. Of course, I insisted that I should come some Thursday when she returned to London— which appeared to relieve the mind of my old friend of a difficult negotiation. The next day Lord Redesdale drove us over to see the Ashbees' works, and in the afternoon she left.

October 5th.—A refreshing holiday in Normandy and Brittany—lasting the best part of three weeks—first a week with the Bertrand Russells, and then two weeks alone together. The Russells we found settled in uncomfortable lodgings in a little Normandy village—riding and reading together but not serenely happy—a tragic austerity and effort in their relations. They are both so good in the best and most complete sense, Alys has so much charm and Bertrand so much intellect, that it is strange they cannot enjoy light-hearted happiness in each other's love and comradeship—but there is something that interferes, and friends can only look on with respect and admiration and silent concern. Perhaps, they will grow into a more joyful union; certainly, they have the big essential condition—a common faith so far as personal conduct is concerned.

We two thoroughly enjoyed our time—cycling abroad is a new discovery to us—sight-seeing completes each day, and alternating with lively exercise rests instead of tiring one. And here we are back in London and thoroughly fit for an autumn's work.

November 1st.—Haldane dined with us alone: gather that events are pointing (in that circle) to Asquith as Prime Minister with Rosebery serving under him as Foreign Secretary. Our friend was very vague as to politics. Not very definite as to the " Charlottenburg " scheme, which Professor Ramsay is crabbing in all directions, and the low state of South African finance making more difficult of attainment. Had secured young Lord Lytton to run about for him, and wanted us to come and meet him—but that proved impossible.

November 3rd.—Dined at the Asquiths'. Lord Hugh Cecil, the Lyttons, Sir A. Lyall and the Birrells—our host and hostess most gracious; Lord Hugh disappointing—a bigot even on fiscal questions, dominated entirely by a sort of deductive philosophy from *laisser-faire* principles held as theological dogma; the Lyttons a charming young couple with the delightful gracious deference of the well-bred aristocrat; Sir Alfred glowing, the Birrells somewhat hack diners out; but on the whole a pleasant party gratifying to one's social vanity. Margot (Mrs. Asquith) certainly has vitality and was full of fervour for the free-trade cause and scepticism of all other aspects of the progressive programme—told us plentiful gossip about " Arthur " and called all the élite of high political society by their Christian or pet names. It is a strange little *clique*—in which the bond of union is certainly not common conviction or desire for any kind of reform. (I fancy we are admitted to it—strange to say—not as reformers and experts, but as persons with a special kind of *chic*.) I suggested that why Chamberlain would make headway, in spite of his bad arguments, was because he had a vision;

desired to bring about a new state of affairs; and was working day and night for a cause—that no one else wished anything but a quiet life and the *status quo*. Whereupon Lord Hugh and Margot exclaimed, " Why change the present state of things—all was well ". Whereupon I burst out " That's all right for you, Lord Hugh—a convinced ultra-Tory—but is that a possible attitude for the leader of the Liberal Party who, one would think, was, or ought to be, ' professionally ' aware of the mass of misery, vice and distorted human nature of our present state of society? " But, conscious of the absurdity of indignation whilst eating and drinking at the Asquiths' table, I calmed down and tried to make up for my useless and somewhat self-righteous indignation. I suppose it is well to be on good terms with these people, but I come back from their society to our shabby little home and regular hard work with a deep sigh of gratitude that I am an outsider, and have not the time nor the energy to become one of them, even if they opened wide their doors. Probably the door is kept open because we do not try to enter in.

Alfred Cripps called in splendid form. Very discontented with the Archbishop's attitude towards Education Act. Gave him the names of the bitterest opponents of the Act on L.C.C.—the rotten part of the Progressive Party which would be best lopped off. Took care not to compromise Sidney.

Reading Gladstone's Life. Interesting to note that when, after ten years' political experience, he became convinced that the state had to be an infidel state, and could not be used to promote religious truth— he turned straight away into a *laisser-faire* democrat holding persistently to the policy of diminishing the function of government and doing nothing but what every individual consented to in advance. Hence, his doctrine of nationalities and, in the end, Irish Home Rule. Add to this genuine alteration of intellectual creed, the heady emotion of feeling himself in accord with crude democracy and, owing to his superlative talent as a revivalist preacher, leading it; and you have the Gladstone of 1869–80. After 1880, he was out of sympathy with the collectivist trend of the newer democracy of town workmen, and became a reactionary, appealing pathetically to the Nonconformist middle-class in terror of the new creed and hating the new apostles. His soul was wrapped up in his own principles—religious and economic—each set in a water-tight compartment; he never realised the new order of ideas. Moreover, he was socially an aristocrat and disliked the *parvenu* in riches and political power—such as Chamberlain.

Progressives gained considerably, as I predicted, at [November] borough council elections—which will perhaps wake up the Catholics and Church to action, and possibly lull the Progressives into confidence for L.C.C. election in March. We shall lie low and say nothing, and look after our own constituency. It is vital to London education that the Nonconformists should be chastened; if they come back triumphant, the outlook will be serious. At present, the L.C.C. Progressives feel confident that there will be no turnover, and the Nonconformists are playing their game with discretion.

November 18th.—A strange piece of luck! J. R. MacDonald knocked off the register [during his absence abroad] and thus disabled from standing for the L.C.C. at the next election—an iniquitous flaw in the law, but not for us an ill wind.

November 26th.—Bryan, the late Democratic candidate for the U.S.A. presidency, dined with us last night. A most attractive personality, a large bodied and large brained man, with great simplicity and directness of nature, a delightful temper and kindly attitude towards life. Knew nothing of administration and was, in all the range of political and social questions, dominated by abstractions—by words and not by things as they actually are. A Jeffersonian democrat like Altgeld. But shrewd in his estimate of men and women, and with a strong unselfconscious and vivid faculty of speech.

November 28th.—Kept my pledge against coffee and alcohol for the month—treated myself to a cup after lunch to-day, and retake the pledge for two months from this evening. I am better without either and, though coffee is a temptation, I have practically got over the worst part of giving it up and might as well stick to it. Have taken cream inadvertently two or three times in the month, but shall avoid it in future, without insisting on total abstinence. Should like to get into the habit of never taking a mouthful more after I feel that my hunger is satisfied. I have reduced myself as a rule to three cigarettes a day. Health better than ever before.

December 1st.—Mr. Arthur Acland has been in once or twice lately to talk over education with Sidney and to arrange for interviewing Austen Chamberlain and Morant. We got on to Rosebery—Acland not cordial to his leadership; intimated that he had been intolerable as head of the Cabinet 1894–5, shy, huffy and giving himself the airs of a little German king towards his Ministers. Had neither the equality of public-school Englishmen nor the courteous and punctilious formality of the well-trained *grand seigneur*, which is the best substitute for it. " He complained that his colleagues never came to see him, but when we did go he had hurried off to the Durdans or to Dalmeny. Then after a Cabinet he might ask one of us to come to lunch—but of course we had, as busy Ministers, already mapped out our day with deputations and parliamentary work. If we pleaded a previous engagement, he would seem offended." Then he gave us a vision of the strange weird ways which Rosebery indulged in at home —delighting in surrounding himself with some low fellows and being *camarades* with them—then suddenly requesting one of his free-thinking colleagues to go to church with him, or insisting that some elderly conventional guest should drive out at 10 o'clock at night for a couple of hours in an open victoria, with a postillion galloping at high speed through the night air. "Always posing," was Acland's summary, " imagining himself to be an extraordinary being with special privileges towards the world." It is odd how that impression exactly corresponds to my memory of him on board the *Russia*[1] thirty years ago, and with my estimate of his attitude towards us during the last four years. For instance—a very considerable amount of pose—fictitious senti-ment obviously a source of enjoyment to himself. He is certainly unique—whether for good or for evil—an asset or an incubus to the Progressive Party is a question.

December 6th.—Haldane looked in this afternoon to consult on University business. Reproached him half-seriously and half in chaff about Rosebery's attitude. " If Joe were to take up the notion of a national minimum of wages, health and education, and run it alongside of preferential duties or a protective tariff, you would be done, Mr Haldane." " But *Joe* won't do that," he retorted with a self-complacent emphasis, " he would break up his party if he did." Obviously the Liberal leaders do not seriously want social reform, and would only take it up in a practical manner if they were forced to do so by com-petition. They are, in fact, relying on the stupid Conservatism which they profess to despise and to fight. And I fear our friends the " Limps " are in this respect the worst sinners. The others have some sort of hazy notion that, after pulling down existing structure, they would build up something in its stead on the basis of more equal distribution of wealth. We cannot join with them because we don't want to pull down the existing structure—all we want is slowly and quietly to transform and add to it. So that we remain isolated from all political parties, so far as party cries are concerned, though willing and eager to work with any party who are consciously or unconsciously engaged in constructive work. But it is unpleasant, this perpetual transit from camp to camp, however bitterly hostile these camps feel to one another. It is perilously near becoming both a spy and a traitor—or rather, being considered such by the camp to which we officially belong. No

[1] 1937: Father, Kate and I crossed the Atlantic with him on the *Russia*, Christmas, 1873, and he and I sat opposite each other on either side of the Captain.

wonder the Progressives are beginning to feel uncomfortably disposed towards Sidney!

December 18*th*.—Bertrand Russell published a short article, " The Free Man's Worship ", in the *Independent Review* which throws an illuminating light on his character and conduct. In it he adopts, as a starting point, the pessimistic hypothesis of the universe—that it is " blind, mechanical, cruel ", lower than man, that man alone has, by accident, attained to morality and intelligence (much the same hypothesis as that in Metchnikoff's *Nature of Man*). Upon this hypothesis he bases, by a process of reasoning which it is not easy to follow, a fine morality, tender towards others, stoical towards self— a morality devised to sustain us in this tragedy of life. The interest of the article does not lie in the fine passages on conduct but in his betrayal of the purely agnostic attitude, and his deliberate acceptance of an hypothesis which cannot be proved to be true by the scientific method. This course he has always declared to be immoral in cases in which the choice has fallen on the religious hypothesis—hence his indignation at William James's *Varieties of Religious Experience*, or at such Hegelians as McTaggart, Haldane, Schiller. I thought he held that, as pure reason and scientific verification could not be applied to anything but phenomena, it was a betrayal of the integrity of the intellect to accept *any explanation* of the universe as a whole. But it is clear that his personal bias towards the tragic in life has made him select and dogmatically affirm the most tragic of all the hypotheses of the nature of the great " unknown "—the one in which man poses as the supreme martyr of life—condemned to suffer until extinguished as an individual or a race. Realising this bias towards the tragic explana- tion of the universe, one feels less perturbed at what he conceives to be the concrete tragedy of his present life. Tragedy is a pose with him, and both the facts of the universe and the facts of matrimony must live up to it. As a matter of fact, his marriage is an amazingly fortunate one —but if the facts are not such as make up a tragedy so much the worse for the facts! Fortunately his splendid morality outweighs his tragic propensities and I doubt whether Alys realises that he thinks his married life an heroically lived tragedy.

The Nature of Man, by Metchnikoff—a book just now causing some sensation—is based on the same pessimistic hypothesis. But it is more practical in its deductions: which are to find out " the secret of physical health ", " longevity ", and " the desire for death, when death becomes inevitable ". And towards the solution he throws out a brilliant scientific hypothesis—that, owing to bad regimen, we never attain physiological old age but always die a violent death, eaten up prematurely by our own phagocytes; and, therefore, we object to and resist the process—exactly as a healthy-minded man usually does object to violent death. His moral is a simple life—above all things simple food and little of it. . . . I believe both in his account of what does happen, and his suggestion of what would happen if we lived the wisest kind of life. But he seems to me to transcend the sphere of the scientific method when he asserts that science alone will discover " the goal of human existence ". The book, of course, is rank materialism of the crudest sort, and Metchnikoff would have as little patience with Russell's " The Free Man's Worship " as he would have of Catholic Christianity. Indeed, he hints that the teaching of any *unverified knowledge* should be prohibited like the consumption of poisons. How far his own book with its daring excursions into the land of conjecture would survive the application of this principle is doubtful?

December 20th.—The effect created by the accession of Charles Booth to the protectionist ranks proves what power, nowadays, is wielded by a non-party expert who is free to throw himself on one side or the other, and who is widely known to be personally disinterested, if not, indeed, philanthropic in his ends. Intrinsically, I do not attach much importance to C. B.'s opinion on the fiscal question— he has no special knowledge, a great deal of prejudice, and by no means any marked capacity for intricate reasoning. But for the world at large his credentials are 17 volumes, a public life of 30 years' service, and a great expenditure of private means for public objects. A platform which even a more powerful politician might well envy. Such a position is the sort of thing I aim at for Sidney.

1904

In December 1903, the Other One published a handbook on *London Education* which was freely circulated to all whom it might concern. In its 200 pages, he foreshadowed the establishment of a systematically co-ordinated educational system from the infant school to the university, including polytechnics, research institutes and public libraries ; and he pleaded for a whole-hearted endeavour to bring this new national culture within the reach of every inhabitant of the metropolis. Here are a few extracts:

The new authority [the author declared] is called upon to endow London with a complete educational system. To give to each of London's 800,000 children during the years of compulsory school attendance the most effective physical, moral, and intellectual training; to develop in them the utmost mental acquisitiveness; to arouse in as many as possible of them the indefinable quality that we call resourcefulness, initiative, inventiveness, or the capacity for meeting new conditions by new devices; to provide for the whole of them the widest possible opportunities for continuing their studies after leaving the day school; to carry on, by a " capacity-catching " scholarship system, all whose brains make it profitable for the community to equip them with more advanced instruction; to organise, as well for these scholarship-holders as for all others able to benefit by it, an efficient and duly varied system of secondary and university education, whether predominantly literary, scientific, artistic, commercial, technological, or professional in type; to provide the best possible training for teachers of every kind and grade; and so to organise the whole machine, as, while increasing knowledge and efficiency, to promote everywhere the development of character and culture, and ultimately to encourage the highest scholarship and the most advanced research—all this, and nothing less than this, is the duty which Parliament has committed to the London County Council [pp. 10-11].

In a final chapter on " The Lion in the Path " he visualises the one big obstacle to the vigorous administration of the new service.

But it would be idle to ignore the fact that, at this juncture, there are forces at work which may make the carrying-out of any efficient policy absolutely impracticable. It is a peculiarity of educational politics that, in some countries, at some stages of their development, the clash of religious controversy rouses feelings of such intensity that the rival partisans would occasionally rather wreck the whole machine, waste all the millions of public money, and even let the little children suffer, than permit their respective adversaries to gain a seeming triumph. Keeping strictly to my standpoint as an administrator, I end this little book by a few words with regard to the fundamental conditions without which London can have no efficient administration in education or in any other public service.

The first condition of administrative efficiency is the loyal co-operation of the whole administrative machine, from the humblest official up to the directing committee, in carrying out the purpose for which it is framed, *and no other*. If we consider the extreme case of absolute refusal, on the part of a member of the civil service, to execute the policy laid down by his official superior, or his setting himself deliberately to thwart it, we see at once that such conduct makes impossible any sort of efficiency. What is not so clearly perceived is the disastrous effect which is produced on the whole administrative machine, when any part of it seeks, not to fulfil the purpose of its being, but to twist or contort the law in order to bring about some other result. This is true no less of the controlling and directing committee-men than of the officials who serve them. When the law seeks to effect one result and the administrator another, the whole service suffers. The knowledge of any such duality permeates to the minutest ramifications of the organisation. Every officer, however humble his sphere, feels himself entitled to interpret the law and the administrative policy according to his own predilections, it may be his own conscientious conviction as to what Parliament ought to have decided; it may be, on the other hand, the interpretation which he thinks likely to serve his personal interest. This anarchic influence will be intensified by the fact that the attempts made by this or that section of the administration to twist or evade the law cannot be openly avowed, and must remain (unless they pass into the phase of sheer rebellion, which is the negation of administration) in the plane of suggestion, favouritism, or intrigue. Nor is it only the majority in power, or their executive officers, who are demoralised. The members in a minority feel that, in addition to being outvoted at the polls, they are being outwitted in the committee room, and their resentment of this fraud adds acrimony to their enforced submission. They are tempted to adopt similarly illegitimate devices of covert obstruction, intrigue with officers of their own way of thinking, and illicit connivance with outside authorities. Thus, in such an atmosphere, whilst the salaried staff becomes honeycombed with suspicion, uncertainty, and disloyalty, the directing committee itself becomes the scene, not of honest working together and mutual enlightenment, but of " sharp practice " of one sort or another, mutual antagonism and a partisan favouritism in promotion which, in its destructive results on administrative efficiency, is nearly as bad as pecuniary corruption itself. The Lion in the Path of London education is this peril of administrative perversion [pp. 196-8].

I resume the diary extracts:

January 17th, 1904.—Seven letters he [S. W.] wrote yesterday to editors enclosing his book and turning their minds to an anti-Nonconformist movement—to end in a considerable reduction of the Progressive majority, if not in a Moderate victory. If he brings off his plan and becomes responsible for the administration of the Act, I shall get still less of his time and thought for the book. Fortunately, I keep splendidly fit and can work steadily every day—but I am deplorably slow in getting over the ground and have to be constantly stopping to call for clearer and more copious evidence.

Except for four dinners of the staff of the School of Economics with gatherings of the students afterwards, which I have arranged for February and March, I am keeping myself free from social engagements. It is not the time but the energy I lack—unless I deliberately abstract it from my work. In the afternoons I take exercise, ponder and read—about twice a week I walk along the Embankment to St. Paul's and listen to the anthem and join in the beautiful liturgy of the evening prayer. Sidney's news, letters and newspapers, an occasional friend or student to lunch, now and again a few friends to dinner, or a dinner out, are sufficient from the standpoint of the greatest output. How any sane mortal with resources of their own and a few intelligent friends can exert themselves to get into " society " passes my comprehension. And yet I have just expended 21 guineas on an evening dress! I hasten to add that it is four years since I paid the same amount for my present evening garment. Still I might have done without it— if I had been quite single-minded in my indifference to social glamour. The cold-drawn truth is that though I am honestly indifferent as to whether or not I see the great world, when I do enter it I like to do credit to my reputation—an unworthy desire I own—unworthy of an ascetic student and a collectivist reformer!

February 27th.—Sidney and [Robert] Phillimore returned unopposed for Deptford—a somewhat striking comment on the threats of last summer that " he shall lose his seat ". He is now turning his attention to getting G. B. S. in for St. Pancras. What effect G. B. S.'s brilliant slashing to the right and the left among his own nominal supporters will have, remains to be seen—the party organisers have long ago given up the seat as lost. Sidney has written to every clergyman in the St. Pancras constituency (about 21), sending them a copy of his book and imploring them to go hard for Shaw; he has even got the Bishop of Stepney's blessing sent to the Rural Dean. He has now taken charge of two-thirds of the constituency, installed the Spencers [our own secretaries] in a committee room, and called up the whole of the Fabian Society on Shaw's behalf. Whether this effort will win what would be a forlorn hope to any other Progressive candidate, and will counteract the enemies G. B. S. makes in our own ranks, we cannot tell. The Shaws have been good friends to us, and we would not like them to have a humiliating defeat. What that erratic genius will do, if he gets on the L.C.C., heaven will know some day—but I am inclined to think that in the main he will back up Sidney. And he will become the *enfant terrible* of the Progressive Party, and make Sidney look wisely conventional. In the Fabian Society, they have certainly managed to supplement each other in a curiously effective way—let us hope it will be the same on the L.C.C. But he is not likely to get in!

March 1st.—Dined with the Munro Fergusons one day, Haldane the next; little parties of " Limps ". There is a depression in those ranks; within the Liberal Party, the Campbell-Bannerman, [Lord] Spencer, Morley crew followed by Reid, Lloyd George, Macnamara, are in the ascendant and are asserting their right to make the future Cabinet, and include as much or as little of the Roseberyites as they choose. Specially against Haldane is there a set; Rosebery, also, is at a discount—a heavier discount than he has been since he came back to speech-making politics. Partly due to growing discredit of the results of the war (Chinese labour!), dislike for expenditure on the forces; partly to Rosebery's disclaimer of social reform and to the quite opposite reason—the rehabilitation of *laisser-faire* by the free trade propaganda. Little Englandism, crude democracy, economy, secularism, are all again to the front in the official Liberal Party—are, in fact, the only actively militant forces with a policy to push. The vacuum over which the " Limps " have zealously watched cannot be kept intact; and the old creed and the old cries are rushing in, in default of better stuff.

The success of Sidney in wheeling the Progressives round to promise the energetic and prompt administration of the Act has been enormously helped by the publication of his little book with its extensive and detailed constructive programme. It has made it quite impossible for anyone to fight him as an obstructive or reactionary as the C. B. Liberals are fighting Rosebery and Haldane. Whatever space there is in the mind of the enquirer for thoughts about London education, Sidney has filled it up—packed one proposal on the top of the other, till the question whether or not Anglican or Nonconformist Christianity is to be taught for a few hours every week in certain elementary schools seems of quite minor importance.

March 3rd.—As I sat at home this morning, working at the book (Sidney having gone up to G. B. S.'s committee room), three typical interruptions occurred. Gomme, the clerk of the L.C.C., came down in haste to consult Sidney on new information before the committee met this afternoon, as to exact wording of the reference to the education committee by the new L.C.C.; a messenger came with a note from the editor of the *Daily Mail* urgently begging Sidney to write the leader telling the citizens of London how to vote on Saturday; and Robert Harcourt broke in to beg Sidney's advice and help to stave off a Labour candidate against his brother in Rossendale—the latter an altogether mistaken estimate of our influence with Labour leaders! But the discreet guidance of important officials, and hidden influence in the press, are both characteristic of Sidney's peculiar gift for " getting his own way " without anyone quite realising how.

March 5th.—Sidney wrote a signed Progressive article for the *Daily Mail*—mildly and impartially Progressive, ending with a puff of G. B. S. Now off to work for a more than doubtful result.

March 7th.—G. B. S. beaten badly; elsewhere the Progressives romping back with practically undiminished numbers. As to the first event, we are not wholly grieved. G. B. S., with a small majority, might have been useful; with an overwhelming one, would simply have been compromising. He certainly showed himself hopelessly intractable during the election: refused to adopt any orthodox devices as to address and polling cards, inventing brilliant ones of his own; all quite unsuited to any constituency but Fabians or " Souls ". Insisted that he was an atheist; that, though a teetotaller, he would force every citizen to imbibe a quartern of rum to cure any tendency to intoxication; laughed at the Nonconformist conscience; chaffed the Catholics about transubstantiation; abused the Liberals, and contemptuously patronised the Conservatives—until nearly every section was equally disgruntled. His bad side is very prominent at an election—vanity and lack of reverence for knowledge or respect for other people's prejudices; even his good qualities—quixotic chivalry to his opponents and cold drawn truth, ruthlessly administered, to possible supporters, are magnificent but not war. Anyway, we did our best for him, Sidney even puffing him outrageously in the *Daily Mail*—and he and Charlotte are duly grateful. He will never be selected again by any constituency that any wire-puller thinks can be won.

As for the general result—it is perturbing. The Church and the Catholics have apparently exercised no kind of influence—those sent to Coventry by the ecclesiastics being apparently no whit the worse. The Moderates in many constituencies, deserted by the official Conservatives, have had to bear the full brunt of the Government's unpopularity—they come back as they went out, virtually powerless. Of course, the Progressives have vowed to administer the Act impartially —but if they do so they will show real statesmanship and patriotism. I confess to a lively admiration for the " junta " who have beaten us in our underground attack on the size of the Progressive majority. For, to be absolutely honest, it was only when he [S. W.] saw that the " game was up " that he slipped down in the columns of the *Daily Mail* (Sidney would say I exaggerate his disaffection) on the Progressive side. Now it is his turn to be a " good boy " and be content with what's given him!

Yesterday Morant came to dine, and he and Sidney are working to get the pedantic Anson to approve the scheme (for the L.C.C. Education Committee) so that the Council may get to work without any sense of obstruction from the Education Department. To rebellion in Wales and hostile administration in the West Riding, there is no reason to add a newly elected and overwhelmingly popular but recalcitrant London County Council. Moreover, co-opted members would be futile if forced on the present County Council.

March 11th.—To our delighted surprise the Progressives—so far as the leaders are concerned—have returned to Spring Gardens in admirable temper, they seem literally *chastened* by their prosperity. At the lengthy party committees that have been held prior to the party meeting to-day, they have welcomed Sidney back into their counsels with great cordiality—quite disposed now that they see that the party is safe and sound, to listen to his advice on educational matters. They have even gone the length of suggesting that he should be chairman of the education committee, though they realise the difficulties; but he has decidedly negatived that notion, if anyone else can be found who will take the job on and let him work under them. It would be adding insult to injury to appoint the executioner as executor or trustee of the dead man's property—an insult which might jeopardise the smooth working of the concern. But what is really surprising is the almost unanimity with which the party committee has decided *not* to make Lord Stanley an alderman, but only to offer him co-option on the committee as a late School Board member—an offer which we know he won't accept. As for Macnamara, there has not been a whisper of having him on in any capacity—not even as a co-opted member. Meanwhile, within the party committee there has been much more trouble on what seems to us to be the unimportant question—whether Cornwall or Benn should be chairman of the Council this year—a question which seems immaterial since the other will be chairman next year! But they are both candidates for London constituencies, and both want to run as " Chairman of the Council ". The Progressive Party would like to pass both over—but there is a strong feeling, which Sidney has always upheld—that they have both earned the right, by hard administration and party work, to sit in the chair.

Meanwhile, we have been pulling the strings to get the Government to sanction the scheme, and I think we have succeeded in overcoming Anson's pedantry—Haldane, Cripps, the Bishop of Stepney and the Archbishop of Canterbury have been moved to intervene. Altogether matters look far more promising than we could have hoped with a thumping Progressive majority—it really seems as if Sidney had converted his own party by his book, at the infinitesimal cost of not being chairman for the first year, or perhaps not at all—in many ways a positive advantage. Going to open an educationist address book of persons likely to be useful in that sphere. I must *organise* our contact with them—we must learn the facts ourselves and spread our own ideas.

March 19th.—The last week there have been continuous sittings of the selection committee of the L.C.C., comprised of the party committee of each side *plus* a few others—a committee nominally elected by the L.C.C. at its first sitting but practically selected previously by the party whips. This committee is like an American Congress committee in that it never meets except formally—the two halves of it, Progressive and Moderate, meeting separately to select their respective members to serve on all the Council's committees. Sidney describes the Progressive meetings as extraordinarily frank and friendly; the dozen select members canvassing, with perfect candour, the qualities of all the others and planting them out where they will do most good or least harm. Jephson, an old member of the School Board, and new member of the L.C.C., who had been put on the selection committee, told me that he had never heard such a barefaced " assessment " of colleagues, and was taken aback at the autocratic manner in which the party " cabinet " disposed of or dispensed with the services of their fellows. Sidney reports great friendliness towards him and anxiety to accept his suggestions as to the education committee—Wood and Dickinson especially being somewhat remorseful over making Collins chairman—a remorse which is strengthened by their jealousy, in the political sphere, of Sir William. But, assuming that the latter bears out his reputation of letting others do the work and taking all the credit, Sidney will think it an excellent bargain—for all he wants is to have an outlet for his thought and experience and policy in London education—and, if he can get this without creating jealousy and hostility, so much the pleasanter and more effectual. Moreover Collins, being an able man, with great weight on the Council—liking, moreover, ceremonial occasions, will really free Sidney from a good deal of work and leave him free to think out the detail of educational administration, or to get on with the book. The disadvantage is that in the next weeks of transition the chairman will almost necessarily have to decide things off-hand, without consultation, and it is not yet apparent whether Collins will be able and willing to make Sidney into a deputy or at least a confidential adviser in these crucial new departures. But looked at from the point of view of efficiency and consent . . . I doubt whether the party leaders could have handled the matter more wisely than they have done. They have secured Sidney's service without raising the hostility which his chairmanship would have caused among the rank and file. They have " placed him out " in the way in which he will do most good and least harm! Certainly McKinnon Wood has shown, within the sphere of municipal administration on party lines, real statesmanship, and the party have had the sense to follow his leadership both as to policy and as to persons. " After all, Webb," he said in soothing and confidential tones, " with the exception of the somewhat unimportant matter of the co-opted members, we have done exactly what you said we ought to do; which, considering the composition of the party and their temper last spring, is more than you were justified in expecting."

The truth is the Progressives have come back very pleased with themselves, having converted themselves in the course of their electioneering to the pose they took up, for the purposes of the election, of the plain man refusing to be moved by the clamour of Church or Chapel—the Turk guarding the Holy Sepulchre of the child's intellect. Moreover, the more they look at the Education Act the more they like it, and the less fault they are inclined to find in it even with regard to denominational teaching. So Sidney is back in their favour and they all turn to him to instruct them in their new duties; not caring to take their instructions from the members of the School Board. Nine of the leading men among them dined last night at Evan Spicer's to discuss a way out of the religious difficulty, and it is significant that none of the school board L.C.C. members were invited. " The truth is," said Cornwall, " I see no better solution than the *status quo*—we must keep some denominational schools as a safety valve, else there will be a perpetual struggle to get hold of the provided schools. So far as London is concerned it is a very good Act!" " Look at Webb smiling", chaffed Williams Benn, the new chairman of the L.C.C. and a stalwart Nonconformist.

March 25th.—" The committee has gone adversely ", reported Sidney of the first meeting. Collins had insisted on Shepheard being elected vice-chairman, and had showed signs of letting everything slide, whilst keeping Sidney at arm's length. His old antagonism to Sidney, partly jealousy and partly real disagreement on university policy—a matter on which he has been beaten—is rising pretty obviously to the surface and may develop into a nasty business. Hitherto, however, Collins has never come into the open, we have heard rumours of his unfriendliness to the London School of Economics and to the lines of Sidney's educational policy, without this hostility bearing much fruit in positive opposition. What is, perhaps, more serious is his disinclination to grasp the matter himself, so that it is inevitable that the School Board members will, by their superior assiduity and knowledge, capture large parts of the organisation and keep on the old tradition. However, so long as the new committee keeps its reputation intact as a sane and efficient administrative body, and no retrogression about higher education takes place, we must be content to mark time until a more balanced Council gives the experts a chance. In watching a public body it is amusing to note that each success or failure brings about an almost immediate reaction—we are now suffering the reaction from excluding Lyulph Stanley and Stewart Headlam. Moreover, the rank and file of the Progressives, feeling themselves in the majority, but at the same time face to face with an extremely complicated business which they don't understand, are suffering from a fear of being " bossed ". At first it was Stanley, yesterday it was Webb, to-morrow it is as likely as not they will react against the School Board members. Middle-class demos is very sensitive as to its equality in capacity for administrative work, even compared with the most experienced expert. At the finance committee a few days ago, when Lord Welby (the chairman) turned to consult Sidney on an important item in the education estimates, the worthy but stupid Leon burst out into a hot protest. " The matter has not yet been discussed by the education committee, I don't see that Mr. Webb can have any opinion as to what should be done." But, as the question had to be settled, Lord Welby quietly accepted Sidney's proposals, and passed on to other business.

I tell Sidney he had better sit back in his chair and take it easy— he has changed the form of the authority and enormously extended its powers—the substance of its action had better remain as it is until a more seasonable time. Let Collins and Shepheard and the School Board men manage elementary education as they will—if they do it with efficiency so much the better, if they muddle it up there will come an inevitable reaction. Meanwhile, we can get on with the book, and he can keep an eye on university and secondary education. It will be as much as he can do to prevent a bad reaction in that quarter—and a possible withdrawal of the University grant or of the subsidy to the School.

April 15*th*.—Ten days at Felixstowe—and only one lazy one— Good Friday. For the first three, we worked hard finishing the chapters on *Nuisances*—the last five or six we spent on county, town and vestry records with the Spencers at Ipswich and Woodbridge—a happy and really restful time because it turned the current of Sidney's thoughts away from the little intrigues and jealousies of the L.C.C. and its education committee, on to the bigger currents of past developments in local government. We have quite settled to devote the next year and possibly three years to the book. Sidney to slack off the L.C.C.; I intend to take him off the scene early in July as it is clear that, so long as he is there, there is always a tendency on the part of officials and even on the part of the malcontents of the education committee, to make him do the work of drafting and negotiating. That won't suit our present book—in the metaphorical sense—and will not help to get the future book—in the real sense—finished. So I am considering Scotland and the possibility of a really long sojourn there with our material, and the Spencers looking up things for us in London. The next five weeks we shall devote to getting our material on municipal enterprise into order so as to see what we require for completion.

April 19th.—We have had a couple of days with H. G. Wells and his wife at Sandgate, and they are returning the visit here. We like him much—he is absolutely genuine and full of inventiveness—a " speculator " in ideas—somewhat of a gambler but perfectly aware that his hypotheses are not verified. In one sense, he is a romancer spoilt by romancing—but, in the present stage of sociology, he is useful to gradgrinds like ourselves in supplying us with loose generalisations which we can use as instruments of research. And we are useful to him in supplying an endless array of carefully sifted facts and broad administrative experience.

I asked him to tell me frankly why Wallas and some others were so intensely suspicious of us, and seemed bent on obstructing every proposal of Sidney's. He threw out two suggestions: first, that Sidney (and no doubt I) was too fond of " displaying " his capacity for " tactics ", that he gave a " foxy " impression—that he had better fall back on being an enthusiast; secondly, that we were always regarded as a " combination " working into each other's hands, but not impelled by *quite* the same motives, or inspired by quite the same purpose—that I was regarded as a " reactionary " with an anti-Radical creed, and it was suspected that Sidney would eventually veer round to my side.[1] Of course, we have got to be ourselves, whatever

[1] Here is a kindly characterisation of the Webbs and their methods by one of the most distinguished journalists of his time, A. G. Gardiner:

" Among the acolytes of the Fabian order there is a constant controversy as to which of the two is before or after the other. It is an idle theme, for you can never tell where one ends and the other begins—how much you are yielding to the eloquence of Mrs. Webb, and how much to the suggestion of Mr. Webb. It is she who weaves the spells, but he who forges the bolts. Between them they have an uncanny power of persuasion. Their knowledge overwhelms you, their sweet reasonableness disarms you. You are led captive in the chains of their silken logic, and they have the victories that fall to those whose knowledge is the instrument of relentless purpose, whose patience is inexhaustible and whose urbanity is never ruffled. . . . It is this sleuth-like pursuit of their purposes that makes them so powerful and so often distrusted. There is nothing that men dislike so much as being ' managed '. And Mr. and Mrs. Webb are always ' managing ' you. They sit behind the scenes, touching buttons, pulling wires, making the figures on the stage dance to their rhythms. To their modest table come the great and the powerful to learn their lessons, and to be coached up in their facts. Some fear to enter that

may be the drawbacks, but his criticism increased my inclination for a somewhat severe abstinence from trying to " run the show "—for a quiet and unselfconscious withdrawal into other work for the next three years. Directly the grant for the School is safe we will go into retreat with our papers and books until the October session.

April 20th.—For the Wellses we had a little dinner—carefully selected—Mr. Balfour, the Bishop of Stepney, the Bernard Shaws, Mrs. Reeves, and a Mr. Thesiger, a new L.C.C. Moderate. The P.M., finding himself in a little party of intimates (Thesiger was the only stranger), belonging to a strange world completely detached from party politics, let himself go, and, I think, thoroughly enjoyed the mixture of chaff and dialectic which flew from G. B. S. to Wells and round the table to Sidney, the Bishop of Stepney and myself. There is always method in our social adventures, and at my instigation Sidney, after we had left, backed up by the Bishop and Wells and Shaw, gave an elaborate argument in favour of our half-time scheme for boys.[1] As I had told Mr. Balfour that the grand distinction between him and the Liberal leaders was that his attitude towards proposals of social reform could be expressed by " Why not? " and theirs by a grudging " Why? " he felt bound to be sympathetic and was, I think, somewhat taken with the notion. He is honestly concerned about the alleged degeneracy of the race, and inclines to, at any rate, " flirt " with new proposals. And in these days, when the mind of every Liberal leader is as closed as a live oyster, one must be grateful for small mercies.

May, Bramdean.—In the life of a little village one notes how far happier and more dignified is the existence of the hard-working daughter of the middle-class farmer or shopkeeper than that of the rich young woman who drifts through life in the big upper middle-class houses dotted about the country. There are seven Miss Legges—in the big house next door—there are five Meinertzhagens at Brockwood—

parlour of incantations, and watch the Webbs with unsleeping hostility. A mere suspicion that they are prompting behind the curtain is enough to make them damn the most perfect play " (*Pillars of Society*, by A. G. Gardiner, pp. 204-6).

[1] In our *Industrial Democracy*, 1897 (vol. ii. p. 769), we had suggested that (instead of pleading for an extension for one or two years of the compulsory attendance at the elementary school, at that time ending, as regards some occupations, at 10 years of age) there should be demanded universal compulsory, all-round training, including physical and technological, for both boys and girls up to 18 years of age, but only half time, either by alternate days or half-days, or by alternate seasons. It could be assumed, we urged, that such a halving of the supply of labour between 10 and 18 would lead to an increase in the hourly rate of wages which would render unnecessary any but a tiny scholarship in partial maintenance. We had discovered such an idea in the apprenticeship laws of certain Swiss Cantons; and it had somehow (!) found its way into the Report of the Trade Union Minority of the Royal Commission on Labour, C. 7421, 1894.

there are countless young ladies all " awaiting " with more or less self-possession the lot of the marriage market, or a useless old-maidenhood. Compare these listless young persons to pretty energetic Dolly Hawkins who " runs " our little lodgings, helps her father the post-master, and thoroughly enjoys her casual flirtations, restricted to her few spare hours or afternoons. The cottager lives at too low a level of health and intelligence—the men are brutalised, the women prematurely old; but the respectable and successful lower middle-class country-bred person now combines physical comfort, personal freedom and a considerable education, and stimulus to activity—a rising standard of ease and comfort, but not too high for efficiency. . . .

In the middle of our stay we ran up to London to take the Joseph Fels' to the University reception to the foreign academies—for once breaking our rigid rule of refusing to appear at evening parties. One reason for so doing was the desire to be polite to the Fels'. Dowdy little Americans to look at—he a decidedly vulgar little Jew with much push, little else on the surface, she a really refined and intellectual and public-spirited little body who, by mere force of character, has dragged her husband and his partner into the Fabian Society and other advanced movements. The partner, Coates, who lives with them, is a mild-mannered and dowdy Yorkshireman—a refined and gentle-spirited young clerk who has been made by Fels a partner in his concern—the concern being *Fels Naptha Soap*. Perhaps, after all, it was to the soap that we gave the dinner? Certainly, if it could have been demonstrated to us that the soap was a lie that would be found out—that dinner would not have been given. But a subscription of £100 to the Fabian Society and the report of golden soap-suds, set us thinking of the Fels' as possible founders, yet uncaptured; while the lunch made us take a genuine fancy to her, and not finding him repulsive, so we speculated an evening on them—more than that, a journey up to London!

I note a certain change in our surroundings. Some of our old comrades of ten or even eight years ago have become indifferent or even hostile to our ideas. . . . On the other hand, there is a new group of friendly young men disposed to take our views seriously—Masterman, Morgan, Ensor, Bray, Isaac Mitchell, T. E. Harvey, Basil Williams, Bron Herbert, and with a certain reservation, George Trevelyan, are all anxious to see more of us. What is, perhaps, a less wholesome sign is the accession of " society " folk—the Hubert Parrys, Batterseas, Elchos, Lyttons, [Munro] Fergusons, Monteagles, Alfred Lytteltons, Asquiths, Thesigers, Stamfords, Sydney Buxtons, Bryces and Gorst, have been added to those who ask and are asked to dinner—but all of these have a certain usefulness. Some new *friends* we have made within the same period—H. G. Wells the foremost, and the George Protheros; H. J. Mackinder is a new colleague and then there are the outer circle of senators, L.C.C., and school lecturers, and educational administrators, and bishops and distinguished foreigners. On the whole, it is an extraordinarily varied and stimulating society. The dominant note in our intercourse with these people is *social reconstruction*—in all the little dinners at Grosvenor Road and the *tête-à-tête* talk at other people's dinners—it is always round some project that the conversation ranges. What is utterly lacking is art, literature for its own sake, and music—whilst physical science only creeps up as analogous and illustrative matter; history appears in much the same aspect. The relation of man's mind to the universe is constantly present as a background in my own thought and with some of our more intimate acquaintances—with T. E. Harvey, Masterman, Haldane, Russell—I have long talks; but the subject bores Sidney as leading nowhere and as not capable of what he considers valid discussion—exactly as he dislikes discussing what train you will go by, before he has got hold of the Bradshaw. He prefers reading a statistical abstract, or an L.C.C. agenda. His relation to the universe—in the spiritual sense, he mockingly suggests, consists in his relation to me!

June 8th.—Turned from roads to help Sidney to write an article on *The Policy of a National Minimum.* Before we left London we had a little series of young progressives to discuss the possibility of pushing the policy of creating an artificial bottom to society by collective regulation and collective expenditure—" canalising " the forces of competition so that all the individuals in the community should be pressed upwards not cast downwards. The upshot of this was that we had an urgent request for an article to embody our doctrine—five thousand words, necessarily topical, are a poor medium; we were tired and disinclined to turn from our own proper business, but we felt obliged to accept. I thought it better for Sidney to sign the article singly—the double signature overloads so slight a thing, and it is too political in its tone to warrant the intervention of the female partner. I believe in mere " wife's politics "—only in research do I claim equality of recognition!

June 17th.—We lunched yesterday with the Chamberlains—to introduce the Irvines—others there were the Bonar Laws and a certain Sweet-Escott, Governor of British Honduras. I sat on one side of my old friend and we talked without constraint. He is obsessed with the fiscal question—has lost his judgement over it—refuses to think or talk of anything else. He looks desperately unhealthy, rather thin too; a restless look in his eyes, bad colour, and general aspect of " falling in ". But I should imagine that there is plenty of force in the man yet; an almost mechanically savage persistence in steaming ahead. I tried to suggest the " national minimum " as a complementary policy to import duties. " I have no prejudice against it," he answered, " but it would not do for me to suggest it—it would be said that I was trying to bribe the working-class. But there is no reason why it should not be added on by someone else." Then we drifted on to the Education Acts 1902 and 1903, which he clearly does *not* favour—he is afraid of the advent of the bureaucrat. The trail of the profit-maker in industry is in everything that Chamberlain proposes or opposes—he detests the salaried expert. Like many others who share this dislike he tries to ignore the inevitability of the officials' (salaried administrators) government of society, instead of devising safeguards against the evils of it. " If I had been Prime Minister, you would not have had the Education Act." " The one and only reason for my not regretting that you are *not* Prime Minister ", I answered pleasantly; and we passed on to other things. Sidney says that after the ladies left, Chamberlain urged on Irvine almost passionately the need for preferential tariffs (S. W. devoting himself to Sweet-Escott, as it was clear that Chamberlain wanted to talk confidentially to Irvine. Bonar Law had left). Upstairs, we four ladies had conversation—gossip about Rosebery and the Liberal Cabinet—and discussing the relative merits of Protestantism and Catholicism. I like Mrs. Chamberlain; there is a lot of sincerity and simple feeling in her face—a somewhat pathetic expression, as if life were too much for her, though she obviously enjoys, to its full, the social side of the position. I imagine she worships her great man. But there must be times when the great personage with his irritability, one-sidedness, pitiful unhealthiness and egotism and vulgarity, is rather a heavy handful for that refined and charming little lady.

All goes well with the L.C.C. and the education committee. First-rate officials are being selected, the routine administration is being digested and the plain man is learning his lesson. Sidney finds himself on agreeable terms with all parties: the School Board women being apparently the only persons who bear him a grudge. I have been somewhat assiduous in my cultivation of the Progressives—successfully, so I think; and, by leaving London at the end of June, we have at least convinced them that Sidney does not want to run the show. Antagonisms are being developed between some of the members, but Sidney has kept well outside them. He has been re-elected on the party committee, the grant to the University and the School went through without a word, and some of the leading Progressives have signified that they think he has acted " nobly " in subordinating his claims to the chairmanship of the education committee. He has given the impression that he really does not care for the distinctions of office, and as we have other work which we actually prefer doing, we are glad enough that he should be absolved from close attendance. So we go off to Scotland with our books and our papers for our three months' recess, with a good conscience and good hope.

June 20*th.*—Sidney's influence on the joint-life is wholesome in curbing my lower desires. There have been three separate entertainments that I should like to have gone to—Lady Wimborne's, Mr. Balfour's and the Duchess of Sutherland's evening parties. Feeling secure in the possession of an attractive garment I should have liked to have paraded myself. But S. was obdurate. " You won't be able to work the next morning, and I don't think it is desirable that we should be seen in the houses of great people. Know them privately if you like, but don't go to their miscellaneous gatherings. If you do, it will be said of us as it is of Sir Gilbert Parker—in the dead silence of the night you hear a distant but monotonous sound—Sir Gilbert Parker climbing, climbing, climbing." And I recognised the better voice and tore up the cards.

The last weeks Sidney's days have been over-filled with committees and the work arising from them. Yesterday, for instance, 8.45–11.0, drafting a report for the chairman of one of the sub-committees of the education committee of the L.C.C.; 11 o'clock Royal Commission on Trade Disputes; 12.30 sub-committee at School Board offices; 1.30 took train to South Kensington, lunching in the train, for 2 o'clock Departmental Committee on Royal College of Science; 4.30 took the chair at the London School of Economics at meeting of railway magnates to decide on railway department (secured £1000 a year to start department); 6 o'clock arrived late at higher education committee at School Board office and transacted, as chairman, remainder of business; 8 o'clock dinner here—Bernard Shaws, Jack Tennants, John Burns, Munro Fergusons and Stephen Hobhouse; after dinner group of young Progressives to be introduced to John Burns and G. B. S.; to bed 12 o'clock; began work again at book at 8.45. Very naturally there is not much brain left for the book, and until we get right away from London we shall only muddle on. But muddling on is better than leaving off; the stuff one gets on to the paper contains the necessary quotations and gives one something to bite.

October 16*th.*—The three months in Scotland were so completely a joint existence that there was neither the desire nor the opportunity to record it in this book. When Sidney is with me I cannot talk to the other self with whom I commune when I am alone—" it " ceases to be present and only reappears when he becomes absent. Then the old self, who knew me and whom I have known for that long period before Sidney entered into my life—who seems to be that which is *permanent* in me—sits again in the judgement seat and listens to the tale of the hours and days, acts, thoughts and feelings, which the earthly one has experienced.

Beautiful and peaceful have been the scenes of our long working holiday—especially enchanting the hill-side of Fyrish, with heather and fir-clad mountains rising up behind us, and Cromarty Firth and the North Sea rolled out beneath us; the " Golden Gate ", as we called the North and South Suters, will remain in my memory as one of the most beautiful expanses of water, land and sky. Especially beautiful the week before we left when the sun rose midway between the two promontories, right out of the ocean, its rays lighting up, one by one, each feature of the Firth until the whole landscape of cornfields, heather and rich foliage was one soft glow of gold, brown and green.

Except for four days' cycling on the West Coast and the two days broken by our change of quarters at the end of July (from Nethy Bridge near Grantown, to Fyrish near Evanton), we worked steadily six days out of seven at the book, for the four morning hours—spending the afternoons in reading and exercise. Once a week we would take a Sabbath and go some thirty miles to see friends or explore the mountains of the Black Isle. Excellent health, and greater bodily and mental vigour than I have ever known before, made me feel as if I were still in the very prime of life, and Sidney too seemed unreservedly happy. We saw a good deal of neighbours; made friends with the elementary teachers and ministers in both places, and at Fyrish had, as agreeable acquaintances, the mother and daughter of the Laird of Novar—Munro Ferguson.

We made some superficial and scattered observations on Scottish education and social life, but I doubt whether they are worth recording. I brooded, in lonely walks, over the book, or over the new philosophy which is gradually taking shape in my mind; or praised the unknown for our exceeding happiness; or prayed for strength to be abstemious, persistent in work, and clear-sighted and constantly kind to others. But I was working so hard at technical detail (roads, pavement and cleansing) that I had little strength left over for other reading or writing, and was glad to let myself be absorbed in the mere enjoyment of light, air and colour.

November 8th.—Sidney has been busy drafting his *scholarship scheme* and getting it accepted by his higher education committee. He has found his Progressive colleagues in a most kindly humour. Cornwall thanked him the other day for his self-abnegation—intimating that the junta recognised his delicacy in so retiring from view that it could not be said that he was " running them " and practically asking him to continue the same policy for a little longer, and then all would be well. And the policy has at least the advantage of enabling him to spend half his time in reading at the British Museum—all to the good of the book.

We spent last Sunday at the Sydney Buxtons with Haldane and the Birrells—endless discussions as to the future of the Liberal Party. It is clear that they are unrepentant in their determination to run into place on the old lines of economy and freedom of trade, and anti-priest bias— they refuse even to contemplate any other policy—dismiss all social reform from their minds except, perhaps, a revision of the incidence of taxation in favour of the small consumer.

They are not optimistic—look forward to a bare majority over the Irish and a tenure of one or two years—" let us get a front bench " is their cry. Haldane told us as we drove to the station early on Monday morning, that there had been a move to exclude the " Limps " last spring, but that it had collapsed and the dominant note now was a Cabinet of all sections.

December 6th.—We stayed Saturday and Sunday with the Thesigers, an attractive young couple, he a son of the General, Lord Chelmsford, and she a daughter of Lord Wimborne, both tall and pleasant to look at, intelligent, public-spirited, and versed in all the little amenities of hospitality and conversation. He is a leading Moderate on the L.C.C., also a member of the Dorset County Council; together they run the church, the school, the library, the glee-club, of their hamlet—all activities which militate against his getting on over much at the Bar. Indeed, it is this willingness to spend themselves on social service, this apparent absence of political, professional or social ambition, which lends a peculiar attractiveness to the *ménage,* in spite of a lack of any special distinction in the way of forceful administrative capacity or intellectual curiosity or subtlety. Our fellow-guests were Professor Ker—professor of English and English literature at University College, and a young Cecil [1]—a son of Lord Eustace Cecil. The former was distinctly of the *owl* type—his qualifications to teach the higher forms of his own language judged by his own conversational powers were not considerable. He was mostly silent, when he did speak one barely understood him; sometimes there seemed to glimmer through his badly chosen words and awkward sentences a sort of pawky Scotch humour, but one had to puzzle it out. Sidney says that on the Senate he never gets his proposals carried from lack of power of lucid or even correct expression. Imagine a university professor of French in Paris being

[1] Note, 1936.—Algernon Cecil; he joined the Roman Catholic Church some years afterwards.

remarkable for an utter absence of the power to talk good French![1]
Young Cecil was interesting because he was able to describe or imply
the Cecil philosophy of life. For him society was cloven in two—the
Church and the world. The Church was governed by spiritual illumination; the world outside of this radius was exclusively dominated by
the motive of pecuniary self-interest. To attempt to run the secular
world on any other motive was not only contrary to the commandment
" Give unto Caesar the things which are Caesar's " but was almost
blasphemy. All real progress was confined to *progress of the individual
soul under the influence of the Church.* Any increase of honesty or
kindliness, of honour, public spirit or truth-seeking brought about
otherwise, was merely a higher stage of self-interest (equally damnable
as the lower stages)—merely the discovery by each individual that those
qualities paid better. Accompanying, and to some extent coinciding
with this cleavage, was that between the hereditary and landed aristocracy represented by the Cecils, and " the others ". The Cecils
governed by spiritual illumination (inherited through a long line of
noble ancestors) were to direct the policy of the state, making use of
the lower motives of vulgar folk to keep the state going on its material
side. The odd part of the whole scheme was the almost fanatical objection to any attempt to alter the motives of human nature, otherwise
than by the action of the Church on the individual soul—and a
complete complacency with the one secular motive of enlightened self-
interest as the basis of everyday life. It was almost as wicked to tamper
with this motive by introducing other considerations into the industrial
or political organisation of the state, as it was to introduce the pecuniary
motive into the Church—as for instance in the sale of indulgences or
simony. Altogether I began to see the current Radical objection to the
Toryism of the Cecil type. The boy himself was both pure in heart
and intellectual in tastes, and with that delightful modesty of manner
and easy deference which robbed the creed of any *appearance* of class
insolence or religious intolerance. He was suffering from an extremity
of bad health—appendicitis and its results—and was quite obviously
being villainously treated on the physic and " much food " plan of the
ordinary doctor. I did my best to upset both his philosophy and his
régime by a combination of serious discussion and rap-dazzle repartee

---

[1] Later I realised that this hasty and superficial impression did injustice to a fine
intellect, the master of massive erudition in fields of which I knew nothing. Walter
Paton Ker (1855–1923) held the Chair at University College, London, in
English Language and Literature, and published many learned books and articles
on the mediaeval literature of England, which had a great reputation. He was a shy
and unassuming, but very kindly teacher; and I have been told that, with intimate
friends, he was witty as well as wise. He was elected a Fellow of the British Academy
in 1903.

—but I doubt success in either direction—the philosophy and the regimen were both too congenial to the fastidious and subtle self-indulgence of his temperament to be undermined in 48 hours by an elderly free-thinking woman. If the creed and the regimen remain unqualified he will be a waste product in society—interesting only as an obsolete type.

December 22nd.—An outburst of jealousy among the leading Progressives at the scholarship scheme, which has attracted much attention and is almost universally praised. Collins, Cornwall and Dickinson have not been making much of a success of their special functions—getting a good deal of odium for sins of commission and omission from Non-conformists and Church alike—Sidney on their instructions lying low. Then out he comes as chairman of the higher education committee with his great scholarship scheme carefully thought out in detail, with arguments showing that it is inevitable. They don't like to oppose it because the need for more teachers is urgent and the trend of opinion all in favour of increased facilities for the lower middle-class—they can't object to the detailed proposals because they don't know sufficient to suggest others to take their place—but it is offending the N.U.T., backing up the secondary schools, and spending the rates. Moreover, as Collins naïvely remarked to the Council, " If it is a success, the credit will be Mr. Webb's "—he said it in a complimentary tone but it was clearly an uncomfortable thought. However, though it is adjourned, Sidney thinks it is certain to go through because of the general outside approval, and because they cannot suggest an alternative. But he was a wee bit hurt at the lack of frankness and generosity on the part of the governing *clique.* I have given up trying to propitiate them as I don't find my cordiality makes any difference to their jealousy of Sidney's influence with the press and the powers that be. I tell him that he must put up with the defects of his qualities: if he goes in for hidden influence he must expect hidden obstruction. It is worth while " preparing positions " so as to carry measures one believes in—if one's talent lies in that direction one *ought* to do it. But very naturally the persons who find themselves in these prepared positions—unable to get out except through his way—naturally do not like it, and try to make the way as unpleasant as they can for him personally. Our amazing good fortune and perpetual happiness an ample reward for these vexations.

Kate Courtney remarked the other day that she always wondered, in reading the published diaries or confidential writing of private persons, why they seemed so little concerned with the great question of peace and war—so infinitely more important than their own little doings or narrow range of interests, solemnly recorded in their diaries.

And I bethought me that there is hardly a reference to the Russia-Japanese war in these pages. The answer I gave on the spur of the moment, is, I think, the true one: "The private person *has* no specialist knowledge, no particular or exceptional experience as to world politics—his thoughts and feelings would be a mere reflection of his morning newspapers and worthless both to him and to those who might some day read the story of his life". And yet, if one looks back on the past year and thinks how much one has brooded over the Far-Eastern drama—how eagerly one has read each morning's news and how one has stumbled into foreshadowing the effect of the " Rising Sun " on our Western civilisation—it is hardly fair to leave it wholly unnoticed. For instance, I watch in myself and others a growing national shamefacedness at the superiority of the Japanese over our noble selves in capacity, courage, self-control, in benevolence as well as in all that makes up good manners! They shame our Christianity, they shame our administrative capacity, they shame our inventiveness, they shame our leadership, and alas! they shame our " average sensual man ". Perhaps, it makes the matter worse that they have won not by the genius of one man—which might be an accident not likely to recur again—but on the intellectual, physical and moral qualities of the whole people. They seem both more scientific and more religious than ourselves—a nobler purpose and more ably contrived processes wherewith to carry out this purpose. Their success will alter not merely the balance of power, but the balance of ideas—it will tell against Christianity as the one religion, against materialistic in-dividualism, against autocracy, against luxury, in favour of organisation, collective regulation, scientific education, physical and mental training —but on the whole *not* in favour of democracy. They have suddenly raised the standard of international efficiency—exactly in those depart-ments of life where we Western nations imagined ourselves supremely superior to the Eastern races. How far this shock to self-esteem will go in English society—how far it will be neutralised by the vulgar delight of seeing our ally beat our enemy—remains to be seen. But, for many a long day, the reformer will be able to quote on his side the innovating collectivism of the Japanese; the idealist, the self-abnegation of all classes of the community in a common cause. Even in one's own daily life, one is inclined towards greater persistency and more self-sacrifice. So closes 1904 and this book of the diaries.

1905

January 21*st*.—The main excitement [I write on January 21, 1905] is watching events in Russia—likely to prove the essential need for *consent* as an element in stable government. Japan is proving the superlative advantage of scientific methods in the international struggle for existence. How to combine the maximum of consent with the highest degree of efficiency is the problem before us in England: the average sensual man not wanting to be improved!

February 8th.—Dickinson, who is now trying to boss the Council's policy in *elementary* education, told Sidney quite frankly that he intended to get by *administration* what he despaired of getting by an amendment of the Act—I suppose the extinction of denominational schools through a combined policy of impossible requirements and starvation. He very naïvely added that he could not take Sidney into his confidence since he might use the knowledge to thwart him—a declaration which absolves Sidney from loyalty to the party counsels. They were most friendly with each other, but it was clear that Dickinson had got the governing *clique* to back him up and was going to keep Sidney at arm's length. However, in regard to secondary and university education, they are letting Sidney have his own way, and he is preparing some interesting situations for them to wake up to presently. The ratepayer, too, will have something to say to a policy of supersession. I have confidence that Dickinson will turn out too stupid—will fail to bring about a reaction. But it all means lack of efficiency—mutual obstruction instead of co-operation.

We have Sir Oliver Lodge staying here for two or three days. A delightful personality—large and fresh in his thought and feeling, but suffering from a bad fit of intellectual dissipation after a long life of specialism, made more acute by introduction to the Balfour-Elcho-Wyndham set—a fascinating temptation to an attractive person condemned to live in a provincial town. He is another instance of the fallacy that physical science is an outfit for the psychological and social sciences. It never occurs to us economists and political science students to imagine that our long-standing study of the complicated structure and function of society fits us to be astronomers or physicists—but the physical science man plunges head foremost into the discussion of our questions, armed with the four rules of arithmetic and the instruments of a laboratory.

For his entertainment we had a little party consisting of the Bertrand Russells, Granville-Barkers (the intellectual actor), Mackinder, Lion Phillimore, Wernher (Wernher & Beit) and Balfour. I begged the P.M. to talk to Bertrand and placed them next each other, and they got on famously—I sacrificed myself during some part of dinner to the millionaire (who is endowing London University); Lodge, Granville-Barker, Sidney and the two charming ladies kept up a lively talk at the other end. There was a subtle antipathy of Balfour to Mackinder and Wernher—mere philistine materialist administrators he would feel —there was sympathy between him and Russell and Barker, and of course he and Lodge are affectionate friends and fellow synthetic philosophers. Lodge got on with all the company—Mackinder and Wernher chummed up and walked away together—the intellectual young actor wrote me enthusiastically that he had walked home with the great man. Mr. Balfour likes both the Webbs—that is clear— finds them stimulating and attractive. To-day I took our guest to lunch with the Courtneys—to meet John Morley, the Spenders, George Trevelyan, etc. John Morley eyed me suspiciously, but insisted on listening to my lively talk to Spender.

February 29th.—Sidney gleeful as to the acceptance of his scholarship scheme—the only piece of constructive work done as yet by the education committee of the L.C.C. Without in the least being aware of it, the dear Progressives have let themselves in for supporting all the existing secondary schools (under separate management, and some, decidedly, and nearly all, theoretically, denominational) and for providing others under the direct management of the L.C.C. And the amusing part of it is that those who, like Graham [Wallas], object to the existing schools, will push all they know how, to get L.C.C. secondary schools started, whereas timid Progressives, like Torrance and the party leaders, who don't like to run up the rates for higher education, will find themselves forced to defend the denominational schools as the cheapest way out of the dilemma. " I can now leave the two forms of obstruction to fight it out," chuckles Sidney, " they will both be pushing on the machine in the direction that I want it to go." The scholarship scheme is, in fact, going to dominate the whole policy of the committee. Meanwhile, the five big officials have coalesced satisfactorily and are constantly coming to Sidney for advice. So that he really loses very little by not being chairman, and escapes both the odium and the responsibility. " The glory of it " he is quite content to leave to others! If the Progressives had dared to do it, they would really have been able to control him better by placing him in the chairmanship and then forcing him to accept the whole responsibility. And, of course, the administration would have been more efficient and more economical. But in view of the violent suspicion of the Nonconformists and the N.U.T., that was politically impossible.

March 5th.—The Wallases and Bray came to dine last night, and the three men sat for two hours discussing education policy, whilst I listened dreamily to Audrey's gentle chatter in the drawing-room. Sidney and Bray tried to get Graham to enter into a *concordat*— Sidney prepared to back him up with regard to the elementary education if he, Wallas, would back Sidney up in secondary and university matters. But Graham will not budge from his principle of starving out the secondary schools under separate management—he will not agree to run both systems, provided and non-provided, side by side. Sidney, on the other hand, whilst ready to provide as many secondary and university institutions as the ratepayers will pay for, wants gradually to acquire sufficient control over all the others to raise their standard to the required level. However, though Graham refused to give up his principle, he agreed to consult with Sidney and Bray as to the application of it, and not to wantonly obstruct without consideration or warning. What is clear is that the present constitution of the L.C.C. as educational authority is transitional, and unstable in the last degree. The men who know most and are most patiently persistent will, however unpopular their policy may be, in the end rule the roost. The next three years, with the parliamentary election to take some of the foremost Progressives into higher spheres, and the L.C.C. elections two years hence to lose some Progressive seats, will clear off a good many of the present obstructions. But when exactly we shall feel free to go off for our eight months' trip to the Far East remains in dim obscurity —a vision of rest and refreshment at the end of many more months and years of sustained drudgery. I am beginning to hanker after a period of fallowness.

March 31*st.*—Another old friend passed away—Marie Souvestre. A brilliant woman, handsome, warm-hearted—the very soul of veracity—and keen-witted. A school mistress for nearly half-a-century, she must have counted for much in the lives of many women coming from the best of the governing class in England, America, France and Germany. But she was not only a school mistress: she was an habituée, during middle life, of intellectual society in Paris, Berlin and London: she had known most of the advanced politicians and thinkers springing from the professional and middle-class. Twenty years ago, in York House days, I used to meet her at the Chamberlains, Harrisons, Morleys—it was she who introduced me to the Creightons.

It is strange to think of that passionate nature—with her scorn of what she felt to be mean, her bitter criticism of what she did not understand, her devoted service to those she loved, her exalted enthusiasm for what was noble in her eyes—to think of that force passed away into the unknown silence of death. A few weeks ago I visited her twice, and thought I saw the hand of death on her face; she seemed quite as alive in spirit as when I first met her at Frederic Harrison's—and now where is she?

Veracity, an undeviating directness of intelligence, faithfulness and warmth of affection, were her most delightful qualities; dignity of manner and brilliancy of speech her chief ornaments. An amazing narrowness of vision for so intelligent a person; a total inability to understand religion; a dogmatism that was proof against the spirit of scientific investigation; a lack of charity to feelings with which she did not sympathise—in short, an absence of humility was, perhaps, the most disabling of her characteristics. It narrowed her influence to those whom she happened to like and who happened to like her. Others refused to listen; and with some she roused evil feelings.

It is hard for those born in the modern England to understand the passionate hatred of ecclesiasticism—of religion—which seems to dominate French free-thinkers; it is so hard not to count it as an evil thing. Yet this feeling is not mainly evil—it has in it an element of idealism—of faith in noble qualities which were, far back in history, trampled under foot by organised Christianity; and which they still believe are in danger from the existing Church. The shackling of the spirit of investigation into the processes of life, the attempt to stereotype the purpose of life—the suppression of the inner light by mere formalism, the assumption of individuals of better motives than are actually present —all these various shades of disloyalty to truth seem to these militant secularists still rampant in any body of men knit together by the religious spirit. This conviction may have a grain of truth in it, since this lack of veracity is the special temptation which besets the religious mind. But, on the other hand, the absence of religious impulse seems to leave most of these natures blind and infirm even in their intellectual judgements. Marie Souvestre was not a wise woman—she was hard on the great mass of common people—occasionally even unjust; she always insisted, like Herbert Spencer, on being judge in her own case. She could not tolerate the idea that *she* might be wrong. And it was a strange irony that she was almost as ignorant of the persistent industry, patience and humility, involved in the scientific method, as she was of the religious impulse. All knowledge appeared to her as a series of intuitions, as sparks struck by the instantaneous contact of the mind with its environment—not as the slow adjustment of the order of thought to the order of things. Observation and conjecture, yes, but verification, no.

April 2nd.—Sidney is happier in his L.C.C. work than I have known him since the first Council. He has, in his special department of education, the maximum of power with the minimum of responsibility. He has no personal enemies on the Council, and the bulk of the Progressives, feeling that they have behaved rather shabbily in keeping him out of all prominent places, are really anxious to " oblige him " on questions of policy. The Moderates, whilst acknowledging his separate standpoint, feel him to be an ally of their best side—*i.e.* of their endeavour to develop the neglected parts of the educational system. The officials, one and all, consult and trust him, regarding him almost as one of themselves. And as regards the future, it is rather a case of " heads you lose, tails I win ". If the Progressives, by insisting on direct administration and county provision of all education, run up the rates, then there will be a reaction in favour of the Moderates. If the Moderates come in, there will be better organisation and more delegation; if the Progressives maintain themselves, there will be more expenditure; in short, the Progressives will find it impossible not to improve the *function* and the Moderates to improve the *structure* of the educational authority—and both parties must more or less accept his policy. Meanwhile, he is completely in the background—a free-lance ready to engage in a skirmish with either side, and relieved from the worry and strain of getting things through the Council in which he is not specially interested. He is thus free to give time and thought to the book.

April 17*th.*—Three or four weeks, day after day, spent either amassing new material at the British Museum for our chapters on the county or in analysing our twelve boxes of material at home. Some days I have spent a good six hours at work—seeing no one until Sidney returned in the evening—just going for a constitutional after lunch or walking along the Embankment to call on Kate Courtney in the hour or so before supper. But most weeks we have had a twelve-person dinner at home; dined out twice or three times; lunched casual persons on intermediate days; and, on three occasions, we have entertained at dinner the staff of the School, with gatherings of 50 to 70 students coming in afterwards. Then my work the next day has suffered either in quality or quantity or both, and I have felt disheartened at the length and complexity of our task. Our life tends, however, to become more and more the student's life and to be less interrupted by social engagements—partly the pressure of completing these two first volumes disinclines me to accept dinners, makes me neglect calls, and absolutely prohibits evening parties other than our own. With such persons as we do see, we find ourselves on the pleasantest of terms—the result of the privilege of living with a companion who knows neither malice nor envy, nor desire to excel, nor the remotest tinge of what the world calls " snobbishness ". Sidney is simply unconscious of all the little meanness which turns social intercourse sour: he is sometimes tired, occasionally bored, but never unkindly or anxious to shine, or be admired, and wholly unaware of the absence of, or presence of, social consideration. I verily believe that if he were thrown, by chance, into a company of persons all of whom wanted to snub him, he would take up the first book and become absorbed in it, with a sort of feeling that they were good-natured enough not to claim his attention, or that they did not perceive that he was reading on the sly. And the greater

personages they happened to be, the more fully satisfied he would be at
the arrangement; since it would relieve him of any haunting fear that
he was neglecting his social duty and making others uncomfortable.
On the other hand, whether in his own house or in another's, if some
person is neglected or out of it, Sidney will quite unconsciously drift
to them and be seen eagerly talking to them.

H. G. Wells came for the night: he had sent us his *Utopia*. " The
chapters on the Samurai will pander to all your worst instincts ", he
laughingly remarked when I congratulated him. He is full of intellectual
courage and initiative, and is now settling down to psychological novels
—I fancy somewhat inspired by Henry James's late success.

A pleasant little dinner at the Talbots' (Bishop of Rochester) on
Saturday. The P.M., the Dean of Westminster, Lady Gwendolen
Cecil and ourselves. Mr. Balfour's plaint, " There is no need for the
newspapers to tell me my faults, I know them all, but I can't alter
them ". A long talk with the Bishop afterwards. Sidney hopeful about
the future, he somewhat pessimistic. Lady Gwendolen Cecil, like her
sister, Lady Selborne (whom we met at a large and fashionable dinner
the other day, and with whom I talked much), exactly the same
philosophy as young Algernon Cecil. Utterly sceptical of any reform
of society brought about by altering the environment of individuals—
the boy brought up by drunken parents in the worst slum of London,
Lady Gwendolen maintained, was as likely to turn out satisfactorily
as the most favoured person. " It is surely a question of experience," I
suggested, " your experience of life leads to one conclusion, my experience leads me to another." But, in some subtle way, this reference
to experience, as the test of our rival assumptions, did not satisfy
her.

May 11th.—A happy three weeks with the Playnes at Longfords.
Wrote about one-third of our part on the " County ", taking the two
last days off for long rides in glorious weather—to Malmesbury one
day, and then a lovely day in the Standish woods alone with my boy.
We hid our bicycles in the leaves at the top of the beech woods and
wandered down, hand in hand, to the dear old field overlooking the
house—the scene of childish sorrow and joy and all the stirrings and
strivings of young womanhood. The valley was shrouded in heat mist,
the broad surface of the Bristol channel glimmering through and the
hills behind in faintest outline—these only to the eye of knowledge.
Then a lovely walk wheeling our iron round the crest of the Cotswolds
to the Beacon Hill, overlooking a more glorious view of the greatest
breadth of the Severn Valley bordered by the Malverns, on one side,
and the Channel, on the other. A ride back through the deep lanes of
the valley—cottages, churches and farms, that one knew long ago—

even some familiar faces grown old and furrowed. A delicious ending to our Easter recess!

We worked away for four or five hours a day in our little sitting-room, and chatted with the family in the intervals. There was a German nephew [1] and his wife—a young doctor—lying up with a bruised back. He was quite the typical good sort of *gebildeter* German—self-complacent, materialist, well-instructed, but appallingly ignorant of anything outside what he himself had read and observed. He was intensely nervous about his health, selfish with his excellent little wife, lacking in public spirit; or even of any notion of duty other than being a respectable doctor, father, husband. He was completely satisfied with everything German—from the German elementary education to the German Emperor, believing that Germany's pre-eminence was unquestioned in industry, in government, in knowledge, in poetry and in sentiment. Beyond the fact that he was a " nice " fellow, he had no distinction, except only a desire to improve his professional knowledge. What young English doctor, in mid-career as a consultant at a fashionable watering-place, would dream of spending his winter months at one or other university to work under specialist professors—and yet he is considered merely a commonplace young man.

Then we had a Chinese lady and her brother down for a couple of days—the lady in native costume, the gentleman in European. They spoke English volubly but badly. They belonged to the wealthy class—the uncle the Chinese Governor of Shanghai, the father brought up to be a Mandarin but preferring the free-er position of a capitalist at large. He owned the pawnshops of Shanghai and much real estate, and had married the daughter of a large rice planter. They gave us a vision of the residences of the wealthy Chinaman; it contained within its own walls 40 maid servants, 20 men servants, 6 private secretaries and tutors, 4 tailors, all serving a family of 15, including two married sons and their babies and two unmarried daughters—the ladies and children living in the ladies' apartments in the inner walls of the establishment. These two young people represented the most emancipated of rich persons: both were supremely discontented with the government of China, the education of China, the society of China—without in the least admiring any other race or civilisation. For the Japanese they had envy and the irritation of mortified vanity at being considered their inferiors—perhaps, just a glimmer of satisfaction at their " cousins " beating the detested foreigners. They were crass materialists, regarding all religion as so much folly, fit only to eke out legal compulsion in respect to uncivilised races or classes. They had no notion of science; they were conscious there was some trick of Western civilisation which

[1] Dr. Geise. (Ed.)

they wanted to learn—which led to mechanical invention profitable to men—but the discovery of truth for its own sake was to them an unknown impulse. Honour of parents and love of children seemed their best quality, perhaps, just the first signs of philanthropy. They lacked the symptoms of health, they had no courage either physical or mental, and one would not trust their veracity. Their manners were excellent, and they were sensitive to every change of expression in those with whom they consorted—adaptable yet dignified. We have promised to visit them in China.

The little lady was the more intelligent of the two; she told us of the futility of Chinese education—how it took three years to learn the mechanical art of writing, and ten years to learn to express yourself in literature, owing to the inconceivable complication of the Chinese language. And as children they worked eight hours a day, chiefly learning books by heart—no physical exercise, no freedom, no intercourse with the world. And rich young men smoked and gambled, read and sometimes kept " seraglios "—the last was very bad, she thought. The poor worked incessantly to become rich. Some foolish persons took to " prayer ", but that occupation struck her as " only something a degree less undesirable than opium smoking ". She wanted to write a book to tell the Chinese how the Western people lived, and to get the Chinese ladies out of their habit of perpetual chatter about their dresses and their pearls. She was a good little soul, but I suspected that she said to us what she thought would please us, not her real opinions. She told us that this brother was not married—a thumping lie as she afterwards admitted—because an English missionary's wife had told her a married man was never spoken to in England!

A long talk with H. G. Wells at Sandgate: two articles of our social faith are really repulsive to him—the collective provision of anything bordering on religious or emotional training, and the collective regulation of the behaviour of the adult. As to the latter, we are not really at variance, for we would willingly accept his limitation of this intervention to all such behaviour as impinges on the non-adult (heaven knows, that little scheme would give us enough regulation of the adult and to spare). But he is obdurate as to education: no form of training must be provided out of common funds that he personally objects to. My plea for variety and experiment, for leaving the door open for new religions or morality, by permitting those who believe in the old to have it provided for their children; Sidney's plea for tolerance strikes a deaf ear. " The child is not fit for emotional training until after adolescence ", he dogmatically asserts. " There is no injustice in not giving one form of training ", he insists. But he went further than this: " I don't believe in tolerance, you have got to fight against anything being taught anybody which seems to you harmful, you have got to struggle to get your own creed taught." We all got hot and exaggerated in our arguments and were no nearer agreement when we parted.

I suppose it is inevitable that we who believe in extending the functions of the state in all directions should be keenly desirous of making this activity as catholic as possible; of safeguarding each new departure by deliberate provision for dissenters from the established view. Clearly, the whole of Liberalism in England is swinging into rigid conformity—both in the structure and formations of the social organism. As you cannot have each individual separately provided for according to his needs, therefore, you must have identical treatment to all—seems their present dogma.

June 10*th.*—The Progressives have turned Sidney off the party committee. Some of the rump are very angry with him for entangling them in secondary education. The leaders are always civil to him; the rank and file find themselves accepting his proposals; but neither the leaders nor the ordinary members really like his policy and are vexed to find themselves pursuing it. So they try to keep him down *personally*; and would, I think, be relieved to get rid of him. Sidney, meanwhile, is in the best of humours—his scholarship scheme is working admirably, and forcing by its mere weight the Council either to subsidise existing secondary schools or to build and manage new ones. It is " heads I win, tails you lose ". And, as he cannot get control of the whole machine of London education—elementary, secondary and university—and make it really efficient, he is glad enough to be *obviously* out of office, to hang loosely to the Progressive Party. It absolves him of any responsibility to the public, and of any excessive loyalty to the party. When McKinnon Wood, *I think* sincerely, expressed his regret that he had been knocked off the party committee, Sidney answered smilingly that he thought that " there was really a cleavage of opinion between himself and the party, and that therefore it was well that this should be acknowledged: he was glad to feel at liberty to take his own line, which he could hardly do if he belonged to the inner circle ". Whereupon McKinnon Wood looked thoughtful and not over-pleased. They don't want to break with him.

July 30*th.*—One or two friends we have seen in a quiet way. A Sunday with Cyril Jackson of the Education Department, in his agreeable bachelor establishment at Limpsfield—to meet us, Masterman and Beveridge (a leading Toynbee-ite), his secretary Napier and a young friend of his about to become an Indian civil servant. This latter young man (whose name I have forgotten) struck me as typical of the coming civil servant. A " double first ", clean in looks and mind, strong-willed but unselfconscious, deprecating enthusiasm, critical of ideas and projects, and above all abstemious—given up tobacco, alcohol, meat—all because the doctor who passed him for the civil service remarked that his organs were not perfectly in good order. What his views are one could not tell, since he and Napier sat silent, listening to the torrent of discussion between Masterman, Beveridge and ourselves—with Jackson intervening as an official Conservative in a party of disputing Progressives. Masterman, an attractive journalist, combines being a religionist of the high Anglican order with sentimental and pessimistic Radicalism—in theory, he is collectivist, by instinct an anarchist individualist—above all, he is a rhetorician. Beveridge an ugly-mannered but honest, self-devoted, hard-headed young reformer of the practical type, came out well in comparison ,with Masterman; and, from disliking him, as we had formerly done, because of his ugly manners, we approved him. There was no hope of the Liberal Party in either of these young men; but intense dislike of the Tories, and the usual anger with Balfour for remaining in.

We have slipped into a sort of friendliness with Balfour. He comes in to dinner whenever we ask him, and talks most agreeably—perhaps our vanity is flattered by his evident interest in our historical and philosophical paradoxes and enjoyment of our conversation. I have not yet discovered any consistent attitude towards private and public life which comes to the surface in dinner-party conversation: there is merely a rather weary curiosity as to other people's processes of reasoning and feeling, lit up, now and again, with a very real interest in human character—where it is distinguished. The bulk of men bore him, whether regarded as individuals or as an electorate, or a Parliament, and all the common thoughts and feelings of common folk seem to him ineffably banal—fit only for the subject-matter of Bernard Shaw's derisive wit. I raised the question, whether the derision embodied in *John Bull's Other Island*—derision unaccompanied by any positive faith or hope—counted for good? He seemed quite surprised at my doubt—thought it better to clear away humbug at any cost. I suggested that, though I personally loathed both the Irish and English " home rule " shibboleths—yet, surely, with many Irish home rulers and English Liberals, these formulas embodied honest effort towards a better state of things? " Question whether we may not be too intellectually aristocratic," I urged, " whether we may discourage right effort because it happens to express itself—not in bad grammar, because that is often picturesque, and since board schools somewhat unusual—but in fluffy thought and silly sentiment? " He acquiesced in his courteous way, but I could see he was not convinced.

October 5th.—A week or so disturbed by too much society. First

309

the visit of the French deputies [members of the Paris Municipal Council, whom the London County Council had invited]. We cut all the parties and I had not even to go to the dinners, while Sidney felt obliged to attend. But we had long talks with the brilliant journalist quartered on us (Dausset) who suffered our voluble bad French gladly for the sake of informing himself as to English society and English public opinion. In return, he expounded to us the work of the Paris Municipal Council. " More a debating society, and that disorderly, than an administrative body ", was his verdict. " When I was president I was younger than I am now, and an enthusiast—I imagined that I was really going to help to govern Paris. What I gradually discovered was that, whenever I differed from the Préfet de la Seine, I was beaten hopelessly by his policy of passive resistance. Everything the council proposed to do or not to do was practically under his veto. He always refused to discuss the proposed policy when he disliked it. He was never ' at home '; never once did I succeed in seeing him." But this not all. Evidently it is the officials of the council who draw up all the reports—reports which M. Dausset admitted he seldom read—it is officials (many of whom are not removable without the consent of the Préfet) who execute all the orders. It would be a somewhat analogous position if the L.C.C. had to get most of its work done by the police under the Home Office. Then we gathered that all the deputies lived in terror of their constituents and he admitted voting for *les bêtises*, because he feared to lose his seat. The question arises, why he is a member on these conditions. And the general impression left by the deputies on their English hosts was that they were individuals " on the make " and there for other reasons than the good government of Paris.

Interesting to observe how intensely nervous all were about Germany—anxious to ascertain whether we genuinely intended to back them up in case of German aggression.

Mary Playne came up for ten days; and, knowing she liked to see folk, I took the opportunity to ask people to dine. George Trevelyan and his wife—excellent and interesting young people, with the charm of a strenuous and conscientious life and considerable talent, spent an evening alone with us. Among the young Liberals he is the most promising, because he has some conviction and a fervent desire for more. He is to spend the next years of his life in a history of England, 1790–1810, which is to be the glorification of Fox and rehabilitation of the French Revolution—one would think a somewhat conventional and banal task—a modernised replica of his father's book. Still, he has enthusiasm and industry, and that is better than paradoxical originality without those qualities.

On Sunday afternoon G. B. S. and Granville-Barker dropped in and spread out before us the difficulties, the hopes, the ridiculous aspects of their really arduous efforts to create an intellectual drama. Granville-Barker has suddenly filled out—he looks even physically larger than a year ago—he has grown extraordinarily in dignity and knowledge of human nature. But he dislikes the absorption in mere acting and longs to mix with persons actually in affairs or intellectually producing. G. B. S.'s egotism and vanity are not declining; he is increasing his deftness of wit and phrase, but becoming every day more completely iconoclastic—the ideal derider. In the evening we dined with the Courtneys. On Monday John Burns and Mrs. J. R. Green dropped in about 7 o'clock and stayed to share with Mary and ourselves half a pheasant! They talked at each other—Alice raging against the Liberals —John raging against the priest. Incidentally, Burns showed his dislike of the notion of a larger Labour Party, and his rooted suspicion of even his present colleagues. Keir Hardie, Crooks and Henderson " would all be out of Parliament " if he were providence. It is pitiful to see the lack of any good comradeship between these men.

On Tuesday, there dined with us Wernher (the South African capitalist), a heavy, good-natured, public-spirited and scientific-minded millionaire, Lord Lytton, Bernard Shaw and Mrs. Prothero (the mates of these three were ill)—a somewhat crooked party, that was only straightened out by sheer energy on my part into a comfortable affair. Wernher stumbled heavily along in his broken German, G. B. S. scintillated, Mrs. Prothero listened with Irish scepticism of Irish wit, Lord Lytton hung on G. B. S.'s words—looking the beautiful, fastidious young artist-aristocrat—a party of interesting types, but not mixing well. Meanwhile, I had got note after note from the Duchess of Marlborough who apparently has been seized with a whim to hear Sidney lecture and get us to dine with them afterwards. It would have been discourteous to refuse—so there was another evening of talk— the other guests being George Peel and Mrs. Craigie (John Oliver Hobbes). The Duke and Duchess corresponded exactly to the account given of them by the private secretary during our visit to Blenheim— somewhat futile young persons floating aimlessly on the surface of society, both alike quite unfit for their great position, swayed to and fro by somewhat silly motives—neither good nor bad. The little Duke is, I should imagine, mildly vicious—the Duchess has charm and, I think, goodness. I wondered how he came to be dragged by his wife to a technical lecture, and into entertaining two dowdy, middle-aged, middle-class intellectuals uncomfortably at a restaurant—for quite obviously they had come up to London on purpose. Was it G. B. S. they were after? They reminded us of H. G. Wells' " little white people " in *The Time Machine*.

On Friday we had a really entertaining and useful party—Lord Milner, the Morants, the Albert Grays, Mackinder and Alfred Cripps. This was a real success, everyone was glad to meet the others, and the conversation was sustained in subject as well as bright. I had a long talk with Milner after dinner. He has grown grim and (perhaps temporarily) bitter—obsessed too with a vision of a non-party Government without having invented any device for securing it. His grimness may be the result of fatigue and lonely work—with a life among friends and after rest, it may work off. His thesis is that the war itself, the dragging out of it, the unsatisfactory character of the settlement, the barely averted disaster—all were the result of the party system which forced half the political world to be against him. He is sufficient of a fanatic not to see that there was a genuine cleavage of opinion among the thinking people—that it was not merely a knot of cranks that disapproved his policy. He would take colonial affairs " out of politics ", but he does not suggest how. He is a strong man and an intensely public-spirited man—but he is harder and more intolerant, more distinctively the bureaucrat than when he left England. And he is sore, and bitter to opponents—not a good state of mind with which to enter politics. A little religion, or a purely intellectual pursuit, or perhaps some emotional companionship, is needed if he is to get back his sanity—his sense of proportion. So ended our week's dissipation. On all but *one* day I managed to work, though the sleeplessness which always follows on talking late made the work of poor quality. This next week has to be diverted to preparing my lecture—so alas! the book will be hung up.

The smart world is tumbling over one another in the worship of G. B. S., and even we have a sort of reflected glory as his intimate friends. It is interesting to note that the completeness of his self-conceit will save him from the worst kind of deterioration—he is proof against flattery. Where it will injure him is in isolating him from serious intercourse with intimate friends working in other departments of life —whenever he is free there is such a crowd of journalists and literary hangers-on around him that one feels it is kinder to spare him one's company—and that will be the instinct of many of his old friends engaged in administration, investigation or propaganda.

What a transformation scene from those first years I knew him: the scathing bitter opponent of wealth and leisure—and now! the adored one of the smartest and most cynical set of English " society ". Some might say that we, too, had travelled in that direction: our good sense preserve us! Fortunately, the temptation is at present slight and quite easily evaded. Curiosity about us is quickly satisfied and the smart ones subside, after one interview, into indifference. And Sidney steadily discourages my more sociable nature. " By all means be courteous but keep clear of them " is his perpetual refrain, in tone, if not in words. He is a blessed mate for me.

November 23rd.—Appointed to the Royal Commission on the Poor Law: awaiting anxiously the names of my colleagues—Charles Booth being the only one I know of.

Yesterday evening we dined with Lord Lucas (Bron Herbert that was) in his great mansion in St. James's Square: Mrs. Willie Grenfell, and Mrs. Lindsay, flippant but clever little lady, and a pleasant young Tory lawyer made up the party. Our host interests me as the son of my dear old friend Auberon Herbert; as a boy, I remember he eyed me with hostility, when I came to stay with his father twenty years ago—perhaps he thought I was going to become his stepmother! But, since he has come into the political world, first as a young Liberal candidate, now as a peer, he has cultivated our friendship. He is an attractive creature, dreamy and vague, with a charming veracity and gentleness of nature, with (for a *grand seigneur*) simple tastes and ways, and public-spirited and philanthropic impulses—the sort of ideal young aristocrat pictured in Bulwer Lytton's novels. But, from our point of view, he is no good. He is steeped in his father's individualist philosophy (he is a mere child in knowledge and thought on social and economic questions) and the only direction in which he has broken away from his father's influence is in the desire for an Empire—dragged thither by the Rosebery and millionaire associates among whom he lives. Moreover, he has no notion of work; he has great possessions and a most attractive personality. I fear that he must be written off as useless though not dangerous. His cousin, Mrs. Willie Grenfell, struck me last night as something more than the fashionable and pretty woman I took her to be. But, when I sat with her and the other smart little woman in that palatial room, I felt a wee bit ashamed of myself. Why was I dissipating my energy in this smart but futile world in late hours and small talk? Exactly at the moment this feeling was disconcerting me, the door opened and Mr. Balfour was announced. I confess that the appearance of the P.M. dissipated my regrets. It is always worth while, I thought, to meet those who really have power to alter things—should I be on the Poor Law Commission (the tempter said) if it were not for my friendship with this great one? And I collapsed into complacency. He was looking excited and fagged, on the eve of resignation. We chatted over the fire—Mrs. Grenfell, he and I—in a disjointed fashion until twelve o'clock, when Sidney and I left the tiny party to talk, perhaps more intimately.

November 29th.—Yesterday A. J. B. lunched with us, and went

afterwards to G. B. S.'s new play *Major Barbara*. The vanishing
Prime Minister was looking particularly calm and happy—compared
to six months or even six days ago; seemed like one with a load lifted
off his mind. Quite unexpectedly the conversation drifted on to the
whole underlying argument of the tariff question—the possibility of
continuous exports, should a prohibition tariff, say, 100% be raised
against us by the whole world. Though apparently dead against
ordinary protection as unsound, he seems haunted by a somewhat
theoretical fear of *universal hostile* discrimination against us. I think
he accepts the rate of exchange reaction as a solution of the ordinary
tariff war when each country blindly raises walls against all other
countries, whilst insisting on importing from other countries. But, in
that extreme case, he had the support of even Sidney. He cross-
examined Sidney as to the rise in the price of commodities brought
about by a tariff, and discussed the whole matter with perfect frankness
and ease. Sir Oliver Lodge and Sir Arthur Rucker, and a nice young
Conservative lawyer—L.C.C.—were the party; after lunch he asked
somewhat anxiously *who* the young man was, and looked reassured
when I told him he was of the right colour. On the way to the play
he told me " as a friend " all his difficulties with the Royal Commission
—his refusal to have any politicians, and difficulty on finding a chairman. " George Hamilton is not the fool he looks ", he apologetically
explained.

G. B. S.'s play turned out to be a dance of devils—amazingly clever,
grimly powerful in the second act—but ending, as all his plays end
(or at any rate most of them), in an intellectual and moral morass.
A. J. B. was taken aback by the force, the horrible force of the
Salvation Army scene, the unrelieved tragedy of degradation, the disillusionment of the Greek professor and of Barbara—the triumph of
the unmoral purpose: the anti-climax of evangelising the Garden City!
I doubt the popular success of the play: it is hell tossed on the stage—
with no hope of heaven. G. B. S. is gambling with ideas and emotions
in a way that distresses slow-minded prigs like Sidney and me, and
hurts those with any fastidiousness. But the stupid public will stand a
good deal from one who is acclaimed as an unrivalled wit by the great
ones of the world.

December 2nd.—To-day, I called on the Shaws and found G. B. S.
alone in his study. He was perturbed—indeed, upset by the bad acting,
as he thought, of Undershaft and generally of all in the last scene—
and by a virulent attack on the play in the *Morning Post*. Calvert, he
said, had completely lost his nerve over Undershaft—could not understand or remember his part and was aghast at what he considered its
blank immorality. I spoke quite frankly my opinion of the general

effect of his play—the triumph of the unmoral purpose. He argued earnestly and cleverly, even persuasively, in favour of what he imagines to be his central theme—*the need for preliminary good physical environment before anything could be done to raise the intelligence and morality of the average sensual man.* " We middle-class people, having always had physical comfort and good order, do not realise the disaster to character in being without. We have, therefore, cast a halo round poverty, instead of treating it as the worst of crimes—the one unforgiveable crime that must be wiped off before any virtue can grow." He defended Undershaft's general attitude towards life on the ground that, until we divested ourselves of feeling (he said malice), we were not fit to go the lengths needed for social salvation. " What we want is for the people to turn round and burn, not the West End, but their own slums. The Salvation Army with its fervour and its love might lead them to do this and then we really should be at the beginning of the end of the crime of poverty."

I found it difficult to answer him—but he did not convince me. There is something lacking in his presentment of the crime of poverty. But I could honestly sympathise with his irritation at the suggested intervention of the censor—not on account of the upshot of the play, but because Barbara in her despair at the end of the second act utters the cry, " My God, my God, why hast thou forsaken me ". A wonderful and quite rational climax to the true tragedy of the scene of the Salvation Army shelter.

Meanwhile, Governments are changing in England and government of any sort is coming to an end in Russia.

CHAPTER VII

ROYAL COMMISSION ON THE POOR LAW AND THE RELIEF OF DISTRESS

· 1905–1909

Two events are casually noted in the concluding pages of the foregoing chapter: the one of outstanding national importance—the advent of the Liberal Government in December 1905; and the other of major significance in the life story of Our Partnership—my appointment, in November of the same year, to serve on the Royal Commission on the Poor Law and the Relief of Distress. Seeing that this book is, in the main, an autobiography and only incidentally material for British political history, I shall give premier place to the day-to-day working of this remarkable public enquiry ending in the publication, in January 1909, of the Majority and Minority Reports of the Royal Commission of 1905–9. In this recital will be included entries relating to our continued personal investigation into English local government, leading to the publication of three volumes during these very years; a ponderous volume on *The Parish and the County* in 1906, and two volumes on *The Manor and the Borough* in 1908. Hence this chapter is closely linked up with Chapter IV. describing our enquiry into English local government from the seventeenth century onwards. For it was, I venture to think, exactly this continuous six years' hard work on our own account, from 1899 to 1905, that qualified us to see further into the past, present and possible future of that unique institution—the English Poor Law—than was practicable to some of my colleagues. For the rest, the reader will find in the following pages a veritable hodge-podge of diary entries, relating to the Other One's activities on the L.C.C., the Senate of London University, the Technical Education Board and the London School of Economics, together with chance characterisations of our social and political environment, intermingled with my own meditations on the destiny of mankind.

Why did the Prime Minister (Arthur Balfour), at the close of the session of 1905, announce in reply to an evidently prearranged question in the House of Commons, that the Government had come to the conclusion that the time had come for a full enquiry into the whole question, adding with significance that there had been no such enquiry since that of 1832–34? Why did the Cabinet, on the very eve of its resignation, put itself to the trouble of choosing the members of a large and representative Royal Commission; and charge it " to enquire into (1) the working of the laws relating to the relief of poor persons in the United Kingdom; (2) the various means which have been adopted outside of the poor laws for meeting distress arising from want of employment, particularly during periods of severe industrial depression; and to consider and report whether any, and if so what, modification of the poor laws, or changes in their administration, or fresh legislation for dealing with distress, are advisable "?

Our own impression at the time was that the Commission owed its creation to the coincidence of there being, as newly appointed head of the poor law division, an energetic man of affairs (James Stewart Davy) intent on reaction; and, as President of the Local Government Board, a philosopher (Mr. Gerald Balfour) who recognised the public advantage of a precise discrimination between opposing principles. There was, in fact, in official circles, an uneasy feeling that there had been, during the last two decades, an unwilling drift away from the principles of 1834, and one which sooner or later had to be decisively stopped.

The underlying principles advocated by the Royal Commission on the Poor Law of 1832 and embodied straight away in the Poor Law Amendment Act of 1834, are herewith summarised: [1]

___

[1] For a further and more elaborate description of the principles of 1834, see *English Poor Law Policy*, by Sidney and Beatrice Webb, published in 1910. This book was an enlargement and completion of the report which I circulated to the

(1) That the public relief of destitution out of funds raised by taxation—as distinguished from the alms of the charitable—devitalised the recipients, degraded their character and induced in them general bad behaviour.

(2) That the operation of the Malthusian law of population, accentuated by the theory of a wage fund, rendered all such relief, not only futile in diminishing the miseries of the poor, but actually harmful in the creation of a wider pool of destitution.

(3) That it was imperative for a department of the national government to direct and control the actions of the local authorities concerned so as to impose on them a policy which would diminish, if not abolish, the disease of pauperism.

Hence, the famous principle of " less eligibility ". Out of these ardently held assumptions, springing from this tenaciously held principle of " less eligibility ", sprang the officially recognised policy of the Local Government Board from 1834 to 1905.

The first and most essential of all conditions, the Commissioners of 1832–34 tell us: " A principle which we find universally admitted, even by those whose practice is at variance with it, is, that his [the able-bodied person's] situation, on the whole, shall not be made really or apparently so eligible as the situation of the independent labourer of the lowest class. Throughout the evidence it is shown that, in proportion as the condition of any pauper class is elevated above the condition of independent labourers, the condition of the independent class is depressed; their industry is impaired, their employment becomes unsteady, and its remuneration in wages is diminished. Such persons, therefore, are under the strongest inducements to quit the less eligible class of labourers and enter the more eligible class of paupers. . . . Whole branches of manufacture " [to cite a much-quoted passage] " may thus follow the course, not of coal mines or of streams, but of pauperism; may flourish like the funguses that spring from corruption, in consequence of the abuses which are ruining all the other interests

Commission in July 1907, on the poor law policy of the Central Authority from 1834 to 1905, and which is referred to in the diary entries.

See also *History of the English Poor Law* in two volumes, by Sidney and Beatrice Webb.

of the places in which they are established, and to cease to exist in the better administered districts, in consequence of that better administration." The converse is the effect when the pauper class is placed in its proper position, below the condition of the independent labourer. In short, by making the alternative plainly penal, the whip of starvation was to be placed securely in the hands of the employers.

The second principle insisted on by the Report of 1834 is the principle of " national uniformity "—that is, of identity of treatment of each class of destitute person from one end of the kingdom to the other, for the purpose of reducing the perpetual shifting from parish to parish, of preventing discontent, and of bringing the parochial management effectually under the control of a government department carrying out the principles of 1834. The third principle, commonly known as the " workhouse system ", that is the complete substitution of indoor for outdoor relief, was no part of the recommendations of the 1834 Report for any but the ablebodied. It was, however, adopted by the strictest of the reformers of 1834–47, and again by those of 1871–85, as the only effective method of applying the principles of less eligibility and of reducing pauperism. The workhouse, on this principle, was not to be regarded as a place of longcontinued residence, still less as an institution for beneficial treatment, but primarily (if not exclusively) as a " test of destitution ", that is, as a means of affording the actual necessities of existence under conditions so deterrent that the pauper would rather prefer to maintain himself independently than accept the relief so offered.

So much, or rather so little, about the principles underlying English poor law policy during the seventy years preceding 1905. Now let us consider the make-up of the Royal Commission of 1905–9. Like its predecessor in 1934, it was to a marked degree a reforming commission, but unlike the Poor Law Commission of 1832–34, that of 1905–9 was largely composed of persons who had actually taken part in the administration of the poor law. There were on it no fewer than five guardians of the poor, four of whom were, or had been, chairmen of their boards.[1] Even more influential was the presence of the permanent heads of the Local Government Boards of England, Scotland and Ireland respectively, who were personally directing the poor law administration of the three countries, together with the senior medical inspector of the English poor law division.[2] These nine experienced poor law administrators were reinforced by half-a-dozen prominent members of the Charity Organisation Society, all of whom began the enquiry as convinced adherents of the principles of 1834; notably, the Society's general secretary, C. S. Loch; one of its founders, Miss Octavia Hill; and two other distinguished exponents of its doctrines, Mr. Hancock Nunn and Mrs. Bernard Bosanquet.[3] There were two political economists, belonging to what was then called the orthodox school, Professor William Smart of Glasgow and the Rev. L. R. Phelps of Oxford. With the Rev. Prebendary Russell Wakefield, afterwards Bishop of Birmingham, the Church of England had three representatives, and the Roman Catholic Church in Ireland one (the Bishop of Ross).[4] This predominantly *stand pat* composition of the Commission was emphasised by the appointment of a Conservative ex-Cabinet Minister as chairman: Lord George Hamilton. Out of the twenty members there were only three who belonged to the Labour and Socialist movements—Mr. George Lansbury, and Mr. Francis Chandler (general secretary of the old-established Amalgamated Society of Carpenters), and myself. But the unique characteristic of this Commission was the inclusion in it of members who had proved their capacity for the work of social investigation. There was Charles Booth,[5] who

[1] The poor law guardians were F. H. Bentham, George Lansbury, T. Hancock Nunn, the Rev. L. R. Phelps and F. Chandler (subsequently added to represent the trade union movement).

[2] Sir S. B. Provis, K.C.B., J. Patten-MacDougall, C.B., Sir Henry Robinson, K.C.B., and Dr. A. H. (now Sir Arthur) Downes.

[3] The C.O.S. members included the above-mentioned together with Rev. T. G. Gardiner and the Rev. L. R. Phelps.

[4] The Bishop of Ross (Dr. Kelly) was added to the Commission in place of the O'Conor Don, who died in 1906.

[5] The Right Honourable Charles Booth (1840-1917), shipowner and merchant, had devoted many years of thought and work, and large drafts upon his income, to

might be termed the inventor of one of the leading methods of sociological research; there were the ablest members of the Charity Organisation Society—a society whose activities were avowedly based, in a far-reaching survey of social results, on exhaustive enquiry into individual cases; and there was one of the leading researchers of the Fabian Society. The Commission was, in fact, predominantly a body of experts, either in poor law administration or social investigation. Indeed, one of the few members of the Commission who had neither an extensive knowledge of the subject, nor experience in research, was its chairman, Lord George Hamilton. Fortunately for the amenity of the Commission's internal life, and perhaps even for its efficiency as an instrument of research, this experienced politician and attractive *grand seigneur* combined exceptional personal charm and social tact with an open mind and a willingness to give free play to the activities of his fellow-commissioners. Regarded as an instrument of reform, what the Commission seemed to lack was the guiding hand of an experienced lawyer, who might have kept the enquiry strictly within the terms of reference, and insisted on all evidence being brought before the Commission as a whole, and tested by some common standard of relevance and validity; and who might, in the end, have negotiated a unanimous report on all those issues—and there proved to be many—upon which there was common agreement.[1]

statistical investigation of social conditions, for which he had a passion, and in which he became an inventor of a new technique. Public recognition of his achievements came in a privy councillorship, a fellowship of the Royal Society, and doctorates of the Universities of Liverpool, Oxford and Cambridge. For his life, see *Charles Booth—A Memoir*, 1918 (by his widow); and for an account of his great work, *Life and Labour of the People in London*, 17 vols., 1902 (of which the first volume in the original edition had been published in 1889), see *My Apprenticeship*, by Beatrice Webb, 1926, chap. v., "A Grand Inquest into the Condition of the People of London", pp. 216-56.

I may add that he had married my cousin Mary Macaulay, daughter of Charles Macaulay, a distinguished civil servant and brother of the historian, hence my intimate connection with this great enquiry into the condition of the people of London.

[1] The Poor Law Commission of 1905-9 exceeded, in the volume of published proceedings, memoranda, reports and (especially) statistics, even the Poor Law Inquiry Commission of 1832-34. Besides the lengthy Majority and Minority Reports (Cd. 4625)—these were also published in three octavo volumes from which

The entries in the diary revealing the activities of the Royal Commission open in the first days of December 1905.

December 2nd.—A pleasant visit to Gracedieu colloguing in the old way with Charles Booth as to the proper course of the poor law enquiry. I had extracted from Davy, the assistant secretary of the L.G.B., in a little interview I had had with him, the intention of the L.G.B. officials as to the purpose and procedure they intended to be followed by the Commission. They were going to use us to get certain radical reforms of structure; the boards of guardians were to be swept away, judicial officers appointed and possibly the institutions transferred to the county authorities. With all of which I am inclined to agree. But we were also to recommend reversion to the principles of 1834 as regards policy; to stem the tide of philanthropic impulse that was sweeping away the old embankment of deterrent tests to the receipt of relief. Though I think the exact form in which this impulse has clothed itself is radically wrong and mischievous, yet I believe in the impulse, if it takes the right forms. It is just this vital question of what and which forms are right that I want to discover and this Commission to investigate. Having settled the conclusions to which we are to be led, the L.G.B. officials (on and off the Commission) have predetermined the procedure. We were to be spoon-fed by evidence carefully selected and prepared; they were to draft the circular to the board of guardians; they were to select the inspectors who were to give evidence; they were virtually to select the guardians to be called in support of this evidence. Assistant commissioners were to be appointed who were to collect evidence illustrative of these theories. And above all we were to be given *opinions* and not *facts*. Charles Booth and I consulted what line we should take. To-day at lunch I put Lansbury (the working-man on the Commission) on his guard against this policy.

At the first meeting this afternoon, Lord George laid the scheme before us: the circular had been drafted, the witnesses had been selected, the assistant commissioner had almost been appointed: it remained for us to ratify. Fortunately, the scheme did not meet with approval and

our quotations are taken—there were issued no fewer than 47 folio volumes of appendices ending with a specially elaborate " General Consolidated Index " of 1086 pages. For Scotland (Cd. 4922) and Ireland (Cd. 4630) there were also Majority and Minority Reports.

The Commission was greatly aided in its work by the ability and devotion of its secretariat, notably by its secretary, R. G. Duff, then an assistant general inspector, and subsequently a general inspector of the Local Government Board (now Ministry of Health); and by its assistant secretary, John Jeffrey, then in the Scottish Local Government Board and subsequently secretary to the Scottish Health Insurance Commission and afterwards Permanent Secretary of the Scottish Health Department.

was virtually defeated; the only point settled on is the calling of the experts of the L.G.B. for which we are all quite prepared. I suggested *all* the inspectors should be called, a suggestion to which Lord George made no answer. And no other commissioner supported me at the time —but the seed had fallen on some prepared ground. It will need all my self-command to keep myself from developing a foolish hostility, and becoming self-conscious in my desire to get sound investigation. Certainly, the work of the Commission will be an education in manners as well as in poor law. I was not over pleased with my tone this afternoon and must try to do better. Beware of showing off superior knowledge of irrelevant detail. To be single-minded in pursuit of truth, courteous in manner, and kind in feeling—and yet not to betray one's trust for the sake of popularity and be modestly persistent in my aim must be my prayer. Meanwhile, we must get on with the book and not sacrifice our own work to what, at least, can only be co-operation in a joint task with seventeen persons, with almost as many aims—and, therefore, certain to be a partial failure.

But how interesting will be this conflict of wills. I will certainly describe it as it goes along. For instance, there are four big officials on the Commission, two from England, one each from Ireland and Scotland respectively. The English officials think they are going to direct and limit the enquiry, the Scotch and Irish officials told us pretty plainly that they did not want any enquiry, and they had already investigated the whole subject by departmental committees! And as there were no Irish and Scotch representatives of the anti-official view the enquiry into Irish and Scotch poor law has been indefinitely postponed, and will probably hardly take place. On the other hand, Charles Booth and I want a real investigation of English administration as well as an examination into pauperism, though C. B. is more concerned with the question of right treatment than of prevention by better-regulated life. Lansbury, on the other hand, is willing and anxious to enquire into the initial causes of pauperism, not so keen to investigate the effect of different methods of relief. C. S. Loch wants to drag in the whole question of endowed charity, in which he has the support of Mrs. Bernard Bosanquet. She and I, and possibly Miss Octavia Hill, may combine on the question of a rate-in-aid of wages to women workers—the need for discovering how far it actually obtains —and there will be a good deal of common ground, as far as the enquiry goes, between Loch and myself. Certain other commissioners such as Smart and Phelps are going to look on, I think, and intervene as the spirit moves them.

December 15th.—Certainly, the procedure imposed on us by Lord George was amazing. There was no agenda; a cut and dried scheme was laid before us, we were not asked to vote on it, only to express our opinion on half-a-dozen points ranging from the hour of luncheon to the appointment of assistant commissioners. The only subject really discussed was the issue of the preliminary circular to the boards of guardians. On this point there was almost unanimity against the course proposed. Whereupon Lord George called up, out of the Commission, the guardians of the poor; and we left these five persons under the chairman's eye, sitting discussing the matter. Yesterday, I got a formal announcement that unless the commissioners dissented by post the circulars would be sent out.

This was rather intolerable. I wrote a courteous but firm dissent and enigmatically suggested that I wished for some procedure that would enable those who objected to record that objection. I did not stop there. I went and unburdened my soul to the secretary, Mr. Duff. He is an attractive and sensible young civil servant, who gave me to understand that he had been against Lord George's high-handed action. So I elaborately complained to him of the absence of agenda, of concrete resolutions, of any formal appointment and authorisation of the committee; and I claimed to have a formal procedure in future; with the circulation of all proposals, of the names of witnesses, of the précis of their evidence. Apparently, our chairman had decided against all those suggestions on the ground that " we should know too much "! " I don't want to make myself disagreeable," I ventured to add; " it is extraordinarily unpleasant for a woman to do so on a commission of men. But I don't, on the other hand, intend to hide my intentions. If a procedure and methods of investigation are adopted or slipped into the Commission, which I think incompetent to elicit the truth, it will be my obvious duty to report such procedure and to describe and analyse such methods one by one. To enable me to do this, without incurring a charge of bad comradeship, I must express, clearly and emphatically, my dissent. That is why I asked for a formal procedure for the business of the Commission." I begged Mr. Duff to report the gist of the conversation to Lord George. I await the result with some amusement, and a little anxiety. It is a new experience for me to *have* to make myself disagreeable in order to reach my ends. In private life, one can only get one's way by being unusually pleasant. In official life—at least as the most insignificant member of a Commission overwhelmingly against me in opinion—I shall only get my share of control by quietly and persistently standing on my rights as an individual commissioner and refusing altogether to be overawed by great personages who would like to pooh-pooh a woman who attempts to share in the control of affairs.

Whilst I am busy with my little teacup of a Royal Commission, a

324

new Ministry has been formed[1] [I write on December 15, 1905]. It is a strong Government and felt to be so. All the possible actors have been included, and the parts have been skilfully allotted. Our friends the " Limps " have romped in to the leading posts under Campbell-Bannerman; Morley and Bryce being marooned on India and Ireland respectively. To put Asquith and Lloyd George and Winston Churchill dead in front of Joe on the tariff and the colonies; to place John Burns to look to the unemployed; to give Birrell the Education Office; are all apt placements. But the great *coup* is to get Haldane to take the War Office—the courtly lawyer with a great capacity for dealing with men and affairs, and a real understanding of the function of an expert, and skill in using him.

Two of the new Cabinet have already come in to talk over their new life. The very day of his introduction to the Cabinet, John Burns arrived, childishly delighted with his own post. For one solid hour he paced the room expanding his soul before me—how he had called in the permanent officials, asked them questions. " That is my decision, gentlemen ", he proudly rehearsed to me once or twice. " Don't be too doctrinaire about the unemployed, Mr. Burns ", I mildly suggested. " Economise your great force of honesty, Mrs. Webb," he rejoined solemnly, " I am a different man from what I was a week ago. You read what I say to-morrow when I stand by C. B. at the deputation. You will see I shan't give myself away." What he and the big officials will do with each other remains to be seen. To listen to him talking one would think he was hopelessly confused and blurred in his views and intentions. His best chance will be to refuse to be overwhelmed with routine administration, to devote himself to one or two points, and strike dramatic effects in one or two unconventional decisions. A sort of working-class Roosevelt is his rôle. The story goes that, when C. B. offered him the L.G.B. with a seat in the Cabinet, he clasped the Premier by the hand. " I congratulate you, Sir Henry: it will be the most popular appointment that you have made."

Yesterday afternoon Haldane came in. *He* also was in a state of

[1] Campbell-Bannerman accepted office on December 5, 1905. The Cabinet he formed included the leading Liberal Leaguers and the leading pro-Boers. Among the former were Asquith as Chancellor of the Exchequer; Grey as Foreign Secretary; Haldane as Secretary for War; together with Sydney Buxton, Post Office. Among the pro-Boers were Reid, afterwards Lord Loreburn, as Lord Chancellor; John Morley as Secretary for India; John Burns, Local Government Board; Lloyd George, Board of Trade; whilst Reginald McKenna, Winston Churchill, Herbert Samuel, Walter Runciman, appeared as under-secretaries. In the general election beginning January 12, 1906, the Liberals obtained 377 seats, a majority of 84 over all other parties combined. The Conservatives and Liberal Unionists secured only 157, the Irish Nationalists 83, and Labour members, 24 supporting the Liberal Party, and 29 styling themselves the Labour Party, with their own organisation and their own whips.

exuberant delight over his new task. " I chose the War Office out of three offices. Asquith, Grey and I stood together; they were forced to take us on our own terms. We were really very indifferent," he added sublimely, " Asquith gave up a brief of £10,000 to defend the Khedive's property that very week; I was throwing away an income of £15,000 to £20,000 a year; and Grey had no ambition and was sacrificing his fishing. But it was a horrid week—one perpetual wrangle. The King signified that he would like me to take the War Office; it is exactly what I myself longed for. I have never been so happy in my life ", and he beamed all over. And then he poured into my sympathetic ear all his plans. " I shall spend three years observing and thinking. I shall succeed: I have always succeeded in everything I have undertaken." I confess I was a little surprised at the naïveté of this last remark. Alas! what hideous failures the wisest of us makes. But, of course, it was merely the foam of his excited self-complacency, in the first novelty of power. He came straight from a whole day talking over matters with Arnold-Forster [preceding Secretary for War]—a thoroughly English proceeding, showing the essential solidarity of the governing class.

The lower ranks of the Government are filled with young men we know, or have known. Herbert Samuel, an old friend . . . has made a surprising advance in obtaining the under-secretaryship of the Home Office, leaving poor C. P. Trevelyan behind. Lough, McKenna, Runciman, all friendly acquaintances. We gather that as regards the non-Cabinet offices there is a sort of panel constructed by the Prime Minister, from which the Cabinet Ministers select subordinates for their respective offices. Burns said he had selected Runciman out of those submitted to him—Trevelyan and Jack Tennant being the other two—so there is still a chance for C. P. For some mysterious reason, Macnamara has refused office: it is said he could not afford to take an inferior berth or give up the editorship of the *Schoolmaster*; and he was offered no position equal to his expectations, and in that sense he is a disappointed man.

A satisfactory interview with the chairman of our Commission, arranged by the secretary whom I apparently alarmed by my rebellious attitude. For a whole hour I listened to his somewhat weak proposals, quietly insisting on a regular procedure, the appointment of a committee to consider and report on methods of investigation and the concentration of our efforts on ascertaining the facts about the relief of destitution, and not merely collecting casual opinions as to defects in law and practice. I felt strengthened by the fact that Sidney had helped me to draft a series of concrete proposals which I succeeded in making him ask me for. What upset his aristocratic mind was the notion that the Commission should appoint its own committees and regulate its own procedure. " I saw the democratic method worked out on the London School Board when I was chairman," he naïvely remarked, " and I was not impressed with its results." I tried to convince him that consent was a preliminary requirement to efficiency. " Moreover," I urged, " you will find that you practically appoint the committees even if you submit the names formally to the Commission; it may be that one or two others will be added, but when the first flush of energy has exhausted itself we shall suffer not from too large but too small a membership of the working committee." So we chatted on, getting more and more friendly. " You must remember, Lord George, that we are all rather awed by our *grand seigneur* chairman," was my parting shot, " and with a nondescript body like the Commission awe some-times gets transformed into suspicion of being bossed. With a per-tinacious spirit like C. S. Loch, for instance, this feeling might have inconvenient results."

Meanwhile, I have sent my suggestions to one or two of the com-missioners: and have had a most friendly chat with Loch who, so far as investigation goes, will, I think, be a sturdy ally.

1906

January 9th.—Second meeting of Commission went off well. The chairman introduced the motion for a committee on procedure and methods of investigation: Charles Booth (to whom I had sent my suggestions) backed it up: Loch somewhat demurred, Mrs. Bernard Bosanquet objected, seeing, I think, an insidious proposal of mine which would give the London members and the experts in investiga-tion complete control over the Commission. But the Commission on the whole was favourable. At any rate, I have made friends with the chairman, and shall now be careful not to excite the jealousy of those who feel themselves opposed to me in doctrine. The C.O.S. are far more suspicious of me than I am of them. I believe that they *do* want investigation and should be glad if we could co-operate against those who do not. But I see that, at first at any rate, they will keep both Charles Booth and me at arm's length. C. B. made a useful suggestion that no one need cross-examine Adrian [legal official of L.G.B.] until we have the proof of his evidence. The wisdom of this was quickly apparent. Adrian, a heavy, dull but conscientious official, began, in monotonous tone, to read a verbose disquisition on the law from the very beginning of poor relief to the end. The room was cold, and we all, I think, failed to take any intelligent interest in what he said. I stayed for lunch and chatted pleasantly with Lord George and then

327

escaped and went for a walk and service at Westminster Abbey. Thory (T. G.) Gardiner came to tea and I impregnated him with our views of investigation. I stay away to-day, and see clearly that my most important work will be done outside the Commission room. I will give my best *thought* but scamp attendance.

Third meeting of Commission. I did not attend, as Adrian's evidence in chief consisted of his reading from copious notes, or long legal disquisitions, which, as it was all taken down in shorthand and served to us in printed form in two days' time, and before his cross-examination began, it was sheer waste of time to sit there listening to it. On Monday (4th meeting) the cross-examination began, and on that afternoon and the following morning I tried to make him admit that we must see and study the general and special orders, circulars, etc., for ourselves, before we could understand the body of law and regulation under which the guardians acted. In this endeavour I was stopped by the chairman and Sir Samuel Provis, and I had a little tiff across the table as to whether he, or we, should judge whether documents were important or not. But I got a specific promise from the chairman that all the documents that we needed should be at the disposal of the Commission.

However, as the Commission seemed still in a rudderless condition, at the mercy of the little clique of officials, Sidney and I prepared a memorandum on methods of enquiry, which I have asked to be circulated to the whole Commission. That done I feel that I have striven to get the enquiry on the right lines, and can now rest a bit. To reform the procedure of royal commissions would be worth delaying the completion of our book. But, up to now, I find attendance at the Commission a most disagreeable business—it is extraordinarily unpleasant when one has to force people's hands and make them attend to one by sheer ugly persistency at the cost, of course, of getting back a certain insolence of attitude on the part of hostile men.—*This is exaggeration!* (a week after).

Thought it wise to let the two secretaries see both our proof of *The Parish* and also our first draft of *The History of the Poor Law, 1689–1835*. The publication of the work before the Report of the Commission is one of the trump cards in our hand and, as our object is to make them throw up the game of obstruction to investigation, it is well to put the card on the table.

January 28th.—Hewins and his wife came to lunch here after many months' interval owing to preoccupation on all sides. Both were very depressed: he was somewhat bitter against all the Unionist leaders, even including Joe; she was merely " down on her luck "—dreary—poor little soul! The result of the election has evidently been a terrible disillusionment for Hewins: it never occurred to him that the reaction might be so complete as to keep the Tories out for six years. From his private point of view it is a catastrophe: he thought, I am convinced, that in a few years, if not immediately, he would be arranging tariffs, and tariff wars, and tariff treaties, at the Board of Trade—hurrying from continent to continent, in close and confidential intercourse with ministers and great financial personages—one long delightful intrigue with a World Empire as the result. From the public point of view, it appears to him also as a disaster. " It depends on the next six years whether or not we lose Canada: six years hence it will be too late ", he exclaimed in his mysterious way. His autumn visit to Canada has convinced him that the Canadians will range themselves under the American flag, unless we give them a substantial preference. " A great people with great resources—just chucked away through sheer ignorance and petty selfishness."

Of course, he is contemptuous of Balfour and those who surround him. But he is also irritated against Joe—for reasons I do not understand; except when there has been a gigantic fiasco, all concerned condemn " the others ". Poor Hewins, with his grand castles in the air that he has been, for the last three years, inhabiting— now lying in ruins about him! I suppose he will become a paid organiser of the protectionist cause—an occasional leader-writer in protectionist papers. Meanwhile, it is conceivable that he is right about Canada. Sidney regards it as a " mare's nest ": " if Canada leaves us because she cannot get a tariff she will leave us anyhow ".

February 5th.—The memorandum I sent in on methods of enquiry led the chairman to ask all the other commissioners for memoranda. And some six or seven responded. Whereupon all have been referred to a committee consisting of Lord George, Provis, Booth, Bentham, Smart, Loch, Phelps, Mrs. Bosanquet and myself, and we meet on Monday 12th to consider them. This morning I spent taking out all the questions which the L.G.B. witnesses had told us we ought to enquire into, with a view to trying to persuade the committee to start on a systematic survey of all the unions, with a view to more detailed investigation of some. Yesterday, Bentham—the ablest person (except perhaps Provis) on the Commission—came here, and we talked poor law from 5.30 to 11 o'clock. Result, bad headache this afternoon!

Dear Charles Booth is as delightful as ever, but he is losing his intellectual grip and persistency of purpose—is not much use on the Commission. Happily, he is unaware of it. Alas! for the pathetic strivings of age—more pitiful to the onlooker than those of youth, because without hope of amendment.

Want to get the Commission, sooner or later, to undertake:

(1) Survey of all English unions, with regard to difference of constitution and methods of administration of union.

(2) Analysis of the whence and whither of pauperism in some among them.

(3) Clear vision of course of legislation.

(4) Analysis of developments of policy of central authority.

It would be natural to begin with numbers three or four: but owing to the fact that we shall be fully occupied until next autumn in completing our book, I shall suggest beginning at the other end. We want, if possible, to superintend, or at any rate supplement, three and four.

February 9th.—About nine o'clock yesterday evening, in walked John Burns. He had an indefinable air of greater dignity—a new and perfectly fitting jacket suit, a quieter manner, and less boisterous vanity in his talk. The man is filling in with good stuff. He described the three committees of the Cabinet upon which he had that day sat—one on the Trade Disputes Bill, the other on the unemployed, and the third on the Workmen's Compensation Extension Bill. He was naïvely delighted with his share in the proceedings, especially his insistence that workmen's compensation should include provision for illness or death from unhealthy occupations. He had filled in his time with seeing all and sundry—philanthropists, Labour representatives, great employers and asking their advice. "They are all so kind to me," he said, in glowing appreciation—"especially the great employers, just the men who might have objected to my appointment." Oh! the wisdom of England's governing class!

He pulled out a set of cards, upon which he had written the measures which he had decided to bring forward in the first two years—mostly measures that the L.G.B. had long ago pigeon-holed—the abolition of overseers, further equalisation of rates in London, amendment of the Alkali Act, and finally (as a concession to the Labour Party), an amendment of the Unemployed Act of last session in the direction of greater contributions from the rates. " I want to be efficient," he said, with youthful fervour, " if you and Sidney can give me a tip I am always ready to listen. I am ready to take tips from anyone so long as they mean business in my direction." If good intentions, and a strong vigorous and audacious character, can make up for lack of administrative experience and technical knowledge, John Burns may yet be a success as President of the Local Government Board.

Altogether Sidney and I are in better spirits as to the course of political affairs than we have been for many years. We do not deceive ourselves by the notion that this wave of Liberalism is wholly progressive in character—much of its bulk is made up of sheer conservatism aroused by the revolutionary tariff policy of Chamberlain. But it looms as progressive in its direction and all the active factors are collectivist. Moreover, it is clear that Joe is going to try to outbid the Liberals by constructive social reform. It is an interesting little fact that a fortnight ago he wrote in his own hand to W. P. Reeves to beg him to send all the Acts, and literature about the Acts, relating to old-age pensions and compulsory arbitration [in New Zealand]—as if he desired to convince himself of their feasibility as an adjunct to his tariff policy. Whether or not this socialistic addition will make for the popularity of protection, it will come at any rate as pressure on the Liberals to do something for raising the standard of life of the very poor—it will bar the way to a policy of the *status quo*.

February 12th.—I sent another memorandum to the chairman sketching out the work of three committees—on statistics, local administration and central policy respectively—a scheme which in his gentlemanly way he pressed on the acceptance of the committee on procedure. The committee on statistics was agreed to, so was a committee on blue-books, etc., to which the documents of the L.G.B. might be added; and, in the course of the discussion, it became clear that a committee on local administration would, in the end, be required. But most of the members were against taking any steps towards a positive scheme until after the inspectors' evidence. Charles Booth wants one committee only; Mrs. Bosanquet objects to any but temporary committees; no members want a systematic investigation but myself. I threw out the notion of a statistical officer and an assistant commissioner to undertake the investigation into local administration —but as yet, it is not responded to. Meanwhile, Sir Samuel Provis will not agree to anyone looking through the L.G.B. documents— insists that we must call for those we want to see and not have the run of the whole. In an interview we had at the L.G.B. he lost his temper and asserted that he "would not have a picking enquiry into L.G.B. policy ". I kept my temper and we parted on friendly terms. Charles Booth blames me for having raised the hostility of the L.G.B. He may be right—the other policy would have been to wheedle my way into the place. On the other hand, if one begins by being disagreeable, one may come in the end to a better bargain. It is, however, clear that I shall not have the support of the Commission in my desire for scientific research into the past seventy years.

There is one very pleasant feature about the Commission. We are all of us after public objects, however much we may disagree as to what these objects are and how to arrive at them. There is hardly any personal vanity, or personal ambition, and no personal interest at work in the Commission. A little jealousy of those who take the lead—but very little of that. And we are all getting fond of our chairman—who, like many a *grand seigneur*, can afford to be modest and unassuming.

He and his wife dined with us yesterday, meeting Rowntree (author of *Poverty*), the Barnetts, the clerk of the Westminster Board of Guardians, Mrs. Sydney Buxton and Henry Hobhouse—a most pleasant and useful party. Rowntree, who stayed the night here, is to help me to get an analysis of 1000 applications—the whence and the whither of pauperism. I am beginning to enjoy the Commission work: but the grind of combining it with our own enquiry keeps one at a low level of strength and good spirits. Book III., *Seignorial Franchise and Municipal Corporations*, is in some ways the hardest of all.

Meanwhile, Balfour has succumbed to Chamberlain, and the Conservative Party has become definitely protectionist—for the time—so long as Chamberlain lives. In so far as it commits the most *laisser-faire* party to the policy of state control and increase of taxation, we rejoice in it. Sidney still thinks that import duties are a wasteful device, though agreeing to the expediency of deepening the channels of trade between Anglo-Saxon communities. Personally, I don't believe much in the injuriousness of tariffs to a prosperous wealth-producing country like England. And, if a tariff were part and parcel of a deliberately conceived scheme of raising the standard of life by collective regulation and public expenditure, I should be willing to pay for this scheme in a slight rise in the price of commodities. And, other things being equal, I would rather pay more for commodities produced by our colonists under fair conditions of employment than fractionally less for commodities produced under unknown conditions by an oppressed people. This, as a matter of sentiment, and as an argument for bettering conditions here. However, for the next six years we have to look to the Liberal Party for any reforms. It is well that Sidney is a " free importer ". As for my private predilection " mum's the word ".

February 19*th*.—Dined last night with Tommy Lough (now promoted to the parliamentary secretaryship of the Education Department) and met three other minor members of the Ministry—the Lord Chancellor of Ireland, Lord Advocate for Scotland, and Solicitor-General for Ireland, as well as two or three ministerial M.P.'s. The minor Ministers were all on their best behaviour, with that peculiar combination of new-born discretion and modesty with obvious self-complacency at being within the mystic circle of the Government. Tommy Lough was great on the reforms he intended to introduce in the financial transactions of the Education Department—horror-struck at the notion of 80,000 separate cheques a year on behalf of separate institutions. " We might as well have a separate cheque for each packet of tea sold by the Tower Company." The mysteries of education are still above and beyond him. "As for the Government's intention," he whispered to me, " about education or any other matter, I know less than I did as a private member. You see I may not gossip and no one gossips with me." He added sadly, " We under-secretaries are just set down to do some departmental job and, as we know nothing of the subject, we have got to stick to it, instead of amusing ourselves in the lobby, picking up news. But it is interesting", he continued with glowing enthusiasm, " to feel yourself right inside the machine. Morant is a fine fellow and we get on splendidly—but the office from a mere business point of view *does* want reforming."

A boisterous tea dealer, whose business career has been divided between advertising packets of tea and starting doubtful companies— whose public interests are wholly Irish or working-class, who has neither literary culture nor scientific knowledge—as one of the heads of our Education Department! A rum thing is English government.

For all that I like Tommy Lough, he has energy, he is no respecter of persons, he wants, in a philistine way, to make society more prosperous and happier, and he never says what he does not think. He is a rough, ugly instrument, but so far as he cuts at all he cuts in the right direction.

February 22nd.—Had a party of young Liberals dining here last night: Herbert Samuel and Reginald McKenna, Masterman and John Simon, Massingham and Sydney Olivier. Of these Simon, the young lawyer, is by far the most brilliant—making a big income as the rising junior at the Bar. He has a conventional mind but excellent working intellect, a charming person, agreeable voice and manner. But his spirit has been broken and his whole life made arid by the loss, some three years ago, of his young wife. He declares himself already " bored " by Parliament after three days of it. " Rufus Isaacs has shown me a quiet corner to which I retire and work at my briefs." He is an individualist Liberal of the Morley type, without Morley's idealism.

I sat between the two new under-secretaries, both full of the work and dignity of office—neither of them exciting personalities, but McKenna a genuine reformer of the ordinary kind—and both as respectable and hard-working as Cabinet Ministers could desire in subordinates. Masterman exuberant in his half-cynical, half-sentimental talk; Sydney Olivier full of the possibility of going out to South Africa in an important post, all of them full of themselves and rather impatient of each other's obsessions.

This morning I took off—the first holiday for a fortnight or more. I walked along the Embankment to St. Paul's for the 10 o'clock service. The beauty of the music and the old-world charm of the words, the great space of the dome, are always the best recreation when I am weary with straining my poor little mind. I prayed for strength to order my effort rightly and keep my motives pure, to preserve the patience and persistency of purpose needed to carry through our intentions. These next three years are going to try my strength of body, intellect and character: I sometimes wonder whether I shall keep going, or whether some day I may not find that I have stopped for repair. And yet it is little that I really accomplish with all my abstinence and cutting down of all but business intercourse. Sidney can do about four times as much as I, whether measured in time or in matter.

Sidney thoroughly satisfied with the secondary education side of L.C.C. work: he gets through all his grants without opposition: he is building up a system of provided and non-provided schools side by side. He is happy in his work, as all antagonism to him personally has subsided. The little jealousies between the leading Progressives are now transferred from Spring Gardens to Westminster—and Sidney does not appear in this higher sphere. Spring Gardens has become a mere backwater in which the remaining big fish of the old gang can swim without fear of creating disturbance. Thirty-two of the Progressives, including all the leaders, now in the House of Commons! There is actually some talk of making Sidney vice-chairman of the education committee! Collins even pressed him to accept the great position: Sidney modestly put himself at the " disposition of his party " and acquiesced in the suggestion that he should work under Shepheard (who is to be promoted to the chairmanship) if the majority of the party actually desire it.[1] It is a great luxury to feel that he is beyond all question of dignity and personal position. If you are content to accept any position that is forced on you and never to compete, there is a good deal of excellent and happy work to be done in the world.

March 1st.—Meanwhile, my Royal Commission grinds slowly on. The three committees that I pressed for on the procedure committee have been appointed and have set to work: statistics, documents (on central policy and on local administration). I am trying to guide the committee on documents into making an analysis of all the documents of the central authority—statutes, orders, reports, with a view of writing a memorandum on the attitude of the state towards each class of pauper. Lord George gives me unhesitating support: my difficulty is with Sir Samuel Provis. But I had the most friendly chat with him this afternoon, and he comes to dine to meet a carefully selected party on Wednesday. Charles Booth has the statistical committee well in

[1] They did not wish it, so he remains chairman of the higher education committee—a post he prefers.

hand: Bentham has elaborated and improved my question as to the working constitution of the boards of guardians: I hope that investigations will be presently set on foot as to the life history of paupers in different unions. And I no longer find the association with my fellow-commissioners disagreeable. But it is a somewhat disastrous interruption of work on the book, which drags on painfully.

We are trying to avoid dining out except when it seems absolutely desirable that we should be present (*e.g.* Liberal Ministers). We wish to be on friendly terms with the administrators and to make ourselves as useful as possible. Mr. Haldane came in this morning—first to discuss with Sidney and Mackinder the organisation of London University—and, when Mackinder had left, to consult us about his scheme of army reform. So far as we could understand it, this scheme provides for a small and highly expert professional army with the militia in attendance for foreign service (a reduction of 50,000 men). Then, in the background, as material for reinforcements, in time of war, a mass of half-trained material under a semi-civil authority—probably a county authority bearing some sort of likeness to the joint committee for police —with " grants in aid " to promote extension and efficiency. Of his secretaries young Acland is attending to the labour side (contracts, etc.), Lord Lucas to Buckingham Palace, Widdows to army education, Colonel Ellison to army organisation. We are to meet all of them at dinner on Tuesday; young Acland comes to lunch to-morrow to consult Sidney about army contracts and their conditions.

A brilliant dinner for the Students' Union [London School of Economics]—A. J. B. and Sir John French as guests. One of those academic discourses from the ex-Premier in which he delights, and in which he delights his hearers. In our talk together I gathered that he is set on continued leadership: would not hear the suggestion that he should take a holiday. " It is exactly now that they are beaten and demoralised that they need me: I shall be with them as continuously as if I were Prime Minister." Like all great personages there creeps out, now and again, a little horn of egotism—a sensitiveness, more than with the ruck of men, to any depreciation of his past work and present position. He pressed me to come, both of us, to stay at Whittingehame—perhaps, we may go. I should like to talk out some matters of government with him and some aspects of the philosophy of public conduct. Is he an ingrained individualist incapable of change? Tariff reform has, at any rate, shaken the *laisser-faire* side of his philosophy.

At the meeting of Tuesday, 27th February, of the Royal Commission, Charles Booth attempted the use of the method of the interview which seemed to me illegitimate and was hotly resented by the chairman, Sir S. Provis and others. He happened to be in the chair when Preston-Thomas (inspector for South Wales District) was to be cross-examined on his printed statement. This statement concerned the district as a whole (I had urged that the inspectors should be asked to supply separate particulars about each union, but, largely because Charles Booth backed down, I was defeated and the inspector was asked to describe his district as a whole). But Charles Booth insisted on taking him right through the whole of the unions—one by one—asking him questions for which the man was not prepared and could only give hearsay evidence. Five hours were thus spent without the other members having a chance of asking questions arising out of his printed statement. I had left after lunch, but I hear that there was a hot dispute as to the relevancy of the questions and the chairman seems determined to put a stop to it. That sort of wholesale interviewing is all very well if the man is prepared and is speaking of facts within his own knowledge. But it is hardly worth the £100 which each weekly meeting of the Commission costs the national exchequer. I am inclined to think that a statement of the cost of the different methods of investigation ought to be submitted to the commissioners by the chairman—it is a case where efficiency would be actually promoted by some attention to economy. A Royal Commission drifts into stupid, lazy and costly ways through sheer inadvertence and lack of forethought as to means and ways.

The documents committee, consisting of Smart (chairman), Russell Wakefield, MacDougall, Provis and myself, met for the first time. I had circulated suggestions proposing to limit ourselves, in the first instance, to discovering what policy had been laid down by the central authority [1] as to the relief of various kinds of paupers since 1834, and proposing that the work should be undertaken by an efficient clerk under Jeffrey (clerk to the committee), according to definite plans decided on by the committee. To show what I meant, I circulated an analysis of the 1834 report, the first three statutes and two general orders, made by Mrs. Spencer. Professor Smart, on the other hand, proposed that he and Wakefield should undertake the blue-books, and that I and MacDougall should undertake the general orders and circulars—each selecting what we thought fit and doing it in the way we thought best. I was beaten, though Sir Samuel Provis supported my suggestion that the work should be done systematically under direction. The simple truth was that I had a majority against me on both counts. MacDougall, Wakefield and Provis did not want an

---

[1] By the term " central authority " is always meant the unbroken succession of government departments dealing with the Poor Law : first the Poor Law Commissions of 1834–48; then the Poor Law Board, 1849–71; then the Local Government Board, 1871–1930, when it was succeeded by the Ministry of Health. See *English Poor Law History*, by S. and B. Webb.

historical retrospect—they desired only to enquire into the laws of to-day—and Smart, MacDougall and Wakefield did not want the work done systematically under a deliberate plan. Seeing myself beaten, I suggested that Smart and Wakefield should do their job first and that, if that were satisfactory, we could then decide whether we would do the circulars and statutes in the same way. So the committee has adjourned for two or three months; which has the incidental advantage of leaving my Monday mornings free for our own work. The longer the Commission delays the better for me. Meanwhile, I will put Miss Longman on to the " general orders " and circulars. In all probability we shall have to do the work ourselves—a plan that has its advantages.

March 19th.—Attended a meeting of the Poplar Board of Guardians, held at 6.30. About 30 were present, a rather low lot of doubtful representatives of Labour, with a sprinkling of builders, publicans, insurance and other agents. The meeting was exclusively engaged in allotting the contracts for the year, which meant up to something between £50,000 and £100,000. I did not ascertain the exact amount. The procedure was utterly reckless. The tenders were opened at the meeting, the names and prices read out, and then, without any kind of report of a committee or by officials, straight away voted on. Usually the same person as heretofore was taken, nearly always a local man— it was not always the lowest tender, and the prices were, in all cases, full, in some cases obviously excessive. Butter at 1s. 2d. a lb., when the contracts ran into thousands of pounds worth, was ridiculous. Milk at 9d. a gallon—the best and most expensive meat, tea at 2s. 8d. " Give Bow a chance " was one of the relevant considerations urged successfully in favour of a change in the contractor. Will Crooks sat in the chair and did nothing to check the recklessness. Even Lansbury, by constitution a thorough-going sentimentalist, and with no other experience of public affairs, protested, and was clearly ashamed of the procedure.

March 20th.—Two dinners, that well illustrated a subtle distinction of atmosphere—one at the Asquiths, the other at the George Hamiltons. The former consisted of the Russian Ambassador, the Desboroughs, Lord Goschen, the Dickson Poynders, Mrs. Lowther (the Speaker's wife), Lord Hugh Cecil, Mrs. Lester (Mrs. Cornwallis West's sister), one or two aristocratic young men, and the Asquiths' daughter and Raymond. The large garish rooms, the flunkeys and the superlatively good dinner, gave a sort of " Second Empire " setting to the entertainment. Lady Desborough, Margot, Mrs. Lester and Lady Dickson Poynder were all very *décolletée* and highly-adorned with jewels. The conversation aimed at brilliancy—Margot's sparkling little disjointed sayings, kindly and indiscreet, Lady Desborough's somewhat artificial grace, Lady Dickson Poynder's pretty folly, Mrs. Lester's *outré* frankness, lending a sort of stagyness to the talk; we might have all been characters brought on to illustrate the ways of modern " society "—a twentieth-century Sheridan's play. They were all gushing over G. B. S., and I had to entertain the ladies after dinner with a discourse on his philosophy and personality—mostly the latter. We came away feeling half-flattered that we had been asked, half-contemptuous of ourselves for having gone. And not pleased with the entourage of a democratic Minister.

Very different the George Hamiltons. Here the party consisted of the Neville Lytteltons, Lady Arthur Russell, the Herbert Jekylls, Sir Francis Mowatt—persons belonging to much the same set as the Asquith party though of a dowdier hue. But the reception in the cosy library was homely, and the dinner without pretentiousness—the George Hamiltons treating us as if we were part of a family party— no attempt to shine, just talking about the things that interested each of us in a quiet simple way. It would have been almost impossible to show off, so absolutely sincere and quiet was the tone. And yet the conversation was full of interest and lingered willingly on each subject. After we ladies had left, Sidney said that he listened with eager interest to a long interchange of official experience between Lord George, Mowatt and Lyttelton, as to the administration of the War Office and the relations between Cabinet, War Minister and permanent staff—Jekyll and Sidney listening and occasionally intervening. And, as we drove away, we felt that we had had a restful evening, learnt something and gained stimulus from the refinement and public spirit manifest in our hosts and their guests. The Tory aristocrat and his wife were, in relation to their class, living the simple life; and the Yorkshire manufacturer's son was obviously " swelling " it, to use the vulgar expression for a vulgar thing.

April 6th.—Towards municipalisation. Edgar Speyer, the millionaire promoter of the electric tubes, and undertaker of the electrification of the underground railway, with his general manager Sir George Gibb, dined here last night to meet McKinnon Wood, and discuss a deal with the L.C.C. He wants the L.C.C. to raise five millions for him, he paying 4% and inserting a purchase clause for the whole undertaking at 21 or 40 years. A shrewd little Jew—taciturn and almost gloomy, but lighting up at the end of the evening when he thought he had impressed McKinnon Wood and Sidney. Sir George Gibb (late general manager of N.E.R.), a courtly official of great capacity and considerable charm, to whom Speyer gives £10,000 to manage his undertakings—a personage typical of the present time, when the enterprise of syndicates is managed on Civil Service lines and big officials are perpetually transferring themselves from company to company, or from company to Government, and from Government to company. McKinnon Wood and Sidney, unpaid organisers of society, Gibb and Speyer heavily-remunerated organisers—though the difference is more apparent than real since the two L.C.C. members are pensioners on the nation's industry exactly as Gibb and Speyer—the only difference being that, in Sidney's and McKinnon Wood's case, the income is small, not much more than a livelihood and working expenses. Sidney helped to bring Speyer and Wood together because he approves of the L.C.C. becoming a sleeping partner in London transport—eventually taking it over. Also Speyer may, in return, help forward the School. We are looking out for a donor of £40,000 to enlarge the building: Speyer seems the most likely of the millionaires.

Haldane has asked Sidney to join a little committee consisting of Lord Esher, Monro (L.G.B. official), and one or two military experts, with young Lord Lucas as a sort of secretary, to consider the carrying out of his scheme of " voluntary conscription ",[1] and we are trying to introduce the Secretary for War to various county and city administrators. We hope, by involving county organisations in the volunteer movement, we may pave the way for the half-time movement, by which half the working hours and all the leisure of the boys up to eighteen will be absorbed in some sort of training.

April 15*th.*—Decided to publish our three volumes separately: *The Parish and the County*, October 1st; *Seignorial Franchises and Municipal Corporations*, January 1st; and *Statutory Authorities for Special Purposes and some Conclusions*, May 5th. We think in that way we shall get almost continuous advertisement for the whole work for six months. There is such a mass of new stuff—both facts and theories—that the reviewer would be unable to grasp the whole. Moreover, though we do not want to hurry the work, it is essential that we get the kudos of our publication in time for the L.C.C. election and for my work on the Royal Commission.

These last three months my work has been slacker and, I fear, less good quality than last year, owing to the rival interest of the P.L.C. But we are well on with Book III., having finished the *Lord's Court and Manorial Boroughs* and beginning our analysis of *Municipal Corporations*. Most of Book IV. is done: Book V., *Some Conclusions*, is as yet but dreamt of! Toothache and nervous exhaustion somewhat spoils

---

[1] This was a phrase indignantly hurled at me by a Radical member who disapproves of Haldane and all his works.

the prospect of our Easter holiday at Longfords. But, perhaps, a few days' complete rest and more generous diet may re-establish a painless equilibrium.

April 16th.—A happy time at Longfords, and some progress with our chapter on the *City of London*—taken out of turn as the analysis and the constitution of the MS., 1835, is not yet completed by our secretaries. But there will be a stiff pull over that analysis and I must sacrifice all my other work to getting a grip of the material, which is overpowering in quantity and complexity.

Mary Playne growing every year more benign: lost all her old cynicism and worldliness—not all her old restlessness. The spirit of religion becomes every day a more potent influence in her life— presently she will be a veritable saint. Will she end in the Catholic Church? There are signs that her inward eyes are turning that way. She prophesies great accessions to the Church universal through the virtual disestablishment of the English Church, by the Education Bill if it passes into law. The saintly Prior of Woodchester is a frequent visitor, and the unselfconscious and gentle devoutness of some neighbouring Catholics are telling on her mind. But, on the whole, I think she will remain satisfied with a mystical Christian science and conformity to the Church of England. She and I become increasingly sympathetic: we discuss, in moony fashion, the need for a new order embodying faith in a spiritual force, the obligation to love and thankfulness, and abstemiousness from all harmful, if not unnecessary, physical indulgence or vain display. We are too old and worn to start it. Some younger woman may.

Sidney thinks the Education Bill[1] a harsh measure, but takes no part in the agitation against it; does not care to discuss it since it is clear he cannot influence the result. We have no kind of influence, either on Birrell or those behind him, or on any of the parliamentary groups that are likely to carry amendments in committee. And, as we belong neither to the Church nor to the Catholics, we have no place in either of the movements in the country against it. If it is defeated, it will be through using the indifference of the bulk of parents and ratepayers to the whole question of religious education, combined with their objection to the cost of buying out the denominational schools: if that issue were separately put to the country, I think the Catholic and Church schools would be allowed to continue on the present basis. But I doubt the skill and persistency of the Church. Half, or at any

[1] This was the measure by which the Liberal Government sought to reverse the scheme of 1902, which placed the cost of the staffing and the incidental expenses of the Anglican and Roman Catholic elementary schools upon the shoulders of the Local Education Authority out of the rates.

rate a large fraction, like the Bill as a curb on Anglican priestcraft; whilst a powerful minority even among the clergy are really rationalists and desire the suppression of distinctively dogmatic teaching—Canon Henson for instance. The Catholics are fervent, logical and unanimous: their plea unanswerable since to them undenominational teaching is the very devil.

May 15th.—A baffling time divided between superintending two secretaries at work on the City of London records, and drafting a memorandum on the policy of the central authority of the Poor Law, 1834–47, from Miss Longman's notes.

The Royal Commission lumbers along; chaotic and extravagant in its use of time and money, each committee doing as it seems fit in its own sight. There is a lack of method and discipline with which some of us get impatient and, I fear, I sometimes offend by my easygoing ways—intervening when I ought to hold my peace. " You did not behave nicely yesterday," said Lord George in kindly reproof, " you should not have referred to current politics." So I thanked him warmly for the hint, and promised to be " seen and not heard " in future. I find it so difficult to be official in manner. However, I really will try. Dignified silence I will set before me, except when the public good requires me to come forward. Ah! how hard it is for the quick-witted and somewhat vain woman to be discreet and accurate. One can manage to be both in the written word—but the " clash of tongues " drives both discretion and accuracy away.

May 22nd.—C. S. Loch completely lost his temper yesterday at my cross-examination of Lockwood. He is always making *ex parte* statements in his questions, and yesterday he made Lockwood—a weak witness—advocate the prohibition of compounding, on the ground that the occupier, if he were conscious of paying rates, would be more severe on expenditure. So I made Lockwood say that the landlord, whatever the arrangement, really paid the rates and that the occupier would, therefore, prefer to pay the economic rent to the local authority in the form of rates, from whom he received services, than to the landlord from whom he received nil. Loch got white with rage, and protested against my questions as misleading statements of economic doctrine. All this dialectic seems to me a foolish business: but it is important to let the commissioners know that we shall challenge all the current assumptions. However, in the little tiff, the Commission was on my side. What makes him angry is that the enquiry is drifting straight into the *causes of destitution* instead of being restricted to the narrower question of *granted destitution is inevitable, how can we best prevent pauperism?* And the answer that is being extracted by our enquiry into the causes of destitution takes the form of *more regulation and more public provision without the stigma of pauperism*—probably compulsory provision which *must* be given and *cannot* be refused.

May 22nd.—An agreeable Sunday with Sir Charles Eliot, late Governor of East Africa and now Principal of Sheffield University, and Lady Elcho who had persuaded us to go thither. Poor Sir Charles, having chucked away his prospects by indiscreet and unbecoming resistance to the policy of the Foreign Office, has taken on a wholly uncongenial task. To be more or less subordinate to a second-rate town council, to be organising lectures by fifth-rate professors for clerks and unemployed young women, is somewhat riling to a distinguished diplomatist and bureaucrat of the Empire. So he takes refuge in " beasties ", spending more time in his little laboratory—describing, dissecting, and discoursing about slugs of the sea and the earth—than in the committee room or the class room. He is a strong man— observant and executive—but without subtlety or charm. Nevertheless, if I were Secretary of State I should get him back into the administration of the Empire.

Lady Elcho, a kindly sympathetic, interested but somewhat weary woman—her friendship with " Mr. Arthur ", as he is called in that set, the romance of her life, but a romance which has become somewhat faded. Now, at any rate, no sign of anything beyond old friendliness between them: " Mr. Arthur " having had a good many fancies, I imagine. We met him at dinner at her house the other night, and I was allotted to him. If it were not for the glamour that envelops a man of charm who has been Prime Minister and the leader of a great party—should I like him? One thing I know, I should dislike the set.

June 15th. Bramdean.—The last days of the Whitsun recess spent in this little country hamlet, close to Brockwood Park—whither we came for rest and work, and a sight of Georgie [Meinertzhagen] and her children. A happy peaceful time: good work done though less of it than we hoped—*The City of London*, with our wealth of material, proving a longer job than we expected.

Meanwhile, the Commission is developing in what seems a most favourable direction. They have actually given us two assistant commissioners to enquire into the connection between sweating and pauperism and have practically permitted me to select them—Steel-Maitland and Rose Squire. This is more than I should have dared to do even if I had been chairman, and is another sign of the lack of proper control of the commissioners by the chairman or staff. The commissioners have, in fact, been run away with by those commissioners who have been sufficiently pertinacious without thought of the enquiry as a whole. Charles Booth has scampered off with the statistics of to-day, I have seized upon the historical survey and have secured the marking off of sweating as a cause of pauperism. Mrs. Bosanquet has captured her own little corner of outdoor relief as a rate-in-aid of wages to women. Whether we three shall meet together in the same place, at the end of our respective enquiries, I do not know. Possibly, other commissioners feel that they are having their look in. C. S. Loch seems to have gone *caput*. But quite clearly there is no one directing purpose shaping the enquiry to a predetermined end. Which of the many conflicting or diverging purposes will prevail remains to be seen. Meanwhile, it means that, besides our own big task of history of local government, 1689–1834, we have two investigations to direct —the policy of the central authority, 1834–1906; and the connection between bad conditions of employment, or insanitary and overcrowded houses, with pauperism. All these investigations will have to go slow and be partially sacrificed the one to the other.

All this while Sidney is giving at least half his time and thought— perhaps more—to the organisation of secondary and higher education in London. This year, four wranglers (Camb.) from the L.C.C. scholars selected nine years ago! He is very happy in the success of his unseen work; all his little schemes, or at any rate the most dearly cherished of them, have come off—the scholarship ladder, the in-numerable educational institutions, secondary to university, which he has kept alive and under a semi-voluntary management; and, lastly, the London School of Economics has grown in size, significance and grace. These successes are a constant source of half-conscious satisfaction and make up a good part of his happiness.

Indeed, we both of us live in an atmosphere of gratitude to each other, to the community which gave us such an extraordinary good start in life, and to that undefined *providence*. There is nothing we lack in our lives, and we have far more than we deserve. Now and again, I long to rest and have time to look round and enjoy beauty, or to dissipate in purposeless thought, yet I doubt whether, with my in-grained habits of methodic work, I could be long out of the tracks without dissatisfaction and displeasure. Moreover, we have, as a matter of fact, an easy time of it, at least I have. Whenever I am really fagged I break off, lie on bed or sofa, and just let my mind go blank. It is this capacity for going blank that gives me, I think, my power for rapid and intense thought when I am in good condition. For the best intellectual effort of which a given brain is capable I suggest two habits of body are needful—abstinence in indulging appetites and the trick of complete relaxation of muscle and obliviousness of mind. With these two habits, you can get the greatest output of mental energy of which your particular brain is capable. And, with John Stuart Mill, I am inclined to think that the exercise of intellect—perhaps suffused with love—is the highest happiness of which we poor mortals are capable. " Love without intellect ", the Eastern might assert is the Nirvana. To this state I have not attained—death may it be?

. . . This long entry in my diary I have written this morning, by the open window, looking out on to the park-like meadow—a dull warm rainy grey day after a fortnight of glorious weather. Sidney has run up to London, on L.C.C. administrative business, just as I ran up on Monday for two meetings of the Commission. And, as he is away, and I have been somewhat tired, I am treating myself to a day off, or two days off, so as to go back fresh to London. Before we settle down in the Bertrand Russells' little house near Oxford six weeks hence we want to have completed *The City of London*, the memorandum on the policy of the Central Authority, 1834–1849, to have despatched Vol. I. for striking off, to have finished the records of Norwich, and, for me, to have got forward with the analysis of the constitution of municipal corporations. The last, I fear, will remain undone, which worries me. " Keep your hair on, missus " is Sidney's somewhat inelegant advice—reminiscent of the London street boy.

. . . After a 12.30 lunch I cycled off in a grey windy afternoon, up the Winchester hill along the ridge of the highland towards West Meon through fields of red clover and hay grass, under avenues of beech and fir—delighting in the sense of a holiday and in the physical vigour springing from the morning's rest. This countryside is like a beautiful but pale and somewhat stately lady—the white undertone yielded by the chalk, and the long unbroken lines of undulating down and wide stretches of valley, lack warmth and interest unless the landscape is flushed with sun or made glorious by thunder clouds. Still there is a sort of gentle unassuming sympathy—restful and meditative—in the rolling hill and dale, whilst in the high-hedged lanes, bordered with flowering broom and tall field flowers, there are delightful touches of intimacy. Always the same background of wonder, wistful wonder whether or not there is a spiritual force towards which we humans are tending, or whether we are mere animals, as we think animals to be, which are to-day and to-morrow are not—like the leaves of a tree or the blades of the grass. No more reason that we are the beginning of another and higher stage of the life force than that we are the end of this world's development, not likely to be bettered in our best types even in the one hundred million years deemed to be before our race on this earth. And we all of us—or at any rate many of us—go through this world, asking this question, perpetually, persistently, asking it and getting no answer, unless we are willing to turn our back on reason.

" I have taken service under reason," pitifully exclaimed Henry Sidgwick in explaining the pessimistic agnosticism of his later years, " I cannot now desert her." And so, in spite of every gift of artifice and nature, there remained behind all the effort of this intellectual saint, behind the love of his friends and the devotion to and from his wife, behind all the delightful intercourse and attractive surroundings of his daily existence, a background of gloom and world melancholy. Without true faith in a spiritual force, if not in personal immortality, human life seemed to Sidgwick, and seems at times to most of us, like a shallow stagnant pool of somewhat dirty water. Perhaps, it would be better for it to be entirely dried up one hundred million years before the last catastrophe? Sidney would prosaically answer: " It will not be so. Hence, we must labour to embank and cleanse waters, to drain off the overflow, stay a creeping morass." " The world can wait for political science ", bitterly moaned Professor Sidgwick. " No it cannot," urges Sidney, " for, meanwhile, lives are wrecked, and men and women and little children grow mean or suffer pain without redemption. To lessen, by one iota, physical pain or mean motive is a sufficient good for me." And he goes on his way rejoicing in his love for me, and my love for him, untroubled with the meaning of the universe, and slightly bored by those who are or think themselves so to be.

Grosvenor Rd., June 20th.—A useful little dinner here last night to help forward Haldane's territorial army scheme—R. B. H., Lord Esher, Lord Lucas and Sidney (representing the War Office committee) and Colonel Hughes (Lord Mayor of Sheffield), Sir H. Bell (Lord Lieutenant, North Riding), Bickersteth (Clerk of C.C. East Riding), Harcourt Clare (Clerk of C.C. Lancashire). After dinner Haldane enthused them all—though the clerks of the county councils were somewhat cynical as to the efficiency of the representative members of the joint committees.

July 2nd.—A freakish dinner—arranged before Lallie's death and one I did not like to put off. Balfour and Lady Elcho to meet four young Liberal M.P.'s, Masterman, Simon, Gooch and Carr-Gomm, with Sir Oliver Lodge and Beatrice Creighton thrown in. I am wondering whether Balfour will recover his position as a leader—at present there is a note of contempt in most persons' opinion of him— his charm and reputation for charm increasing the irritation at his intellectual indecision. I asked him after dinner, when we sat on the balcony, whether there had ever been a cause (apart from general good government) about which he had been really concerned. " Have you ever wished to bring about another state of affairs to what at present exists? " I insisted, perhaps somewhat rudely. " I am a Conservative," he rejoined quietly, " I wish to maintain existing institutions." Then, presently, he added: " There are some things about which I have been keen: take for instance the clause in the Scotch Free Church Bill enabling the established Church of Scotland to change its formulas—freeing it from the dead hand—I worked very hard to secure that ". I sympathised and we dropped the subject. Afterwards, I wondered whether it is not exactly this basis of pure Conservatism combined with extraordinary ingenuity and resourcefulness in evading demands for advance, whether it is not this combination that leads to an appearance of shiftiness. It is characteristic that the liberty for an association to change its opinion, seemed among the most important reforms to be secured. I imagined he might have added a Catholic university for Ireland—another reform affecting the opinion or the creeds of men—all in the direction of tolerance for varieties of opinion. Perhaps faith in this sort of freedom of mental development is the most positive side of Balfour's political opinions. Mixed up with his Conservatism and with his over-subtle opportunism there is a solid layer of Whig doctrine. By birth and tradition he is a Conservative, by conviction he is a Whig, whilst by temperament he is a manipulator, delighting in finesse. An unpopular combination just at present.

Altogether I have had this week thirty persons to lunch or dinner, as well as half-a-dozen in the afternoon—nearly all of the lot being on business of some sort. Assistant commissioners coming to be instructed in the art of investigation, and the scope of their enquiry; the secretary of the Commission to talk over the former; a German lady needing information on education, a clever woman requiring advice as to her career; also nephews, nieces. For the next six weeks my days will be taken up in much the same way, tiring and leading to little result that is apparent to oneself. But I never like to refuse to see those who think I can help them when they are in any way connected with my side of things. It all distracts one from our main work.

Dined at the house of a millionaire—Sir J. Wernher, Bath House. We went there, partly because of Sidney's connection with him over the " Charlottenburg " scheme, partly from curiosity to see inside such an establishment, partly because we both respect and like the man. He is a German giant, not unduly self-indulgent, and a real drudger at his business. But he is better than that. He is noted for generosity inside his own circle; regarding the South African commercial world as something for which he is responsible, perpetually carrying the weaker men on his back—he is good, that is to say, to his own community. He is also public-spirited in his desire for the efficiency of all industry, and the advancement of its technique. Moreover, he is obviously unconcerned with social ambition or desire to push himself by his wealth. " I have no time, even to know that I am wealthy: the only result of

my millions is to make me dread being introduced to a new person lest
they should begin to beg from me. The really happy person is the man
with £10,000 a year, reputed to have £2000."

But, though our host was superior to his wealth, our hostess and her
guests were dominated by it. . . . The company was composed, either of
financial magnates, or of the able hangers-on of magnates. The setting
in the way of rooms and flowers and fruit and food and wine and music,
and pictures and works of art, was hugely overdone—wealth—wealth
—wealth—was screamed aloud wherever one turned. And all the
company were living up to it, or bowing down before it. There might
just as well have been a Goddess of Gold erected for overt worship—
the impression of worship in thought, feeling and action could hardly
have been stronger. Always excepting Wernher himself. He looked
wistful as I suggested that the fallacy of wealth was becoming apparent.
" My husband and I have all the wealth we could possibly make use of
without diminishing our delightful happiness. Four private secretaries
on £1000 a year: a fifth would break me down. What you enjoy ", I
ventured to add, " is not your wealth but the power it gives you to
organise the affairs of the world." " Yes, perhaps, that is so ", he
answered wearily.

A French lady factory inspector was billeted on us for the International Sociological Congress (of which we were members who did
not attend). A large heavily-scented, well-dressed, clever person, with
a sort of personal attraction that one could hardly associate in England
with fastidious conduct—cool but agreeable in manner, direct in
language, and quite clearly grasping in disposition. With extraordinary
frankness she displayed to me, one by one, articles of clothing bought
at absurd prices—the longest kid gloves 6 fr., an evening dress 40 fr.,
and a perfectly fitting grey evening cloak 29 fr.—from factories and
shops which she inspected! With regard to the cloak, she explained
how she had seen a model at a fashionable purveyor to smart shops in
the course of her inspection, and had then and there asked the price of
a similar one. " Mais, Madame, 5 frs.", the proprietor had politely suggested would be the cost of making it; 14 fr. the cloth, another 10 fr.
the lace, total 29 fr. for a 250 fr. cloak. Towards us her behaviour has
been extraordinary: she was asked to stay five days, and has stayed nine.
To-day, when all the other congressists are departed, she is running
round London with an attaché of the French Embassy with whom she
seems *très amie*. Altogether, an astonishing glimpse of the possibilities
of French officialism. I am wondering whether she will leave the
house without borrowing money. All the same, she is not merely well-
informed and hard-working, but she is cultivated, ready to tell you,
and in correctly turned phrases, the whole development of legislature,

metaphysical thought, French literature, the theatre, politics—doubtless superficial information but distinctly lucid and comprehensive. She is a vigorous feminist—has nothing but bad to say of the position of women in France. Frenchmen have, according to her, an innate contempt for women—both for their intellects and their conduct. And, if she is a representative type of the professional woman and advanced reformer, one is hardly surprised at a certain dislike and suspicion of anything but the conventionally pious and " innocent " lady. But she must be an exception—a product perhaps of the shoddiness of sociology.

July 17th.—Yesterday we had a field day on the Royal Commission discussing our future procedure. Various memoranda had been circulated—conflicting, overlapping and irrelevant, from the chairman, the evidence committee, the secretary, C. S. Loch and myself—a fine confusion to serve instead of a compact agenda. The chairman opened the proceedings by a long rambling statement: he had interviewed John Burns [then President of the Local Government Board], who was willing to delay dealing with the unemployed otherwise than by an extension of the Act, until the autumn session of 1908. From which Lord George deduced that our report on the whole of our reference must be in the hands of the Government by August 1908. After some preliminary sallies, we settled down to consider evidence for October. Settled by lunch time. At the afternoon sitting, we roamed over the whole field—spreading out our enquiry into the furthermost points that any individual commissioner desired to reach; Lord George always giving way with a weak protest against doing any one investigation " too thoroughly ". I confined my effort to keeping open for further consideration questions which he, or the Commission as a whole, wished to close—old-age pensions, the condition of the 200,000 children now receiving outdoor relief, the administration of relief by boards of guardians, and more important than all, the relation of poor law medical treatment to public health.

This is a new hare that I have recently started. In listening to the evidence brought by the C.O.S. members in favour of restricting medical relief to the technically destitute, it suddenly flashed across my mind that what we had to do was to adopt the exactly contrary attitude, and make medical inspection and medical treatment compulsory on all sick persons—to treat illness, in fact, as a public nuisance to be suppressed in the interests of the community. At once, I began to cross-examine on this assumption, bringing out the existing conflict between the poor law and public health authorities, and making the unfortunate poor law witnesses say that they were in favour of the public health attitude! Of course Sidney supplied me with some instances, and I hurried off to consult M.O.H.s—Dr. McCleary (Fabian), Dr. Newman (infant mortality expert). As luck would have it, Dr. Downes [member of the Commission] had to give evidence and was puzzled to know what to talk about. He had dined here, and I brought forward all my instances of conflict. In the witness box, he made this conflict part of his thesis, though taking the poor law attitude and complaining of the public health authorities pauperising tendencies. With S.'s help, I drew up a memorandum emphasising all my points. Yesterday Dr. Downes, who is frightened at his own action, tried to stifle the question and to refuse to call evidence on the public health side. I purposely did not press it more than to insist on keeping the question open. I am elaborating an enquiry on my own—with funds supplied by Charlotte Shaw—so I merely said that I should, in the course of the next six months, present the Commission with a further memorandum. " You might elaborate with a few more details the one you have already presented ", said Lord George in a frightened way. And so it was left. At present I am engaged in finding a medical woman to undertake the enquiry, and on rousing the interest of the M.O.H.s throughout the country.

Meanwhile, despairing of any action on the part of the Commission, I have undertaken, unknown to them, an investigation into the administration of boards of guardians. I shall put Mrs. Spencer to analyse the documents that are pouring in to me by every post, and Miss Bulkeley shall go through minutes.

I, therefore, look forward to at least three memoranda handed in by me, (1) *Central Policy*, (2) *The Relation of Poor Law Medical Relief to Public Health*, (3) *Administration of Relief by Boards of Guardians*, as well as the report of the assistant commissioners on the relation of bad conditions of employment to pauperism. On these documents I shall base my report.

My relations to my fellow-commissioners are quite pleasant. I am completely detached from them and yet on most agreeable terms. I just take my own line, attending for just as long as it suits me, cross-examining witnesses to bring out my points and conducting the enquiries that I think important independent of the Commission's work. The lines of reform both in constitution and policy are gradually unfolding themselves to me. Whether I shall embody them in a report of my own, or give up part of my way in order to bring the whole Commission along, will be a question of expediency and delicate negotiation—about which nothing can at present be foreseen.

July 31st.—Out of the blue Lord Cromer wrote to ask to see Sidney. We invited him to lunch. " Shall we begin our talk now or wait until after lunch? " he opened abruptly, as he sat himself down. " What I want, Mr. Webb," he continued, on Sidney's acquiescence to proceed immediately to business, " is for you to come to Egypt for six weeks and report to me on an education system." Then he described his dissatisfaction with it—feeling that it was hollow and, perhaps, not the best suited to the natives. When he had delivered himself, Sidney quietly explained that he was not the man for the job. " I am a mere administrator making use of experts; what you want, Lord Cromer, is someone who understands the whole machinery of education— buildings, plant, curriculum, time tables, etc." " It would have been a fraud if I had taken it," Sidney said, after Lord Cromer had left, " besides we have not the time."

Lord Cromer impressed us both. He was so strong and direct, and lacking in all " side " or pretension. He had even a distinct flavour of the amateur, informal and unconventional, almost unofficial—not the suspicion of a bureaucrat. But he was evidently accustomed to rely entirely on experts for methods and processes, was deferential to Sidney exactly on those questions in which Sidney excelled him in knowledge. Beyond all things (though an attractive and somewhat sensual man) he was impersonal in his attitude, apparently quite unconcerned about the impression he was making on others. In this respect he reminded me of my father. A great administrator of the English type. The exact opposite in methods and temperament to Lord Milner.

On Saturday, a luncheon party to meet Mr. W. J. Bryan, Sidney Buxton, Horace Plunkett. Exactly the same impression as before of the wide-mouthed democrat, upright and kindly, but infantile in his administrative notions. Thought he could solve the question of administration by allotting all offices after each election to the political parties according to their voting strength. Was going to parcel out all the railways among the States—proposed to deal with trusts by making it penal to do more than 50% of the trade in one article. Sydney Buxton appeared quite a statesman comparatively. Mrs. Bryan a plain, middle-aged woman of the assertive American type, full of the shibboleths and self-deceptions of the ordinary American political metaphysician. Bryan took very much the same view as H. G. Wells of the prospects of great social reforms in America, with this difference that he is not a collectivist, all good is to come by ultra-democratic machinery— election, election, election, the cure for all evils.

August 4th. Lower Copse, Bagley Wood.—On August 1st, we arrived here after a lazy morning in London: the day after we rested. We spent yesterday writing the preface of Vol. I. This morning I started to survey the material for the chapters on the municipal cor-poration, and its statutory developments—the two pivotal chapters of Vol. II. Sidney busy on the article on the birth-rate and one on trade unionism for Mackinder's American encyclopaedia. Julia Faulder and

Stephen Hobhouse staying Sunday here. Before we began work Sidney drafted my letter to the M.O.H.s asking for information *re* medical relief public health enquiry. It goes out in the next few days to 600 M.O.H.s.

September 4th.—Five weeks passed like one day—all the more like one day because even the sun, moon and star-lit nights have been continuous—the darkness just sufficient for the five hours' sleep. A happy day, with no cares, no sorrow, no irritation—just the interest of our work, each other's companionship, pleasant converse with friends, and dreamy restful hours in the garden and the wood, or walking or cycling through lanes and by sleepy villages, wandering by the river or gazing at church towers and empty Oxford colleges. The net result: Vol. I. through the press; the whole material for the two pivotal chapters of Vol. II. sorted, together with our ideas as to the substance and order of these chapters; the sections on the legal instrument, the officers, the courts, court of record, court leet, court of quarter sessions, roughed out in first draft; the circular to the M.O.H.s sent out and some hundred replies received; the plan of the investigation of the relation of poor law medical relief and public health settled with Dr. Woodcock; the article on the birth-rate written (I contributing only part of the final section of it); articles on factory legislation and trade unionism finished by Sidney for Mackinder's encyclopaedia; three boards of guardians attended; five poor law institutions inspected by me—not a bad record for five weeks' holiday time. We do not feel fagged —we are both in excellent health and good spirits—having really " lazed " considerably.

Among the friends who have visited us are the Granville-Barkers; he stayed for ten days, she for Sunday. G. B. is a most attractive person, young and good-looking—good-looking in a charming refined fashion—with a subtle intellectual expression, faculties more analytic than artistic? I think with self-control, industry, freedom from vulgar desires and common fears, with varied interests, good memory, a sharp observer of human nature and above all a delicate appreciation of music, poetry and art—a medley of talents of which I do not yet see a very definite whole. He has not yet emancipated himself from G. B. S.'s influence, or found his own soul.

We took G. B. [Granville-Barker] to see Lord Milner. An old Tudor house—giving almost the impression of an inhabited ruin, a garden surrounded by a deserted backwater of the Thames—seemed a fit setting for that stern, rigid man, brooding over the South African victory or disaster. At first he was constrained, but after lunch he unbent; and, from democracy to the present Government, from the present Government to their policy in South Africa, from this to the war and its results, we drifted on until we reached intimate conversation. We tried to cheer him by suggesting that after all the friction and abuse after the war and its devastation, there still remained the two republics merged in the Empire. That was (if you believed in its rightness) a sufficient accomplishment for one man. This Government would not last more than four years, and they could undo little of the past. But he would not be comforted. " It is well for you to be optimistic," he retorted; " you say you are always in a minority, but events are moving your way; whilst my house of cards is tumbling down." And then he explained that he had started all kinds of elaborate enterprises and experimental governmental organisations of agriculture and industry in South Africa, whereby the country might really become independent of gold production; all this good work would, under self-government, certainly be dismantled—salaries reduced, officials dismissed, plant disused. He practically admitted the mistake of the introduction of Chinese labour (given the crass stupidity of the English elector and wicked lies of the Radical agitators), but he defended its introduction as inherently right on the ground that you had to create material wealth before you could give the start to higher things. " Blood and money " (the philosophy that G. B. S. tried to dramatise in *Undershaft's* character and career) had, in fact, been the underlying philosophy of Milner's government. Like Mackinder, he seems to me to enormously overestimate the value of the purely material forces, he is willing to rely on those forces though they be necessarily joined with at least a temporary demoralisation of character. Milner, though a public-spirited, upright and disinterested man, does not believe in the supremacy or even in the relevance of the spiritual side of things— goodness is a luxury to be arrived at after a course of money-getting, by whatever means, and of any blood-letting that may be necessary to the undertaking. As I listened to his feeble, forceful voice, watched his rigid face and wrinkled narrow brow, noted the emphasis on plentiful capital, cheap labour and mechanical ingenuity, I thought that perhaps, after all, there was some justification for Leonard Courtney's hard epithet " a lost mind ". A God and a wife would have made Milner, with his faithfulness, persistency, courage, capacity and charm, into a great man: without either he has been a tragic combination of success and failure. " He would have been made by being loved ", summed up G. B. as we rode away.

Among our frequent visitors have been the Ruskin Hall men, and their principal, Lees-Smith. These working-men students with their good conduct, their public spirit and their naïve enjoyment of the college life of learned leisure, were refreshing to look at and listen to. All I.L.P. in politics, enthusiastic admirers of Keir Hardie and

J. R. MacDonald, believers in the advent, as a permanent force, of the Labour Party, bitter against John Burns, Isaac Mitchell and the Liberal-Labour men—perpetually discussing, as Lees-Smith shrewdly remarked, not problems of administration but policy in its narrowest sense of getting your men *there*. Once there, the remedies for social ills would come of themselves—to them they seem almost *too* obvious to be discussed. Lees-Smith is an exceptionally attractive person, gentle and cultivated, with a strong will, high purpose, excellent manners and temper, and intelligence, lucid and slight in texture—sufficient for an instructor of the ordinary man. We have taken him on as lecturer on local government in Percy Ashley's place at the School of Economics. He has not Percy Ashley's broad knowledge, and amazing memory and capacity for work, nor his ambition, but I fancy we shall find his intellectual inferiority outweighed by his superior charm and finer moral nature. We need some moral distinction in the professoriate—at present there is a note of hard efficiency. Percy Ashley remains as lecturer on economic history: he has been promoted to an expert's place in the Board of Trade and has married a rich Jewess.

September 16th.—Whittingehame is an unattractive mansion, with large formal rooms and passages, elaborate furniture and heavy luxury totally without charm, somewhat cold in the fireless September phase. The atmosphere of gracious simplicity, warm welcome, intellectual interest, is all the more strikingly personal to the family that inhabits it. The four women, sisters and sisters-in-law, are in themselves remarkable—Alice Balfour neither brilliant nor very capable, but singularly loving, direct and refined, with talents both artistic and scientific wholly sacrificed to the endless detail entailed by her brother's political career and patriarchal establishment; Mrs. Sidgwick, weirdly silent but also the soul of veracity and moral refinement, open-minded, too, in a limited way; Lady Betty (Gerald's wife) a woman of quite unusual delightfulness, good to look at, sweet to listen to, original in purpose and extraordinarily gracious in disposition. Even Lady Frances, whom I expected to dislike, was attractive in her impulsive indiscretions and straightforward friendliness, with her vivid wit and large experience of political affairs. As kind as kind could be were these four women to me on the day of our arrival. In the afternoon " Prince Arthur " arrived from North Berwick—a veritable prince of the establishment —the mediaeval and saintly knight Gerald, and the boor, Eustace, completing the party. Some dozen children hovered round at intervals, but did not join us.

What shall I say of our visit? Too self-consciously Arthur's " latest friend " to be quite pleasant, the party each night becoming a watched *tête-à-tête* between us two—the rest of the company sitting round, as

Sidney said, " making conversation ". In fact, the great man is naturally enough too completely the centre of the gathering—without perhaps deserving the position of pre-eminence—all the family worshipping him and waiting on his fancies. " A Prime Minister of the ' little white people '," I said sometimes to myself, " without any guiding social purpose, floated to leadership without any strong desire to lead anywhere in particular." Charm he has—almost too obviously —a genius for destructive criticism of the logic of other people's ideas, but not the remotest desire to verify his own by testing his order of thought by the order of things. It is always theories that he is building up or pulling down in his mind, when he is not merely playing the game of office-holding or office-getting. Does he ever think of the state of affairs and wish to alter it? He was contemplating a treatise on economics. I suggested that there were only two things to be done in economics: either a mere sweeping away of fallacies—comparatively easy and somewhat futile, but a task for which he was extraordinarily fitted; or a concrete study of phenomena, say, the course of trade and the effect of different kinds of taxation on it—a task that demanded the devotion of a lifetime and, therefore, one which he could *not* undertake. But I pressed him to undertake a quite other work—a careful account of his own experience of political life and great administrative affairs— to be published after his retirement and, perhaps, even after his death. But I doubt whether he takes my suggestion either negative or positive. I learnt little about him on this visit except that he is self-absorbed and lonely, seldom consulting anyone. " Brother Arthur is independent of human companionship ", sighed Lady Betty, somewhat hurt perhaps that even Gerald was not admitted to his complete confidence. Gerald is really a more attractive nature, though far less substantial than Arthur—a dreamy, poetic, metaphysical soul, saintly in his motives and subtle in his thoughts, but with small capacity for transacting business and lacking broad sympathies. He is unspoilt—has none of the self-consciousness and egotism which lies beneath Arthur's perfect manner—has not developed the cunning of the leader, fearing deposition, or the sentimentality of the lifelong philanderer, never thoroughly in love. For philanderer, refined and consummate, is Prince Arthur, accustomed always to make others feel what he fails to feel himself. How many women has he inspired with a discontent with their life and life companion, haunted with the perpetual refrain " if only it had been so ". Not a good or wholesome record, and demoralising to the man himself—and not a worthy substitute for some sort of social fervour. But this is a harsh judgement—one aspect only of the man. Deeper down there are other and better things—but they were hidden from me in these hours of philandering!

From the glamour and charm of Whittingehame we cycled with Lady Betty to Berwick—a happy ride chatting over " brother Arthur ", Gerald and his literary and philosophical tastes, social questions— altogether the opening of a pleasant friendship. The dirty crowded railway station from which we saw her off to Whittingehame was a fit prelude to our five days in Berwick.

Dirty stuffy lodgings [at Berwick]—seven hours a day working at records in a cellar without windows and lit only by three gas jets brought us back to our work-a-day life. But the hours in the cellar passed rapidly in the fascinating pursuit of tearing the facts out of volume after volume of MS. minutes—far more voluminous and interesting than we had expected. The Berwick of to-day is a god-forsaken place, inhabited by a dull and somewhat drunken population, no municipal amenities, no leadership, the freemen demoralised by their share in the common land (about £8 a year) which serves merely as a sort of outdoor relief, the corporation no better for its £10,000 a year from rents—these simply making the rates lighter for the other landlords. All the private enterprise seems run with insufficient capital and brains; the pretty coast scenery has been spoilt by mean rows of cottages and smoky works, the only attractive feature being the ramparts made by the national Government.

A Sunday at Hutton Castle with the Jack Tennants—restful and unexciting—and then on to Alnwick. Here again we reposed in dirt— this time at the inn, but we found useful material in the records, and enjoyed the novelty of lunching with the ducal family—a courtesy we owed to Lady Frances Balfour. This glimpse of " high life " interested us. . . .

Of course, I got nothing to eat but peas and apricot tart—the six men servants, finding I did not take the regulation dishes, refused to hand me anything else, denied me the bread sauce, the plain pudding or another piece of bread. His Grace was far too much absorbed in his own dignity to note that I was unprovided with the necessaries of life. The poor man was in fact struggling to keep us at a distance, scared by the assumed attempt of these notable Socialists to get access to the records of his manor courts. He had, owing to the pressure of Lady Frances, secured for us access to the records of the Alnwick Borough (now a private company of freemen) and he was determined that he would do no more. This determination made him, at first, almost dis-courteous to me—which I, discovering, turned round and talked to the daughters. At the other end of the table, I heard Sidney discoursing pleasantly with the Duchess—indeed, if it had not been for ourselves it seems to me the party would have eaten its meal in heavy silence. When the Duke awoke to the fact that we were not otherwise than well-bred people, not likely to push our desires on an unwilling host, and that we were ready to talk pleasantly on other subjects, he relaxed a little, and after lunch discussed county council business with Sidney— self-important but not otherwise objectionable. Before we left, the Duchess most graciously showed us the most beautiful of the pictures and handed us on to a uniformed gentleman to show us the dungeon. It never occurred to her to introduce us to their librarian—an eminent historian of the county—whom she had told me was in the castle! As we strode away through the embattled portals of the Percys—with its pretentious magnificence—we felt we were leaving behind the atmosphere of a tomb in which several worthy and one distinguished soul (the poor Duchess) were shrinking up, day by day, into puppets walking their respective parts in the ducal establishment, with a strange combination of grandiose self-complacency and dull melancholy.

And what has been the result of the castle of the Percys on the life of the little town? That problem interested us because at Berwick there was no social leadership—but otherwise much the same condition past and present. The Percys have at any rate held up the standard of personal morality and physical self-control—they are a pious, dutiful and decorous family—prone to good works. They are public-spirited —the stupid stiff Duke being a competent chairman of the county council and an active magistrate, appearing when he ought to appear, and saying what he ought to say. Moreover, his property is well-managed; the house property which he owns in Alnwick is not only sanitary and well-built but positively charming in its varied architecture and well-kept gardens. Instead of the dirty crowded station of Berwick, there is a dignified erection to welcome the traveller, with spacious, clean public rooms. Surrounding the little town are the beautiful gardens and parklands of Alnwick Castle—much of which is open to the townsfolk. All this counts for good. On the other hand, the castle officials are, if they are of superior grade, aloof and somewhat insolently indifferent to the town life; if they are inferior, perpetually touting for shillings and sixpences to give admission to this or that sanctuary—even when it is known to be open to the public. There is a heavy atmosphere of snobbishness—all folk having their eyes fixed on the castle, fearful of its displeasure and anxious for the slightest sign of approval. And, in spite of his eminent worthiness, the Duke, who is seated on a pinnacle, is just a stupid, commonplace Englishman—made stupider and more commonplace by his lifelong entombment in the magnificence of the Percys of Northumberland.

September 22nd.—This day we begin our autumnal session and, except for three or four days' visits, shall not be away from London until Christmas. I start Mrs. Spencer on Monday on her enquiry into administration by boards of guardians; Miss Woodcock and Miss Phillips I have already started off on the medical relief and public health enquiry. Miss Longman is hard at it, preparing her memorandum on central policy (1847–71) on the plan of mine. What I have to arrange is to oversee all this investigation without interfering with my own absorption in the second volume of our work, which must come out this time next year. Refreshed by our fortnight's change we are setting out to cast, in final form, the first chapters; our work at Lower Copse having given us enough inkling of those two pivotal chapters to enable this to be done. Apart from my own enquiries, I do not intend to let the Commission take up much of my time—I shall slack it, in respect to listening to evidence, and bother neither myself nor the Commission with cross-examination. But all my self-control and new-found strength will be needed to pull this programme through.

October 1st.—First meeting of the Commission after the recess—all very friendly—to discuss our future plans. Lord George brought forward some proposals to delegate to committees the formulating of provisional general ideas which might be the basis of our report. He threw out for consideration the abolition of the boards of guardians and the creation of an authority for a larger area in order to run segregated institutions, a new machinery for determining under which class a pauper came, the drawing together of charitable agencies under a statutory authority, the possible abolition of outdoor relief, the compulsory detention of certain classes of paupers; consideration of the conditions which lead to pauperism; settlement—all these were to be considered by two committees into which the whole Commission might be divided. He invited us to discuss.

Charles Booth opened with an almost passionate denunciation of the policy of patching. He wanted to go back to the principles of 1834, start fresh from those principles and apply them drastically. This could not be done by the Poor Law Commissioners of 1835–47. They had enough to do to reduce the 15,000 parishes to 600 unions and introduce some measure of uniformity. We must at all hazard get rid of out-relief.

Mr. Phelps continued the discussion on the chairman's suggestion. He began by saying that the agreed with Mr. Booth. But he immediately started an entirely different line which will bring him, if he follows it, very much to mine. In the North of England he had found that the whole question of pauperism was a small matter: what people were thinking about was how to improve and raise the whole of the population by the advancement of public health and education. In this effort, whether or not persons were destitute, was an irrelevant issue; if it was desirable that they should be treated, then they had to be treated, whether they were rich or poor. He should favour taking large classes of cases out of the poor law.

This brought C. S. Loch to the rescue of the principles of 1834. He did not understand Mr. Phelps's suggestion, he agreed with Mr. Booth. We must have a national organisation of relief with local charitable agencies.

Bentham followed him. We must mark off for stigma the dependants of the state—there must be no blurring of the lines between persons who were supporting themselves and those that were being supported out of the rates—whether on account of old age, sickness or unemployment.

Hancock Nunn followed suit with an eloquent defence of a rigid test of destitution *plus* organised charitable agencies and provident societies. Quite a little sermon, in admirable words, did the little man give us on the principles of 1834 *plus* the C.O.S.

No other member of the Commission spoke at length: Provis warned the Commission that it would be very difficult to rearrange areas because of local jealousies; Downes protested that we had as yet no evidence warranting the abolition of the guardians. But it was evident the Commission as a whole was still on the old lines of restricting all collective provision to the technically destitute, with a view to diminishing collective expenditure on the poor. Two committees were proposed —one on indoor and the other on outdoor relief—to consider proposals. As I wanted to keep my Monday mornings free, and as I thought the time had not arrived for pushing my views, I quietly said that I did not feel sufficiently at one with the Commission to co-operate usefully in the discussion at this early stage, rather giving them to understand that I should have to have my own report. This is the line I am now taking. As I fancy they will be more anxious to meet me if I do so, even if I eventually decide to throw in my lot with the Commission or any section of it. Discussion now is premature and I think a waste of time. But it is pleasant to find that there is no tension between myself and any of the other commissioners. It is generally understood that I am undertaking a good slice of work on documents, exactly as Charles Booth is on statistics. The first part of my memorandum on central policy is to be circulated to the whole Commission.

The week before the Commission met we had a most pleasant two days with the George Hamiltons at Deal Castle. Certainly those two are the simplest-mannered, kindest and most public-spirited aristocrats I have ever come across—not intellectual but quite open-minded and anxious to understand the point of view of other classes of the community. I think we and they thoroughly like each other in private life —though the chairman finds the " trusty and well-beloved Beatrice Webb, wife of Sidney Webb " somewhat of a handful. He talked much about his former colleagues in late Conservative Governments: Dizzy is his hero—Salisbury's memory he respects, Joe he has a " sentiment " for as a warm-hearted, impulsive and forceful enthusiast —somewhat of the " vulgar boss " in his manners, but genuinely a patriot. Towards Arthur Balfour he is cool: thinks that his ingrained laziness, encouraged by his contact with the brilliant but silly " Souls ", and his tendency to regard politics as only one part of a somewhat amusing game, has resulted in devious ways, disloyal to colleagues and upsetting to the party. Also, his sense of decorum in public affairs was offended by Balfour's cliquey friendships. " When Salisbury sat at the head of the table at 10 Downing Street we were all addressed by our official designations—the Secretary for the Colonies, the President of the Board of Trade and so on. When Balfour took his place, Cabinets degenerated into cliquey conversations between ' Arthur ' and ' Bob ' and ' George '—sometimes almost unintelligible in their intimate allusions, to the outer circle of the Cabinet. I was one of the old gang of youthful friendships, but I always felt such an atmosphere to be objectionable in the conduct of great affairs by a group of men representing different interests and coming from different sections of the governing class—perhaps in some instances even hostile to one another —at any rate not on the terms of personal friendship."

Public spirit, good feeling and unselfconscious dignity, seem to me to characterise our chairman: large views or capacity for transacting business on a great scale he has not, and no inkling of technical knowledge or even much appreciation of it in others. In administration he must have been a caretaker, but a modest caretaker ready to listen to those whose character and intelligence he respected—he may therefore have arrived at some reforms and not have got much credit for them— but I suspect he usually remained in the rut.

October 18*th.*—H. G. Wells gave an address to the Fabian Society on Socialism for the middle-classes, ending up with an attack on the family. Some of the new members welcomed his denunciation, but the meeting, which was crowded, was against him, for the simple reason that he had nothing constructive to suggest. Since then I have read *The Days of a Comet*, which ends with a glowing anticipation of promiscuity in sexual relations. The argument is one that is familiar to most intellectuals—it has often cropped up in my own mind and has seemed to have some validity. Friendship between particular men and women has an enormous educational value to both (especially to the woman). Such a friendship is practically impossible (or, at any rate, impossible between persons who are attractive to each other—and, therefore, most remunerative as friends) without physical intimacy; you do not, as a matter of fact, get to know any man thoroughly except as his beloved and his lover—if you could have been the beloved of the dozen ablest men you have known it would have greatly extended your knowledge of human nature and human affairs. This, I believe, is true of our present rather gross state of body and mind. But there remains the question whether, with all the perturbation caused by such intimacies, you would have any brain left to think with? I know that I should not—and I fancy that other women would be even worse off in that particular. Moreover, it would mean a great increase in sexual emotion for its own sake and not for the sake of bearing children. And that way madness lies. This is omitting the whole social argument against promiscuity, which is the strongest. Regarding each individual as living in a vacuum with no other obligations than the formation of his or her own character, I still reject " free love " as a method of development. I suggested to Sidney for consideration whether our philosophy was not tending to the restriction of all physical desires to the maintenance of health in the individual and the race—meaning by health, the longest continued and greatest intensity of mental activity —and to the continuance of the species at its highest level of quality?

H. G. Wells is, I believe, merely gambling with the idea of free love—throwing it out to see what sort of reception it gets—without responsibility for its effect on the character of hearers. It is this recklessness that makes Sidney dislike him. I think it important *not* to dislike him: he is going through an ugly time, and we must stand by him for his own sake and for the good of the cause of collectivism. If he will let us—that is to say. I am not sure he is not getting to dislike us in our well-regulated prosperity.

Sidney's articles on the birth-rate published in the *Times* were a great popular success—a stroke for collectivism. It is strange that no one of the correspondents suggested that voluntary restriction was wrong—Bradlaugh and Besant justified at the bar of public opinion of to-day—perhaps, not of to-morrow!

The following correspondence published in the *Times*, and attached to the diary entry of November 5, 1906, needs a word of explanation. In the spring of 1889, I took what afterwards seemed to me a false step in joining with others in signing the then notorious manifesto, drafted by Mrs. Humphry Ward and some other distinguished ladies, against the political enfranchisement of women, thereby arousing the hostility of ardent women brain-workers; and, in the eyes of the general public, undermining my reputation as an impartial investigator of women's questions. When pressed by Frederic Harrison and James Knowles (the well-known editor of the *Nineteenth Century*) to write a reasoned answer to Mrs. Fawcett's indignant retort to this reactionary document, I realised my mistake. Though I delayed my public recantation for nearly twenty years, I immediately and resolutely withdrew from that particular controversy. Why I was at that time an anti-feminist in feeling is easy to explain, though impossible to justify. Conservative by temperament, and anti-democratic through social environment, I reacted against the narrow outlook and exasperated tone of some of the pioneers of women's suffrage, with their continuous clamour for the *Rights of Women*. Also, my dislike of the current parliamentary politics of the Tory and Whig " ins " and " outs " seemed a sort of argument against the immersion of women in this atmosphere. But the root of my anti-feminism lay in the fact that I had never myself suffered the disabilities assumed to arise from my sex. Quite the contrary; if I had been a man, self-respect, family pressure and the public opinion of my class would have pushed me into a money-making profession; as a mere woman, I could carve out a career of disinterested research. Moreover, in the craft I had chosen a woman was privileged. As an investigator, she aroused less suspicion than a man, and, through making the process entertaining to the persons concerned, she gained more inside information. Further, in those days, a competent female writer on economic questions had, to an enterprising editor, actually a scarcity value. Thus, she secured immediate publication and, to judge by my own experience, was paid a higher rate than that obtained by male competitors of equal standing.

November 5th.—For some time I have felt the old prejudice evaporating [I write in my diary]. And as the women suffragists were being battered about rather badly, and coarse-grained men were saying coarse-grained things, I thought I might as well give a friendly pull to get the thing out of the mud, even at the risk of getting a little spattered myself. What is, perhaps, more likely is that I shall be thought, by some, to be a pompous prig. The movement will stand some of that element now!

Times, November 5th, 1906

" SIR,—I have just received the enclosed letter from Mrs. Sidney Webb. As she generously allows me to make any use of it I like, may I beg the favour of its insertion in *The Times*?

" Those who have been working for many years for women's suffrage naturally regard with extreme satisfaction the adhesion to the movement of two of the ablest women who have hitherto opposed it, Mrs. Creighton and Mrs. Sidney Webb. Mrs. Creighton's change of view was chronicled in your columns about a week ago.—Yours obediently,

" MILLICENT GARRETT FAWCETT."

41 GROSVENOR ROAD
WESTMINSTER EMBANKMENT, NOV. 2

" DEAR MRS. FAWCETT,—You once asked me to let you know if I ceased to object to the grant of the electoral franchise to women. The time has come when I feel obliged to do so.

" My objection was based principally on my disbelief in the validity of any ' abstract rights ', whether to votes or to property, or even to ' life, liberty and the pursuit of happiness '. I prefer to regard life as a series of obligations—obligations of the individual to the community and of the community to the individual. I could not see that women, as women, were under any particular obligation to take part in the conduct of government.

" I have been told that the more spiritually minded Eastern readily acquiesces in the material management of his native country by what he regards as the Anglo-Saxon ' man of affairs '. In the same way, I thought that women might well be content to leave the rough and tumble of party politics to their mankind, with the object of concentrating all their own energies on what seemed to me their peculiar social obligations, the bearing of children, the advancement of learning, and the handing on from generation to generation of an appreciation of the spiritual life.

" Such a division of labour between men and women is, however, only practicable if there is among both sections alike, a continuous feeling of consent to what is being done by government as their common agent. This consciousness of consent can hardly avoid being upset if the work of government comes actively to overlap the particular obligations of an excluded class. If our Indian administrators were to interfere with the religious obligations of Hindus or Mahomedans, British rule in India would, I suppose, come to an end. It seems to me that something analogous to this is happening in the Europe of to-day with regard to the particular obligations of women. The rearing of children, the advancement of learning, and the promotion of the spiritual life—which I regard as the particular obligations of women—are, it is clear, more and more becoming the main preoccupations of the community as a whole. The legislatures of this century are, in one country after another, increasingly devoting themselves to these subjects. Whilst I rejoice in much of this new development of politics, I think it adequately accounts for the increasing restiveness of women. They are, in my opinion, rapidly losing their consciousness of consent in the work of government and are even feeling a positive obligation to take part in directing this new activity. This is, in my view, not a claim to rights or an abandonment of women's particular obligations, but a desire more effectually to fulfil their functions by sharing the control of state action in those directions.

" The episodes of the last few weeks complete the demonstration that it is undesirable that this sense of obligation should manifest itself in unconstitutional forms. We may grant that persistent interruption of public business is lowering to the dignity of public life. But it is cruel to put a fellow-citizen of strong convictions in the dilemma of political ineffectiveness or unmannerly breaches of the peace. If the consciousness of non-consent is sufficiently strong, we can hardly blame the public-spirited women who by their exclusion from constitutional methods of asserting their views are driven to the latter alternative, at the cost of personal suffering and masculine ridicule. To call such behaviour vulgar is an undistinguished and I may say an illiterate use of language. The way out of this unpleasant dilemma, it seems to me, is to permit this growing consciousness among women—that their particular social obligations compel them to claim a share in the conduct of political affairs—to find a constitutional channel.

" The reasoning involves, of course, the admission to the franchise of women as women, whether married or single, propertied or wage-earning.

" It is, I feel, due to you that I should tell you of my change of attitude, and I thought you would perhaps be interested in my reasons.—Yours very truly,

" BEATRICE WEBB."

November 21st.—Haldane came in for a quiet talk—during an enlarged dinner hour. He is completely absorbed in his office, thinking out the problems of army administration and attempting to adapt the experience of Germany to the character and ways of the English officer. Among other developments, there is that connected with the School of Economics—a permanent departmental committee of business magnates, distinguished soldiers, Sidney and H. J. Mackinder. We are to have forty officers to instruct in business methods, and, in return, to receive about £2000 a year. It all goes to build up the School as a national institution for administrative science, which is, perhaps, an aspect of the scheme which appeals to us more than the honour of instructing the army. On general politics, Haldane gave us the impression that the P.M. offers no lead to his Cabinet—allows each Minister to go his own way and relies on his personal popularity, and perpetual concessions, when a whip reports disaffection, to carry his huge majority in favour of the policy, or no policy, of each department. " But I see little of the House of Commons ", beamingly remarked our War Minister. " My own department takes up all my thought and time." He was very much interested in my poor law medical relief and public health enquiry; in Sidney's report as to the Progressives and London education, and the possibilities arising out of the Lords' amendments of the Education Bill. He hinted (perhaps that we might report it to our friends the churchmen) that the Government would not accept the Lords' amendments, and that, if the Lords refused to pass the Bill, the Commons would refuse to vote the education grants. Sidney said afterwards to me that this refusal of supplies would be impracticable.

Meanwhile, it looks like a *débâcle* of the Progressive forces at the March L.C.C. election. We always thought that the first Liberal Ministry would see us defeated. We are even getting anxious about the Deptford seat. But Sidney is really very unconcerned. " I have done my level best for London these last fourteen years, and, if London does not desire my services, there are plenty of causes to which I could devote my energies." He would like, for instance, to give more time both to our own research and also the School of Economics. Nevertheless, he is putting a good deal of thought into the organisation of the election, and means to make a hard fight for it. Administrative work in the afternoons exactly suits his temperament. And, during the last year or so, he has been singularly happy in the L.C.C. work. He feels without responsibility for the general Progressive policy, since they have turned him off the party committee and never consult him. And yet he has got all his pet schemes through and feels that in the last three years he has placed both university and secondary education on a thoroughly sound public foundation. " Most of my work they can't undo even if I am turned out ", he chuckles to himself. But it is sad to see the complete break-up of the old gang who have worked together so loyally and heartily these last fourteen years. For it is not only Sidney who is separated from the rest—among themselves there is no good-comradeship; and, whenever any of them talk confidentially with Sidney, it is to abuse the other. Wood, Dickinson, Collins, Benn and even Cornwall, all have their eye on the Treasury bench—and it is clear that only one will be taken. Alas! for human jealousies. What a privilege to have work—and work one loves,—without the sordid element of competition.

Dined the other night with Herbert Samuel at the House—now a sedate young Minister. Talked to Whitelegge of the Home Office about my scheme, and to young Acland about general politics. The day after A. J. B. came in for the dinner hour—tried to make him friends with Alfred Cripps, but it did not come off. The great personage dislikes my " little jewel of an advocate " and the latter feeling this dislike was singularly unattractive—both too free in his manner and too anxious to please. They touch on each other's worst sides: Alfred's self-assertiveness, and A. J. B.'s intolerance for anyone or anything that does not, at the moment, please him. But, in spite of the friction, it was a display of Prince Arthur's admirable manners—and the party went off with superficial pleasantness and ease. He hurried off when I left the dining-room. Apparently, the hard fighting with small forces is far more agreeable than thinking out an administrative policy. He is, in the main, a negative man and shines most in opposition.

November 22nd.—Lord Milner, dining here last night again, laid bare his materialist view of a nation's policy. He was upholding the Bismarckian axiom that a statesman had no right to go beyond the pecuniary or, at any rate, the material interests of his country. " It is exactly like the position of a trustee in private life. As a trustee you have no right to consider anything else than the business interests of your clients—you have no right, for instance, to satisfy some philanthropic impulse out of trust funds—it is positively immoral." For the time I was somewhat nonplussed: all I could retort was that you were at liberty to act according to the highest business honour and that this intangible " business honour " did, as a matter of fact, rule out a good deal of action dictated by bare pecuniary consideration. But I see now there is a more fundamental answer to this materialist view of statesmanship. Who decides that the statesman shall be the trustee of the *business interests of the community* to the exclusion of other matters? Why should he not consider himself the trustee of the national character, or the national intellect, or for that matter of the spiritual advancement of the people? The analogy of the " business trust " is a false one. Here, the character of the trust is exactly specified. It need not be so. If a child is left you, with full power to do what you think right for its welfare, still more if you were specifically required to make it into a saint, or a man of science, you might be justified in advising it to devote the whole of its energies and its property to religion, or the discovery of truth. The statesman has no *specified* trust: he is assumed to be trustee of the good of the community. He may choose to interpret the good spiritually or intellectually, or in terms of simple happiness, or in terms of wealth or in terms of Empire. All he is required to do is to state to the people what he conceives to be " the good " so that he shall not wield power on false pretences. But I see no reason to accord pre-eminence to material wealth, or to the extent of dominion, as the purpose of the statesman's trusteeship.

But though Lord Milner has a low ideal of the national purpose—and curiously enough no consciousness that there could be any other ideal—he is a strict believer in the " rules of the game "; he would, I think, be far more scrupulous in his personal methods of carrying out his ideal than many a man whose aim was higher. And, undoubtedly, he is disinterested and public-spirited. That is why my dominant feeling towards him is one of personal respect.

November 30th.—H. G. Wells, who was staying here for two nights, first justified the last chapters of *The Days of the Comet* by asserting that it was a work of art and, therefore, could not be criticised from the standpoint of morality. " When Michael Angelo displayed groups of nude figures in stone or colour, it does not follow that he desired to see all his acquaintances sprawling about without clothes "—a specious retort to my criticism. However, he afterwards admitted that he thought " free-er love " would be the future relation of the sexes when we had got over the sordid stage of the masculine proprietorship of the woman. " At present, any attempt to realise this free-er love means a network of low intrigue, assumes and, therefore, creates an atmosphere of gross physical desire—but this is only an incident of a morality based on the notion of private property in women. No decent person has a chance of experimenting in free-er love to-day—the relations between men and women are so hemmed in by law and convention. To experiment you must be base; hence to experiment starts with being damned." There is, of course, truth in this argument: it has a negative value,—detracts from the argument against free love based on the disastrous results of present-day experience. But I cling to the thought that man will only evolve upwards by the subordination of his physical desires and appetites to the intellectual and spiritual side of his nature. Unless this evolution be the purpose of the race, I despair—and wish only for the extinction of human consciousness. Without this hope—without this faith—I could not struggle on. It is this purpose, and this purpose only, that gives a meaning to the constantly recurring battles of good and evil within one's own nature—and to one's persistent endeavour to find the ways and means of combating the evil habits of the mass of men. Oh! for a Church that would weld into one living force all who hold this faith, with the discipline and the consolations fitted to sustain their endeavour.

As it is, I find myself once or twice a week in St. Paul's—listening to the music of the psalms and repeating, with childlike fervour, the words of the old Elizabethan prayers. It is this recreation that sustains me in these days of murky feeling. Perhaps I am suffering from a sort of brain fag. I long for the rest of a long and complete change of thought and scene. But there is no holiday for us until 1910.

Sidney making up his mind to retire from the L.C.C. in 1910 before we go abroad for our Sabbatical year. " I want to be rid of electioneering and all the devious ways of the elected person. Eighteen years is a fair term of service." His desires turn more and more to investigation and constructive thinking, and to the organisation of the social sciences. Administration he is willing to go on with, if those concerned are ready to have him as a co-opted colleague. " But I am weary of doing harmless things for ulterior motives: it is, after a time, irksome to distribute prizes because an election is at hand." He feels he has earned a right to be fastidious in his methods and single-minded in his aims. A luxury, I think, we elderly folk ought to be allowed.

December 14th.— This is an interesting vision of the Webb attitude towards religion by a learned and saintlike Dominican.[1] Clearly he has himself very much the same body of thought and feeling that is represented by that most remarkable epistle of Father Tyrrell to a Catholic professor in trouble about his soul—*A Much Abused Letter.* In this letter the passage, pp. 67-83, expressed my own faith in a spiritual force and the need for a Church—a communion of those who hold the faith—far more beautifully and completely than I could express it myself. Where I begin to doubt and differ is when he insists, pp. 83-8, on Christ as the central figure round which the faith of all races, and all ages, must necessarily revolve. Jesus of Nazareth seems to me only one and, perhaps, not the most perfect embodiment of the ideal of faith. It is, in fact, more difficult for me to accept the *Person* than the *Institution*—the person is limited by circumstances, temperament and capacity for expression, and even by the day in which he lived—the institution is indefinite in its power of experience of expression, comprehension and growth. But Tyrrell's letter is a plea for conformity to the church you are born in, not a plea for joining the Catholic Church.

December 18th.—A general palaver—the last day of the autumn session of the Poor Law Commission. The two committees—on indoor and outdoor relief respectively—brought up the interim reports containing certain abstract proposals—definitions of a most controversial

---

[1] This was the Dominican, Father Vincent McNabb, afterwards transferred to the headship of a more important London Monastery, who has [1937] remained an occasional friendly correspondent of " the Webbs " on public affairs.

character. These reports were apparently to lie on the table—being neither rejected nor confirmed—and the two committees proposed to continue their labours. The chairman, however, had taken fright at the thought of half the Commission accepting these abstract resolutions: it would, he suggested, shackle them in the consideration of any report he might eventually draft. So he proposed that the committees should cease to meet. This naturally did not please the one or two members of each committee who had drafted these propositions—they were delighted with their definitions and felt they were laying down the lines upon which the majority report should proceed. And it certainly did seem hard on Loch and Bentham, who had both slaved to get these propositions drafted and passed, that they should not be permitted to finish their work of determining upon what principles outdoor and indoor relief should proceed—since they had been expressly commissioned to do this. " If we don't continue meeting, all our labour will be wasted ", they plaintively remarked. I managed to make my own position clear in refusing to take part in their deliberations, and said I did not agree with either report. " But if any members of the Commission feel that they are gaining light by these discussions, why should not they go on discussing? If one committee met one Monday morning, and the other committee met the other Monday, the rest of the Commission can go on taking evidence." But the members of the committee did not like this way of looking at their labour. " If the Commission is not going to attend to our recommendations," said Bentham testily, " it is not much use our wasting our time over them." So no decision was arrived at and I assume we shall drift on as before. Meanwhile, Loch has got on the scent of my various enquiries. He objected to my circularising the M.O.H.s. I retorted that, anyhow, I had a perfect right to ask for information as an individual commissioner, and, as regards public health I had actually been deputed to prepare a memorandum. " We were not very wise when we put the matter into the hands of an individual commissioner ", Lord George sadly remarked. The odd thing is that now they are calling M.O.H.s selected by me—four for Lancashire out of twenty witnesses—and the whole enquiry is drifting in the direction of sickness as a cause of pauperism. But I shall be surprised if, sooner or later, I don't get into hot water over my special enquiries, and the means I am taking to get facts. Poor Lord George—what between Charles Booth, C. S. Loch and me, he is going to have a hard time.

1907

From the entries of the diary of 1906, the reader will have gathered that, during its first year of office, the Royal

Commission on the Poor Law drifted away from being an enquiry into the disease of pauperism, into an investigation of the disease of destitution. For, while it was clear that the only direct way of restricting relief out of the rates to the destitute, and thus diminishing pauperism, was by making their condition less eligible than that of the lowest-paid labourer, this policy not only left undiminished the mass destitution outside the poor law, but also, in the case of the infant, the child, the child-bearing mother, the sick and the mentally defective, actually increased it. Moreover, so far as the able-bodied worker was concerned, all that the deterrent policy did was to induce him to accept any job which afforded more freedom and comfort than the able-bodied " test " workhouse, which was, in fact, a penal establishment of a peculiarly repulsive character. But what if there were no jobs offering for hundreds of thousands of workers, men and women, young and old? If so, the abolition of relief, except under penal conditions, not only increased mass destitution, with its inevitable mendicancy and vagrancy, but, as many witnesses asserted, actually multiplied the number of criminals; the energetic and self-willed man preferring a life of theft or fraud, with its off-chance of prison, to the certainty of daily existence in one of the able-bodied " test " workhouses established by some boards of guardians with the approval of the Local Government Board. Hence some members of the Royal Commission insisted, in season and out, on an immediate investigation by the Commission itself, and by assistant commissioners, of all the various types of destitution.

January 10th, 1907.— . . . Meanwhile the evidence is coming in nicely—my paper on poor law medical relief and public health has started a ball rolling, and it promises, I think, to be a snowball. The idea of universal medical inspection and medical treatment was already afloat: all I have done is to make the Poor Law Commission into a landing-stage. The reports of the assistant commissioners are all pointing away from bad administration as *the* cause of pauperism and towards bad conditions among large classes of the population as the overwhelmingly important fact—conditions which, if we are to check destitution, must be changed, and if we do not see that destitution is checked, it is, thanks to democracy, too late in the day to check pauperism. That is the little lesson the C.O.S. will have to learn through the Commission. But, if I am to carry the majority along with me any part of the way, I shall have to be discreet—I do not altogether despair of getting my transference of poor law medical relief to the public health authorities accepted by the majority. Meanwhile, whilst I am more or less engineering the evidence in my direction, C. S. Loch is continuing his outdoor relief committee—against the strongly expressed desire of the chairman. He evidently feels that he is gaining something tangible by drafting these propositions and getting a section of the Commission to agree to them. I am clearly better out of this business: the less I say on abstract questions the better—it only irritates or frightens the bulk of my fellow-commissioners. I lack discretion in the spoken word—to that extent I lack manners.

January 28th.—The medical investigator is appointed—and turns out to be Mr. McVail, M.O.H. for Dumbartonshire—nominated obviously by my friend Jeffrey (the Scotch secretary). Certainly, the ways of the Commission are past explanation. They appoint an investigator to look after and counteract me and my machinations to transfer medical relief to the public health authority, and they appoint an M.O.H.! I should not have dared to suggest it: it is *almost* sufficiently unfair to the other side to make me protest. And a Scotchman too, naturally biased in favour of *domiciliary treatment*.

At the palaver this morning there was a protest against any more evidence from M.O.H.s. "They are all for one scheme," one member plaintively said; "we know their view now." I compromised on printed précis from eight more—two only to be cross-examined. And, apparently, I am to have the choosing of both those who send in their statements and those who are to be called. I am completely puzzled by the collapse of the C.O.S.—it almost makes me wonder whether I am not under some extraordinary delusion. Is it that they intend to ignore the evidence as quite irrelevant to their report? In that case why don't they hurry to close the enquiry? Or are they getting converted?

February 16th.—Alone in Beachy Head Hotel with a hurricane roaring around. Came here with Sidney completely exhausted—so exhausted that he hardly liked to leave me and return to his electioneering—which is imperative. The exhaustion was brought on by the events—a most tiring five days with the Commission in Yorkshire, and a tempestuous upset in the evidence committee with regard to my special enquiries. As for the first, to a "short hour" worker like myself it was suicidal—running about from 9 A.M. to 5 P.M., then writing a report, then discussion from 9 P.M. to 11 P.M., consequently no sleep. Moreover, my inveterate social instincts always mean that I lavish entertainment on my companions. I don't simply do my work. Following on that, and partly because I was deliberately or carelessly frank about the enquiries I had on hand, I received from the chairman a somewhat curt and crude request to give up investigating on my own account—a sort of badly-delivered message from the evidence committee. I seized the opportunity to regularise the whole situation. Whilst gently complaining that my action had been discussed and condemned in my absence, I laid bare all my doings and ended up by saying politely but firmly that I intended to continue—basing myself on the practice of the Royal Commissions and select committees that I had known. " Splendid," said R. B. Haldane (to whom I submitted the correspondence), " *they* won't encounter you in a hurry again." But all this took a good deal out of me. A Sunday at the Elchos'— pleasant enough but late hours and talk—finished up my strength. I lasted out two days' Commission evidence, and a dinner to some M.O.II.s, and then fled here and completely collapsed with sleeplessness and indigestion. If it were not for my reliance on Sidney's strength, I should almost retire from business. I tremble to think how utterly dependent I am on him—both on his love and on his unrivalled capacity for " putting things through ". When he is late, I get into a panic of fear lest some mishap has befallen him. This fear of losing each other is always present—more with me, I think, than with him. " I don't think about it ", he often says. Sometimes we try to cheer each other in advance by remembering that we have had a happiness which death cannot take from us.

What has again been troubling me is the question of social engagements. I go out hardly at all, and except for business interviews at lunch and dinner entertain even less. But such society as we have, apart from professional society, is tending to become of an aristocratic and fastidious character. This partly because I like brilliant little parties, and interesting folk versed in great affairs, and partly because my reputation of knowing them helps forward the various works we have on hand. But there are grave disadvantages to this " dallying with fashion ". Least of them, perhaps, is the spiteful things that are said— partly by envious folk, partly by fanatics. More important is the drain on energy both financial and personal, that any association with the great world involves. Better clothes, fares to country houses, and most of all the exhaustion of living up to a reputation, or even of " letting myself go ". It seems ludicrous to bother about the question—the amount we do is very little—and any day we could give that little up without a pang. For all that, my conscience about it is not quite easy.

What exactly will be gained by two days' motoring with A. J. B. at Stanway? The only reply is that I have asked him to dinner to meet the two most accomplished of my M.O.H.s—the keenest for a new idea—and I have even bored him by sending him the pamphlet on poor law medical relief and public health. " It is the sort of reform that the Conservatives might bring about ", say I—and go to Stanway.

February 24th.—A week to-day, and we shall know the fate of the Progressive majority in general, and Sidney in particular. There has been a torrent of malicious denunciation of the Progressives by the " yellow " press, backed discreetly by the respectable Conservative papers. This time the Moderates are being run by the " yellow " press —almost run on commercial lines—the *Daily Mail* and the *Daily Express* taking command of the campaign. The aid of the Conservative Party has not been invoked, the L.C.C. Moderates, themselves, are completely overlooked—almost snubbed. But the Harmsworth-Pearson gang are shovelling out money, using their daily and evening papers as great advertisement sheets for the Municipal Reformers and against the Progressives. It will be an amazing testimony to John Bull's steady head if there is not a complete smash of the Progressives. How exactly Sidney stands compared to other Progressives, it is difficult to say. On the figures of past elections, he ought to be in, if there are forty Progressives left—perhaps even if there are thirty. But there is Non-conformist disaffection to his personality, a split between Liberals and Labour over the last parliamentary and borough council elections, leaving soreness; and also, the fact that he is identified with high rates —the 20s. in every £ cry which is being used as malignantly as the enemy knows how. On the other hand, he has the Church and the Catholics on his side: he is personally popular with all sections of the Progressive Party at Deptford, he has a record of long service and he is distinguished. In electioneering, I fear, I am useless to him. I loathe the whole business, the mechanical office work tires me out of all proportion to the amount I do, finally Sidney does not encourage me to sacrifice strength to it. The result is, I fear, a certain feeling of discouragement on the part of the women workers down at Deptford— very naturally they feel, " if the wife does not work, why should we? " The fact that I send down a private secretary does not quite make up for it. If he is beaten I shall regret my apathy—feel that I have been an indifferent helpmate. And a beating I think we are going to get. He is singularly calm, almost indifferent. If the London elector decides against him, he is willing to turn to other work, accepting the check as part of the day's work. Moreover, most public-spirited persons, including ourselves, think it would be better for the other side to come into office: it is clear that some Progressives have to lose seats. There would be a certain abstract justice in Sidney, who has been a bad party man, doing so. You can't both push unpopular opinions, and remain popular. It is only his skill as a manipulator that has enabled him to do it so far. It would be pleasanter if this state of things would last just three years more. But it is unreasonable to expect it.

March 3rd.—Escaped with our bare lives in the general rout. But still here they are, Phillimore and Webb—L.C.C.s again! On Wednesday, the seats were, I am convinced, lost. But we poured some three hundred Fabians into the constituency on polling day, admirably marshalled under eleven captains in eleven committee rooms, and by their dogged work we won the constituency back again by a two hundred and one hundred majority for Webb and Phillimore respectively. A narrow margin, but sufficient. From 8.30 to 8 P.M. I toiled, organising the bringing-up of the slum wards—and G. B. S., W. P. Reeves, E. Pease, Galton, the Spencers and one or two other friends did the same for the other wards. At the end, I felt singularly indifferent as to the result. We had fought hard and really it was a toss-up which ending was the best for us personally. But, now it is all over and we see that the Progressives have been completely smashed, I am proud that my man has survived in spite of his independent attitude. It is a tribute to my boy's personality. How will he find a Council run by the Moderates? And by an overwhelming majority. Not quite so satisfactory as government by a weak majority—the result we desired.

March 18th.—A nasty trick by the remaining " rump " of the Progressives—leaving R. A. Bray off the education committee. A clear case of spite. Bray was on the School Board, then on the education committee—was chairman of a sub-committee. An old member who had only recently come on to the education committee, and who had never been on the School Board, or taken an active part in education, and one new member have been put on by the selection committee. When Sidney protested, one of the committee remarked that Bray was not a good party man. Sidney was very much depressed and almost paralysed. But egged on by me he telegraphed and wrote all over the place, and is arranging for the Moderate majority to intervene, if necessary, to save Bray. That " rump " will have to be kicked and brought to heel—if we fail to give them a kicking over this business of Bray, good-bye to our influence with the Progressive Party. They are a mean lot—arranging the whole thing secretly and springing it on a hurried meeting of the selection committee—expressly and obviously hurried in order to stop Sidney's protest.

A delightful Saturday and Sunday with the Elchos at Stanway,

A. J. B. bringing down his motor. An answer to the last words of my description of the visit to Whittingehame. In his courtly devotion to Lady Elcho, in the intimate and sincere talk about men and thought that seems to be natural to him in her presence, Prince Arthur is at his best. It is clearly an old and persistent sentiment—good sound friendship, with just that touch of romantic regret that it could not have been more, that deepens sex feeling and makes such a relation akin to religious renunciation. One can believe that the relation between these two has always been at the same high level of affectionate friendship, without taint of intrigue. With this background, the intellectual camaraderie of the Conservative leader with the Webbs, dropped also its right place as a slight new thing agreeably stimulating to all concerned. Round about the central figures of the party were a dozen or so accomplished men and maidens, and intermediate between these and the distinguished elders came the fascinating Lady Desborough. " No intellect, but great organising capacity, ought to be the head of a great institution ", was my suggestion as to her characteristics to which her friends agreed. To outward appearance, she is a smart, handsome, cleverish woman—beneath it she has an iron will, excellent temper and methodic mind, but with neither wit nor reasoning power! She was an admirable foil to the beautiful-natured Mary Elcho— neglected wife, devoted and tenderly-loved mother, and adored friend —a beautiful soul in a delicately refined form. Brilliant and pleasant was the talk, as we whirled through the countryside in A. J. B.'s motor, or lounged in the famous hall of Stanway. Amused and interested we undoubtedly were (but hardly rested). What was, I think, achieved, was a wholesome settling of our new friendship. The sensationalism apparent at Whittingehame had wholly departed.

But shall we advance matters by our friendship with A. J. B.? A week ago, I had him to meet the two most eminent of the M.O.H.s, and the two most distinguished of the poor law medical officers. The dinner delighted the medical men, who found themselves subject to A. J. B.'s deferential curiosity on all scientific questions. So far it was wholly to the good, because they were more likely to become Mrs. Webb's whole-hearted allies after that most pleasant evening. But, whether the talk made the slightest practical impression on the leader himself, I could not tell. What interested him clearly was not the side of the discussion which touched the public welfare (with this aspect he was slightly bored), but the merely pathological problems, such as, the relative parts played by bacteria and constitutional tendencies in contracting of disease, the interchangeability of bovine and human tuberculosis, etc. Now and again, I fancy I interested him on the human side; but then he seemed to drift away eluding the issue—

sceptical or indifferent. No virility, either of thought or feeling, in respect to the constitution of society as it affects a human development. That makes one wonder whether, except " for the honour and glory of it ", there is any good purpose served by his friendship? (The very notion of there being a purpose in social intercourse other than amusement and recreation would repel him!) And so we may be playing an elaborate game of cross-purpose, out of which nothing can come but waste of energy—beyond gratified vanity and a little pleasure.

March 22nd.—A brilliant little luncheon, typical of the " Webb " set. Dr. Nansen (now Norwegian Minister), Gerald and Lady Betty Balfour, the Bernard Shaws, Bertrand Russells, Masterman and Lady Desborough, typical in its mixture of opinions, classes, interests—all as jolly as jolly could be—a rapid rush of talk. The present diplomat and past explorer, a fascinating Viking of simple character and romantic strength, a hero out of a saga, perhaps even too much so—with the philosophy of the secularist of 1870, holding that religion is no more than folk-lore and that there is nothing worth considering but the scientific method, the spirit of adventure and a bureaucratic government.

April 10th. Bramdean.—Two weeks and three days happy recess in these little lodgings. For two days (brilliant warm weather) we rested —spending the hours lying out of doors dreaming and reading pleasant literature—lunching and chatting with Georgie [Meinertzhagen] and her children at Brockwood, or toddling round the lanes on our cycles. As a recreation from the wear and tear of the Royal Commission and L.C.C. I plunged into mysticism—mainly Father Tyrrell's *Oil and Wine, Much Abused Letter*, Maeterlinck's *Flower*, Lodge's *The Substance of Faith*, whilst Sidney read books of all degrees and kinds borrowed from Brockwood, with intervals of the fifty volumes of L.G.B. reports that we brought down.

During these two weeks Sidney and I have been hard at work on Royal Commission business. First, we drafted a memorandum on the unemployed—getting out all the expedients that have been tried since 1834, with the evidence we need for coming to a conclusion about them. This is for the palaver on the unemployed that we are to have on the 22nd April—to decide on the course of an enquiry next winter. Then we set ourselves to finish the memorandum on the policy of the central authority—completed the period from 1847 to 1871, and began that of 1871–1906. This we expect to end in about a fortnight's time. Then, I shall have seriously to take up the memorandum on medical relief and public health.[1] I mean to make this as good as I know

---

[1] Afterwards published as *The State and the Doctor*.

375

how. But really the threat of it has already served the original purpose. The statements of the eight M.O.H.s that were called for are rolling in—long elaborate essays in favour of transferring poor law medical relief to public health authorities, and free medical assistance by these. Through fear of it, the Commission has appointed McVail to investigate poor law medical relief, and it is said that he will report in favour of my scheme or something like it. The Scotch evidence, largely owing to Jeffrey's keenness, seems likely to be in the same direction. There is no need for my memorandum. But they shall have it as a supplementary document.

The only set-off against me is a proposal by Duff that we should ask for a new member to be added to the Commission—a medical man —who presumably would stop this wild scheme in the interests of the private practitioner. This I doubt the chairman agreeing to. I have written to Burns to suggest that, if such a person is asked for, he might appoint Newsholme or Newman or McCleary. C. S. Loch threw out a suggestion of another investigator to look into the overlapping of medical agencies in London with a view to proving, I assume, that there is already too much medical assistance of the poor, not too little. But a proof of overlapping and extravagant granting of free medical treatment will help my argument. If, in some places, you have unsystematic lavishness, in other places, actual deficiency—all the more reason for some order in the chaos.

Meanwhile, the row over my special investigations has settled down quite satisfactorily to me. I, generously, offered to hand over my two investigators into widows with children on outdoor relief, with all the material these investigators had collected, to the Commission. This the Commission has accepted, and Miss Longman and Miss Phillips will now get comfortable salaries amounting to £7 a week in all and expenses, instead of the £2 Miss Phillips was drawing from me. The Commission has appointed an old acquaintance of mine, Dr. Williams (a lady doctor), to undertake an enquiry into all children under the poor law, and my assistants are to work under her. Responsibility for the condition of these children, and for their adequate maintenance and training, has therefore been accepted. This responsibility was refused by the Commission last summer on the ground that it rested with the parent. For the first time, these 160,000 children on outrelief become part and parcel of the so-called " children of the state ".

The enquiry into the policy of boards of guardians since 1834 goes on apace—no one objecting. But it is characteristic of the chairman's nerveless handling of the Commission's work that he would not let the minute of the documents committee, authorising me to conduct this enquiry, come up before the Commission. This minute was *ultra vires*

—as the documents committee had no authority to enquire into anything else but the policy of the central authority. When the storm broke over my investigations, Jeffrey, the secretary of the committee, felt it necessary to report this minute to the Commission as a whole. Lord George first delayed the report and then suppressed it! So the minute stands, and has been reported to the Commission by the secretary. " You will go on as before," whispered my friend Jeffrey, " the minute has been officially reported and you are authorised to conduct the investigation into the documents of the local authorities and to present a memorandum." And, as this is one of the enquiries that I detailed in my letter to the evidence committee, there can be no more said about the matter.

My fifth enquiry has also turned out well. This was an investigation into all the applications for relief in two unions—Hitchin and York—which began at the opening of the Commission. It was believed that Mrs. Bosanquet and Professor Smart were doing the same enquiry elsewhere. The question of such an investigation—especially in a town such as York—was brought up by C. S. Loch at our last meeting. I quietly observed that this enquiry was nearly complete—600 cases carefully investigated by a lady guardian who was also a trained enquirer. Charles Booth remembered the authorisation, and called for the results of the others. But mine were the only two that had been followed up, and were ready for consideration. So *that* material becomes part of the evidence before the Commission. . . .

What interests me as an observer of human nature is that I have become wholly indifferent to the Commission. I merely work as hard as I know how in my own direction without caring much what happens. I find myself perpetually watching my colleagues, dashing in when I see an opening—I sometimes push or squeeze through, sometimes the door is jammed in my face—and I accept either fate (with equal equanimity). At first, I was so horribly sensitive to their dislike. Now I watch the chairman's expression of puzzled displeasure, or listen to C. S. Loch's rude ejaculations (I heard him say " what cheek " to one of my questions to a witness), and find myself calmly calculating on how much they will stand, or wondering whether Loch is really seriously ill, since he so often loses his temper. I sometimes ponder over whether this aloofness is quite a good quality. But then I recollect that, after all, I am in a minority, and that it is my business to be hostile to the Government—and if I can be comfortably and good-naturedly hostile, so much the better. With Sidney, this attitude of indifference to his colleagues on public bodies is habitual—perhaps I am merely becoming masculine—losing the " personal note " which is the characteristic of the woman in human intercourse. What is rather disconcerting is that I catch myself " playing the personal note " when it suits my purpose—playing it without feeling it. Is that a characteristic of the woman on public bodies? I do try to check myself in this mean little game; but it has the persistency of an inherited or acquired habit.

April 23rd.—Royal Commission palaver on the lines of our enquiry next autumn into unemployed question. Smart and I had each of us circulated a good memorandum—either would have been a businesslike basis for a discussion. But the chairman made up, out of ours, one of his own which sprawled over the subject without sequence or order, with the result that we found ourselves discussing relief works, the motives of Messrs. Walter Long and Gerald Balfour in bringing in the Unemployed Act, and the amounts of casual labour employed by the railway companies on bank holidays, in an equally futile way. What exactly was decided on we none of us know—something, I suppose, will appear as minutes out of the fertile brains of two secretaries and the statistical officer—all in attendance. In spite of a protest, the out-relief " labour test ", which is the standard of dealing with the able-bodied men, was excluded from the investigation to be conducted next winter. The worst of it is that I do not quite see my way to do the needful work myself. And I am blest if I know yet what to do with the able-bodied!

Meanwhile, I am more than satisfied with the course of the children's enquiry. My two young ladies and all their material have been handed over to Dr. Williams—a new investigator. The latter stayed with me yesterday to talk the whole matter over. She is exactly what I remembered—an able progressive and attractive medical woman of broad views and even broader sympathies—ready for any change that could be shown to be, in itself, desirable. She welcomes the idea of transferring medical relief to the public health authorities, and she is quite prepared to welcome the proposal to hand over the children of school age to the education authorities. I suggest that the infants would naturally go to the public health authority concerned with infant mortality. Thus, the public health authority would continue to look after the physical condition of the children of school age and the education authority the mental training of the infants. In the same way, the public health authority might take all aged and infirm persons who were not fit to receive their pension, exactly as they would take imbeciles and other non-able-bodied poor. All this might be done gradually—step by step.

April 27th.—Dined alone with Morant to talk over the handing over of poor law children of school age to the education authority—infants to the public health authority. He agreed to both, and was much pleased with the latter idea because it chimes in with his notion of taking the ordinary infants away from the school, and placing them under the public health authority. He would like to go to the L.G.B. and we must see whether it could not be managed. He says he will be forced to start a medical department because of the incapacity of the L.G.B. to do the necessary work. But we pressed on him the desirability of placing the new medical officers under the M.O.H. in each locality and, if possible, doing likewise with the central inspectors and the L.G.B.

Went for a friendly chat with McKenna at the B. of Education —also to ventilate the handing over of the children to the education authority. He was taken aback by the notion—feared it would mean additional expense. Wanted to know whether the Commission as a whole would take that view. Asked me what we proposed about old-age pensions. He was up to his neck in that question. I told him we had taken no evidence and had not discussed the matter; we thought it would be settled for us. I gathered from him that the Government plan is a non-contributory scheme—something between the New Zealand and Danish plan. How were they to limit the number of applicants to the sum they were prepared to put down? If they suggested anything below 65, they would be laughed at. Could they make character a test? I suggested not—except perhaps criminal conviction—anything less was too intangible in our densely-crowded populations. Then he suggested some proof of destitution—inability to earn. I proposed the New Zealand limit of income. How were they to discover whether a person was fit to live out of an institution? That I vigorously maintained must be settled by the public health authority—it was, in the last resort, a question of a public nuisance, a dirty or neglected old person. He took that point. " The worst of all your proposals, Mrs. Webb, is that though each one seems excellent, they all mean more expenditure. And where are we to get the money? "

At lunch at the Commission, I asked Lord George what he meant to do about old-age pensions. He replied that certainly the evidence was in favour of old-age pensions—non-contributory—but where was the money to come from? Asquith has not the money for it, he said, in a weakly tone. " That's his look-out—all we have to say is whether old-age pensions are desirable from the standpoint of character and health ", I retorted. He seemed to agree; and, apparently, he is drifting towards recommending some form of pension—in the main because he sees it is coming.

May 3rd.—Dined alone with Haldane, his two brothers and sister, to talk poor law report. He is completely absorbed in his own department—and singularly aloof in his attitude both towards Parliament and towards his colleagues. " Not a good Parliament," he remarked, " no constructive ideas, merely objections to other people's ideas. I spend very little time there ", he continued (I thought he added, but I could not be quite sure, " Nor does the Cabinet interest me "). I suggested that he, at any rate, had got his reforms over the footlights, but that it was impossible to make a success of a Government that was made up of men, either with no settled opinions, or with contrary opinions on the questions with which they had to deal. " You are not even agreed as to whether you want public expenditure, assuming it to be right expenditure, or object to it." " No," he answered in a detached tone, " we are not agreed on root questions." The only person he volunteered kindly interest in was the leader of the opposition! " I see a good deal of Balfour ", he genially remarked. " What do you think of Churchill? " he asked with a note of anxiety. I gathered that Mr. Churchill is the only man who arouses R. B. H.'s anxious interest—a mixture of respect for capacity and suspicious dislike. He feels in him the man that may push him on one side.

The same aloofness from his colleagues, and absorption in his own career, I noted in McKenna. I gather also from Morant who has seen a good deal of Birrell and McKenna and heard from them about the others, that the Cabinet is an incoherent body—intensely individualistic —each man for himself—C. B. presiding merely. There is not even a *clique* of intimate friends round the Premier, or a *clique* of enemies concerting against him, as in A. J. B.'s case. The separate individuals forming the Government have neither repulsion not attraction for each other, so I suppose the Cabinet will hold together so long as the outside pressure of a great House of Commons majority, Liberal public opinion in this country, and their separate desires to keep in office, bind them together.

R. B. H. asserted that, as with the Government, so with the public —there was no common opinion about anything—he was conscious merely of chaos and indifference leading to the massing of electors now on this side, now on that. Moved more by impatience of what was than by any clear notion of what state of affairs they desired to bring about.

The little boom in the Fabian Society continues, and Sidney and I, G. B. S. and H. G. W. sometimes ask ourselves, and each other, whether there is a bare possibility that it represents a larger wave than we think—are we, by our constructive thought, likely to attract considerable numbers of followers in the near future? If this pleasant suspicion grows, it will consolidate the Society and draw the leaders nearer together. There are no personal jealousies to keep us apart since we none of us have political ambition, and our literary spheres are wholly distinct. Indeed, as a matter of fact, we stand to gain by each other's success—each one introducing the other two to new circles of admirers. With the Shaws our communion becomes ever closer and more thoroughly complementary and stimulating—and I hope and believe it will be so with H. G. W.

Meanwhile, Sidney and I are living at the usual high pressure. We are seeing little or nothing of general society. But, whilst he is working hard at my memorandum on the central policy, I am somewhat distracted with the two days' Commission meetings, seeing M.O.H.s and other medical experts, directing our secretaries, interviewing students and generally fussing around. When I see him settling down every morning to my work, I feel rather a fraud. Just now our usual positions are somewhat reversed: it is he who sits at home and thinks out the common literary work, it is I who am racing around dealing with men and affairs! And " the book " is completely shelved until these two memoranda are out of the way.

May 15th.—Launched my scheme of poor law reform in strict confidence to the chairman, H. Nunn, Smart, and Thory Gardiner, C. Booth, Phelps and Sir H. Robinson. Wakefield and Lansbury are practically agreed, and Chandler will have to agree to everything we three decide on. The Bishop of Ross will probably prepare to sign an advanced report. These eight commissioners represent the largest possible contingent that I might win over -the chairman would only come if he saw I was going to get a majority without him. But to get even eight would be almost inconceivable with the packed Commission, probably four only will sign my report, and of course I might be left with Wakefield and Lansbury only. What I have to aim at is to draw up a rattling good report, vivid in statement of fact, and closely reasoned with a logical conclusion and immediately practicable proposals of a moderate character.

June 4th.—Sent my scheme of poor law reform to Lord Fitzalan, Alfred Cripps, Henry Hobhouse (all coming to give evidence as to areas), to F. A. Hyett, Canon Barnett and Morant and some of the M.O.H. friends. Dined with Sir V. Horsley (the great surgeon), to try and interest the B.M.A., or at any rate to stop their being hostile. What I have not got clear is the constitution and formation of the " distress committee ". We have now finished the two memoranda— as to policy of the central authority and the relation of poor law medical relief to public health. I go to Scotland with the Commission on Monday and leave Sidney at work on our book.

June 11th.—Sidney and I spent Sunday with the Gerald Balfours— A. J. B. joining us on Sunday morning. Took my scheme down to lay before Gerald as a past and possible future President of the L.G.B.

381

" If anything like this issues from the Commission, it will be as great
a reform as the 1834 Commission." On the whole, he was favourably
impressed, especially with the " stipendiary ". He agreed that curative
treatment must be applied to all classes, if we could find sufficient
administrative capacity to do it; he was sympathetic to free medical
assistance. From what he said I should think he by no means expects
to be out of office in any future Conservative Government; and,
perhaps, he expects to resume the L.G.B. Anyway, he seemed to spend
more time in considering the results of the Commission than would
have been the case if he had made up his mind to retire from politics.

I did not attempt to talk to A. J. B. about it: he regards himself
too much as the general manager of the party—the party tactician—
to even consider a purely departmental topic. Sunday evening the
brothers Balfour, Lady Betty and we two talked of many things—all
of us at our best—the central topic being political philosophy of one
kind or another. Certainly, we and they are sufficiently sympathetic to
be absolutely frank and free to range at large—Sidney is more at home
with these men than with almost any others, except G. B. S. Full of
charm and stimulus was this visit: on the whole, I prefer Gerald—a
finer and purer temperament than the greater brother. But for sheer
charm, for that delightful combination of intellect, public spirit,
artistic sense and moral refinement, this family of Balfours has no
equals. It is the oddest fact in English politics that they should be mixed
up—predominantly mixed up—with democratic politics.

Edinburgh, June 21st.—Here a fortnight with the Commission at
Edinburgh. Scotch poor law is in just as bad a mess as English poor law.
The principle of " less eligibility " more deeply rooted in the administration: that of curative treatment less understood. The boarding-out
of children the only bright spot in the system—twenty years behind us
in institutional treatment. But, on account of facts of structure, Scotland
is almost more ripe for my scheme than England.

I am not impressed with Scotch local government: there is less
capacity, public spirit and integrity in the unpaid representatives than
in England—especially those of the greater towns—more graft, I think.
On the other hand, the officials are good, perhaps better than in the
ordinary English town. Hence, the officials occupy a more predominant
position than in England. I suppose it is the deep-rooted individualism
of the Scotch—they don't believe in government; it is only when they
are actually paid for performing its functions that they take it seriously
—unpaid governmental work is left to the busybodies, to vain people
and corrupt self-interested folk.

I have been reading in the morning hours Edward Carpenter's *Art
of Creation.* Here is another helpful book—not a great work but

adequately resumes the trend towards a sort of synthesis of the scientific with the mystical spirit—opening up vistas to human thought and feeling, the vision of which gives me hope and courage, assurance in a reality underlying one's own and every other life.

" Love shining through knowledge " might be the summing-up of his teaching. . . . This little book has helped me much—has given me a lift up—has made bad feelings and silly thoughts more difficult to me, and good feelings and strenuous but peaceful thought more easy. It is strange how ideas change feelings, and feelings change outward expression and action of all sorts. Ideas seem to be almost as actual as physical food, or physical poison, running their course through the body—they produce not merely states of mind, but states of body? Edward Carpenter has consoled me with his ideas, made me feel not merely morally better but physically stronger—more ready to work and to pray.

To-night, I rush back to my boy—just for two days and one night —and then begin again at Aberdeen for the inside of a week. It is hard to be away from him—apart we each of us live only half a life, together we each of us have a double life.

July 3rd.—Back from Scotland in state of exhaustion. Five days with Dr. Downes and a Scotch inspector (a kindly nonentity whom we quite unconsciously ignored—Dr. Downes and I—parcelling out the work between us). I had some long talks with my medical colleague— broke to him the coming of my report on medical assistance of the poor. He is a deep-rooted voluntaryist, timid of new things, fearful of expense, always anxious to make the existence of some little voluntary enterprise the excuse for official non-intervention—a type of official who was common twenty years ago, but is now being brushed on one side by forceful young bureaucrats eager to extend their activities. But he is apparently anxious to have a report of decided hue—something strong and vigorous in one direction or the other. He is attracted by my " stipendiary " and the notion of altering much without making a new authority or new area. On my way home, I stayed with Dr. Leslie Mackenzie, the medical member of the Scotch L.G.B.—the official of the progressive ambitious imaginative type—full of strong philanthropic feeling and an innovator. He is my most ardent supporter and the most important witness on my side—important because it is clear he had the whole idea of medical reform long before I had; he has merely been strengthened in his opinion by my independent movement towards this reform. With him also this particular proposal is only one application of the theory of mutual obligation between the community and the individual—merely one little offshoot from a general philosophy of social life. He is one of the remarkable men with whom this enquiry has brought me into contact—the other is Andrew Young, the head-master of Canongate board school—a moral genius of a man—one I should like to see more of, but shall not.

July 5th.—Had the Bishop of Stepney to lunch, also Percy Dearmer, separately to start propaganda in the Church in favour of our scheme of poor law reform. I want to make an atmosphere favourable to it—partly to influence Lord George, and partly to influence possible witnesses. The Bishop of Stepney, a wily ecclesiastic, was cautious but encouraging—he is inclined to trust us in social matters. I gave him both my memorandum on " central policy " and that on " medical relief ", to take away and read, besides having sent him my scheme. Percy Dearmer is the Fabian in Christian Social Union—an attractive, enthusiastic propagandist—easily tuned because in general harmony with us.

July 9th.—Had five medicals to meet Haldane and the Gerald Balfours to discuss my scheme—also to convert McVail, the investigator, at any rate not to be hostile to it. G. B. and R. B. H. much impressed by it—the former even enthusiastic. I tried to explain to both of them the policy of clearing up the base of society—equally necessary for a sound individualist, or a sound socialist state. Nathan Raw, the head of the Liverpool poor law infirmary, told me that some of the Royal Commission had asked him to meet them at Liverpool with a view to trying to get him to make out a list of diseases that might be " dispauperised ", leaving all the rest in the poor law. Clearly the Commission is getting perturbed at the advance of the doctrine of free medical assistance—I gathered that this surreptitious consultation was between Bentham, Phelps, Nunn and Nathan Raw—but he would not tell me the names.

July 18th.—McKenna dined with us alone last night to discuss the old-age pension scheme. Office has hardened him—developed both capacity and cynicism. To him has apparently been entrusted the task of drafting an Old Age Pension Bill. The scheme he thrashed out with us was universal non-contributory pensions to all over 65 with less than 10s. a week from property, with sliding scale from 5s. upwards, income under 5s. not to be taken into account. No disqualification from pauperism present or future, some contribution from the rates on account of potential paupers. To be administered evidently by a stipendiary. He calculates that it will cost the national exchequer £7,000,000 to £10,000,000. He also adumbrated his Education Bill of next session which he means to pass! All denominational schools to depend on a three-quarter parents' majority, and then to be supported wholly by the Government grant and voluntary contributions; on the other hand, to be emancipated from all local control. Cowper-Temple religion to be swept away, and in its stead, hymns, prayers and Bible reading—difficult to understand exactly what he meant. He said that he hoped the Lords would throw the Bill out because if they did the Liberals would come back to power. If they passed it, there would be nothing to bind Liberal and Labour together. But I am not sure he did not express his hope to impress me with the impolicy of throwing out the Education Bill. School Medical Inspection Bill sure to pass: said he intended to appoint Newman as he heard nothing but good of him. He impressed Sidney with the rapidity of his mind and both of us with his hard businesslike tone—I think he has goodwill too, of a somewhat common sort.

July 19th. Ayot St. Lawrence.—The Bernard Shaws have lent us their little week-end house for two-and-a-half months, they having migrated to a large mansion in Wales close to the Fabian Summer School. Now we are going to set to work to finish up our volume on *The Manor and the Borough*, laid aside for six whole months in order to complete the report for the Poor Law Commission. This somewhat abstruse historical work is restful after the contriving of schemes, and the drafting of analyses, meant to affect action. And I am convinced that this intimate knowledge of what past generations of one's own race have actually done—of the motives upon which they have acted—of the potential machinery they have invented, or cast on one side, gives larger scope to one's imagination as a reformer of the present state of things. Moreover, history teaches one the impermanence during one generation, even during one decade, of any kind of social structure, and it gives one leading ideas as to what is practicable. For example, the whole theory of the mutual obligation between the individual and the state, which I find myself working out in my poor law scheme, is taken straight out of the nobler aspect of the mediaeval manor. It will come as a new idea to the present generation—it is really a very old one that has been thrust out of sight in order to attain some measure of equality in political rights. There are some who wish to attain to a socialist state by the assertion of economic equality—they desire to force the property-owners to yield to the non-property owners. I prefer to have the forward movement based on the obligation of each individual to serve, not merely by making commodities and fulfilling services, but by being healthy, intelligent and loving.

The reader of the interminable diary entries for the first eighteen months of the proceedings of the Royal Commission will have noticed that the Commission during this period was almost entirely concerned with two questions. First, we were led to enquire how far the boards of guardians were administrating the poor law according to the principles of 1834 which, so the officials of the L.G.B. assured us, had been from 1834 to 1906 the official policy prescribed by the central authority, alike for the able-bodied pauper and the non-able-bodied. The second subject emerging from the discussions and investigations of the Commission was the scheme put forward by a minority of the commissioners for taking all the non-able-bodied (the infants and children, the sick and the mentally defective) out of the poor law with its framework of repression, in order to transfer their treatment to the already existing framework of prevention, imperfectly embodied in the public health and education acts, administered by the county and county borough councils. To this it was proposed to add a national system of old-age pensions, paid for and carried out, free from any stigma of pauperism, by a department of the central government.

But the consideration of how best to treat the non-able-bodied poor was not the most important task set before us by the reference of the Commission. We had also to enquire into " the various means which have been adopted, outside of the poor laws, for meeting distress arising from lack of employment, particularly during periods of severe industrial depression; and to consider and report whether any, and if so what modification of the poor laws, or changes in their administration, or fresh legislation for dealing with distress, are available ". Successive Governments, led by Joseph Chamberlain when President of the Local Government Board in 1886, had recognised that there was a social disease of unemployment which ought, somehow or other, to be treated outside the poor law administered according to the principles of 1834. It was this question of the "disease of unemployment " that, at any rate, so far as the Socialist minority was concerned, dominated the procedure of the Commission from July 1907 to December 1908.

July 31st.—Final meetings of the Commission for settling the first weeks of the unemployed witnesses in October, and hearing five rural experts—the three stupid ones were in favour of the *status quo*, the two clever ones in favour of the county authority for poor law and not against distributing the services among the existing committees. At the private meeting of the Commission, a queer little episode over the reception of my report on the policy of the central authority. Lord George, before proposing that it should be circulated, made a little speech which seemed to me wholly unnecessary. In a loud high voice, he recited the circumstances under which it was drafted by an individual commissioner, and not by a committee, and explained in a somewhat ungracious way that the Commission must not in any way be bound by its conclusions, that it must not influence their report. (He apparently forgot, in his anxiety to repudiate its conclusions, to thank me for the labour of it.) I responded to the challenge by explaining that I had suggested that the documents committee should undertake the work as a committee with a salaried officer to do the drudgery, but that Sir Samuel Provis and I had been over-ruled, and that I had been forced to undertake the whole labour of the analysis and the final drafting and that, of course, it represented my opinion only, and that I had carefully stated this fact in the first paragraph. " If that be understood," said the chairman rather grumpily, " I propose that it be circulated." " Rather ungracious, the chairman's reception of your report," said the astute Sir Henry Robinson to me at lunch, " if I could get someone to draft a report like that, I should be willing to pay £500 " (Sir Henry is a consummate flatterer). " Yes," said I, pretending to be a little hurt, " I *did* think it rather unkind after having all that immense task forced on me against my better judgement! " Honestly, I thought the discomfort of the chairman and my fellow-commissioners somewhat justified. The last part of the report is a compelling document, and whether they like it or not, it will, as a matter of fact, influence their final report. And, protesting that it won't do so, will not diminish this influence. Altogether, I am satisfied with the course of events on the Commission—so far as I can see everything is working up towards my solution. Meanwhile, having my own scheme settled, I amuse myself by promoting every dissension among my colleagues, backing up every proposal that separates one from the other—my bundle of commissioners! At present they feel themselves to be bound up against me—but we shall see! What I have got to discover during the next year resolves itself into two questions: (1) Must we have a national authority for dealing with the able-bodied? (2) If national or mainly national, what must be the constitution of the body? It is the one new authority that we have to create, and I have not at present the remotest notion of how to constitute it. I have arranged to set Mrs. Spencer to work on it in October. I shall tell the documents committee that I propose to break up my report on the policy of the local authorities into classes, and that I shall present them with the report on the able-bodied about Easter of next year. This will include all past treatment of able-bodied destitution and end up with definite proposals. I shall then proceed to a report on children and finish up with one on the aged.

September 28th. Ayot St. Lawrence.—The time here has been enjoyable and unexpectedly fruitful. We have sent off the last word of *The Manor and the Borough* to the printer (we have written what equals 174 pages), we have corrected a good deal of the proof, I have organised with Mrs. Spencer the " able-bodied " enquiry and Sidney has fixed up many small jobs—we have had all three secretaries down here—the two assistant investigators (Miss Longman and Miss Phillips), Jeffrey of the Poor Law Commission, Beveridge, Pringle, [Cyril] Jackson (enquirer into " able-bodied "), the Barnetts, Leslie Mackenzie and the Granville-Barkers, and numerous young Fabians. Altogether our society has been of the useful kind—doing business—chiefly poor law—always excepting the fascinating Granville-Barker.

I gathered from Jeffrey that there has been a row about my " central policy " report—that Lord George had actually thought of not circulating it. What he has done is to issue a ukase that we are none of us to show even our own productions to other people. This I do not mean to obey—he has no right to lay it down. At present my two reports are being read by a committee of the Cabinet. Lord George has, however, issued strict orders that we are not to have copies supplied to us. But you cannot treat commissioners like children, and I shall find some way of getting all the copies I require. What is more serious is that Dr. Ethel Williams is proving incapable of methodical investigation, that she has become estranged from the two assistant investigators, that Duff is trying to baulk the enquiry. The plain truth is that the Commission is becoming deadly sick of the facts and I must be prepared for a possible wind-up in twelve months' time. Meanwhile, I think trouble is brewing between the chairman and the C.O.S. over outdoor relief—clearly my best policy is to go on quietly preparing reports on the able-bodied and keeping an eye on the material being collected by the assistant investigators on the children. About Easter I must prepare the report on the able-bodied, before the recess I must have the report on children, and later on a short one on the aged and the whole question of insurance. Whether this hemming-in of the Commission by reports will at all paralyse their activity remains to be seen—I have hopes that it will. But we shall see. In any case the game is extraordinarily exciting.

October 8th.—The first meeting of the Commission was a stormy one. The chairman took it upon himself to order the deletion of three or four paragraphs in Crooks' statement about Poplar—because they reflected on the impartiality of Inspector Davy's enquiry. Directly I got notice that this had been done, I thought it only right to stand by Lansbury and Crooks—who are fellow-Fabians. Moreover, it seemed a good opportunity to assert the right of individual commissioners to publish anything that was rejected by the Commission as a whole. So I advised Crooks to refuse to permit his statement to be mutilated, and Lansbury to protest against the chairman's action and to state his intention, if he thought fit, of inserting the whole of Crooks' statement in his report or supplementary report. At the first meeting of the Commission, the chairman made a kindly statement of the case and the correspondence was read and Lansbury made his protest. He asked me to speak: so I simply reiterated Lansbury's right to report anything he chose " on his own view and knowledge ". Thereupon Phelps cut in with the suggestion that, after all, Crooks' statement might be printed in its entirety. I quietly maintained that, if that was decided, Mr. Crooks must be informed, as he might, after all, like to give evidence. "Then you will have to get another chairman ", said Lord George. " I did not suggest that your ruling should be over-ruled, it was Mr. Phelps who did so—all I ask is that it should be definitely decided whether or not those paragraphs are to be deleted and, if they are not to be deleted, that Mr. Crooks be informed." It was referred to the evidence committee and we all quickly recovered our temper.

Meanwhile, an astonishing memorandum has been circulated from the chairman. This proposes the evisceration of the poor law by taking out the sick, the aged and the vagrant, but proposes to set up a new *ad hoc* elected poor law authority for each county and county borough. The sick are to be transferred to the public health authority, the aged to be dealt with by pensions, and the vagrants to be managed by the police. Children are not mentioned, nor are the unemployed. The whole scheme is impracticable—but it is all in the right direction and, incidentally, sweeps on one side the " principles of 1834 ". The remarkable feature about it is the adoption of the public health authority for the treatment of all sickness, though he rejects a salaried service, and favours the B.M.A. plan of free choice of doctors. This memorandum we were to discuss in an informal way. At the discussion to-day, there were present Phelps, Smart, Bentham, B. W., Lansbury, Nunn, Wakefield, MacDougall, Loch, Hill, Bosanquet, Chandler, T. Gardiner and Downes. No protest was made by the C.O.S. members against the tendency of the proposed reforms. Loch talked a good deal, but no one could gather what his proposals were—he is evidently very ill, poor fellow. There appeared to be five solid votes for my scheme, though this scheme was not mentioned: Phelps, Smart, B. W., Lansbury and Chandler—all agreed that the poor law had to be swept away; Wakefield and Nunn in a state of indecision—inclining our way; Bentham in favour of an indirectly elected *ad hoc* body, with all the old functions; Hill and MacDougall for the *status quo*; Bosanquet for an elected county *ad hoc* body, also with all the old functions; Downes in favour of a nominated body for institutions and an *ad hoc* elected smaller area for outdoor relief; and poor Loch simply fumbling. For the dissociation of medical relief from the poor law there was, I think, just a majority,—Wakefield, Nunn and the chairman joining our five, making eight out of the fourteen present. To this might be added, I imagine, the two Irishmen, making a majority of the Commission in favour of the transfer of all medical relief to the public health authority. In the course of the discussion, the chairman remarked that he had looked through McVail's draft report and that " he corroborated Mrs. Webb's conclusions as to the impossibility of maintaining the poor law as the medical authority ". It shows how well worth while it was to do that report. But it is curious to note that not a single commissioner raised the question of the children—it would be really comic to keep a poor law authority, with the deterrent principles and the stigma of pauperism, alive for the children and a few of the able-bodied! After the discussion to-day, it is clear that there is nothing between the *status quo* and my scheme.

At the meeting on Tuesday, we had as witnesses Long and Beveridge. I managed to land Walter Long on to the essentials of my scheme [1]— the county council and county borough council as the authority, and the withdrawal of some of the functions from the stigma of pauperism and the deterrent test. It is certainly amusing that the class which these Conservative statesmen wish to withdraw from the principles of 1834 is exactly the able-bodied male wage-earners! exactly the class to which *a priori* you would say the principles of 1834 were most applicable. Wishing to get Wakefield definitely on my side, I brought him home to lunch; and, when I had discovered that he was quite sound, I

---

[1] Here is a kindly account of my cross-examination of Walter Long, by the accomplished journalist, A. G. Gardiner: " There is no cross-examiner at the bar more suave or subtle than Mrs. Webb. When I was called to give evidence before the Poor Law Commission I entered the room in the midst of her examination of Mr. Walter Long. The subject was the finance of the unemployed committees. Step by step she led him unconscious to his doom with gentle, innocent-seeming questions. Suddenly he saw he was being made to admit that voluntary effort was a failure and that the rates must be used. But it was too late to retreat. With a quiet ' Thank you, that is all ', she snapped the ' bracelets ' on his wrists, folded her hands, and sat back in her chair, the picture of demure, unexultant triumph " (*Pillars of Society*, by A. G. Gardiner, pp. 204-6).

suggested that he should suggest to Phelps and Smart the circulation of something approximating my scheme and their own. " The Commission won't take it from me—it had better come from a middle party, and you and Professor Smart and Mr. Phelps are the right people to launch it." " It must be something much less elaborate than your scheme, Mrs. Webb—a few simple propositions." Acting on this suggestion, Sidney and I drafted a series of propositions beginning piano and ending piano, with the substance in the middle, and I sent three copies of these to Wakefield asking him, if he approved, to approach Smart and Phelps. I offered to sign with Lansbury and Chandler, but suggested that they were " better without us "—at any rate in the first instance. I await the result of my little machination with interest.

Meanwhile, I am trying to create " an atmosphere " in favour of the scheme. Haldane, who came in this morning, is adumbrating it in the Cabinet, but he wants me to get hold of Burns. " He is vain and ignorant, and in the hands of his officials, and opposes everything and talks so much that we find it difficult to get to business; if you could get him to take up the scheme as his own, then I could follow, but he is at the head of the department concerned, and would resent a lead off by another member of the Cabinet." What I want to secure is that, when old-age pensions are discussed next year, the " break-up of the poor law " should be quietly taken for granted by both front benches. That would be immensely impressive to Lord George and the less resolute members of the Commission—it would make it almost impracticable to set up a new authority with the stigma of pauperism and the test of destitution.

Morant came to lunch to talk over the children question—he is quite in favour of the poor law children going over to the education authority. What he really rather demurs to is heaping up the county and county borough councils with other work—medical relief, etc., so as to increase the pressure in favour of an *ad hoc* education authority. He agrees to help me with my enquiry into the poor law and industrial schools and to put on Miss Longman as an unpaid inspector. That will just suit my book.

Gerald Balfour, Beveridge, Mackinder and Dr. Newman (new head of the medical department) dined here on Tuesday to discuss the " labour exchange " and other ways of dealing with unemployment. They stayed from 7.30 to 12 o'clock—which left me rather a rag the next day. Altogether, I can foresee that this year's work is going to be straining, and I shall have to economise my strength in all directions, but the Commission's work must take the front place. I have succeeded so well up to now in my enveloping movement that I must do the job completely and tumble down humpty-dumpty so it will never get set on the wall again.

October 22nd.—Paid John Burns a visit to get some particulars about stoneyards—left my scheme with him. " I shall be going to the Home Office next summer, Mrs. Webb." " All the more reason for saying, in general terms, what you *would* have done if you had remained at the L.G.B.", I suggested. " You read my scheme and, if you agree with it, you might give a sort of lead-off to your colleagues on the question of poor law reform."

Meanwhile, Russell Wakefield has circulated the memorandum which I drew up for him (with one or two tiny alterations) as his own: he clearly did not want to share the glory of the new idea with Smart and Phelps. " Jeffrey tells me that it will be a bomb", he said to Lansbury. " That's splendid," I rejoined sympathetically, " I only hope we shall be able to agree with it." Oh! the vanity of men! How far is it wrong to play with it?

October 29th.—Another row on over my investigations.[1] Not the able-bodied, in the very midst of which I am, not the children for whom I am quietly arranging—but the medical which is completely done with. A brilliant idea has struck Mrs. Bosanquet: why not ask Mrs. Webb for her " correspondence with M.O.H.s " upon which she has manifestly based her report on the medical services? Can we not extract something from this correspondence which will discredit her? she can hardly refuse to let us have it, as she expressly said she was glad to put the material she collected at the disposal of the Commission. Probably we shall find that the M.O.H.s were not predominantly in favour of the transfer, thought the little woman. " I shall be charmed to send the material connected with public health for inspection ", I said cheerily. That evening I looked through the correspondence, took away all letters that were at all compromising to the authors (I had to remember Provis and Downes) and a due proportion of stupid conservative ones, and bundled the letters and reports off to the Commission. To be frank, I had qualms of conscience in making any kind of selection of those I did and did not send. But it was clear that Mrs. Bosanquet was not playing the game fair. She did not want to see my correspondence in order to " inform her own mind "—which was the

---

[1] Elizabeth Haldane refers to this misdemeanour on my part in *From One Century to Another*: " Mrs. Webb did valiant service for poor law administration, but she was much criticised by some of her fellow-commissioners for getting private evidence for her own satisfaction, for not attending the meetings when she did not think it worth her while to do so, and in general organising her own activities. On the whole, she came out triumphantly, and the Minority Report, which was mainly hers, has been a sheet-anchor for the more advanced reformers " (p. 231).

only legitimate ground for the request; she wanted, as has been proved since, to incriminate me by documents which I supplied of my own free will to the Commission. So I swallowed the tacit deception and sent exactly what I thought fit—without, be it added, in any way giving the Commission to understand that I had sent them the whole or the part. I had, however, left quite enough adverse letters in the bundle to encourage Mrs. Bosanquet in her plan. In spite of the fact that I said quite distinctly that all the correspondence must be regarded as confidential, she persuaded the evidence committee to ask my permission to have the whole printed with the circular letters written to the M.O.H.s. To this request I sent a dignified refusal, pointing out that the Commission could obtain the statements of fact and opinion direct from the persons concerned. I stuck to the undeniable position that I had no authority from my correspondents to circulate their letters in a printed form which might get to the authorities concerned. I said I had no objection to the statements of fact and opinions being analysed (though I failed to see the advantage to the Commission of one year old casual letters), and the Commission could use my correspondence to put them on the track of persons whom they would like to consult. But, what relevance this mean little tricky attempt to trip me up has to a defence of the principles of 1834, I fail to see. Moreover, this particular battle of medical relief is fought and won as far as I can win it. It is my other movements they ought to be now counter acting. Meanwhile, and it is this that has made the C.O.S. so angry, I have issued a slashing memorandum on *Some Historical Considerations Bearing on the Reconstruction of the Poor Law*, backing up the chairman's " alternative scheme " and R. Wakefield's suave proposals. The Commission's atmosphere is getting very hot, and it will be hotter before we have done. " The *status quo* or the break-up of the poor law ", I tell all the colleagues I am friendly with, is the inevitable issue. Nothing intermediate can survive discussion.

October 30th.—John Burns has become a monstrosity. He is, of course, a respectable hard-working man, who wants, when he is not blinded by vanity and malice against those who have abused him, to see straight. But this faculty of seeing facts as they are is being overgrown by a sort of fatty complacency with the world as it is: an enormous personal vanity, feeding on the deference and flattery yielded to patronage and power. He talks incessantly, and never listens to anyone except the officials to whom he *must* listen, in order to accomplish the routine work of his office. Hence, he is completely in their hands and is becoming the most hidebound of departmental chiefs, gulled by an obstructive fact or reactionary argument, taken in by the most naïve commonplaces of middle-class administrative routine.

Almost unconsciously one treats him as a non-responsible being—a creature too unintelligent to be argued with, too crazily vain to be appealed to as one self-respecting man appeals to another. What *is* the right conduct towards such a man? When issues of the gravest character are at stake, ought one to damage the chance of his taking the right course by frankness that offends him? Ought one to increase the chances of his taking the right course by ministering to his vanity—by at any rate allowing for it? Or ought one to forego all influence by merely avoiding any connection with him? Will mere genuine kindliness and charity get over the difficulty? Ought one resolutely to refuse to see a fellow-creature's faults? Ought one to treat every man as if he were a saint? Or at any rate had the makings of a saint? What casuist will answer?

November 12*th. Beachy Head.*—The row about my investigations developed: the chairman coming on the track of my investigations into the Unemployed Workmen's Act. Unfortunately I was, at the moment, in a state of high fever, and there ensued a somewhat angry correspondence between us—he censoring me and I asserting my right to get at facts for myself. All this has meant, on the top of a year's hard work, a bad nervous breakdown, and I am here for ten days' absolute quiet—a truce having been proclaimed in my absence on sick leave. Perhaps when I return it will all have blown over.

Meanwhile, I think, I have just saved the situation with regard to the L.G.B. public health department. For the last year I have set my heart on getting Newsholme to succeed the present man. But I had no notion that a change was imminent. Fortunately, John Burns came in to lunch about a fortnight ago to meet H. G. Wells. He casually mentioned that Dr. Power was going in December. " And are you going to appoint Newsholme? " I asked. " No, I know two better men than Newsholme—and I shall get them both too." I dared not then pursue the subject. But, after the others had gone, I went in hot and strong in favour of Newsholme. He looked pensive. " Newsholme is a publicist," he said, evidently repeating what his officials had told him: " he would do better as Registrar-General." " No, no," I said, " he is an administrative genius, with an entirely new outlook on the whole question of public health. If you appoint him, you will make your reputation as a public health reformer." He left looking thoughtful. I thought it better to strike hard, so I wrote him a long letter. I also got Morant in motion, to set Newman in motion. I believe I have just saved it—but, if so, it will have been a near shave. J. B. really wants to do right in his appointments—but how can he judge? However, he will like to make " a striking and original appointment " and I think it is all right.

But I am low and disheartened. I don't like all this intriguing. I should prefer to play with my cards on the table. It is partly remorse for my little lack of straight dealing with regard to the M.O.H.s' correspondence that has brought about my nervous collapse. Was I bound to hand over everything? Not legally certainly; but, perhaps, I ought simply to have refused to give up *any* private correspondence? I was surprised into acceding to an unwarrantable demand and then did not choose to fulfil it completely. Another time I will ask for " notice of the question " and will accept or refuse deliberately and fully.

November 15th.—Taken up a fresh position before putting in my appearance at the Commission. I have, with Sidney's help, written a kindly but dignified letter to Professor Smart begging to be released from the task of reporting on the policy of the local authorities between 1834–1907. It is clear, from what has happened lately, that such a series of reports as I intended, under this heading, would not be tolerated by the Commission, or if they were, would create an enormous amount of ill-feeling. By retiring from a position which is, at present, untenable, on the ground of wounded feelings at the ungrateful reception of the other reports, I immediately set them thinking whether they would not, after all, do well to get me to make these reports! In my letter to Smart I have given the Commission to understand that I am going on investigating, as I assume they all are, with a view to solving the problems set to us. What with offended feelings and delicate health, I shall be able to withdraw myself from the silly business of endless cross-examining, and devote my whole energy to solving the questions of able-bodied destitution. I am wondering whether Lord George will be mollified by my withdrawal from making unwelcome reports, or whether he will insist on discussing my *right* to make personal investigations.

November 26th.—Reappeared at the Commission yesterday for the general palaver. Colleagues kindly, but not specially on-coming. I gather from Jeffrey that there has been a row of an acute character between Loch and the documents committee, over my report on the " central policy ". Loch has raised the question that the documents committee has not itself reported on the central policy, and has consequently disobeyed its reference. He has not been able to complain of *my* action, as Jeffrey has pointed out that I desired the documents committee to do the work by its paid official, and that I was over-ruled and ordered to do it myself. The documents committee, meanwhile, refuses to write another report on the policy of the English central authority, no one being willing to supervise the work, and it being hardly worth while doing it again, now I have done it. It was this row that has been so disturbing to the chairman's peace, not that about the M.O.H.s' correspondence, or my new enquiry into the able-bodied.

Meanwhile, a most unexpected development has taken place. The general palaver on all the memoranda revealed the fact that I was the only person with a compact following of four or five and that various other members were veering round to me. Hence, at a certain point of the discussion, there was a call for my scheme from many quarters. To this I gracefully responded. So I am now submitting a fully formed scheme of reform—the *Break-up of the Poor Law*—in all its detail. I propose to submit myself to cross-examination, so as both to convert my colleagues, if possible, and also to learn the exactly weak points in my own armour. It is a bold move, on my part, but I think on the whole a wise one. The majority of the Commission are tired of wandering about the subject without a leader and, though I may not attract many more than I have already, the planking down of an attractive and logical scheme of reform will make the other members nervous of being contented with muddle-headed generalisations.

Beginning to prepare an atmosphere for our able-bodied proposals: Sidney put our proposals into a Christian Social Union tract (signed by Donaldson, a Leicestershire clergyman), and I am submitting them to General Booth of the Salvation Army to get that organisation on my side. One reason for attempting to rush the Commission on the *Break-Up of the Poor Law* is to clear the decks for the more revolutionary scheme of dealing with unemployment. That scheme is so drastic that I cannot conceivably get a majority, but I may get an influential minority. But its very completeness will injure my chance of getting a majority for the break-up of the poor law, if it is thrust on their attention simultaneously. It will be amusing to see how much " Webb " this Commission will stand—what exactly will be saturation point? They have absorbed a good deal already, with the transference of medical relief to public health authorities, and the county and county borough as the authority for the treatment of all destitute persons. How much more will they stand?

November 30*th.*—Lunched to-day with Miss Anderson, the factory inspector, to meet Smith Whitaker, the secretary, and Dr. Ford Anderson, a leading member of the British Medical Association, to discuss my medical report. Glad to find that they were not unfavourable to the transfer of poor law medical relief to the public health authority —even regarded it as inevitable—and also preferred a salaried whole-time service to a " free choice of doctor " scheme. Quite clearly my report had convinced them that something had to be done and that a greatly extended public health service was certain to come. " The question is," I ventured to suggest, " is the B.M.A. going to dominate the new service or is it not? If the Association throws itself at once on the side of the new regime then it will dominate it, if it opposes its development the new scheme will organise itself as a rival." " That is what I tell them ", said Mr. Smith Whitaker.

December 9th.—Lord George scored a great victory to-day, and I a great success. The scheme for the break-up of the poor law, which the Commission had hastily demanded, was, as is usual with my productions, received in stony silence, no reference being made to it in the course of the discussion. Lord George had circulated another memorandum denouncing my scheme as " anti-democratic ", but accepting a large part of it—transference of poor law to county and county borough councils swallowed; county stipendiary officer, the principle of curative and preventive treatment—everything, in fact, except the distribution of the services among the county council committees and the stipendiary officer for the administration of outdoor relief. In their hatred of me, all the C.O.S. members rallied to him, giving up the *ad hoc* poor law body, the principle of deterrence, the strict administration of outdoor relief—a real stampede from the principles of 1834. I insisted on taking a vote on the crucial question of a poor law statutory committee of the county council *versus* a distribution between the education committee, the health committee, etc. Lansbury and Chandler voted with me, Smart and Phelps refused to vote, all the others present (not present Booth, Robinson, Wakefield, Nunn) voted for Lord George's scheme of a statutory committee. Thereupon, I gave them to understand that we considered the issue vital and should have our minority report. Short of getting a majority report written by ourselves, this large measure of conversion to our proposals on the part of the majority, with freedom for a great report of my own, is exactly the position which I prefer. I shall lose Phelps and, perhaps, Wakefield and not gain any others. On the other hand, the report will be a thoroughly Webbian document—in tone, statement of fact, and proposals. Meanwhile, our chairman is overjoyed at the victory and received my hearty congratulations most graciously. He and I are excellent friends. With my other colleagues, there is a most distinct consolidation against me—amounting almost to boycott, at any rate, to a discourteous coldness. Honestly, I think they are somewhat justified in their dislike of me—I have played with the Commission. I have been justified in doing so, because they began by ignoring me— but it is unpleasant to be played with, especially by a person whom you want to despise.

The activity of the majority will be on the Commission: my activity will be outside it—investigating, inventing, making an atmosphere favourable to my inventions; and, where possible, getting the persons with right opinions into high places, and persons in high places in the right state of mind. The two reports on the able-bodied and the children must be finished by the summer, and we must be thoroughly equipped to turn off, on short notice, a first-rate minority report.

December 12*th*.—The next day's meeting was like pleasant sunshine after drifting storm. The chairman was enjoying an unaccustomed sense of personal power, the C.O.S. was chuckling over the defeat of my scheme, I was thoroughly complacent with having dragged the whole Commission so far in my direction whilst preserving my freedom for a minority report; others like Nunn, Wakefield, Smart and Phelps, felt that they alone were free of any decision, since they had either been absent or not voted. Perhaps it was this undeterminate party that was least comfortable. Among these and the office staff, there was a reaction in my favour—a feeling that I had been treated somewhat cavalierly in having my elaborate report peremptorily dismissed without any kind of discussion. So we all parted for the month's recess the best of friends—and, so far as I am concerned, this attitude will persist. Whether the majority will fall out among themselves and split into factions, it is impossible to foretell. Now that the pressure brought about by fear of a " Webb majority " has been removed, it is doubtful whether the chairman's party will hold together. All I have to do is to get on with my own work and leave them alone to settle their own report; merely use the Commission to get the information I need and they can give me, be pleasant with each and all of them personally, without troubling myself about the Commission as a whole. By persistent discourtesy, they have absolved me from obligations of good-fellowship.

1908

January 13*th*.—A weird Christmas recess at Hollesley Bay Colony, investigating the daily routine of the 300 men's lives, getting particulars about their former occupations and present views, having long talks with the superintendent, the works' manager, the farmer and the gangers, with a view to ascertaining the possibilities of the working colony as an element in any scheme for dealing with unemployment. The atmosphere—the impression of the place was mournfully tragic—half-educated, half-disciplined humans, who felt themselves to have been trampled on by their kind, were sore and angry, every man of them in favour of every kind of protection, protection against machinery, protection against female, boy and foreign labour, protection against Irish, Scotch and country men, protection against foreign commodities, protection against all or anything that had succeeded whilst they had failed. There was a growing assumption in their minds that they had the *right* to 30s. a week—in London the rate for borough council work, though this assumption was, as yet, tall talk to most of them. They were a faint-hearted, nerveless set of men, their manner sometimes servile, sometimes sullen, never easy and independent.

January 30th.—Now we have decided to take a whole four days to discuss new editions of the chairman's memorandum defining the constitution and powers of the central and local nominated committees. This seems, from the standpoint of the majority, rather a slow procedure, since the whole question can be reopened when we have the draft report before us—but the chairman seems quite unaware that there is any distinction between casual discussions on casual memoranda and binding decisions on the actual draft report. I propose to take little or no part in these discussions—just stand by in a pleasant and kindly attitude, and await events. C. S. Loch is seriously ill, which, if he recovers, will delay matters (he will want to reopen any decision), if he does not recover will help on the chairman with the other C.O.S. members. About Newsholme's appointment there is a certain sullenness on the Commission—altogether the body is in a moody leaderless state. I do not understand where exactly they are drifting to. There is no sign of any policy on unemployment or on any other question.

Meanwhile, we are working at high pressure, collecting our information—most of my activity being the direction of the research conducted by our secretaries.[1] At present we can barely see the forest for the trees—but I have ample confidence in our method. Without Sidney's help I should not persist in this terrific effort to clear up the whole question, to cut a way through the tangle of existing facts. Fortunately, we have already discovered our principles of 1907, and we have already devised our scheme of reform. What we are now manufacturing is the heavy artillery of fact that is to drive both principles and scheme home.

We have remitted our unemployment scheme to the leading members of the Labour Party (barring MacDonald), and have met with quite unexpected response—almost a promise of active support. I have also sent this scheme with a long letter to A. J. B. and he has suggested coming to discuss it. And Haldane and Asquith have had the poor law scheme and we are to meet them to-night at Haldane's house to discuss details of it. The Christian Social Union is circulating

[1] So far as I remember, it was Charlotte Shaw's generosity that made it possible for us to have four or five research secretaries during this period.

both schemes as tracts and we are putting them in circulation elsewhere—so that they will be cropping up in altogether unexpected
quarters. Shall we advance matters by all this tireless investigation,
invention and propaganda—at times one gets disheartened—if it were
not for the comradeship of our effort, I should be tempted to give up
the struggle. It will be a real relief when the Commission is closed and
we can go back to the peaceful life of research.

February 2nd. Hadleigh Farm Colony.—Here for a week-end watching the Salvation Army at work among the unemployed and un-
employable. The most interesting fact is the Salvation Army itself. I
have seen something of the officers in London; Colonel Lamb, Colonel
Iliffe, Commander Cox and others, all belonging to the social side of
the army. On the colony are some half-dozen other officers engaged
in philanthropic administration, and two spiritual officers (women); two
" specials " came down for Sunday—Brigadier Jackson and his wife.
In respect to personal character, all these men and women constitute
a *Samurai* caste, that is, they are men and women selected for their
power of subordinating themselves to their cause, most assuredly a
remarkable type of ecclesiastic: remarkable because there is no in-
equality between man and woman, because home life and married life
are combined with a complete dedication of the individual to spiritual
service. A beautiful spirit of love and personal service, of content and
joy, permeates the service; there is a persistent note of courtesy to
others and open-mindedness to the world. The men, and some of the
women, are far more cultivated than is usual with persons of the same
social status—one can talk to them quite freely—far more freely than
you could talk to an elementary school teacher, or trade union official;
there is a curious feeling that they are, in some ways at any rate, citizens
of the world. All the officers carry a power of command and have the
personal dignity which springs from this, especially when it is combined
with the habit of obedience. This is especially true of the officers
engaged in the social work, the officers on the spiritual side have more
the characteristics of the artist or public performer—more emotion
and less intelligence.

How does Hadleigh differ from Hollesley? A more mixed lot of
men—ex-convicts, ex-tramps, workhouse-able-bodied and men picked
up in shelters, far more human wreckage, but, on the other hand, less
the ordinary ruck of casual labourers. Here they are, I think, more
successful in getting the men to work, there is less foul talk, perhaps
less discontent and jeering. The self-devotion of the officers counts for
something in raising the tone of the colonists. On the other hand, there
is tremendous religious pressure—far more than I had realised. The
colonists must attend the Saturday evening social and the Sunday

evening religious service, whilst they are invited—almost implored—to come to prayer meetings all day on Sunday and on the other evenings. The Sunday evening service is a stirring and compelling ceremony, at which every act is used to attract the colonists to the penitent's form. Music, eloquence, the magnetic personality of the trained salvationist preachers—a personality that combines the spiritual leader with that of the refined variety artist—all these talents are lavished on the work of conversion. And would it be very surprising if the ignorant and childishly suspicious men, who make up the colonists, should imagine that they would do better, even from the worldly point of view, if they accepted the creed of their governors? The Saturday entertainment, though permeated with religious feeling, even the Sunday morning and afternoon services, did not transgress the limits of reasonable influence. But the intensely compelling nature of the appeal to become converted made to-night by Brigadier Jackson and his wife, I confess somewhat frightened me off recommending that the Salvation Army should be state- or rate-aided in this work of proselytising persons committed to their care for secular reasons! Is it right to submit men, weakened by suffering, to this religious pressure exercised by the very persons who command their labour?

The Salvation Army ritual is certainly a wonderful work of art. The men and women who conduct it are thoroughly trained performers —well modulated voices, clever gestures, all the technique of an accomplished artist, something between melodrama and the music-hall. But this technique is possessed by no mere performers. The men and women are, for the most part, real living saints, who feel intensely all they are saying and acting. To those who do not hold their faith and who look at them critically, their passionate pleadings, their dramatic gestures, their perpetual impromptus, sometimes speaking, sometimes singing, sometimes playing on various instruments, calling to each other, all this wonderful revivalist business, leaves on the outsider a feeling of amazement that these wondrous beings should be ordinary English citizens brought up in ordinary English traditions; they seem possessed with some weird faith belonging to another civilisation. And yet once the meeting is over the salvationist is a particularly shrewd, kindly, courteous, open-minded individual, eminently easy and satisfactory to do business with.

February 10th.—A series of political dinner parties—Haldane and A. J. B. to meet the advisory committee on army education, with the thirty young officers already at the school coming in after dinner! [I remember, on this occasion, when A. J. B. came up after dinner and saw the company of young officers, he asked with a smile, " And what am I here for to-night, Mrs. Webb? " " To show that the School is not a Socialist institution ", I laughingly replied.] Dinner with Haldane, at which I went in with Asquith, and had some talk with Winston Churchill—renewed our acquaintance; dining to-night with Sydney Buxton and on Monday with Asquith and seeing such folk as Masterman, Lyttelton and other M.P.'s. The net impression left on our mind is the scramble for new constructive ideas. We happen just now to have a good many to give away, hence the eagerness for our company. Every politician one meets wants to be coached—it is really quite comic—it seems to be quite irrelevant whether they are Conservatives, Liberals or Labour Party men—all alike have become mendicants for practicable proposals. Hence, our life has become somewhat too exciting. We have the hard grind of the poor law enquiry and, on the top of it, speculative investments in the minds of rival politicians. We are inclined to plunge heavily in all parties, give freely to anyone who comes along—the more the merrier. Asquith actually asked me whether he should adumbrate the " break-up of the poor law " in the budget speech, when he introduces pensions. What effect would that little bomb have on my Commission I am wondering? Would it blow them forward or blow them back? Meanwhile, life is decidedly too exciting: it is hard to keep one's head cool and free for real downright grind. And yet it is the grind that tells far more than the gamble.

February 17*th.*—These two meetings of the Commission, the first of which is just over, settles the fate of the majority report. The majority have definitely decided to abolish the board of guardians and set up the county council and county borough council as the supreme authority. But this authority is to be exercised by a poor law statutory committee of the council itself, as regards institutions, and by local committees, nominated by the council, as regards outdoor relief. To-day, they decided to retain poor law medical relief in the poor law; to-morrow they will, I think, decide to throw back the unemployed into the poor law. Clearly, I cannot get them any further along my road. But there is every sign that they will " stay put " in their present position. I shall have at most four signatories to my minority report, possibly only two besides myself (Lansbury and Chandler)—Phelps contemplates the possibility of signing both! Russell Wakefield will revert to the chairman (mean dog that he is!). [This was an unjust aspersion as the event proved.] After to-morrow I shall not bother to attend their palavers and must grind at my own report as they evidently *mean* to hurry the report on to the finish before the autumn recess. They are, as a body, so light-headed and careless of form and substance that I think it conceivable that they will accomplish it. But what a document it will be! The unanimity of the Commission outside my clique is a personal triumph for the chairman, if he manages to preserve it through the actual discussion of the draft. I like the man so much that I am inclined to be pleased with his success—since it pleases him and doesn't hurt me! His one failure has been to convert the majority to any change in the *status* of medical relief. But that failure was, I think, inevitable, when once he had decided on *one* statutory poor law committee of the county council. If you withdraw one class from the authority of the committee, the whole structure falls to pieces. The reflection of my cry to abolish the poor law is viewed in the desire of the majority to alter the name into " public assistance "; they are already talking of the " old poor law " (*i.e.* the present poor law) as a thing of the past, which is to be superseded by a completely transformed service. The spirit of change possesses them, without any clear conception of whither they wish to go.

February 18*th.*—Half the morning's discussion on the unemployed question. Unanimity in favour of a system of labour exchanges—really half-hearted on the part of the C.O.S., regarded as a safe futility, not compulsory or nationally managed. Such relief as is given to be doled out by the public assistance authority. What was interesting was Loch's proposal to abolish the class of " able-bodied " altogether, with all the L.G.B. restrictions on the relief of this class, and to let the relieving authority deal with each case " on its merits ". " But this goes against the fundamental principles we have adopted in favour of uniformity and classification ", protested poor Lord George. " Would not the system of treating each case on its merits be rather difficult to work with nominated committees spending the county rate? " I asked innocently of Sir Samuel Provis. " Impossible ", was the reply.

What, however, is clear, is that the C.O.S. party are desperately anxious to slur over everything which distinguishes one destitute person from another destitute person—the category of the destitute is to be kept absolutely separate from the rest of the population. Yesterday it looked like a possible report by the end of this summer; to-day we were again in the morass of unsettled opinions, and were surrounded by big controversies. A majority report became again a nebulous affair —but with this extreme muddleheadedness on the part of the chairman and most of the members, there is no saying where the Commission may be dragged by the C.O.S. faction. Just at present they are in the ascendant. Having given way to the chairman as regards the constitution of the authority, they are forcing him to accept their policy with regard to each class of destitute person, *i.e.* rooted objection to the curative policy and determination to stand by the principle of merely *relieving destitution*, whether that destitution be due to childhood, age, illness, unemployment or vagrancy.

Note that the curative principle is absolutely inconsistent with national uniformity of treatment. The only possible sphere for the principle of uniformity is the economic sphere: the question whether a person is within the income-limit for treatment at the public expense, or treatment without charge, or treatment in the home (the latter assumes that outdoor relief is economically pernicious and must be guarded against).

February 22nd. Leeds.—Off on a tour round able-bodied work-houses and labour yards in Lancashire and Yorkshire—an unpleasant and costly business (Commission won't allow me even my travelling expenses), but necessary to my work. The Sheffield " test " house and " test " yard represent the most deterrent poor law practice. But it is interesting to note that neither the master of the workhouse, nor the superintendent of the yard, feel satisfied that they are doing more than shift the problem for others to deal with. It is a horrid business: ah me! When will all this wicked misery cease—misery that leads to wicked-ness and wickedness that leads to misery? An abomination. Oh! ye politicians, what a work before you if you could only be forced, every-one of you, to realise the needlessness of this abomination.

March 11th.—Winston Churchill dined with us last night, together with Masterman, Beveridge, Morton: we talked exclusively shop. He had swallowed whole Sidney's scheme for boy labour and unemployment, had even dished it up in an article in *The Nation* the week before. He is most anxious to be friendly and we were quite willing to be so. He and Masterman seem to be almost sentimental friends. Rhetoricians both are, but Winston has a hard temperament, with the American's capacity for the quick appreciation and rapid execution of new ideas, whilst hardly comprehending the philosophy beneath them. But I rather liked the man. He is under no delusions about himself. And I am not sure that he is not beginning to realise the preposterousness of the present state of things—at any rate he is trying hard to do so, because he feels it necessary that he should do so, if he is to remain in the Liberal ranks. Will he remain in the Liberal ranks?

March 17th.—Two more palavers over a wonderful scheme of Mrs. Bosanquet's for medical relief. A fantastic constitution—" cycle upon epicycle " of nominated committees, all to start going a scheme of provident associations to which the whole world below a certain wage limit is eventually to belong. But I pricked the bubble by reminding them that " free choice of doctor " by destitute persons meant some millions of compensation to the 3500 poor law medical officers. Moreover, they could not make up their own minds, whether or not these provident associations were to be subsidised out of the rates, and whether any kind of compulsion was to be exercised on poor persons to belong to them; eventually they decided *against* all four conditions of success; *i.e.* free choice of doctors by destitute persons, subsidy from the rates, compulsion to belong, most important of all, prohibition of free medical treatment by hospitals and charitable agencies. So the whole business fell to the ground. " A profitless meeting", said Sir Henry Robinson to me angrily. " Here I have been called all the way from Ireland to discuss a silly memorandum, and we have come to no conclusions." He did not appear on the following day, and I thought it not worth while to put in an appearance. Apparently, they were all very angry with each other and the second day's discussion ended in a quagmire. Such resolutions as they did pass have been circulated, though apparently neither Provis nor Robinson believe that they bind the majority of the Commission. I gather that there are to be no more palavers until Easter: yet the report is to be ready by August! But the atmosphere is quite peaceful, and we are the best of friends among ourselves.

March 24th.—Gave A. J. B. my poor law scheme whilst we were staying at Stanway. Lord Elcho had read it and been captivated by it, and begged me to hand it on, in A. J. B.'s presence. " If he will really read it and remember to return it to me ", I graciously remarked. " I promise on both counts, Mrs. Webb." So having reported to H.M. Government, I report to H.M. Opposition (A. J. B. kept it for some weeks and returned it with an encouraging letter).

Meanwhile, the L.C.C. with its Moderate majority has plumped down in its statement of evidence on my side, much to the dismay of the majority. And an enterprising journalist has adopted the L.C.C. scheme to the whole country and issued it as a forecast of the Commission's report. Fortunately it is *not* exactly my scheme, as the minor local authorities (metropolitan borough councils and urban district councils) are retained for outdoor relief and there is no stipendiary. But the children are to be managed by the education authority, and the sick by the health authority, etc. etc. The chairman is much perturbed and begs us to be discreet. If the forecast had been inspired (which it had not), it could not have been more discreetly indiscreet—more likely to raise the right sort of expectations. Will they persist in their stupid plan? The coils are winding round them—they must be beginning to feel a bit stuffy—though they look quite happy and self-complacent. No sign of a draft report.

For my part I have returned to the anti-Commission state of mind. The meetings seem no longer to concern me; and, if I look in after lunch, it is only to show that I bear no ill-will. Moreover, the Commission has run dry, both in evidence and in capacity for palavers—on two successive Tuesdays we have not met at all, and Monday's meetings have been very perfunctory and ill-attended. Sidney and I are hard at work on the treatise on " able-bodied destitution ", its prevention and treatment, and we foresee that for the next six months or a year we shall be absorbed in preparing the various reports arising out of the Commission. Just at present, the bulk of the work is falling on him, as I feel dreadfully tired—habitually tired, not ill—merely physically and mentally weary. Owing to his blessed strength and capacity, I can lie back in these times, just giving him all the suggestions and help that I can, and waiting calmly for returning strength. And, in order to store the strength up, we are not entertaining or being entertained; one day after another passing in its regular routine of early hours, simple meals and regulation work—I just luxuriating by the side of my boy, encouraged and encouraging.

Matters are disconcertingly slack on the Commission. A draft of the headings of the report has been prepared—a most extensive document covering the whole field of poor law and unemployment. The sort of report which would take us six months to *write*. If Lord George really means to have a report of that sort, we shall be discussing it this time next year—at least we shall if the Commission gets out of its chronic state of paralysis. I don't believe we shall have the completed draft by October. There is the possibility of the C.O.S. rucking up and going back in favour of an *ad hoc* authority, when they realise that municipalisation means distribution of services. They have already broken away from the chairman, as to London. Also, they may begin to see that they had better play for delay so that this Government shall not touch the question. On the whole, I incline to think that this Government will *not* be able to do either poor law or unemployment. In some ways it would be better that they should not, if we can get Morant settled at L.G.B. and both front benches impregnated with the idea of the break-up. But as Sidney says, " A Bill in the hand is better than a Bill in the bush. . . ."

April 22nd. Kilteragh, near Dublin.—Four days with Horace Plunkett in his charming and restful home—the perfect ease of a most comfortable but easygoing bachelor establishment, seeing officials and his little clique of the Irish Agricultural Organisation Society. He is the same dear, good man—painstaking and with delicate insight into human nature—but not wanting in little human weaknesses. He is, at present, smarting at his dismissal and at the iconoclastic disposition of the Russell-Birrell administration. Hence, he is dead on all their doings and trying to nullify their action as they have nullified his. For instance, he is fomenting opposition to Birrell's Catholic University Bill on the ground of its unworthy governing body; he is trying to discount, in advance, the report of the Commission on the congested districts. On the whole, as far as I understood his contention, I agree with his dislike of the mechanical and materialist views of social reform which the English Liberal metes out to the Irish. Mechanical relief is to them the only alternative to *laisser-faire*. Plunkett, like ourselves, wishes to grow a new set of obligations for the individual in return for increased state aid. How far he has been too nervous in taking action, too anxious to put education in front of assistance—one cannot say.

April. Rian Hotel, Co. Galway.—A pleasant and useful time with eight or nine colleagues at Dublin—chairman, Phelps, Bentham, Downes, Robinson, Bishop [of Ross], Smart, H. Nunn, MacDougall— all most friendly. The chairman is quite satisfied that the Commission, as a whole, has accepted the resolutions agreed to as a final basis for the report, and is now beginning to write it, with the help of his three secretaries. He believes he can get the whole draft ready for discussion by the end of July—and that he will get it passed by the middle of August. If necessary he proposes to adjourn to Deal. " We must settle It before we part: if we don't we shall come back in October with new ideas, and shall have to begin all over again." Such is the stability of these proposals. But the other members of the Commission are not so confident. Phelps, it is true, thinks we shall muddle through somehow, and intends to stick to the chairman and the majority, whatever they propose. But Downes is determined to abide by the boards of guardians, and will have his own report. H. Nunn is going for the abolition of outdoor relief and a minor authority, made up of charitable agencies, to grant admission to institutions. Robinson and Smart feel wholly uncommitted and are attracted by my scheme—Robinson determined not to put his name to anything that is unworkable and fantastic. MacDougall is resolved, like Downes is for England, to stand on the *status quo* for Scotland, though he is indifferent as to what happens in the other kingdom. The Bishop does not think he can sign my report, as our ideas are " so fundamentally opposed " on the family—but he also feels himself uncommitted by the resolution. Meanwhile, the chairman thinks his greatest difficulty will be Loch, and I believe I have Wakefield in addition to Lansbury and Chandler, so that it is difficult to see where exactly is the majority on which the chairman relies! The members may be paralysed by their own inability to draft a report and their fear of tumbling into my arms, into accepting the chairman's draft. But my impression is that the end of August will see us in a morass of conflicting ideas.

Meanwhile, Morant has had my scheme reprinted with another front page, to circulate to experts and no doubt the Cabinet. Directly

I get back, we must put all else on one side and devote ourselves to the general report. Every word of the report must be devised to lead to the conclusion. It must be a work of art in the best sense, admirably adapted to its " end ", the conversion of the reader to the " break-up of the poor law ".

May 3rd.—Henry Robinson (the Vice-President of the L.G.B. of Ireland), who is escorting our party, is one of the most agreeable companions I have ever run across. He comes of an Irish garrison family that has produced a bevy of admirals, governors and army officers of considerable distinction. He was bred, with his brother, for the public service. He is tall and thin, with a retreating forehead, large ears, straight dark hair, long foxy nose, and somewhat foxy expression in his dark grey eyes. He has an agreeable and accomplished manner and a most pleasant faculty of mimicry and an endless flow of Irish stories. He knows his Ireland through and through, and looks at its life with kindly good sense. His enemies say he is " slim " and a " time server ". So he is, but he has developed these qualities, without a lack of uprightness, and with a measure of good intention. So far as I have carried my investigation, during our long motor rides together, I have discovered no kind of preference for one state of society over another. After trying to elicit a positive principle, or a positive prejudice, I asked him outright what kind of society he desired in Ireland, assuming he had complete power to bring it about. A dull look came into his grey eyes—giving the impression of a sort of film—an expression of deadness which he has whenever one gets away from the facts of to-day, and after a moment's silence he said, " Well, Mrs. Webb, I have lived all my life at concert pitch, and I really never thought of all these questions in which you are interested. What has concerned me is to keep my successive chief secretaries out of trouble." To keep the chief secretary out of trouble in all matters coming within the purview of the Irish L.G.B. is, in fact, Robinson's chief aim. He looks at each successive chief secretary, both with regard to his past pledges, the exigencies of his party in England, and with regard to Irish affairs, as a problem to be solved. He naturally prefers the Unionist chiefs as these have a freer hand—they can ignore their own allies and need have no consideration for the " Irish Party "; but I could not discern any real personal opinion as to reform, one way or the other, except a preference for law and order. His only personal concern is the agreeableness of the holder of the office—he liked Balfour and Long and he likes Birrell; he detested Wyndham, Hicks-Beach; found Bryce a bore, and so on. He has the characteristics of all very clever officials; he seems indiscreet and is a monument of discretion.

Just now he is thinking a good deal of the probable successor to

Antony Macdonnell. This last, he says, like all Indian administrators coming to Ireland, has been a complete failure—not one of his schemes has come off. He came as a great land expert, and intended to take up and reform each department of Irish administration on Indian lines. But he found the law, the customs, the habits of the people wholly different. Moreover, he was face to face with a new factor—one he had never before encountered—the democratic institutions of Great Britain, which baffled and perplexed him; which he began by ignoring and which, therefore, were always straight in his road stopping his way. So poor Antony is now a broken man, broken in health, broken in spirit and much worsened in fortune. And he is on the point of resigning. Who is to succeed him? The next to succeed is an old man— Dougherty—with one year to run, and he may and probably will be appointed for next year. But who next? asks H. R. If it were not for politics, undoubtedly Robinson would get the place. But he is reputed a Unionist, and the Irish nationalists detest him. Will Birrell dare, if he should be in office, to make him under-secretary in spite of nationalist pressure? That is the question.

H. R. has told me much about Irish local government and the doings of various chief secretaries; but from these casual sketches, it is difficult to construct even an outline of what happened. I cannot even make out whether the countryside is better or worse for all this subsidising activity—there is less misery but more dependence. Feeling the impossibility of getting any kind of knowledge—even the most casual—from my trip, I have taken it as a holiday jaunt at the Treasury expense, with just the excuse of investigation to give a flavour to our touring. These days of motoring and steaming along coasts, and between islands, have been a most delightful rest to me. The beauty of the scenery, the freshness and pathos of Irish life, the complete break into the continuous routine grind of the last two years, have done me a world of good. But this very enjoyment shows how hopelessly irresponsible I feel with regard to Irish affairs—no more responsible than if I were travelling in Norway or Sicily. For the misery is genuine—the men, women and children who crouch in those filthy huts and toil hour by hour on those bog lands in a listless fashion, are in this their beloved country hopeless and helpless with regard to this world's affairs. There is heaven and there is America—and, according to whether they are the children of this world or of the next, they desire to escape to one or the other. Until this escape opens to them, they are drearily indifferent to varying degrees of squalor and want— mechanically day after day they toil, but they do not struggle to survive the ordeal. In the West of Ireland, one realises for the first time the grim fact of the existence of a whole community on the margin of cultivation. All the expedients resorted to seem but to prolong the misery of the mortally sick.

May 5th. Mallarany.—The last day of the Irish holiday. Yesterday, we continued our unblushing jaunt at the Treasury's expense by a most delightful steam in the Congested Districts' boat to Clare Island, and afterwards up Killary Bay—the most beautiful part of the Connemara scenery. At Clare Island we shipped a loquacious priest, Father Nally, a rebel against the authority of Bishop or Irish party— a denouncer of the " Gombean Man " who now rules these western coastal islands. I suggested to him a co-operative store run by the district board, or the abolition of prosecutions for debt so as to destroy the credit system. I am not sure that the abolition of debt is not the best measure for these folk—to force them to rely on character among neighbours for fulfilling their obligations.

I seem to have converted both Robinson and Downes to the notion that the alternatives before the Commission are the *status quo* and my scheme. That is what I have aimed at—steadily to press to that conclusion. Professor Smart has maintained throughout the little trip what Robinson called " a mad dog " habit of wandering off by himself, jotting down little facts about the countryside—the number of public-houses in a village street, the character of the crops on the wayside, and every other morsel of disjointed fact that he can pick up—in the intervals of heavy eating. He is a dull fellow without intellectual purpose—and with precious little intelligence, with all the less attractive qualities of the Scotchman. The gentle Downes, the lively Robinson and I have made up a jolly party, and we all part with regret from each other's company.

Directly I get back we must start on the general report—every word must tell. If every word in every sentence tells towards the conclusion, then I can afford to circulate it freely to my colleagues, without fear that some of it shall be taken and the rest left.

May 15th.—Yesterday we met for the last time before adjourning for the chairman to write the report. This he believes, he and the secretaries, with Mrs. Bosanquet and Professor Smart's help, will accomplish by the first week in July. He then proposes to sit every day until the report is passed; even into August; it will then be handed over to someone to smooth out inconsistencies and we shall meet to sign it in October. Meanwhile, the minority and minorities, or partial dissentients, will be expected to produce their documents equally ready for signature in October.

Meanwhile, Morant has provided me with some 100 copies of my scheme for breaking up the poor law, which he has had printed for his own consideration. I have sent or given it in confidence to Asquith, Lloyd George, Haldane, Winston Churchill, McKenna, Sydney Buxton, Runciman, Harcourt, H. Samuel, John Burns, McKinnon Wood of the present Government, and Balfour, Long, Austen Chamberlain, Lyttelton, Gerald Balfour, of the late Government, and to a select few important civil servants, journalists and local administrators. I have a notion that, when we have got our " unemployed " scheme drafted in its final form, we will get Winston Churchill to print it at the Board of Trade and do ditto with that. Such big schemes require careful consideration by many brains, they have to sink in to the minds of those likely to carry them out, if they are to become practical politics within a generation.

May 19th.—I had a talk with John Burns at the L.G.B. about the Commission and the possibility of his bringing in a big poor law scheme. He went over the scheme of the " break-up of the poor law " very carefully. When we came to the able-bodied, I explained that you could either revert to the principles of 1834 and establish an able-bodied " test " workhouse under police committees, or go forward towards a great national authority for the unemployed. " That's no good, Mrs. Webb: I should prefer to make the police the authority for vagrants and able-bodied men. Now the rest of your scheme I see clearly." He brought up the name of Morant, evidently to see what I should say. I again assured him that Morant was the only man who could carry out the job, and bring order into the L.G.B. He is clearly considering the matter and said that, any day, I might hear of great changes. He is clearly uncomfortable about his loss of popularity in the Liberal ranks, but consoles himself with cuttings from the *Daily Mail* and *Express*.

From John Burns we went to lunch alone with R. B. Haldane and found him as friendly as ever. Clearly his *bête noire* is Lloyd George—and after him Winston Churchill—the young generation knocking at the door. He is full of confidence in his Territorial Army and in all the reforms he has brought about at the War Office. " I shall have finished my work there in eighteen months and then I should be prepared to take on the L.G.B." I impressed on him that Asquith must see to the appointment of Morant at the L.G.B. (Burns by the way actually suggested Sidney, but I pooh-poohed the idea as impossible on account of his views), and told him how delighted we should be to have him at the L.G.B. Both Burns and Haldane declared that it would be impossible to bring in a big poor law scheme next session, even if the Commission did report by December or January. This would certainly be so, unless the report were practically unanimous. If two or three courses were suggested, there would have to be a year's consideration of the alternatives opened out by the Commission.

What interested me, somewhat sadly, in both these men, was the manner in which their own personalities and their own careers loomed large before them; with Burns, blocking out everything else; with Haldane, detracting from the charm of his public-spirited intelligence. This was shown in both cases by an extraordinary anxiety to prove to us that they were the important factors in the Government, and to run down other members of the Cabinet. Probably every poor mortal suffers from this obsession with self; but actors and actresses, and politicians, seem really plagued by it. Fine-natured men like Haldane, fastidious-natured men like A. J. B., neither of whom, as *littérateurs* or as lawyers or as doctors, would be self-conscious, are in their character as politicians teased by the spirit of competitive fame.

July 27th.—Exactly two months since I have reported progress. Three weeks we spent happily at the Playnes', then a fortnight in London, then four weeks at the Hermitage, Luton, all the time working day in day out at the report, and not yet nearly finished Part I., *The Non-Able-bodied.* To survey the whole field and lead up, step by step, to the break-up of the poor law, in such a way as to make any other policy impossible, is a very big task. Whether we shall not overreach ourselves in the elaborateness of our statement and our argument, is a serious question. Many people will think so. But so momentous a change—one needing so large an expenditure of thought and money—can only be brought about by an exhaustive process. Anyway, when it is finished we can throw over any parts which seem really superfluous —and on this we may take advice. Meanwhile, I have sent all we have written to be printed at the request of the secretaries of the Commission who seem most anxious for the privilege of reading it. After considering this anxiety, we decided that, on the whole, it would suit us better to have it in print.

Our stay in the cottage of the millionaire, whilst we were composing this great collectivist document, was really rather comic. Sir Julius Wernher wrote in May to offer us " The Hermitage ", a pleasant little house in its own grounds, but in his park, for as long as we cared to accept it. From the extreme corner of the millionaire's park, we surveyed a machine for the futile expenditure of wealth. Wernher himself is big in body and big in mind, and even big in his aims. To make wealth was his first aim; to carry on great enterprises because he delights in industrial construction was his second aim, and now to advance technology and applied science has been his latest aim. It was over the establishment of the London " Charlottenburg " scheme that Sidney came across him, and found him the best of fellows according to his own lights. Hence, we felt free to accept his hospitality. Part of the minor convention of his life has been the acquisition of a great country mansion, with an historic name as counterpart to Bath House, Piccadilly. This was no doubt to please his " society "-loving wife—a hard, vainglorious woman, talkative and badly bred, but not otherwise objectionable. The family spend some Sundays at Luton Hoo and a few months in the autumn, but all the rest of the 365 days the big machine goes grinding on, with its 54 gardeners, 10 electricians, 20 or 30 house servants and endless labourers for no one's benefit, except that it furnishes dishonest pickings to all concerned. The great mansion stood, closed and silent, in the closed and silent park—no one coming or going except the retinue of servants, the only noises the perpetual whirring and calling of the thousands of pheasants, ducks and other game that were fattening ready for the autumn slaughter. At the gates of the park, a bare half-mile distant, lay the crowded town of Luton— drunken, sensual, disorderly—crowded in mean streets, with a terrific infant mortality. The contrast was oppressingly unpleasant, and haunted our thoughts as we sat under the glorious trees and roamed through wood and garden, used their carriages, enjoyed the fruit, flowers and vegetables, and lived for a brief interval in close contact with an expenditure of £30,000 a year on a country house alone.

September 15th.—After another six weeks at the little house in Herefordshire, and four days at the Fabian Summer School, we are again back in London. Not yet finished the " non-able-bodied " report, though nearly through with it. Meanwhile, I am again in disgrace with the Commission, this time somewhat seriously. As part of the newspaper campaign for " the break-up of the poor law ", we gave our poor law scheme to Amery[1] of the *Times*, telling him he could use the idea, but was *not* to mention either our names or the Royal Commission. About the middle of August, there appeared special articles on the breaking-up of the poor law, giving the whole scheme— the last part verbatim. This really indiscreet use of our composition roused Lord George Hamilton to fury, and he fired off angry letters denouncing a breach of confidence. The last of these letters is not only amazingly indiscreet, but contains a malicious fib. There are no two separate series of propositions before the Commission, there is only his draft report. He stuck this statement in in order to make it appear that there had been a breach of confidence; and, of course, to anyone who knows the make-up of the Commission the evil one must be the Webbs, in the combined capacity of commissioner and publicist. To this attack, there was no public rejoinder possible. I circulated a letter to the Commission saying that neither Sidney nor I had contributed the articles, but that we had circulated freely our scheme of reform, and that the writer had evidently had a copy of it beside him. I was

[1] Afterwards the Rt. Hon. L. Amery, member of Conservative Cabinets.

worried about the business, but Sidney remained imperturbable. Of course, the publication in the *Times*, together with Lord George's indiscreet letter, have boomed the scheme enormously, the *Morning Post*, *Standard* and many provincial papers accepting it as the obvious reform. The net result of our indiscreet, or, as some would say, unscrupulous activity, has been to damage the Webbs but to promote their ideas. We seem destined to use ourselves up in this breaking-up of the poor law—the fate of capacity and good intentions combined with bad manners! And the worst of my temperament is, that I have far more audacity than I have passive courage—I do this thing with splendid dash and then tremble with fear afterwards. All of which means nervous strain. Fortunately, there is always Sidney to fall back on with his genuine indifference to what the world says. " They say, what say they, let them say ", might be his motto—except that he is unaware of his indifference, it is too complete.

The *Times* episode breaks, I think, finally any friendly relations with my colleagues—with all except Chandler, Lansbury and possibly Wakefield. Fortunately, no further co-operation is necessary—I am known to be writing the minority report, and they will be discussing the majority report. I already announced my intention in the spring of not joining in their discussions, and shall only put in a formal appearance on the first days. Afterwards, I shall leave the guerilla warfare to Lansbury and Chandler. What we want now is some months' delay to perfect our report, both in form and substance—we want, in fact, till Easter. So far as I hear from Lansbury, who has been abroad with Loch, Nunn and Bentham, there is a great desire to finish the business by Christmas, partly to be rid of it, partly to counteract the Webb propaganda by definite contrary proposals. If they are really both united and determined, they could do it. We should then have to consider whether we would issue our " non-able-bodied " report with this, and issue the " able-bodied " separately, or hurry through with both in a less perfected form than would be desirable. Probably, however, they will *not* finish their discussion by Christmas and will adjourn for re-drafting. Even when the majority proposals are in their final shape, there will be dissentient paragraphs and supplementary reports to be drafted and printed. But I shall have to keep in the best training, refuse to worry over the coldness of my colleagues, or the censorious remarks of other people, with my mind fixed on the one aim (whatever happens to the Webbs). The position is unpleasant, but it will be soon over.

The Fabian Summer School has become an odd and interesting institution. Two or three houses on the mountainous coast of North Wales are filled to overflowing for seven weeks with some hundred Fabians and sympathisers—a dozen or so young university graduates and undergraduates, another strain of lower middle-class professionals, a stray member of Parliament or professor, a bevy of fair girls, and the remainder—a too large remainder, elderly and old nondescript females, who find the place lively and fairly cheap. The young folk live the most unconventional life, giving the quaker-like Lawson Dodd, who rules the roost, many an unpleasant quarter of an hour—stealing out on moor or sand, in stable or under hayricks, without always the requisite chaperone to make it look as wholly innocent as it really is. Then the gym costume which they all affect is startling the methodist Wales, and the conversation is most surprisingly open. " Is dancing sexual? " I found three pretty Cambridge girl graduates discussing with half-a-dozen men. But mostly they talk economics and political science in the intervals of breaking off the engagements to marry each other they formed a year ago. Meanwhile, there is some really useful intellectual intercourse going on between the elders, and between them and the younger ones. The Cambridge men are a remarkable set— quite the most remarkable the Fabian Society has hitherto attracted— fervent and brilliant.

I had seven of the Cambridge Fabians to stay with me on their way to Wales. Two are remarkable men—Keeling and Dalton—the one a fervent rebel (who reminds me of sister Holt in his generous vitality and incontinent intelligence), and the other an accomplished ecclesiastical sort of person—a subtle wily man with a certain peculiar charm for those who are not put off by his mannerism. The other five were, I think, commonplace—Schloss, Strachey, Brooke [1] (a poetic beauty) and Shove—perhaps Dudley Ward was a little over the line of medium capacity and character.

October 2nd.—Sidney and I are living at the highest pressure of brain-work. We are working against time on the report—fearing lest the majority should agree to their report before Christmas. Sidney has to give six lectures on " currency " at the School in November—a subject with which he is not familiar: he has also to help Reeves to get into the saddle.

There is the usual medley of business at the L.C.C., the Central Unemployed Body and Fabian Society, and we have to write the chapter on social movements for the *Cambridge Modern History*. To enable me to fill my part of the work, I am living on the most rigorous hygienic basis—up at 6.30, cold bath and quick walk or ride, work

[1] This was the afterwards famous Rupert Brooke who put me off the track of his distinction by delivering a super-conceited lecture on the relation of the university man to the common herd of democracy. Also I am poetry blind like some persons are colour blind.

Ben Keeling was killed in the war; Hugh Dalton is now a member of the Labour Party (December 1923).

from 7.30 to 1 o'clock, bread and cheese lunch, short rest, another walk, then tea and work until 6 or 6.30, sometimes as much as seven hours' work in the day. I feel it is too much, and am sleeping badly from brain excitement. But short of breaking down, I must continue at it until Christmas. After the report is done with we *must and will* have a complete rest—Egypt or Italy—somewhere where we shall rid our minds of the whole business.

October 5th.—First meeting of the Commission after the recess. I came in when they were just beginning business. A letter from me offering the "infant mortality" material had been circulated and lay on the table. But they evidently did not intend to discuss it while I was there. The chairman somewhat haltingly described the difficulties in drafting the Majority Report, and desired a general discussion on its reception by the Commission. The Bishop endorsed it fully: R. Wakefield and H. Nunn hedged; Lansbury and Chandler stated their general objection to it, but would move amendments; Bentham agreed, with minor amendments; Smart pleaded that the whole report, including his long-winded history, should be retained and not curtailed; Phelps dryly agreed to it generally; ditto Provis, Loch, Bosanquet and Gardiner. Dr. Downes and Miss Hill stated that they were not in agreement as to the machinery and constitution. No member objected to the doctrines contained in it, but everyone held themselves free to alter it. Settled that we are to meet twice a week, and that we are to try and get finished by Christmas, so far as discussion is concerned, leaving one month to get the report revised and out before the session begins. There was coldness towards me, and Lansbury says they are very angry both at the *Times* episode and at the length of my report. They were not pleased with the offer of the "infant mortality" material[1] and will, I think, refuse to receive it. Lansbury and Chandler are going to attend all the sittings and move some amendments. I shall seldom intervene. We have now a clear three months to complete our report in, that ought to suffice to make a really good job of it. On the whole, I doubt the majority getting through by Christmas—if they do it will be an odd document.

October 16th.—Meanwhile, we are seeing something of Ministers. On Sunday we lunched with Winston Churchill and his bride—a charming lady, well bred and pretty, and earnest withal—but not rich, by no means a good match, which is to Winston's credit. Winston had made a really eloquent speech on the unemployed the night before

---

[1] The statistics of infant mortality for a certain number of workhouses were actually compiled and analysed for me by Dr. (afterwards Sir Arthur) Newsholme, the principal medical officer of the L.G.B.

and he has mastered the Webb scheme, though not going the whole length of compulsory labour exchanges. He is brilliantly able—more than a phrase-monger I think—and he is definitely casting in his lot with the constructive state action. No doubt he puts that side forward to me—but still he could not do it so well if he did not agree somewhat with it. After lunch Lloyd George came in and asked us to breakfast to discuss his insurance scheme.

On Friday, we fulfilled the engagement at 11 Downing Street, meeting Haldane, Blain of the Treasury, two secretaries, Harold Cox and, after breakfast, Winston. We had a heated discussion with the Chancellor about the practicability of insurance against invalidity; tried to make him see that the state could not enter into competition with the friendly societies and insurance companies, that it could hardly subsidise a voluntary scheme without becoming responsible for the management, and that any insurance scheme would leave over all the real problems of public assistance. I tried to impress on them that any grant from the community to the individual, beyond what it does for all, ought to be conditional on better conduct and that any insurance scheme had the fatal defect that the state got nothing for its money— that the persons felt they had a right to the allowance whatever their conduct. Also, if you did all that was requisite for those who were uninsured, there was not much to be gained by being insured, except more freedom. No; insurance against unemployment had the great advantage that you could offer more freedom to the person who insured compared with the person whom you maintained and forced to accept training. Hence, insurance against unemployment *might* be subsidised by the state as a sort of " set off " to the trade unionists to get them to accept " maintenance with training " for all the others.

He is a clever fellow [Lloyd George], but has less intellect than Winston, and not such an attractive personality—more of the preacher, less of the statesman. Haldane intervened, as the peace-maker, and suggested that insurance had to be part of a big scheme with conditional relief for those at the bottom, and insurance for those struggling up. We begin our report on the unemployed to-morrow—it must be finished by the end of November—which means sharp work with our tendency to elaboration.

November 15*th.*—The Prime Minister wrote about a fortnight ago to Lord George Hamilton to ask for the evidence taken before the Commission. Without any notice, Lord George brought the matter before the Commission and persuaded those who were present to refuse to supply the evidence, but to offer the draft report after it had passed the drafting committee. Lansbury happened to be present, and after the resolution had been passed stated that he assumed the minority would be at liberty to send their report when they considered it sufficiently ready. This seemed to take the chairman by surprise, but the Commission reluctantly agreed that our dissent should be *sent by the secretary* after it had been discussed by the Commission, thus keeping in their hands the power to withhold it until they could find a day to discuss it in. I happened to meet McKenna the next morning outside the Commission office, he gleefully told me that the Cabinet was going to get the evidence. " Don't be too sure of that," I said, " you will get neither the evidence nor my report—only their own silly nonsense." On Saturday, Haldane came round in his motor. " I have come to ask you whether you would object to our seeing your report? " " Certainly not ", I replied. " I feel quite at liberty to give you all I have as I understand that the majority are sending you their draft— but get the evidence and the investigators' reports ", I added. " Asquith has written again for it, and he quite hopes to get it." " Well, if they *don't* give it you, I shall feel free to do so, as I know John Burns has had some of it—I saw it on his table a year ago." This morning Haldane again appeared. " I want another copy of your report: I have given mine to a young man to master,[1] and I want one for myself. Also *could* you possibly give the Cabinet a loan of the evidence? " " I will get you Lansbury's, if possible." Poor dear ninnies of a Commission: a futile refusal producing the worst impression. And not to realise that the Government had only to ask me for it!

Haldane explained that he had been deputed by the P.M. to get up the whole subject, with a view to drawing up a comprehensive scheme of reform. They would bring in some portions of it next year and the year after (I understand Winston's labour exchanges, and Lloyd George's invalidity pensions), and go the year after that to the country on the whole scheme. He was rather woolly about it. But we chaffingly told him that, if the Liberals did not " break-up the poor law ", we would give the whole business to the tariff reformers—they were in want of a good social reform cry wherewith to go to the country. My own idea is that the Liberals will adumbrate the scheme, but the Tories will carry it out. Which I should prefer in many ways—there would be no nonsense about democracy!

About a fortnight ago, we were invited to breakfast at the Board of Trade. We found assembled some half-dozen of the Labour M.P.'s —Shackleton, Barnes, Curran, Henderson, Appleton, the principal officials of the Board of Trade, Winston and Lloyd George and

---

[1] The young man turned out to be Harold Baker, a brilliant Oxford graduate, at that time a frequenter of political society. He reported, so I was once told, against the minority, and in favour of the Majority Report, which accounts for the coolness of the Liberal Cabinet towards poor law reform in the last years of the administration.

Masterman. After breakfast, we sat round a table and discussed this agenda for a couple of hours—Winston using us to explain the theory of labour exchanges to the Labour men. They were cordial, but strongly urged that the organisation for casual labour by labour exchanges should not be given them as a provision for unemployment.

We are working at terribly high pressure. The way seems clear as regards the organisation of the labour market—the difficulty lies in the character of the provision we make for those thrust out by this very organisation. Having ascertained our surplus and isolated it, how are we going to treat it? That's the question. *We* answer, training. But the Labour men laugh at the notion of training adult men. They want employment at good wages, not to interfere with ordinary employment. In despair, when they realise the danger of displacement of the ordinary workers by unemployed labour, they sometimes suggest unemployed benefit paid by the state *with no conditions.* That is, of course, under the present conditions of human will, sheer madness, whatever it may be in good times to come.

The difficulty of solving the question oppresses me. I dream of it at night, I pray for light in the early morning, I grind, grind, grind, all the hours of the working-day to try to get a solution. Our task is made more difficult by the obligation to carry Lansbury, Chandler and Wakefield with us. I have got to satisfy those men, both in our statements of fact and in our proposals. And there is the consciousness of being hurried and scurried by that blessed old Commission, which is bungling through its report at a great rate, though it seems to order almost as much to be rewritten as it accepts as final. Also, though in a way the fight between my colleagues and myself adds to the excitement and amusement, it also adds to the strain. Their last little pin-prick is to suggest that I am only to have one proof to work on. " Tell the chairman ", I said to Jeffrey yesterday, " that on the day that I am refused the number of proofs that I think necessary for efficient working the report goes off to my private printer, *and if that happens I will not be responsible for the consequences.*"

The poor old Commission—and it is getting more old and weary, if not actually senile, with every week's sitting. It is floundering about in its morass of a report. Everyone is disgusted with the report but no one dares get up and openly rebel. " What is the alternative? Mrs. Webb's draft dissent from the chairman's draft report ", says one disconcerted commissioner to the other. For our document stares at them in a fine blue cover; and, though it is only Part I., yet there it is, 300 pages of reasoned stuff with a scheme of reform at the end. Their report is still in scraps, and each week makes these scraps more discordant with each other. The majority commissioners are getting so tired and irritated with each other that they may break up any day. But I guess they will stick together in so far as mere formal signing is concerned. Are all men quite so imbecile as that lot are? I sit and watch them and wonder. They play about, altering commas and capitals and changing the names of things, but leaving to mere accident whether or not the vagrants or the mentally defective are to be dealt with under the poor law. What puzzles me is that Provis goes into fits of laughter,[1] and Loch is beginning to be hysterically hilarious, when the chairman is more than usually muddled and inconsequent. I should have thought that a report which everyone is waiting for is not quite a laughing matter. On the other hand, they talk quite seriously of their scheme coming into existence, in so many months, and discuss for hours the interim arrangements. As they have not yet settled their scheme, in a form that is intelligible, their discussion seems somewhat " previous ". If I ever sit again on a Royal Commission, I hope my colleagues will be of a superior calibre—for really it is shockingly bad for one's character to be with such folk—it makes me feel intolerably superior.

To these entries of the 1908 diary I add two from that of January 1909, a somewhat cat-like description of the last scenes of the Royal Commission on the Poor Law and Unemployment of 1905–9.

January 1st, 1909.—Our report is finished and we await only the revise of the majority, so as to correct our references and keep in or omit our criticism according to their decision to keep in or omit the paragraph on " The Break-up of the Poor Law ". On Saturday, we are all to attend and be photographed and sign a blank piece of paper. So ends the Commission of 1905–9. I am in a state of complete exhaustion, made worse by nervous apprehension of more indiscretions in the press in the interests of the dissentient minority. The Minority Report has been pretty considerably read, and one or two copies are flying about. However, my colleagues will now melt back into the world at large, and we shall know each other no more. The relation has not been a pleasant one, for either side.

---

[1] After his retirement I became a colleague of Sir Samuel Provis in the Statutory Committee for Pensions of Disabled Soldiers, and we became warm friends. Hence, when the reconstruction committee appointed a sub-committee to recommend as to poor law reform, Provis and also Lord George Hamilton were among my colleagues, and the report of that committee, which was in favour of the break-up of the poor law, was drafted by Sir Samuel Provis, Sir Robert Morant and myself, and accepted by the committee. This reform was, however, not carried out until the Poor Law Amendment Act of 1929.

January 17*th*, 1909.—A scrimmagy meeting on Saturday ended the Royal Commission as far as I am concerned. I was dead beat, and in that state gave Duff a bit of my mind as regards the procedure of the Commission. We are all commanded to sign. But the report from which we had to sign our dissent is still in the making—a new piece of it came round to-day, which apparently is to be inserted into the *signed* document without any meeting of the signatories. It happens to be a somewhat vital part, as it lays down the principle that all applications are to be made, in the first instance, to the " voluntary aid committee "!

Meanwhile, everything looks favourable for the reception of the Minority Report. The majority are counting on the reviewers never getting to that document, and damning it as Socialist. We naturally are taking care, so far as we can, that they get at it—not later than to the Majority Report. We believe that the Majority Report will get a bad reception from all sides. We shall see.

Now I am resting for a week with sister Playne before pulling myself together and clearing up all the mess left over by the report. Then we are going off for a month's holiday. The next months may be stormy. " You have declared war," wrote one of the inspectors of the Local Government Board, " and war this will be."

CHAPTER VIII

THE PLUNGE INTO PROPAGANDA

1909–1911

THE next two years, from the spring of 1909 to the summer of 1911, when we started on our second tour round the world, were spent in an incessant propaganda of the legislative and administrative proposals of the Minority Report of the Poor Law Commission. For this purpose, in May 1909, we inaugurated the National Committee for the Promotion of the Break-Up of the Poor Law, a cumbrous and equivocal title which was changed in the following year to the National Committee for the Prevention of Destitution. This association was presided over by the senior signatory of the report, the Dean of Norwich (Russell Wakefield, afterwards Bishop of Birmingham), with myself as honorary secretary, and the Other One as chairman of the executive committee.

We started out with a small staff of paid assistants and rapidly enrolled a large body of voluntary organisers, journalists and lecturers, together with some 20,000 members, contributing an income for office expenses of over £5000 a year. Within this organisation were not only leading Labour men and Socialists, but also distinguished persons belonging to the Conservative and Liberal parties; also Nonconformist ministers, Anglican dignitaries, and even Catholic priests. In short, the National Committee claimed to be a non-party organisation.

Here it may be well to note that this plunge into propaganda entailed two grave consequences which, if we had realised at the time, might have deterred us from taking this new departure. First and foremost, our research into social institutions had to be suspended: the history of English Local Government during the nineteenth century which we had planned to write in 1899 was never completed, except

Days of the Poor Law Campaign

the history of the English Poor Law, for which my membership of the Royal Commission on the Poor Law enabled us to collect a mass of new material.

The second untoward consequence is less easy to explain. Perhaps it may be summarised in the axiom, you cannot at one and the same time exercise behind-the-scenes influence over statesmen, civil servants and newspaper editors, while you yourself engage in public propaganda of projects which these eminent ones may view with hostility or suspicion.

Thus during 1909–11 we lost touch with Liberal Cabinet Ministers, and later on with the Conservative leaders and superior civil servants. Thereby hangs another tale to be told in a future volume: our rapidly increasing participation in the Labour movement, largely brought about by our success as propagandists of a definite scheme of social reorganisation. This led to the Other One's active participation, during the Great War, in the consolidation of the Labour Party as His Majesty's Opposition; with the result that he himself became a Labour M.P.; then a member of the two Labour Cabinets; and eventually one of the Labour representatives in the House of Lords. Being wise after the event, I sometimes regret this turning-point in Our Partnership. Personally, I should have preferred a life of continued research and non-party social intercourse. But has one, however free one may seem from other people's orders, any real choice between rival calls to action? Is the future as irretrievably fixed as the past seems to be viewed by the historian? Is the career of every mortal settled in advance by character and circumstance? Who knows?

1909

The first entries in the MS. diary after the final meeting for the signature of the two reports reveal utter exhaustion of body and mind, followed by balked self-esteem, blank disappointment at the superior publicity and approval accorded by the press to the Majority over the Minority Report. A restful six weeks' holiday in Italy swept away these unhealthy symptoms and I returned to the daily work of Our Partnership, happy and self-confident, with just a spice of renewed combativeness.

January 17th.—Looking back on those autumn months [I write early in January] I wonder how I managed to come through it—it was sheer will power induced by prayer. Every morning I trudged out between 6.30 and 7.30—an hour of sharp physical exercise combined with intense prayer for help to solve the problem before us each morning. And solutions *did* come to me in those morning walks. How they came I do not know; but, by the time I sat down to work, the particular knot was undone. Now I am in a state of collapse because there is nothing to pray for, nothing particular to do, which seems *beyond* my power—for which I need inspiration. Perhaps, there will be another call. I must be strong enough to answer: " Yes, we will come and do it ".

February 5th.—Still in the depth of depression—the reaction from the pressure of the last eight months. But already I am beginning to foresee that presently I shall revive, and that I shall find myself back again in the quiet atmosphere of the student's life, with no public responsibilities, and with none of those horribly difficult questions of conduct that have been a sort of nightmare to me since I joined the Royal Commission. The plain truth is, that the position of a minority on a hostile Royal Commission is rather intolerable; it has no chance of fighting openly. With no publicity, no appeal from the decision of a preponderant majority, with no regular procedure, so that it is impossible even to know what is being done, leave alone oppose it, the minority is thrown back on the device of working outside the Commission and in defiance of it. Throughout the whole business, Lord George has considered the Commission analogous to a Government of which he was Prime Minister, and those who agreed with him, Secretaries of State, and the minority members sort of Under-Secretaries to be told as much, or as little, as he chose and to obey orders. This has led me to look elsewhere for my forces, and to undermine and circumvent the commissioners' will by calling in those forces. This, of course, has not been nice on my side, and I have from time to time felt horribly miserable about it—especially, I am afraid, when I have been found out. Such are the infirmities of half-civilised human nature! Sidney, of course, takes a different view and has no kind of qualms: he is *self-less* and does not mind doing what he decides it is right to do, whatever other people may think about it. And in all these ways he has a robust conscience. It is immaterial to him whether or not he is found out, or even whether or not he is rightly or wrongly accused. " If I have not done this particular thing," he says cheerily, " I have done something else just as bad, so rough justice is done. *I think I am quite right to do it, or I should not do it* ", he adds.

February 18th.—The day after the reception of the reports of the Poor Law Commission. We turned out to be quite wrong as to the reception of the Majority Report. So far as the first day's reviews are concerned, the majority have got a magnificent reception. We have had a fair look in, but only in those papers which had got to know of the existence of a Minority Report before the issue late on Wednesday night. If we had not taken steps, we should have been submerged completely, by the great length of the Majority Report, coupled with their revolutionary proposals, the largeness of their majority and the relative weight of the names. Roughly speaking, all the Conservative papers went for the majority proposals, and the London Liberal papers were decidedly for ours. We secured, in fact, belligerent rights, but not more than that. The majority hold the platform. Perhaps we feel a trifle foolish at having crabbed the Majority Report to our family and intimate friends, and exalted our own. That has certainly not proved to be the estimate of public opinion.

We have had an amusing little encounter with the majority over the separate publication of our report—by the Fabian Society and Longmans. We thought we had the copyright: or that Sidney had it. I told the Royal Commission staff that we intended to publish immediately after the Royal Commission published. A few days before the publication, the Fabian Society received a peremptory letter from the Treasury solicitor forbidding the publication of the Minority Report as an infringement of the crown copyright. This was, I think, clearly instigated by Lord George or Duff; and it was apparently unwarranted bluff, as there is a Treasury minute (1887) permitting re-publication unless the public has been notified otherwise. We did not know of this minute, and got a bit flustered. But an appeal to Haldane settled the matter, and the Treasury letter was withdrawn. Both editions were published on Thursday, the day on which the Reports were reviewed in the press. It is a most interesting experiment in book-selling.

10,000 Minority Report: encumbered with Majority Report! and notes and references in a ponderous blue-book.	5s. 6d.	
3000 ditto: without references, Fabian pocket edition, two vols.	3s.	
1500 ditto: again without notes and references, Longmans bound, two volumes.	12s. 6d.	

It is scarcely conceivable that separate publication of the Minority Report can injure the blue-book sale of the whole report, but will this amazingly cheap blue-book injure sales of the cheap edition, or stop the 12s. 6d. edition selling?

In another fortnight we sail for Italy for a good five or six weeks' holiday. We need it to refresh us from the hard grind of these years, and to cleanse the thoughts that are in us—at least, I do—at present, I am morbidly sensitive, quite unworthily so.

February 22nd.—I am recovering my equilibrium slowly. It is always interesting to analyse one's mistakes and successes. In our depreciation of the Majority Report and our false expectation of its failure to catch on, we overlooked the immense step made by the sweeping-away of the deterrent poor law, *in name, at any rate*, and, to some extent in substance, by municipalising its control. Every now and again, I realised this; but then, when I considered the chaotic proposals of the Majority Report, I lost sight of it in my indignation at their attempt to present a new appearance while maintaining the old substance underneath. In a sense, the Majority Report meant success to our cause, but not victory to ourselves. However, I am inclined to think the distinction between the two reports—the fact that only by re-distribution of the services can you obtain curative and restorative treatment—will become gradually apparent to the nation. What is certainly most surprising is the absence of any kind of protest from the adherents of the old order—the believers in the principles of 1834— against the iconoclastic effect of the Majority Report. That the principles of 1834 should die so easily is certainly a thorough-going surprise. Even the *Spectator* acquiesces.

April 20th.—Home again after the most refreshing six weeks' holiday. It began badly. The life on board the steamer was horribly unpleasant for the first two days, and boresome, though wholesome, for the last six days. The three days at Naples before we had acquired the habit of the tourist were chaotic; we were real innocents abroad, not knowing exactly what to do with ourselves. But the three weeks at Rome were unexpectedly delightful. Our bedroom at the Hotel Flora looked straight on to the tops of the pines of the Borghese Gardens, to the northern hills of the Campagna. The ruins, the sculptures, the Campagna and the Alban hills, all yielded hours and days of interest and enjoyment. A pleasant little circle of Italians—the Scipio Borgheses, Contessa Pasolini, Count Balzani, Marchesa de Vita, the Sodarinis, and various Monseigneurs and other cultivated men and women, belonging to the " White " and the " Black " sets, just gave the touch of intimacy with native things that prevents one from sinking into the guide-book attitude and feeling the mere tourist. Then four heavenly days at Assisi, a week with the Playnes in Florence, revelling in the pictures I loved so well thirty years ago, a not unpleasant journey home pondering on all the beauty we had seen, on the movements in the old world of Rome, its republica, its empire, its mediaevalism, its renaissance and its nationalism, and its church, and we are back to find our little home cleaned up and re-decorated and our work awaiting us.

Above all, I have a completely rested brain, and the Commission, with all its hateful friction, has practically ceased to concern me. Good intention is now dominant, and I have recovered the habit of prayer. What I have to avoid is all silly worry and self-consciousness. We have to go straight for our object, to clean up the base of society, single-minded, without thought of ourselves or what people think of us or our work. Sidney has this talent of unselfconscious effort—" the soldier's pay if not the victor's meed ", he is always content; our pay, he suggests, is a very handsome one. But I need deliberately to oust from my mind other feelings. Now that I am strong again and my brain thoroughly re-created with new thoughts and feelings, rested by thoughts about great things, unconnected with my own little spark of life, I can go back to my daily work with real enjoyment in the routine grind, and without thought of any other reward than the doing of the work itself, in loving companionship with my boy, and kindly inter-course with fellow-workers. We may have another fifteen or twenty years of working life; may we use these years well, with zeal, discretion, kindliness and straightforward integrity.

So far as we can foretell [I enter a few days later] the work of the next eighteen months will consist of (1) propaganda of the Minority Report, (2) bringing out of books connected with these proposals, and also (3) finishing up our eighteenth-century study of English local government. We are starting a committee for pushing the Minority Report; and we are lecturing considerably; five days next week in the big north-country towns, and odd lectures in London, Oxford, etc.— all before we go for a week to the Fabian School in Wales. Beyond this work I mean, during the next ten months, to turn my attention on to the Fabian Society and the London School of Economics, and to cultivate the young people who are members of either organisation— more especially the Fabian Society. There is coming over the country a great wave of reaction against Liberalism and Labour, and the Fabian Society will probably lose in membership. The Minority Report, and the kudos which the Society has got out of it, will stay that reaction but not wholly prevent it. By our personal influence we have to keep the flag flying—the flag of steady, persistent pressure for

levelling up the bottomest layer of society. We think in the Minority
Report we have a clear consistent scheme which can be worked out by
any sensible and well-intentioned body of administrators. The wave of
political reaction need not prevent this—the Conservatives are, for this
purpose, quite as good as the Liberals and we have as much influence
over them.

May 15*th.*—Enter the National Committee for the Break-Up of
the Poor Law. Started on our campaign for forming public opinion.
My first attempt at organisation. I am trying a new experiment—an
executive committee for consultative purposes and a secretariat of
young men and women who will initiate policy and carry it out, I
acting as chairman, and reporting to the executive committee. We
start, with very little money and a good deal of zeal, on a crusade
against destitution. It is rather funny to start at my time of life, on the
war-path, at the head of a contingent of young men and women. What
I have got to aim at is to make these young people do the work, acting
as moderator and councillor, and occasionally suggesting new departures
for them to carry out. I have to teach them how to work, not work
myself. All the same, it is a horrid nuisance: I long to get back to the
quiet life of research and pleasant friendship, long days and weeks in
the country, which we enjoyed before the Royal Commission came
in to upset our life.

June 18*th.*—A month's grind at preparing forms, letters, membership cards, leaflets, tracts and other literature, for the National Committee. It looks as if Sidney and I will be absorbed in directing the
propaganda—probably entirely, for three or four months at any rate—
and for most of our time for the next year or so. What I am trying to
set on foot is a real comradeship in this crusade—an intensive culture
of the membership with a view to enrolling others and getting everyone
to give of their best. My band of volunteers are devoted; and we are
trying to do the utmost with a small sum of money—£600. I have a
vision of a permanent organisation growing out of the temporary
propaganda; an organisation to maintain the standard of life in all its
aspects, and to co-ordinate voluntary effort with the action of the
public authorities responsible for each service. Time will show. Meanwhile, we have been quite strangely dropped by the more distinguished
of our acquaintances and by the Liberal Ministers in particular. I have
never had so few invitations as this season, and this in spite of the
advertisement of the Minority Report. No doubt this is partly due to
our growing reputation for being absorbed in our work, but largely,
I think, because there is a return of active fear of Socialism, and of
being assumed to be connected with Socialists, though Lord George

Hamilton's bad word (and I hear he " foams at the mouth " whenever I am mentioned) counts. Altogether I am rather in disgrace with the great folk!

June 18*th*.—In response to an invitation to dine, Haldane called yesterday—excused himself from dining here and asked us to come and dine that very evening with Elizabeth and himself alone. Last evening we told him, in a friendly way, of our new plunge into propaganda, and suggested that a crusade against destitution was a really fine complement to " the Great Budget ". He welcomed neither the news of our work, nor the reference to the magnitude of his colleagues' success. Both displeased him. We gathered from what he said, or left unsaid, that he had become indifferent, if not actually hostile, to the minority scheme, or felt that the Cabinet intended to be so. There does not seem to be any chance of the majority scheme being accepted—rather an inertia and a willingness to accept John Burns' assurance at the Local Government Board, that the *status quo* was the best of all possible worlds. Haldane actually stood up for J. B. as an efficient Minister!

A curious little episode at this dinner. The conversation drifted on to religious teaching in secondary schools, and I casually remarked that I liked a definitely religious atmosphere and the practice of prayer as part of the school life. " Nonsense—Mrs. Webb ", blurted out the usually calm Elizabeth, with a sort of insinuation in her voice that I was not sincere. I fired up and maintained my ground; and, in a moment of intimacy, asserted that prayer was a big part of my own life. Whereupon both the Haldanes turned round and openly scoffed at me, Haldane beginning a queer kind of cross-examination in law-court fashion as to what exactly I prayed to, or prayed about, and Elizabeth scornfully remarking that prayer was mere superstition. It was a strange outburst met by another vehement assertion on my part that the two big forces for good in the world were the scientific method applied to the process of life, and the use of prayer in directing the purpose of life. Being well-bred persons, we all saw our mistake—I in introducing a note of too great intimacy, and they in scoffing at it. But the jar produced between us lingered through the remaining part of the evening, and I went away with somewhat hurt feelings.

What the ill-success of that evening proved to me was that my instinct to keep clear of the Liberal Ministry was a wise one; it would have been better if I had *not* invited Haldane and had *not* accepted his *pis aller* invitation. For some reason which we do not appreciate, the Haldanes are constrained or estranged. Possibly because they feel obliged to go back on their former agreement with the Minority Report; possibly because they have heard that we admire Lloyd George and Winston Churchill and openly state that they are the best of the party (I always put in a saving clause for Haldane, out of old affection).

Unfortunately, our estrangement from the Whigs does not mean comradeship with the Radicals: we are wrong, and likely to become wronger, with Lloyd George and Winston Churchill over immediate issues. We do not see our way to support their insurance schemes. We shall not go against them directly, but we shall not withdraw our criticisms in the Minority Report. If their schemes can be carried out we should not much object. Both have good consequences. But we still doubt their practicability, and some of the necessary conditions strike us as very unsatisfactory. The *unconditionality* of all payments under insurance schemes constitutes a grave defect. The state gets nothing for its money in the way of conduct, it may even encourage malingerers. However, we shall honestly try not to crab the Government schemes: they are thoroughly well-intentioned.

We remain friends with the Balfours. Arthur dined here a day or two ago and was as friendly as ever. Gerald has accepted the presidentship of the Students' Union of the London School of Economics—a very kindly action. But then they are not in office (!) and any agitation for the Minority Report does not affect them except that it may be an inconvenience to the Liberals and, therefore, welcome—so says the cynic. I am inclined to believe in their genuine friendliness.

As a set-off to the estrangement from the Liberal leaders, many Progressives who have shunned both us and the Fabians are trooping in to the National Committee—Leonard Hobhouse, J. A. Hobson, G. P. Gooch, Graham Wallas, Gilbert Murray, H. G. Wells and others—and the Liberal editors are friendly.

What I have to keep intact is my health and my nerve. All this office organisation, writing ephemeral tracts, preparing speeches and talking to all sorts of different persons, is soul-destroying; excites but does not satisfy. There is none of that happy alternation of strenuous work and complete rest which made such a pleasant life. However, the life of agitator lies before me for many months, perhaps years.

June 22nd.—I met Winston on the Embankment this afternoon. "Well, how do you think we are doing, Mrs. Webb?" "*You* are doing very well, Mr. Churchill, but I have my doubts about your Cabinet: I don't believe they mean to do anything with the poor law." " Oh! yes, they do ", said Winston. " You must talk to Haldane about it, he has it in hand. We are going in for a *classified* poor law." I muttered something about *that* not being sufficient, which he half understood and then turned the conversation. I had obtained the clue to Haldane's displeasure. He and Asquith have decided against *the break-up of the poor law*. We have a formidable fight before us. They are contemplating, not the majority scheme, but a new poor law authority of some kind or another. We shall have to fight hard, and we may be beaten. We must not talk big, or boast or brag. We must just go persistently on, taking every opportunity of converting the country. Meanwhile, the less we see of the Liberal Ministry, the better. We had better not *know* they are against us.

We had further information that the Liberal Ministers have settled on London to start their new poor law. We shall see!

July 6th.—A pleasant episode: delighted to get my doctorate, and from Manchester, the birthplace of my family as members of the governing class. Dear old Father, how pleased he would have been.[1]

July 22nd.—We are living in a veritable turmoil. The little office we took is crowded with literature and active workers: members are streaming in and a good deal of money. Sidney and I spend our lives writing, talking, organising. After all, we are not far off the end of our working life; and, if we could really start a great social drainage scheme before we leave the scene, it would be something for which to die content. It is no use shrinking from this life of surface agitation—

---

[1] " There were ringing cheers as Mrs. Webb ascended the platform and was presented by Professor Alexander for the degree of Doctor of Letters. Whatever changes in the structure or the methods of industry and society, Professor Alexander said, the future may hold in her lap, they prepare the way not least to a prudent and beneficent result who, like the lady whom I have the honour to present to you, set themselves the task of tracing the growth and the tendency of the forces which are now at work. Trying her young wings over the field of co-operation, she spread them, in the company of her distinguished husband, for a wider and more sustained flight, in order to survey the history of trade unionism, the present operation of the principle of collective bargaining, and its scope and possibilities for the future; and later, with an even greater courage of enterprise, to take in, in one comprehensive view, the whole history and condition of English local government. Let timorous politicians complain that these studies by their persuasiveness of interpretation insinuate a particular ideal of political reform, and warn us that ' Subtle wiles are in her smiles, to set the world a-wooing '; it is for us rather to praise their learning, their devotion to enquiry, the large and luminous sweep of their observation. Of her report upon the poor law I cannot tell whether it is destined to be known hereafter as the report of the minority of a commission or as the judgment of the majority of a people. (Applause.) But, individualists or socialists or Fabians, we are all of us Fabians in the tribute of admiration which we pay to the breadth, the consistency, the singleness of conception displayed by its authors. In all these vast undertakings she has maintained with pertinacious modesty that her own share in the joint labour is less than an equal one. But I crave your permission, Mr. Vice-Chancellor, to follow a world unconvinced in counting this belief of hers in the class of illusions generated by the affections. (Laughter.)

" Though we cannot claim her as one of our own former students, she belongs to a family associated intimately with the life of Manchester, whose tradition of eminent public service she has continued and enlarged. And it is therefore a daughter of our own house whom I ask you to inscribe upon our rolls when in the name of the Senate I present to you Beatrice Webb for the degree of Doctor of Letters in this University " (*Manchester Guardian*, July 5, 1909).

431

from this perpetual outgiving of personality—we have just got to use ourselves up at it. I have taken to it too late to make more than a mediocre success, but I have our joint name as a sort of jumping-off place. It is a curiously demoralising life, if one did not realise the essential conditions of it and guard one's mind from taking them otherwise than conditions that all agitators are subject to—the subservient and foolish admiration of followers. Just as during those last months of the Commission I was working in the atmosphere of perpetual hostility and disparagement, here I am working in the atmosphere of admiration and willing obedience to my will. One has to accept this atmosphere, even to foster it, otherwise an organisation does not flourish. But one must be perpetually reminding oneself that the attitude of followers does not depend on one's own excellence but on the exigencies of leadership.

July 23rd.—As I sat in my office this morning—the three rooms crowded with volunteers—Bentham [a leading member of the majority of the Commission and chairman of the Bradford Board of Guardians] was announced. I gave him the warmest welcome, introduced Colegate [the secretary] to him, and asked him what we could do for him. He seemed almost dazed with the bustle of the office. " I wanted to see your literature ", he said. " You seem as busy here as if it were a general election." " Perhaps it is ", I laughingly replied. " I wish we had someone to organise our side—like you; no member of the Majority cares enough about it." He seemed much perturbed by Willis-Bund's leaflet [the chairman of the Worcestershire County Council who had been converted to our report] and by Shackleton's adhesion [a Labour M.P., afterwards a Government official], collected all the literature he could get hold of, paid for it, and retired, after I had shown him our third room full of stock and literature. Now they have realised that we are at work, what will the majority do? Will they start a rival organisation, or will they issue a manifesto warning the world against us; or will they subside into apathy?

We have three forces against us besides the *status quo* or 1834 school: the *British Medical Journal*, the British Medical Association (*i.e.* the inferior medical practitioners fearing the encroachments of preventive medicine in physic-mongering); the busy-body relief-of-distress philanthropist who likes the " voluntary aid committee " of the majority; and the Hegelians, led by Bosanquet, clinging to the " category of the destitute "! On our side we have organised Labour, the Liberal press, the officials of the new preventive services, and a large section of the disinterested public who long for a radical and comprehensive scheme for *preventing destitution*, and many administrative minds of all creeds and political views. We also have the huge unpopularity of the poor law with its stigma of pauperism. If we can stop any re-establishment of a poor law authority for a couple of years, I think we shall win; we shall commit the country to a policy of complete communal responsibility for the fact of destitution. For many years that responsibility will be imperfectly fulfilled, but it will never again be repudiated. That will be an immense step forward, worth a big sacrifice of time and energy—the best way to spend the remainder of our two little lives.

There won't be much left of us when this work is done! Seventeen years to-day we were married: another such period, and probably only one will be left, if one. If only we could look forward to going out together, hand in hand, as we have pressed through the active period of our lives, trying each day to complete some little part of the common task, but always close together in body and mind, day and night, night and day. This union in death is too great a prize to win—in nature's way?

Sidney has also been thoroughly happy, partly because our comradeship has never been so complete. Hitherto, we have had only one side of our work together: our research and book-writing. But, this last year, we have organised together, spoken together, as well as written together. And he has been extraordinarily generous in not resenting, in the very least, my having nominally to take the front place, as the leading minority commissioner, and ostensible head of the National Committee. Fortunately, in spite of his modesty, everyone knows that he is the backbone of the " Webb " firm, even if I do appear, on some occasions, as the figure-head.

September 27th.—The whole political world is convulsed with excitement as to whether or not the Lords will throw out the budget. No one quite knows what will happen to the finances of the country if they do—the tea duty and the income-tax will lapse, and unless the Government takes some extraordinary measures the public revenue will be in the most amazing confusion. That in itself seems to prove that the constitution does not provide for the Lords throwing out a budget! Hence, wiseacres who are not party men, like Courtney and Sidney, say the Lords won't throw out the budget. On the other hand, two considerations drive them to do so—the exigencies of tariff reform, and the fear of future onslaughts on their power over money bills. All advance in Socialism might, perhaps even must, take the form of money bills, now that the cleavage between parties is chiefly a cleavage with regard to the ownership of property. Hence, if the Lords do *not* throw out the budget, they admit that they are powerless to fulfil their main function—the protection of property and the *status quo*. On the other hand, by throwing out the budget they raise the old, old issue of the right of the Commons to tax the commonalty—an issue that dates back to Charles I and Hampden; they also set themselves against the rapidly growing feeling against great holdings of land and capital by individuals. And, if the country declares overwhelmingly against them, they may lose their veto, not merely over money bills but over all legislation whatsoever. In forcing the Lords to fight on a budget, and a budget which taxes land and great accumulations of capital, the Liberals have chosen the only position from which they may win a victory. And, even if they were to lose, they have a splendid question upon which to work up democratic fanaticism against a *tax-the-food-of-the-people* Government. I am inclined to think that, whatever the result of an election on the budget, it will land the Lords in their last ditch. But have they an alternative?

Meanwhile, our agitation booms along in its own little way. Our membership rises rapidly; a good deal of fluff of course, but a good deal of good material mixed in with it. The manufacture of this movement is really like the manufacture of the School of Economics—it depends on untiring ingenuity in organising power, perpetually inventing new devices, stepping from stone to stone. Though the blatant budget agitation overshadows our propaganda in the public mind, I am not altogether sure that this is not something of an advantage. We don't seem to belong to any party—and each party is inclined to look at us beneficently. We are, in fact, creeping into the public mind much as the School of Economics crept into the University, into the City, into the railway world, into the Civil Service, into the War Office—before anyone was aware of it. Our little office, wedged between the Fabian office close on its right, and the London School of Economics a few yards to its left, is a sort of middle-term between avowed Socialism and non-partizan research and administrative technique. The staff of the three organisations and the active spirits of their management are all the same persons, and they exchange facilities with the utmost freedom. It is only in London that this triangular activity of the Webbs could occur—London with its anonymity, with its emphasis on personal likings, and its contempt for intellectual principles—a state of things which favours a rapid but almost unconscious change in the *substance* of the structure of society.

On the day before his great Bingley Hall meeting A. J. B. dined here. I had to meet him five men—Sir Gilbert Parker, J. W. Hills (M.P. for Durham), Major Wardle, all Conservatives who have joined our Committee, Dr. Macdonald, president of the British Medical Association, and Dr. Newman of the Education Department. We really had a brilliant talk, and sat over dinner until 10.15 o'clock, continuing the discussion upstairs. It all raged over the principles of the Minority Report, and A. J. B. egged us on, evidently vastly interested and amused. I believe he is *with us*, but he is naturally very discreet. Anyway, his presence and obvious intimacy was a proper sight for my two friendly Conservative M.P.'s and my unfriendly Tory president of the British Medical Association.

October 3rd.—Winston and his wife dined here the other night to meet a party of young Fabians. He is taking on the look of the mature statesman—*bon vivant* and orator, somewhat in love with his own phrases. He did not altogether like the news of our successful agitation. " You should leave the work of converting the country to us, Mrs. Webb, you ought to convert the Cabinet." " That would be all right if we wanted merely a change in the law; but we want ", I added, " to *really change* the mind of the people with regard to the facts of destitution, to make them feel the infamy of it and the possibility of avoiding it. That won't be done by converting the Cabinet, even if we *could* convert the Cabinet—which I doubt. We will leave that task to a converted country ! "

In the course of the evening he took a fancy to my organising secretary, Colegate, and told him to apply to the Board of Trade. And I have secured a position for Fred Keeling. Winston Churchill said that anyone, if really recommended " on my honour ", he would take on. I felt justified in recommending Keeling and Colegate.[1]

November 14th.—We are carrying on a raging, tearing propaganda, lecturing or speaking five or six times a week. We had ten days in the North of England and in Scotland—in nearly every place crowded and enthusiastic audiences. In Scotland, our special end was to establish the Scottish National Committee; that is a somewhat difficult task as we have no personality as yet in the movement except, perhaps, that gentle and intellectual Professor James Seth. And the Scottish people are cautious and wait to have the credentials of a new movement before they join. But so far as interested and enthusiastic audiences are concerned, and large sales of literature at our meetings, we could hardly have done better. In some ways Scotland is more ripe for our scheme than England. The school boards are far keener than the education committees to take full reponsibility for the children, and the fact that the children of able-bodied parents cannot be legally relieved out of poor rates adds to this tendency. The public health authorities have already been charged with phthisis. Its unemployed and vagrancy problems are outside the poor law at present, and could hardly be thrust into it as the majority proposes.

[1] As managers of Labour Exchanges which he was just starting.

435

November 14th.—We had a delightful three days at Whittingehame with Arthur Balfour, Lady Betty, Miss Balfour and Professor Lodge. Sidney had far more talk with A. J. B. than ever before. He was more than sympathetic about the Minority Report. I made him read the whole of the latter part of the Scottish Report and he asked Sidney what could be said against the minority scheme; it almost seemed self-evident. Of course, we must not build too much on such sympathetic sayings from a man of Mr. Balfour's temperament. But it means that, if the Liberals did bring in a new poor law, they would probably be opposed by the Labour Party and by the front opposition bench only too glad to find itself advanced. The odd thing is that, this being the attitude of the leader of the opposition, the *Times* should continue so bitterly hostile as it showed itself in its leader about the Scottish Report. The *Morning Post* is already beginning to tack—but it is the only Unionist paper that is ever decently impartial towards the Minority Report and its authors.

A. J. B. is much concerned with all the crude promises about tariff reform as a cure for unemployment that are being made by his following —from his tone I should think there had been ructions.

November 22nd.—As usual, A. J. B. has capitulated to the tail and repeated the shibboleth that tariff reform will diminish unemployment. What can be the attraction of leadership when you are led!

December 1st.—Another two spells of lecturing—Sheffield, Leeds, Bradford and Hereford last week, Bristol, Newport, Cardiff this week, Worcester, Birmingham, Manchester next week, a wearing sort of life, but we do seem to be impressing the Minority Report on those who are interested in the poverty problem.

Meanwhile, we are on the eve of the great political match—Lords *v.* Commons. I am inclined to think the Lords are in for a bad beating; and, through them, the tariff reformers are going to get a set-back. To the onlooker it looks rotten business for the very section of the party— the extreme tariff reformers—who have pushed the Lords over the precipice. Tariff reform would have won handsomely at the next general election coming in its ordinary course. But, allied with Lords and land monopoly, I cannot conceive that the tariff reformers will get any better result than some considerable reduction of the Government majority—which will leave the Government in power for another five years, and Lloyd George and Winston Churchill in command of the Government majority with the backing of the Labour Party.

We feel now much more content with the prospects of an election. We have sixteen thousand members and we are printing one hundred thousand questions for candidates. Whatever happens, John Burns leaves the Local Government Board. He will probably lose his seat, but anyhow, the fact that, if he remains at the Local Government Board and Winston at the Board of Trade, neither of them can draw the £5000 salary, means that there will be a general post of Ministers. If by any chance the Tories come in, we think that the personal friendship of A. J. B. and Lyttelton, combined with the anxiety of the tariff reformers for an advanced programme, will entail a continuation of the breaking-up process, even if they do not deliberately adopt the whole scheme straight away.

Sir R. Morant came to supper with us the other day. Apparently, if the Liberals do come back, Winston means to go to the Local Government Board and to take Morant with him, with the intention of carrying out the Minority Report. Morant is printing our Bill, at his private press, and is getting to work to study the question. He is nervous that J. B. will appoint the legal expert in Adrian's place before leaving, but I hardly think that likely. Altogether everything looks most promising. But there is a good eighteen months' grind, before we can get free of this agitation.

December 10th.—When at Birmingham for our Town Hall meeting we stayed a night with Clara Ryland and met Beatrice Chamberlain. The family is fully satisfied that they are in for a great victory. Apparently the " Master " regards the passing of the budget as a real disaster—as beginning a method of raising money that leads straight away from tariff reform and straight into Socialism. I thought I detected both in Clara Ryland and Beatrice Chamberlain a growing feeling for the protection of property—a growing fear of encroachments on the wealth of the wealthy which I had not noticed before. Hence, rather than pass the budget they are willing to risk a re-invigorated Liberal Party. And, unlike A. J. B., they have no sort of doubt that a tariff reform Government will recommend itself to the people—they have not the shadow of a fear that they would have growing up underneath such a Government an exasperated body of discontent, based on a really revolutionary propaganda against a propertied class and a hereditary second chamber. It seems to me that the welding together of old Radicalism and modern Socialism, which this pro-budget-anti-Lords movement means, will get more and more dangerous the longer it lasts—and it is bound to last until it gets its Government into power. On that reasoning, a victory for tariff reform, *unless it were absolutely overwhelming*, would be the most dangerous issue of the present campaign for Conservatism. Partly because moderate counsels will prevail, we prophesy the return of the Liberals with a much reduced majority—sufficient to pass the budget but not sufficient to permanently handicap the House of Lords *for all purposes.*

December 20th.—We are all awaiting breathlessly the issue of the great battle. The progressives of all shades are in mind united, however Labour and Liberal Party exigencies may make them fight among themselves in particular cases. To the outside observer, it is amazing that the Lords should have dared democratic feeling at one and the same time on the political and economic side! Those who have led them, men of the type of Hewins, Milner, Garvin, Curzon (encouraged by the old politician of Highbury [1]), have apparently relied on the ignorance and snobbish prejudice of the non-political elector—the man *without social purpose* of any kind—the reader of the *Daily Mail* and *Express* intent only on keeping all he has, and leading his life undisturbed by social obligations. No one knows how big this class is, how many persons are actually without any social purpose and can be swayed by vulgar cries of alarm for their property or their personal freedom, or by admiration for the " sporting Lord ". We believe that English public opinion is still sound and healthy, and that there will be at the polls a considerable majority in favour of steady popular control over the life of the community. Even if the polls go against us, the battle will have only just begun and will be of the longest and bitterest that England has experienced since the first Reform Bill. The wisely moderate man should dread a Tory victory. The whole Liberal Party would become extremists. There would be no turning back for the Greys and the Haldanes, the lines would be drawn; political Radicalism would be finally merged into " economic collectivism "; the Fabian Society would be, in fact, triumphant. Perhaps it is an instinctive perception of this fact that has made both Courtney and Henry Hobhouse throw in their lot with the Liberals. The moderate men must, if wise, desire a moderate Liberal victory. That alone will keep the Liberals, for another spell, from falling into the arms of the Socialists.

New Year's Eve, 1909. *Southsea.*—Sidney had to come and speak for Sanders (the Fabian candidate for Portsmouth), so I came too, for three days' walking in the Isle of Wight, a rest before beginning the new year's work.

Very happy we have been since the close of the Commission and our Italian holiday. Since we took up this propaganda we have had a straightforward job, with no problems of conduct, but with a great variety of active work; organising office work, public speaking and personal persuasion of individuals, work which absorbs all one's time without any severe strain on one's nerves. I enjoy it because I have the gift of personal intercourse and it is a gift I have never, until now, made full use of. I genuinely *like* my fellow-mortals whether as individuals, or as crowds; I like to interest them, and inspire them, and

[1] Joseph Chamberlain. [Ed.]

even to order them in a motherly sort of way. Also, I enjoy leadership. Everyone has been kind and appreciative; and money has come in when I asked for it, and volunteers have flocked round us. Of course, we have had a clear field and have just romped in. Our two sets of opponents—the *status quo* and the *majority*—prefer being, until just lately, inert. Now both the one and the other are up and doing. The guardians who have been spending their time in denouncing the Majority Report, are now concentrating all their guns on the " break-up committee " and the Minority Report—the majority commissioners are forming a committee to fight us, and the *British Constitutional Association* is spending all the force it possesses on taking the field against us. So that we shall have this year to fight the forces we have called out. But I think we are getting our defences into good order and are preparing a new campaign, offensive as well as defensive. A good deal depends on the larger political fight; if the Liberals come in, they must take up a modified version of the Minority Report; if the Conservatives come in, we have nothing to depend on but A. J. B.'s personal friendship, and, if they are in with a small majority, the desire of the tariff reformers to get hold of something advanced. If the Tories get in with a large majority, the rank and file reactionaries could either prevent anything being done, or would prefer the Tory report. On the other hand, in such a case, we should have the whole of the Liberal Party wheeling into our movement and probably nothing would be done until they came back again to do it. So we think the game is with us, in the end, on all eventualities; *if we continue to fight in the country* so as to keep the question alive.

From the last entries in the diary of 1909 it will be apparent that we no longer had the field of propaganda to ourselves. During the first year of our propaganda we had been far too optimistic. In the first article of the first number of our monthly *The Crusade*,[1] we had blithely asserted that " the Majority Report, with its proposals to thrust the unemployed and the underfed school children back into the poor law, to give non-elected bodies uncontrolled power over public funds, and to reinstate the old poor-law system under a new name,

[1] *The Crusade*, being the organ of the National Committee of the Prevention of Destitution, first appeared in February 1910 (12 pages), and continued under the editorship of Clifford Sharp as a monthly of larger and larger size until February 1913 (35 pages). On the last page of *The Crusade* of February 1913 appeared the first advertisement of *The New Statesman*, a weekly review of politics and literature to begin on April 12th, 1913, of which Clifford Sharp was appointed the editor.

The Crusade during these two years contains many articles by distinguished medical men, education officials and social researchers.

is to all intents and purposes dead ". And we add: " The character of the membership [of the National Committee for the Break-up of the Poor Law] is, perhaps, even more satisfactory than its size, for it shows that the ordinary party cleavages do not apply to the question of poor-law reform, and that men and women of all parties, classes and creeds are ready and anxious to combine for the purpose of inaugurating a serious and determined campaign against destitution. . . . Our real opponents are the party of the *status quo*, a party which, though as weak in controversy as we could wish, has behind it all the forces of political inertia. It is always easier in this country to resist changes than to bring them about."[1] Unfortunately, that vital fact was exactly what Lord George Hamilton and his colleagues had discovered and acted on.

Hereafter, wherever we penetrated, by word or by script, we were confronted by a powerful organisation doing likewise in an opposite direction. This new association—the National Poor Law Reform Association—presided over by Lord George Hamilton, included not only the members and supporters of the Majority Report but also the far more formidable representatives of the existing boards of guardians. Moreover, this organised opposition to our proposals had the official support of the President of the Local Government Board, John Burns, together with the newly appointed permanent head, Horace Monro, and the staff of local government inspectors, all of whom were dead against any tampering with the structure and working of the existing poor law.

" I do not ask or expect all joining this organisation to consider themselves pledged to every proposal of that report [the Majority Report of the Royal Commission] ", stated Lord George Hamilton. ". . . We propose only one authority, with power to give relief from public funds; the minority propose five authorities, with separate objects and separate sets of officials, and each such authority is to be under the control of a different department of the state.

" We propose to deal with the family as a whole; the

[1] See *The Crusade against Destitution*, February 1910, p. 2.

minority propose to disintegrate it by sending each item of it to a separate committee.

" We propose to place the granting of relief and its recovery in the hands of the authority who gives relief; the minority propose to separate the two functions. The giving of relief is to be in the hands of an elected authority; its recovery is to be subsequently adjudicated upon by a paid official in the employ of the authority giving the relief. All who have experience of these matters know what this means —the recovery will be *nil*, and in a short time all relief given will become gratuitous.

" The majority, whilst admitting that deterrence under our existing system has been pushed too far, propose to retain it in the sense that those who are helped out of public funds, in consequence of an inability to maintain themselves or their dependants, should not be in a position of perfect equality with those who maintain others as well as themselves. The minority would obliterate any such distinction.

" We propose that those requiring relief should apply and prove their application. The minority propose that each authority should send out an army of officials to search out and enforce relief upon all who in nurture, medical attendance, and general surroundings, are not up to the standard which that particular authority may consider to be necessary. The relief given to all such individuals will not be confined to a period of want, but is to be given in anticipation of it and subsequently to it."

Such being the character of the forces arraigned against us, we quickly realised that we must change the direction of our propaganda from a destructive to a constructive policy; from " the break-up of the poor law " to " the prevention of destitution ". Only in this way could we walk round our opponents and ally ourselves with another form of governmental authority, the education and public health departments of the county and county borough councils, with their medical officers of health, their directors of education, school visitors, inspectors and teachers, nearly all of whom were in favour of extending their sphere of beneficent social service.

Here, also, we found supporters in Whitehall to counterbalance the weight against us of John Burns and his Department;—Robert Morant of the Education Department and his energetic medical officer George Newman, and even the gifted Arthur Newsholme, recently appointed chief medical officer for that home of reaction, the Local Government Board.

This change of tactics, embodied in the new title, the National Committee for the Prevention of Destitution, compelled us to explain exactly what we meant by destitution. Destitution, we argued, was being without one or other of the necessaries of life, in such a way that health and strength, and even vitality, is so impaired as eventually to imperil life itself. Nor is it merely a physical state. It is, indeed, a special feature of destitution in modern urban communities that it means not merely a lack of food, clothing and shelter, but also a condition of mental degradation. Destitution in the desert may have been consistent with a high level of spiritual refinement. But destitution in a densely-crowded modern city means, as all experience shows, not only on-coming disease and premature death from continued privation, but also, in the great majority of cases, the degradation of the soul. Massed in mean streets, working in the sweating dens, or picking up a precarious livelihood by casual jobs, living by day and by night in overcrowded one-room tenements, through months of chronic unemployment or persistent under-employment; infants and children, boys and girls, men and women, together find themselves subjected—in an atmosphere of drinking, begging, cringing and lying—to unspeakable temptations to which it is practically inevitable that they should in different degrees succumb, and in which strength and purity of character are irretrievably lost. Anyone acquainted with the sights and sounds and smells of the quarters of great cities, in which destitution is widely prevalent—especially anyone conversant with the life histories of families below the " poverty line "—learns to recognise a sort of moral malaria, which undermines the spiritual vitality of those subjected to its baleful influence and, whilst here and there a moral genius may survive, saddened but otherwise unscathed, gradually submerges the mass of each generation as it grows up, in coarseness and bestiality, apathy and cynical scepticism of every kind. When considerable numbers of people in such a condition are found together—still more when they are practically segregated in cities of the poor—this means that the community of which they form part is, to that extent, diseased. It is in this sense that we are entitled to say that destitution is a disease of society itself.

1910

January 8th.—A set-back for the Webb influence. John Burns has appointed Monro to succeed Provis, and his own private secretary Jerred to succeed Monro, and thus ruined the Local Government Board as a possible instrument of reform. This is serious, and curiously unexpected. All we know about it is that we understood that J. B. had been bound over by Asquith *not* to appoint a successor to Provis without his (Asquith's) consent, and Morant clearly expected to go there. It is an interesting constitutional point as to whether the P.M. has a right to veto big appointments. Lowell, in his big book on the constitution, states that he has. From our standpoint, it means one of two things. If Asquith has consented to these appointments, the Liberals do *not* intend to break up the poor law in a big way, however much they may nibble at the subject. If Asquith has *not* consented, it will widen the rift between J. B. and Winston backed up by Asquith, and may lead to J. B. being excluded from the Cabinet in the reconstruction. This depends on how much Asquith cares for unquestioned supremacy, or whether he merely wants to keep the two parties in his Cabinet balancing and counteracting each other.

Meanwhile, we have to go steadily on converting the country to the *philosophy* of our scheme. The application of it will follow (whatever persons are in power) on the conversion of men of intelligence and good intention.

January 27th.—After the elections. The coalition back with something over 100 majority, a clear anti-Lords majority and, abstracting the Irish, a majority for the budget.

What is remarkable is the dividing of England into two distinct halves each having its own large majority for its own cause—the south country, the suburban, agricultural, residential England going Tory and tariff reform, and the north country and dense industrial populations (excluding Birmingham area) going Radical-Socialist, self-conscious Radical-Socialist. The conversion of Lancashire from chronic Conservative to Liberal-Labour is a big fact; the fidelity of Scotland, in spite of the scare of Socialism, to the anti-Lords-pro-budget party is another asset for our party. On the other hand, tariff reform has got hold of large masses of working-men and lower middle-class men and has become the shibboleth of the upper and upper-middle classes.

On the Saturday before the polling we went to tea with Haldane, who has been seriously ill with gout in the eye. He and Elizabeth were most friendly. From what he said he seems to have looked forward to some such result as has happened. Interesting to hear from a Conservative dame, who was calling, that Lord George Hamilton felt certain of a Conservative majority of forty over all parties. That is why, perhaps, he went out of his way to insult Lloyd George as " a little Welsh solicitor "—which has pretty well done for his blessed report as far as Liberals are concerned. Imagine my insulting Carson or Milner!

We are considering mending our fences on the tariff reform side. The more active spirits see that they must find something that will take with the industrial classes, other than tariff reform. By sheer ignorance they *might* plunge on *poor law reform*, we must see to it that they do not do so. These troubled waters are somewhat disturbing to our little bark: but if she be skilfully steered into the right currents of party interests, she will get all the quicker into harbour.

February 15*th*.—A week-end at Stanway with A. J. B., the Salisburys, Hugh Cecil and George Wyndham. A real " Hotel Cecil " party. All these, including the leader, were anxious to understand the reason of the rout in Lancashire and Yorkshire. We naturally improved the occasion and tried to awaken them to the evil consequences of letting tariff reform be associated with anti-social reform. But Hugh Cecil (who is an attractive creature) was already desperately alive to the peril to their souls from any alliance with reformers of our colour. We shall not get the tariff reform party to take up the Minority Report; all we shall do is to prevent them from throwing their whole weight *against it*. To many of the more upright minds, failure at the polls would be the lesser evil compared with the downward course towards a collectivist organisation. They have a *blind* fear of any increase of social responsibilities; and, if they are to accept any measure of it, they would positively prefer to hide their heads in the sand and *refuse to see it*. Arthur Balfour is, if anything, attracted by our scheme; but he is too unconcerned and sceptical to be more than *negatively beneficent*.

Lord George Hamilton has issued his call to arms against the minority. It is interesting to note that he cannot muster a committee in favour of the majority scheme: he has had to include persons like Charles Booth, Bailward,[1] Clay,[2] Lord Cromer and all definitely pledged to an *ad hoc* elected poor law authority. He explicitly states that membership of his anti-minority committee does not entail agreement with the machinery of the Majority Report. We have, in fact, forced the majority back to the *status quo*; after they have smashed this up by their unanimous condemnation.

Sometimes, in moments of physical depression, I wonder whether we can keep up this agitation, all of which revolves round our joint personality. On Friday, I start off for six days' continuous lecturing in the west country, whilst Sidney is dashing about in other parts of the country. Shall we be able to keep it up?

February 25th. Plymouth.—A sleepless night after the six lectures in seven days. What is worse is that my last lecture, the most important one at Plymouth, was only a qualified success owing to very great fatigue. Once or twice I lost control of the big audience—I was too utterly fagged to keep the verve of the lecturer right to the end. And, now and again, I felt I might suddenly give way and faint or collapse— it was an effort of sheer will-power to keep myself on my feet and talking. However, the difference between a lecture which one feels to be first-rate (as I felt the lectures at Exeter and Falmouth) and a lecture that one feels was a failure, is not so marked to others as it is to oneself; the one not so good, and the other not so bad as it appears to the speaker himself. What I most fear is that I may lose my nerve if I have that unpleasant sensation that I had the other night at the Exeter P.S.A. of coming over faint in the midst of what I am saying.

March 1st.—Another five days' continuous lecturing in Lancashire. On the whole, very successful.

Meanwhile, there have been political crises that have disposed of

---

[1] One of the most prominent members of the new organisation was W. A. Bailward, who declared that: "Speaking generally the Majority Report would enormously extend the functions of state relief, and it would, in fact, bring about a sort of system of state-organised charity which would probably eventually be almost wholly dependent upon public funds. . . . I end as I began, by saying that there are, in my opinion, only two possible policies for the future. The one is that of independence, upon which the reforms of 1834 were based. The other that of the Minority Report, which frankly adopts universal provision by the state. The majority try to steer a middle course. I think that they will fail. I cannot help thinking that the majority of guardians will prefer the old policy, under which this country has made such enormous strides, under which the great friendly societies have been born and flourished, under which rural able-bodied pauperism has practically disappeared " (*Poor Law Conferences*, 1911–1912, pp. 183, 187).

[2] Sir Arthur Clay, a well-known artist; his son, Sir Felix Clay, married my niece Rachel Hobhouse.

most persons' respect for the Liberal leaders. It is almost inconceivable that Asquith should have gone off to the South of France, with no clear idea of what he was going to propose to Parliament as the Liberal policy. But, from what one gathers, that seems to have been the case. At the subsequent Cabinets, Grey insisted on introducing the policy of reforming the House of Lords; a policy which no one but he himself had even mooted during the election. In this he was backed up by Haldane and opposed by Lloyd George and Churchill (?). Partly out of jealousy of the two Radical leaders, the Cabinet gave way to him. No attempt was made to gauge the opinion of the three groups upon whom Asquith depends for his Government's existence.

The King's speech came like a thunderclap over the head of the whole of the progressives—and after a moment's stupefaction, produced an ultimatum from Redmond, a threat from the Labour Party, and vigorous expostulations from the advanced Radicals. Thereupon more Cabinet meetings and a sudden retreat on to the position advocated by the *Daily News* and *Nation*—a complete capitulation to the advanced party. There is a wild rumour that the King intervened in favour of the Veto Bill and not reform. But Asquith has shown himself careless, unintelligent and cowardly—without foresight or firmness. It is a great triumph for Winston and Lloyd George who have behaved with loyalty and discretion, whilst letting it be quietly understood that they disagreed with the King's speech policy, and had opposed the complicated policy of attempting to reconstitute the House of Lords.

Sidney lunched with Haldane the Sunday before the King's speech and his host then adumbrated the policy of " reform " [of House of Lords] *versus* " veto ". " If you do that," Sidney remarked, " you will be preparing for yourselves an ignominious funeral." But R. B. H. turned a deaf ear. I gathered that Haldane had not grasped the policy of the Minority Report though he suggested that the Cabinet was favourable to it. It is clear that, if we had left it to the Cabinet to decide yea or nay, mere jealousy of Lloyd George and Winston might have turned the scales against the minority in favour of a new poor law. By the time any Government is ready to tackle the question, no other course but to break-up shall be open to them.

This week Sidney quietly slips out of the L.C.C. to which he has devoted so much time, thought and feeling. The last three years the L.C.C. has been rather dead to him. The Progressive movement, which the Fabian Society started in 1889, has spent itself. The machine that has been created goes grinding on all in the right direction —but it has become more or less automatic. A fresh impetus will, I think, come from our propaganda, from the new principle of the national minimum and the joint responsibility of the individual and the community, for a given standard of individual life. Possibly he may return to the Council to carry out such a programme—but for the present we can do more by persuading the country at large than by administration of London's municipal business.

March 13th.—We met the Prime Minister, Grey and Birrell at dinner the other day, interesting to note that we had met none of these personages since they were in office—Grey I had not seen for years. We neither of us spoke to any of them, though it was a small party—Asquith was somewhat marked in his non-recognition of either of us. He is much older, and, in a sense, commoner, in appearance; at dinner he was talking scandal with Mrs. Crawshay about " the Pasolini " who has recently eloped (the daughter-in-law of our friend in Rome). After dinner he was ogling Lady Ripon of fashionable and fast fame. Grey looked the same charming aristocrat that he has always been—slim in figure, and young and refined in expression—but somewhat of a " stick " in general attitude. Birrell was the same jovial *littérateur*—pleasantly sparkling about nothing with a group of admiring women. I was quite entertained with a thoughtful Russian—Count Constantine Benckendorff[1] at dinner, and Raymond Asquith afterwards. But it was a somewhat odd sensation to see these three Ministers for the first time since they were in office, and to be conducting an agitation in the country which must eventually affect their policy, and yet not have even a good-day from them! Each of them would, I think, have been supremely bored to have exchanged one little word about poor law or any other social-economic question. Contrasting it with the talk down at Stanway, even with the interest shown in all these questions by Lord Salisbury and George Wyndham, the Liberal Ministers' indifference, not to say distaste, is amazing and makes one wonder what exactly is happening to the leaders of the Liberal Party. Here we are making the bed they will have to lie in—and yet they seem wholly unconcerned with this happening. Strange!

I went to Granville-Barker's *Madras House* this afternoon. After listening to this and to G. B. S.'s *Misalliance*, one wonders whether these two supremely clever persons are not obsessed with the rabbit-warren aspect of human society? G. B. S. is brilliant but disgusting; Granville-Barker is intellectual but dull. They both harp on the mere physical attractions of men to women, and women to men, coupled with the insignificance of the female for any other purpose but sex attraction, with tiresome iteration. That world is not the world I live in, or indeed, think to exist outside a limited circle—at the top and

---

[1] Son of the Russian Ambassador: after the October Revolution he served for a time the Soviet Government in a diplomatic capacity.

at the bottom of the social strata. In the quiet intermediate area of respectable working-class, middle-class and professional life, and in much gentle society, there is not this over-sexed condition. The women are almost as intelligent as, and certainly a good deal more spiritual than, the men, and their relations to the other sex are those of true friendship and intelligent comradeship in the transaction of the affairs of life, and in the enjoyment of the interests and beauty of life. *The male and the female have become the man and the woman.* It is mischievous to be perpetually drawing society as being worse than it is, just because most persons are stupider than such clever mortals as G. B. S. and Granville-Barker, and fail to express their good thoughts and feelings otherwise than in stereotyped and banal phrases which bore these clever ones.

At Exeter, for instance, I stayed with a commercial traveller in a one-servant house. He was a very ugly man, with a red nose and great unshapely, protruding ears; he did not eat nicely, and his accent was harsh. But he was full of goodwill and public spirit, and had wide intellectual and artistic interests. His wife was a gentle pious lady of sound sense and discretion and charming manners, and his daughter played Chopin to me for two hours on end, and gave me a vivid and broadminded account of the life of her sister as a Chinese missionary. They all lived together in affectionate, happy harmony, and had endless friends in Exeter of like temperament and interests. Of course, their house was dull-coloured and dowdy, and not over-clean; the food was of the plainest and had the look of being always on the table. But where was the rabbit warren? Their thoughts and feelings were in the main engaged in spiritual, intellectual, artistic or philanthropic matters. In this set the women folk were treated exactly like the men folk— and all were Christian gentlefolk, in spite of belonging to the lower middle-class. Neither G. B. S., nor Granville-Barker, seems to realise that these people represent the English middle-class far more truly than their surreptitious or avowed polygamists, with women running after them, that they are so fond of producing on the stage as representative of English society. Let us hope that future historians will not take the play, even of the new school of intellectuals, as really representing English society as a whole at the beginning of the twentieth century.

Where I think G. B. S., Granville-Barker, H. G. Wells and many other of the most modern authors go wrong, from the standpoint of realism in its best sense, is their complete ignoring of religion. By religion, I mean the communion of the soul with some righteousness *felt to be outside and above itself.* This may take the conscious form of prayer: or the unconscious form of ever-present and persisting aspirations—a faith, a hope and a devotion to a wholly disinterested purpose. It is this unconscious form of religion which lies at the base of all Sidney's activity. He does not pray, as I often do, because he has not acquired so self-conscious a habit. But there is a look in his eyes when he patiently plods on through his own and other people's work, when he unwittingly gives up what other people prize, or when he quietly ignores the spite or prejudice of opponents, that tells of a faith and a hope in the *eventual* meaning of human life—if not for us, then for those who come after us. He refuses to put his aspiration into words, because he would fear the untruth that might be expressed in those words—he has a dread of being even remotely irrational or superstitious. But, for all that, he believes.

Not one of G. B. S.'s men or women, or Granville-Barker's or H. G. Wells's, have either the conscious or unconscious form of religion. The abler of these puppets of their thoughts deny it; the stupider are oblivious of it—a few are blatant hypocrites. And, that being so, there is nothing left for them to be but intellects or brutes— and for the most part they are both. It is strange that, whatever these clever men may think and feel themselves, they don't perceive that there *is* such a thing as religion and that it is a force which moulds many lives and makes the mere rabbit warren an inconceivable horror.

March 15*th.*—Sidney and I went to Galsworthy's *Justice*—a great play, I think—great in its realistic form, great in its reserve and restraint, great in its quality of pity. Its motive, that all dealings with criminals should be treatment *plus* restraint in the interest of the community, are all worked in with the philosophy of the Minority Report. But what is to be done with the incurable?

April 12*th.*—Last Friday was a great day for the National Committee, our Bill being discussed in a crowded House by A. J. B., Asquith and Burns (besides picked men on all three sides). The first-named was extraordinarily friendly; the second coldly appreciative; the last as hostile as he dared be. The Labour Party gave the Bill a full-blooded support—the rank and file Liberals are obviously inclined to it. But the net impression of the debate was that, though the majority proposals were dead, the *status quo* had the hot approval of J. B., and that Asquith was sceptical of the possibility of change, and A. J. B. hesitating as usual. One big advance has been the sweeping away by A. J. B. of the Socialist bogy and the intimation to the Conservative press that the Conservative Party does not want to be pledged against the Minority Report scheme in the country. That was *real* kind of A. J. B.! And, I think, wise from the standpoint of his party.[1]

[1] " The whole scheme of the minority report was brought before the House of Commons on Friday, April 8, 1910, by Sir Robert Price, where it attracted an

Next session we shall have a litter of Bills embodying the different parts separately, while keeping one complete one on the stocks.

April 28th.—Enter Royal Commission No. 3.

At four o'clock yesterday afternoon a messenger came from Lloyd George asking Sidney to let him submit his name to H.M. as one of the commissioners of the new Development Act, and to announce it that very evening in Parliament. Sidney naturally accepted the honour —rather liking the prospect of new work. So enters Commission No. 3 —this time an executive and permanent Commission in all probability. I bargained that it should not prevent our Eastern travel a year hence.

May 19th.—The King's death has turned politics topsy-turvy— and robbed the Liberals of their cry. Whether they will be able to get up the steam again seems very doubtful. London and the country

unusually large attendance of members, and elicited speeches from the Prime Minister (H. H. Asquith), the President of the Local Government Board (Mr. John Burns) and the leader of the Opposition (Mr. Arthur Balfour). No division could be taken " (*Hansard*, April 8th, 1910).

". . . After his speech and Wyndham's, A. J. B., Long, Lyttelton and myself retired to Balfour's room to consider our attitude to a private members' bill which embodies the policy of the Minority Report of the Poor Law Committee. Balfour, who had not read it or given much consideration to it but who had seen the Webbs, was the most favourably inclined to it. The rest of us, who had gone a little deeper into it, were agreed that it would not do, though I confessed to having been greatly attracted by it before I studied it. I think that our line will be that the first work for parliament (and quite enough for one parliament) is to carry out the recommendations on which both the majority and minority are agreed. These alone will work an enormous change and require all the care parliament can give to them. The popular and sound objections to the minority scheme in its entirety are: (1) That it would cost about 50 millions! (2) That it established an intolerable bureaucratic tyranny. Five separate inspectors from the Local Authority might descend on any working man's home and carry off himself, his wife or any or all of his children to a municipal institution, feed, clothe or otherwise care for them, utterly ignoring both parental rights and parental responsibility, whilst it would rest with a sixth inspector not appointed by or under the control of the Local Authority to decide without appeal whether any and, if so, what part of the cost of this public assistance should be recovered from the family. And all the inspectors might act without any call for help from the individual, without there being any destitution and without there being anything in the nature of a criminal act or default on the part of the parents. (3) The whole tendency of the report is to make the position of the State-aided better than that of the ordinary decent working man taxed to support them. "'The Webbs', said Vivian to Lyttelton, 'carry you on logically and imperceptibly from one point to another; but when you look at the whole, it's moonshine!' " Not a bad criticism " (The Rt. Hon. Sir Austen Chamberlain, K.G., P.C., M.P., *Politics from Inside*, pp. 238-9, March 30th, 1910). " A curious episode: last Friday week Burns rose as soon as Asquith sat down after speaking in the Poor Law discussion. Everyone was surprised at this unusual arrangement of ministerial speeches, especially as Asquith had fairly covered the departmental ground, giving the departmental statistics, etc. "'But no one', said Asquith to Balfour subsequently, 'was more amazed than I was. Burns hadn't said a word to me about it!' What a Cabinet! " (*ibid.* p. 253, April 17th, 1910).

generally is enjoying itself hugely at the royal wake, slobbering over the lying-in-state, and the formal procession. Any collective thought and feeling is to the good; but the ludicrous false sentiment which is being lavished over the somewhat commonplace virtues of the late King would turn the stomachs of the most loyal of Fabians. But is it possible for a *crowd* to be anything but exaggerated in its manifestations, with a popular press playing up to it? " The crowd on the press " and the " press on the crowd ".

One year of our organisation over. We have been at the job continuously lecturing, organising, writing—one long-sustained exposition. And we mean to spend another year at it. Here again, there is a curious process of action and reaction. We have made a following, and now our followers are making us into professional leaders. " How shall we be able to retire? " is what I ask myself. The office with its eleven salaried persons, and its twenty or thirty volunteers, the corps of four hundred lecturers, the three thousand five hundred contributing members, the twenty-five thousand non-contributing members, the twenty or so branches, make up a machine which at present depends on us for its motive force. It is clear that we are making great headway in the country, we are rolling up a great body of enthusiasm. And it is all centring round our joint personality. Will it be possible for us, when we think the idea is safely launched, simply to step back and say —cease, or go on without us?

What we have to do in the next twelve months is to construct machinery that will go on without us! At any rate for a time. We must consolidate, and not merely roll on.

One great success we have had is at the St. James's Hall lectures— six successive Mondays we have had a full house of good material— majority of men of the governing and professional classes—we have actually cleared a profit of three hundred and fifty pounds!

Meanwhile, the co-operators have declared in our favour, and even the friendly societies are unexpectedly in our favour.

May 24th. Edinburgh.—It is better to be dead beat after making a success than dead beat after making a failure—or, to put it more correctly, when one *feels* one has made a success—because I daresay the feeling of success is as exaggerated as that of failure. But holding a big meeting of Scottish ministers for an hour's lecture and answering of questions is a feat of endurance—the giving out of vital energy.[1]

The question is: Where is this going to end? Having discovered in myself the faculty of the preacher and the teacher, shall I be able to withdraw to the life of research?

[1] This was the Church Assembly presided over by the Master of Polwarth.

THE PLUNGE INTO PROPAGANDA

May 27th.—It is just one year since we started the National Committee and we have had one long grind of lecturing and organising. We go now for a month's holiday before directing the Fabian Summer School and entering on another campaign of talking and office organisation. It is well to take stock of our undertaking.

We have done what we set out to do. A year ago, the Minority Report was one among many official documents; now it is a movement which is obviously spreading from one section to another. The co-operative movement is the last of the great Labour organisations to join us; we have practically the whole of the social service side of Nonconformity, and a large and increasing section of the Church. Two Cabinet Ministers have been willing to preside at our meetings, and we were able to prevent a Tory ex-Cabinet Minister (Walter Long) from speaking for the Majority Committee; while Mr. Balfour was extraordinarily favourable to us in the debate of our Bill.

And we do seem to be attracting the devoted service of a large body of volunteers. We are moving out of our five little rooms into more spacious offices, and we are developing a highly-organised staff out of salaried workers and some thirty or forty unpaid office-helpers and some four hundred lecturers.

I am trying to construct out of the volunteers a subordinate organisation—an interesting experiment. There is the executive of fifty members with its three committees—finance, meetings and membership, and literature. These are the spending committees which Sidney and I run. Then there is the office committee of the six staff officers presided over by Sanders of the Fabian Society, to whom we give a small honorarium. But, besides this ordinary organisation, I have now a volunteers council with a press committee, a social committee, a propaganda committee, and an office improvement committee, which revolves round myself and Mrs. Surrey Dane. We ought also to have a lecturers' council revolving round [C. M.] Lloyd and Mrs. Carter. Our difficulty is with our local branches, which are always getting into debt or relapsing into vacuum. We have *not* solved the question of branch organisation—even the Scottish branches being insolvent and raising barely enough money to pay postage and stationery.

Now the question is: Can we develop this organisation into a really big national movement to do away with destitution as a chronic and wholesale state of millions of our people? Here seems an opportunity. The Minority Report has the extraordinary advantage of being a platform at once concrete, comprehensive, and yet unconnected with any one political party. It has a philosophic basis in the whole theory of an enforced minimum of civilised life: and yet it is part and parcel of an urgently-needed reform which must come up for consideration by whichever party is in power. But, at present, the whole organisation depends on us—and is limited by the defects of our joint-personality and the prejudices which this personality arouses. So long as this is the case, the life of the movement will be precarious; not merely because our strength and means might fail, but because the distrust and dislike of us might blaze out into a powerful hostility to the spread of the philosophy which lies at the base of the minority scheme. Sidney and I *are* Socialists; there is no denying the fact. In Scotland, this fact has prevented the Minority Report making any substantial headway with the upper and professional classes, and that means no money for propaganda. Owing to our social prestige and Sidney's administrative reputation—largely owing to Arthur Balfour's personal friendship—this stigma of socialism has not stood in our way in England. But, at any time, the fear of Socialism might deplete our moneyed membership, and then our organisation would necessarily collapse. The problem before us in the next few months is: Can we give this organisation an existence independent of our leadership—exactly as we have done in the case of the London School of Economics? If not, it will have its day—a quite vigorous and useful day—and then be wound up with the first instalment of the reform of the poor law on the lines of the Minority Report. Of course, we *might* fail even to carry this—but that amount of failure I do not contemplate. We have already made it impossible, either to set up a new poor law or to maintain for an indefinite time the present state of things.

I often wonder whether I like this life of propaganda or not. I enjoy the excitement of successful leadership, I like the consciousness of the use of faculties which have hitherto been unused—the faculty for public speaking and the faculty for organisation. On the other hand I feel harassed—I don't like financial responsibilities, I am perpetually haunted by the fear of failure to live up to the position I am forced into. And I grudge the quiet study and thought with its output of big books. I sometimes wonder whether the expenditure of money and energy on mere passing propaganda is as socially useful as research. And I positively dislike the feeling of being dragged along by the movement we have created—almost mechanically dragged along—not able to refuse to respond to a demand we have ourselves stimulated. And, now and again, I wonder with regard to the unemployment scheme whether we could really carry it through. One ought never to propose any public action which one could not, *if called on*, carry out. About the non-able-bodied part of our scheme, I am supremely confident that we are almost *blatantly right*. But, with regard to certain parts of the unemployment scheme, I am not quite so sure—*e.g.* the regularisation of government work and the technique of training establishments both give me pause. Also, I am convinced that Sidney underestimates the expense. However, that last point does not upset me—the more of the national wealth we can divert from the rich to the regular outgoings of the poorest class, *so long as it is accompanied by an increase in personal responsibility on the part of these benefited classes*, the wholesomer for the state. Only one does not like to mislead the public, even for its own good!

July 8th.—A vigorous holiday in Switzerland: walking with Colegate and Lloyd or both—perhaps rather too vigorous for an old lady like myself. But, though it tired my body, I believe it really rested my mind. Now that we are immersed in this movement we cannot get the old half-term holidays in the country. So long as we are in England we stand to be shot at by all our followers and opponents. It is rather a breathless business—a perpetual sense of insufficiency to meet the demands of a perpetually growing clientèle. A reading public has to wait until the author produces the book; and is wholly unknown to the author, not only before the book is produced but, except in rare cases, after it is produced. But, when once one takes to organising public opinion, there is no peace; the unconverted, the half-converted, even the converted are bombarding one for arguments, additional facts, counter-arguments, and orders for personal service to the cause. We have risen to the opportunity which the Royal Commission has opened out before us for the conversion of England.

During the next nine months we have to consolidate our following into a sufficiently self-sufficing organisation to go on without us. The month we were away a certain amount of disorganisation set in, which showed that very unstable equilibrium which exists at present. If we can give the organisation an independent life, nine or ten months' absence a year hence will be all to the good. It will permit it to settle down on its own foundations instead of depending so much on us. Can we do this?

July 12th.—Lord George Hamilton has scored two points against the Webbs. First he has, through his personal friendship with Lord Belper and the Duke of Northumberland, turned the poor law committees of the County Councils Association away from the Minority Report proposals which our friend Chapman had got them to accept. This is largely due to Henry Hobhouse who, in a quiet way, has always been hostile to us, especially to me, and who proposed a scheme of his own with marked majority features. We have advised Chapman to amend and accept it, as it is of the utmost importance that the County Councils Association should seem willing that the county councils should take over the work. Moreover, even H. H.'s scheme proposes that the feeble-minded, the vagrants and the unemployed, should be taken out of the poor law, that the medical services should be unified under the county medical officer, and that the poor law school should be handed over to the education committee. That is good enough for a beginning, and the fantastic constitution of the county poor law board, the body which is to manage the rest, could not pass any Cabinet. The other matter is more serious—though it does not concern the poor law. My late chairman has persuaded Lord Balfour of Burleigh and his Departmental Committee on Royal Commissions to recommend that there should be no more minority reports of the Webb brand! It is odd that Royal Commissions have been going on muddling about all these seventy years, but that no enquiry is made into their procedure until a Labour-Socialist group puts forward a really powerful report upon which a popular movement can be based! No one suggests that the Minority Report is not worth the printing bill. As a matter of fact, the Government have sold more Minority Reports than Majority, in spite of our sale of twelve thousand. So the country thinks the report valuable. In fact, its *power* is exactly the reason why future ones are to be suppressed before they are born. It is rather a mean proceeding. But our enemies have got into a panic—highly complimentary no doubt, but inconvenient. Another sign of this was a three-column review of the Minority Report in the *Times* with a leader calling attention to it— all to the effect that the Minority Report *was* the French Revolution in another form! This gave us an opportunity for a column and a half answer in our best style of modest moderation.

August 19th. *Caermeddyg Llanbedr.*—Half through the very exhausting performance of directing the Fabian Summer School.

On the whole more satisfactory than I expected. The first fortnight, with the somewhat remarkable party we had here and the many interesting and influential persons who had congregated at the National Conference [on the Prevention of Destitution], was really profitable from the standpoint of propaganda and personal influence. But I cannot say that even this fortnight was exactly enjoyable. To keep house for twenty persons and be accessible to another hundred, as well as lecturing three or four times in the week, is a strain on nerves. Since our more especial friends and supporters have left, we have been surrounded by a miscellaneous crowd—all kindly and well-bred and interested, but not exciting in themselves, and some of them ugly and crude in mind and manners. Still, my dominant impression is the well-bredness of this extraordinarily mixed assembly—I.L.P. organisers, M.O.H.s, teachers, minor officials of all sorts, social workers, literary men, journalists and even such out-of-the-way recruits as auctioneers and unregistered dentists—all living in extremely close quarters, and yet not getting on each other's nerves through a too great disparity of speech and behaviour. It is a wonderful instance of the civilising effect of a common purpose and a common faith. Of course, every now and again one longs to escape for a day or two; the whirl of constant talk and discussion and the answering of questions is too much for physical or mental comfort. Sidney is simply splendid—his perpetual courtesy and kindness and willingness to be helpful to all and sundry without distinction of persons. And, I suppose, one gains facility of experience and thrashes out one's own thoughts.

What appalls me is the fear that we may never be able to get quit of leadership again. Is our existence going to be one perpetual round of talking and organising for the rest of our working lives? It is a terrifying prospect! The two of us, taken together, seem to constitute a leader at the time when the English political world is singularly without definite leadership on social and economic questions. And no one has yet attempted to make a political movement without being in politics or desiring to be in politics. I wonder whether it will succeed?

We have planned a big effort for the second National Conference to be held in London next Whitsun. We mean to run it on the constructive side of the Minority Report, and to run it in sections—all sitting concurrently—*unemployment, public health, care of children,* etc. This little start down in Wales has whetted our ambition, and we have secured a nucleus of persons who will assist in getting it up. We have all the winter to work it up, and we mean to make it a real big affair. Meanwhile, we have a hard winter's lecturing before us as well as settling our National Committee on a permanent basis.

September 4th.—Within sight of the end of our six weeks' directorship of the Fabian School—only one more week and the ordeal is over.

The attempt to attract university Fabian Societies has failed and, perhaps, we alone are to blame. We quite casually decided to put on the programme—Conference of University Fabian Societies—without much consulting these societies as to time, place or subjects, and without getting sufficient college celebrities to attract any number of the members. A little group of half-a-dozen Cambridge men—Hugh Dalton, Rupert Brooke, James Strachey, Clifford Allen, Foss—came for a week, and Clifford Allen has stayed on as our guest. One or two other university or ex-university Fabians dribbled in from Edinburgh, Manchester, London—but at the most liberal calculation there cannot be more than forty or fifty university men and women here. Hence, the rather elaborate programme of two discussions every day has been a frost bordering on the ridiculous. We have had interesting and useful talks with these young men: but the weather, being detestable, must have made the trip appear rather a bad investment for them, and they are inclined to go away rather more critical and supercilious than they came. Quite clearly we must not attempt it again unless we can ensure the presence of twenty or thirty leading dons and attractive celebrities. "They won't come, unless they know who they are going to meet", sums up Rupert Brooke. And I gathered that, even if they *did* come, they would only talk together and to us. So that it would not be much use. They don't want to learn, they don't think they have anything to learn. They certainly don't want to help others; unless they think that there is something to be got in the way of an opening and a career, they won't come. The egotism of the young university man is colossal. Are they worth bothering about?

Apart from this specific failure, what is apparent from this six weeks' experience is that there are two conceptions of the school which are really incompatible with each other—the Webbs' conception, and that of the general manager, Miss Hankinson. She and Miss Atkinson desire a co-operative country holiday—made up, in the main, of organised games, excursions and evening entertainments—with a few lectures and discussions thrown in to give subjects for conversation. Our conception is that of an organised school—teaching, learning and discussing, with some off days, and off hours, for recreation and social intercourse. This involves getting at least one hundred to one hundred and twenty persons, and having a real bond of union based on a particular philosophy of life, with many specialised sections—like the several parts of the Minority Report.

For the first fortnight *our* conception was carried out; for the second fortnight there was a rather unsatisfactory compromise. But this third fortnight has been practically given over to Miss Hankinson's pleasuring—and the lectures and discussions have suffered in consequence. Moreover, the sixty or seventy members left have not constituted an audience that is much worth addressing. If there had been no pretension in the last fortnight to be anything in particular, there would have been no note of failure. But, pretending to be a University Fabian Societies' conference, the failure has been obvious. And, as I began, so I end by saying that we are to blame. We presumed on a greater importance and popularity than we possessed with the university Fabians.

One thing stands out as the net result. If we again think of undertaking this sort of business, we must run it deliberately ourselves, with our own staff. Miss Hankinson is most valuable as an organiser, but she is, in a sense, too much of the expert, and will not carry out any policy but her own. Secondly, six weeks is far too long—we must limit the session to a fortnight or three weeks—at most four weeks. Thirdly, we must try and solve the question of a compromise between studiousness and a certain amount of carefully devised entertainment. It is *not* desirable to exclude games, exercise, music, but these must not be permitted to absorb the whole energies of any section of the company. And for this reason I am rather against having professional gymnastic instructors (?), or letting any lively man or woman absorb a large part of the company in a play or a pageant. Exercise, like walking, cycling, golf, bathing, tennis, are all right if they are taken when convenient. But regular lessons or highly organised games, the learning of parts in plays, and the preparation of dresses and scenery, become an occupation in themselves and turn the mind away for good and all from listening to lectures and quiet fireside discussion. Hence, another time we must, somehow or other, select our staff and even our guests, and take a great deal more trouble to plan out an intellectually varied bill of fare, and a far more *technical* and *specialised* kind of discussion which will attract a better type.

To sum up the result: National Conference was an *unqualified* success: the Fabian Summer School partially a financial success, and, I think, a moral success, because we have raised the standard of manners and intellectual atmosphere. Some most valuable friends made, among whom Alfred Ollivant [the well-known novelist] will, I think, prove the best. And finally, a considerable increase of general interest in the Minority Report among some three hundred men and women of more than average intelligence and good-will. Against this we have to set the disappointment of perhaps half-a-dozen persons with the School, together with the harmless but somewhat absurd failure of the Fabian University Conference. Taken as a whole, the experiment has been worth trying, for it has taught us a good deal and has been, *as regards its main purpose* (the promotion of our crusade), decidedly successful. Points to be remembered:

1. Sessions should be two, three or at most four weeks.
2. August the best month.
3. Fee for lectures should be *separate*, and the payment of it should constitute the qualification for residence. (When lectures are thrown in they are regarded as necessary evils and discipline, instead of being the main purpose.) This latter device has selective effect on guests.
4. The whole staff should be under the direction of one head, and should be inspired with the same purpose as the director.
5. The character of the exercise, etc. and all provisions for entertainments should be deliberately organised by the director.
6. The boarding arrangements should be differentiated with regard to *quiet*, accommodation and extra luxuries, according to the diverse wishes of the guests. Of all the differentiations *quiet and freedom from noise* is the *most* important. Some people delight in noise. Would it

be possible to exclude the more boisterous, larky entertainments and substitute, or at any rate include, something of the nature of religious music—or time for meditation? Could you have this and keep the bracing free thought of the Fabian Summer School?

7. Every member of the conference or school should be *formally* introduced to the director and should have an opportunity for some little personal intercourse.

8. Seminars or special classes, to which admission might be considered a privilege, might sometimes take the place of the *second lecture* of the day (technique of public speaking or investigation, metaphysics).

9. Careful attempts should be made respecting literature and sale of literature.

The director ought to have a *secretary* whose business it is to get to know every person and find out whether that person is comfortably settled, and is getting what they want out of the School. The general manager should be restricted to the special province of catering, etc., and the secretary should consider herself as a whole-time official. There should be organisers of games, etc.—there should be a business secretary as well as a social secretary.

A certain selective process should be applied to the guests—proper proportions between men and women, exclusion of undesirable or completely careless people, due admixture of persons of high standing at the same table or in the same house. Persons of high standing should be always persons of good-will and friendly to the School. The purely critical element must not be allowed to set the tune. It has been a misfortune that C. H. Norman, an enemy of Webbs and the Minority Report, settled himself at Caermeddyg. We could not prevent it because the custom of the School is that every guest chooses his own accommodation. The three or four critical *Cambridge* Fabians were also a bad element: on the other hand, Lady Betty Balfour was wholly advantageous.

Finally, there is the financial basis. Quite clearly here, as elsewhere, education of the university type cannot be made self-supporting. The fees or the boarding arrangements cannot pay for the intellectual direction and the lectures—I doubt whether it can be made to cover the necessary machinery for the smooth running of the School in respect to social intercourse and housekeeping. It may be possible to get a few persons to give their time and thought—but holidays are very sacred institutions with English persons; the more leisure they have, the less they will devote to other people (we have not merely given our services but we have been paying guests the whole time). Hence, I do not see that any experiment could be likely to succeed without a fund set apart for the educational side of the School.

The last days of the School have left the pleasantest impression. E. D. Simon and Dr. Saleeby—some thirty or forty pleasant men and women—delightful weather, lively discussions—all this has contributed to a feeling of successful accomplishment. Lawson Dodd is enthusiastically hopeful of a great future for the School, and we complete our directorate amid mutual congratulations with the staff. The one unpleasant result is persistent neuralgia—a bad beginning to a busy autumn.

Perhaps one of the important results of the School is the alliance between ourselves and Dr. Saleeby. The eugenists have always been our bitter opponents on the ground that all attempts to alter environment are not only futile, but positively mischievous, as such improvements in environment diminish the struggle for existence and retard the elimination of the unfit. Eugenics have, in fact, been used as a weapon against Socialism. Dr. Saleeby, who is one of the most prominent of the apostles, now joins not only the National Committee, but the Fabian Society. We spent two days talking with him and eventually proved to him that changes in the environment were a necessary accompaniment to even negative eugenics, whereas *positive* eugenics can only be brought about by collective control and collective expenditure. He has even invented the term preventive engenics, which includes all action against racial poisons and all checks to the deterioration of good stocks by bad environment.

September 17th.—Position in the political world is most unsatisfactory for the progressive movement. The financial basis of the Labour Party has been smashed by the Osborne Judgement.[1] The Labour members are being attacked by a considerable section of the I.L.P. The trade union movement is distracted by the insurrection of large bodies of its members against their officials—the insurrection which involves repudiation of agreements made by the officials. Meanwhile, Tom Mann, recently returned from Australia, is preaching general trade unionism and the general strike, and running down political action. And behind it all there is the likelihood of a compact between the front benches which will keep the Liberal Cabinet in power, in spite of the Labour and Irish parties, till after the coronation, and bring the tariff reformers back in strength at the next election. It looks as if Asquith and Co. had rucked up, and were determined to ally themselves with the Tories rather than let themselves be goaded by Labour. However, there will be old-age pensions, the budget, and a weakened House of Lords as the net result. No break-up of the poor law. I

[1] See " The Osborne Judgement ": *The History of Trade Unionism*, 1920 edition, p. 608, by Sidney and Beatrice Webb.

doubt the passing of the insurance schemes. Neither Labour nor the Tories will accept them. And, if Labour breaks away, many Radicals will follow. The Liberal Cabinet will have to depend on Tory support; and will, therefore, if it remains in, sit still. More probably there will be an explosion in November, and an election in January. Balfour may come in: but not with a *bona fide* tariff reform majority. In fact, my impression is that tariff reform itself has lost ground these last months and that a Conservative majority will be simply an anti-Liberal Cabinet majority. The time might come for a genuine Socialist Party—if we had this sort of smash-up of the Liberal Party.

October 6th.—A. J. B. has done for the chances of a Tory Party at the next election, if this takes place in January, by his Edinburgh speech—a courageous and sincere speech but one of complete scepticism on the constructive side, and a non-possumus attitude towards the Osborne Judgement and payment of members. Now is Asquith's chance! Break up the Conference,[1] and go to the country on House of Lords and Labour representation. The North Country and Scotland would be absolutely firm.

October 9th. Auchterarder.—Started on our autumn campaign. After lecturing at Bournemouth and Southampton, I returned to London for three days and then journeyed to Hull, Middlesbrough and Darlington, arriving here on Saturday and leaving again for Inverness on Monday. I felt ill when I left for Hull, and on the day I travelled to Middlesbrough I thought the end had come, and that I should find myself the next day in bed with a bad breakdown. But, by fasting and prayer (this literally!), I pulled through, and to-day for the first time I feel decently fit for the work—though not over-much so. Splendid meeting at Middlesbrough—speaking for one hour to two thousand persons, with questions afterwards. Small but influential meetings at Darlington and Hull. Now I am spending the Sunday with the Haldanes before opening the Scottish campaign at Inverness and Edinburgh.

I find the Haldanes as kindly as ever; the dear old lady is very frail—Elizabeth is the same sturdy, kind and direct woman. R. B. H. is rapidly ageing and looks as if he were on the verge of another breakdown. He is terribly stout and pasty, and eats enormously and takes no exercise. He is worried and depressed about his War Office administration—in a very different state of mind from the buoyant self-confidence and delight with which he undertook it. He is conscious of hostility to his beloved Territorials from the National Service League, of indiffer-

---

[1] The Constitutional Conference between leaders on both sides of the House, which broke down (Oct. 16th) on the Irish question. (Ed.)

ence from his own party, and of limpness and inefficiency in the W.O. itself. " I can't depend on my orders being carried out—there is slackness directly I turn my back."

He takes the same philosophically cynical but good-natured view of the progressive politics. He is really in favour of the Osborne Judgement and against payment of members—but he is prepared to come down with many qualifications on the advanced side. He would like the party to stay in for another year, and then make way for the Tories, and then come in again in five years' time. He would like the Conference [on the Prevention of Destitution] to succeed. He is inclined to take a benevolent view of a Tory Government; he is contemptuous of the Labour Party and altogether sceptical about the growth of Socialism. His eyes are still fixed on the city as an index of public opinion. All this is not very hopeful. On the other hand, both from my talk with him and with Elizabeth, I gather that they are favourable to the Minority Report. " Both Asquith and Lloyd George want me to go on the Local Government Board, if there is another Liberal administration, and to carry out a large reconstruction." He would evidently be prepared to give us the substance so long as he could keep some semblance of compromise with those favourable to a poor law authority. But I should very much doubt whether our old friend had very much longer to work in the world of edibles—there will be another flare-up presently which may attack something more vital than the eyes. After such a warning as his illness last year—within an inch of total blindness—it is strange he should go on eating himself into the grave, or at any rate into permanent invalidity.

What makes one despair is the atmosphere in which these leaders live. Their lives are so rounded off by culture and charm, comfort and power, that the misery of the destitute is as far off as the savagery of central Africa. To R. B. Haldane the irritation at " Form 4 " in the mind of the landlord is a far more *real grievance* than the absence of employment or the virtual starvation of a family. They don't realise either the misery itself or the possibility of preventing it. And the atmosphere of Cloan is practically identical with that of Whittinge-hame—there is no difference at all in the consciousness of the front benchers. What differs is the rank and file behind them—one made up of reactionaries, and the other of progressives. But as a set-off, the Tory front bench has complete control of their party and they have no effective opposition to any of their schemes, *if they are progressive*, whilst the Liberal front bench has always the Tories and the House of Lords to stem their progress. So really I don't know from what party we shall get the most. We may have, in the end, to establish a real Socialist Party if we want rapid progress.

Edinburgh. October 10*th*-11*th.*—2 P.M. Sleepless! Made a failure of the opening lecture of the Edinburgh course. I had prepared it very carefully—spent the whole day at it. I found my St. James's Hall lecture did not do for Scotland and so had to construct an entirely new one. Unfortunately, the task of preparing it exhausted my remaining strength, and consequently I did not give the lecture I had prepared, but ground out a mechanical reflection of it. Once or twice I wondered whether I could go on—I kept repeating myself and I was conscious of my best friends in the audience being disappointed and concerned at my evident fatigue. However, I daresay it was not so bad as it seemed to me—*some* of the value was there.

On this tour I have had two successes, Middlesbrough and Inverness; two quite decent performances, Hull and Darlington; one failure, Edinburgh. What concerns me is whether I shall get through, especially the one on unemployment, and the one on voluntary agencies. Ah me! What a grind it is, this propaganda; research is not in it. *Shall I pull through?* That is the question which frightens me. This cursed sleeplessness, especially when I have not got my boy with me just to tell me it is all right. " The soldier's pay, if not the victor's meed." But sometimes to march, march, march is wearisome, and one feels one will fall on the way.

October 19*th.*—A bomb thrown into the School by the railway magnates led by Lord Claud Hamilton! A demand for Sidney's resignation of the chairmanship of the School of Economics, in the form of resignation of the position of governor and an implied threat to withdraw the railway class and denounce the School as " socialistic ". The ostensible reason is a speech by Sidney some six weeks ago to the railway servants—the *real* reason is the Minority Report campaign, as the *Times* let out in a leader which actually drew me into the business. The Hamiltons know that we care for the School and that it is our child, so to speak. George Hamilton has also some silly notion that Sidney gains *social status* by being chairman!

It is an awkward corner to turn. We *do* value our connection, and *authoritative* connection with the School, and if Sidney were to retire presently from the chairmanship it would endanger the tie. On the other hand, we value more the continued prosperity of the School so long as it remains unbiassed and open to collectivist tendencies. Moreover, Sidney will be going away for a year presently. And there *is* a danger that, as we succeed more and more in our agitation and as we develop the other parts of our programme, the hostility to us will grow and would make the position untenable. The question therefore arises whether it would not be better to accept the situation gracefully and not stand for re-election in December. If when we come back we return to the life of administration and research, then we can resume our connection. If, on the other hand, we are still in the toils of agitation, we are likely to become more and more prominent and be more and more hated. What is desirable is to keep a good majority on the governing body to back up Reeves. We have put an imprint on the School which it will not easily lose. It is always sad when a favourite child grows up and *seems* to escape influence and control. But one has had one's day and we must not repine. In some ways, the School has been too successful, it has outgrown our tutelage. Still I think it will retain the Webb method of concrete investigation, and the Webb bias in favour of expert administration in all human affairs.

November 5th. Grosvenor Road.—The Claud Hamilton episode seems to be closed. The governors met, and (though there was an undercurrent of disapproval of Sidney's speech) passed a unanimous resolution of confidence in Sidney. There seems a possibility of the return of the four errant knights of individualism. I don't think that the School has been damaged. But clearly, if, when we come back, we are to continue an agitation on a great scale as at present, we shall have to drop into the background in the School's life.

The Scottish tour has, I think, been an unqualified success. We have got through the whole programme and the new lectures on *voluntary agencies, unemployment* and *education*, which I was rather dreading, were the most successful of those which I gave. Indeed, the one drawback was the repetition of the old lectures on the break-up of the poor law in different parts of the country. It is very difficult to invent a new way of stating the old thing.

One Sunday we spent at the Yarrows (who afterwards subscribed one hundred pounds); another we spent at Whittingehame, with that most charming of families. A. J. B. and I had a long argument as to whether the stately charm of Whittingehame was compatible with either feeling or knowing about the problem of destitution. As a " holyday " it is extraordinarily refreshing, there is a delightful atmosphere of intimacy, a freedom to say anything to anybody—to be yourself. Sidney feels it just as much as I do—so evidently do the other guests. But Lady Betty realises that it is gained at the expense of aloofness from the world, from the countryside, from the world of experts and administrators, even from the world of Conservative politicians. A. J. B. works hard as a politician, is nearly always in his place, dominates his front bench, but, save for this work, he is as aloof from all intercourse as if he were a lonely college don. Gathered around him are his family, his intimate friends, and every now and again a new-comer chosen for some personal charm or interest. Within this circle all is friendliness, frankness and equality, without it, all men and women are kept at an equally remote distance, not from any feeling of superiority, A. J. B. is far too philosophical to be conscious of class—but merely from sheer indifference—" No doubt these people are as nice as any others, but life is not long enough to think of knowing them ", is the sort of attitude he takes towards the whole world outside the little circle of friends.

November 30th.—The autumn lecturing is well-nigh over—only four more lectures before Christmas—another four in January (put off on account of election) and we shall have carried out the whole programme of eighty meetings for the two of us in two-and-a-half months. I am not much the worse for it except for a threatening of neuritis of the leg which I hope to walk off. I have had a varied experience—all types of meetings from gatherings of seventy to one hundred and fifty persons, all keen supporters, to great popular meetings of two thousand strong. Everywhere, I see an opening for a different kind of propaganda —conferences of experts on the various kinds of preventive agencies on the lines of the Minority Report. Exactly as the poor law and the guardians have their conferences, we must organise a meeting place where medical officers, teachers, inspectors, labour exchange officials, working-class representatives and voluntary agencies may discuss and resolve with regard to the new preventive authorities. To the teachers must be devoted the next three months.

Meanwhile, we are again in the turmoil of an election. The sensational counter-stroke of the Lords is a clever dodge which will, if it does not succeed, do much to damage their prestige as sober folk. The violent abuse by the Tory press of the Liberals and Lloyd George, on the ground of Socialism and Irish nationalism, is an old game which everyone tires of. But it is hardly to be expected that the Liberals will do more than hold their own. If they do not lose at the election it will be a triumph, and the Lords will have to go as a permanent drag on progressive legislation. If they gain seats, then we are in for a time of rapid changes in our direction. The tariff reformers will become very desperate; they will have played every card and will have either to wait for the inevitable reaction or invent some more taking programme. At present they refuse as a party to declare themselves for any specific proposal except the silly business of occupying ownership of land. " They all say ", remarked our one devoted tariff reform M.P., J. W. Hills, " they are in favour of social reform, but when you urge them to declare in favour of any single item they shrink back with a cry ' That is Socialism! ' In which of course they are right."

The big thing that has happened in the last two years is that Lloyd George and Winston Churchill have practically taken the *limelight*, not merely from their own colleagues, but from the Labour Party.

They stand out as the most advanced politicians. And, if we get a Liberal majority and payment of members, we shall have any number of young Fabians rushing for Parliament, fully equipped for the fray—better than the Labour men—and enrolling themselves behind these two Radical leaders.

December 1st. The eve of the election.—Balfour's sudden advocacy of the referendum, whatever effect it may have, at the eleventh hour of the election, completely alters our constitutional system. Now that a responsible party has proposed the referendum, it will have to come; unless, of course, the responsible party were to drop it, which it will not. It is a bad method of government if the country could trust its representatives to play fair. But elections have been run on such rotten issues lately that the referendum may be the only way out of the difficulty. And, from the point of view of the leader of a party, it has one inestimable quality. It delivers him from the domination of a political sect that has got hold of the caucus. That advantage must appeal to A. J. B., who has been suffering from having had tariff reform foisted on him. It is the last move in his duel with Chamberlain; it is a final checkmate to tariff reform. And it is a superlatively fine stroke in his duel with Asquith—though it may be it has been delivered too late for this time.

What other effect will the referendum have on our political life? If we have it coupled with the payment of members, it will hasten the advent of a class of expert representatives paid to carry out the will of the people. It will be the death knell of the caucus supported only by small and energetic minorities capable of making themselves troublesome to the elected representatives. It will, therefore, delay some types of social reform—the more recondite advances in social control—unless the advocates of these can get them *accepted by both parties.* And will it not delay indefinitely women's suffrage?

For us it points to increased propaganda among all classes of the community. Also, we must devote more energy to a propaganda of the *ideas* of the Minority Report apart from its shibboleth. And, hence, we must push forward with the conception of conferences, and the elaboration of *The Crusade* into a technical journal. Sidney and I have exhausted the effect of our own lecturing and writing—at any rate in the big centres of population. Now we must get other people at work —ostensibly unconnected with the Minority Report, but all preaching the same doctrine and developing the technique of the same purpose—the abolition of extreme poverty.

December 10th.—Sidney and I are both feeling weary and somewhat dispirited. In spite of all our work the National Committee does not

466

seem to be gaining many new members and our friends are beginning to melt away. One wonders whether we have not exhausted the interest in the subject, and whether our dream of a permanent organisation inspiring a large sustained movement on a broad philosophical basis, is possible at present? Is public opinion ripe for a synthesis taking the place of chaotic endeavours of public authorities and voluntary agencies? We shall go on steadily for another six months, devoting ourselves for the next two months to collecting money sufficient to carry the National Committee through our absence, and to organising the National Conference at Whitsun. If we fail, we shall have to cut down the work of the Committee to an expenditure of some £2000 a year—of this income, I think, we are pretty well secure for another two years. That will mean dropping the enlarged *Crusade* and dismissing half our staff and giving up our political propaganda. It will also mean the abandonment of all notion of a permanent organisation. As far as we personally are concerned, probably that would be a pleasanter prospect than the development of the National Committee into a big and permanent business. I should regret it because, I think, a permanent organisation would have immense value, and also on the lower ground that some of my staff would be on their beam ends. One never likes to have attracted men and women into work which ends in a *cul-de-sac*, though of course I warned each of them that the job would be probably temporary. In case we had to wind up the National Committee, I should throw the remnant and some of our energy into revivifying the Fabian Society. Whether that would be possible with E. Pease as secretary I do not know.

But whilst I am depressed on some counts, I am supremely grateful that I have been able to struggle through, with no nervous breakdown, the severe ordeal of this autumn's lecturing. An attack of influenza, or even a bad cold, might have made the Scottish tour a costly fiasco: and it would have been serious to have not been able to fulfil our North Country and Midlands engagements. Sidney too has gone on with his lecturing and all his other work—a quite incessant activity—and though strained and weary sometimes, on the whole happy in the intensity of our comradeship.

December 30th. Fishers' Hill, Woking.—We are spending a fortnight in the charming house of the Gerald Balfours, lent us whilst they are at Whittingehame. I have been lazing (Sidney working as usual), alternating long walks, twelve to fifteen miles, across the Surrey hills with days writing casual letters, reading, and talking to a succession of young friends we have had with us. . . .

During the next six months we have to get through three tasks—(1) make the position of the National Committee secure, both financially and constitutionally so that it will outlast our ten months' absence; (2) organise the first of a series of National Conferences; (3) write a short book on *The Prevention of Destitution*, summing up the lectures we have given in the last eighteen months. If we succeed in carrying out this programme we can go away with a clear conscience. I think it is even best that we should go away so as to see whether the movement has independent life.

1911

January.—The general election has brought the Liberals back with far greater power because they have not lost but slightly gained on balance. They have also got a clear mandate in favour of the " veto " and " home rule ", payment of members and a complete reform of the constitution. As Lloyd George said to the press interviewers, we are in for a period of rapid social reconstruction unless foreign complications turn the nation away from its quarry. Whether the complete supersession of the poor law will be one aspect of that reconstruction depends on whether or not John Burns stays at the Local Government Board. And the schemes of insurance are not really helpful to our scheme. Doling out weekly allowances, and with no kind of treatment attached, is a most unscientific state aid; and, if it were not for the advantage of proposing to transfer the millions from the rich to the poor, we should oppose it root and branch. As it is, we shall stand by quietly suggesting criticisms of the schemes to the Labour Party and the Conservatives. The unemployment insurance might bring inadvertently the compulsory use of the labour exchange, and the standardisation of the conditions of employment. But the sickness insurance as expounded in the communicated scheme of the *Times* (January 4th) is wholly bad, and I cannot see how malingering can be staved off except that the amount given is so *wholly inadequate* that it will be only the very worst workmen who will want to claim it and remain out of work (the low-paid women, by the way, and the inhabitants of Irish and Scottish country districts, may find it better than their wages, especially as it will be impossible to prevent their doing home-work). The invalidity scheme may be only an extension of old-age pensions, to which there could be no objection. What the Government shirk is the extension of *treatment* and *disciplinary supervision*— they want merely some mechanical way of increasing the money income of the wage-earning class in times of unemployment and sickness. No attempt is made to secure an advance in conduct, in return for the increased income. What we should like would be for Lloyd George to make the financial provision, but to find his scheme so criticised that he had to withdraw it for reconsideration. Of course, we are handicapped in our criticism by the fact that Lloyd George and Winston are the most favourable to the supersession of the poor law, and that it is these Ministers who are responsible for the insurance schemes. We have to dance on eggs without cracking them—we shall have to try and invent some way out for Lloyd George.

January 16th.—We are organising the Whitsun National Conference with great care, whilst keeping our names well out of it. Our draft prospectus has met with universal approval, and it looks as if the conference would take on considerably. Our object is two-fold: (1) to provide opportunities for discussion between the different experts and stimulus to each department of prevention; (2) to give out to the public the new synthesis, in a non-partizan and expert form—by making all the authorities engaged in preventive works, aware of themselves and each other, and the public aware of them and expectant of great thing . It is a bold idea to exclude the poor law from a conference on destitution! Then I should like, having started this Conference, to gradually transfer the whole staff and organisation of the National Committee to this Conference organisation. In this way we shall get a much wider circle of adherents to the policy of prevention than is possible by the Minority Report campaign. We want, in fact, to slip out of this movement, or at any rate from the leadership of it. After our Eastern tour I should like to get back to our research and finish up all those volumes. And there may have come the time for a big campaign for a Socialist Party with a self-conscious collectivist programme. Payment of members and election expenses may entirely revolutionise English politics. Hosts of able young men, well trained in Fabian economics and administrative lore, will be crowding into the political arena, and if they succeed in squeezing themselves through a many-cornered election they will make Parliament hum! The young men are with us.

March 6th. Eastbourne.—Let our house for one year to the William O'Briens, in order to get it off our hands for our Eastern tour, and retired first to a little house here for five weeks, then to Luton Hoo for two-and-a-half months.

It is a relief to get out of London with its perpetual whirl of talking and organising, and occasional lecturing. After two lectures this next week I am free to turn to the writing of our little book on *The Prevention of Destitution*, summing up all our lectures of the last two years to be left as a legacy to the National Committee for the next session's propaganda.

Since Xmas we have been seeing a good many political personages—we have had both Haldane and Churchill to dinner; we have breakfasted with Lloyd George and had A. J. B. to meet various M.O.H.s.

The front bench Liberals have, in fact, been softening towards us—partly because we are going away, and partly because we could, if we chose, wreck their schemes of insurance by rousing the Labour hostility to them. What we are trying to achieve is to direct the sickness insurance scheme into a big reconstruction of public health. It is clear that public opinion has got firmly into its silly head that insurance has some mystical moral quality, which even covers the heinous sin of expenditure from public funds. It is an amazingly foolish delusion—the only moral advantage of insurance was its voluntary character; when that is superseded by compulsory contributions all the moral characteristics vanish, and you are left with a method of provision which is provocative of immoral motives. But there comes a time when it is useless to argue with an obsession of the public mind; you have to accept it, and by skilful devising of the scheme see that it does as little harm as possible. In the public health scheme, which we have put into the hands of the M.O.H.s to press on Lloyd George and to give to leading politicians in the three parties, we have accepted the contributory side of insurance and attempted to supersede the provision characteristic of insurance, by the provision characteristic of public health administration. We talked to Lloyd George about it, and then suggested that he should see persons who were more expert than ourselves—the little group of M.O.H.s who are in our confidence. Meanwhile, the scheme is published simultaneously under Lyster's name in the *British Medical Journal*, *Public Health Journal* and *The Crusade* of this month. It has been given to all the Cabinet Ministers favourable to our views; to A. J. B. and the Labour Party and to Llewellyn Smith and other officials.

March 7th.—Last night I was dead tired when I gave my last lecture in London. To-morrow I have to speak to the Free Church Council at Portsmouth. After that I am free from this strain of public speaking. For the remainder of our time in England I shall be writing and, to a small extent, organising. And then our holiday, that supreme luxury of the propertied brain-worker! If the National Conference turns out a success, I believe we shall have practically converted England to the obligation of preventing destitution. What will remain is seeing that the obligation is fulfilled by the different public authorities, and the voluntary agencies attached to them. But oh! I am tired—deep down tired. I shall just last out, but not more than last out.

The Fabian Society is going through a crisis, not of dissent, but of indifference. Sidney thought that, as he was leaving England, he had better resign for a year. Thereupon G. B. S. not only announces his intention of resigning, but persuades some half-a-dozen others of the old gang to resign also. All with the view to making room for young men who are not there! Clifford Sharp, who is a loyal and steadfast member of the executive, is in despair, and Sidney is remaining on if G. B. S. and the others persist in going. Charlotte Shaw told Sharp that G. B. S. had got sick of the Fabian Society and cared for nothing but his own productions, that he felt himself too important to work in harness with anyone else. It is largely her fault as she has withdrawn him from association with us and other Fabians in order not to waste his intellectual force in talk and argument. It is clear to me that the Fabian Society has to get a new impetus, or gradually dwindle to a mere name. I am not sure that the time may not have arrived for a genuine Socialist Party with a completely worked-out philosophy, and a very detailed programme. When we come back from the East we will see how the land lies. If the prevention of destitution movement is safely in other hands, I am not sure whether we had better not throw ourselves into constructing a party with a religion and an applied science. In that case, I should devote half the year to public speaking and organising, and half the year to thinking and writing.

March 8th, 4 a.m.—The non-brain-worker has little conception of the misery of the over-excited brain. Yesterday night I lay right through the long hours twisting every domestic detail or incident of our organisation into a giant of evil, a monster of unpleasant things. And it is in the night that I suffer from remorse for lack of consistency between conduct and conviction. All my little self-indulgences—the cup of tea or occasional coffee after a meal, the regular five or six cigarettes consumed daily, the extra expenditure on pretty clothes—all seem sins from which I can never shake myself free. Ought one ever to do anything that is against an ideal of perfect health, equality of income and the noblest use of money? When the morning comes and one returns to the rough and tumble of a hard day's work, or the necessities of human intercourse, these scruples seem mere weaknesses, and one goes forward without thought of justification with the habits and customs of one's daily life. Still, there lies at the back of one's mind a discontent with these compromises, a longing to be completely at peace with one's own ideal even in the smaller details of life. To a great extent Sidney and I are at peace with our ideal—in all the larger determinations of our life we do conform to our perception of what is best for the community, and we have the extraordinary joy of complete agreement as to this purpose. But I still fail in some of the minor matters because I am not sufficiently convinced of the wrongness of the action to overcome my self-indulgence. As for Sidney, he sweeps on one side as irrelevant and foolish all consideration of these trifles! By nature and training economical in personal expenditure, abstemious without being faddy, untroubled by vanity or large appetite, he goes on his way of sane temperance, without temptation or scruple, and with one settled opinion that he wants *me* to indulge myself to the top of my bent! He is the most perfect of lovers, by night and by day, in work and in play, in health and in sickness!

March 12*th. Eastbourne.*—Sidney has gone up to London, summoned by the M.O.H.s to counsel them what next to do. They had a formal interview with Lloyd George, Buxton and Masterman, at which Lloyd George explained his scheme of wholesale subsidy to friendly societies; and, for the excluded residuum, an artificial friendly society managed by the state nominees, with far lower benefits relatively to the contributions. They report that Masterman seemed a bitter opponent of the public health administration, and that he even suggested that the poor law was not " half bad ". Lloyd George, having explained his scheme, asked the M.O.H.s to consider it and send him a memorandum on it, and he would see them again. So they wrote begging Sidney to meet them and draft the memorandum. They have now their chance. Alone among medical men they have been consulted. It is characteristic of the public contempt for the medical profession that it should be so, a contempt largely justified since the B.M.A. has only one idea—to protect the pecuniary interests of the worst type of medical man by a futile insistence on free choice of doctors by the beneficiaries of state insurance—an obvious administrative absurdity, as absurd as free choice of teachers by the school children or their parents, rather more so, as the parents would be a better judge of a teacher than of a medical man as they would have *far less reason for choosing a bad one.*

The whole attitude of the Government about the destitution question, together with the leaderless state of the democratic movement, makes me feel more strongly every day that our duty, when we return, *may be* to throw ourselves into the democratic movement. Hitherto Sidney and I have kept ourselves almost exclusively for the work of expert guidance of the expert. Sidney has had a repulsion for public speaking and public agitation, partly because he is impatient of stupidity, and partly because he really hates putting himself forward; he far prefers working quietly in the background and he does not like the intercourse entailed by leadership. The life he really enjoys is to sit in a room and draft things for other people, and then to spend his spare time reading endless books and being with me without anyone there to bother him. Added to that he would like to go on writing great books of wisdom and research, and enjoy the mild pleasure of an academic reputation. Popular approval he does not enjoy, it bores him; he has no glow of satisfaction at the applause at a public meeting. He is the ideal " man at the desk "—thinking, devising, scheming and drafting ideas and devising actions for subordinates to carry out, and other public speakers to advocate. And this is in spite of the fact that he is a most persuasive advocate and speaker himself; and, if he had chosen to push forward, might have been a notable leader of public opinion and acknowledged as such in his own generation. There may still rise up some master-man in the Labour Party or the Fabian Society, or the leaders of the Liberal Party may prove themselves to have both conviction and knowledge. But unless this does happen, I am afraid we are doomed to offer ourselves as officers of the larger crusade to conquer the land of promise.

April 21st. The Hermitage, Luton Hoo.—In retreat here, toiling at our book on destitution and finding the task a tediously stale one. But we had to present the old story in a new form, with all the main objections answered and all the new developments noted. Moreover, with the National Conference at hand, it was all-important to have a book coming out entitled *The Prevention of Destitution*, giving the minority scheme in a non-controversial form—a textbook practically for the persons who attend the Conference, or for future Conferences. Having patented the name, and then getting it adopted as the name of a larger article of commerce than we can provide, we proceed to suggest that our patent is that larger article of commerce! And the odd thing is that few are taken in, but they all believe the others are taken in! Here is Lord George Hamilton accepting the vice-presidency of the Conference, and C. J. Hamilton reading a paper at one of the sections. I imagine that they have not the remotest objection to the ideas of the Minority Report, which are rampant in each one of the sections—all they desire is that we should not get the credit of them—that they should not be *credited* to the Minority Report. And, of course, we are only too glad to oblige them. If we were quite certain that our proposals would be accepted if we withdrew ourselves and our book, we would retire at once, and for good and all, and devote our energies to pushing on further up in the Socialist movement. In fact, that is what we rather hope may happen during the next year or so.

May 13th.—The splendid reception by all parties of Lloyd George's scheme of sickness insurance is a curious testimony to the heroic demagogy of the man. He has taken every item that could be popular with anyone, mixed them together and produced a Bill which takes some twenty millions from the propertied class to be handed over to the wage-earners *sans phrase* to be spent by them, as they think fit, in times of sickness or unemployment. If you add to this gigantic transfer of property from the haves to the have-nots the fact that the tax is to be collected in the most costly and extravagant fashion, and that the whole administration of the fund is to be put into the hands of the beneficiaries who are contributing only one-third, there is enough to make the moderate and constitutional Socialist aghast.

The first asset he started with was the word *insurance*. To the governing class insurance has always meant the voluntary contributions of the persons benefited—a method of raising revenue which has saved the pockets of all other persons. During the controversy about old-age pensions, insurance gradually acquired a compulsory element, and the Conservative Party became pledged to raising money from wage-earners, employers and the general taxpayer, as an alternative to non-contributory pensions. Hence, by using this word Lloyd George secured the approval of the Conservative section of the community. Then there were the friendly societies who stood in the way. So he puts them into possession of the whole machinery of distribution: a fund that is mainly contributed by non-beneficiaries is to be wholly administered by the beneficiaries. This scheme has the adherence of the friendly society world and of the larger part of the working class.

" What is a communist? " " A man who pockets your shilling and forks out his twopence." When one knows the liability to malingering, even in a friendly society in which all members stand to lose by the misconduct of one member, when one thinks of all the diatribes levied at unconditional outdoor relief, one is simply amazed at the " Simple Simon " of upper and middle-class optimism.

Now the question is: Can he hustle it through this session? If he does not, the scheme won't survive the criticism of all the interests imperilled by it. He has extraordinary luck. The Coronation shortens the time, distracts the attention, and makes everyone inclined to a sentimental gift to the working-class. The Parliament Bill paralyses the opposition—they dare not oppose any popular scheme. The Labour and Irish parties stand to gain—the Liberals are naturally averse to even criticising their leader's magnificent demagogy. If the Cabinet backs him up, the scheme will go through. The only way of stopping it would be for all the outraged interests to make the ordinary M.P. feel that he would lose votes heavily. But they have precious little time to organise this pressure.

Sidney, on the whole, wishes the Bill to go through. I am not sure that I do. He believes that the big and difficult matter is to get the money voted, and that the inanities of both the method of raising the revenue, and the character of the provision given, could and will be altered by subsequent legislation. I fear the growth of malingering and the right to money independently of the obligation to good conduct. I cannot dismiss my rooted prejudice to relief instead of treatment. Anyway, our duty is clear—just to say what we think about it. In our chapter on insurance in our forthcoming book we have done this faithfully. And, by the time it comes out, the Bill will have been read a second time, and we shall be out of the country. But where are the professional champions of sound administration?

The Unemployment Bill is on quite a different basis. If it is carried through, it will lead to increased control of the employer and the wage-earner by the state. We are not against this, so long as this control is exercised on the wage-earners' behalf. On the other hand, it might smash up trade unions and not give anything in return. I should imagine the opposition will concentrate on this far more statesmanlike proposal, just because it is statesmanlike. Public opinion takes the sloppy and sentimental schemes and dislikes anything that looks like increased efficiency and control. Even the propertied class are ready to spend public money, but they are not ready to exact the corresponding conduct, even when it is the conduct of the non-propertied class on whom the money is being spent. Administrative nihilism has its partizans; slovenly administration has its adherents; good administration has no public opinion on its side. That is the principal danger in front of us.

If only we could have a leader, or a body of opinion, that would undertake to redress the whole of the grievances and yet insist on redressing them in such a way as to improve conduct.

One result of the Sickness Insurance Bill, if it passes into law as now drafted, is that it will sweep away innumerable voluntary agencies —act as a great scavenger. We shall have a sort of bastard organisation, neither a properly constituted organ of the state, nor a voluntary agency. The only good feature being that it will be in such a state of unstable equilibrium that it will tumble the Government of the country sooner or later.

May 26th.—George Lansbury was down here consulting with us about the amendment or postponement of Lloyd George's rotten scheme of sickness insurance. The more we examine, the less we like it, both for what it does and what it omits to do. We have written in our new book what is virtually a scathing indictment of insurance in general and the Government scheme in particular—but it will come out after the Bill is well in committee and will probably not be much attended to except by our own followers. Lansbury told us that Masterman came up to him after Lloyd George's triumphant exposition of his scheme with a pleasant jeering expression: " We have spiked your guns, eh? " showing that he is hostile to the whole conception of the Minority Report and that the Government schemes are intended as an alternative method of dealing with the question of destitution. John Burns also goes about saying that insurance has finally " dished the Webbs ". All of which is interesting. What remains to be seen is whether the Minority Report has come too late to stop insurance, or whether the Government scheme of insurance has come too late to stop the Minority Report! The issue is fairly joined—complete state responsibility with a view of prevention, or partial state responsibility by a new form of relieving destitution unconnected with the poor law, but leaving the poor law for those who fall out of benefit. It is a trial of strength between the two ideas. In our new book we have said our say. By the time we get back from our holiday, the matter will probably be settled one way or the other—possibly for a generation. However, if the nation finds sickness increasing and premiums going up, they may turn more quickly than we expect to prevention. And it is still possible that opposition may grow to Lloyd George's scheme and that, if he cannot get it through this session, he will have to abandon it altogether. On the whole, I should prefer the scheme abandoned rather than passed in its present form. But we do not feel inclined to agitate against it.

June 3rd.—Probably my last entry in this tag-end of a period of my life, finishing with the National Conference on the Prevention of Destitution [1]—a great success, doing credit to Robert Harcourt and John W. Hills, Clifford Sharp, and the staff and volunteers. " What organisation is at the back of this? " was the question which everyone asked each other. We kept ourselves carefully in the background—the three secretaries evidently desired us to do so, and we were only too glad to be relieved from attendances and responsibility. Sidney will write the preface to the proceedings and then we are quit of the whole business. I have advised Sharp to steer the National Committee into the National Conference, and see what subscribers to the old organisation he can keep for the new. When we come back next spring we shall have to decide what is to be done—whether we are to close up or go on, or to divide the work between the National Conference and the Fabian Society. We shall know, too, how this insurance is going to affect us. If it is carried, it alters the whole situation and we shall have

[1] This remarkable Albert Hall meeting, which opened the National Conference for the Prevention of Destitution, in Whitsun Week, 1911, was presided over by an old friend of the Webbs, the Bishop of Southwark (Dr. Talbot). The following resolution :

" the formation of a National Conference of a non-party and non-sectional character, to promote the working of the various agencies for the prevention of destitution . . . as a valuable means of bringing together municipal representatives and social workers from all parts of the country "

was proposed by Mr. Arthur Balfour, seconded by Sir John Simon (then Solicitor-General) and supported by Mr. Ramsay MacDonald. To get these three leaders of the three political parties to formally adopt the policy of the national minimum of civilised life, was an apparent success for our cause. But looking back on it, I am inclined to think that it was a little too clever. It lost us the friendship of the Conservative leader, and did little to gain us any general support from the Liberal and Labour leaders, neither of whom were our personal friends.

to begin a new kind of propaganda. And, even if it does not pass, the issues have been so much bigger that the Minority Report propaganda sinks into insignificance for the present. I think it will rise up as the only alternative to a hopeless muddle.

A. J. B. spoke with his usual charm and distinction at the Albert Hall meeting. But he held himself back considerably and appeared less friendly than he has done before. In talking with me at the Cripps's dinner, he was inclined to be pleased with Lloyd George's Bill (before I explained matters to him), he thought it excellent to make the wage-earners " pay ", and he thought it would be unpopular! (Oh! ye politicians!) Everywhere among the governing class one meets the naïve delight at making the men pay—a delight which makes them overlook all the other circumstances—the heavy state contributions, the cost of collection, the absence of prevention, the exclusion of the weakest, and even the danger of malingering—all these real evils are to be cancelled by the extracting of the pennies from the workman's disposable income, extracting them so that he shall feel extraction.

Can I sum up the success or failure of this plunge into propaganda by word and by script? For this purpose, I must answer two separate and distinct questions: Did we get the specific recommendations of the Minority Report actually implemented by law and administration? Moreover, in making these recommendations, were we right or were we wrong in assuming that they would or could, without any more fundamental change in the structure of society, lead to the prevention of mass destitution in all its forms, whether due to old age or sickness, illiteracy or unemployment, so as to ensure to the workers by hand and by brain steady progress in health and happiness, honesty and kindliness, culture and scientific knowledge, and the spirit of adventure?

First, was the Minority Report carried out by Parliament and the Government? So far as immediate events were concerned, our propaganda ended in failure. For another eighteen years the defenders of the *status quo* maintained their position all along the line. Indeed, during the next few years, propaganda to retain and enlarge the powers of the boards of guardians altogether eclipsed the allied propaganda for the Majority Report. This aspiration to become the sole authority dealing with all classes of necessitous persons was emphatically endorsed by Charles Booth in his presidential address to the Central Poor Law Conference of 1912. " It is essential ", stated this experienced philanthropist, " that the elective character of the boards of guardians should be retained, and that the authority of the guardians and their responsibilities should suffer no diminution." He urged the guardians not to shrink " from any consistent development in the work or its responsibilities; holding that, whatever may be the cause of distress—whether moral, mental or physical, depravity, incompetence, or ill-health, or pure misfortune— its public relief lies within the proper sphere of the poor law ". The poor law, as established by the Royal Commission of 1834 and administered by directly elected boards of guardians, under the supervision of the poor law department, first of the Local Government Board, and then by the newly established Ministry of Health, remained intact and practically unaltered until the Local Government Act of 1929.[1]

Meanwhile, in 1911–12, there was established by Act of Parliament a system of compulsory insurance, financed by a triangle of taxation, deduction from wages, contribution from employers and a Treasury grant. This Insurance Act was divided into two sections, unemployment and sickness: Part I., dealing with unemployment, being passed through Parliament in December 1911, and Part II., dealing with sickness, during the following session of 1912. Neither of these measures are to be found in the Minority proposals. If not actually opposed by the National Committee for the Prevention of Destitution, this way of taking the destitute out of

[1] We note, in our *History of the English Poor Law*, that our agitation " powerful as it became, was destined to be unfruitful in the political field. The Liberal Cabinet remained unfriendly to any legislative reform of the poor law, to which the Minister primarily concerned (Mr. John Burns from 1906 to 1914) was resolutely opposed. Meanwhile Mr. Lloyd George, the most powerful force in the government, had become enamoured of an entirely distinct method of dealing with poverty, and was pressing forward the vast scheme of sickness insurance, to which the initial experiment in unemployment insurance promoted by Mr. Winston Churchill was eventually attached. Although these schemes of social insurance left untouched both the evils and the cost of the poor law, and thus gave the go-by to all the proposals of the Royal Commission, they presently absorbed the whole attention, not only of the Cabinet and the legislature, but also of the public. All the steam went out of the movement for extinguishing the boards of guardians and transferring their powers to the county and municipal authorities and to the national government, whether according to the prescriptions of the majority or those of the minority " (pp. 722-3)

the poor law received a very half-hearted support. To us the compulsory insurance with automatically distributed money allowances, during illness or worklessness, with free choice of doctor under the panel system, would not and could not prevent the occurrence of sickness or unemployment. Indeed, the fact that sick and unemployed persons were entitled to money incomes without any corresponding obligation to get well and keep well, or to seek and keep employment, seemed to us likely to encourage malingering and a disinclination to work for their livelihood.

But some of the proposals embodied in the Minority Report were carried out by the Liberal Government in the next few years. A non-contributory old-age pension scheme, financed by the Treasury, opened its payments in January 1909: a measure advocated by the Other One in 1890 and popularised a few years later by Charles Booth. And here I come to a paradoxical event which certainly we had not foreseen. The section of the Minority Report which was most vehemently denounced, alike by the defenders of the *status quo* and by the Majority Reporters, was our detailed plan for taking the able-bodied out of the penal poor law and transferring them to a Ministry of Labour designed not to prevent able-bodied pauperism, but to prevent the cause of this type of destitution—unemployment and under-employment, as well as low wages and long hours. And I must admit our opponents were justified. The 280 pages of Part II. of the Minority Report concerned with the able-bodied was a far more revolutionary document than Part I. dealing with the old, the sick, the disabled and the mentally deficient, for the good reason that it was a direct challenge to the epoch-making report of the Royal Commission on the Poor Law of 1834; which, it will be remembered, was almost exclusively concerned with the abolition of able-bodied pauperism, and not with the prevention of able-bodied destitution. Moreover, our propaganda of this new scheme for preventing unemployment and under-employment was apparently effective. " The history of modern unemployment policy ", states an authoritative writer on British unemployment policy, " really begins before the Great War. This is not so much because of the extent of the pre-war problem, as because there was a fundamental change in the attitude of the community towards its unemployed citizens about the years 1909 to 1911. It was then that the new sense of social responsibility took shape in the creation of a national system of employment exchanges and a limited experiment in compulsory unemployment insurance. The former were to reduce unemployment to the minimum, whatever the state of the labour market; the latter was to compensate the genuine worker for unavoidable interruptions of wage-earning." [1]

Our main proposal—the axle round which all our other recommendations turned—was the creation of a national authority for the exclusive purpose of organising the labour market, so as to prevent unemployment and under-employment as well as enforcing a minimum standard of earnings and hours by factory legislation and wages boards. " The task of dealing with unemployment is altogether beyond the capacity of local authorities having jurisdiction only over limited areas ", the Minority Report dogmatically asserts. The first step in this direction taken by the Liberal Government was the establishment of a national system of labour exchanges in the spring of 1909, as a department of the Board of Trade, a seemingly harmless proposal which had been endorsed by the majority commissioners. These labour exchanges proved to be the thin edge of the wedge which ultimately lifted the destitute able-bodied out of the poor law. In 1916, a Ministry of Labour was created which took over from the Board of Trade all questions relating to labour, whether regulative or administrative. But neither the labour exchanges, nor unemployment insurance with its continuously enlarged sphere and increasing benefits, sufficed to prevent the wholesale able-bodied destitution which arose during the great depression of 1929–33. Hence the National Government took the final step of taking the able-bodied out of the poor law, by passing the Unemployment Act of 1934; Part I, establishing the Unemployment Assistance Board,

[1] *British Unemployment Policy since 1930*, by Ronald C. Davison, 1938. 136 pp.

to relieve all able-bodied persons who had fallen out of benefit, an authority more or less under the control of the Ministry of Labour; and Part II., constituting the Unemployment Insurance Statutory Committee, which was " to advise the Government and Parliament how to make the insurance scheme financially self-contained, and self-adjusting, without legislation, and to block the channel of indefinite borrowing from the Treasury ".[1]

Meanwhile, by the Local Government Act of 1929, the boards of guardians were abolished and all their duties and powers relating to the non-able-bodied destitute persons were transferred to the county and county borough councils, these authorities being enjoined, somewhat haltingly, to deal with the children and the sick through their education and public health committees, with the co-operation of a newly established public assistance committee, in so far as money allowances were concerned. Hence, it is only the non-able-bodied person who is now within the poor law, and that to an ever-decreasing extent, according to the capacity and public spirit of the local authority concerned.[2]

And now for the second question: Were we right, or were we wrong, in assuming that our recommendations would or could, without any more radical change in the structure of society, lead to the prevention of mass destitution in all its forms?

The sole purpose of the Minority Report, so we told listeners and readers, was to secure a national minimum of civilised life (note the word minimum) open to all alike, of

[1] *The Unemployment Insurance Statutory Committee*, by Sir William Beveridge (" Politica " Pamphlet No. 1).
[2] In our epilogue to volume ii. of *English Poor Law History: The Last Hundred Years*, we observe: " In a thousand pages we have followed the doings of these Destitution Authorities, and estimated the successes and failures, from 1834 to 1928, of the deterrent Poor Law that they were set to administer. We are grateful to Mr. Baldwin's Cabinet for enabling us to finish the story with dramatic completeness. For in this Epilogue we recount the sentence of death passed by Parliament in December 1928 on the century-old Boards of Guardians. Is there not also a policy, conscious or unconscious, implicit in this upsetting of existing institutions? Can it be doubted that the transfer of the obligation to relieve the destitute, from the ' Guardians of the Poor ' to the Local Authorities primarily concerned, each in its own sphere, with the prevention of destitution, finally disposes of the ' Principles of 1834 '? " (p. 985).

both sexes and all classes, by which we meant sufficient nourishment and training when young, a living wage when able-bodied, treatment when sick, and a modest but secure livelihood when disabled or aged. Could these conditions be obtained without altering fundamentally the existing system of wealth production, distribution and exchange; without sweeping away the landlords and the capitalists, and penalising the profit-making motive? We implied, if not openly asserted, that they could. How otherwise should we have sought the support of Conservative and Liberal leaders and of the majority of the working-class who certainly were not at that time convinced Socialists? And in doing so were we sincere? I think we were. In the years before the Great War, and for some time afterwards, we did not foresee the collapse of Western Civilisation: that is, of the strange and mutually destructive trilogy of the Christian religion, profit-making capitalism and political democracy. To-day, it is crystal-clear that the code of conduct taught by Jesus of Nazareth, and presumably accepted by the Christian churches, is hopelessly inconsistent with the dominance of the profit-making motive in the direction of production, distribution and exchange; whilst the addition of political democracy to a capitalist system of industry, sooner or later, leads to class war, hidden or naked. But, though we ourselves were convinced Socialists, we did not assert, or even imply, in our propaganda that the proposed enforcement of a national minimum of life for all the inhabitants, all the time, was impracticable under profit-making capitalism. Rightly or wrongly, we believed in " the inevitability of gradualness ". We were content to leave the future to take care of itself.

First, about our proposals with regard to the non-able-bodied. In so far as the infants and the children, the sick, mentally deficient, and aged were concerned, I think our proposals, if fully implemented, could, even under capitalism, prevent the occurrence of mass destitution and secure a minimum standard of life for all the persons concerned. But this result would depend on whether the capitalist system could or would supply the large sum needed for the requisite development of these social services. To-day, this is not the case. There are literally millions of infants and children in the United Kingdom growing up without either the nutriment or the training for regular employment and effective citizenship in adult life. There is a vast amount of preventable disease due to bad housing, poisoned atmosphere, noise and dirt, and the maintenance and treatment afforded by the sickness insurance and panel practice are totally inadequate and of bad quality.

The pension provided for old age is so low that many aged persons who have led respectable and hard-working lives find themselves compelled to seek extra assistance from the poor law. Meanwhile, in every period of trade depression, wages tend to be reduced and hours lengthened, so that the able-bodied who are in employment can afford to spend less on their dependants. Indeed, according to the most influential economists, whether in the City or in the universities, the only way of meeting a chronic state of trade depression has been by deliberate measures to lower the money wage or to raise prices; either policy resulting in a lower standard of life, whether in respect to nourishment, housing or recreation. Finally, there has arisen in the offing, so the statisticians tell us, the menace of a declining birth-rate, which, if not checked by generous endowment of child-bearing and rearing, may lead, if not to the gradual extinction of our race, to lost leadership among the nations of the world. But there is one comforting thought for the authors of the Minority Report. Whether or not the plenty can be produced or will be distributed under a capitalist system of society, our proposal to take all the non-able-bodied out of the poor law and transfer them to deliberately organised social services, administered by the central and local authorities, has proved to be the right road to a better state of things. For, whether we have a capitalist, a Socialist or a Communist organisation of production, distribution and exchange, it is imperative to have all the various classes of non-able-bodied persons dealt with on the lines of preventive service rather than on those of a stigmatised poor law relief. In short, so far as the non-able-bodied are concerned, the supersession of the penal poor law by highly specialised preventive social services, is to-day accepted as a sound principle by public opinion whether Conservative, Liberal or Socialist.

No such complacence can be justified in respect of Part II. of the Minority Report on the destitution of the able-bodied. Here, I admit, we unwittingly misled public opinion. We asserted in the Minority Report, and reaffirmed in our propaganda during 1909–11, that, without any substantial change in the social and economic order, the mass destitution arising from unemployment could be prevented. "*We have to report that, in our judgment, it is now administratively possible, if it is sincerely wished to do so, to remedy most of the evils of unemployment;*[1] to the same extent, at least, as we have in the past century diminished the death-rate from fever and lessened the industrial slavery of young children. It is not a valid objection that a demonstrably perfect and popularly accepted *technique*, either with regard to the prevention of unemployment or with regard to the treatment of the unemployed, has not yet been worked out."

" That unemployment, even under present industrial conditions, is to a very large extent preventable was perhaps the most unexpected and certainly the most welcome piece of information which the Minority Report of the Poor Law Commission had to give to the world. Practically all previous writers, with the exception of Mr. Beveridge, whose book on unemployment appeared a few weeks before the reports of the Royal Commission, accepted the phenomenon of unemployment as an inevitable accompaniment of capitalism

---

[1] *Report of the Royal Commission on the Poor Law and Relief of Distress*, 1909, *Vol. III.: Minority Report*, p. 685. The following note is added to the text of the report: " if . . . by a solution is meant that no man able and willing to work should come to degradation or destitution for want of work, then a solution is not indeed within sight, but by no means beyond hope. Its direction is certain, and its distance not infinite. . . . It is a policy of industrial organization, of meeting deliberately industrial needs that at present are met wastefully because without deliberation. Fluctuations of demand are now provided for by the maintenance of huge stagnant reserves of labour in varying extremities of distress. There is no reason in the nature of things why they should not be provided for by organized reserves of labour raised beyond the reach of distress (*Unemployment: A Problem of Industry*, by W. H. Beveridge, 1909, p. 236)."

and competitive industry, and confined their attention to the problem of how to provide for the ' out-of-work ' and his family. The minority commissioners, however, after a more extensive and searching investigation than had ever before been undertaken, came to the conclusion that unemployment was mainly due to defects of industrial organisation which it is fully in the power of the state to remedy, if and when it chooses. As a consequence of this new knowledge *we are now as a nation morally responsible for the continued existence of the great army of ' out-of-works ' in our midst in a far more direct and unmistakable sense than ever before.*" [1]

To-day (1938) we look back on two decades of continuous mass unemployment in times of good trade, never falling below one million, and at the peak of the last depression in 1933 rising to near three millions of workers actually unemployed, which, including dependants, means nearly nine million persons destitute of livelihood. What is even more disturbing is the appearance of a new type of the disease, unknown or at any rate undetected prior to the Great War: what has been termed *long unemployment*. To quote the authoritative report of the Pilgrim Trust on *Men without Work* (1938): " There is a ' hard core ' of long unemployment which will not be resolved by recovery alone, in every town of this country, however prosperous, however diversified its range of industries or however much its main industry benefits from industrial trends, and wherever it is situated. The problem is of increasing social importance throughout the country and is not entirely bound up with the problem of economic activity and depression." And further on in this report: " It is evident that this hard core of long unemployment carries within itself another hard core of very long unemployment which proves even more obstinate to re-employment than the hard core itself. In the summer of 1935, out of 100 long unemployed men 8 were very long unemployed, but within a year this number had doubled to 16. It is a vivid reminder of the changed conditions when it is realised that in 1936 the number of men who had been

[1] Article by Sidney Webb in *The Crusade*, January 1911.

without work for fully five years was the same as the number of men before the depression who were unemployed and had been without work in the previous year. The ' hard core within the hard core ' in 1936 was the same size as the total hard core of 1929. Evidently this ' hard core within the hard core ' consists of thousands of men who are being passed on from year to year and finally accumulate in that remotest of all backwaters, ' five years or more out of work '. . . . It seems desirable ", the report continues, " to get a clearer insight into the working of this paradoxical fourth factor; that long unemployment tends to be self-generating, and that the longer a man stands in the queue, the less likely he is to get out of it again; and that long unemployment (in addition to age, a home in a depressed district, and connection with a contracting industry) is in itself a bar to re-employment."

Moreover, the most intractable group of this " hard core " of unemployment are found to be not the " too old to be taken on ", but young men in their twenties, who have never yet been regularly employed, and who are adapting themselves in body and mind to a life of idleness—of undeveloped bodies and vacant minds. " Yet this problem of the young unemployed man remains serious, perhaps the most serious of all the problems of the long unemployed. It is especially aggravated by the conditions of Liverpool, the depression, the casual character of much employment and the low standard, material and non-material, at which the Liverpool long unemployed are living. . . . What is most depressing ", sum up the authors of the report, " is to find from the figures of both Category II. and of Category III. that the young men are those who are most ready to accept long unemployment. It is hard to exaggerate the importance of this for the future. One other point must be mentioned here concerning the attitude of these young men. That association with an unemployed community, which can be so powerful a factor in reconciling a man to unemployment, is present probably more extensively here than in any other age group. Though they tend not to belong to specific organisations, the number who spend most of their time with other young men who are also out of work is large. In Liverpool these associations take chiefly the form of ' cellar clubs '. In Leicester, it is the ordinary unemployed club which the young men patronise. But, whatever the form, we find this feature regularly through the various areas into which the sample took us. It suggests at once one of the reasons for their continual unemployment, and also perhaps the possibility of a more effective institutional approach to them than has been made in the past."[1]

It is this pernicious adaptation of the individual to his environment—this thoughtless manufacture of a parasitic class —that leads to a tragic paradox. For, in spite of there being nearly three million unemployed, the enterprising employers in the most progressive industries bitterly complain of a shortage in skilled and reliable labour which prevents fulfilment of pressing orders at home and from abroad.

Confronted with this dismal tragedy of mass unemployment, with its constantly increasing core of manufactured parasitism, it is futile to suggest that the recommendations of the Minority Report of the Poor Law Commission of 1906–9, even if fully implemented, would or could prevent mass destitution of the able-bodied. Labour exchanges for the better organisation of the demand and supply of labour, subsidised trade union insurance for organised workers, maintenance with training for those who fall out, or are never included in the insurance scheme, with a modicum of public works during temporary depressions, might have

---

[1] An even more striking testimony is given by Sir Ronald Davison, whose admirable book on the unemployed I have already quoted, in a communication to the fortnightly *News Letter*, December 3rd, 1938, which is the organ of the National Labour Party: " Unheeded by the general public, a terrible malaise is spreading among many thousands of our younger unemployed. They are being degraded to an almost sub-human way of life, not merely through lack of work, but also as the direct result of our relaxed systems of allowances and doles, doles without end and without conditions. Human nature, or a large part of it, cannot stand the strain of an easy-going official system which freely offers perpetual maintenance, even though a pittance, without exacting any return in self-help and without imposing any ultimate sanction. History has proved in the past and we are proving again to-day that such a system is bound to be abused. But my point in this article is that we are proving it on the bodies and souls of some 100,000 men still under 35 years of age and that we are too complacent about it. The ruin is steadily increasing. Some, alas! perhaps over a third of these men, are already irretrievably damaged, yet we do nothing. Many of us, including our politicians, simply turn away from the forbidding problem."

sufficed to prevent the destitution of the able-bodied during the rapidly expanding capitalist system in Europe and the U.S.A., characteristic of the last decade of the nineteenth century and the first decade of the twentieth century. Where we went hopelessly wrong was in ignoring Karl Marx's forecast of the eventual breakdown of the capitalist system as the one and only way of maximising the wealth of the nations. Karl Marx foresaw that the exploitation of land and labour by the private owners of the means of production, distribution and exchange would lead inevitably and universally to a corruption and perversion of the economic system; that it would divide the community into two nations, the rich and the poor; that it would concentrate power in the hands of the wealthy, and keep the wage-earners and the peasants in a state of poverty and dependence; that it would produce a disastrous alternation of booms and slumps, with a permanent army of unemployed persons, tragically deteriorating in health and happiness, skill and character. This profit-making motive may even lead to the destruction of natural resources, and turn forests and fertile plains into sand-swept deserts. But this was not all. Intent on securing new markets, new lands and minerals, new peoples to exploit, the profit-making motive would lead surely and inevitably, not to the peaceful emulation between individual capitalists to lower prices and improve quality for the community in which they live, but to a trustified and imperialist capitalism crushing out the little man, restricting production at home when it suited them, and transferring capital and brains to undeveloped countries where better prices could be obtained. Moreover, whilst the early nineteenth-century capitalists were almost to a man free-traders and pacifists, the City of London and the manufacturers of certain centres became not only protectionists but imperialists, instigating successive Governments to use force in the conquest of lower races in Asia and Africa. What a significant fact was the appearance of the South African millionaire gold-diggers, who dominated London " society " as well as the City, in the last years of the nineteenth century. I must admit that even the Webbs accepted their gracious hospitality in return for their bene-factions to the London University, the London School of Economics and the Imperial College of Science! Finally, the rule of the capitalist and the landlord has proved to be hopelessly inconsistent with political democracy. There can be no permanence of social peace in a situation in which we abandon production to a tiny proportion of the population, who own the means of production, and yet give the workers the political power to enforce demands on the national income which capitalism has neither the ability nor the incentive to supply. This hopeless contradiction between the economic power of the few and the political power of the many is shown in its most vivid form in the problem of the treatment of the involuntarily unemployed. How far is it practicable to relieve the destitution of the able-bodied, according to the principles of a minimum standard of civilised life under profit-making capitalism? Are you, by giving sufficient nutriment, decent housing, not to mention the amenities of civilised life, to millions of unemployed persons and their descendants, making the conditions of the workless more attractive and secure than those of the regularly employed worker? Can the capitalist system in the period of its decadence, when there are no longer fresh markets, fresh lands and lower races to exploit, afford the high wages, shorter hours, and holidays with maintenance, which would make the conditions of the regularly employed persons more agreeable than that of the man on the dole, or still more than the family claiming public assistance assumed to be full maintenance? If not, the core of permanently unemployed persons will grow steadily larger with each successive depression of trade; the alternative is to throw back the able-bodied into a penal poor law. Is it likely that political democracy will accept a return to the able-bodied " test " workhouse and the stone-yard?

At this point I break off my argument, otherwise I should be anticipating future chapters of *Our Partnership*. But, in case I should not live to finish this autobiography, here is a short indication of the successive stages of our conversion to the Marxian theory of the historical development of profit-making capitalism. It may be recalled that Marx held that though, as an alternative to feudalism, the free enterprise of the profit-making capitalist was the most efficient way of increasing the wealth of the nation at the end of the eighteenth and the beginning of the nineteenth century, it inevitably passed first through a period of stabilisation, and then into the period of trustified imperialist capitalism, which would restrict production and create the paradox of masses of unemployed capital with a host of unemployed men.

First, on our return from our Far Eastern tour in June 1912, we discovered that our propaganda of a national minimum of civilised life within the capitalist system was out-of-date. In the three great political democracies of the United Kingdom, France and the U.S.A., the workers were, from 1912 to the outbreak of the Great War, in open revolt. Anarchist workers in the U.S.A. were blazing out into multitudinous strikes and were being suppressed by armed forces, the leaders being hung or sentenced to life imprisonment; whilst, in France and Great Britain, the syndicalist and the guild socialist movement was promoting general strikes in all the main industrial activities, in order to secure complete "workers' control" as an alternative to the rule of the capitalist profit-maker. Then came, in the autumn of 1914, the Great War, ostensibly started to protect a little state against absorption by a big Empire; but, in fact, the outcome of a long-standing bitter struggle between capitalist states; some having extended dominions and colonies, others wanting new territories, new markets and new native populations to exploit for the purpose of making profit for their financiers, manufacturers and traders. There followed the disastrous peace of Versailles, breaking up defeated Empires, annexing their colonies, and imposing impossible reparations which could only be paid by the exportation of capital from the victorious countries to the victims. . . . It was in the years immediately following the disastrous war, and still more disastrous peace, that we published our first indictment of the capitalist system *The Decay of Capitalist Civilisation*, supplemented by our forecast of *A Constitution for the Socialist Commonwealth of Great Britain*.

The next event to disturb our faith in a modified capitalism was the great depression of trade which began in the 'twenties, first in Europe, and then in 1929 with even greater intensity in the United States of America, a depression which shows every sign of being recurrent, each depression leaving a larger residuum of permanent unemployment, judged by the statistics of unemployment, home production and foreign trade. Meanwhile there had arisen out of a tumultuous but successful revolution a new social order, in a vast territory, one-sixth of the earth's surface, with 160 millions of inhabitants, of many races, languages and religions—the Union of Socialist Soviet Republics. A detailed examination and description of this new social order, in two ponderous volumes published in 1935, entitled *Soviet Communism: A New Civilisation*, was the final and certainly the most ambitious task of " Our Partnership ". Whether we were right or whether we were wrong in acclaiming Soviet Communism with its multiform democracy, its sex, class and racial equality, its planned production for community consumption, and above all its penalisation of the profit-making motive and insistence on the obligation of all able-bodied persons to earn their livelihood by serving the community, the event will prove: perhaps I ought to substitute *will have been proved* or disproved before *Our Partnership* is published and read, or not read, by students of social institutions.

NOTE TO BIOGRAPHICAL INDEX

THIS volume, like its predecessor *My Apprenticeship*, is much more than a mere personal record; it is a slice of English social history during a deeply interesting and important period, and so is bound to be used as a standard work of reference by students for many years to come. In the course of the years which it covers, the Webbs' work and interests brought them into contact with an enormous number of persons of importance in Society, in politics and in the social services, many of whom will be but names even to the present generation, or, if they are remembered at all, their connection with the events of 1892 to 1912 will have been forgotten. In order, therefore, to help make this book of permanent value as a record, to save its readers from the burden of hunting in elderly works of reference—and to avoid littering the text with innumerable footnotes—the Editors decided to add to it a biographical index, compiled by one of them, of everyone mentioned in its pages whom it has proved possible to trace; some have proved to date untraceable and their names are omitted. The notes which follow are not, of course, biographies; but it is hoped that they will date and identify for students the persons mentioned, and, in the case of well-known figures, indicate their special connection with Beatrice's life and work.

Every endeavour has been made with the generous help of others to check the facts. Errors, however, will have undoubtedly crept in, particularly in the present rather difficult circumstances, and we shall welcome any additions or corrections for future editions.

M. I. C.

BIOGRAPHICAL INDEX

ABERDEEN and TEMAIR, ISHBEL MARIA, Marchioness of (1857–1939). Sister of Lord Tweedmouth and wife of the Marquess of Aberdeen who was Governor-General of Canada and Lord-Lieutenant of Ireland. Lady Aberdeen was a public figure, President of the International Council of Women from 1893 to 1899 and from 1904 to 1936, and of several other bodies.

ABRAHAM, MARY (Mrs. Tennant) (1870–1946). Factory inspector, at one time Superintending Inspector of Factories; an authority on factory legislation and women's problems and member of several Government commissions. Married, as his second wife, Harold John Tennant, *q.v.*

ABRAHAM, WILLIAM (1842–1922). Known as " Mabon ", and celebrated as a Methodist preacher and for his fine singing voice, Abraham, the miners' leader from the Rhondda, was first elected to Parliament for that area in 1885, and held it for many years, first as Lib-Lab and then as Labour.

ACLAND, SIR ARTHUR HERBERT DYKE (1847–1926). Liberal politician and educationalist, grandfather of the present Sir Richard Acland. M.P. for Rotherham, Vice-President of the Privy Council Committee on Education and Cabinet Minister, 1892–95; in this capacity he did much to promote higher education, through the Science and Arts Department, effective inspection and better conditions in schools. After his retirement he devoted himself to the cause of co-operation—his wife was a leading co-operator—and education, particularly adult education; he established the Acland scholarships.

ACLAND, SIR FRANCIS DYKE (1874–1939), "young Acland". Liberal politician; M.P. successively for Richmond, North Cornwall and Tiverton; Chairman of the Devon County Education Committee. Parliamentary Private Secretary to Haldane, 1906–8; afterwards held various under-secretaryships. Father of Sir Richard Acland.

ACWORTH, SIR WILLIAM MITCHELL (1850–1925). Barrister and railway economist; member of several commissions of enquiry into railway affairs.

ADLER, DR. CYRUS (1863–   ). American scholar and authority on Jewish history and comparative religion. One of the editors of the *Jewish Encyclopaedia.*

ADRIAN, ALFRED DOUGLAS (1845–1922). Civil servant; Assistant Secretary to Local Government Board, 1883–89, and its legal adviser, 1899–1910.

ALEXANDER, SAMUEL (1859–1938). The philosopher; from 1893 to 1924 Professor of Philosophy in Manchester University; especially effective in marrying philosophy with modern scientific thought.

ALLAN, WILLIAM (1813–74). Founder, with William Newton, of the Amalgamated Society of Engineers, the new model Union of its time, and forerunner of the present Amalgamated Engineering Union. Allan was elected its general secretary in 1851 and retained this position until his death. He was, however, primarily interested in administration and though he built up a very strong organisation, he took less part in the moulding of opinion in the mid-century than men like Newton and Applegarth.

ALLEN, CLIFFORD, afterwards Lord Allen of Hurtwood (1889–1939). Fabian Socialist, and member of the I.L.P. Secretary and General Manager of *Daily Citizen*, 1911–15. Pacifist and conscientious objector (absolutist) during first world war; imprisoned three times. Chairman of I.L.P., 1922–26; promoter of *Socialism in Our Time* programme; sided with MacDonald in 1931 crisis.

ALTGELD, JOHN PETER (1847–1902). American politician, served in the Civil War on the Union side. Governor of Illinois, 1893–97, and pardoned the Chicago anarchists; prison reformer and bimetallist.

AMERY, LEOPOLD STENNETT (1873–   ). Secretary for India in the National Government of 1931. On editorial staff of *The Times*, 1899–1909; in his youth a Fabian Socialist.

ANDERSON, ADELAIDE MARY (1868–1936). Australian-born factory inspector. Principal woman inspector of factories under the Home Office, 1897–1921; during the inter-war years did much work for the International Labour Office in China, and wrote several books.

ANDERSON, ELIZABETH GARRETT (1836–1917). First English woman doctor, friend of Emily Davies of Girton College and sister of Mrs. Fawcett. A pioneer of women's rights and founder of the hospital which bears her name.

ANDERSON, DR. JOHN FORD. Doctor, with a large general practice in Hampstead, medical officer to the Haverstock Hill Provident Dispensary. During the period of the Royal Commission on the Poor Law he was a member of the Council of the British Medical Association.

ANSON, SIR WILLIAM REYNELL (1843–1914). The distinguished jurist, author of *The Law and Custom of the Constitution*. Parliamentary Secretary to Board of Education, 1902–5.

APPLETON, WILLIAM ARCHIBALD (1859–1940). Trade Unionist, a lacemaker by craft, then Secretary to the Lace-makers' Union, 1896–1907, and from 1907 Secretary of the General Federation of Trade Unions; never in Parliament. He was a strong supporter of the Lloyd George insurance proposals.

ARNOLD, SIR ARTHUR (1833–1902). Liberal, Chairman of the L.C.C., 1895–97, and President of the Free Land League.

ARNOLD-FORSTER, HUGH OAKLEY (1855–1909). Tory politician and author, grandson of Arnold of Rugby, adopted son of W. E. Forster of the 1870 Education Act; much interested in education and social questions. Secretary of State for War, 1903–5.

ASHBEE, C. R. (1862–1942). Architect, designer and town planner; Founder and Director for twenty-five years of the Guild of Handicrafts. His wife was Janet Elizabeth Forbes.

ASHLEY, SIR PERCY WALTER LLEWELLYN (1876–1945). Historian who became a civil servant. Lecturer at London School of Economics till 1906, then joined Board of Trade and became Assistant Secretary, 1918–28, and Secretary to Import Duties Advisory Committee, 1932–39. Wrote text-books on local government.

ASQUITH, EMMA ALICE MARGARET, " MARGOT " (d. 1945). Countess of Oxford and Asquith, leading spirit of the " Souls " and London political hostess of Beatrice's early married life. (See her autobiography.) Notwithstanding their political connections, Mrs. Webb did not like Mrs. Asquith, and the sentiment was reciprocated.

ASQUITH, HERBERT HENRY (1852–1928). Earl of Oxford and Asquith, Liberal Prime Minister, 1908–16. Asquith in the years between 1895 and 1905 was a friend of Haldane's and one of the Liberal imperialist group which the Webbs hoped to make use of for Socialist purposes. Beatrice never, however, felt for Asquith the instinctive sympathy which she had for Balfour the Tory.

ASQUITH, RAYMOND (1878–1916). Eldest son of the Prime Minister, killed in action. He married a daughter of Lady Horner, q.v.

ATKINSON, MABEL. Fabian, journalist on the *Daily News*, and lecturer on economics, on which she wrote a text-book with a Miss McKillop. Very active in the Fabian Society and its Women's Group before the first world war. She married an Australian named Palmer, but they soon separated; and in 1920 she left England to lecture in economics at the University of Durban.

AUSTIN, MICHAEL (1855–   ). Irish Nationalist and Trade Unionist, M.P. for West Limerick, 1892–1900. Member of the Royal Commission on Labour; signed the Minority Report.

BACON, SIR HICKMAN (1855–1945). Premier baronet of Britain. Very much interested in the Webbs' projects.

BAILWARD, WILLIAM A. Member of the Charity Organisation Society and a Poor Law Guardian for Bethnal

African financier and diamond merchant. Partner in firm of Wernher, Beit and Co. Life Governor of De Beers Consolidated Mines. Director of Rand Mines, Rhodesian Railways and other companies. One of the rich men whom Beatrice tried to " milk " for particular projects.

BELL, SIR HUGH (1844–1931). The great coal and ironmaster of the Tyne area, director of Brunner Mond, Dorman Long, the L.N.E.R., etc. His wife (*née* Frances Oliffe) was author of many books, including the social study entitled *At the Works*.

BELL, JAMES. Town Clerk of Leicester, 1894–1902.

BELPER, HENRY STRUTT, second Baron (1840–1914). Chairman of Nottingham County Council and Quarter Sessions.

BENN, SIR JOHN WILLIAMS (1850–1922). Member of the L.C.C. from its formation until his death; Chairman in 1904, and connected with all its activities. Liberal M.P. for Devonport, 1904–10.

BENTHAM, F. H. Chairman of Bradford Poor Law Guardians, member of the 1905 Royal Commission on the Poor Law, and editor of the *Poor Law Conferences*, 1910–11.

BENTHAM, JEREMY (1748–1832). The founder of the school of Philosophic Radicalism, to which the early Fabians owed so much.

BERENSONS, The. Relatives of Bernhard Berenson, the American art critic, who married a sister of Alys Russell and Logan Pearsall Smith.

BESANT, ANNIE (1847–1933). Annie Besant, married young to a clergyman, left him on becoming a convert to Secularism and birth control, for which she and Charles Bradlaugh were the most popular and effective propagandists in the 'seventies. In the early 'eighties she became a Socialist; she was an early member of the Fabian Executive, one of the seven contributors to *Fabian Essays* in 1889, and a brilliant speaker and lecturer for Socialism; in 1888 she led a successful strike of miserably-paid matchgirls at Bryant & May's. In 1889 she suddenly abandoned Socialism for theosophy and became a passionate advocate of Indian nationalism.

BEVERIDGE, WILLIAM HENRY, Lord Beveridge (1879–   ). The author of the Beveridge Report. Originally a civil servant, he was Director of Labour Exchanges at the Board of Trade; during the first world war served in the Ministry of Munitions and the Ministry of Food. Director of the London School of Economics, 1919–37, and Master of University College, Oxford, 1937–45.

BICKERSTETH, JOHN JOSEPH (1850–1932). Son of the Bishop of Durham and married to a daughter of Lord Ashburnham. Clerk of the Peace and Clerk to the East Riding County Council from 1889.

BIRRELL, AUGUSTINE (1850–1933). Liberal politician, lawyer and writer of biography and *belles lettres*. President of the Board of Education, 1905–7, and Chief Secretary to the Lord-Lieutenant of Ireland, 1907–16. His wife was a Locker by birth and widow of the Hon. Lionel Tennyson.

BIRTWISTLE, THOMAS. One of the first Trade Union secretaries to be selected by competitive examination. He was Secretary of the Lancashire Weavers from 1861 to 1891, and in the following year, although he was very old, he was appointed inspector under the new Factory Act as being the only man who understood the methods of wage-payment in the weaving trade.

BLACKIE, JOHN STUART (1809–95). Philosopher and humanist. Professor of Greek at Edinburgh University, 1852–82.

BLAIN, WILLIAM (*d.* 1908). Civil servant; Assistant Secretary to the Treasury, 1907, and Auditor of the Civil List.

BLAND, HUBERT (1856–1914). Socialist. Journalist and author, a founder-member of the Fabian Society, whose Honorary Treasurer he remained from 1884 to 1911. Bland was married to E. Nesbit, the writer of many children's books; they had an unorthodox and interesting household which was enjoyed by many young Fabians.

BOOTH, CHARLES (1840–1914). Shipowner and manufacturer who carried through at his own expense the great eighteen-volume enquiry into the

Life and Labour of the People of London at the end of the 'eighties. Beatrice learned her own trade in this enquiry (see *My Apprenticeship*), and recorded that " for the fifteen hardest years of my life they [Booth and his wife, Mary Macaulay, cousin of Beatrice] were my best and most faithful friends ". They disapproved strongly, however, of her marriage to a Socialist and the former intimacy was interrupted.

BOOTH, WILLIAM (1829–1912). " General Booth ", founder in 1865 of a Christian Mission in Whitechapel which in 1878 became the Salvation Army.

BOSANQUET, MRS. HELEN DENDY. Wife of Professor Bernard Bosanquet (1848–1923), the Hegelian philosopher who also did much work in connection with University Extension and the Charity Organisation Society, in which she played a considerable part. Mrs. Bosanquet was a noted social worker and member of the 1905 Royal Commission on the Poor Law.

BRADLAUGH, CHARLES (1833–1891). The great Secularist leader and birth-control propagandist. Friend and colleague of Annie Besant before she became a Socialist.

BRAY, REGINALD ARTHUR (1879–). Fabian, writer on apprenticeship and other kindred subjects. Member of L.C.C. (Progressive), 1904–19.

BROADHURST, HENRY (1840–1911). General Secretary of the Stonemasons' Union, and from 1875 to 1890 secretary of the Parliamentary Committee of the Trades Union Congress. In 1875 he was secretary of the Labour Representation League. He sat himself as a Liberal from 1880 to 1886 and again from 1894 to 1906, and was Under-Secretary to the Home Office in 1886. Broadhurst in his youth was a vigorous Trade Unionist of the " new model " kind; but events caught him up, and he lived to be the strongest opponent of efforts to convert the Unions to Socialism.

BROOKE, RUPERT (1887–1915). The Cambridge poet and Socialist who wrote *Grantchester* and the war sonnets and died on active service at Lemnos.

BROWNE, MRS. CARRIE, *née* Darling (*d.*

1900). Beatrice met Miss Darling when she was a Newnham student and was captivated by the freshness of her mind. She left England for Australia in 1882, but returned, having parted from her husband, to become a successful elementary teacher in England at the age of fifty.

BRYAN, WILLIAM JENNINGS (1860–1925). American Democratic politician, Presidential candidate in 1896 and 1900, beaten by McKinley. The passionate bimetallist, who declared that America " should not be crucified upon a cross of gold ".

BRYANT, SOPHIE (1850–1922). Educationalist, succeeded Frances Mary Buss as headmistress of the North London Collegiate School for Girls, and remained there from 1895 to 1918. An ardent worker in the cause of London higher education.

BRYCE, JAMES, Viscount Bryce (1838–1922). The historian and Liberal politician, Chairman of the Royal Commission on Secondary Education, and holder of various offices under Liberal Governments. British Ambassador to U.S.A., 1907–1913.

BUCKLE, GEORGE EARLE (1854–1925). Editor of *The Times*, 1884–1912. Author (with Monypenny) of the *Life of Disraeli* and editor of Queen Victoria's letters.

BULKLEY, MILDRED E. Economist and research worker, research secretary to Beatrice from 1906 to 1909, and from then till 1912 secretary to the National Committee for the Prevention of Destitution. Afterwards held office in the Ministry of Munitions and the Carnegie Endowment. Research secretary to Professor Tawney, 1923–1946.

BURDETT-COUTTS, ANGELA GEORGINA (1814–1906). Millionairess philanthropist. Baroness Burdett-Coutts makes a link with the eighteenth century. Daughter of Sir Francis Burdett, Radical M.P. of pre-Reform days, and Sophia Coutts of the great banking family, she inherited a share in the Coutts bank when only twenty-three. She entertained enormously royalty, politicians and literary men; and the Burdett-Coutts charities became almost legendary—they did not

CECIL, ALGERNON (1879–   ), second son of Lord Eustace Cecil.

CECIL, LORD EUSTACE (1834–1921), fourth son of the Marquess of Salisbury, Tory M.P. for Essex divisions, 1865–85.

CECIL, LADY GWENDOLEN (d. 1945). Second daughter of the Marquess of Salisbury, whose Life she wrote up to 1892.

CECIL, LORD HUGH, later Lord Quickswood. (1869–   ). The friend of Balfour and brother of Viscount Cecil of Chelwood; a strong supporter of resistance to the Home Rule Bill.

CHADWICK, EDWIN (1800–90). Poor Law and public health reformer. As secretary of the famous Poor Law Commission of 1834, which set up the New Poor Law, Chadwick laid down the principle of " less eligibility " for paupers, which caused the Poor Law to be so bitterly hated by the working classes. Later, impressed by the disease due to poverty and bad conditions, he became an enthusiastic advocate of public health legislation.

CHAMBERLAIN, AUSTEN (1863–1937). Tory politician, son of Joseph. Foreign Secretary, 1922–29, and negotiator of the Locarno Pacts.

CHAMBERLAIN, BEATRICE (1861–1918). Eldest child of Joseph Chamberlain, half-sister to Austen and Neville. Beatrice Chamberlain was only a year or two younger than Beatrice Webb—whose stepdaughter she might have been—and they kept up for a long while the friendship made before the Webb marriage.

CHAMBERLAIN, JOSEPH (1836–1914). Radical politician in his early days. Mayor of Birmingham, 1870–73, during which period he introduced many municipal reforms. The local government programme of the early Fabians — the " gas - and - water " Socialists — owed a great deal to Chamberlain. He split with Gladstone over Home Rule in 1886 and formed the Liberal Unionist group; was Colonial Secretary in the Salisbury Government of 1895 (and therefore at the time of the Jameson Raid), but quarrelled with his colleagues on the Tariff Reform issue and resigned in 1903. Beatrice was much impressed by Chamberlain in his Radical days

(see My Apprenticeship). He eventually married Mary Endicott, daughter of an American judge.

CHAMPION, HENRY HYDE (1859–1928). Artillery officer and Socialist organiser. A leading member of the S.D.F., and its first Honorary Secretary, Champion took part in the great London demonstrations, and in the columns of his Labour Elector agitated continually for Socialist M.P.s. He believed in the imminence of social revolution and drilled its would-be participants; he was violently opposed to Liberalism and Lib-Lab politics and caused a storm by running Socialist candidates with the aid of " Tory gold " to keep the Liberals out. In 1893 he left England for Australia.

CHANDLER, FRANCIS W. (1849–1938). Woodworker, General Secretary of the Amalgamated Society of Carpenters and Joiners, and put on the 1905 Royal Commission on the Poor Law as representing the industrial workers.

CHAPLIN, HENRY, Viscount Chaplin (1841–1923). Tory politician, M.P. for many years and " Father of the House ". President of the Local Government Board, 1895–1900.

CHAPMAN, SIR ARTHUR WAKEFIELD (1849 – 1926). Chairman, Surrey County Council, 1911–17, and Vice-Chairman of County Councils Association.

CHELMSFORD, LORD. See Thesiger.

CHURCHILL, LORD RANDOLPH HENRY SPENCER (1849–95). Father of Winston Churchill, founder of the "Fourth Party " and the Primrose League. Chancellor of the Exchequer, 1886; but resigned immediately after a quarrel. Anti-Home Ruler, invented phrase " Ulster will Fight and Ulster will be Right ".

CHURCHILL, WINSTON LEONARD SPENCER (1874–   ). Son of Lord Randolph Churchill, he first entered Parliament as a Tory, but broke away on the Tariff Reform issue, and became President of the Board of Trade, Home Secretary and finally First Lord of the Admiralty in Asquith's Government; returned to the Tories after the first world war. Churchill was always a perplexity to Beatrice, whose personal and political estimate of him varied amusingly from time to time. Mrs. Churchill was *née* Clementine Hozier.

CLARE, SIR HARCOURT E. (1854–1922). Town Clerk of Liverpool and then Clerk to the Lancashire County Council. A man of much local government experience; member of several Royal Commissions.

CLAY, SIR ARTHUR TEMPLE FELIX (1842–1928). Artist, who also wrote against Syndicalism; his son married the daughter of Beatrice's sister Margaret.

CLERKE, AGNES MARY (1842–1907). Historian of astronomy, wrote many articles for the *Encyclopaedia Britannica*. Fifth woman to be elected an honorary member of the Royal Astronomical Society.

CLIFFORD, DR. JOHN (1836–1923). Baptist, Minister of Praed Street and Westbourne Park Church, 1858–1915, and for many years the most powerful figure in the Nonconformist churches. Led the resistance to aid from the rates to Church schools and had his goods distrained for refusal to pay rate demands. First President of the Christian Socialist League.

COLE, GEORGE DOUGLAS HOWARD (1889–   ). Professor of Social and Political Theory in the University of Oxford, and author of a very large number of books on Socialism, Trade Unionism, and other social and economic subjects, from *The World of Labour* (1913) to *An Intelligent Man's Guide to the Post-War World* (1947). Soon after Cole had joined the Fabian Society, he, as a supporter of Syndicalism and Guild Socialism, came into vigorous collision with the views of the Webbs, which were at that time purely collectivist, and resigned in 1915 after a stormy battle. Subsequently this particular controversy died down, and he and his wife became friends of the Webbs and frequent visitors to Passfield Corner. See Margaret Cole, *Beatrice Webb*.

COLEGATE, W. ARTHUR (1884–   ). At first a civil servant, joining the Board of Trade in 1909; Joint Secretary to 1916 Committee of Reconstruction. In 1927 he became director of Brunner Mond, and later Tory M.P. for the Wrekin until 1945.

COLLINGS, JESSE (1831–1920). Liberal-Radical politician, faithful follower of Joseph Chamberlain. Founder and Honorary Secretary of the National Education League. A passionate supporter of small agricultural holdings (under the slogan " Three Acres and a Cow "), he was responsible for carrying in 1886 an Amendment to the Royal Address which resulted in the fall of Salisbury's government.

COLLINS, SIR WILLIAM JOB (1859–1946). Surgeon and London County Councillor, 1892–1907. Chairman of Council, 1897–98, member of many committees and did much work for London government. Twice Vice-Chancellor, University of London, member of many Government committees, tribunals, etc.

COLSON, ALFRED (*d.* 1910). Engineer and Manager of the gas department of Leicester from 1882 to his death. Colson was an able man who greatly improved the gasworks, introduced electric lighting and became Manager of the combined Gas and Electric Light Department, and also gained a reputation as a chemist.

COMTE, ISIDORE AUGUSTE MARIE FRANÇOIS XAVIER (1798–1857). The French philosopher, founder of the Positivist system, to which many of the friends of Beatrice's youth subscribed.

CORNWALL, SIR EDWIN (1863–   ). Member of L.C.C. (Progressive), 1892–1910, for eight years Whip to the Progressive Party, and Chairman, 1905–6. Liberal M.P. for Bethnal Green, 1906–18, followed Lloyd George in the 1918 election. Deputy Speaker, 1919–22.

COSTELLOE, BENJAMIN FRANCIS COWAN (1855–1899). Barrister; member of L.C.C. (Progressive), 1891–99; and lecturer for the Fabian Society. He married Mary Pearsall Smith, and was father of Dr. Karin Stephen and the late Mrs. Ray Strachey.

COURTNEY, KATE (1847–1929). Beatrice's second sister, married Leonard Courtney in 1885, and collaborated with him in much of his work. Their house in Chelsea became a centre of Liberal and internationalist thought and so continued after his death.

Crook was the Secretary of the Eighty Club, a group of young Liberals founded by Haldane and others in 1880.

CROOKS, WILLIAM (1852–1921). Trade Unionist and Socialist, member of the Coopers' Union, early Fabian. Mayor of Poplar, 1891, and Chairman of the Poplar Board of Guardians, 1898–1906. Labour M.P. for Poplar, 1903 till his death. A moving speaker on social conditions.

CUNNINGHAME - GRAHAM, ROBERT BONTEEN (1852–1936). One of the most colourful personalities of the early Socialist movement, artist, author, son of a Scottish landowner. He first stood for Parliament as a Liberal of the extreme left, but soon afterwards joined the Social Democratic Federation, sat for North Lanark from 1886 to 1892, and played an active part in all the S.D.F.'s attempts to agitate for the London unemployed in the 'eighties. With his friend John Burns he was imprisoned for six weeks for breaking through the police cordon in Trafalgar Square on "Bloody Sunday", 1887.

CUNYNGHAME, SIR HENRY HARDYNGE (1848–1936). Civil servant, Assistant Under-Secretary, Home Office, 1894–1913. Secretary to Parnell Commission on riots at Featherstone Colliery, etc.

CURRAN, PETER (1860–1910). Socialist and Trade Union leader, member of the I.L.P., organiser of the Gas Workers' and General Labourers' Union from 1891, and first Chairman of the General Federation of Trade Unions. Labour M.P., 1906–10.

CURZON, GEORGE NATHANIEL, Marquess Curzon of Kedleston (1859–1925). The Empire-builder, Viceroy of India, 1899–1905; Foreign Secretary, 1919–22.

DALTON, HUGH (1887–). Chancellor of the Exchequer, 1945; at the date of this book student of King's College, Cambridge, and a leader of the Cambridge Fabian Society.

DAUSSET, LOUIS JEAN JOSEPH (1866–). Senator for the Seine; Agrégé des lettres and professor of rhetoric, Paris. Paris Municipal Councillor, 1900–22, and President, 1901–2,

rapporteur général du budget de la Ville, Paris, 1908–19; président du Conseil général de la Seine, 1919–20.

DAVEY, HORACE, Baron Davey of Fernhurst (1833–1907). Lawyer and Liberal politician, Solicitor-General, 1886; became Lord Justice of Appeal. Chairman of the Committee which drew up the constitution of the University of London, 1897, and member of the Senate.

DAVIES, MRS.—not Miss—MARY (1855–1930). Distinguished soprano, retired from concert-singing to devote herself to teaching; became president of the Welsh Folk Song Society.

DAVISON, SIR RONALD CONWAY (1884–). Civil servant, Board of Trade and Ministry of Labour until 1928; then retired in order to become writer and lecturer on social questions, particularly unemployment and unemployment insurance.

DAVY, SIR HUMPHRY (1778–1829). The great inventor was director and professor at the Royal Institution from 1801 onwards.

DAVY, SIR JAMES STEWART (1848–1915). Civil servant, sternest upholder of "the principles of 1834" in the Poor Law, which, as an inspector, he put forward in evidence before the Commission of 1888. Became Chief Inspector, 1905, and endeavoured to guide the 1905 Royal Commission. (See S. and B. Webb, English Poor Law History.)

DEARMER, REV. PERCY (1867–1936). Broad Churchman, Fabian and social reformer. Vicar of St. Mary's, Primrose Hill, 1901–15; Secretary of London Christian Social Union, 1912–15; later Canon of Westminster. Chairman of the League of Arts from 1920; wrote, edited and contributed to a great many publications.

DESBOROUGH, WILLIAM HENRY GRENFELL (1855–). Created Baron Desborough in 1905. Tory M.P. for Salisbury, Hereford and Wycombe (1900–5), member of the Tariff Commission of 1904. His wife, née Ethel Fane, was co-heiress to the barony of Butler, a noted Society hostess, and one of Mrs. Asquith's "Souls".

DEVONSHIRE, SPENCER COMPTON CAVENDISH, eighth Duke (1833–1908). Liberal politician of many years' standing. Lord President of the Council, 1895–1905, and as such President of the Privy Council Committee on Education until the establishment in 1902 of the Board of Education.

DICKINSON, WILLIAM H., Lord Dickinson (1859–1924). Liberal M.P., elected to L.C.C. as Progressive, 1889; Deputy Chairman, 1892, and subsequently Chairman. An ardent internationalist, Dickinson joined the Labour Party in 1930, but left on the formation of the National Government in the following year.

DIGGLE, REV. J. R. Chairman of the London School Board, 1885–94, defeated in that year. Diggle was a London curate until he left the Church in 1879 on his election to the London School Board. The fight of the Progressive Party against the policy of the Church in education, known as " Diggle-ism ", raged for a long time.

DILKE, SIR CHARLES WENTWORTH (1843–1911). The Liberal Imperialist politician, author of *Greater Britain*.

DILKE, EMILIA FRANCES (1840–1904). Lady Dilke's first husband, Mark Pattison, the Rector of Lincoln College, died; and in 1885 she married Sir Charles Dilke. Lady Dilke was a distinguished author and journalist on painting, sculpture and architecture, but she entered Beatrice's life through her interest in the conditions and organisation of working women. She was Chairman of the Women's Trade Union League and one of its principal speakers.

DILLON, JOHN (1851–1927). Irish Nationalist, M.P. for Tipperary and East Mayo. Leader of the anti-Parnellite faction in the Irish Party; after its reunion became lieutenant to Redmond, and leader after the latter's retirement in 1918. His wife (*d.* 1907) was Elizabeth Mathew.

DISRAELI, BENJAMIN (1804–81). Prime Minister, 1868 and 1874–80.

DODD, FREDERICK LAWSON (1868–). Dentist, Surgeon to Royal Dental Hospital, London. Played a prominent part in the Fabian Society in the days of this book, more particularly as he belonged to a profession in which Socialists have not been

numerous. First Chairman of the Fabian Society's Summer School, and at one time its Honorary Treasurer.

DONALDSON, FREDERIC LEWIS. Archdeacon of Westminster. An enthusiastic Christian Socialist, Vicar of St. Mark's, Leicester, from 1896 to 1918; one of the first members of the Christian Social Union and Chairman of its Leicester branch for many years; a founder of the Church Socialist League and its Chairman, 1913–16; made Canon of Westminster by the first Labour Government.

DONNELLY, SIR JOHN FRETCHEWILL DYKES (1834–1902). Started his career as a soldier, served in the Crimean War and retired as a Major-General. After his retirement became secretary to the Science and Arts Department, 1884–99.

DOUGHERTY, SIR JAMES BROWN (1844–1934). Liberal politician. Under-Secretary to the Lord-Lieutenant of Ireland, and Clerk to the Privy Council in Ireland; M.P. for Londonderry City, 1914–18.

DOWNES, SIR ARTHUR HENRY (1851–1937). Doctor and administrator. Senior Medical Inspector for the Poor Law under the Local Government Board,1889 onwards;member of many departmental committees and of 1905 Royal Commission on the Poor Law.

DUFF, ROBERT HAROLD AMBROSE GORDON (1871–1946). Civil servant, mainly in Local Government Board; private secretary to its President, 1903 – 5. Secretary to 1905 Royal Commission on the Poor Law, and appointed General Inspector, 1909. Subsequently Secretary to the Mesopotamia Commission and to the Maclean Committee on Local Government.

DUGDALE, MRS. ALICE (1843–1902). Daughter of Sir Charles Trevelyan and in 1893 widow of William Stretford Dugdale. She was a connection of the Potter family, and her son later married Blanche, daughter of Eustace and Lady Frances Balfour.

DUKE, SIR HENRY EDWARD (1855–1939). Lord Justice Duke, afterwards Lord Merrivale. Lawyer, Recorder of Devonport, 1897–1914. Tory M.P. for Plymouth. Chief Secretary for Ireland, 1916–18.

EDGEWORTH, FRANCIS YSIDRO (1845–1926). Economist and statistician; from 1891 Professor of Political Economy, University of Oxford. Assisted London School of Economics in its early days.

EDWARDS, ALLEN CLEMENT (1869–1928). Liberal politician and journalist, writer for the *Daily News*. A Fabian for many years and author of several Fabian Tracts.

ELCHO, LORD. Hugo Richard Wemyss Charteris, later 11th Earl of Wemyss (1857–1937). M.P. for Haddington, 1883–85, and for Chiswick, 1886–95. His wife (*d.* 1937) was Mary Constance Wyndham, grand-daughter of Lord Leconfield, a Society lady and one of the hostesses of the " Souls ").

ELIOT, SIR CHARLES NORTON EDGECUMBE (1864–1931). Diplomat; Commissioner and Commander-in-Chief, British East Africa Protectorate, 1900–4; resigned and became Vice-Chancellor (not Principal) of Sheffield University, and in 1913 Principal of University of Hong Kong. Later Ambassador to Japan.

ELLISES. The last Leicester representative of this family, William Henry Ellis, moved to Hucknell in the next-door county, where his son, Francis Newman Ellis (1855–1934) became a colliery director and Sheriff of Nottingham.

ELLISON, SIR GERALD FRANCIS (1861–). Soldier, Secretary to War Office Reconstruction Committee, 1904; Private Secretary to Haldane, 1905–8, and Director of Organisation, Army Headquarters, 1908–11.

ENSOR, ROBERT CHARLES KIRKWOOD (1877–). Journalist, Fabian, political theorist and historian; member of L.C.C., 1910–13. Leader-writer on *Daily News* and *Daily Chronicle*, 1906–30, now " Scrutator " of the *Sunday Times*. Author of *England, 1870–1914*, etc.

ESHER, REGINALD BALIOL BRETT, second Viscount (1852–1930). Secretary to the Office of Works, 1895–1902. The friend of Edward VII, wrote Memoirs in four volumes. A friend of Haldane's; chairman of the War Office Reconstruction Committee, 1904.

FARADAY, MICHAEL (1791–1867). The great scientist was taken on by Sir Humphry Davy as his assistant at the Royal Institution, and was its superintendent at the time of his death.

FARRER, KATHERINE EUPHEMIA. Wife of Baron Farrer, a Vice-Chairman of the L.C.C.

FAULDER, JULIA (1880–1921). Daughter of Beatrice's sister Blanche Cripps and wife of Tom Faulder, surgeon.

FAWCETT, MILLICENT GARRETT (1847–1929). Sister of Elizabeth Garrett Anderson and wife of Henry Fawcett, the blind Postmaster-General. The leader for many years of the constitutional movement for women's suffrage.

FELS, JOSEPH (1854–1914). Millionaire Socialist and single-taxer; built up the huge Fels-Naptha plant which sold its products all over the world. Afterwards Fels came to England, made friends with Keir Hardie and George Lansbury and other Socialist leaders, and became very interested in the Back-to-the-Land Movement. He bought 1300 acres of land at Hollesley Bay and 600 at Maylands (both in Essex), for the settlement of unemployed men as agricultural workers, and gave generously to many social movements.

FISHER, MRS. ARABELLA, *née* Buckley. Secretary to Sir Charles Lyall; her brother later became Lord Wrenbury. She was one of the friends of Beatrice's girlhood, and " encouraged me in my lonely studies ".

FITZALAN, EDMUND BERNARD FITZALAN-HOWARD, first Viscount (1855–). Son of the Duke of Norfolk. Tory M.P. for Chichester, 1894–1921, a Lord of the Treasury, 1905, and Chief Whip, 1913–21.

FOSS, W., of Emmanuel College, Cambridge, Secretary of the Cambridge University Fabian Society in the autumn of 1909.

FOWLER, SIR HENRY, later Viscount Wolverhampton (1830–1911). Liberal politician and leading Wesleyan. President of the Local Government Board, 1892–94.

FOXWELL, HERBERT SOMERTON (1849–1936). Professor of Political Economy, University College, London, and owner of a unique library of books on political and social questions —now in the possession of the Univer-

BIOGRAPHICAL INDEX

sity of London. Foxwell's political views were strongly conservative, and his appointment as lecturer to the London School of Economics helped to give the lie to the suggestion that the Webbs intended to use that body as a vehicle of crude Socialist propaganda.

FRAMPTON, SIR GEORGE JAMES (1860–1928). The sculptor who made the Edith Cavell Memorial as well as many statues of Queen Victoria, Queen Mary and other works. One of the art advisers to the London Technical Education Board.

FRENCH, SIR JOHN DENTON PINKSTONE, later Earl French of Ypres (1852–1925). Commander-in-Chief in France, 1914–15, and in England, 1915–18.

GALTON, FRANCIS W. (1867–). Fabian Socialist; joined Morris's Socialist League in 1885 and the Fabian Society in 1891. Secretary to the Webbs, 1892–98, and to London Reform Union, 1898–1918. General Secretary to Fabian Society, 1920–39.

GARDINER, ALFRED G. (1865–). The Liberal writer and journalist, editor of the Daily News from 1902 to 1919, and author of many pen-portraits of the men and women of his day.

GARDINER, REV. THORY GAGE (1857–). Churchman, Co-operator, and Poor Law administrator. Secretary to Education Committee of the Co-operative Union, 1891–95. Member of Charity Organisation Society and of several Boards of Guardians; served on Royal Commission on the Poor Law, 1905. Residentiary Canon of Canterbury.

GARNETT, DR. WILLIAM (1850–1932). Mathematician, physicist and educationalist. Planned the Durham College of Science, Newcastle, of which he became Principal and Professor. Secretary and adviser to the London Technical Education Board, 1893–1904, and Education Adviser to L.C.C., 1904–15.

GARVIN, JAMES LOUIS (d. 1947). The journalist, editor of The Observer, 1908–42, and of the 1929 Encyclopaedia Britannica; author of the three-volume Life of Chamberlain.

GIBB, SIR GEORGE STEGMAN (1850–

1925). Solicitor, professional man and arbitrator. General Manager L.N.E.R., 1891–1906, and its Chairman, 1906–10. Managing Director, London Underground Railways, 1906–10, Chairman of the Road Board, 1910–19, a member of the war-time Committee on Production, 1915–18.

GLADSTONE, HERBERT, Viscount Gladstone (1854–1930). Son of the Liberal leader. Chief Liberal Whip, 1899–1906, and Home Secretary, 1906–1910, during the early part of the suffrage agitation; he was then sent out to South Africa as Governor-General.

GLADSTONE, WILLIAM EWART (1809–1898). Gladstone (whose last Premiership was from 1892 to 1894) represented the part of the Liberal tradition with which the Webbs had least sympathy. He was very old when they entered politics, and neither the modified Socialism of the Newcastle Programme nor the modified Imperialism of Haldane and his friends had any appeal for him.

GOMME, SIR GEORGE LAWRENCE (1853–1916). In the service of the Metropolitan Board of Works until 1889, when he was transferred to its successor, the L.C.C., whose Clerk he was from 1900 to 1915. Gomme was also an antiquary of some note.

GOOCH, GEORGE PEABODY (1873–). The Liberal historian, Fellow of Trinity College, Cambridge, joint-editor of the Contemporary Review and of the Cambridge History of British Foreign Policy; author of many books on history and on the problems of peace and democracy.

GORE, CHARLES (1853–1932). High Church leader, Christian Socialist and social reformer, Bishop of Worcester, 1902–5, of Birmingham, 1905–1911, and of Oxford, 1911–19.

GORST, SIR JOHN ELDON (1860–1911). Liberal M.P. who went over with Joseph Chamberlain to Liberal Unionism. Vice-President of the Privy Council Committee on Education, 1895–1902; hence responsible for the piloting through Parliament of the 1902 Education Act.

GOSCHEN, GEORGE JOACHIM, first Viscount (1831–1907). The Liberal

506

anti-Home Ruler, became Liberal Unionist. Chancellor of the Exchequer, 1886–92, and First Lord of the Admiralty, 1900–5; a strong supporter of University Extension.

GRANVILLE-BARKER, HARLEY GRANVILLE (1877–1946). The actor and dramatist, author of *The Madras House, The Voysey Inheritance*, etc. In 1894 entered on management at the Royal Court Theatre, and later the Savoy. Fabian and associate of Shaw in the early years of the century; his wife at that time was the actress Lillah McCarthy.

GRAY, SIR ALBERT (1850–1928). Lawyer, Counsel to the Chairman of Committees in the House of Lords from 1896 onwards. His wife was Sophie, daughter of S. Wells Williams of the U.S. Legation, Peking.

GREEN, ALICE SOPHIA AMELIA (*d.* 1929). Wife of John Richard Green, the historian of England, and herself a writer on historical subjects. A member of the Frederic Harrison group, and a friend and neighbour of the Webbs. She was a passionate Irish Nationalist, and became a member of the first Senate of the Irish Free State. Of her Beatrice wrote in her diary: " She chose me as a friend, and not I her, but she was good to me in the springtide of my good fortune, and she was one of the first to appreciate and like Sidney ".

GREEN, JOSEPH FREDERICK (1855–1932). Originally a curate, became a Positivist, Fabian and Secretary of the International Arbitration and Peace Association from 1886 to 1917. It that year, however, he became violently opposed to all attempts to end the war, and, in the ensuing general election, stood as National Labour candidate against Ramsay MacDonald, beat him and became P.P.S. to Sir Eric Geddes of "Geddes Axe " fame.

GRENFELL, MRS. WILLIE, see DESBOROUGH.

GREY, EDWARD, Viscount Grey of Fallodon (1862–1933). Liberal politician, Foreign Secretary from 1906 to 1916. Grey was one of the group of Liberal Imperialists in the early years of this century, which included Asquith and Haldane. See his auto-

biography. His wife, who died in 1906, was a Widdrington from Northumberland.

HALDANE, ELIZABETH SANDERSON (1862–1937). Sister of Haldane of Cloan and herself a distinguished public woman, writer on philosophy, ethics and Scottish history, and the first woman magistrate in the whole of Scotland.

HALDANE, RICHARD BURDON, Lord Haldane of Cloan (1856–1928). Lawyer, philosopher, leader among Liberal collectivists and Liberal Imperialists, educationalist, Army reformer, and lifelong friend of the Webbs. Most noted as effective founder (with the Webbs) of the modern University of London, and as Secretary of State for War and subsequently Lord Chancellor in the 1906 Liberal Government (from which he had to resign upon accusation of pro-German sympathies), Haldane became gradually converted to Labour and was Lord Chancellor to the first Labour Government of 1924. The " dear old lady " mentioned on p. 461 was Haldane's mother; she lived to be 100.

HALL, SIR BENJAMIN, afterwards Baron Llanover (1802–67). Whig politician, first returned to Parliament for Monmouth Boroughs in 1831; in the new House sat for Marylebone, and supported many projects for reform. In 1855, as Chief Commissioner of Works, he brought in the Bill which established the Metropolitan Board of Works, and settled the area of the present L.C.C.

HAMILTON, CHARLES JOSEPH (1878–). Economist; Professor of Economics at Calcutta, 1912–18; and later at Patna University, India.

HAMILTON, LORD CLAUD JOHN (1843–1925). Son of the Duke of Abercorn and grandson of the Duke of Bedford; Tory M.P. for various divisions, 1865–88, and 1910–18. Chairman of the Great Eastern Railway.

HAMILTON, SIR EDWARD WALTER (1847–1908). Civil servant, Treasury, from 1870; rose to be Joint Permanent Secretary, 1902.

HAMILTON, LORD GEORGE FRANCIS (1845–1927). Tory politician who held a number of offices between 1874 and 1903. Chairman of the London School Board, 1894–95, and of the Royal Commission on the Poor Laws, 1905–9. His wife was Maud, daughter of the Earl of Harewood.

HAMMILL, FREDERICK (1856–1901). Engineer from the North-East coast and member of the A.S.E. An early Fabian, and a prominent worker with Keir Hardie in the I.L.P.

HANKINSON, MARY. Socialist and prominent member of the Fabian Women's Group. By profession a gymnastic instructor in schools. Miss Hankinson was for many years manager of the Fabian Summer School and captain of its cricket team.

HARBEN, HENRY DEVENISH (1874–). Socialist and Fabian of many years standing, member of Executive Committee, 1911–20. As a recruit from the Liberal League organised a Fabian enquiry into land problems, which was published as *The Rural Problem*. Harben had many arguments with the Webbs and the Fabian Society before the last war, but remained their firm friend and admirer.

HARCOURT, LEWIS, Viscount Harcourt (1863–1922). Son of Sir William Harcourt; Liberal M.P. for Rossendale, 1904–17, and First Commissioner of Works, 1905–10.

HARCOURT, ROBERT VERNON (1878–). Brother of Lewis Harcourt, and a more Radical Liberal. M.P. for Montrose Burghs, 1908–18; journalist, and also wrote plays.

HARCOURT, SIR WILLIAM (1827–1904). Liberal politician ; imposer, as Chancellor of the Exchequer in the 1892 Government, of the first death duties, and author of the phrase " we are all Socialists now ". Leader of the Commons in Rosebery's Adminstration. The rivalry between him and Lord Rosebery accounted for much of the weakness of Liberal leadership around the turn of the century.

HARDIE, JAMES KEIR (1856–1915). The Scottish miners' leader who founded the I.L.P. and was the chief influence in the formation of the Labour Representation Committee which became the Labour Party. Hardie—whom John Burns so strongly disliked— stands for the emotional appeal of Socialism in the British working-class

movement; but his mind was out of tune with the Webbs, and they never really got on terms with him.

HARKNESS, MARGARET. A second cousin of Beatrice's and about the same age. Daughter of a parson, she ran away from home to work with the Salvation Army, became a Socialist and joined the S.D.F., earning her living as a free-lance journalist. Beatrice found her " greatly improved " by social work. (MS. diary, 1883.)

HARMSWORTH, ALFRED CHARLES WILLIAM (1865–1922). Lord Northcliffe of *Answers* and the *Daily Mail*. The founder of modern popular journalism.

HARRISON, AMY (Mrs. Spencer). One of the Webbs' earliest secretaries, married another—see note on p. 153 of this book; also wrote on factory legislation.

HARRISON, CHARLES (1835–97). Liberal politician, solicitor and advocate of leasehold enfranchisement. M.P. for Plymouth; elected to L.C.C. in 1886 and became Vice-Chairman and member of its Parliamentary Committee.

HARRISON, FREDERIC (1831–1923). The Radical leader of the English Positivists, free thinker and staunch supporter of Trade Unionism in the latter part of the nineteenth century. Harrison never succeeded in converting Beatrice to Positivism, but he and his wife were among her oldest friends. (See *My Apprenticeship*.)

HARRISON, JANE ELLEN (1850–1928). The distinguished classical scholar and archaeologist; author of *Prolegomena to the Study of Greek Religion*.

HART, SIR ISRAEL (1835–1911). Chairman of Hart & Levy, wholesale manufacturers of Leicester, four times Mayor of Leicester; presented the city with a free library and an ornamental fountain.

HARVEY, ALFRED SPALDING (1840– 1905). Originally a civil servant, in 1880 Harvey left to become secretary to the banking house of Glyn, Mills, Currie & Co., and retained this position until his death: he was a member of two Royal Commissions and was often consulted by the Treasury. He was a strong Liberal and free-trader and welcomed economic education on those lines.

HOBHOUSE, MARGARET (" MAGGIE "), (1854–1921). The sister next above Beatrice in age, married to Henry Hobhouse, and a convert to her son Stephen's pacifist opinions. Beatrice often differed from her, but always admired her courage, integrity and outspokenness. (See *My Apprenticeship*.)

HOBHOUSE, STEPHEN (1881–   ). Son of Henry and Margaret Hobhouse, became a Quaker and refused to inherit his father's property. A conscientious objector during the first world war, he was imprisoned and became concerned in prison reform. The book *English Prisons To-day* (1922; preface by Bernard Shaw) which he wrote with Fenner Brockway is a classic of its time.

HOBSON, JOHN ATKINSON (1858–1940). The Radical pacifist economist and internationalist, author of *The Evolution of Modern Capitalism, Imperialism, Work and Wealth*, and many other important books. Anticipated much of the Keynesian economic theory, for which he never received adequate recognition.

HOBSON, SAMUEL GEORGE (1864–1940). Author, journalist and Socialist; a foundation member of the I.L.P. and an early member of the Fabian Society, on whose Executive Committee he sat from 1900 to 1910. He was often, however, at odds with the policy of Shaw and the Webbs, particularly during the years immediately preceding the first world war, when as a leading Guild Socialist and author of the chief text-book, *National Guilds*, he was violently opposed to the collectivists. After the war he was Secretary of the National Building Guild.

HOGG, SIR JAMES MACNAGHTEN MCGAREL, later Baron Magheramone (1823–90). Soldier who became a Tory politician; M.P. successively for Bath, Truro and Middlesex. In 1867 Hogg became a member of the Metropolitan Board of Works, and was its Chairman from 1870 until its abolition in 1889.

HOLMES, DAVID (1843–1906). A cotton worker. President of the Burnley Weavers' Association; in 1896 Chairman of the Parliamentary Committee of the T.U.C.

HOLT, LAURENCINA (" Lallie ") (1845–1906). Beatrice's eldest sister, married to Robert Holt, the big Liverpool shipowner.

HOOKER, SIR WILLIAM JACKSON (1785–1865), and HOOKER, SIR JOSEPH DALTON (1817–1911). The reference in the text may be to either father or son. Both were Directors of Kew Gardens, the younger also President of the Royal Society from 1872 to 1877.

HORNER, SIR JOHN FRANCIS FORTESCUE (1842–1927), married Frances Graham (*d.* 1940). Lady Horner was a great beauty in her day and one of the leading lights of the " Souls ", and mother-in-law to Raymond Asquith.

HORSLEY, SIR VICTOR ALEXANDER HADEN (1857–1916). The famous surgeon, practising at the National Hospital for the Paralysed and Epileptic in Queen Square. A leader of the British Medical Association and a strong supporter of women's rights.

HOWELL, GEORGE (1833–1910). Former Chartist and Trade Union Leader in mid-nineteenth century; member of the " Junta " and secretary to the Parliamentary Committee of the T.U.C. Howell's books of reminiscence are invaluable for students of working-class history; he also collected the large George Howell library.

HUBBARD, EVELYN (1852–1934). Son of the first Lord Addington, married to a daughter of Sir Wyndham Portal. M.P. for Brixton, 1896–1900. Alderman of L.C.C. (Moderate), 1895–98.

HUBBARD, N. W. Progressive member of L.C.C., 1889–1907; Alderman, 1895–1901.

HUGHES, COLONEL HERBERT (1853–1917). A solicitor by profession, Councillor and Alderman of Sheffield from 1892, and Lord Mayor in 1906.

HUTCHINS, BEATRICE. Fabian, writer on factory and social questions, including the employment of women. Author of *Women in Modern Industry* and *History of Factory Legislation* (with Amy Harrison).

HUTCHINSON, HENRY H. (*d.* 1894). An early member of the Fabian Society and one of its financial pillars, related to the Clerk to the Justices of Derby.

On his death the Fabian leaders were astonished to find that he had left £10,000 for Fabian purposes, to be spent in ten years. Half of this sum went to pay travelling Hutchinson Lecturers; the other half founded the London School of Economics.

HUTTON, SIR JOHN (1842–1903). Chairman of L.C.C., 1892–95.

HUXLEY, THOMAS HENRY (1825–93). The great scientist was professor at the Royal Institution as well as the Royal College of Surgeons.

HUYSMANS, CAMILLE (1871–). Belgian Socialist politician, Prime Minister to the Coalition Government of 1946. Huysmans entered international politics in 1905, as Secretary to the Second International, and at the end of the first world war played the chief part in its reorganisation; he was strongly opposed to both German and Russian Communists. The Webbs had a high opinion of his abilities, and it was at his request, in his official international capacity, that they wrote *A Constitution for the Socialist Commonwealth of Great Britain*.

HYETT, SIR FRANCIS ADAMS (1844–1941). Gloucestershire landowner; Deputy Chairman of Quarter Sessions, 1886–1904, and Chairman, 1904–20. Vice - Chairman, Gloucestershire County Council, 1904–18, and Chairman, 1918; also wrote bibliographical and other mono graphs.

ILIFFE, WILLIAM H. (*d.* 1938). Lieutenant Commissioner of the Salvation Army, and an officer in the Army from 1886 (?) to his death. He served in India, was at one time in charge of the Army's Land Colony at Hadleigh and of its Boxsted Small Holdings Settlement, and later commanded its Men's Social Work throughout Great Britain.

IRVINE, SIR WILLIAM HILL (1858–1944) is almost certainly the individual referred to. He was a British-born Australian politician, Attorney-General and later Premier of Victoria, afterwards Attorney-General to the Commonwealth and Lieutenant-Governor of Victoria, 1918–35.

ISAACS, RUFUS DANIEL, afterwards Marquess of Reading (1860–1935). The lawyer and politician. Attorney-General, 1910–13, at the time of the Marconi scandal.

JACK, JAMES M. (1848–1912). Secretary of the Associated Ironmoulders of Scotland.

JACKSON, BRIGADIER, afterwards Colonel (*d.* 1930). In the Salvation Army from 1886 to 1930. For many years Chief Accountant at the Army's headquarters, and later its Auditor-General. He was only a visiting officer at the Hadleigh Colony, but went there often as conductor of the International Staff Songsters — also an Army venture.

JACKSON, SIR CYRIL (1863–1924). Educational administrator; head of Education Department, Western Australia, 1896–1903, then Chief Inspector of the Board of Education until 1906. Member of London School Board, 1891–96, and of L.C.C. (Progressive), 1907–13; Chairman, 1915. One of the expert investigators employed by the 1905 Royal Commission on the Poor Law; and member of many commissions.

JAMES, WILLIAM (1842–1910). The American philosopher and psychologist, brother of Henry James.

JAMESON, SIR LEANDER STARR (1853–1917). " Dr. Jim " of the Jameson Raid, which he organised while administrator of Rhodesia for the Chartered Company of South Africa. After the South African War he was Premier of the Cape from 1904 to 1908, and in 1913 was made Chairman of the British South African Company.

JEFFREY, SIR JOHN (1871–1947). Civil servant, joined as boy clerk in 1888. 1905–9, Assistant Secretary to Royal Commission on the Poor Law, subsequently Secretary to Scottish National Health Insurance Commission, Scottish Board of Health, Department of Health for Scotland, and from 1933 to 1937 Permanent Under-Secretary for Scotland.

JEKYLL, SIR HERBERT (1846–1932). Soldier (retired 1901), Private Secretary to the Earl of Carnarvon and to Lord Houghton. Assistant Secretary, Board of Trade, 1901–11. His wife was Agnes Graham, daughter of William Graham, M.P.

JEPHSON, ARTHUR W. (1853–1935). Canon of Southwark. Member of

McCLEARY, GEORGE FREDERICK (1867–   ). Doctor and public health expert. Deputy Senior Medical Officer, Ministry of Health, and Principal Medical Officer to the National Health Insurance Commission; M.O.H. for Battersea. Specialist in maternity and child welfare, and an authority on population.

MACDONALD, DR. J. A. Doctor; district Poor Law Officer at Taunton; from 1907 onwards held high office in the British Medical Association.

MACDONALD, JAMES RAMSAY (1866–1937). Labour Prime Minister, 1924 and 1929–31; then Prime Minister in the National Government until 1935. During the period of this book MacDonald was a writer and lecturer on Socialism, member of the I.L.P., and first Secretary of the Labour Representation Committee; he resigned from the Fabian Society at the time of the Boer War. The Webbs never really liked or trusted MacDonald, nor he them.

MACDONALD, MARGARET ETHEL (1870–1910). Wife of Ramsay MacDonald, daughter of Dr. Gladstone, a professor of chemistry and member of the London School Board—and herself a steadfast worker for women's labour organisations. Her death at so early an age was a disaster in more ways than one.

MACDONNELL, SIR ANTONY PATRICK, later Lord Macdonnell (1844–1925). Indian and Irish administrator, Lieutenant-Governor of Accra and Oudh, organiser of Indian famine relief in 1897, and author of the famous Famine Report. In 1903 he became Irish Under-Secretary under Wyndham with special administrative powers, but his indiscretions led to Wyndham's resignation, and though he remained in office until 1908 he lost his special powers.

McKENNA, REGINALD (1863–1933). Liberal politician; Financial Secretary to the Treasury, 1905–7, thereafter President of the Board of Education, First Lord of the Admiralty, Home Secretary, and Chancellor of the Exchequer (1915–16). After retirement from politics he became Chairman of the Midland Bank.

MACKENZIE, SIR LESLIE (1862–1935).

The distinguished doctor and public health practitioner. M.O.H. for Kirkcudbright and Wigtown, and for Leith; medical member of Scottish Local Government Board, 1904–19, and of Scottish Board of Health, 1919–28.

MACKINDER, SIR HALFORD JOHN (1861–1947). Geographer, Reader in Geography, University of Oxford, 1887–1905; Reader and afterwards Professor, University of London, 1900–25. Director of London School of Economics, 1903–8; member of many Government committees.

McNABB, FATHER VINCENT (d. 1943). Dominican priest, born at Portaferry, County Down; an untiring worker and preacher in the cause of social and economic morality; the first Dominican father to become an extension lecturer for the University of London. He continued lecturing for more than twenty years until his death, and wrote many books, pamphlets, and articles on Christianity, literature, etc.

MACNAMARA, THOMAS JAMES (1861–1931). Elementary school teacher who became a Liberal politician. Member of London School Board, 1896–1902, and M.P. for North Camberwell, 1900–18; Coalition Liberal in 1918 election and Minister of Labour, 1920–22. A strong Nonconformist, and editor of The Schoolmaster from 1892 to 1907.

MACROSTY, HENRY W. Civil servant; member of the Fabian Executive from 1895 to 1907; Assistant Director of the first Census of Production, 1907; writer on trusts and combines.

McTAGGART, JOHN McTAGGART ELLIS (1866–1925). Hegelian philosopher; Fellow of Trinity College, Cambridge.

McVAIL, JOHN CHRISTIE (1849–1926). Scottish doctor; M.O.H. for Stirling and Dumbarton. Examiner in medical jurisprudence and public health for Scottish Universities. President, Society of M.O.H.s of Great Britain; on General Medical Council. Medical investigator for the 1905 Royal Commission on the Poor Law.

MAETERLINCK, MAURICE (1862–   ). The Belgian playwright and mystic published his L'Intelligence des Fleurs, the book to which Beatrice refers in the text, in 1906.

MANN, TOM (1856–1941). Best known of the orators and organisers of left-wing Trade Unionism. An engineer by trade and member of the A.S.E., he joined the S.D.F., threw himself into the "new Unionism" of the 'eighties, and played part in the unemployed demonstrations and the London Dock Strike. From 1910 onwards he was active in the Syndicalist movement and in the great strikes of 1911–13; and after the war was connected with various "minority movements" among Trade Unionists and with the Communist Party. He was a member of the Royal Commission on Labour of 1891.

MARLBOROUGH, CHARLES RICHARD JOHN SPENCER-CHURCHILL, ninth Duke (1871–1934). Held minor office in Tory administrations. His wife, Consuelo Vanderbilt of New York, obtained a divorce in 1920.

MARLOWE, THOMAS (1868–1935). Journalist, editor of Northcliffe's Daily Mail, 1899–1926. Chairman of Associated Newspapers, 1918–26.

MARSHALL, ALFRED (1842–1924). Professor of Economics, University of Cambridge. Member of the Royal Commission on Labour. Marshall had been a friend of Beatrice before her marriage and was much interested in her social investigations—though he tried to discourage her from tackling the Co-operative Movement. (See My Apprenticeship.)

MARSHALL, SIR JOSEPH HERBERT (1851–1918). Music and pianoforte dealer of Leicester. Chairman of the local Conservative Association and leader of his party. Member of the Town Council from 1888 onwards and Mayor in 1896.

MARTIN, JOHN W. Member of the Fabian Society in its early days and of the Executive Committee from 1894 to 1899. Author of the Tract State Education at Home and Abroad (1894). Subsequently went to New York, where he married the leading exponent of Fabianism in the U.S.A.

MARX, KARL (1818–83). In her earlier days Beatrice came across Marx's economic theories—not his theory of

history—and criticised them strongly. (See appendices to My Apprenticeship.) The Webbs did not take at all kindly to Marxism until they went to the U.S.S.R.

MASSIE, JOHN (1842–1925). Liberal and Congregationalist; M.P. for Cricklade, 1906–10. Professor of New Testament Exegesis at Mansfield College, Oxford; Chairman of Council of Congregational Union; Treasurer of National Liberal Federation, and member of many other educational and political bodies. Assistant Commissioner, Royal Commission on Secondary Education, 1894.

MASSINGHAM, HENRY WILLIAM (1849–1924). Liberal journalist, editor of the Daily Chronicle till 1899, the Star, and from 1907 to 1923 of the weekly Nation, since amalgamated with the New Statesman. A member of the Fabian Society in the 'nineties, Massingham did a great deal to put across Fabian propaganda, until he quarrelled with the Society over its policy during the Boer War.

MASTERMAN, CHARLES FREDERICK GURNEY (1873–1927). Radical politician. Extension lecturer and journalist; Liberal M.P. for West Ham, 1906–11, and for Bethnal Green, 1911–14. Parliamentary Secretary to Local Government Board, 1908–9, and held various other offices; but his political career came to an end soon after the outbreak of war.

MAWDSLEY, JAMES (1848–1902). One of the most conservative of Trade Unionists, leader for many years of the Lancashire cotton spinners; in 1906 he stood for Parliament as a Tory. He was a member of the 1891 Royal Commission on Labour, in which capacity, in spite of his conservatism, he signed, with Abraham, Austin and Tom Mann, the Minority Report for which Webb was largely responsible.

MEINERTZHAGEN, DANIEL (1842–1910). Senior partner in a leading firm of foreign bankers and merchants, married to

MEINERTZHAGEN, GEORGINA (1850–1914), Beatrice's fourth sister. Editor of records of the Potter family, e.g. From Ploughshare to Parliament, and writer of plays for children.

MERRIMAN, JOHN XAVIER (1841–1926). South African politician, entered the Cape Parliament in 1869, and obtained office in 1881. Merriman was a member of the Committee on the Jameson Raid and drew up its report; subsequently he was a member of the National Convention for Union (of South Africa) and Prime Minister from 1908 to 1910 in the United Government.

MERZ, JOHN THEODORE (1840–1920). Scientist and engineer, of a well-known Newcastle family. Wrote a monumental work on the development of European thought in the nineteenth century, stressing the importance of the growth of science and scientific method.

METCHNIKOFF, ILYA (1845–1916). The Russian biologist who became assistant director of the Pasteur Institute at Paris, and did much work on the possibility of prolonging life by preventing intestinal putrefaction. Beatrice, who had a lifelong interest in dieting, was naturally influenced by Metchnikoff's work.

MILL, JOHN STUART (1896–73). The great Utilitarian philosopher who bridged the gap between Benthamism and Socialism, sat as an Independent for Westminster from 1865 to 1868, and introduced into Parliament the first petition for Women's Suffrage. The social philosophy of the Fabians owed a great deal to Mill.

MILNER, ALFRED, Viscount Milner (1854–1925). Journalist and civil servant; Under-Secretary for Finance in Egypt, 1889–92, then Chairman of the Board of Inland Revenue till 1897. A member of the Rhodes school of Imperialists, as High Commissioner for South Africa from 1897 to 1901, Milner bears responsibility for much of the policy which led to the South African War.

MITCHELL, H. ISAAC (1867–   ). A leading official of the Boilermakers' Society and wrote its history. He subsequently became an official of the Labour Department of the Board of Trade.

MONRO, SIR HORACE CECIL (1861–   ). Civil servant; entered Local Government Board, 1884; was secretary to several Presidents. Assistant Secretary to the Board, 1897–1910, and Permanent Secretary, 1910–19.

MONTEAGLES, The. THOMAS SPRING RICE, second Baron Monteagle (1849–1926), and his wife Elizabeth Butler (d. 1908), daughter of the Bishop of Meath and sister of Lady Prothero.

MORANT, SIR ROBERT LAURIE (1862–1920). Civil servant; chief author of the 1902 Education Act. Morant started his career by laying (as tutor to the Crown Prince) the foundation of an educational system in Siam; on returning to England he entered the Education Department in 1895 and wrote special reports for Sir Michael Sadler. In 1902 he became private secretary to the Duke of Devonshire and in 1903 Permanent Secretary to the Board of Education, where he had great influence. Differences with his colleagues led him to leave in 1911 and to become Chairman of the National Health Insurance Commissioners, and in 1919 Secretary to the new Ministry of Health.

MORGAN, JOHN HARTMAN (1876–   ). Lawyer and journalist; wrote for *Daily Chronicle* and *Manchester Guardian*; Liberal candidate in 1910 election; published many books on legal and political subjects. He married Helen Mary Cracknell.

MORLEY, ARNOLD (1849–1916). Liberal politician. Chief Liberal Whip, 1886–1893, and Postmaster-General, 1892–1895.

MORLEY, JOHN (1838–1916). Lord Morley of Blackburn, biographer of Gladstone, Secretary of State for India during the Morley-Minto reforms, resigned from the Asquith Cabinet in 1914 on pacifist grounds. Morley was a close friend of the Leonard Courtneys (*q.v.*), although not of the Webbs.

MOWATT, SIR FRANCIS (1837–1919). Civil servant; appointed Clerk in the Treasury, 1856; Assistant Secretary, 1888, and Permanent Secretary, 1888–1903; member of many Royal Commissions. Alderman L.C.C., 1903, and member of the Senate of London University.

MUNDELLA, ANTHONY JOHN (1825–1897). Progressive Radical politician. Originally a hosiery manufacturer in Nottingham, Mundella set up the first conciliation board in industry; he supported the New Model Unionism of Allen, Applegarth, etc., and worked continuously for Parliamentary reform, for universal education and for Factory and Housing Acts. As President of the Board of Trade in 1886 he established its Labour Department and he was a member of the 1891 Royal Commission on Labour.

MUNRO FERGUSON, RONALD CRAUFURD (1860–1934). Later Viscount Novar. Large Scottish landowner and Liberal politician; M.P. for Leith, 1886–1914; at one time Private Secretary to Lord Rosebery.

MURRAY, GEORGE GILBERT AIMÉE (1866–   ). Gilbert Murray, Professor of Greek, translator of Euripides; Liberal and internationalist; Chairman of the League of Nations Union until there was no longer a League of Nations.

MURRAY, GRAHAM, Viscount Dunedin (1849–   ). Scottish lawyer and Tory politician. Secretary of State for Scotland, 1903–5. Chairman, 1903–6, of the Royal Commission on Trade Union Law, set up as a result of the Taff Vale judgment.

NANSEN, FRIDTJOF (1861–1930). The explorer who nearly reached the North Pole in the *Fram* in 1893. He became Professor of Oceanography at Oslo, director of the repatriation of prisoners after the first world war, when he introduced the " Nansen " passport; and High Commissioner for Relief in the Russian famine of 1921.

NAPIER, SIR ALBERT EDWARD ALEXANDER (1881–   ). Youngest son of Lord Napier of Magdala; lawyer, Assistant Secretary in the Lord Chancellor's Office, 1919–44, and Permanent Secretary since 1944. At the time of this book he was private secretary to Cyril Jackson (*q.v.*) and lived in his house at Limpsfield.

NAPIER, THOMAS BATEMAN (1854–1933). Lawyer, County Court Judge, Derbyshire, from 1912 onwards. Ph.D. of London University, on its Senate in 1895; member of L.C.C. (Progressive), 1893–1906, and three times chairman of its Parliamentary Committee.

NASH, VAUGHAN (1861–1932). Jour-

nalist who became a civil servant. Nash's interest in Trade Unionism and social questions began early; with Llewellyn Smith he wrote the standard history of the 1889 Dock Strike; he was on the editorial staff of the *Daily Chronicle* and the *Daily News*. In 1905 he became private secretary to Campbell-Bannerman and subsequently to Asquith; and was Secretary to the Ministry of Reconstruction in 1917–1919.

NEVILL, LADY DOROTHY FANNY (*d.* 1913). Daughter of the third Earl of Oxford, married R. M. Nevill, a grandson of the Earl of Abergavenny. She was a great Society hostess, and wrote entertaining memoirs.

NEWMAN, SIR GEORGE (1870–   ). Doctor and public health administrator. Chief Medical Officer to Ministry of Health, 1919–35, and to Board of Education, 1907–35. Chairman of the Health of Munition Workers Committee during the first world war, member of many Government committees, and author of Government Reports and other publications.

NEWSHOLME, SIR ARTHUR (1857–   ). Doctor and public health administrator; for many years Principal Medical Officer to the Local Government Board. Author of many books and important Government Reports.

NORMAN, CLARENCE HENRY (1886–   ). Expert shorthand writer and author, and a Fabian Socialist. Conscientious objector during first world war; twice imprisoned; on Executive of No-Conscription Fellowship.

NORTHUMBERLAND, HENRY GEORGE PERCY, seventh Duke (1846–1918). M.P. for North Northumberland, 1868–85. Lord-Lieutenant of the County and Custos Rotulorum, Chairman of Northumberland County Council and Chancellor of the University of Durham. The Duchess (*d.* 1913) was Lady Edith Campbell, daughter of the Duke of Argyll.

NUNN, THOMAS HANCOCK (1859–1937). Member of the Charity Organisation Society, a Poor Law Guardian and member of the 1905 Royal Commission on the Poor Law; signed the Majority Report. A pioneer in the

1934), "Imperial Perks". Railway engineer and lawyer; Wesleyan (Treasurer of the Wesleyan Twentieth-Century Million Fund); Liberal M.P., 1892–1910. Perks, the Founder and Treasurer of the Liberal League, was the wire-puller *par excellence* of the Liberal Imperialist group (the " Limps ") formed by Haldane and his friends; but the Webbs did not find him congenial.

PERRY, SIR EDWIN COOPER (1856–1938). The distinguished physician, consultant to Guy's Hospital. Much interested in the University of London, of which he was Vice-Chancellor, 1917–19, and thereafter Principal Officer.

PERTHES, FRIEDRICH CHRISTOPH (1772–1843). German Liberal and Nationalist, who founded a famous publishing house at Gotha. Justus Perthes, the geographical publisher, was his uncle.

PHELPS, LANCELOT RIDLEY (1853–1936). Fellow and Tutor of Oriel College, Oxford, and Provost, 1914–1929. Interested in social reform; a Poor Law Guardian and member of the C.O.S. and of the 1905 Royal Commission on the Poor Law.

PHILLIMORE, MRS. LUCY (" Lion "), *née* Fitzpatrick. Wife of R. C. Phillimore. A prominent member of the Fabian Society and associated with many causes.

PHILLIMORE, ROBERT CHARLES (1871–1919). Eldest son of the first Lord Phillimore, one of the rich young adherents of the Webbs in their early work. Member of L.C.C. for Deptford, 1898–1910 and 1913–19.

PHILLIPS, MARION (1881–1932). Australian-born, she came to the London School of Economics and became an investigator for the 1905 Royal Commission on the Poor Law; then took up work in the Labour movement, and became in 1918 Chief Woman Officer to the reorganised Labour Party.

PLAYNE, ARTHUR (1845–1913). Country squire and owner of a cloth mill in Gloucestershire, married to Beatrice's third sister, Mary.

PLUNKETT, SIR HORACE CURZON (1854–1932). The great promoter of the Irish Co-operative movement; founded in 1894 the Irish Agricultural Organisation Society. M.P. for Dublin County, 1892–1900, and Commissioner for the Congested Districts Board, Ireland, 1891–1918. In later years Plunkett became a much closer friend of the Webbs and took them for their first ride in an aeroplane.

POLLOCK, SIR FREDERICK (1845–1937). The distinguished judge and legal authority, editor for many years of the *Law Reports*. Member of the 1891 Royal Commission on Labour.

POWER, DR. W. H. Doctor and public health specialist. Chief Medical Officer to the Local Government Board until 1907.

POYNDER, SIR JOHN POYNDER DICKSON, later Lord Islington (1869–1936). Tory landowner and politician, member of L.C.C. (Moderate), 1898–1904, M.P. for Chippenham, 1892–1910; held various minor offices. His wife was Anne, daughter of Lord Napier of Magdala.

PRESTON-THOMAS, HERBERT. Civil servant in Local Government Board; entered the service in 1859, and in 1894 was appointed Inspector under the Poor Law.

PRICE, SIR ROBERT JOHN (1854–1926). Liberal M.P. for East Norfolk, 1892–1918.

PRINGLE, REV. JOHN CHRISTIAN (1872–1938). For many years secretary to the Charity Organisation Society; during 1902–9 was assistant curate in East End parish. Expert investigator (on distress due to unemployment) to 1905 Royal Commission on the Poor Law.

PROTHERO, SIR GEORGE WALTER (1848–1922). The historian; Professor of History at Edinburgh University, 1894–99; editor of the Cambridge Historical Series and co-editor of the *Cambridge Modern History*; a member of the British Peace Delegation, 1919. Best known to Beatrice, however, as the editor of the *Quarterly Review*. His wife was Mary Frances Butler, daughter of the Bishop of Meath; they had a large circle of literary, scientific and political friends.

PROVIS, SIR SAMUEL BUTLER (1845–1926). Lawyer and civil servant;

Permanent Secretary to Local Government Board, 1898–1910. Member of 1905 Royal Commission on the Poor Law.

PYCROFT, ELLA. Social worker, worked with Beatrice in her early days as a rent collector for St. Katharine's Buildings. (See *My Apprenticeship*.) Subsequently turned her attention to education and became chief organiser of domestic economy under the Technical Education Board of the L.C.C.

RAMSAY, SIR WILLIAM (1852–1916). Chemist, Professor of Chemistry at University College, London, 1887–1912. In 1904 he received the Nobel Prize for chemistry.

RATHBONES. The great Liverpool family of merchants and philanthropists, founded by William Rathbone (1757–1809), whose son William (1787–1868) was Mayor of Liverpool and a great benefactor of education. The late Eleanor Rathbone, the protagonist of family allowances, was granddaughter to the second William, and the family includes many well-known names.

RAW, NATHAN (1866–1940). Doctor and tuberculosis expert; M.P. (Tory) for Wavertree, 1918–22. Head of various asylums and hospitals, O.C. first Western General Hospital, Lancashire.

REDESDALE, ALGERNON BERTRAM FREEMAN-MITFORD (1837–1916), first Baron Redesdale, diplomatist and M.P.

REDMOND, JOHN ARTHUR (1851–1918). The Irish Nationalist, leader first of the Parnellites and then of the reunited Nationalist Party from 1900 to his death.

REEVES, WILLIAM PEMBER (1857–1932). Director of the London School of Economics, 1908–19. Reeves was a New Zealander who became Minister of Labour, Education and Justice in the colony, and resigned to come to London as Agent-General; from 1905 to 1909 he was its High Commissioner. Socialist and Fabian, wrote books on State experiments in Australia and New Zealand, etc., father of Amber Blanco White. His wife, *née* Magdalen Stuart Robison, was a social investigator, author of the

famous *Round About a Pound a Week*.

REID, ROBERT THRESHIE, later Lord Loreburn (1846–1923). Lawyer and Liberal politician; Lord Chancellor, 1905–16.

RHODES, CECIL (1853–1902). Rhodes of South Africa, whose estate founded the Rhodes Scholarships. Though they did not take the pacifist line during the Boer War, the Webbs never accepted Rhodes' imperialism.

RICHARDS, HENRY CHARLES, K.C. (1851–1905). Lawyer; Tory M.P. for Finsbury from 1895, had previously fought hard against Bradlaugh at Northampton; frequent speaker in favour of the Constitution.

RIPON, FREDERICK OLIVER ROBINSON, 2nd Marquess of (1852–1925). Large landowner in Yorkshire and Liberal politician, friend of Rosebery; at one time Liberal leader in the House of Lords. He married Constance Gladys, widow of the Earl of Lonsdale.

RITCHIE, CHARLES THOMSON, Baron Ritchie (1838–1906). Tory politician, M.P. from 1874 onwards, held various Government posts, rising to Chancellor of the Exchequer, 1902–3. As President of the Local Government Board (1886–92) played a considerable part in the formation of the London County Council.

ROBERTS, SIR OWEN (1835–1915). Magistrate; Clerk for forty years to the Worshipful Company of Clothfounders, and thereafter its Master; Lieutenant for the City of London and High Sheriff of Carnarvonshire.

ROBERTSON, JOHN G. (1867–1933). Professor of German Language and Literature, University of London.

ROBINSON, SIR FREDERIC LACY (1840–1911). Inland Revenue official, 1857–1902, during his last ten years Deputy Chairman of the Commissioners. Thereafter member of L.C.C. (Moderate).

ROBINSON, SIR HENRY AUGUSTUS (1857–1927). Vice-President, Local Government Board for Ireland, from 1898 until its abolition. Member of 1905 Royal Commission on the Poor Law.

ROBINSON, JOSEPH ARMITAGE (1858–1933). Churchman and author. Professor of Divinity at Cambridge,

Morant; thereafter Vice-Chancellor of the University of Leeds. Father of Michael Sadleir, the novelist and publisher.

SALEEBY, DR. CALEB WILLIAM (1879–1940). Doctor, eugenist, Fabian, divorce law reformer, etc. Founder of the Sunlight League, and propagandist and organiser for a large number of associations connected with hygiene, sociology and racial health.

SALISBURY, JAMES EDWARD HUBERT GASCOYNE-CECIL (1861–1947), fourth Marquess, son of the third, first took office in 1909 as Under-Secretary for Foreign Affairs, and thereafter held many other posts, ending his political career as Lord Privy Seal, 1924–29, and Leader of the House of Lords, 1925–29.

SALISBURY, ROBERT ARTHUR TALBOT GASCOYNE-CECIL, Marquess of Salisbury (1830–1903), "the Markiss" as *Punch* called him. Three times Conservative Prime Minister, retiring in 1902 to be succeeded by Arthur Balfour.

SALT, HENRY STEPHENS (1851–1937). Eton master, writer, humanitarian, vegetarian, Fabian, Socialist; secretary for thirty years of the Humanitarian League. Salt married a relative of J. L. Joynes, another Eton master who was a Socialist and friend of William Morris, and served humanitarian causes all his life; his best-known book is his autobiography, *Seventy Years Among Savages*.

SAMUEL, HERBERT LOUIS, Viscount Samuel (1870–). An intimate friend of the Webbs in the early years of this century. First held office in the Liberal Government of 1906; High Commissioner for Palestine, 1920–25; Home Secretary in the National Government, 1931–32, and leader of Liberal Parliamentary Party, 1931–35.

SANDARS, JOHN S. (1869–1934). Private secretary to Arthur Balfour from 1892 to 1905.

SANDERS, WILLIAM STEPHEN (1876–1942). Fabian Socialist who started life as a farmer's boy and later became a Fabian lecturer under the Hutchinson Trust. Secretary of the Fabian Society, 1914–20, and Honorary Treasurer thereafter. L.C.C. Alderman, 1904–10, and Labour M.P. for North Battersea, 1929–31.

SAUER, J. W. (*d.* 1913). South African lawyer and politician. Colonial Secretary to the Cape Government under Rhodes; after the Union became Minister of Railways and subsequently of Agriculture. Sauer described himself as a "philosophic radical" and refused a knighthood.

SCHILLER, FERDINAND CUNNING SCOTT (1864–1937). The leading English Pragmatist philosopher: not a Hegelian, as stated in the text.

SCHLOSS, DAVID F. Civil servant, on the staff of the Labour Department of the Board of Trade; prepared important Reports on *Gain - sharing* and on *Profit - sharing and Co - partnership*. Schloss also wrote on *Methods of Industrial Remuneration* and pioneer studies in unemployment, and lectured for the Fabian Society.

SCHREINER, WILLIAM PHILIP (1857–1919). South African politician; Attorney-General to the Cape Government, 1893, and its Prime Minister from 1898 to 1900. From 1914 to 1919 he was High Commissioner for South Africa: his sister was Olive Schreiner, the novelist, author of *The Story of an African Farm*.

SELBORNE, LADY. Lady Beatrix Maud Cecil, daughter of the Marquess of Salisbury and wife of the second Earl of Selborne, the Liberal politician.

SELLICKS, ALFRED (1845–1902). Woolwich member of the A.S.E. and delegate to national conferences of that organisation.

SETH, JAMES (1860–1925). Professor of Moral Philosophy, University of Edinburgh, from 1898; and co-editor of the *Philosophic Review*.

SHACKLETON, SIR DAVID JAMES (1858–1940). Trade Unionist and Labour M.P. who became a civil servant. A cotton operative, President of the Weavers' Amalgamation, he was elected to Parliament as Labour M.P. for Clitheroe in 1902; in 1910 he became Labour Adviser to the Home Office, and was later Permanent Secretary to the Ministry of Labour.

SHARP, CLIFFORD DYCE (1883–1935). Journalist and Fabian; editor of *The Crusade*, and of the *New Statesman* from its foundation until 1931. He married the daughter of Hubert Bland, treasurer of the Fabian Society.

SHAW, FLORA LOUISE (*d.* 1929). Author and journalist, friend of Rhodes and Joseph Chamberlain; Special Commissioner for *The Times* in South Africa. In 1902 she married Sir Frederick Lugard (Lord Lugard, the great colonial administrator).

SHAW, GEORGE BERNARD (1856–   ). Playwright, Socialist, very early member of the Fabian Society, to which he introduced Sidney Webb. Editor of *Fabian Essays*, and one of the " Big Four " who ran the early Fabian Society. Shaw, whom Beatrice Webb described as a " Sprite ", was the lifelong friend of both of them, as well as being the Fabian Society's most brilliant pamphleteer. See Shaw, *Early History of the Fabian Society*.

SHAW-LEFEVRE, GEORGE JOHN, Baron Eversley (1832–1928). Liberal politician; as Postmaster-General, 1882–84, introduced the sixpenny telegram. First Commissioner of Works and later President of the Local Government Board in Rosebery's government of 1892–95, in which capacity he carried the first London Equalisation of Rates Act. Sat on the L.C.C. as a Progressive.

SHEPHEARD (not Shepherd), A. J. Member of L.C.C. (Progressive), 1901–13.

SHIPTON, GEORGE (1839–1911). By trade a builder, Shipton's chief claim to fame is his long secretaryship of the London Trades Council in the latter days of the Junta. (See Webb, *History of Trade Unionism*.) He gave evidence before the 1874 Royal Commission on the Labour Laws, which produced important and far-reaching changes. He was an opponent of Burns and Tillett and the " New Unionists ", but eventually became converted to the regulation of hours of work by law.

SHOVE, GERALD FRANK (1887–1947). Economist; lecturer in economics at Cambridge University and Fellow of King's College; in early days a strong left-wing Socialist and Syndicalist.

SIDGWICK, ELEANOR MILDRED (1845–1936). Widow of Henry Sidgwick and sister of Arthur Balfour the Prime Minister; Principal of Newnham College, 1892 – 1910, and Bursar, 1880–1919.

SIDGWICK, HENRY (1838–1900). The philosopher, influenced by John Stuart Mill, who wrote text-books on ethics and political economy. A strong advocate of higher education for women; promoted Newnham College, Cambridge.

SIMON, ERNEST DARWIN, afterwards Baron Simon of Wythenshawe (1879–   ). Manufacturer of gas engines; Liberal, later Labour politician and expert on housing and local government. Member of Manchester City Council, 1911–25, and Lord Mayor, 1921. Twice Liberal M.P. for Withington, author of several books on housing, city government, democracy, etc. Chairman of B.B.C., 1947.

SIMON, JOHN ALSEBROOK, first Viscount (1873–   ). Lawyer, Liberal and then National Liberal politician; M.P. for Walthamstow, 1906–18, and thereafter for other divisions. Solicitor-General, 1910–13; Foreign Secretary, 1931–35; Lord Chancellor, 1940–45. His first wife, Ethel Mary Venables, died in 1902, after three years of marriage.

SMART, WILLIAM (1853–1915). Economist; Professor of Political Economy at Glasgow University from 1896 to his death; author of Smart's *Economic Annals of the Nineteenth Century*. Member of 1905 Royal Commission on the Poor Law.

SMITH, FRANK S. (1854–1940). Furnishing trades worker who became a journalist and Salvationist. Lifelong Socialist and member of I.L.P.; close friend of Keir Hardie. Member of L.C.C. (with intermission) from 1892 to 1913.

SMITH, LOGAN PEARSALL (1865–1946). Writer of books, of essays and belles-lettres, of which *Trivia* is the best known. Brother of Alys, first wife of Bertrand Russell, and a friend of the Webbs from their early married days.

SOMERSET, LADY HENRY (1851–1921). Unhappily married when quite young, Lady Henry Somerset ran away from her husband. The social ostracism thus incurred turned her mind to philanthropic work; she became an ardent temperance advocate (Chairman for a time of the World Women's Temperance Organisation) and interested herself in the problem of " fallen " women.

SOUVESTRE, MARIE (*d.* 1905). Brilliant French intellectual, daughter of the French Academician Émile Souvestre, in the last quarter of the nineteenth century owned and ran a fashionable boarding-school, first at Fontainebleau and then at Wimbledon. Mlle. Souvestre was a radical free-thinker, intimate with the set which surrounded the Frederic Harrisons; Beatrice in youth greatly admired her intellect.

SPENCER, FREDERICK HERBERT (*d.*1946). One of the Webbs' earliest secretaries, who rose to become Chief Inspector to the L.C.C. (See note on p. 153 of this book.)

SPENCER, HERBERT (1820–1903). The philosopher who was Beatrice's earliest friend and preceptor and who so violently disliked her conversion to Socialism. (See the amusing account in *My Apprenticeship*.)

SPENCER, LORD (1835–1910). Liberal peer; First Lord of the Admiralty, 1892–95.

SPENDER, E. HAROLD (1864–1926). Liberal journalist; editor between 1891 and 1914 in succession of the *Pall Mall Gazette*, the *Daily Chronicle*, the *Manchester Guardian* and the *Daily News*; brother of J. A. Spender, the biographer of Asquith. Spender was a Fabian, and his London editorships afforded many good openings for Fabian facts and propaganda. His wife was Violet Hilda Schuster.

SPEYER, SIR EDGAR (1862–1932). Millionaire, partner in Speyer Bros. in three countries, Germany, America and England; became director of the London house in 1887; responsible for electrification of London railways. Speyer was also a patron of music and art and one of the founders of the Whitechapel Art Gallery.

SPICER, SIR EVAN (1849–1937). Of a well-known philanthropic family, Liberal, Congregationalist and interested in education. Alderman of L.C.C., 1889 onwards, and its Chairman, 1906–7.

SQUIRE, ROSE ELIZABETH (1861–1938). Civil servant. Inspector of Factories, Home Office, 1896, and Senior Woman Inspector, 1903; Principal in Home Office, 1921–26. Special Com

missioner to 1905 Royal Commission on the Poor Law.

STACY, ENID (*d.* 1903). One of the most effective women speakers and lecturers in the 'nineties. A Socialist from Bristol, she joined the Fabian Society in 1891, became lecturer to the Hutchinson Trust and a member of the Council of the I.L.P. She married a Socialist curate in Newcastle, the Rev. P. E. T. Widdrington; but unfortunately died very young.

STAMFORD, WILLIAM GREY, ninth Earl (1850–1910). Married Elizabeth Theobald. He was a strong churchman, a Chairman of the Charity Organisation Society, and member of the councils of many religious organisations.

STANLEY, ARTHUR PENRHYN (1815–1881). Dean of Westminster from 1864 to his death. The famous " Dean Stanley ", who defended Dr. Jowett and Bishop Colenso against the orthodox. A connection of Lord Stanley of Alderley.

STANLEY, EDWARD LYULPH, Lord Stanley of Alderley, later Lord Sheffield (1839–1925). Educationalist and authority on social questions, sat on Government Commissions on housing, etc. Member of London School Board, 1876–85 and 1886–96. M.P. for Oldham, 1880–85.

STEADMAN, W. C. (1851–1911). Secretary of the Barge-Builders' Union, and in 1905 Secretary to the T.U.C. Sat on L.C.C. for many years representing Stepney; Lib-Lab M.P. for Tower Hamlets, 1898–1900, and for Central Finsbury, 1906–10. An early Fabian.

STEEL, MRS. FLORA ANNIE (1847–1929). The popular novelist—mostly on Indian themes. She lived in India until 1889, and was inspector of schools in the Punjab.

STEEL-MAITLAND, SIR ARTHUR HERBERT DRUMMOND RAMSAY (1876–1935). Tory politician; M.P. for Birmingham seats, 1910–29; Minister of Labour, 1924–29. Special Commissioner to 1905 Royal Commission on the Poor Law.

STEPHEN, SIR LESLIE (1832–1904). The Rationalist, first editor of the *Dictionary of National Biography* and author of *The English Utilitarians* and

English Thought in the Eighteenth Century, etc. Father of Virginia Woolf.

STEYN, MARTINIUS THEUNIS (1857–1916). South African politician. Attorney-General to the Orange Free State, 1889, and its President from 1896 to 1900. At first he was friendly to Great Britain, but joined with the Transvaal Republic at the outbreak of war.

STONE, SAMUEL. The first Town Clerk of Leicester after the Municipal Corporations Act, 1835. Stone was both Town Clerk and Clerk to the Magistrates from 1836 to 1872.

STOREY, JOHN. Town Clerk of Leicester, 1874–94.

STRACHEY, LIEUTENANT-GENERAL SIR RICHARD (1817–1908). Distinguished Indian Army officer and administrator, Secretary to the Government of the Central Provinces during the Mutiny; was subsequently member of the Council for India. President of the Famine Commission, 1878–80, and held many other offices. Lytton Strachey was one of his five sons, and St. Loe Strachey of the *Spectator* his nephew. Lady Strachey was a daughter of Sir John Grant of Rothiemurchus; she wrote poetry and memoirs.

STRACHEY, JAMES B. The psychoanalyst, brother of Lytton Strachey. As an undergraduate of Trinity College joined the Cambridge University Fabian Society in 1908.

STUART, SIR JAMES (1843–1913). Professor of Mechanics at Cambridge, 1875–89; Liberal M.P. for Hoxton, 1885–1900, and for Sunderland, 1906–10. Founded the University Extension system at Cambridge.

STURGE, MILDRED. Of an old Quaker family, of whom three sisters married three brothers, Stephens by name, all descended from one great-great-grandfather. Mildred Sturge became Mrs. Arthur Stephens, and had six children.

SUTHERLAND, MILLICENT, Duchess of Sutherland. Wife of the fourth Duke (who *d.* 1913). Author, social worker and Society hostess; a prominent and distinguished lady in her day.

SWEET-ESCOTT, SIR ERNEST BICKHAM (1857–1942). Colonial administrator, entered the service in 1881 and rose to be Governor of British Honduras, 1904–6, of the Leeward Islands, 1906–1912, and Governor of Fiji and High Commissioner and Consul-General for Western Pacific, 1912–18.

TALBOT, EDWARD STUART (1844–1934). Bishop of Rochester, 1895–1905, of Southwark, 1905–11, and of Winchester, 1911–23. A moderately high churchman who supported many social reforms and worked for agreement among the various sections of Church opinion.

TENNANT, HAROLD JOHN (1865–1935). Liberal politician; Private Secretary to Asquith, who married his sister Margot; held various offices. His wife was May Abraham, the inspector of factories.

TERRY, ELLEN (1847–1928). The actress. See Bernard Shaw's *Letters to Ellen Terry*.

THESIGER, FREDERIC AUGUSTUS. Baron Chelmsford (1827–1905). Soldier, served in Crimean War, Indian Mutiny, Kaffir and Zulu Wars. Lieutenant of the Tower, 1884–89.

THESIGER, FREDERIC JOHN NAPIER, afterwards Viscount Chelmsford (1868–1933). Member of the London School Board, 1900–4, and of L.C.C. (Moderate), 1904–5. Viceroy of India, 1916–21, and First Lord of the Admiralty in the first Labour Government. His wife was Frances Charlotte Guest, a daughter of Lord Wimborne.

TILLETT, BENJAMIN (1860–1943). One of the principal organisers of the Transport Workers. Started work in a brickyard, subsequently served in the Navy and in merchant shipping. As Secretary of the Tea Porters' Union, Tillett played a considerable part in the 1889 Dock Strike, and became Secretary of the Dock, Wharf, Riverside and General Workers' Union. He ran the London Dock Strikes of 1911 and 1912, and prayed on Tower Hill that "God would strike Lord Devonport dead". Labour M.P., 1917–24 and 1929–31.

TORRANCE, SIR ANDREW M. (*d.* 1909). Member of L.C.C. (Progressive), 1889–1907. Liberal M.P. for Central Glasgow, 1906.

TOWNSHEND, CHARLOTTE PAYNE (*d.* 1944). Fabian, the "Irish millionairess with green eyes ", who became the wife of Bernard Shaw. (See Shaw's *Letters to Ellen Terry*, etc.)

TREVELYAN, SIR CHARLES PHILIPS (1870–). Eldest son of Sir George Otto Trevelyan. At first a Liberal M.P., holding office in the last Liberal Government, but resigned in 1914 on pacifist principles, and became a strong pacifist and internationalist. Joined the Labour Party, and was President of the Board of Education in the Labour Government of 1929.

TREVELYAN, GEORGE MACAULAY (1876–). The historian and Master of Trinity College, Cambridge, younger brother of the above. His wife was Janet Penrose, daughter of Mrs. Humphry Ward.

TREVELYAN, ROBERT CALVERLEY (1872–). Poet and man of letters. Younger brother of Sir Charles Trevelyan, and associated with him in the Webbs' Socialist and Poor Law projects.

TUCKWELL, GERTRUDE. Niece of Lady Dilke. Honorary Secretary of the Women's Trade Union League, 1892–1904, and thereafter Chairman. Miss Tuckwell was one of the most fervent promoters of Trade Unionism among women, and of labour legislation. She was for many years Honorary Treasurer of the British Section of the International Association for Labour Legislation; she was also one of the first women magistrates.

TWEEDMOUTH, EDWARD MARJORIBANKS, Baron Tweedmouth (1849–1909). Rich Liberal landowner and politician, held various offices. When First Lord of the Admiralty (1906–8) he wrote an indiscreet letter to the Kaiser which led to the termination of his political career.

TYNDALL, JOHN (1820–92). The great scientist who succeeded Faraday in 1867 as Superintendent at the Royal Institution.

TYRRELL, GEORGE (1861–1909). Father Tyrrell, the modernist priest who in 1906 was turned out of the Society of Jesus for an unorthodox " Letter to a Professor of Anthropology ". Writer of many books and articles, and a strong influence in the early twentieth century.

VANDERVELDE, ÉMILE (1866–1939). For many years leader of the Belgian Labour Party and President of the Labour and Socialist (" Second ") International. His best-known book is *Le Socialisme contre l'État*. Several times a Minister in Belgian Governments.

VINCENT, SIR WILLIAM WILKINS (1843–1916). Hat and cap manufacturer of Leicester; member of the Town Council from 1891; Mayor in 1902 and 1910.

VIVIAN, HERBERT (1865–1940). Traveller and journalist; correspondent for *Morning Post*, *Daily Express*, *Daily Mail*; strongly Conservative in politics.

WAKEFIELD, REV. HENRY RUSSELL (1854–1933). Broad churchman, member of the London School Board, 1897–1900; Rector of St. Mary's, Bryanston Square, 1894–1909, and Bishop of Birmingham, 1911–24. Chairman of the Central Committee on the Unemployed, member of the 1905 Royal Commission on the Poor Law, where he signed the Minority Report.

WALLAS, AUDREY (1859–1934), *née* Ada Radford. Wife of Graham Wallas and herself a writer.

WALLAS, GRAHAM (1858–1932). Sociologist, author of *Human Nature in Politics* and other books, and lecturer at the London School of Economics. With Webb, Shaw and Olivier, Wallas made up the " Big Four " of the early Fabian Executive, on which he sat from 1888 to 1895. He was a member of the London School Board from 1894 to 1904, and of the L.C.C. from 1904 to 1907.

WARD, DUDLEY (1885–). Banker and expert on bridge; Director and Manager of British Overseas Bank. In Treasury during the first world war and represented it at the Peace Conference and the 1921 Brussels Conference.

WARD, MARY AUGUSTA. Mrs. Humphry Ward (1851–1920), the author, her most famous novel being *Robert Elsmere*. Mrs. Humphry Ward was a strong opponent of women's suffrage and in 1889 induced Beatrice to sign a letter to the Press objecting to it. (See *My Apprenticeship*.)

WELBY, REGINALD EARLE, first Baron

1937. Previously Clerk in House of Commons, 1892–1901, and Secretary of Transvaal Education Department.

WILLIAMS, DR. ETHEL MARY NUCELLA (1863–   ). Doctor; President of the British Federation of Medical Women, in practice in Newcastle-on-Tyne from 1913. Active in local government, education and women's emancipation; Treasurer of the first Socialist Medical League.

WILLIAMS, JOSEPH POWELL (1840–1904). Liberal-Unionist politician; M.P. for South Birmingham. Chamberlain's right-hand man, Chairman of the Management Committee of the Liberal-Unionist Association.

WILLIS-BUND, JOHN WILLIAM BUND (1842–1928). Chairman of Worcester County Council and Worcester Quarter Sessions, and of Cardigan Quarter Sessions.

WILSON, JAMES HAVELOCK (1858–1929). Creator in 1887 of the National Sailors and Firemen's Union, which for many years was a vigorous fighting Union. Wilson, however, disliked the I.L.P. type of Socialism; elected to Parliament in 1892 as a Lib-Lab he refused to co-operate in any way with Keir Hardie, and during the first world war, on his instigation, members of his Union refused to carry MacDonald, Henderson and others to meet Russian Socialists and to discuss the re-formation of the International. Thereafter Wilson broke completely with the Labour Party.

WIMBORNE, LADY. Daughter of the seventh Duke of Marlborough and wife of Ivor Bertie Guest, Baron Wimborne. A famous Society hostess.

WOOD, SIR EDWARD (1839–1906). Boot and shoe manufacturer of Leicester; member of the Town Council from 1880 to his death, and Mayor in 1888, 1895, 1901 and 1906.

WOOD, THOMAS MCKINNON (1855–1927). Liberal politician, member of the L.C.C., 1892–97; Chairman, 1898–99, and Leader of the Progressive Party. Liberal M.P., 1906–1918; Parliamentary Secretary to Board of Education, 1908.

WOODCOCK, DR. Her Christian name was not Julia. The only woman Dr. Woodcock on the Medical Register at the date mentioned was Dr. Louisa Woodcock of Portman Square, an eye specialist.

WOODS, SAMUEL (1846–1915). A Lancashire miner by origin, Woods was a Trade Unionist of some note, Secretary to the London Trades Council from 1894 to 1904, and Lib-Lab M.P. from 1892 to 1895 and from 1897 to 1900. He was one of the four delegates sent by the T.U.C. to take part in the Conference of 1900 which resulted in the formation of the Labour Party.

WYNDHAM, GEORGE (1863–1913). One of the most brilliant of the aristocratic Tory politicians, a descendant of Lord Edward Fitzgerald and private secretary to Balfour for five years. From 1900 to 1905, Chief Secretary for Ireland, passed Irish Land Purchase Act; but died young.

YARROW, SIR ALFRED FERNANDEZ (1842–1932). Founder and Chairman of Yarrow & Co., shipbuilders, on the Clyde. His wife was née Minnie Florence Franklin.

YOUNG, ANDREW (1858–   ). Socialist schoolmaster, co-operator. Head for 27 years of North Canongate School, Edinburgh; Edinburgh Town Councillor. Labour M.P. for Partick, 1923–24.

INDEX

THE END